About the cover image

Emigrants Moving West

This anonymous family, photographed while searching for a homestead in central Nebraska, was drawn to the Loup Valley during an era of high rainfall that would soon give way to a prolonged drought. Their particular fate is unknown. But in packing up all their belongings and striking out into an unknown landscape, they followed a path taken by hundreds of thousands of European and American migrants before them who risked everything in a quest for opportunity, improvement, and independence.

Available Volumes

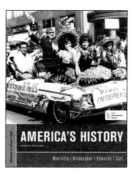

Volume 1: To 1877   **Volume 2: Since 1865**

CANADA

MINNESOTA

Lake Superior

WISCONSIN

St. Paul
Minneapolis

Lake Michigan

MICHIGAN
Lansing

Milwaukee
Madison

Lake Huron

Detroit

IOWA

Des Moines

CENTRAL
LOWLAND

Chicago

Lake Erie

Cleveland

Wheeling

Pittsburgh

PENNSYLVANIA

Lake Ontario

NEW
YORK

Buffalo

St. Lawrence River

MAINE

Augusta

VERMONT

Burlington   Montpelier
                                      Portland
Mt. Washington   Concord
(6,288 ft.; 1,917 m)   NEW
                    Manchester   HAMPSHIRE

Albany   Boston
                                      MASS.
          Hartford
                          Providence
                              R.I.
New York   CONNECTICUT

OHIO

Columbus

INDIANA

Indianapolis

Cincinnati
Charleston

MISSOURI
Springfield

Kansas City
St. Louis

ILLINOIS

Frankfort

Louisville

KENTUCKY

Cumberland
River

Ohio River

Missouri River

Omaha

Topeka

Jefferson
City

W.
VA.

APPALACHIAN MTS.

Trenton
Harrisburg   Philadelphia
                                    NEW JERSEY
Baltimore   Dover
                              DELAWARE
              Annapolis
Potomac   WASHINGTON, D.C.
River   MARYLAND
Richmond   Chesapeake
                              Bay
VIRGINIA
              Norfolk

ATLANTIC
OCEAN

Raleigh

Knoxville

Mt. Mitchell
(6,684 ft.; 2,037 m)

NORTH CAROLINA

Nashville

TENNESSEE

Charlotte

Memphis

SOUTH CAROLINA

TIDEWATER

Tennessee River

Atlanta

ARKANSAS

Little
Rock

Birmingham

Columbia

Charleston

Tulsa

ALABAMA

GEORGIA

MISSISSIPPI

Alabama River

Montgomery

Dallas

LOUISIANA

Jackson

Jacksonville

Tallahassee

Baton Rouge

Orlando

Houston

New Orleans

FLORIDA

Gulf
of
Mexico

Lake
Okeechobee

Miami

B
A
H
A
M
A
S

**THE
UNITED STATES**

Elevation

Feet	Meters
Over 13,001	Over 3,001
6,561–13,000	2,001–3,000
3,281–6,560	1,001–2,000
1,641–3,280	501–1,000
661–1,640	201–500
0–660	0–200
Below sea level	Below sea level

ATLANTIC OCEAN

San Juan

PUERTO
RICO

VIRGIN
ISLANDS

Caribbean Sea

0   50   100 miles
0   50   100 kilometers

67°W   65°W

18°N

CUBA

N
W   E
S

0   150   300 miles
0   150   300 kilometers

ARCTIC OCEAN

NORWAY

SWEDEN

FINLAND

ESTONIA
LATVIA
LITHUANIA

DEN.
NETH.
GER. POLAND
LUX. BELARUS
CZ. REP.
AUS. SLK. UKRAINE
SLN. HUNG. MOLDOVA
CR. B.H. ROMANIA
ITALY SER.
MONT. BULGARIA
MAC.
KOS.
ALB. GREECE
MALTA

TUNISIA

LIBYA

EGYPT

NIGER

CHAD

SUDAN

ERITREA

YEMEN

DJIBOUTI

NIGERIA

BENIN
TOGO CENTRAL
AFRICAN REP.
CAMEROON
EQ.
GUINEA
GABON
CONGO
DEM. REP. OF
THE CONGO
SÃO TOMÉ BURUNDI
& PRÍNCIPE

ANGOLA

ZAMBIA

NAMIBIA
BOTSWANA

ZIMBABWE

SOUTH
AFRICA

MOZAMBIQUE
SWAZILAND
LESOTHO

RUSSIAN FEDERATION

KAZAKHSTAN

GEORGIA
ARMENIA
TURKEY
SYRIA
CYPRUS LEBANON
ISRAEL IRAQ
JORDAN
KUWAIT
SAUDI ARABIA
QATAR
UNITED ARAB
EMIRATES

UZBEKISTAN
TURKMENISTAN

AZERBAIJAN

AFGHANISTAN

IRAN

BAHRAIN

OMAN

KYRGYZSTAN
TAJIKISTAN

PAKISTAN

INDIA

MONGOLIA

CHINA

N. KOREA
S. KOREA

JAPAN

BHUTAN
NEPAL

BANGLADESH

MYANMAR
(BURMA)

THAILAND

CAMBODIA

LAOS
VIETNAM

TAIWAN

PACIFIC OCEAN

Mariana Is.
(U.S.)

Guam
(U.S.)

MARSHALL
IS.

PHILIPPINES

BRUNEI

MALAYSIA

SINGAPORE

MALDIVES

SRI
LANKA

SOMALIA

ETHIOPIA

UGANDA
RWANDA
KENYA

TANZANIA

MALAWI

COMOROS

SEYCHELLES

INDIAN OCEAN

MADAGASCAR

MAURITIUS

PALAU

FEDERATED STATES
OF MICRONESIA

NAURU

KIRIBATI

INDONESIA

EAST TIMOR

PAPUA
NEW
GUINEA

SOLOMON
IS.

TUVALU

VANUATU

FIJI

New Caledonia
(Fr.)

AUSTRALIA

NEW
ZEALAND

Tasmania
(Aust.)

ABBREVIATIONS

ALB.	ALBANIA
AUS.	AUSTRIA
BEL.	BELGIUM
B.H.	BOSNIA AND HERZEGOVINA
CR.	CROATIA
CZ. REP.	CZECH REPUBLIC
DEN.	DENMARK
GER.	GERMANY
HUNG.	HUNGARY
KOS.	KOSOVO
LUX.	LUXEMBOURG
MAC.	MACEDONIA
MONT.	MONTENEGRO
NETH.	NETHERLANDS
SER.	SERBIA
SLK.	SLOVAKIA
SLN.	SLOVENIA
SWITZ.	SWITZERLAND

ANTARCTICA

20°E   40°E   60°E   80°E   100°E   120°E   140°E   160°E

AMERICA'S HISTORY

VOLUME 1: TO 1877

AMERICA'S HISTORY

EIGHTH EDITION

VOLUME 1: TO 1877

James A. Henretta
University of Maryland

Eric Hinderaker
University of Utah

Rebecca Edwards
Vassar College

Robert O. Self
Brown University

BEDFORD / ST. MARTIN'S
Boston • New York

For Bedford/St. Martin's

Publisher for History: *Mary V. Dougherty*
Executive Editor for History: *William J. Lombardo*
Director of Development for History: *Jane Knetzger*
Senior Developmental Editor: *Laura Arcari*
Production Editor: *Annette Pagliaro Sweeney*
Senior Production Supervisor: *Jennifer Peterson*
Executive Marketing Manager: *Sandra McGuire*
Associate Editor: *Robin Soule*
Editorial Assistant: *Victoria Royal*
Copyeditor: *Susan Zorn*
Indexer: *Leoni Z. McVey, McVey & Associates, Inc.*
Cartography: *Mapping Specialists, Ltd.*
Photo Researchers: *Pembroke Herbert and Sandi Rygiel, Picture Research Consultants, Inc.*
Senior Art Director: *Anna Palchik*
Text Designer: *Maureen McCutcheon*
Cover Designer: *Marine Miller*
Cover Art: *Emigrants Moving with Covered Wagon © Bettmann/CORBIS*
Composition: *Jouve*
Printing and Binding: *RR Donnelley and Sons*

President, Bedford/St. Martin's: *Denise B. Wydra*
Director of Marketing: *Karen R. Soeltz*
Production Director: *Susan W. Brown*
Director of Rights and Permissions: *Hilary Newman*

Manufactured in the United States of America.

8	7	6	5	4	3
f	e	d	c	b	a

For information, write: Bedford/St. Martin's, 75 Arlington Street, Boston, MA 02116   (617-399-4000)

ISBN: 978–1–4576–2816–0 (Volume 1)
ISBN: 978–1–4576–2900–6 (Loose-leaf)

Preface
Why This Book This Way

History classrooms present a unique dilemma. How do we offer our students a basic understanding of key events and facts while inviting them to see the past not as a rote list of names and dates but as the fascinating, conflicted prelude to their lives today? How do we teach our students to think like historians? As scholars and teachers who go into the classroom every day, we know these challenges well and have composed the eighth edition of *America's History* to help instructors meet them. *America's History* has long been known for its breadth, balance, and ability to explain to students not just what happened, but *why*. The latest edition both preserves and substantially builds upon those strengths.

The foundation of our approach lies in our commitment to an integrated history. *America's History* combines traditional "top down" narratives of political and economic affairs with "bottom up" narratives of the lived experiences of ordinary people. Our goal is to help students achieve a richer understanding of politics, diplomacy, war, economics, intellectual and cultural life, and gender, class, and race relations by exploring how developments in all these areas were interconnected. Our analysis is fueled by a passion for exploring big, consequential questions. How did a colonial slave society settled by people from four continents become a pluralist democracy? How have liberty and equality informed the American experience? Questions like these help students understand what's at stake as we study the past. In *America's History*, we provide an integrated historical approach and bring a dedication to *why history matters* to bear on the full sweep of America's past.

One of the most exciting developments in this edition is the arrival of a new author, Eric Hinderaker. An expert in native and early American history, Eric brings a fresh interpretation of native and colonial European societies and the revolutionary Atlantic World of the eighteenth century that enlivens and enriches our narrative. Eric joins James Henretta, long the intellectual anchor of the book, whose scholarly work now focuses on law, citizenship, and the state in early America; Rebecca Edwards, an expert in women's and gender history and nineteenth-century electoral politics; and Robert Self, whose work explores the relationship between urban and suburban politics, social movements, and the state. Together, we strive to ensure that energy and creativity, as well as our wide experience in the study of history, infuse every page that follows.

The core of a textbook is its narrative, and we have endeavored to make ours clear, accessible, and lively. In it, we focus not only on the marvelous diversity of peoples who came to call themselves Americans, but also on the institutions that have forged a common national identity. More than ever, we daily confront the collision of our past with the demands of the future and the shrinking distance between Americans and others around the globe. To help students meet these challenges, we call attention to connections with the histories of Canada, Latin America, Europe, Africa, and Asia, drawing links between events in the United States and those elsewhere. In our contemporary digital world, facts and data are everywhere. What students crave is analysis. As it has since its inception, *America's History* provides students with a comprehensive explanation and interpretation of events, a guide to why history unfolded as it did and a roadmap for understanding the world in which we live.

Of course, the contents of this book are only helpful if students read and assimilate the material before coming to class. So that students will come to class prepared, they now receive access to **LearningCurve** — an adaptive, game-like online learning tool that helps them master content — when they purchase a new copy of *America's History*. And because we know that your classroom needs are changing rapidly, we are excited to announce that *America's History* is available with **LaunchPad**, a new robust interactive e-book built into its own course space that makes customizing and assigning the book and its resources easy and efficient. To learn more about the benefits of LearningCurve and LaunchPad, see the "Versions and Supplements" section on page xvii.

A Nine-Part Framework Highlights Key Developments

One of the greatest strengths of *America's History* is its part structure, which helps students identify the key forces and major developments that shaped each era.

A four-page part opener introduces each part, using analysis, striking images, and a detailed **thematic timeline** to orient students to the major developments and themes of the period covered. New **Thematic Understanding** questions ask students to consider periodization and make connections among chapters. By organizing U.S. history into nine distinct periods, rather than just thirty-one successive chapters, we encourage students to trace changes and continuities over time and to grasp connections between political, economic, social, and cultural events.

In this edition, we have reengineered the part structure to reflect the most up-to-date scholarship. Precontact native societies and European colonization are now covered in two distinct parts, allowing us to devote comprehensive attention to the whole of North America before the 1760s. We have also added an additional part bridging the nineteenth and twentieth centuries, bringing fresh perspectives on industrialization, the "long Progressive Era," and the growth of American global power. Together, the nine parts organize the complex history of North America and the United States into comprehensible sections with distinct themes.

Part 1, "Transformations of North America, 1450–1700," highlights the diversity and complexity of Native Americans prior to European contact, examines the transformative impact of European intrusions and the Columbian Exchange, and emphasizes the experimental quality of colonial ventures. **Part 2, "British North America and the Atlantic World, 1660–1763,"** explains the diversification of British North America and the rise of the British Atlantic World and emphasizes the importance of contact between colonists and Native Americans and imperial rivalries among European powers. **Part 3, "Revolution and Republican Culture, 1763–1820,"** traces the rise of colonial protest against British imperial reform, outlines the ways that the American Revolution challenged the social order, and explores the processes of conquest, competition, and consolidation that followed it.

Part 4, "Overlapping Revolutions, 1800–1860," traces the transformation of the economy, society, and culture of the new nation; the creation of a democratic polity; and growing sectional divisions. **Part 5, "Creating and Preserving a Continental Nation, 1844–1877,"** covers the conflicts generated by America's empire building in the West, including sectional political struggles that led to the Civil War and national consolidation of power during and after Reconstruction. **Part 6, "Industrializing America: Upheavals and Experiments, 1877–1917,"** examines the transformations brought about by the rise of corporations and a powerhouse industrial economy; immigration and a diverse, urbanizing society; and movements for progressive reform.

Part 7, "Domestic and Global Challenges, 1890–1945," explores America's rise to world power, the cultural transformations and political conflicts of the 1920s, the Great Depression, and the creation of the welfare state. **Part 8, "The Modern State and the Age of Liberalism, 1945–1980,"** addresses the postwar period, including America's new global leadership role during the Cold War; the expansion of federal responsibility during a new "age of liberalism"; and the growth of mass consumption and the middle class. Finally, **Part 9, "Global Capitalism and the End of the American Century, 1980 to the Present,"** discusses the conservative political ascendancy of the 1980s; the end of the Cold War and rising conflict in the Middle East; and globalization and increasing social inequality.

Hundreds of Sources Encourage Comparative and Critical Thinking

America's History has long emphasized primary sources. In addition to weaving lively quotations throughout the narrative, we offer students substantial excerpts from historical documents — letters, diaries, autobiographies, public testimony, and more — and numerous figures that give students practice working with data. These documents allow students to experience the past through the words and perspectives of those who lived it, to understand how historians make sense of the past using data, and to gain skill in interpreting historical evidence. Each chapter contains three source-based features.

American Voices, a two-page feature in each chapter, helps students learn to think critically by comparing texts written from two or more perspectives. New topics include "The Debate over Free and Slave Labor," "Jewish Immigrants in the Industrial Economy," "Theodore Roosevelt: From Anti-Populist to New Nationalist," and "Immigration After 1965: Its Defenders and Critics."

New **America Compared** features use primary sources and data to situate U.S. history in a global context while giving students practice in comparison and data analysis. Retooled from the Voices from America feature from the last edition to include data in addition to primary sources, these features appear in every chapter on topics as diverse as the fight for women's rights in France and the United States, an examination of labor laws after emancipation in Haiti and the United States, the loss of human life in World War I, and an analysis of the worldwide economic malaise of the 1970s.

Finally, we are excited to introduce a brand-new feature to aid you in teaching Historical Thinking Skills. A **Thinking Like a Historian** feature in every chapter includes five to eight brief sources organized around a central theme, such as "Beyond the Proclamation Line," "Making Modern Presidents," and "The Suburban Landscape of Cold War America." Students are asked to analyze the documents and complete a Putting It All Together assignment that asks them to synthesize and use the evidence to create an argument. Because we understand how important primary sources are to the study of history, we are also pleased to offer for **free**, when packaged, the all-new companion reader, *Sources for America's History*, featuring a wealth of additional documents.

As in past editions, an outstanding **visual program** engages students' attention and gives them practice in working with visual sources. The eighth edition features over 425 paintings, cartoons, illustrations, photographs, and charts, most of them in full color and more than a quarter new to this edition. Informative captions set the illustrations in context and provide students with background for making their own analysis of the images in the book. Keenly aware that students lack geographic literacy, we have included dozens of **maps** that show major developments in the narrative, each with a caption to help students interpret what they see.

Taken together, these documents, figures, maps, and illustrations provide instructors with a trove of teaching materials, so that *America's History* offers not only a compelling narrative, but also—right in the text—the rich documentary materials that instructors need to bring the past alive and introduce students to historical analysis.

Study Aids Support Understanding and Teach Historical Thinking Skills

The study aids in the eighth edition have been completely revised in the new edition to better support students in their understanding of the material and in their development of Historical Thinking Skills. New **Identify the Big Idea** questions at the start of every chapter guide student reading and focus their attention on identifying not just what happened, but why. A variety of learning tools from the beginning to the end of each chapter support this big idea focus. As they read, students will gain proficiency in Historical Thinking Skills via **marginal review questions** that ask students to "Identify Causes," "Trace Change over Time," and "Understand Points of View," among other skills. Where students are likely to stumble over a key concept, we boldface it in the text where it is first mentioned and provide a **glossary** that defines each term.

In the Chapter Review section, a set of **Review Questions** is given for the chapter as a whole that includes a new Thematic Understanding question, along with new **Making Connections** questions that ask students to consider broader historical issues, developments, and continuities and changes over time. A brief list of **More to Explore** sources directs students to accessible print and Web resources for additional reading. Lastly, a **Timeline** with a new **Key Turning Points** question reminds students of important events and asks them to consider periodization.

New Scholarship Includes Latest Research and Interpretations

In the new edition, we continue to offer instructors a bold account of U.S. history that reflects the latest, most exciting scholarship in the field. Throughout the book, we have given increased attention to political culture and political economy, including the history of capitalism, using this analysis to help students understand how society, culture, politics, and the economy informed one another.

With new author Eric Hinderaker aboard, we have taken the opportunity to reconceptualize much of the pre-1800 material. This edition opens with two dramatically revised chapters marked by closer and more sustained attention to the way Native Americans shaped, and were shaped by, the contact experience and highlighting the tenuous and varied nature of colonial experimentation. These changes carry through the edition in a sharpened continental perspective and expanded coverage of Native Americans, the environment, and the West in every era. We have also brought closer attention to the patterns and varieties of colonial enterprise and new attention to the Atlantic World and the many revolutions — in print, consumption, and politics — that transformed the eighteenth century.

In our coverage of the nineteenth century, the discussion of slavery now includes material on African American childhood and the impact of hired-out slaves on black identity. The spiritual life of Joseph Smith also receives greater attention, as do the complex attitudes of Mormons toward slavery. New findings have also deepened the analysis of the war with Mexico and its impact on domestic politics. But the really new feature of these chapters is their heightened international, indeed global, perspective.

In the post–Civil War chapters, enhanced coverage of gender, ethnicity, and race includes greater emphasis on gay and lesbian history and Asian and Latino immigration, alongside the entire chapter devoted to the civil rights movement, a major addition to the last edition. Finally, we have kept up with recent developments with an expanded section on the Obama presidency and the elections of 2008 and 2012.

Acknowledgments

We are grateful to the following scholars and teachers who reported on their experiences with the seventh edition or reviewed features of the new edition. Their comments often challenged us to rethink or justify our interpretations and always provided a check on accuracy down to the smallest detail.

Jeffrey S. Adler, *University of Florida*
Jennifer L. Bertolet, *The George Washington University*
Vicki Black, *Blinn College*
Stefan Bosworth, *Hostos Community College*
Tammy K. Byron, *Dalton State College*
Jessica Cannon, *University of Central Missouri*
Rose Darrough, *Palomar College*
Petra DeWitt, *Missouri University of Science & Technology*
Nancy J. Duke, *Daytona State College*
Richard M. Filipink, *Western Illinois University*
Matthew Garrett, *Bakersfield College*
Benjamin H. Hampton, *Manchester Community College and Great Bay Community College*
Isadora Helfgott, *University of Wyoming*
Stephanie Jannenga, *Muskegon Community College*
Antoine Joseph, *Bryant University*

Lorraine M. Lees, *Old Dominion University*
John S. Leiby, *Paradise Valley Community College*
Karen Ward Mahar, *Siena College*
Timothy R. Mahoney, *University of Nebraska–Lincoln*
Eric Mayer, *Victor Valley College*
Glenn Melancon, *Southeastern Oklahoma State University*
James Mills, *University of Texas, Brownsville*
Frances Mitilineos, *Oakton Community College*
Anne Paulet, *Humboldt State University*
Thomas Ratliff, *Central Connecticut State University*
LeeAnn Reynolds, *Samford University*
Jenny Shaw, *University of Alabama*
Courtney Smith, *Cabrini College*
Timothy Thurber, *Virginia Commonwealth University*
Sarah E. Vandament, *North Lake College of the Dallas County Community College District*
Julio Vasquez, *University of Kansas*
Louis Williams, *St. Louis Community College–Forest Park*

As the authors of *America's History*, we know better than anyone else how much this book is the work of other hands and minds. We are indebted to Mary Dougherty, William J. Lombardo, Dan McDonough, and Jane Knetzger, who oversaw this edition, and Laura Arcari, who asked the right questions, suggested a multitude of improvements, and expertly guided the manuscript to completion. As usual, Denise B. Wydra and Joan E. Feinberg generously provided the resources we needed to produce an outstanding volume. Annette Pagliaro Sweeney did a masterful job consulting with the authors and seeing the book through the production process. Karen R. Soeltz, Sandi McGuire, and Janie Pierce-Bratcher in the marketing department understood how to communicate our vision to teachers; they and the members of college and high school sales forces did wonderful work in helping this edition reach the classroom. We also thank the rest of our editorial and production team for their dedicated efforts: Associate Editors Robin Soule and Jen Jovin; Editorial Assistant Victoria Royal; Susan Zorn, who copyedited the manuscript; proofreaders Arthur Johnson and Lindsay DiGianvittorio; art researchers Pembroke Herbert and Sandi Rygiel at Picture Research Consultants, Inc.; text permissions researcher Eve Lehmann; and Kalina Ingham and Hilary Newman, who oversaw permissions. Finally, we want to express our appreciation for the invaluable assistance of Patricia Deveneau, who expertly suggested topics and sources for the

Thinking Like a Historian features in Chapters 8–14; Kendra Kennedy, for crucial research aid; and Eliza Blanchard and Erin Boss, and especially Michelle Whalen and the U.S. historians — Robert Brigham, Miriam Cohen, James Merrell, and Quincy Mills — for their invaluable help and advice at Vassar. Many thanks to all of you for your contributions to this new edition of *America's History*.

James A. Henretta
Eric Hinderaker
Rebecca Edwards
Robert O. Self

Versions and Supplements

Adopters of *America's History* and their students have access to abundant extra resources, including documents, presentation and testing materials, the acclaimed Bedford Series in History and Culture volumes, and much more. See below for more information, visit the book's catalog site at **bedfordstmartins.com/henretta /catalog**, or contact your local Bedford/St. Martin's sales representative.

Get the Right Version for Your Class

To accommodate different course lengths and course budgets, *America's History* is available in several different formats, including three-hole-punched loose-leaf Budget Books versions and e-books, which are available at a substantial discount.

- Volume 1, To 1877 (Chapters 1–16): available in paperback, loose-leaf, and e-book formats
- Volume 2, Since 1865 (Chapters 15–31): available in paperback, loose-leaf, and e-book formats

Any of these volumes can be packaged with additional books for a discount. To get ISBNs for discount packages, see the online catalog at **bedfordstmartins.com /henretta/catalog** or contact your Bedford/St. Martin's representative.

New Assign LaunchPad — the Online, Interactive e-Book in a Course Space Enriched with Integrated Assets

The new standard in digital history, LaunchPad course tools are so intuitive to use that online, hybrid, and face-to-face courses can be set up in minutes. Even novices will find it's easy to create assignments, track students' work, and access a wealth of relevant learning and teaching resources. It is the ideal learning environment for students to work with the text, maps, documents, video, and assessment. LaunchPad is loaded with the full interactive e-book and the *Sources for America's History* documents collection — plus Learning-Curve, short author video chapter previews, additional primary sources, videos, guided reading exercises designed to help students read actively for key concepts, boxed feature reading quizzes, chapter summative quizzes, and more. LaunchPad can be used as is or customized, and it easily integrates with course management systems. And with fast ways to build assignments, rearrange chapters, and add new pages, sections, or links, it lets teachers build the course materials they need and hold students accountable.

Let students choose their e-book format. In addition to the LaunchPad e-book, students can purchase the downloadable *Bedford e-Book to Go for America's History* from our Web site or find other PDF versions of the e-book at our publishing partners' sites: CourseSmart, Barnes & Noble NookStudy; Kno; CafeScribe; or Chegg.

✓ New Assign LearningCurve So You Know What Your Students Know and They Come to Class Prepared

As described in the preface and on the inside front cover, students purchasing new books receive access to LearningCurve for *America's History*. Assigning LearningCurve in place of reading quizzes is easy for instructors, and the reporting features help instructors track overall class trends and spot topics that are giving students trouble so they can adjust their lectures and class activities. This online learning tool is popular with students because it was designed to help them rehearse content at their own pace in a nonthreatening, gamelike environment. The feedback for wrong answers provides instructional coaching and sends students back to the book for review. Students answer as many questions as necessary to reach a target score, with repeated chances to revisit material they haven't mastered. When LearningCurve is assigned, students come to class better prepared.

Take Advantage of Instructor Resources

Bedford/St. Martin's has developed a rich array of teaching resources for this book and for this course. They range from lecture and presentation materials and assessment tools to course management options. Most can be downloaded or ordered at **bedfordstmartins .com/henretta/catalog**.

Instructor's Resource Manual. The instructor's manual offers both experienced and first-time instructors tools for preparing lectures and running discussions. It includes chapter-review material, teaching strategies, and a guide to chapter-specific supplements available for the text, plus suggestions on how to get the most out of LearningCurve and a survival guide for first-time teaching assistants.

Guide to Changing Editions. Designed to facilitate an instructor's transition from the previous edition of *America's History* to the current edition, this guide presents an overview of major changes and of changes in each chapter.

Computerized Test Bank. The test bank includes a mix of fresh, carefully crafted multiple-choice, short-answer, and essay questions for each chapter. It also contains brand new stimulus-based multiple-choice questions and volume-wide essay questions. All questions appear in Microsoft Word format and in easy-to-use test bank software that allows instructors to add, edit, re-sequence, and print questions and answers. Instructors can also export questions into a variety of formats, including Blackboard, Desire2Learn, and Moodle.

***The Bedford Lecture Kit* PowerPoint Maps, Images, Lecture Outlines, and i>Clicker Content.** Look good and save time with *The Bedford Lecture Kit*. These presentation materials are downloadable individually from the Instructor Resources tab at **bedfordstmartins .com/henretta/catalog** and are available on *The Bedford Lecture Kit* **Instructor's Resource CD-ROM.** They provide ready-made and fully customizable Power-Point multimedia presentations that include lecture outlines with embedded maps, figures, and selected images from the textbook and extra background for instructors. Also available are maps and selected images in JPEG and PowerPoint formats; content for i>clicker, a classroom response system, in Microsoft Word and PowerPoint formats; the Instructor's Resource Manual in Microsoft Word format; and outline maps in PDF format for quizzing or handing out.

All files are suitable for copying onto transparency acetates.

America in Motion: Video Clips for U.S. History. Set history in motion with *America in Motion*, an instructor DVD containing dozens of short digital movie files of events in twentieth-century American history. From the wreckage of the battleship *Maine* to FDR's fireside chats to Oliver North testifying before Congress, *America in Motion* engages students with dynamic scenes from key events and challenges them to think critically. All files are classroom-ready, edited for brevity, and easily integrated with PowerPoint or other presentation software for electronic lectures or assignments. An accompanying guide provides each clip's historical context, ideas for use, and suggested questions.

Videos and Multimedia. A wide assortment of videos and multimedia CD-ROMs on various topics in U.S. history is available to qualified adopters through your Bedford/St. Martin's sales representative.

Package and Save Your Students Money

For information on free packages and discounts up to 50 percent, visit **bedfordstmartins.com/henretta /catalog**, or contact your local Bedford/St. Martin's sales representative. The products that follow all qualify for discount packaging.

NEW *Sources for America's History.* This primary-source collection is designed to complement the textbook. *Sources for America's History* provides a broad selection of over 225 primary-source documents as well as editorial apparatus to help students understand the sources. To support the structure of the parent text, unique document sets at the end of each part present sources that illustrate the major themes of each section. Available free when packaged with the print text and included in the LaunchPad e-book. Also available on its own as a downloadable PDF e-book or with the main text's e-Book to Go.

NEW Bedford Digital Collections @ **bedfordstmartins .com/bdc/catalog.** This source collection provides a flexible and affordable online repository of discovery-oriented primary-source projects and single primary sources that you can easily customize and link to from your course management system or Web site. Package discounts are available.

The Bedford Series in History and Culture. More than 120 titles in this highly praised series combine first-rate scholarship, historical narrative, and important primary documents for undergraduate courses. Each book is brief, inexpensive, and focused on a specific topic or period. For a complete list of titles, visit **bedfordstmartins.com/history/series**. Package discounts are available.

Rand McNally Atlas of American History. This collection of over eighty full-color maps illustrates key events and eras, from early exploration, settlement, expansion, and immigration to U.S. involvement in wars abroad and on U.S. soil. Introductory pages for each section include a brief overview, timelines, graphs, and photos to quickly establish a historical context. Available for $5.00 when packaged with the print text.

Maps in Context: A Workbook for American History. Written by historical cartography expert Gerald A. Danzer (University of Illinois at Chicago), this skill-building workbook helps students comprehend essential connections between geographic literacy and historical understanding. Organized to correspond to the typical U.S. history survey course, *Maps in Context* presents a wealth of map-centered projects and convenient pop quizzes that give students hands-on experience working with maps. Available free when packaged with the print text.

The Bedford Glossary for U.S. History. This handy supplement for the survey course gives students historically contextualized definitions for hundreds of terms — from *abolitionism* to *zoot suit* — that they will encounter in lectures, reading, and exams. Available free when packaged with the print text.

U.S. History Matters: A Student Guide to U.S. History Online. This resource, written by Alan Gevinson, Kelly Shrum, and the late Roy Rosenzweig (all of George Mason University), provides an illustrated and annotated guide to 250 of the most useful Web sites for student research in U.S. history as well as advice on evaluating and using Internet sources. This essential guide is based on the acclaimed "History Matters" Web site developed by the American Social History Project and the Center for History and New Media. Available free when packaged with the print text.

Trade Books. Titles published by sister companies Hill and Wang; Farrar, Straus and Giroux; Henry Holt and Company; St. Martin's Press; Picador; and Palgrave Macmillan are available at a 50 percent discount when packaged with Bedford/St. Martin's textbooks. For more information, visit **bedfordstmartins.com/tradeup**.

A Pocket Guide to Writing in History. This portable and affordable reference tool by Mary Lynn Rampolla provides reading, writing, and research advice useful to students in all history courses. Concise yet comprehensive advice on approaching typical history assignments, developing critical reading skills, writing effective history papers, conducting research, using and documenting sources, and avoiding plagiarism — enhanced with practical tips and examples throughout — has made this slim reference a best-seller. Package discounts are available.

A Student's Guide to History. This complete guide provides the practical help students need to be successful in any history course. In addition to introducing students to the nature of the discipline, author Jules Benjamin teaches a wide range of skills, from preparing for exams to approaching common writing assignments, and explains the research and documentation process with plentiful examples. Package discounts are available.

Going to the Source: The Bedford Reader in American History. Developed by Victoria Bissell Brown and Timothy J. Shannon, this reader's strong pedagogical framework helps students learn how to ask fruitful questions in order to evaluate documents effectively and develop critical reading skills. The reader's wide variety of chapter topics that complement the survey course and its rich diversity of sources — from personal letters to political cartoons — provoke students' interest while teaching them the skills they need to successfully interrogate historical sources. Package discounts are available.

America Firsthand. With its distinctive focus on ordinary people, this primary documents reader, by Anthony Marcus, John M. Giggie, and David Burner, offers a remarkable range of perspectives on America's history from those who lived it. Popular Points of View sections expose students to different perspectives on a specific event or topic, and Visual Portfolios invite analysis of the visual record. Package discounts are available.

Brief Contents

✔️ **LearningCurve** bedfordstmartins.com/henretta

Contents

PART 1   Transformations of North America, 1450–1700   2

Chapter 1
Colliding Worlds, 1450–1600   6

How did the political, economic, and religious systems of Native Americans, Europeans, and Africans compare, and how did things change as a result of contacts among them?

AMERICA COMPARED
Altered Landscapes   *14*

THINKING LIKE A HISTORIAN
Colliding Cultures   *26*

AMERICA VOICES
The Spanish Conquest of Mexico   *32*

Chapter 2
American Experiments, 1521–1700   40

In what ways did European migrants transfer familiar patterns and institutions to their colonies in the Americas, and in what ways did they create new American worlds? How did Native Americans adapt to the growing presence of Europeans among them?

THINKING LIKE A HISTORIAN
Who Was Pocahontas?   *50*

AMERICA COMPARED
Plantation Colonies Versus Neo-Europes   *57*

AMERICAN VOICES
The Causes of Metacom's War   *68*

Maps, Figures, and Tables

(after Francaviglia)

WASHINGTON
Coeur d'Alene
MONTANA
N. DAK.
Helena
Butte
Florence
Virginia City
OREGON
IDAHO
1862
BLACK HILLS
Deadwood 1874
Boise City
Silver City
1861
Custer City
S. DAK.
WYOMING
Weaverville
South Pass
1868
Corinne
NEBR.
Virginia City
1859
Eureka
Central City
Denver
Coloma
1848
Austin
Leadville
COLORADO
San Francisco
Aurora
UTAH TERRITORY
1876
Pike's Peak
1859
Mariposa
NEVADA
Creede
Cripple Creek
1890
CALIFORNIA
ARIZONA TERRITORY
Los Angeles
Wickenburg
1863
NEW MEXICO TERRITORY
Santa Rita
Tubac
1854
Tombstone
1878
TEXAS
Terlingua

● Gold bonanza
▲ Silver bonanza

☐ Gold mining (primarily)
☐ Intermontane region (gold, silver, copper, iron)
☐ Rocky Mountain region (gold, silver, lead, copper)

0   250   500 miles
0   250   500 kilometers

Special Features

THINKING LIKE A HISTORIAN

AMERICA'S HISTORY

Transformations of North America
1450–1700

In 1450, North America, Europe, and Africa were each home to complex societies with their own distinctive cultures. But their histories were about to collide, bringing vast changes to all three continents. European voyagers sailing in the wake of Christopher Columbus set in motion one of the most momentous developments in world history: sustained contact among Native Americans, Europeans, and Africans in dozens of distinct colonial settings. Before the arrival of Europeans, a wide range of complex Native American societies claimed the continent as their own. Although colonization brought profound change, it did not erase what had come before because Native American societies interacted with colonizers from the beginning. They shaped colonial enterprise in important ways, enabling some forms of colonization while preventing others.

Native Americans, Europeans, and Africans were surprisingly similar in many ways, though the differences among them were important as well. Their distinctive ideas about gods and the spirit world informed their political systems and animated their approaches to trade and warfare. Whether they met in peace or war — or whether peaceful interactions quickly turned violent — Native Americans, Europeans, and Africans viewed one another through lenses that were shaped by these ideas.

In Part 1, we compare Native American, European, and African societies on the eve of colonization and then explore how Europeans experimented with various models of colonization in the first two centuries of sustained transatlantic contacts. The story in Chapters 1 and 2 addresses three main developments that are central to this period:

Native American Diversity and Complexity

Popular culture can lead us to think of Native American societies as being substantially the same everywhere in North America: they were organized into tribes, with few material possessions and primitive beliefs and cultures, and reliant mostly on hunting for their subsistence. This impression distorts a much more complicated picture. Native American political organization ran the gamut from vast, complex imperial states to kin-based bands of hunters and gatherers. Patterns of political organization varied widely, and the familiar label of *tribe* does more to obscure than to clarify their workings. Native Americans' economic and social systems were adapted to the ecosystems they inhabited. Many were extremely productive farmers, some hunted bison and deer, while others were expert salmon fishermen who plied coastal waters in large oceangoing boats. Native American religions and cultures also varied widely, though they shared some broad characteristics.

These variations in Native American societies shaped colonial enterprise. Europeans conquered and coopted Native American empires with relative ease, but smaller and more decentralized polities were harder to exploit. Mobile hunter-gatherers appeared politically amorphous, but they became especially formidable opponents of colonial expansion.

Colonial Settlement and the Columbian Exchange

European colonization triggered a series of sweeping changes that historians have labeled the "Columbian Exchange." At the same time that people crossed the Atlantic in large numbers, so too did plants, animals, and germs. Old World grains like wheat and barley were planted in the Americas for the first time, and weeds like dandelions were carried across the ocean as well. Potatoes, maize (corn), and tomatoes, among other foods, crossed the Atlantic in the other direction and transformed dietary practices in Asia as well as Europe. Native Americans domesticated very few animals; the Columbian Exchange introduced horses, pigs, cattle, and a variety of other creatures to the American landscape. Germs also made the voyage, especially the deadly pathogens that had so disordered life in Europe in the centuries prior to colonization. Smallpox, influenza, and bubonic plague, among others, took an enormous toll on Native American populations. Inanimate materials made the voyage as well: enough gold and silver traveled from the Americas to Europe and Asia to transform the world's economies, intensifying competition and empire building in Europe.

Old World diseases devastated Native American peoples. On average, they lost ninety percent of their numbers over the first century of contact, forcing them to cope with European and African newcomers in a weakened and vulnerable state.

Experimentation and Transformation

The collisions of American, European, and African worlds challenged the beliefs and practices of all three groups. Colonization was, above all, a long and tortured process of experimentation. Over time, Europeans carved out three distinct types of colonies in the Americas, each shaped by the constraints and opportunities presented by American landscapes and peoples. Where Native American societies were organized into densely settled empires, Europeans conquered the ruling class and established tribute-based empires of their own. In tropical and subtropical settings, colonizers created plantation societies that demanded large, imported labor forces—a need that was met through the African slave trade. And in the temperate regions of the mainland North America, where neither the landscape nor the native population yielded easy wealth, European colonists came in large numbers hoping to create familiar societies in unfamiliar settings.

Everywhere in the Americas, core beliefs and worldviews were shaken by contact with radically unfamiliar peoples. Native Americans and Africans struggled to maintain autonomy in their relations with colonizers, while Europeans labored to understand—and profit from—their relations with nonwhite peoples. These transformations are the subject of Part 1.

Transformations of North America 1450–1700

Thematic Understanding

This timeline arranges some of the important events of this period into themes. Look at the entries for "Ideas, Beliefs, and Culture" from 1450 to 1700. How did the Protestant Reformation and the response of the Catholic Church influence the colonization of the Americas in these years? In the realm of "Work, Exchange, and Technology," how did colonial economies evolve, and what roles did Native American and African labor play in them? **>**

	WORK, EXCHANGE, & TECHNOLOGY	PEOPLING	POLITICS & POWER	IDEAS, BELIEFS, & CULTURE	IDENTITY
1450	• Diversified economies of Native America • Rise of the Ottoman Empire blocks Asian trading routes of the Italian city-states • Europeans fish off North American coast • Portuguese traders explore African coast	• Christopher Columbus explores the Bahamas and West Indies (1492–1504) • Pedro Alvares Cabral makes landfall in Brazil (1500) • Spanish conquest of Mexico and Peru (1519–1535)	• Rise of monarchical nation-states in Europe • Aztecs and Incas consolidate their empires • Probable founding of the Iroquois Confederacy • Rise of the Songhai Empire in Africa	• Protestant Reformation (1517) sparks century of religious warfare • Henry VIII creates Church of England (1534) • Founding of Jesuit order (1540)	• Castile and Aragon joined to create Spain; the Inquisition helps create a sense of Spanishness • John Calvin establishes a Protestant commonwealth in Geneva, Switzerland
1550	• Growth of the outwork system in English textile industry • Spanish *encomienda* system organizes native labor in Mexico • Inca *mita* system is co-opted by the Spanish in the Andes	• Castilians and Africans arrive in Spanish America in large numbers • English colonies in Newfoundland, Maine, and Roanoke fail	• Elizabeth's "sea dogs" plague Spanish shipping • English monarchs adopt mercantilist policies • Defeat of the Spanish Armada (1588)	• Philip II defends the Roman Catholic Church against Protestantism • Elizabeth I adopts Protestant Book of Common Prayer (1559)	• English conquest and persecution of native Irish • Growing Protestant movement in England
1600	• First staple exports from the English mainland colonies: furs and tobacco • Subsistence farms in New England • Transition to sugar plantation system in the Caribbean islands	• First set of Anglo-Indian wars • African servitude begins in Virginia (1619) • Caribbean islands move from servitude to slavery	• James I claims divine right to rule England • Virginia's House of Burgesses (1619) • English Puritan Revolution • Native Americans rise up against English invaders (1622, 1640s)	• Persecuted English Puritans and Catholics migrate to America • Established churches set up in Puritan New England and Anglican Virginia • Dissenters settle in Rhode Island	• Pilgrims and Puritans seek to create godly commonwealths • Powhatan and Virginia Company representatives attempt to extract tribute from each other
1700	• Tobacco trade stagnates • Maturing yeoman economy and emerging Atlantic trade in New England	• Growing gentry immigration to Virginia • White indentured servitude shapes Chesapeake society • Africans defined as property rather than people in the Chesapeake	• Restoration of the English crown (1660) • English conquer New Netherland (1664)	• Metacom's War in New England (1675–1676) • Bacon's Rebellion calls for removal of Indians and end of elite rule • Salem witchcraft crisis (1692)	• Social mobility for Africans ends with collapse of tobacco trade and increased power of gentry

1

Colliding Worlds
1450–1600

In April 1493, a Genoese sailor of humble origins appeared at the court of Queen Isabella of Castile and King Ferdinand of Aragon along with six Caribbean natives, numerous colorful parrots, and "samples of finest gold, and many other things never before seen or heard tell of in Spain." The sailor was Christopher Columbus, just returned from his first voyage into the Atlantic. He and his party entered Barcelona's fortress in a solemn procession. The monarchs stood to greet Columbus; he knelt to kiss their hands. They talked for an hour and then adjourned to the royal chapel for a ceremony of thanksgiving. Columbus, now bearing the official title *Admiral of the Ocean Sea*, remained at court for more than a month. The highlight of his stay was the baptism of the six natives, whom Columbus called Indians because he mistakenly believed he had sailed westward all the way to Asia.

•

In the spring of 1540, the Spanish explorer Hernando de Soto met the Lady of Cofachiqui, ruler of a large Native American province in present-day South Carolina. Though an epidemic had carried away many of her people, the lady of the province offered the Spanish expedition as much corn, and as many pearls, as it could carry. As she spoke to de Soto, she unwound "a great rope of pearls as large as hazelnuts" and handed them to the Spaniard; in return he gave her a gold ring set with a ruby. De Soto and his men then visited the temples of Cofachiqui, which were guarded by carved statues and held storehouses of weapons and chest upon chest of pearls. After loading their horses with corn and pearls, they continued on their way.

•

A Portuguese traveler named Duarte Lopez visited the African kingdom of Kongo in 1578. "The men and women are black," he reported, "some approaching olive colour, with black curly hair, and others with red. The men are of middle height, and, excepting the black skin, are like the Portuguese." The royal city of Kongo sat on a high plain that was "entirely cultivated," with a population of more than 100,000. The city included a separate commercial district, a mile around, where Portuguese traders acquired ivory, wax, honey, palm oil, and slaves from the Kongolese.

•

Three glimpses of three lost worlds. Soon these peoples would be transforming one another's societies, often through conflict and exploitation. But at the moment they first met, Europeans, Native Americans, and Africans stood on roughly equal terms. Even a hundred years after Columbus's discovery of the Americas, no one could have foreseen the shape that their interactions would take in the generations to come. To begin, we need to understand the three worlds as distinct places, each home to unique societies and cultures.

IDENTIFY THE BIG IDEA
How did the political, economic, and religious systems of Native Americans, Europeans, and Africans compare, and how did things change as a result of contacts among them?

Their greene corne

Corne newly sprong

Their sitting at meate

The place of Solemne prayer

rose wherin the Tombe of their Herounds standeth.

SECOTON

A Ceremony in their prayers wth strange testures and songs dansing abowt posts carued on the topps lyke mens faces.

Village of Secoton, 1585 English colonist John White painted this view of an Algonquian village on the outer banks of present-day North Carolina. Its cluster of houses surrounded by fields of crops closely resembled European farming communities of the same era. White captured everyday details of the town's social life, including food preparation and a ceremony or celebration in progress (lower right). Service Historique de la Marine Vincennes, France/Giraudon/The Bridgeman Art Library.

The Native American Experience

When Europeans arrived, perhaps 60 million people occupied the Americas, 7 million of whom lived north of Mexico. In Mesoamerica (present-day Mexico and Guatemala) and the Andes, empires that rivaled the greatest civilizations in world history ruled over millions of people. At the other end of the political spectrum, hunters and gatherers were organized into kin-based bands. Between these extremes, semisedentary societies planted and tended crops in the spring and summer, fished and hunted, made war, and conducted trade. Though we often see this spectrum as a hierarchy in which the empires are most impressive and important while hunter-gatherers deserve scarcely a mention, this bias toward civilizations that left behind monumental architecture and spawned powerful ruling classes is misplaced. Regardless of size or political complexity, the energies and innovations of Native American societies everywhere profoundly transformed American landscapes. To be fully understood, the Americas must be treated in all their complexity, with an appreciation for their diverse societies and cultures.

The First Americans

Archaeologists believe that migrants from Asia crossed a 100-mile-wide land bridge connecting Siberia and Alaska during the last Ice Age sometime between 13,000 and 3000 B.C. and thus became the first Americans. The first wave of this migratory stream from Asia lasted from about fifteen thousand to nine thousand years ago. Then the glaciers melted, and the rising ocean submerged the land bridge beneath the Bering Strait (Map 1.1). Around eight thousand years ago, a second movement of peoples, traveling by water across the same narrow strait, brought the ancestors of the Navajos and the Apaches to North America. The forebears of the Aleut and Inuit peoples, the "Eskimos," came in a third wave around five thousand years ago. Then, for three hundred generations, the peoples of the Western Hemisphere were largely cut off from the rest of the world.

During this long era, migrants dispersed through the continents as they hunted and gathered available resources. The predominant flow was southward, and the densest populations developed in central Mexico — home to some 20 million people at the time of first contact with Europeans — and the Andes Mountains, with a population of perhaps 12 million. In North America, a secondary trickle of migration pushed eastward, across the Rockies and into the Mississippi Valley and the eastern woodlands.

Around 6000 B.C., some Native American peoples in present-day Mexico and Peru began raising domesticated crops. Mesoamericans cultivated maize into a nutritious plant with a higher yield per acre than wheat, barley, or rye, the staple cereals of Europe. In Peru they also bred the potato, a root crop of unsurpassed nutritional value. The resulting agricultural surpluses encouraged population growth and laid the foundation for wealthy, urban societies in Mexico and Peru, and later in the Mississippi Valley and the southeastern woodlands of North America (Map 1.2).

American Empires

In Mesoamerica and the Andes, the two great empires of the Americas — the Aztecs and Incas — dominated the landscape. Dense populations, productive agriculture, and an aggressive bureaucratic state were the keys to their power. Each had an impressive capital city. Tenochtitlán, established in 1325 at the center of the Aztec Empire, had at its height around 1500 a population of about 250,000, at a time when the European cities of London and Seville each had perhaps 50,000. The Aztec state controlled the fertile valleys in the highlands of Mexico, and Aztec merchants forged trading routes that crisscrossed the empire. Trade, along with **tribute** demanded from subject peoples (comparable to taxes in Europe), brought gold, textiles, turquoise, obsidian, tropical bird feathers, and cacao to Tenochtitlán. The Europeans who first encountered this city in 1519 marveled at the city's wealth and beauty. "Some of the soldiers among us who had been in many parts of the world," wrote Spanish conquistador Bernal Díaz del Castillo, "in Constantinople, and all over Italy, and in Rome, said that [they had never seen] so large a market place and so full of people, and so well regulated and arranged" (see American Voices, p. 32).

Ruled by priests and warrior-nobles, the Aztecs subjugated most of central Mexico. Captured enemies were brought to the capital, where Aztec priests brutally sacrificed thousands of them. The Aztecs believed that these ritual murders sustained the cosmos, ensuring fertile fields and the daily return of the sun.

Cuzco, the Inca capital located more than 11,000 feet above sea level, had perhaps 60,000 residents. A dense network of roads, storehouses, and administrative

IDENTIFY CAUSES
What factors allowed for the development of empires in central Mexico and the Andes?

MAP 1.1

The Ice Age and the Settling of the Americas

Some sixteen thousand years ago, a sheet of ice covered much of Europe and North America. The ice lowered the level of the world's oceans, which created a broad bridge of land between Siberia and Alaska. Using that land bridge, hunting peoples from Asia migrated to North America as they pursued woolly mammoths and other large game animals and sought ice-free habitats. By 10,000 B.C., the descendants of these migrant peoples had moved south to present-day Florida and central Mexico. In time, they would settle as far south as the tip of South America and as far east as the Atlantic coast of North America.

MAP 1.2

Native American Peoples, 1492

Having learned to live in many environments, Native Americans populated the entire Western Hemisphere. They created cultures that ranged from centralized empires (the Incas and Aztecs), to societies that combined farming with hunting, fishing, and gathering (the Iroquois and Algonquians), to nomadic tribes of hunter-gatherers (the Micmacs and Shoshones). The great diversity of Native American peoples—in language, tribal identity, and ways of life—and the long-standing rivalries among neighboring peoples usually prevented them from uniting to resist the European invaders.

centers stitched together this improbable high-altitude empire, which ran down the 2,000-mile-long spine of the Andes Mountains. A king claiming divine status ruled the empire through a bureaucracy of nobles. Like the Aztecs, the empire consisted of subordinate kingdoms that had been conquered by the Incas, and tribute flowed from local centers of power to the imperial core.

Chiefdoms and Confederacies

Nothing on the scale of the Aztec and Inca empires ever developed north of Mexico, but maize agriculture spread from Mesoamerica across much of North America beginning around A.D. 1000, laying a foundation for new ways of life there as well.

Understanding the Cosmos of the Aztecs

Using Aztec sources, German geographers drew this map of Tenochtitlán in 1524. Recent scholarship suggests that the Aztecs viewed their city as a cosmic linchpin, where the human world brushed up against the divine. In the center of the city stand two elevated temples that represent Coatepec, the Serpent Mountain and the mythic birth-place of the Aztecs' tribal god Huitzilopochtli. Priests sacrificed thousands of men and women here, a ritual the Aztecs believed transformed the temples into the Sacred Mountain and sustained the cosmos. Bildarchiv Preussischer Kulturbesitz/Art Resource, NY.

The Mississippi Valley   The spread of maize to the Mississippi River Valley around A.D. 1000 led to the development of a large-scale northern Native American culture. The older Adena and Hopewell cultures had already introduced moundbuilding and distinctive pottery styles to the region. Now residents of the Mississippi River Valley experienced the greater urban density and more complex social organization that agriculture encouraged.

The city of Cahokia, in the fertile bottomlands along the Mississippi River, emerged around 1000 as the foremost center of the new Mississippian culture. At its peak, Cahokia's population exceeded 10,000; smaller satellite communities brought the region's population to 20,000 to 30,000. In an area of 6 square miles, archaeologists have found 120 mounds of varying size,

shape, and function. Some contain extensive burials; others, known as platform mounds, were used as bases for ceremonial buildings or rulers' homes. Cahokia had a powerful ruling class and a priesthood that wor-shipped the sun. After peaking in size around 1350, it declined rapidly. Scholars speculate that its decline was caused by an era of ruinous warfare, exacerbated by environmental factors that made the site less habitable. It had been abandoned by the time Europeans arrived in the area.

Mississippian culture endured, however, and was still in evidence throughout much of the Southeast at the time of first contact with Europeans. The Lady of Cofachiqui encountered by Hernando de Soto in 1540 ruled over a Mississippian community, and others dot-ted the landscape between the Carolinas and the lower

Mississippi River. In Florida, sixteenth-century Spanish explorers encountered the Apalachee Indians, who occupied a network of towns built around mounds and fields of maize.

Eastern Woodlands   In the eastern woodlands, the Mississippian-influenced peoples of the Southeast interacted with other groups, many of whom adopted maize agriculture but did not otherwise display Mississippian characteristics. To the north, Algonquian and Iroquoian speakers shared related languages and lifeways but were divided into dozens of distinct societies. Most occupied villages built around fields of maize, beans, and squash during the summer months; at other times of the year, they dispersed in smaller groups to hunt, fish, and gather. Throughout the eastern woodlands, as in most of North America, women tended crops, gathered plants, and oversaw affairs within the community, while men were responsible for activities beyond it, especially hunting, fishing, and warfare.

In this densely forested region, Indians regularly set fires — in New England, twice a year, in spring and fall — to clear away underbrush, open fields, and make it easier to hunt big game. The catastrophic population decline accompanying European colonization quickly put an end to seasonal burning, but in the years before Europeans arrived in North America bison roamed east as far as modern-day New York and Georgia. Early European colonists remarked upon landscapes that "resemble[d] a stately Parke," where men could ride among widely spaced trees on horseback and even a "large army" could pass unimpeded (America Compared, p. 14).

Algonquian and Iroquoian peoples had no single style of political organization. Many were chiefdoms, with one individual claiming preeminent power in a community. Some were paramount chiefdoms, in which numerous communities with their own local chiefs banded together under a single, more powerful ruler. For example, the Powhatan Chiefdom, which

The Great Serpent Mound

Scholars long believed that this mound was the work of the Adena peoples (500 B.C.–A.D. 200) because of its proximity to an Adena burial site in present-day southern Ohio. Recent research places the mound at a much later date (A.D. 950–1200) and, because of the serpent imagery, ties it to the Fort Ancient culture, which is closely related to the Mississippian complex. The head of the serpent is aligned with the sunset of the summer solstice (June 20 or 21 in the Northern Hemisphere), an event of great religious significance to a sun-worshipping culture. © Bettmann/Corbis.

The Kincaid Site
Located on the north bank of the Ohio River 140 miles from Cahokia, the Kincaid site was a Mississippian town from c. A.D. 1050 to 1450. It contains at least nineteen mounds topped by large buildings thought to have been temples or council houses. Now a state historic site in Illinois, it has been studied by anthropologists and archaeologists since the 1930s. Artist Herb Roe depicts the town as it may have looked at its peak.
Herb Roe, Chromesun Productions.

dominated the Chesapeake Bay region, embraced more than thirty subordinate chiefdoms, and some 20,000 people, by the time Englishmen established the colony of Virginia in Powhatan territory. Powhatan himself, according to the English colonist John Smith, was attended by "a guard of 40 or 50 of the tallest men his Country affords."

Elsewhere, especially in the Mid-Atlantic region, the power of chiefs was strictly local. Along the Delaware and Hudson rivers, Lenni Lenape (or Delaware) and Munsee Indians lived in small, independent communities without overarching political organizations. Early European maps of this region show a landscape dotted with a bewildering profusion of Indian names. European colonization would soon

drive many of these groups into oblivion and force survivors to coalesce into larger groups.

Some Native American groups were not chiefdoms at all, but instead granted political authority to councils of sachems, or leaders. This was the case with the Iroquois Confederacy. Sometime shortly before the arrival of Europeans, probably around 1500, five nations occupying the region between the Hudson River and Lake Erie—the Mohawks, Oneidas, Onondagas, Cayugas, and Senecas—banded together to form the Iroquois.

These groups had been fighting among themselves for years, caught in a destructive cycle of wars of retribution. Then, according to Iroquois legend, a Mohawk man named Hiawatha lost his family in one of these

Altered Landscapes

In the eastern woodlands, Native Americans set fires once or twice a year to clear underbrush and open up landscapes that would otherwise have been densely wooded. The burnings made it easier to plant corn, beans, and squash and drew big game animals into the clearings, where hunters could fell them. As European colonization displaced Indian populations, this practice ended. Some scholars have even suggested that the decline in burning caused a drop of carbon in the atmosphere large enough to account for the Little Ice Age, an episode of global cooling that lasted from about 1550 to 1850, though the claim is controversial.

Thomas Morton, Of the Custome in burning the Country, and the reason thereof (1637)

The Savages are accustomed to set fire of the Country in all places where they come, and to burne it twize a yeare, viz: at the Spring, and the fall of the leafe. The reason that mooves them to doe so, is because it would other wise be so overgrowne with underweedes that it would be all a coppice wood, and the people would not be able in any wise to passe through the Country out of a beaten path.

The meanes that they do it with, is with certaine min-erall stones, that they carry about them in baggs made for that purpose of the skinnes of little beastes, which they convert into good lether, carrying in the same a peece of touch wood, very excellent for that purpose, of their owne making. These minerall stones they have from the Piquenteenes, (which is to the Southward of all the plantations in New England,) by trade and trafficke with those people.

The burning of the grasse destroyes the underwoods, and so scorcheth the elder trees that it shrinkes them, and hinders their grouth very much: so that hee that will looke to finde large trees and good tymber, must not depend upon the help of a woodden prospect to finde them on the uplandground; but must seeke for them, (as I and oth-ers have done,) in the lower grounds, where the grounds are wett, when the Country is fired, by reason of the snow water that remaines there for a time, untill the Sunne by continuance of that hath exhaled the vapoures of the earth, and dried up those places where the fire, (by reason of the moisture,) can have no power to doe them any hurt: and if he would endevoure to finde out any goodly Cedars, hee must not seeke for them on the higher grounds, but make his inquest for them in the vallies, for the Savages,

by this custome of theirs, have spoiled all the rest: for this custome hath bin continued from the beginninge.

And least their firing of the Country in this manner should be an occasion of damnifying us, and indaingering our habitations, wee our selves have used carefully about the same times to observe the winds, and fire the grounds about our owne habitations; to prevent the Dammage that might happen by any neglect thereof, if the fire should come neere those howses in our absence.

For, when the fire is once kindled, it dilates and spreads it selfe as well against, as with the winde; burning continually night and day, untill a shower of raine falls to quench it.

And this custome of firing the Country is the meanes to make it passable; and by that meanes the trees growe here and there as in our parks: and makes the Country very beautifull and commodious.

Source: Thomas Morton, *The New English Canaan* (Boston: John Wilson and Son, 1883 [orig. pub. 1637]), 172–173.

QUESTIONS FOR ANALYSIS

1. What benefits and dangers does Morton attribute to the practice of Indian burning? How did he and his fellow colonists respond to the practice?

2. Since Europeans did not practice widespread burning in the Indian manner, they achieved deforestation only slowly, through many years of backbreaking labor. Think-ing comparatively about European and Native American approaches to landscape management, how would you assess the benefits and challenges of each approach?

wars. Stricken by grief, he met a spirit who taught him a series of condolence rituals. He returned to his people preaching a new gospel of peace and power, and the condolence rituals he taught became the foundation for the Iroquois Confederacy.

Once bound by these rituals, the Five Nations began acting together as a political confederacy. They avoided violence among themselves and became one of the most powerful Native American groups in the Northeast. The Iroquois did not recognize chiefs; instead, councils of sachems made decisions. These were **matriarchal** societies, with power inherited through female lines of authority. Women were influential in local councils, though men served as sachems, made war, and conducted diplomacy.

Along the southern coast of the region that would soon be called New England, a dense network of powerful chiefdoms — including the Narragansetts, Wampanoags, Mohegans, Pequots, and others — competed for resources and dominance. When the Dutch and English arrived, they were able to exploit these rivalries and play Indian groups against one another. Farther north, in northern New England and much of present-day Canada, the short growing season and thin, rocky soil were inhospitable to maize agriculture. Here the native peoples were hunters and gatherers and therefore had smaller and more mobile communities, though they were no less complex than their agriculturally oriented cousins.

The Great Lakes

To the west, Algonquian-speaking peoples dominated the Great Lakes. The tribal groups recognized by Europeans in this region included the Ottawas, Ojibwas, and Potawatomis. But collectively they thought of themselves as a single people: the Anishinaabe. Clan identities — beaver, otter, sturgeon, deer, and others — crosscut tribal affiliations and were in some ways more fundamental. The result was a social landscape that could be bewildering to outsiders. Here lived, one French official remarked, "an infinity of undiscovered nations."

The extensive network of lakes and rivers, and the use of birchbark canoes, made Great Lakes peoples especially mobile. "They seem to have as many abodes as the year has seasons," wrote one observer. They traveled long distances to hunt and fish, to trade, or to join in important ceremonies or military alliances. Groups negotiated access to resources and travel routes. Instead of a map with clearly delineated tribal territories, it is best to imagine the Great Lakes as a porous region, where "political power and social identity took on multiple forms," as one scholar has written.

The Great Plains and Rockies

Farther west lies the vast, arid steppe region known as the Great Plains, which was dominated by the hunting and gathering activities of small, dispersed groups. The geopolitics of the Plains Indians was transformed by a European import — the horse — long before Europeans themselves arrived. Livestock was introduced in the Spanish colony of New Mexico in the late sixteenth century, and from there horses gradually dispersed across the plains. Bison hunters who had previously relied on stealth became much more successful on horseback.

Indians on horseback were also more formidable opponents than their counterparts on foot, and some Plains peoples leveraged their control of horses to gain power over their neighbors. The Comanches were a small Shoshonean band on the northern plains that migrated south in pursuit of horses. They became expert raiders, capturing people and horses alike and trading them for weapons, food, clothing, and other necessities. Eventually they controlled a vast territory. From their humble origins, their skill in making war on horseback made the Comanches one of the region's most formidable peoples.

EXPLAIN CONSEQUENCES
How did landscape, climate, and resources influence the development of Native American societies?

Similarly, horses allowed the Sioux, a confederation of seven distinct peoples who originated in present-day Minnesota, to move west and dominate a vast territory ranging from the Mississippi River to the Black Hills. The Crow Indians moved from the Missouri River to the eastern slope of the Rocky Mountains, where they became nomadic bison hunters. Beginning in the mid-eighteenth century, they became horse breeders and traders as well.

In some places, farming communities were embedded within the much wider geographical range of hunter-gatherers. Thus the Hidatsa and Mandan Indians maintained settled agricultural villages along the Missouri River, while the more mobile Sioux dominated the region around them. Similarly, the Caddo Indians, who lived on the edge of the southern plains, inhabited agricultural communities that were like islands in a sea of more mobile peoples.

Three broad swaths of Numic-speaking peoples occupied the Great Basin that separated the Rockies from the Sierra Mountains: Bannocks and Northern Paiutes in the north, Shoshones in the central basin, and Utes and Southern Paiutes in the south. Resources were varied and spread thin on the land. Kin-based bands traveled great distances to hunt bison along the

Yellowstone River (where they shared territory with the Crows) and bighorn sheep in high altitudes, to fish for salmon, and to gather pine nuts when they were in season. Throughout the Great Basin, some groups adopted horses and became relatively powerful, while others remained foot-borne and impoverished in comparison with their more mobile neighbors.

The Arid Southwest

In the part of North America that appears to be most hostile to agriculture — the canyon-laced country of the arid Southwest — surprisingly large farming settlements developed. Anasazi peoples were growing maize by the first century A.D., earlier than anywhere else north of Mexico, and Pueblo cultures emerged around A.D. 600. By A.D. 1000, the Hohokams, Mogollons, and Anasazis (all Pueblo peoples) had developed irrigation systems to manage scarce water, enabling them to build sizable villages and towns of adobe and rock that were often molded to sheer canyon walls. Chaco Canyon, in modern New Mexico, supported a dozen large Anasazi towns, while beyond the canyon a network of roads tied these settlements together with hundreds of small Anasazi villages.

Extended droughts and soil exhaustion caused the abandonment of Chaco Canyon and other large settlements in the Southwest after 1150, but smaller communities still dotted the landscape when the first Europeans arrived. It was the Spanish who called these groups Pueblo Indians: *pueblo* means "town" in Spanish, and the name refers to their distinctive building style. When Europeans arrived, Pueblo peoples, including the Acomas, Zuñis, Tewas, and Hopis, were found throughout much of modern New Mexico, Arizona, and western Texas.

The Pacific Coast

Hunter-gatherers inhabited the Pacific coast. Before the arrival of the Spanish, California was home to more than 300,000 people, subdivided into dozens of small, localized groups and speaking at least a hundred distinct languages. This diversity of languages and cultures discouraged intermarriage and kept these societies independent. Despite these differences, many groups did share common characteristics, including clearly defined social hierarchies separating elites from commoners. They gathered acorns and other nuts and seeds, caught fish and shellfish, and hunted game.

The Pacific Northwest also supported a dense population that was divided into many distinct groups who controlled small territories and spoke different languages. Their stratified societies were ruled by wealthy families. To maintain control of their territories, the more powerful nations, including the Chinooks, Coast Salishes, Haidas, and Tlingits, nurtured strong warrior traditions. They developed sophisticated fishing technologies and crafted oceangoing dugout canoes, made from enormous cedar trees, that ranged up to 60 feet in length. Their distinctive material culture included large longhouses that were home to dozens of people and totem poles representing clan lineages or local legends.

Patterns of Trade

Expansive trade networks tied together regions and carried valuable goods hundreds and even thousands of miles. Trade goods included food and raw materials, tools, ritual artifacts, and decorative goods. Trade enriched diets, enhanced economies, and allowed the powerful to set themselves apart with luxury items.

Anasazi Ladle
Crafted between A.D. 1300 and 1600 and found in a site in central Arizona, this Anasazi dipper was coiled and molded by hand and painted with a geometric motif. Anasazi pottery is abundant in archaeological sites, thanks in part to the Southwest's dry climate. Clay vessels and ladles helped Anasazi peoples handle water — one of their most precious resources — with care. National Museum of the American Indian, Smithsonian Institution.

Chilkat Tlingit Bowl

This bowl in the form of a brown bear, which dates to the mid-nineteenth century, is made of alder wood and inlaid with snail shells. The brown bear is a Tlingit clan totem. Animal-form bowls like this one, which express an affinity with nonhuman creatures, are a common feature of Tlingit culture. National Museum of the American Indian, Smithsonian Institution.

In areas where Indians specialized in a particular economic activity, regional trade networks allowed them to share resources. Thus nomadic hunters of the southern plains, including the Navajos and Apaches, conducted annual trade fairs with Pueblo farmers, exchanging hides and meat for maize, pottery, and cotton blankets. Similar patterns of exchange occurred throughout the Great Plains, wherever hunters and farmers coexisted. In some parts of North America, a regional trade in war captives who were offered as slaves helped to sustain friendly relations among neighboring groups. One such network developed in the Upper Mississippi River basin, where Plains Indian captives were traded, or given as diplomatic gifts, to Ottawas and other Great Lakes and eastern woodlands peoples.

Across longer distances, rare and valuable objects traveled through networks that spanned much of the continent. Great Lakes copper, Rocky Mountain mica, jasper from Pennsylvania, obsidian from New Mexico and Wyoming, and pipestone from the Midwest have all been found in archaeological sites hundreds of miles from their points of origin. Seashells — often shaped and polished into beads and other artifacts — traveled hundreds of miles inland. Grizzly bear claws and eagle feathers were prized, high-status objects. After European contact, Indian hunters often traveled long distances to European trading posts to trade for cloth, iron tools, and weapons.

Within Native American groups, powerful leaders controlled a disproportionate share of wealth and redistributed it to prove their generosity and strengthen their authority. In small, kin-based bands, the strongest hunters possessed the most food, and sharing it was essential. In chiefdoms, rulers filled the same role, often collecting the wealth of a community and then redistributing it to their followers. Powhatan, the powerful Chesapeake Bay chief, reportedly collected nine-tenths of the produce of the communities he oversaw — "skins, beads, copper, pearls, deer, turkeys, wild beasts, and corn" — but then gave much of it back to his subordinates. His generosity was considered a mark of good leadership. In the Pacific Northwest, the Chinook word *potlatch* refers to periodic festivals in which wealthy residents gave away belongings to friends, family, and followers.

Sacred Power

Most Native North Americans were **animists** who believed that the natural world was suffused with spiritual power. They sought to understand the world by interpreting dreams and visions, and their rituals appeased guardian spirits that could ensure successful hunts and other forms of good fortune. Although their views were subject to countless local variations, certain patterns were widespread.

Women and men interacted differently with these spiritual forces. In agricultural communities, women grew crops and maintained hearth, home, and village. Native American conceptions of female power linked their bodies' generative functions with the earth's fertility, and rituals like the Green Corn Ceremony — a summer ritual of purification and renewal — helped to sustain the life-giving properties of the world around them.

For men, spiritual power was invoked in hunting and war. To ensure success in hunting, men took care

UNDERSTAND POINTS OF VIEW
How did Native Americans' conceptions of the spiritual world influence their daily lives?

not to offend the spirits of the animals they killed. They performed rituals before, during, and after a hunt to acknowledge the power of those guardian spirits, and they believed that, when an animal had been killed properly, its spirit would rise from the earth unharmed. Success in hunting and prowess in war were both interpreted as signs of sacred protection and power.

Ideas about war varied widely. War could be fought for geopolitical reasons — to gain ground against an enemy — but for many groups, warfare was a crucial rite of passage for young men, and raids were conducted to allow warriors to prove themselves in battle. Motives for war could be highly personal; war was often more like a blood feud between families than a contest between nations. If a community lost warriors in battle, it often retaliated by capturing or killing a like number of warriors in response — a so-called mourning war. Some captives were adopted into new communities, while others were enslaved or tortured.

Western Europe: The Edge of the Old World

In 1450, Western Europe lay at the far fringe of the Eurasian and African continents. It had neither the powerful centralized empires nor the hunter-gatherer bands and semisedentary societies of the Americas; it was, instead, a patchwork of roughly equivalent kingdoms, duchies, and republics vying with one another and struggling to reach out effectively to the rest of the world. No one would have predicted that Europeans would soon become overlords of the Western Hemisphere. A thousand years after the fall of the Roman Empire, Europe's populations still relied on subsistence agriculture and were never far from the specter of famine. Moreover, around 1350, a deadly plague introduced from Central Asia — the Black Death — had killed one-third of Europe's population. The lives of ordinary people were afflicted by poverty, disease, and uncertainty, and the future looked as difficult and dark as the past.

Hierarchy and Authority

In traditional hierarchical societies — American or European — authority came from above. In Europe, kings and princes owned vast tracts of land, forcibly conscripted men for military service, and lived off the peasantry's labor. Yet monarchs were far from supreme: local nobles also owned large estates and controlled hundreds of peasant families. Collectively, these nobles challenged royal authority with both their military power and their legislative institutions, such as the French *parlements* and the English House of Lords.

Just as kings and nobles ruled society, men governed families. These were **patriarchies**, in which property and social identity descended in male family lines. Rich or poor, the man was the head of the house, his power justified by the teachings of the Christian Church. As one English clergyman put it, "The woman is a weak creature not embued with like strength and constancy of mind"; law and custom "subjected her to the power of man." Once married, an Englishwoman assumed her husband's surname, submitted to his orders, and surrendered the right to her property. When he died, she received a dower, usually the use during her lifetime of one-third of the family's land and goods.

Men also controlled the lives of their children, who usually worked for their father into their middle or late twenties. Then landowning peasants would give land to their sons and dowries to their daughters and choose marriage partners of appropriate wealth and status. In many regions, fathers bestowed all their land on their eldest son — a practice known as **primogeniture** — forcing many younger children to join the ranks of the roaming poor. Few men and even fewer women had much personal freedom.

Hierarchy and authority prevailed in traditional European society because of the power held by established institutions — nobility, church, and village — and because, in a violent and unpredictable world, they offered ordinary people a measure of security. Carried by migrants to America, these security-conscious institutions would shape the character of family and society well into the eighteenth century.

Peasant Society

In 1450, most Europeans were **peasants**, farmworkers who lived in small villages surrounded by fields farmed cooperatively by different families. On manorial lands, farming rights were given in exchange for labor on the lord's estate, an arrangement that turned peasants into serfs. Gradually, obligatory manorial services gave way to paying rent, or, as in France, landownership. Once freed from the obligation to labor for their farming rights, European farmers began to produce surpluses and created local market economies.

As with Native Americans, the rhythm of life followed the seasons. In March, villagers began the exhausting work of plowing and then planting wheat, rye, and oats. During the spring, the men sheared wool, which the women washed and spun into yarn. In June, peasants cut hay and stored it as winter fodder for their livestock. During the summer, life was more relaxed, and families repaired their houses and barns. Fall brought the harvest, followed by solemn feasts of thanksgiving and riotous bouts of merrymaking. As winter approached, peasants slaughtered excess livestock and salted or smoked the meat. During the cold months, they threshed grain and wove textiles, visited friends and relatives, and celebrated the winter solstice or the birth of Christ. Just before the cycle began again in the spring, they held carnivals, celebrating with drink and dance the end of the long winter (Figure 1.1).

For most peasants, survival meant constant labor, and poverty corroded family relationships. Malnourished mothers fed their babies sparingly, calling them "greedy and gluttonous," and many newborn girls were "helped to die" so that their brothers would have enough to eat. Half of all peasant children died before the age of twenty-one, victims of malnourishment and disease. Many peasants drew on strong religious beliefs, "counting blessings" and accepting their harsh existence. Others hoped for a better life. It was the peasants of Spain, Germany, and Britain who would supply the majority of white migrants to the Western Hemisphere.

Expanding Trade Networks

In the millennium before contact with the Americas, Western Europe was the barbarian fringe of the civilized world. In the Mediterranean basin, Arab scholars carried on the legacy of Byzantine civilization, which had preserved the achievements of the Greeks and Romans in medicine, philosophy, mathematics, astronomy, and geography, while merchants controlled trade in the Mediterranean, Africa, and the Near East. This control gave them access to spices from India and silks, magnetic compasses, water-powered mills, and mechanical clocks from China.

> **COMPARE AND CONTRAST**
> In what ways were the lives of Europeans similar to and different from those of Native Americans?

In the twelfth century, merchants from the Italian city-states of Genoa, Florence, Pisa, and especially Venice began to push their way into the Arab-dominated trade routes of the Mediterranean. Trading in Alexandria, Beirut, and other eastern Mediterranean ports, they carried the luxuries of Asia into European markets. At its peak, Venice had a merchant fleet of more than three thousand ships. This enormously profitable commerce created wealthy merchants, bankers, and textile manufacturers who expanded trade, lent vast sums of money, and spurred technological innovation in silk and wool production.

Italian moneyed elites ruled their city-states as **republics**, states that had no prince or king but instead

FIGURE 1.1

The Yearly Rhythm of Rural Life and Death

The annual cycle of nature profoundly affected life in the traditional agricultural world. The death rate soared by 20 percent in February (from viruses) and September (from fly-borne dysentery). Summer was the healthiest season, with the fewest deaths and the most successful conceptions (as measured by births nine months later). A value of 100 indicates an equal number of deaths and conceptions.

Procession in St. Mark's Square in Venice, 1496

Venice was one of the world's great trading centers in the fifteenth century. Its merchant houses connected Europe to Asia and the Middle East, while its complex republican government aroused both admiration and mistrust. Here, Venetian painter Gentile Bellini (c. 1429–1507) depicts a diplomatic procession celebrating the League of Venice, a union of European states opposed to French expansion into Italy. Galleria dell 'Accademia, Venice, Italy/Giraudon/The Bridgeman Art Library.

were governed by merchant coalitions. They celebrated **civic humanism**, an ideology that praised public virtue and service to the state and in time profoundly influenced European and American conceptions of government. They sponsored great artists — Michelangelo, Leonardo da Vinci, and others — who produced an unprecedented flowering of genius. Historians have labeled the arts and learning associated with this cultural transformation from 1300 to 1450 the **Renaissance**.

The economic revolution that began in Italy spread slowly to northern and western Europe. England's principal export was woolen cloth, which was prized in the colder parts of the continent but had less appeal in southern Europe and beyond. Northern Europe had its own trade system, controlled by an alliance of merchant communities called the Hanseatic League centered on the Baltic and North seas, which dealt in timber, furs, wheat and rye, honey, wax, and amber.

As trade picked up in Europe, merchants and artisans came to dominate its growing cities and towns. While the Italian city-states ruled themselves without having a powerful monarch to contend with, in much of Europe the power of merchants stood in tension with that of kings and nobles. In general, the rise of commerce favored the power of kings at the expense of the landed nobility. The kings of Western Europe established royal law courts that gradually eclipsed the manorial courts controlled by nobles; they also built bureaucracies that helped them centralize power while they forged alliances with merchants and urban artisans. Monarchs allowed merchants to trade throughout their realms; granted privileges to **guilds**, or artisan organizations that regulated trades; and safeguarded commercial transactions, thereby encouraging domestic manufacturing and foreign trade. In return, they extracted taxes from towns and loans from merchants to support their armies and officials.

Myths, Religions, and Holy Warriors

The oldest European religious beliefs drew on a form of animism similar to that of Native Americans, which held that the natural world — the sun, wind, stones, animals — was animated by spiritual forces. As in North America, such beliefs led ancient European peoples to develop localized cults of knowledge and spiritual practice. Wise men and women developed rituals to protect their communities, ensure abundant harvests, heal illnesses, and bring misfortunes to their enemies.

TRACE CHANGE OVER TIME

How did the growth of commerce shift the structure of power in European societies?

The pagan traditions of Greece and Rome overlaid animism with elaborate myths about gods interacting directly with the affairs of human beings. As the Roman Empire expanded, it built temples to its gods wherever it planted new settlements. Thus peoples throughout Europe, North Africa, and the Near East were exposed to the Roman pantheon. Soon the teachings of Christianity began to flow in these same channels.

The Rise of Christianity   Christianity, which grew out of Jewish monotheism (the belief in one god), held that Jesus Christ was himself divine. As an institution, Christianity benefitted enormously from the conversion of the Roman emperor Constantine in A.D. 312. Prior to that time, Christians were an underground sect at odds with the Roman Empire. After Constantine's conversion, Christianity became Rome's official religion, temples were abandoned or remade into churches, and noblemen who hoped to retain their influence converted to the new state religion. For centuries, the Roman Catholic Church was the great unifying institution in Western Europe. The pope in Rome headed a vast hierarchy of cardinals, bishops, and priests. Catholic theologians preserved Latin, the language of classical scholarship, and imbued kingship with divine power. Christian dogma provided a common understanding of God and human history, and the authority of the Church buttressed state institutions. Every village had a church, and holy shrines served as points of contact with the sacred world. Often those shrines had their origins in older, animist practices, now largely forgotten and replaced with Christian ritual.

Christian doctrine penetrated deeply into the everyday lives of peasants. While animist traditions held that spiritual forces were alive in the natural world, Christian priests taught that the natural world was flawed and fallen. Spiritual power came from outside nature, from a supernatural God who had sent his divine son, Jesus

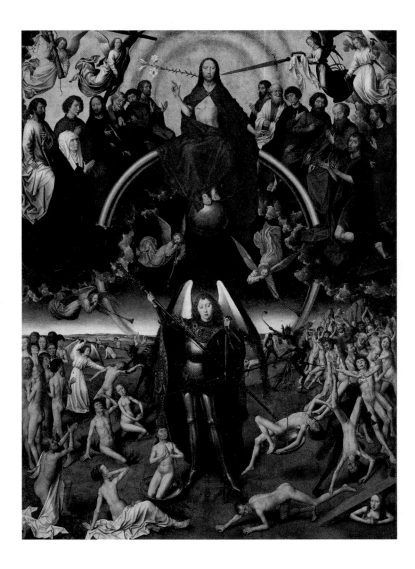

The Last Judgment, **1467–1471**
Death—and their fate in the afterlife—loomed large in the minds of fifteenth-century Christians, and artists depicted their hopes and fears in vividly rendered scenes. In this painting by the German-Flemish artist Hans Memling (c. 1433–1494), Christ and his apostles sit in judgment as the world ends and the dead rise from their graves. The archangel Michael weighs the souls of the dead in a balance to determine their final fate: either eternal life with God in heaven or everlasting punishment in hell. Erich Lessing/ Art Resource, NY.

Christ, into the world to save humanity from its sins. The Christian Church devised a religious calendar that transformed animist festivals into holy days. The winter solstice, which had for millennia marked the return of the sun, became the feast of Christmas.

The Church also taught that Satan, a wicked supernatural being, was constantly challenging God by tempting people to sin. People who spread **heresies** — doctrines that were inconsistent with the teachings of the Church — were seen as the tools of Satan, and suppressing false doctrines became an obligation of Christian rulers.

The Crusades

In their work suppressing false doctrines, Christian rulers were also obliged to combat **Islam**, the religion whose followers considered Muhammad to be God's last prophet. Islam's reach expanded until it threatened European Christendom. Following the death of Muhammad in A.D. 632, the newly converted Arab peoples of North Africa used force and fervor to spread the Muslim faith into sub-Saharan Africa, India, and Indonesia, as well as deep into Spain and the Balkan regions of Europe. Between A.D. 1096 and 1291, Christian armies undertook a series of **Crusades** to reverse the Muslim advance in Europe and win back the holy lands where Christ had lived. Under the banner of the pope and led by Europe's Christian monarchs, crusading armies aroused great waves of popular piety as they marched off to combat. New orders of knights, like the Knights Templar and the Teutonic Knights, were created to support them.

The crusaders had some military successes, but their most profound impact was on European society. Religious warfare intensified Europe's Christian identity and prompted the persecution of Jews and their expulsion from many European countries. The Crusades also introduced Western European merchants to the trade routes that stretched from Constantinople to China along the Silk Road and from the Mediterranean Sea through the Persian Gulf to the Indian Ocean. And crusaders encountered sugar for the first time. Returning soldiers brought it back from the Middle East, and as Europeans began to conquer territory in the eastern Mediterranean, they experimented with raising it themselves. These early experiments with sugar would have a profound impact on European enterprise in the Americas — and European involvement with the African slave trade — in the centuries to come. By 1450, Western Europe remained relatively isolated from the centers of civilization in Eurasia and Africa, but the Crusades and the rise of Italian merchant houses had introduced it to a wider world.

The Reformation

In 1517, Martin Luther, a German monk and professor at the university in Wittenberg, took up the cause of reform in the Catholic Church. Luther's *Ninety-five Theses* condemned the Church for many corrupt practices. More radically, Luther downplayed the role of the clergy as mediators between God and believers and said that Christians must look to the Bible, not to the Church, as the ultimate authority in matters of faith. So that every literate German could read the Bible, previously available only in Latin, Luther translated it into German.

Meanwhile, in Geneva, Switzerland, French theologian John Calvin established a rigorous Protestant regime. Even more than Luther, Calvin stressed human weakness and God's omnipotence. His *Institutes of the Christian Religion* (1536) depicted God as an absolute sovereign. Calvin preached the doctrine of **predestination**, the idea that God chooses certain people for salvation before they are born and condemns the rest to eternal damnation. In Geneva, he set up a model Christian community and placed spiritual authority in ministers who ruled the city, prohibiting frivolity and luxury. "We know," wrote Calvin, "that man is of so perverse and crooked a nature, that everyone would scratch out his neighbor's eyes if there were no bridle to hold them in." Calvin's authoritarian doctrine won converts all over Europe, including the Puritans in Scotland and England.

Luther's criticisms triggered a war between the Holy Roman Empire and the northern principalities in Germany, and soon the controversy between the Roman Catholic Church and radical reformers like Luther and Calvin spread throughout much of Western Europe. The **Protestant Reformation**, as this movement came to be called, triggered a **Counter-Reformation** in the Catholic Church that sought change from within and created new monastic and missionary orders, including the Jesuits (founded in 1540), who saw themselves as soldiers of Christ. The competition between these divergent Christian traditions did much to shape European colonization of the Americas. Roman Catholic powers — Spain, Portugal, and France — sought to win souls in the Americas for the Church, while Protestant nations — England and the Netherlands — viewed the Catholic Church as corrupt and exploitative and hoped instead to create godly communities attuned to the true gospel of Christianity.

TRACE CHANGE OVER TIME
How did the growing influence of the Christian Church affect events in Europe?

West and Central Africa: Origins of the Atlantic Slave Trade

Homo sapiens originated in Africa. Numerous civilizations had already risen and fallen there, and contacts with the Near East and the Mediterranean were millennia old, when Western Europeans began sailing down its Atlantic coast. Home to perhaps 100 million in 1400, Africa was divided by the vast expanse of the Sahara. North Africa bordered on the Mediterranean, and its peoples fell under the domination of Christian Byzantium until the seventh century, when Muslim conquests brought the region under Islamic influence. In its coastal seaports, the merchandise of Asia, the Near East, Africa, and Europe converged. South of the Sahara, by contrast, the societies of West and Central Africa bordering on the Atlantic were relatively isolated. After 1400, that would quickly change.

Empires, Kingdoms, and Ministates

West Africa — the part of the continent that bulges into the Atlantic — can be visualized as a broad horizontal swath divided into three climatic zones. The Sahel is the mostly flat, semiarid zone immediately south of the Sahara. Below it lies the savanna, a grassland region dotted with trees and shrubs. South of the savanna, in a band 200 to 300 miles wide along the West African coast, lies a tropical rain forest. A series of four major watersheds — the Senegal, Gambia, Volta, and Niger — dominate West Africa (Map 1.3).

Sudanic civilization took root at the eastern end of West Africa beginning around 9000 B.C. and traveled westward. Sudanic peoples domesticated cattle (8500–7500 B.C.) and cultivated sorghum and millet (7500–7000 B.C.). Over several thousand years, these peoples developed a distinctive style of pottery, began to cultivate and weave cotton (6500–3500 B.C.), and invented techniques for working copper and iron (2500–1000 B.C.). Sudanic civilization had its own tradition of monotheism distinct from that of Christians, Muslims, and Jews. Most Sudanic peoples in West Africa lived in stratified states ruled by kings and princes who were regarded as divine.

From these cultural origins, three great empires arose in succession in the northern savanna. The first, the Ghana Empire, appeared sometime around A.D. 800. Ghana capitalized on the recently domesticated camel to pioneer trade routes across the Sahara to North Africa, where Ghana traders carried the wealth of West Africa. The Ghana Empire gave way to the Mali Empire in the thirteenth century, which was eclipsed in turn by the Songhai Empire in the fifteenth century. All three empires were composed of smaller vassal kingdoms, not unlike the Aztec and Inca empires, and relied on military might to control their valuable trade routes.

Gold, abundant in West Africa, was the cornerstone of power and an indispensable medium of international trade. By 1450, West African traders had carried so much of it across the Sahara that it constituted one-half to two-thirds of all the gold in circulation in Europe, North Africa, and Asia. Mansa Musa, the tenth emperor of Mali, was a devout Muslim famed for his construction projects and his support of mosques and schools. In 1326, he embarked on a pilgrimage to Mecca with a vast retinue that crossed the Sahara and passed through Egypt. They spent so much gold along the way that the region's money supply was devalued for more than a decade after their visit.

To the south of these empires, the lower savanna and tropical rain forest of West Africa were home to a complex mosaic of kingdoms that traded among themselves and with the empires to the north. In such a densely populated, resource-rich region, they also fought frequently in a competition for local power. A few of these coastal kingdoms were quite large in size, but most were small enough that they have been termed ministates by historians. Comparable to the city-states of Italy, they were often about the size of a modern-day county in the United States. The tropical ecosystem prevented them from raising livestock, since the tsetse fly (which carries a parasite deadly to livestock) was endemic to the region, as was malaria. In place of the grain crops of the savanna, these peoples pioneered the cultivation of yams; they also gathered resources from the rivers and seacoast.

> **COMPARE AND CONTRAST**
> How do the states of the savanna compare to those of the Americas and Europe?

Trans-Saharan and Coastal Trade

For centuries, the primary avenue of trade for West Africans passed through the Ghana, Mali, and Songhai empires, whose power was based on the monopoly they enjoyed over the **trans-Saharan trade**. Their caravans carried West African goods — including gold, copper, salt, and slaves — from the south to the north across the Sahara, then returned with textiles and other foreign goods. For the smaller states clustered

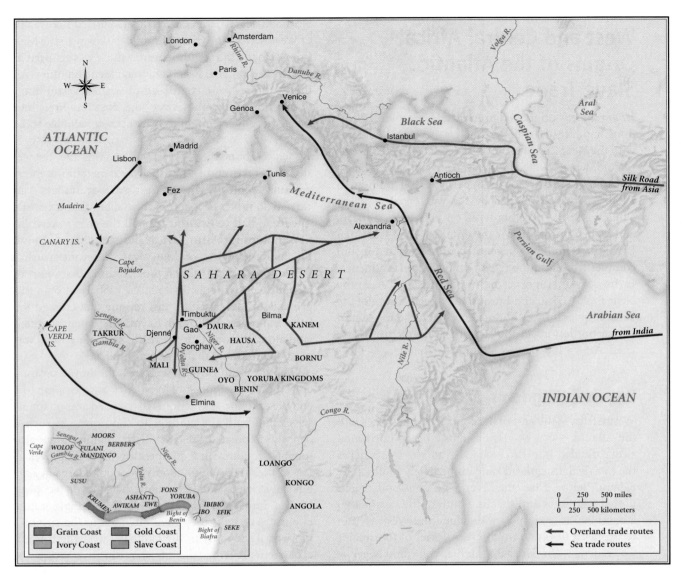

MAP 1.3

West Africa and the Mediterranean in the Fifteenth Century

Trade routes across the Sahara had long connected West Africa with the Mediterranean region. Gold, ivory, and slaves moved north and east; fine textiles, spices, and the Muslim faith traveled south. Beginning in the 1430s, the Portuguese opened up maritime trade with the coastal regions of West Africa, which were home to many peoples and dozens of large and small states. Over the next century, the movement of gold and slaves into the Atlantic would surpass that across the Sahara.

along the West African coast, merchandise originating in the world beyond the Sahara was scarce and expensive, while markets for their own products were limited.

Beginning in the mid-fifteenth century, a newly opening coastal trade with Europeans offered many West African peoples a welcome alternative. As European sailors made their way along the coast of West and then Central Africa, they encountered a bewilderingly complicated political landscape. Around

the mouths of the Senegal and Gambia rivers, numerous Mande-speaking states controlled access to the trade routes into the interior. Proceeding farther along the coast, they encountered the Akan states, a region of several dozen independent but culturally linked peoples. The Akan states had goldfields of their own, and this region soon became known to Europeans as the Gold Coast. East of the Akan states lay the Bight of Benin, which became an early center of the slave trade and thus came to be called the Slave Coast. Bending

Terracotta Figure from Mali
Dating to the thirteenth or fourteenth century, this terracotta figure came from an archaeological site near Djenna. The rider wears a large, ornate necklace, while the horse has a decorative covering on its head. The Mali Empire relied on a large cavalry to expand and defend its borders, and the horse was an important symbol of Mali's wealth and power. Werner Forman/Art Resource, NY.

south, fifteenth-century sailors encountered the Kingdom of Kongo in Central Africa, the largest state on the Atlantic seaboard, with a coastline that ran for some 250 miles. It was here in 1578 that Duarte Lopez visited the capital city of more than 100,000 residents. Wherever they went ashore along this route, European traders had to negotiate contacts on local terms (Thinking Like a Historian, p. 26).

The Spirit World

Some West Africans who lived immediately south of the Sahara—the Fulanis in Senegal, the Mande-speakers in Mali, and the Hausas in northern Nigeria—learned about Islam from Arab merchants and Muslim leaders called imams. Converts to Islam knew the Koran and worshipped only a single God. Some of their cities, like Timbuktu, the legendary commercial center on the Niger River, became centers of Islamic learning and instruction. But most West

Africans acknowledged multiple gods, as well as spirits that lived in the earth, animals, and plants.

Like animists in the Americas and Europe, African communities had wise men and women adept at manipulating these forces for good or ill. The Sudanic tradition of divine kingship persisted, and many people believed that their kings could contact the spirit world. West Africans treated their ancestors with great respect, believing that the dead resided in a nearby spiritual realm and interceded in their lives. Most West African peoples had secret societies, such as the Poro for men and the Sande for women, that united people from different lineages and clans. These societies conducted rituals that celebrated male virility and female fertility. "Without children you are naked," said a Yoruba proverb. Happy was the man with a big household, many wives, many children, and many relatives—and, in a not very different vein, many slaves.

> **PLACE EVENTS IN CONTEXT**
> Why were West African leaders eager to engage in trade with Europeans?

Exploration and Conquest

European engagement with the wider Atlantic world began around 1400, when the Portuguese monarchy propelled Europe into overseas expansion. Portugal soon took a leading role in the African slave trade, while the newly unified kingdom of Spain undertook Europe's first conquests in the Americas. These two ventures, though not initially linked, eventually became cornerstones in the creation of the "Atlantic World."

Portuguese Expansion

As a young soldier fighting North African Moors with the Crusading Order of Christ, Prince Henry of Portugal (1394–1460) learned of Arab merchants' rich trade in gold and slaves across the Sahara. Seeking a maritime route to the source of this trade in West Africa, Henry founded a center for oceanic navigation. Henry's mariners, challenged to find a way through the treacherous waters off the northwest African coast, designed a better-handling vessel, the caravel, rigged with a lateen (triangular) sail that enabled the ship to tack into the wind. This innovation allowed them to sail far into the Atlantic, where they discovered and colonized the Madeira and Azore islands. From there, they sailed in 1435 to sub-Saharan Sierra Leone, where they exchanged salt, wine, and fish for African ivory and gold.

Colliding Cultures

Carefully consider each of the objects or texts below. What meanings might you—thinking like a historian—impart to them?

---

1. Mississippian warrior gorget (neck guard), A.D. **1250–1350.**

Source: The National Museum of the American Indian/George Gustav Heye Center/New York, NY William E. Meyer Collection 15/853.

2. Portuguese officer's account of de Soto's expedition, 1557. *This excerpt describes Indian resistance in the face of de Soto's campaign of conquest against Indians in the southeastern United States.*

[Spanish soldiers] went over a swampy land where the horsemen could not go. A half league from camp they came upon some Indian huts near the river; [but] the people who were inside them plunged into the river. They captured four Indian women, and twenty Indians came at us and attacked us so stoutly that we had to retreat to the camp, because of their being (as they are) so skillful with their weapons. Those people are so warlike and so quick that they make no account of foot soldiers; for if these go for them, they flee, and when their adversaries turn their backs they are immediately on them. The farthest they flee is the distance of an arrow shot. They are never quiet but always running and crossing from one side to another so that the crossbows or the arquebuses can not be aimed at them; and before a crossbowman can fire a shot, an Indian can shoot three or four arrows, and very seldom does he miss what he shoots at. If the arrow does not find armor, it penetrates as deeply as a crossbow. The bows are very long and the arrows are made of certain reeds like canes, very heavy and so tough that a sharpened cane passes through a shield. Some are pointed with a fish bone, as sharp as an awl, and others with a certain stone like a diamond point.

3. Duarte Lopez, *A Report on the Kingdom of Kongo,* **1591.** *A Portuguese explorer's account of his travels in southern Africa in the sixteenth century.*

[T]he Kingdom of Sofala lies between the two rivers, Magnice and Cuama, on the sea-coast. It is small in size, and has but few villages and towns. . . . It is peopled by Mohammedans, and the king himself belongs to the same sect. He pays allegiance to the crown of Portugal, in order not to be subject to the government of Monomotapa [Mutapa]. On this account the Portuguese have a fortress at the mouth of the River Cuama, trading with those countries in gold, amber, and ivory, all found on that coast, as well as in slaves, and giving in exchange silk stuffs and taffetas. . . . It is said, that from these regions the gold was brought by sea which served for Solomon's Temple at Jerusalem, a fact by no means improbable, for in these countries of Monomotapa are found several ancient buildings of stone, brick, and wood, and of such wonderful workmanship, and architecture, as is nowhere seen in the surrounding provinces.

The Kingdom of Monomotapa is extensive, and has a large population of Pagan heathens, who are black, of middle stature, swift of foot, and in battle fight with great bravery, their weapons being bows and arrows, and light darts. There are numerous kings tributary to Monomotapa, who constantly rebel and wage war against it. The Emperor maintains large armies, which in the provinces are divided into legions, after the manner of the Romans, for, being a great ruler, he must be at constant warfare in order to maintain his dominion. Amongst his warriors, those most renowned for bravery, are the female legions, greatly valued by the Emperor, being the sinews of his military strength.

4. **Benin figurine of a Portuguese soldier from the seventeenth century.** *This brass figure would have been kept on an altar or on the roof of the royal palace of Benin.*

Source: © The Trustees of the British Museum/Art Resource, NY.

5. **Sixteenth-century Portuguese coin made from African gold.** *Before the discovery of the Americas, half of the Old World's gold came from sub-Saharan Africa.*

Source: © The Trustees of the British Museum/Art Resource, NY.

6. **Sixteenth- or seventeenth-century Spanish silver real.** *Spain minted enormous quantities of American silver; much of it was shipped to Manila, where it was exchanged for Asian luxury goods.*

Source: © RMN-Grand Palais/Art Resource, NY.

Sources: (2) John E. Worth, "Account of the Northern Conquest and Discovery of Hernando de Soto by Rodrigo Rangel," trans. John E. Worth, in Lawrence A. Clayton et al., eds., *The De Soto Chronicles: The Expedition of Hernando de Soto to North America in 1539–1543* (University of Alabama Press, 1993), 59; (3) Filippo Pigafetta, *A Report of the Kingdom of Congo,* trans. Margarite Hutchinson (London: John Murray, 1881), 117–119.

ANALYZING THE EVIDENCE

1. What can you infer about cultural values among Mississippian peoples from source 1? About the cultural values of the Spanish and Portuguese from sources 5 and 6? What *can't* you infer from these objects?

2. How does de Soto describe the native peoples he encounters in Florida (source 2)? How does that compare to the traits of the African kingdoms that Lopez comments upon in source 3? Why might the king of Sofala prefer a Portuguese alliance to subjection to Monomotapa?

3. What does source 4 suggest about Benin relations with the Portuguese?

PUTTING IT ALL TOGETHER

What do these sources tell us about the ways Native Americans, Europeans, and Africans thought about themselves, perceived one another, and capitalized on cross-cultural exchanges as they came into sustained contact? Write a short essay that considers the connection between the impulses of warfare and commerce, which appear again and again in contact settings.

Banza in the Kingdom of Kongo, c. 1670

The city of Banza, or Mbanza Kongo, was the capital of the Kingdom of Kongo when Portuguese traders first arrived in 1483. Kongo's king, Nzinga a Nkuwu, chose to be baptized to cement an alliance with Portugal and took the name João I. Kongo became officially Christian and Banza came to be known as São Salvador. Duarte Lopez visited and described the city in 1578; this engraving shows the city as it appeared a century later. Banza in the Kingdom of Kongo, San Salvador, from Olfert Dapper, ca. 1668.

Henry's efforts were soon joined to those of Italian merchants, who were being forced out of eastern Mediterranean trade routes by the rising power of the Ottoman Empire. Cut off from Asia, Genoese traders sought an Atlantic route to the lucrative markets of the Indian Ocean. They began to work with Portuguese and Castilian mariners and monarchs to finance trading voyages, and the African coast and its offshore islands opened to their efforts. European voyagers discovered the Canaries, the Cape Verde Islands, and São Tomé; all of them became laboratories for the expansion of Mediterranean agriculture.

On these Atlantic islands, planters transformed local ecosystems to experiment with a variety of familiar cash crops: wheat, wine grapes, and woad, a blue dye plant; livestock and honeybees; and, where the climate permitted, sugar. By 1500,

IDENTIFY CAUSES
How did Europe's desire for an ocean route to Asia shape its contacts with Africa?

Madeira was producing 2,500 metric tons a year, and Madeira sugar was available — in small, expensive quantities — in London, Paris, Rome, and Constantinople. Most of the islands were unpopulated. The Canaries were the exception; it took Castilian adventurers decades to conquer the Guanches who lived there. Once defeated, they were enslaved to labor in the Canaries or on Madeira, where they carved irrigation canals into the island's steep rock cliffs.

Europeans made no such inroads on the continent of Africa itself. The coastal kingdoms were well defended, and yellow fever, malaria, and dysentery quickly struck down Europeans who spent any time in the interior of West Africa. Instead they maintained small, fortified trading posts on offshore islands or along the coast, usually as guests of the local king.

Portuguese mariners continued to look for an Atlantic route to Asia. In 1488, Bartolomeu Dias rounded the Cape of Good Hope, the southern tip of

Africa. Vasco da Gama reached East Africa in 1497 and India in the following year; his ships were mistaken for those of Chinese traders, the last pale-skinned men to arrive by sea. Although da Gama's inferior goods — tin basins, coarse cloth, honey, and coral beads — were snubbed by the Arab and Indian merchants along India's Malabar Coast, he managed to acquire a highly profitable cargo of cinnamon and pepper. Da Gama returned to India in 1502 with twenty-one fighting vessels, which outmaneuvered and outgunned the Arab fleets. Soon the Portuguese government set up fortified trading posts for its merchants at key points around the Indian Ocean, in Indonesia, and along the coast of China (Map 1.4). In a transition that sparked the momentous growth of European wealth and power, the Portuguese and then the Dutch replaced the Arabs as the leaders in Asian commerce.

The African Slave Trade

Portuguese traders likewise ousted Arab merchants as the prime purveyors of African slaves. Coerced labor — through slavery, serfdom, or indentured servitude — was the norm in most premodern societies, and in Africa slavery was widespread. Some Africans were held in bondage as security for debts; others were sold into servitude by their kin in exchange for food in times of famine; many others were war captives. Slaves were a key commodity of exchange, sold as agricultural laborers, concubines, or military recruits. Sometimes their descendants were freed, but others endured hereditary bondage. Sonni Ali (r. 1464–1492),

> **TRACE CHANGE OVER TIME**
> How was the African slave trade adapted to European needs?

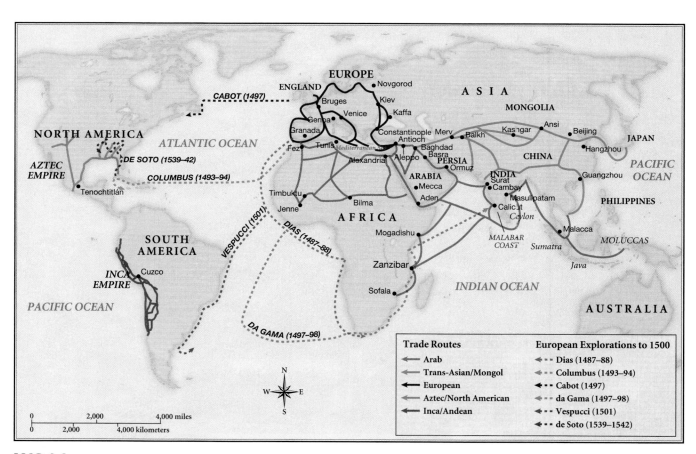

MAP 1.4

The Eurasian Trade System and European Maritime Ventures, c. 1500

For centuries, the Mediterranean Sea was the meeting point for the commerce of Europe, North Africa, and Asia — via the Silk Road from China and the Spice Route from India. Beginning in the 1490s, Portuguese, Spanish, and Dutch rulers and merchants subsidized Christian maritime explorers who discovered new trade routes around Africa and new sources of wealth in the Americas. These initiatives undermined the commercial primacy of the Arab Muslim–dominated Mediterranean.

the ruler of the powerful Songhai Empire, personally owned twelve "tribes" of hereditary agricultural slaves, many of them seized in raids against stateless peoples.

Slaves were also central to the trans-Saharan trade. When the renowned Tunisian adventurer Ibn Battuta crossed the Sahara from the Kingdom of Mali around 1350, he traveled with a caravan of six hundred female slaves, destined for domestic service or concubinage in North Africa, Egypt, and the Ottoman Empire. Between A.D. 700 and 1900, it is estimated that as many as nine million Africans were sold in the trans-Saharan slave trade.

Europeans initially were much more interested in trading for gold and other commodities than in trading for human beings, but gradually they discovered the enormous value of human trafficking. To exploit and redirect the existing African slave trade, Portuguese merchants established fortified trading posts like those in the Indian Ocean beginning at Elmina in 1482, where they bought gold and slaves from African princes and warlords. First they enslaved a few thousand Africans each year to work on sugar plantations on São Tomé, Cape Verde, the Azores, and Madeira; they also sold slaves in Lisbon, which soon had an African population of 9,000. After 1550, the Atlantic slave trade, a forced diaspora of African peoples, expanded enormously as Europeans set up sugar plantations in Brazil and the West Indies.

Sixteenth-Century Incursions

As Portuguese traders sailed south and east, the Spanish monarchs Ferdinand II of Aragon and Isabella I of Castile financed an explorer who looked to the west. As Renaissance rulers, Ferdinand (r. 1474–1516) and Isabella (r. 1474–1504) saw national unity and foreign commerce as the keys to power and prosperity. Married in an arranged match to combine their Christian

The Map Behind Columbus's Voyage

In 1489, Henricus Martellus, a German cartographer living in Florence, produced this huge (4 feet by 6 feet) view of the known world, probably working from a map devised by Christopher Columbus's brother, Bartholomew. The map uses the spatial projection of the ancient Greek philosopher Claudius Ptolemy (A.D. 90–168) and incorporates information from Marco Polo's explorations in Asia and Bartolomeu Dias's recent voyage around the tip of Africa. Most important, it greatly exaggerates the width of Eurasia, thereby suggesting that Asia lies only 5,000 miles west of Europe (rather than the actual distance of 15,000 miles). Using Martellus's map, Columbus persuaded the Spanish monarchs to support his westward voyage. Bildarchiv Preussischer Kulturbesitz/Art Resource, NY.

kingdoms, the young rulers completed the centuries-long *reconquista*, the campaign by Spanish Catholics to drive Muslim Arabs from the European mainland, by capturing Granada, the last Islamic territory in Western Europe, in 1492. Using Catholicism to build a sense of "Spanishness," they launched the brutal Inquisition against suspected Christian heretics and expelled or forcibly converted thousands of Jews and Muslims.

Columbus and the Caribbean Simultaneously, Ferdinand and Isabella sought trade and empire by subsidizing the voyages of Christopher Columbus, an ambitious and daring mariner from Genoa. Columbus believed that the Atlantic Ocean, long feared by Arab merchants as a 10,000-mile-wide "green sea of darkness," was a much narrower channel of water separating Europe from Asia. After cajoling and lobbying for six years, Columbus persuaded Genoese investors in Seville; influential courtiers; and, finally, Ferdinand and Isabella to accept his dubious theories and finance a western voyage to Asia.

Columbus set sail in three small ships in August 1492. Six weeks later, after a perilous voyage of 3,000 miles, he disembarked on an island in the present-day Bahamas. Believing that he had reached Asia — "the Indies," in fifteenth-century parlance — Columbus called the native inhabitants Indians and the islands the West Indies. He was surprised by the crude living conditions but expected the native peoples "easily [to] be made Christians." He claimed the islands for Spain and then explored the neighboring Caribbean islands and demanded tribute from the local Taino, Arawak, and Carib peoples. Buoyed by stories of rivers of gold lying "to the west," Columbus left forty men on the island of Hispaniola (present-day Haiti and the Dominican Republic) and returned triumphantly to Spain (Map 1.5).

 To see a longer excerpt of Columbus's views of the West Indies, along with other primary sources from this period, see *Sources for America's History.*

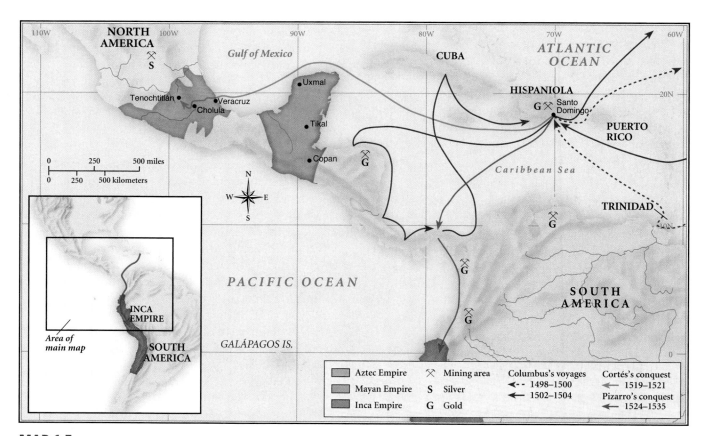

MAP 1.5

The Spanish Conquest of America's Great Empires

The Spanish first invaded the islands of the Caribbean, largely wiping out the native peoples. Rumors of a gold-rich civilization led to Cortés's invasion of the Aztec Empire in 1519. By 1535, other Spanish conquistadors had conquered the Mayan temple cities and the Inca empire in Peru, completing one of the great conquests in world history.

The Spanish Conquest of Mexico

How could a Spanish force of 600 men take control of an empire of 20 million people? That the Spanish had steel swords, armor, some guns, horses, and attack dogs certainly gave them a military advantage. Still, concerted attack by the armies of the Aztecs and their allies would have overwhelmed the invaders before they reached the capital of Tenochtitlán. Why was there no such attack? One reason was that Cortés's force was bolstered by a sizable army from Tlaxcala, an independent kingdom hostile to the Aztecs. A later tradition also suggests that some Aztecs, including Moctezuma, thought that Cortés might be an emissary of their god Quetzalcoatl.

These documents come from people who experienced the conquest. Consider them first as *sources*: How trustworthy are they? Are they biased in any way? Then think about their *contents*: Do their accounts agree? Do they explain why the Spaniards reached the city unmolested?

Bernal Díaz del Castillo
Cortés and Moctezuma Meet

Bernal Díaz was an unlikely chronicler of great events. Born poor, he went to America as a common soldier in 1514 and served under conquistadors in Panama and Cuba. In 1519, Bernal Díaz joined Cortés's expedition, fought in many battles, and as a reward received an estate in present-day Guatemala. In his old age, Díaz wrote *The True History of the Conquest of New Spain*, a compelling memoir written from the perspective of a common soldier. In fresh and straightforward prose, it depicts the conquest as a divinely blessed event that saved the non-Aztec peoples of Mexico from a barbarous regime.

The Great Moctezuma had sent these great Caciques in advance to receive us, and when they came before Cortés they bade us welcome in their language, and as a sign of peace, they touched their hands against the ground. . . .

When we arrived near to [Tenochtitlán], . . . the Great Moctezuma got down from his litter, and those great Caciques [aristocrats] supported him with their arms beneath a marvelously rich canopy of green coloured feathers with much gold and silver embroidery . . . which was wonderful to look at. The Great Moctezuma was richly attired according to his usage, and he was shod with sandals, the soles were of gold and the upper part adorned with precious stones. . . .

Many other Lords walked before the Great Moctezuma, sweeping the ground where he would tread and spreading cloths on it, so that he should not tread on the earth. Not one of these chieftains dared even to think of looking him in the face, but kept their eyes lowered with great reverence. . . .

When Cortés was told that the Great Moctezuma was approaching, and he saw him coming, he dismounted from his horse, and when he was near Moctezuma, they simultaneously paid great reverence to one another. Moctezuma bade him welcome and our Cortés replied through Doña Marina [Malinali, also called Malinche, Cortés's Indian interpreter who bore him a child] wishing him very good health. . . . And then Cortés brought out a necklace which he had ready at hand, made of glass stones, . . . which have within them many patterns of diverse colours, these were strung on a cord of gold and with musk so that it should have a sweet scent, and he placed it round the neck of the Great Moctezuma. . . . Then Cortés through the mouth of Doña Marina told him that now his heart rejoiced having seen such a great Prince, and that he took it as a great honour that he had come in person to meet him. . . .

Thus space was made for us to enter the streets of Mexico, without being so much crowded. But who could now count the multitude of men and women and boys who were in the streets and in canoes on the canals, who had come out to see us. It was indeed wonderful. . . . Coming to think it over it seems to be a great mercy that our Lord Jesus Christ was pleased to give us grace and courage to dare to enter into such a city; and for the many times He has saved me from danger of death . . . I give Him sincere thanks. . . .

They took us to lodge in some large houses, where there were apartments for all of us, for they had belonged to the father of the Great Moctezuma, who was named Axayaca. . . .

Cortés thanked Moctezuma through our interpreters, and Moctezuma replied, "Malinche, you and your brethren are in your own house, rest awhile," and then he went to his palaces, which were not far away, and we divided our lodgings by companies, and placed the artillery pointing in a convenient direction, and the order which we had to keep was clearly explained to us, and that we were to be much on the alert, both the cavalry and all of us soldiers. A sumptuous dinner was provided for us according to their use and custom, and we ate it at once. So this was our lucky and daring entry into the great city of Tenochtitlan Mexico on the 8th day of November the year of our Saviour Jesus Christ, 1519.

Source: Bernal Díaz del Castillo, *The True History of the Conquest of New Spain*, trans. A. P. Maudslay (1632; London: Routledge, 1928), 272–275.

Friar Bernardino de Sahagún

Aztec Elders Describe the Behavior of Moctezuma

During the 1550s, Friar Bernardino de Sahagún published *General History of the Things of New Spain*. His *History* compiled the stories of Aztec elders who lived through the conquest. They told their stories to Sahagún in a repetitive style, according to the conventions of Aztec oral histories, and he translated them into Spanish.

Moctezuma enjoyed no sleep, no food, no one spoke to him. Whatsoever he did, it was as if he were in torment. Ofttimes it was as if he sighed, became weak, felt weak. . . . Wherefore he said, "What will now befall us? Who indeed stands [in charge]? Alas, until now, I. In great torment is my heart; as if it were washed in chili water it indeed burns." And when he had so heard what the messengers reported, he was terrified, he was astounded. . . . Especially did it cause him to faint away when he heard how the gun, at [the Spaniards'] command, discharged: how it resounded as if it thundered when it went off. It indeed bereft one of strength; it shut off one's ears. And when it discharged, something like a round pebble came forth from within. Fire went showering forth; sparks went blazing forth. And its smoke smelled very foul; it had a fetid odor which verily wounded the head. And when [the shot] struck a mountain, it was as if it were destroyed, dissolved . . . as if someone blew it away.

All iron was their war array. In iron they clothed themselves. With iron they covered their heads. Iron were their swords. Iron were their crossbows. Iron were their shields. Iron were their lances. And those which bore them upon their backs, their deer [horses], were as tall as roof terraces.

And their bodies were everywhere covered; only their faces appeared. They were very white; they had chalky faces; they had yellow hair, though the hair of some was black. . . . And when Moctezuma so heard, he was much terrified. It was as if he fainted away. His heart saddened; his heart failed him. . . . [but] he made himself resolute; he put forth great effort; he quieted, he controlled his heart; he submitted himself entirely to whatsoever he was to see, at which he was to marvel. . . . [He then greeted Cortés, as described above.]

And when [the Spaniards] were well settled, they thereupon inquired of Moctezuma as to all the city's treasure . . . the devices, the shields. Much did they importune him; with great zeal they sought gold. . . . Thereupon were brought forth all the brilliant things; the shields, the golden discs, the devils' necklaces, the golden nose crescents, the golden leg bands, the golden arm bands, the golden forehead bands.

Source: From Friar Bernardino de Sahagún, *Florentine Codex: General History of New Spain*, translated by Arthur O. Anderson and Charles E. Dibble. Copyright © 1975. Reprinted by permission of Utah Press.

QUESTIONS FOR ANALYSIS

1. Both Díaz's account and that of the Aztec elders were written in retrospect, and both reflect their authors' awareness of the impending conquest. Compare the tone of these accounts. How does each reflect the author's knowledge of what is to come?

2. Why does Moctezuma pay "great reverence" to Cortés? Why does Cortés return the honor? What is the strategy of each leader?

3. What is Díaz's explanation for the easy entry of the Spanish into the city? What explanation is suggested by the elders' account?

Although Columbus brought back no gold, the Spanish monarchs supported three more of his voyages. Columbus colonized the West Indies with more than 1,000 Spanish settlers—all men—and hundreds of domestic animals. But he failed to find either golden treasures or great kingdoms, and his death in 1506 went virtually unnoticed.

A German geographer soon labeled the newly found continents America in honor of a Florentine explorer, Amerigo Vespucci. Vespucci, who had explored the coast of present-day South America around 1500, denied that the region was part of Asia. He called it a *nuevo mundo*, a "new world." The Spanish crown called the two continents *Las Indias* ("the Indies") and wanted to make them a new Spanish world.

The Spanish Invasion

After brutally subduing the Arawaks and Tainos on Hispaniola, the Spanish probed the mainland for gold and slaves. In 1513, Juan Ponce de León explored the coast of Florida and gave that peninsula its name. In the same year, Vasco Núñez de Balboa crossed the Isthmus of Darien (Panama) and became the first European to see the Pacific Ocean. Rumors of rich Indian kingdoms encouraged other Spaniards, including hardened veterans of the *reconquista*, to invade the mainland. The Spanish monarchs offered successful conquistadors noble titles, vast estates, and Indian laborers.

With these inducements before him, in 1519 Hernán Cortés (1485–1547) led an army of 600 men to the Yucatán Peninsula. Gathering allies among native peoples who chafed under Aztec rule, he marched on Tenochtitlán and challenged its ruler, Moctezuma. Awed by the Spanish invaders, Moctezuma received Cortés with great ceremony (American Voices, p. 32). However, Cortés soon took the emperor captive, and following a prolonged siege, he and his men captured the city. The conquest took a devastating toll: the

Mexican Counterattack

This image, which comes from a history of the Aztecs written in 1570 by the Spanish Dominican monk Diego Durán, illustrates a successful counterattack by Mexica warriors against Spanish soldiers prior to the final conquest of Tenochtitlán. The Spaniards try to hold their position as the Mexicans prepare to strike. Institut Amatller d'Art Hispanic/Arxiu Mas.

conquerors cut off the city's supply of food and water, and the residents of Tenochtitlán suffered spectacularly. By 1521, Cortés and his men had toppled the Aztec Empire.

The Spanish had a silent ally: disease. Having been separated from Eurasia for thousands of years, the inhabitants of the Americas had no immunities to common European diseases. After the Spaniards arrived, a massive smallpox epidemic ravaged Tenochtitlán, "striking everywhere in the city," according to an Aztec source, and killing Moctezuma's brother and thousands more. "They could not move, they could not stir. . . . Covered, mantled with pustules, very many people died of them." Subsequent outbreaks of smallpox, influenza, and measles killed hundreds of thousands of Indians and sapped the survivors' morale. Exploiting this demographic weakness, Cortés quickly extended Spanish rule over the Aztec Empire. His lieutenants then moved against the Mayan city-states of the Yucatán Peninsula, eventually conquering them as well.

In 1524, Francisco Pizarro set out to accomplish the same feat in Peru. By the time he and his small force of 168 men and 67 horses finally reached their destination in 1532, half of the Inca population had already died from European diseases. Weakened militarily and divided between rival claimants to the throne, the Inca nobility was easy prey. Pizarro killed Atahualpa, the last Inca emperor, and seized his enormous wealth. Although Inca resistance continued for a generation, the conquest was complete by 1535, and Spain was now the master of the wealthiest and most populous regions of the Western Hemisphere.

The Spanish invasion changed life forever in the Americas. Disease and warfare wiped out virtually all of the Indians of Hispaniola — at least 300,000 people. In Peru, the population of 9 million in 1530 plummeted to fewer than 500,000 a century later. Mesoamerica suffered the greatest losses: In one of the great demographic disasters in world history, its population of 20 million Native Americans in 1500 had dwindled to just 3 million in 1650.

Cabral and Brazil At the same time, Portuguese efforts to find a sailing route around the southern tip of Africa led to a surprising find. As Vasco da Gama and his contemporaries experimented with winds and currents, their voyages carried them ever farther away from the African coast and into the Atlantic. On one such voyage in 1500, the Portuguese commander Pedro Alvares Cabral and his fleet were surprised to see land loom up in the west. Cabral named his discovery Ihla da Vera Cruz — the Island of the True Cross — and

continued on his way toward India. Others soon followed and changed the region's name to Brazil after the indigenous tree that yielded a valuable red dye; for several decades, Portuguese sailors traded with the Tupi Indians for brazilwood. Then in the 1530s, to secure Portugal's claim, King Dom João III sent settlers who began the long, painstaking process of carving out sugar plantations in the coastal lowlands. For several decades, Native Americans supplied most of the labor for these operations, but African slaves gradually replaced them. Brazil would soon become the world's leading producer of sugar; it would also devour African lives. By introducing the plantation system to the Americas — a form of estate agriculture using slave labor that was pioneered by Italian merchants and crusading knights in the twelfth century and transplanted to the islands off the coast of Africa in the fifteenth century — the Portuguese set in motion one of the most significant developments of the early modern era.

By the end of the sixteenth century, the European colonization of the Americas had barely begun. Yet several of its most important elements were already taking shape. Spanish efforts demonstrated that densely populated empires were especially vulnerable to conquest and were also especially valuable sources of wealth. The Portuguese had discovered the viability of sugar plantations in the tropical regions of the Americas and pioneered the transatlantic slave trade as a way of manning them. And contacts with native peoples revealed their devastating vulnerabilities to Eurasian diseases — one part of the larger phenomenon of the Columbian Exchange (discussed in Chapter 2).

SUMMARY

Native American, European, and African societies developed independently over thousands of years before they experienced direct contacts with one another. In the Americas, residents of Mesoamerica and the Andes were fully sedentary (with individual ownership of land and intensive agriculture), but elsewhere societies were semisedentary (with central fields and villages that were occupied seasonally) or nonsedentary (hunter-gatherers). West and Central Africa also had a mix of sedentary, semisedentary, and nonsedentary settlements. Western Europe, by contrast, was predominantly sedentary. All three continents had a complex patchwork of political organization, from empires, to kingdoms and chiefdoms, to principalities, duchies, and ministates; everywhere, rulership was imbued with notions of spiritual power. Ruling classes relied on warfare, trade, and tribute (or taxes) to dominate those around them and accumulate precious goods that helped to set them apart from ordinary laborers, but they also bore responsibility for the well-being of their subjects and offered them various forms of protection.

As Portuguese and Castilian (later Spanish) seafarers pushed into the Atlantic, they set in motion a chain of events whose consequences they could scarcely imagine. From a coastal trade with Africa that was secondary to their efforts to reach the Indian Ocean, from the miscalculations of Columbus and the happy accident of Cabral, developed a pattern of transatlantic exploration, conquest, and exploitation that no one could have foretold or planned. In the tropical zones of the Caribbean and coastal Brazil, invading Europeans enslaved Native Americans and quickly drove them into extinction or exile. The demands of plantation agriculture soon led Europeans to import slaves from Africa, initiating a transatlantic trade that would destroy African lives on both sides of the ocean. And two of the greatest empires in the world—the Aztec and Incan empires—collapsed in response to unseen biological forces that acted in concert with small invading armies.

European Map of Brazil, c. 1519

This lavishly illustrated map of Brazil is drawn from the Miller Atlas, made by order of King Manuel I of Portugal around 1519. It features images of Indians harvesting brazilwood; macaws and other colorful birds; a monkey; and—improbably—a fire-breathing dragon. Note, too, the dense annotations and place names along the coast—a reminder that Portuguese familiarity with Brazil was confined almost entirely to the seaboard. Bibliotheque Nationale de France.

CHAPTER REVIEW

MAKE IT STICK   Go to **LearningCurve** to retain what you've read.

TERMS TO KNOW   Identify and explain the significance of each term below.

Key Concepts and Events

tribute (p. 8)
matriarchy (p. 15)
animism (p. 17)
patriarchy (p. 18)
primogeniture (p. 18)
peasants (p. 18)
republic (p. 19)
civic humanism (p. 20)
Renaissance (p. 20)
guilds (p. 20)

Christianity (p. 21)
heresy (p. 22)
Islam (p. 22)
Crusades (p. 22)
predestination (p. 22)
Protestant Reformation (p. 22)
Counter-Reformation (p. 22)
trans-Saharan trade (p. 23)
reconquista (p. 31)

Key People

Hiawatha (p. 13)
Martin Luther (p. 22)
Mansa Musa (p. 23)
Vasco da Gama (p. 29)

Christopher Columbus (p. 31)
Hernán Cortés (p. 34)
Moctezuma (p. 34)
Pedro Alvares Cabral (p. 35)

REVIEW QUESTIONS   Answer these questions to demonstrate your understanding of the chapter's main ideas.

1. How did the rulers of Native American, European, and African empires and kingdoms secure and sustain their power? How did ordinary people benefit from, or suffer under, their rule?

2. What role did religious and spiritual ideas play in shaping the experience of ordinary people on the three continents?

3. Why was long-distance trade in exotic goods such an important phenomenon in North America, Europe, and Africa?

4. Compare the societies of the eastern woodlands of North America with the kingdoms of Western Europe. What similarities do you see? Differences? How do you weigh their relative importance?

5. **THEMATIC UNDERSTANDING** Review the events listed under "Peopling" and "Work, Exchange, and Technology" on the thematic timeline on page 5. How did contacts among Europeans, Native Americans, and Africans alter the economies of the three continents?

MAKING CONNECTIONS

Recognize the larger developments and continuities within and across chapters by answering these questions.

1. **ACROSS TIME AND PLACE** The century following the first contacts among Europe, sub-Saharan Africa, and the Americas brought some of the most momentous changes in world history: a dramatic reconfiguration of human populations across the globe, new patterns of trade and warfare, and immense challenges to peoples' worldviews. Thinking about our contemporary world, what monumental changes are currently affecting our lives? How would you compare them with the events described in this chapter?

2. **VISUAL EVIDENCE** Return to the image of *The Last Judgment* on page 21. How does the emphasis on universal truth and everlasting punishment and reward make Christianity different from animism? How might faith in such a religious system shape the values and priorities of believers?

MORE TO EXPLORE

Start here to learn more about the events discussed in this chapter.

Philip D. Curtin, *The Rise and Fall of the Plantation Complex,* 2nd ed. (1998). Traces the long evolution of plantations and slavery in world history.

Peter C. Mancall, ed., *Travel Narratives from the Age of Discovery* (2006). Travelers' accounts from Asia, Africa, the Americas, and Europe.

Charles C. Mann, *1491* (2005) and *1493* (2011). These two books explore the Americas before Columbus and the global changes unleashed by his voyages.

David Northrup, *Africa's Discovery of Europe: 1450–1850,* 2nd ed. (2008). European-African interactions from an African perspective.

Timothy R. Pauketat, *Cahokia* (2009). An evocative account of North America's great city and archaeologists' efforts to unearth it.

"1492: An Ongoing Voyage" (**loc.gov/exhibits/1492/intro.html**). Offers images and analysis of the native cultures of the Western Hemisphere.

TIMELINE

Ask yourself why this chapter begins and ends with these dates and then identify the links among related events.

c. 13,000–3000 B.C.	• Asian migrants reach North America
c. 6000 B.C.	• Domestication of maize begins in Mesoamerica
312	• Roman emperor Constantine converts to Christianity
c. 600	• Pueblo cultures emerge
632	• Death of Muhammad
632–1100	• Arab people adopt Islam and spread its influence
c. 800	• Ghana Empire emerges
c. 1000	• Irrigation developed by Hohokam, Mogollon, and Anasazi peoples
c. 1000–1350	• Development of Mississippian culture
c. 1050	• The founding of Cahokia
1096–1291	• Crusades link Europe with Arab trade routes
c. 1150	• Chaco Canyon abandoned
c. 1200	• Mali Empire emerges
1300–1450	• The Renaissance in Italy
c. 1325	• Aztecs establish capital at Tenochtitlán
1326	• Mansa Musa's pilgrimage to Mecca
c. 1350	• The Black Death sweeps Europe; Cahokia goes into rapid decline
c. 1400	• Songhai Empire emerges
1435	• Portuguese trade begins along West and Central African coasts
1492	• Christopher Columbus makes first voyage to America
1497–1498	• Portugal's Vasco da Gama reaches East Africa and India
1500	• Pedro Alvares Cabral encounters Brazil
c. 1500	• Founding of the Iroquois Confederacy
1513	• Juan Ponce de León explores Florida
1517	• Martin Luther sparks Protestant Reformation
1519–1521	• Hernán Cortés conquers Aztec Empire
1532–1535	• Francisco Pizarro vanquishes Incas
1536	• John Calvin publishes *Institutes of the Christian Religion*
1540	• De Soto meets the Lady of Cofachiqui; founding of the Jesuit order
1578	• Duarte Lopez visits the Kongo capital

KEY TURNING POINTS: The domestication of maize (6000 B.C.), the founding of Tenochtit-lán (1325), and the conquest of the Aztec empire (1519–1521). How did the domestication of maize make the city of Tenochtitlán possible? What characteristics of the Aztec empire and its capital city made it vulnerable to conquest?

2

American Experiments
1521–1700

Beginning in the 1660s, legislators in Virginia and Maryland hammered out the legal definition of **chattel slavery**: the ownership of human beings as property. The institution of slavery — which would profoundly affect African Americans and shape much of American history — had been obsolete in England for centuries, and articulating its logic required lawmakers to reverse some of the most basic presumptions of English law. For example, in 1662 a Virginia statute declared, "all children borne in this country shalbe held bond or free only according to the condition of the mother." This idea — that a child's legal status derived from the mother, rather than the father — ran contrary to the patriarchal foundations of English law. The men who sat in Virginia's House of Burgesses would not propose such a thing lightly. Why would they decide that the principle of patriarchal descent, which was so fundamental to their own worlds, was inappropriate for their slaves?

The question needed to be addressed, according to the statute's preamble, since "doubts have arisen whether children got by an Englishman upon a negro woman should be slave or free." One such case involved Elizabeth Key, a woman whose father was a free Englishman and mother was an African slave. She petitioned for her freedom in 1656, based on her father's status. Her lawyer was an Englishman named William Greensted. He not only took Key's case, but he also fathered two of her children and, eventually, married her. Key won her case and her freedom from bondage. Elizabeth Key escaped her mother's fate — a life in slavery — because her father and her husband were both free Englishmen. The 1662 statute aimed to close Key's avenue to freedom.

The process by which the institution of chattel slavery was molded to the needs of colonial planters is just one example of the way Europeans adapted the principles they brought with them to the unfamiliar demands of their new surroundings. In the showdown between people like Elizabeth Key and William Greensted, on the one hand, and the members of Virginia's House of Burgesses on the other, we see how people in disorienting circumstances — some in positions in power, others in various states of subjection to their social and political superiors — scrambled to make sense of their world and bend its rules to their advantage. Through countless contests of power and authority like this one, the outlines of a new world gradually began to emerge from the collision of cultures.

By 1700, three distinct types of colonies had developed in the Americas: the tribute colonies created in Mexico and Peru, which relied initially on the wealth and labor of indigenous peoples; plantation colonies, where sugar and other tropical and subtropical crops could be produced with bound labor; and **neo-Europes**, where colonists sought to replicate, or at least approximate, economies and social structures they knew at home.

IDENTIFY THE BIG IDEA

In what ways did European migrants transfer familiar patterns and institutions to their colonies in the Americas, and in what ways did they create new American worlds? How did Native Americans adapt to the growing presence of Europeans among them?

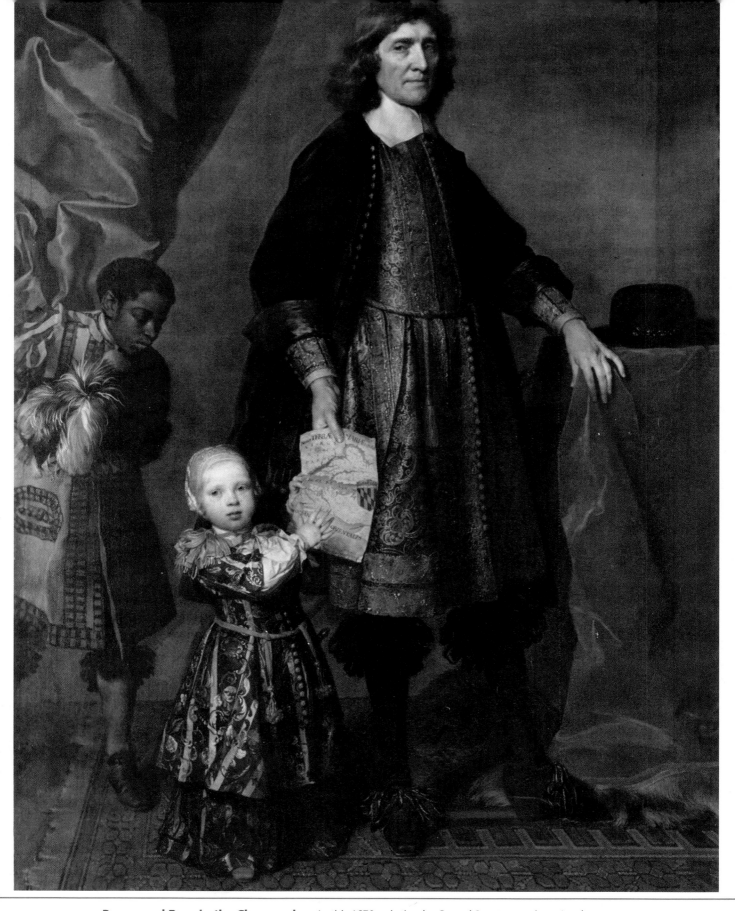

Power and Race in the Chesapeake   In this 1670 painting by Gerard Soest, proprietor Lord Baltimore holds a map of Maryland, the colony he owned and which would soon belong to his grandson Cecil Calvert, shown in the painting as already grasping his magnificent inheritance. The presence of a young African servant foretells the importance of slave labor in the post-1700 economy of the Chesapeake colonies.

Spain's Tribute Colonies

European interest in the Americas took shape under the influence of Spain's conquest of the Aztec and Inca empires. There, Spanish colonizers capitalized on pre-existing systems of tribute and labor discipline to tap the enormous wealth of Mesoamerica and the Andes. Once native rulers were overthrown, the Spanish monarchs transferred their institutions — municipal councils, the legal code, the Catholic Church — to America; the empire was centrally controlled to protect the crown's immensely valuable holdings. The Spanish conquest also set in motion a global ecological transformation through a vast intercontinental movement of plants, animals, and diseases that historians call the Columbian Exchange. And the conquest triggered hostile responses from Spain's European rivals, especially the Protestant Dutch and English (Figure 2.1).

A New American World

After Cortés toppled Moctezuma and Pizarro defeated Atahualpa (see pages 34–35), leading conquistadors received *encomiendas* from the crown, which allowed them to claim tribute in labor and goods from Indian communities. Later these grants were repartitioned, but the pattern was set early: prominent men controlled vast resources and monopolized Indian labor. The value of these grants was dramatically enhanced by the discovery of gold and, especially, silver deposits in both Mexico and the Andes. In the decades after the conquest, mines were developed in Zacatecas, in Guanajuato, and — most famously — at Potosí, high in the Andes. Spanish officials co-opted the *mita* system, which made laborers available to the Inca Empire, to force Indian workers into the mines. At its peak, Potosí

alone produced 200 tons of silver per year, accounting for half the world's supply.

The two great indigenous empires of the Americas thus became the core of an astonishingly wealthy European empire. Vast amounts of silver poured across the Pacific Ocean to China, where it was minted into money; in exchange, Spain received valuable Chinese silks, spices, and ceramics. In Europe, the gold that had formerly honored Aztec and Inca gods now flowed into the countinghouses of Spain and gilded the Catholic churches of Europe. The Spanish crown benefitted enormously from all this wealth — at least initially. In the long run, it triggered ruinous inflation. As a French traveler noted in 1603: "Everything is dear [expensive] in Spain, except silver."

A new society took shape on the conquered lands. Between 1500 and 1650, at least 350,000 Spaniards migrated to Mesoamerica and the Andes. About two-thirds were males drawn from a cross section of Spanish society, many of them skilled tradesmen. Also arriving were 250,000–300,000 Africans. Racial mixture was widespread, and such groups as mestizos (Spaniard-Indian) and mulattos (Spaniard-African) grew rapidly. Zambo (Indian-African) populations developed gradually as well. Over time, a system of increasingly complex racial categories developed — the "casta system" — buttressed by a legal code that differentiated among the principal groups.

Indians were always in the majority in Mexico and Peru, but profound changes came as their numbers declined and peoples of Spanish and mixed-race descent grew in number. Spaniards initially congregated in cities, but gradually they moved into the countryside, creating large estates (known as haciendas) and regional networks of market exchange. Most Indians remained in their native communities, under the authority of native rulers and speaking native

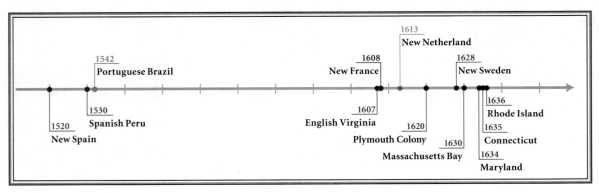

FIGURE 2.1
Chronology of European Colonies in the Americas

languages. However, Spanish priests suppressed religious ceremonies and texts and converted natives to Christianity *en masse*. Catholicism was transformed in the process: Catholic parishes took their form from Indian communities; indigenous ideas and expectations reshaped Church practices; and new forms of Native American Christianity emerged in both regions.

The Columbian Exchange

The Spanish invasion permanently altered the natural as well as the human environment. Smallpox, influenza, measles, yellow fever, and other silent killers carried from Europe and Africa ravaged Indian communities, whose inhabitants had never encountered these diseases before and thus had no immunity to them. In the densely populated core areas, populations declined by 90 percent or more in the first century of contact with Europeans. On islands and in the tropical lowlands, the toll was even heavier; native populations were often wiped out altogether. Syphilis was the only significant illness that traveled in the opposite direction: Columbus's sailors carried a virulent strain of the sexually transmitted disease back to Europe with them.

The movement of diseases and peoples across the Atlantic was part of a larger pattern of biological transformation that historians call the **Columbian Exchange** (Map 2.1). Foods of the Western Hemisphere — especially maize, potatoes, manioc, sweet potatoes, and tomatoes — significantly increased agricultural yields and population growth in other continents. Maize and potatoes, for example, reached China around 1700; in the following century, the Chinese population tripled from 100 million to 300 million. At the same time, many animals, plants, and germs were carried to the Americas. European livestock transformed American landscapes. While Native Americans domesticated very few animals — dogs and llamas were the principal exceptions — Europeans brought an enormous Old World bestiary to the Americas, including cattle, swine, horses, oxen, chickens, and honeybees. Eurasian grain crops — wheat, barley, rye, and rice — made the transatlantic voyage along with inadvertent imports like dandelions and other weeds.

> **PLACE EVENTS IN CONTEXT**
> How did the ecological context of colonization shape interactions between Europeans and Native Americans?

The Protestant Challenge to Spain

Beyond the core regions of its empire, Spain claimed vast American dominions but struggled to hold them. Controlling the Caribbean basin, which was essential for Spain's transatlantic shipping routes, was especially difficult, since the net of tiny islands spanning the eastern Caribbean — the Lesser Antilles — provided many safe harbors for pirates and privateers. Fortified outposts in Havana and St. Augustine provided some

Smallpox Victims

Hans Staden, a German soldier who was shipwrecked in Brazil in 1552, was captured by a Tupinambá Indian named Jeppipo Wasu. Shortly thereafter, Wasu and his family traveled to a neighboring village as smallpox ravaged the population; when they returned, they were very sick. Wasu recovered, but he lost his mother, two brothers, and two children. This engraving, which depicts Wasu's return amid his townspeople's grief, appeared in the third volume of Theodor de Bry's monumental *America*, published in Frankfurt in 1593. Courtesy of the John Carter Brown Library at Brown University.

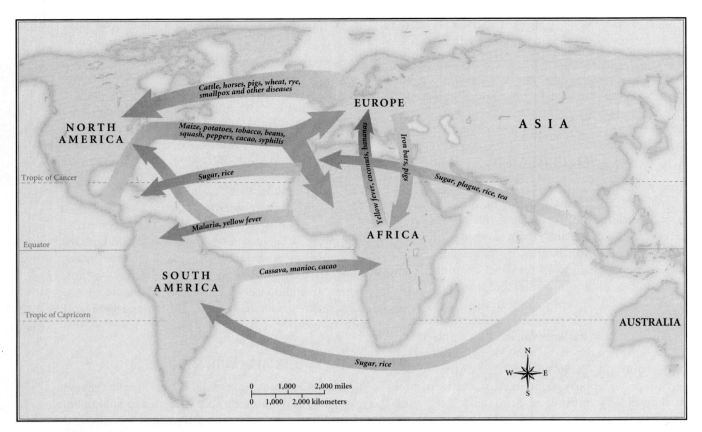

MAP 2.1
The Columbian Exchange

As European traders and adventurers traversed the world between 1430 and 1600, they began what historians call the Columbian Exchange, a vast intercontinental movement of plants, animals, and diseases that changed the course of historical development. The nutritious, high-yielding American crops of corn and potatoes enriched the diets of Europeans, Africans, and Asians. However, the Eurasian and African diseases of smallpox, diphtheria, malaria, and yellow fever nearly wiped out the native inhabitants of the Western Hemisphere and virtually ensured that they would lose control of their lands.

protection, but they were never sufficient to keep enemies at bay.

And Spain had powerful enemies, their animosity sharpened by the Protestant Reformation and the resulting split in European Christendom (see p. 22). In the wake of Martin Luther's attack on the Catholic Church, the Protestant critique of Catholicism broadened and deepened. Gold and silver from Mexico and Peru made Spain the wealthiest nation in Europe, and King Philip II (r. 1556–1598) — an ardent Catholic — its most powerful ruler. Philip was determined to root out challenges to the Catholic Church wherever they appeared. One such place was in the Spanish Netherlands, a collection of Dutch- and Flemish-speaking provinces that had grown wealthy from textile manufacturing and trade with Portuguese outposts in Africa and Asia. To protect their Calvinist faith and political liberties, they revolted against Spanish rule in

1566. After fifteen years of war, the seven northern provinces declared their independence, becoming the Dutch Republic (or Holland) in 1581.

The English king Henry VIII (r. 1509–1547) initially opposed Protestantism. However, when the pope refused to annul his marriage to the Spanish princess Catherine of Aragon in 1534, Henry broke with Rome and placed himself at the head of the new Church of England, which promptly granted an annulment. Although Henry's new church maintained most Catholic doctrines and practices, Protestant teachings continued to spread. Faced with popular pressure for reform, Henry's daughter and successor, Queen Elizabeth I (r. 1558–1603), approved a Protestant confession of faith. At the same time, however, Elizabeth retained the Catholic ritual of Holy Communion and left the Church in the hands of Anglican bishops and archbishops. Elizabeth's compromises angered radical

Queen Elizabeth Receiving Dutch Ambassadors

This sixteenth-century Dutch painting by an anonymous artist depicts a pair of Dutch ambassadors being received by England's Queen Elizabeth I. The seventeen provinces that constituted the Dutch Republic were in rebellion against Spanish rule in the later decades of the sixteenth century and hoped for Elizabeth's support. In 1585 she signed the Treaty of Nonsuch, pledging her support for the Dutch cause. An undeclared war with Spain ensued, punctuated by the defeat of the Spanish Armada in 1588. © Museumslandschaft Hessen Kassel/The Bridgeman Art Library.

Protestants, but the independent Anglican Church was anathema to the Spanish king, Philip II.

Elizabeth supported a generation of English seafarers who took increasingly aggressive actions against Spanish control of American wealth. The most famous of these Elizabethan "sea dogs" was Francis Drake, a rough-hewn, devoutly Protestant farmer's son from Devon who took to the sea and became a scourge to Philip's American interests. In 1577, he ventured into the Pacific to disrupt Spanish shipping to Manila. Drake's fleet lost three ships and a hundred men, but the survivors completed the first English circumnavigation of the globe and captured two Spanish treasure ships. When Drake's flagship, the *Golden Hind,* returned to England in 1580, it brought enough silver, gold, silk, and spices to bring his investors a 4,700 percent return on their investment.

At the same time, Elizabeth supported military expeditions that imposed English rule over Gaelic-speaking Catholic Ireland. Calling the Irish "wild savages" who were "more barbarous and more brutish in their customs . . . than in any other part of the world," English soldiers brutally massacred thousands, prefiguring the treatment of Indians in North America. To meet Elizabeth's challenges, Philip sent a Spanish Armada — 130 ships and 30,000 men — against England in 1588. Philip intended to restore the Roman Church in England and then to wipe out Calvinism in Holland. But he failed utterly: a fierce storm and English ships destroyed the Spanish fleet.

Philip continued to spend his American gold and silver on religious wars, an ill-advised policy that diverted workers and resources from Spain's fledgling industries. The gold was like a "shewer of Raine," complained one critic, that left "no benefite behind." Oppressed by high taxes on agriculture and fearful of military service, more than 200,000 residents of Castile, once the most prosperous region of Spain, migrated to America. By the time of Philip's death in 1598, Spain was in serious economic decline.

By contrast, England grew significantly during the sixteenth century, its economy stimulated, as colonial advocate Richard Hakluyt noted, by a "wounderful increase of our people." As England's population soared from 3 million in 1500 to 5 million in 1630, its monarchs supported the expansion of commerce and manufacturing. English merchants had long supplied European weavers with high-quality wool; around 1500, they created their own **outwork** textile industry. Merchants bought wool from the owners of great estates and sent it "out" to landless peasants in small cottages to spin and weave into cloth. The government aided textile entrepreneurs by setting low wage rates and helped merchants by giving them monopolies in foreign markets.

This system of state-assisted manufacturing and trade became known as **mercantilism**. By encouraging textile production, Elizabeth reduced imports and increased exports. The resulting favorable balance of trade caused gold and silver to flow into England and stimulated further economic expansion. Increased trade

TRACE CHANGE OVER TIME
Why did Spain's economy deteriorate and England's economy improve in the sixteenth century?

with Turkey and India also boosted import duties, which swelled the royal treasury and the monarch's power. By 1600, Elizabeth's mercantile policies had laid the foundations for overseas colonization. Now the English had the merchant fleet and wealth needed to challenge Spain's control of the Western Hemisphere.

Plantation Colonies

As Spain hammered out its American empire and struggled against its Protestant rivals, Portugal, England, France, and the Netherlands created successful plantation settlements in Brazil, Jamestown, Maryland, and the Caribbean islands (Map 2.2). Worldwide demand for sugar and tobacco fuelled the growth of these new colonies, and the resulting influx of colonists diminished Spain's dominance in the New World. At the same time, they imposed dramatic new pressures on native populations, who scrambled, in turn, to survive the present and carve out pathways to the future.

Brazil's Sugar Plantations

Portuguese colonists transformed the tropical low-lands of coastal Brazil into a sugar plantation zone like the ones they had recently created on Madeira, the Azores, the Cape Verdes, and São Tomé. The work proceeded slowly, but by 1590 more than a thousand sugar mills had been established in Pernambuco and Bahia. Each large plantation had its own milling operation: because sugarcane is extremely heavy and rots quickly, it must be processed on site. Thus sugar plantations combined backbreaking agricultural labor with milling, extracting, and refining processes that made sugar plantations look like Industrial Revolution–era factories.

Initially, Portuguese planters hoped that Brazil's indigenous peoples would supply the labor required to

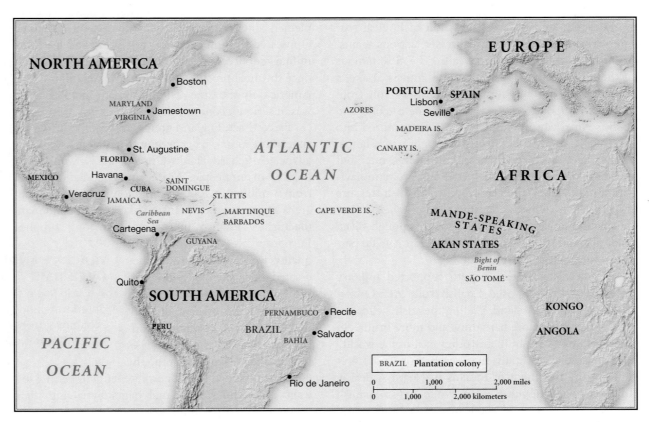

MAP 2.2
The Plantation Colonies
The plantation zone in the Americas extended from the tropical coast of Brazil northwestward through the West Indies and into the tropical and subtropical lowlands of southeastern North America. Sugar was the most important plantation crop in the Americas, but where the soil or climate could not support it planters experimented with a wide variety of other possibilities, including tobacco, indigo, cotton, cacao, and rice.

operate their sugar plantations. But, beginning with a wave of smallpox in 1559, unfamiliar diseases soon ravaged the coastal Indian population. As a result, planters turned to African slaves in ever-growing numbers; by 1620, the switch was complete. While Spanish colonies in Mexico and Peru took shape with astonishing speed following conquest, Brazil's occupation and development progressed more gradually; it required both trial and error and hard work to build a paying colony.

England's Tobacco Colonies

England was slow to embrace the prospect of planting colonies in the Americas. There were fumbling attempts in the 1580s in Newfoundland and Maine, privately organized and poorly funded. Sir Walter Raleigh's three expeditions to North Carolina likewise ended in disaster when 117 settlers on Roanoke Island, left unsupplied for several years, vanished. The fate of Roanoke — the "lost colony" — remains a compelling puzzle for modern historians.

The Jamestown Settlement   Merchants then took charge of English expansion. In 1606, King James I (r. 1603–1625) granted to the Virginia Company of London all the lands stretching from present-day North Carolina to southern New York. To honor the memory of Elizabeth I, the never-married "Virgin Queen," the company's directors named the region Virginia (Map 2.3). Influenced by the Spanish example, in 1607 the Virginia Company dispatched an all-male group with no ability to support itself — no women, farmers, or ministers were among the first arrivals — that expected to extract tribute from the region's Indian

Carolina Indians Fishing, 1585

Though maize was a mainstay of the Indian diet, native peoples along the Atlantic coast also harvested protein-rich fish, crabs, and oysters. In this watercolor by the English adventurer John White, Indians gather fish (in their "cannow," or dugout canoe) in the shallow waters of the Albemarle Sound, off present-day North Carolina. On the left, note the weir used both to catch fish and to store them live for later consumption.
© Trustees of the British Museum/Art Resource, NY.

John White's Map of Virginia

This map, drawn by Roanoke colonist John White, may hold a clue to the fate of the so-called lost colony. The island of Roanoke is right of center, just off the mainland and within the barrier islands. Directly west, on the point where the Roanoke and Chowan rivers join, is a (barely visible) paper patch. When lit from behind, a red fort is clearly visible beneath the patch, suggesting that the Roanoke colonists may already have identified a settlement site there: when he left the colony, John White wrote that the remaining colonists "were prepared to remove from Roanoak 50 miles into the maine[land]." Archaeologists and historians plan to use this discovery to guide further explorations in the area. The Art Archive at Art Resource, NY.

population while it searched out valuable commodities like pearls and gold. Some were young gentlemen with personal ties to the company's shareholders: a bunch of "unruly Sparks, packed off by their Friends to escape worse Destinies at home." Others hoped to make a quick profit. All they wanted, one of them said, was to "dig gold, refine gold, load gold."

But there was no gold, and the men fared poorly in their new environment. Arriving in Virginia after an exhausting four-month voyage, they settled on a swampy peninsula, which they named Jamestown to honor the king. There the adventurers lacked access to fresh water, refused to plant crops, and quickly died off; only

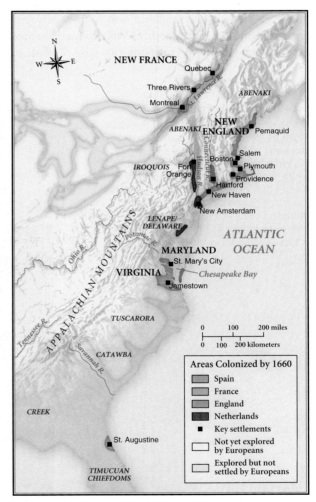

MAP 2.3

Eastern North America, 1650

By 1650, four European nations had permanent settlements along the eastern coast of North America, but only England had substantial numbers of settlers, some 25,000 in New England and another 15,000 in the Chesapeake region. French, Dutch, Swedish, and English colonists were also trading European manufactures to Native Americans in exchange for animal furs and skins, with far-reaching implications for Indian societies.

John Smith and Opechancanough

The powerful Indian warrior Opechancanough towers over English explorer John Smith in this engraving. In December 1607, Smith led a party of Jamestown colonists upriver in search of Indian food supplies. Two hundred warriors intercepted them, captured Smith, and took him to the Powhatan village of Werowacomoco. It was on this occasion that Pocahontas supposedly interceded to save his life (see Thinking Like a Historian, p. 50). The note at the bottom of the engraving is doubly mistaken, as it was Opechancanough (not Powhatan) who took Smith captive. Library of Congress.

C Smith taketh the King of Pamavnkee prisoner 1608

38 of the 120 men were alive nine months later. Death rates remained high: by 1611, the Virginia Company had dispatched 1,200 colonists to Jamestown, but fewer than half remained alive. "Our men were destroyed with cruell diseases, as Swellings, Fluxes, Burning Fevers, and by warres," reported one of the settlement's leaders, "but for the most part they died of meere famine."

Their plan to dominate the local Indian population ran up against the presence of Powhatan, the powerful chief who oversaw some thirty tribal chiefdoms between the James and Potomac rivers. He was willing to treat the English traders as potential allies who could provide valuable goods, but—just as the Englishmen expected tribute from the Indians—Powhatan expected tribute from the English. He provided the hungry English adventurers with corn; in return, he demanded "hatchets . . . bells, beads, and copper" as well as "two great guns" and expected Jamestown to become a dependent community within his chiefdom. Subsequently, Powhatan arranged a marriage between his daughter Pocahontas and John Rolfe, an English colonist (Thinking Like a Historian, p. 50). But these tactics failed. The inability to decide who would pay tribute to whom led to more than a decade of uneasy relations, followed by a long era of ruinous warfare.

The war was precipitated by the discovery of a cash crop that—like sugar in Brazil—offered colonists a way to turn a profit but required steady expansion onto Indian lands. Tobacco was a plant native to the Americas, long used by Indians as a medicine and a stimulant. John Rolfe found a West Indian strain that could flourish in Virginia soil and produced a small crop—"pleasant, sweet, and strong"—that fetched a high price in England and spurred the migration of thousands of new settlers. The English soon came to crave the nicotine that tobacco contained. James I initially condemned the plant as a "vile Weed" whose "black stinking fumes" were "baleful to the nose, harmful to the brain, and dangerous to the lungs." But the king's attitude changed as taxes on imported tobacco

Who Was Pocahontas?

Matoaka—nicknamed Pocahontas—was born around 1596 in the region the English would soon name Virginia. A daughter of Chief Powhatan, her interactions with colonists were important at the time and have been mythologized ever since. Pocahontas left no writings, so what we know of her comes from others. From these accounts, we know that she acted as a mediator with the Jamestown settlers; she was the first Native American to marry an Englishman; and she traveled to England with her husband and son. Pocahontas fell ill and died in Gravesend, England, in June 1617.

---

1. John Smith, *Generall Historie of Virginia*, 1624.
Smith's description of being a captive of Powhatan in 1607.

Having feasted [Smith] after their best barbarous manner they could, a long consultation was held, but the conclusion was, two great stones were brought before Powhatan: then as many as could layd hands on him, dragged him to them, and thereon laid his head, and being ready with their clubs, to beate out his braines, Pocahontas the Kings dearest daughter, when no entreaty could prevaile, got his head in her armes, and laid her owne upon his to save him from death: whereat the Emperour was contented he should live to make him hatchets, and her bells, beads, and copper.

2. Robert Vaughn's engraving of Pocahontas saving Smith's life, from John Smith's *Generall Historie of Virginia*, 1624.

Source: © British Library Board / Robana / Art Resource, NY.

3. John Smith, *Generall Historie of Virginia*, 1624.
Pocahontas visited Jamestown regularly in the years following Smith's capture. Smith returned to England in 1609; four years later Captain Samuel Argall kidnapped Pocahontas and held her captive in Jamestown.

[S]he too James towne [was brought.] A messenger forthwith was sent to her father, that his daughter Pocahontas he loved so dearely, he must ransome with our men, swords, peeces, tooles, &c. he treacherously had stolen. . . . [H]e . . . sent us word, that when we would deliver his daughter, he would make us satisfaction for all injuries done to us, and give us five hundred bushels of Corne, and for ever be friends with us. . . . [W]e could not believe the rest of our armes were either lost or stolen from him, and therefore till he sent them, we would keep his daughter. . . . [W]e heard no more from him a long time after. . . . .

[Long before this, Master John Rolfe, an honest Gentleman of good behavior had been in love with Pocahontas, and she with him. . . . T]his marriage came soone to the knowledge of Powhatan, a thing acceptable to him, as appeared by his sudden consent, for within ten daies he sent Opachisco, an old Uncle of hers, and two of his sons, to see the manner of the marriage, and to do in that behalf what they were requested . . . which was accordingly done about the first of April: And ever since we have had friendly trade and commerce.

4. John Rolfe, Letter to Sir Thomas Dale, 1614.
Pocahontas and John Rolfe married in April 1614. In June, Rolfe defended his motives in this letter to Virginia's deputy-governor.

I freely subject my selfe to your grave and mature judgment, deliberation, approbation and determination. . . . [I am not led by] the unbridled desire of carnal affection: but for the good of this plantation, for the honour of our countrie, for the glory of God, for my owne salvation, and for the converting to the true knowledge of God and Jesus

Christ, an unbeleeving creature, namely Pocahontas. To whom my hartie and best thoughts are, and have [for] a long time bin so intangled, and inthralled in so intricate a labyrinth, that I was even aweariд to unwinde my selfe thereout. . . . [I have often thought]: surely these are wicked instigations, hatched by him who seeketh and delighteth in man's destruction[.]

I say the holy spirit of God has often demanded of me, why I was created . . . but to labour in the Lord's vineyard. . . . Likewise adding hereunto her great appearance of love to me, her desire to be taught and instructed in the knowledge of God, her capableness of understanding, her aptness and willingness to receive any good impression, and also the spirituall, besides her owne incitements stirring me up hereunto. . . .

Now if the vulgar sort, who square all men's actions by the base rule of their owne filthiness, shall tax or taunt me in this my godly labour: let them know, it is not any hungry appetite, to gorge my selfe with incontinency; sure (if I would, and were so sensually inclined) I might satisfy such desire, though not without a seared conscience.

5. Portrait of Pocahontas by Simon Van De Pass, 1616. *In 1616, the Virginia Company of London sent Pocahontas, John Rolfe, and their son Thomas to England, where she met King James and sat for this portrait, the only surviving image of Pocahontas.*

Source: National Portrait Gallery, Smithsonian Institution/ Art Resource, NY.

6. John Smith, *Generall Historie of Virginia*, 1624. *In 1624, John Smith recalled a meeting he had with Pocahontas during her 1616 tour of England.*

[H]earing shee was at Branford with divers of my friends, I went to see her: After a modest salutation, without any word, she turned about, obscured her face, as not seeming well contented; and in that humour her husband, with divers others, we all left her two or three houres. . . . But not long after, she began to talke, and remembred mee well what courtesies she had done: saying, ["]You did promise Powhatan what was yours should bee his, and he the like to you; you called him father being in his land a stranger, and by the same reason so must I doe you:["] which though I would have excused, I durst not allow of that title, because she was a Kings daughter; with a well set countenance she said, ["]Were you not afraid to come into my fathers Countrie, and caused feare in him and all his people (but mee) and feare you here I should call you father; I tell you then I will, and you shall call mee childe, and so I will bee for ever and ever your Countrieman. They did tell us [always] you were dead, and I knew no other till I came to [Plymouth]; yet Powhatan did command Uttamatomakkin to seeke you, and know the truth, because your Countriemen will lie much.["]

Sources: (1, 3, 6) John Smith, *Generall Historie of Virginia* (Glasgow: James MacLehose and Sons, 1907), 101, 218, 220, 238–239; (4) J. Franklin Jameson, *Narratives of Early Virginia* (New York: Charles Scribner's Sons, 1907), 237–244.

ANALYZING THE EVIDENCE

1. Most historians now believe that the event described and shown in sources 1 and 2 was a Powhatan ritual to make Smith an ally and that his life was not actually in danger. What elements of these sources suggest the validity of this interpretation? Why would Pocahontas— a child of eleven or twelve at the time—have had a role in such a ritual?

2. How does Vaughn (source 2) depict power relations and social hierarchy among the Powhatans? Where does Pocahontas fit within this hierarchy? What messages about Pocahontas do you think Van De Pass (source 5) intended to convey? How do these images contribute to the Pocahontas myth?

3. How does Rolfe explain his interest in Pocahontas (source 4)? What is his view of her? How do you interpret the letter?

4. Assess the reliability of sources 1, 3, and 6 and consider Smith's motive in including them in his *Historie*. Source 6 purports to record an actual conversation between Pocahontas and Smith. What is the tone of this encounter, and what might explain Pocahontas's remarks?

PUTTING IT ALL TOGETHER

Imagine the various encounters Pocahontas experienced with the Jamestown Englishmen from her point of view. Reflect on who Pocahontas was as described in these documents—savior and friend, captive, baptized wife, Virginia Company prize, and betrayed ally—and in a brief essay, use Pocahontas's experience to explore the uncertain nature of English-Powhatan relations in the first decade of contact.

bolstered the royal treasury. Powhatan, however, now accused the English of coming "not to trade but to invade my people and possess my country."

To foster the flow of migrants, the Virginia Company allowed individual settlers to own land, granting 100 acres to every freeman and more to those who imported servants. The company also created a system of representative government: the **House of Burgesses**, first convened in 1619, could make laws and levy taxes, although the governor and the company council in England could veto its acts. By 1622, land-ownership, self-government, and a judicial system based on "the lawes of the realme of England" had attracted some 4,500 new recruits. To encourage the transition to a settler colony, the Virginia Company recruited dozens of "Maides young and uncorrupt to make wifes to the Inhabitants."

The Indian War of 1622 The influx of migrants sparked an all-out conflict with the neighboring Indians. The struggle began with an assault led by Opechancanough, Powhatan's younger brother and successor. In 1607, Opechancanough had attacked some of the first English invaders; subsequently, he "stood aloof" from the English settlers and "would not be drawn to any Treaty." In particular, he resisted English proposals to place Indian children in schools to be "brought upp in Christianytie." Upon becoming the paramount chief in 1621, Opechancanough told the leader of the neighboring Potomack Indians: "Before the end of two moons, there should not be an Englishman in all their Countries."

Opechancanough almost succeeded. In 1622, he coordinated a surprise attack by twelve Indian chiefdoms that killed 347 English settlers, nearly one-third of the population. The English fought back by seizing the fields and food of those they now called "naked, tanned, deformed Savages" and declared "a perpetual war without peace or truce" that lasted for a decade. They sold captured warriors into slavery, "destroy[ing] them who sought to destroy us" and taking control of "their cultivated places."

EXPLAIN CONSEQUENCES
How did the proximity of the Powhatan Chiefdom affect developments in early Virginia?

Shocked by the Indian uprising, James I revoked the Virginia Company's charter and, in 1624, made Virginia a **royal colony**. Now the king and his ministers appointed the governor and a small advisory council, retaining the locally elected House of Burgesses but stipulating that the king's Privy Council (a committee of political advisors) must ratify all legislation. The king also decreed the legal establishment of the Church of England in the colony, which meant that residents had to pay taxes to support its clergy. These institutions — an appointed governor, an elected assembly, a formal legal system, and an established Anglican Church — became the model for royal colonies throughout English America.

Lord Baltimore Settles Catholics in Maryland A second tobacco-growing colony developed in neighboring Maryland. King Charles I (r. 1625–1649), James's successor, was secretly sympathetic toward Catholicism, and in 1632 he granted lands bordering the vast Chesapeake Bay to Catholic aristocrat Cecilius Calvert, Lord Baltimore. Thus Maryland became a refuge for Catholics, who were subject to persecution in England. In 1634, twenty gentlemen, mostly Catholics, and 200 artisans and laborers, mostly Protestants, established St. Mary's City at the mouth of the Potomac River. To minimize religious confrontations, the proprietor instructed the governor to allow "no scandall nor offence to be given to any of the Protestants" and to "cause All Acts of Romane Catholicque Religion to be done as privately as may be."

Maryland grew quickly because Baltimore imported many artisans and offered ample lands to wealthy migrants. But political conflict threatened the colony's stability. Disputing Baltimore's powers, settlers elected a representative assembly and insisted on the right to initiate legislation, which Baltimore grudgingly granted. Anti-Catholic agitation by Protestants also threatened his religious goals. To protect his coreligionists, Lord Baltimore persuaded the assembly to enact the Toleration Act (1649), which granted all Christians the right to follow their beliefs and hold church services. In Maryland, as in Virginia, tobacco quickly became the main crop, and that similarity, rather than any religious difference, ultimately made the two colonies very much alike in their economic and social systems.

The Caribbean Islands

Virginia's experiment with a cash crop that created a land-intensive plantation society ran parallel to developments in the Caribbean, where English, French, and Dutch sailors began looking for a permanent toehold. In 1624, a small English party under the command of Sir Thomas Warner established a settlement on St. Christopher (St. Kitts). A year later, Warner allowed a French group to settle the other end of the island so they could better defend their position from the Spanish.

A Sugar Mill in the French West Indies, 1655

Making sugar required both hard labor and considerable expertise. Field slaves labored strenuously in the hot tropical sun to cut the sugarcane and carry or cart it to an oxen- or wind-powered mill, where it was pressed to yield the juice. Then skilled slave artisans took over. They carefully heated the juice and, at the proper moment, added ingredients that granulated the sugar and separated it from the molasses, which was later distilled into rum. The Granger Collection, New York.

Within a few years, the English and French colonists on St. Kitts had driven the native Caribs from the island, weathered a Spanish attack, and created a common set of bylaws for mutual occupation of the island.

After St. Kitts, a dozen or so colonies were founded in the Lesser Antilles, including the French islands of Martinique, Guadeloupe, and St. Bart's; the English outposts of Nevis, Antigua, Montserrat, Anguilla, Tortola, and Barbados; and the Dutch colony of St. Eustatius. In 1655, an English fleet captured the Spanish island of Jamaica — one of the large islands of the Greater Antilles — and opened it to settlement as well. A few of these islands were unpopulated before Europeans settled there; elsewhere, native populations were displaced, and often wiped out, within a decade or so. Only on the largest islands did native populations hold out longer.

Colonists experimented with a wide variety of cash crops, including tobacco, indigo, cotton, cacao, and ginger. Beginning in the 1640s — and drawing on the example of Brazil — planters on many of the islands shifted to sugar cultivation. Where conditions were right, as they were in Barbados, Jamaica, Nevis, and Martinique, these colonies were soon producing substantial crops of sugar and, as a consequence, claimed some of the world's most valuable real estate.

Plantation Life

In North America and the Caribbean, plantations were initially small **freeholds**, farms of 30 to 50 acres owned and farmed by families or male partners. But the logic of plantation agriculture soon encouraged consolidation: large planters engrossed as much land as they could and experimented with new forms of labor discipline that maximized their control over production. In Virginia, the **headright system** guaranteed 50 acres of land to anyone who paid the passage of a new immigrant to the colony; thus, by buying additional indentured servants and slaves, the colony's largest planters also amassed ever-greater claims to land.

European demand for tobacco set off a forty-year economic boom in the Chesapeake. "All our riches for the present do consist in tobacco," a planter remarked in 1630. Exports rose from 3 million pounds in 1640 to 10 million pounds in 1660. After 1650, wealthy migrants from gentry or noble families established large estates along the coastal rivers. Coming primarily from southern England, where tenants and wage laborers farmed large manors, they copied that hierarchical system by buying English indentured servants and enslaved Africans to work their lands. At about the same time, the switch to sugar production in Barbados caused the price of land there to quadruple, driving small landowners out.

For rich and poor alike, life in the plantation colonies of North America and the Caribbean was harsh. The scarcity of towns deprived settlers of community (Map 2.4). Families were equally scarce because there were few women, and marriages often ended with the early death of a spouse. Pregnant women were especially vulnerable to malaria, spread by mosquitoes that flourished in tropical and subtropical climates. Many mothers died after bearing a first or second child, so orphaned children (along with unmarried young men)

formed a large segment of the society. Sixty percent of the children born in Middlesex County, Virginia, before 1680 lost one or both parents before they were thirteen. Death was pervasive. Although 15,000 English migrants arrived in Virginia between 1622 and 1640, the population rose only from 2,000 to 8,000. It was even harsher in the islands, where yellow fever epidemics killed indiscriminately. On Barbados, burials outnumbered baptisms in the second half of the seventeenth century by four to one.

Indentured Servitude   Still, the prospect of owning land continued to lure settlers. By 1700, more than 100,000 English migrants had come to Virginia and Maryland and over 200,000 had migrated to the islands of the West Indies, principally to Barbados; the vast majority to both destinations traveled as indentured servants (Figure 2.2). Shipping registers from the English port of Bristol reveal the backgrounds of 5,000 servants embarking for the Chesapeake. Three-quarters were young men. They came to Bristol searching for work; once there, merchants persuaded them to sign contracts to labor in America. **Indentured servitude** contracts bound the men — and the quarter who were women — to work for a master for four or five years, after which they would be free to marry and work for themselves.

For merchants, servants were valuable cargo: their contracts fetched high prices from Chesapeake and West Indian planters. For the plantation owners, indentured servants were a bargain if they survived the

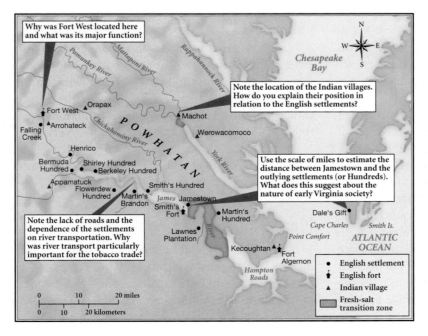

MAP 2.4

River Plantations in Virginia, c. 1640

The first migrants settled in widely dispersed plantations along the James River, a settlement pattern promoted by the tobacco economy. From their riverfront plantations wealthy planter-merchants could easily load heavy hogsheads of tobacco onto oceangoing ships and offload supplies that they then sold to smallholding planters. Consequently, few substantial towns or trading centers developed in the Chesapeake region.

FIGURE 2.2

Chesapeake Whites: Workers, Dependents, and Indentured Servants, 1640–1700

The Chesapeake's white population grew tenfold in the years after 1640, and it also changed significantly in character. As more women migrated to Virginia and Maryland and bore children, the percentage of the population who worked in the fields daily fell dramatically, from 75 percent to 46 percent. The proportion of indentured servants in the labor force likewise declined, from 30 percent to 10 percent.

voyage and their first year in a harsh new disease environment, a process called "seasoning." During the Chesapeake's tobacco boom, a male servant could produce five times his purchase price in a single year. To maximize their gains, many masters ruthlessly exploited servants, forcing them to work long hours, beating them without cause, and withholding permission to marry. If servants ran away or became pregnant, masters went to court to increase the term of their service. Female servants were especially vulnerable to abuse. A Virginia law of 1692 stated that "dissolute masters have gotten their maids with child; and yet claim the benefit of their service." Planters got rid of uncooperative servants by selling their contracts. In Virginia, an Englishman remarked in disgust that "servants were sold up and down like horses."

Few indentured servants escaped poverty. In the Chesapeake, half the men died before completing the term of their contract, and another quarter remained landless. Only one-quarter achieved their quest for property and respectability. Female servants generally fared better. Because men had grown "very sensible of the Misfortune of Wanting Wives," many propertied planters married female servants. Thus a few—very fortunate—men and women escaped a life of landless poverty.

African Laborers   The rigors of indentured servitude paled before the brutality that accompanied the large-scale shift to African slave labor. In Barbados and the other English islands, sugar production devoured laborers, and the supply of indentured servants quickly became inadequate to planters' needs. By 1690, blacks outnumbered whites on Barbados nearly three to one, and white slave owners were developing a code of force and terror to keep sugar flowing and maintain control of the black majority that surrounded them. The first comprehensive slave legislation for the island, adopted in 1661, was called an "Act for the better ordering and governing of Negroes."

In the Chesapeake, the shift to slave labor was more gradual. In 1619, John Rolfe noted that "a Dutch man of warre . . . sold us twenty Negars"—slaves originally shipped by the Portuguese from the port of Luanda in Angola. For a generation, the number of Africans remained small. About 400 Africans lived in the Chesapeake colonies in 1649, just 2 percent of the population. By 1670, that figure had reached 5 percent. Most Africans served their English masters for life. However, since English common law did not acknowledge chattel slavery, it was possible for some Africans to escape bondage. Some were freed as a result of Christian baptism; some purchased their freedom from their owners; some—like Elizabeth Key, whose story was related at the beginning of the chapter—won their freedom in the courts. Once free, some ambitious Africans became landowners and purchased slaves or the labor contracts of English servants for themselves.

Social mobility for Africans ended in the 1660s with the collapse of the tobacco boom and the increasing political power of the gentry. Tobacco had once sold for 30 pence a pound; now it fetched less than one-tenth of that. The "low price of Tobacco requires it should bee made as cheap as possible," declared Virginia planter-politician Nicholas Spencer, and "blacks can make it cheaper than whites." As they imported more African workers, the English-born political elite grew more race-conscious. Increasingly, Spencer and other leading legislators distinguished English from African residents by color (white-black) rather than by religion (Christian-pagan). By 1671, the Virginia House of Burgesses had forbidden Africans to

> **COMPARE AND CONTRAST**
>
> How were the experiences of indentured servants and slaves in the Chesapeake and the Caribbean similar? In what ways were they different?

own guns or join the militia. It also barred them — "tho baptized and enjoying their own Freedom" — from owning English servants. Being black was increasingly a mark of inferior legal status, and slavery was fast becoming a permanent and hereditary condition. As an English clergyman observed, "These two words, Negro and Slave had by custom grown Homogeneous and convertible."

Neo-European Colonies

While Mesoamerica and the Andes emerged at the heart of a tribute-based empire in Latin America, and tropical and subtropical environments were transformed into plantation societies, a series of colonies that more closely replicated European patterns of economic and social organization developed in the temperate zone along North America's Atlantic coast (America Compared, opposite page). Dutch, French, and English sailors probed the continent's northern coastline, initially searching for a Northwest Passage through the continent to Asia. Gradually, they developed an interest in the region on its own terms. They traded for furs with coastal Native American populations, fished for cod on the Grand Banks off the coast of Newfoundland, and established freehold family farms and larger manors where they reproduced European patterns of agricultural life. Many migrants also came with aspirations to create godly communities, places of refuge where they could put religious ideals into practice. New France, New Netherland, and New England were the three pillars of neo-European colonization in the early seventeenth century.

New France

In the 1530s, Jacques Cartier ventured up the St. Lawrence River and claimed it for France. Cartier's claim to the St. Lawrence languished for three-quarters of a century, but in 1608 Samuel de Champlain returned and founded the fur-trading post of Quebec. Trade with the Cree-speaking Montagnais; Algonquian-speaking Micmacs, Ottawas, and Ojibwas; and Iroquois-speaking Hurons gave the French access to furs — mink, otter, and beaver — that were in great demand in Europe. To secure plush beaver pelts from the Hurons, who controlled trade north of the Great Lakes, Champlain provided them with manufactured goods. Selling pelts, an Indian told a French priest, "makes kettles, hatchets, swords, knives, bread." It also made guns, which Champlain sold to the Hurons.

The Hurons also became the first focus of French Catholic missionary activity. Hundreds of priests, most of them Jesuits, fanned out to live in Indian communities. They mastered Indian languages and came to understand, and sometimes respect, their values. Many Indian peoples initially welcomed the French "Black Robes" as spiritually powerful beings, but when prayers to the Christian god did not protect them from disease, the Indians grew skeptical. A Peoria chief charged that a priest's "fables are good only in his own country; we have our own [beliefs], which do not make us die as his do." When a drought struck, Indians blamed the missionaries. "If you cannot make rain, they speak of nothing less than making away with you," lamented one Jesuit.

While New France became an expansive center of fur trading and missionary work, it languished as a

Castor de 26 pouces de longueur entre teste et queue

The Fur Trade

Luxuriant pelts like ermine and silver fox were always desirable, but the humble beaver dominated the early trade between Europeans and Indians in the Northeast. It had thick, coarse hair, but beneath that outer layer was soft "underfur." Those fine hairs were covered in microscopic barbs that allowed them to mat into a dense mass. European hatmakers pressed this fur into felt so strong and pliable that even broad-brimmed hats would hold their shape. As such hats became fashionable in Europe and the colonies, beavers were hunted to near-extinction in North America. National Archives of Canada.

Plantation Colonies Versus Neo-Europes

The prospects for Europeans who traveled to tropical plantations like Barbados differed dramatically from those traveling to neo-European colonies like Massachusetts Bay. In the former, planters employed small armies of servants and slaves; in the latter, the first generation of colonists worked hard, often in cold climates and rocky soils, to eke out a living.

Henry Whistler's Journal, 1655

This Island [Barbados] is one of the Richest Spots of ground in the world and fully inhabited. . . . The gentry here doth Hue [appear] far better than ours do in England : they have most of them 100 or 2 or 3 of slaves[,] apes who they command as they please. . . . This Island is inhabited with all sorts : with English, French, Dutch, Scots, Irish, Spaniards they being Jews : with Indians and miserable Negroes borne to perpetual slavery they and their seed : these Negroes they do allow as many wives as they will have, some will have 3 or 4, according as they find their body able : our English here doth think a negro child the first day it is born to be worth £5, they cost them nothing the bringing up, they go all ways naked : some planters will have 30 more or les about 4 or 5 years old : they sell them from one to the other as we do sheep. This Island is the Dunghill whereon England doth cast forth its rubbish. . . . A rogue in England will hardly make a cheater here : a Bawd brought over puts on a demure comportment, a whore if handsome makes a wife for some rich planter.

Source: *The Narrative of General Venables* (New York: Longmans, Green, and Co., 1900), 145–146.

William Wood, *New England's Prospect*, 1634

But it may be objected that it is too cold a country for our English men, who have been accustomed to a warmer climate. To which it may be answered . . . , there is wood good store and better cheap to build warm houses and make good fires, which makes the winter less tedious. . . . [T]rue it is that some venturing too nakedly in extremity of cold, being more foolhardy than wise, have for a time lost the use of their feet, others the use of their fingers; but time and surgery afterwards recovered them. Some have had their overgrown beards so frozen together that they could not get their strong-water bottles into their mouths. . . . [W]hereas many do disparage the land, saying a man cannot live without labor, in that they more disparage and discredit themselves in giving the world occasion to take notice of their dronish disposition that would live off the sweat of another man's brows. . . . For all in New England must be workers of some kind. . . . And howsoever they are accounted poor, they are well contented and look not so much at abundance as at competency.

Source: William Wood, *New England's Prospect* (Boston: The University of Massachusetts Press, 1993), 28–29, 68.

QUESTIONS FOR ANALYSIS

1. Henry Whistler was a soldier who briefly visited Barbados on a military expedition to the West Indies, while William Wood lived for four years in Massachusetts Bay. How might that difference influence the tone of these two descriptions?

2. What core values does each author ascribe to the colony he writes about? What kinds of people are most likely to end up in each of these two colonies?

farming settlement. In 1662, King Louis XIV (r. 1643–1714) turned New France into a royal colony and subsidized the migration of indentured servants. French servants labored under contract for three years, received a salary, and could eventually lease a farm — far more generous terms than those for indentured servants in the English colonies.

Nonetheless, few people moved to New France, a cold and forbidding country "at the end of the world," as one migrant put it. And some state policies discouraged migration. Louis XIV drafted tens of thousands of men into military service and barred Huguenots (French Calvinist Protestants) from migrating to New France, fearing they might win converts and take control of the colony. Moreover, the French legal system gave peasants strong rights to their village lands, whereas migrants to New France faced an oppressive, aristocracy- and church-dominated feudal system. In the village of Saint Ours in Quebec, for example, peasants paid 45 percent of their wheat crop to nobles and the Catholic Church. By 1698, only 15,200 Europeans lived in New France, compared to 100,000 in England's North American colonies.

Despite this small population, France eventually claimed a vast inland arc, from the St. Lawrence Valley through the Great Lakes and down the course of the Ohio and Mississippi rivers. Explorers and fur traders drove this expansion. In 1673, Jacques Marquette reached the Mississippi River in present-day Wisconsin; then, in 1681, Robert de La Salle traveled down the majestic river to the Gulf of Mexico. To honor Louis XIV, La Salle named the region Louisiana. By 1718, French merchants had founded the port of New Orleans at the mouth of the Mississippi. Eventually a network of about two dozen forts grew up in the Great Lakes and Mississippi. Soldiers and missionaries used them as bases of operations, while Indians, traders, and their métis (mixed-race) offspring created trading communities alongside them.

New Netherland

By 1600, Amsterdam had become the financial and commercial hub of northern Europe, and Dutch financiers dominated the European banking, insurance, and textile industries. Dutch merchants owned more ships and employed more sailors than did the combined fleets of England, France, and Spain. Indeed, the Dutch managed much of the world's commerce. During their struggle for independence from Spain and Portugal (ruled by Spanish monarchs, 1580–1640), the Dutch seized Portuguese forts in Africa and Indonesia and sugar plantations in Brazil. These conquests gave the Dutch control of the Atlantic trade in slaves and sugar and the Indian Ocean commerce in East Indian spices and Chinese silks and ceramics (Map 2.5).

In 1609, Dutch merchants dispatched the English mariner Henry Hudson to locate a navigable route to the riches of the East Indies. What he found as he probed the rivers of northeast America was a fur bonanza. Following Hudson's exploration of the river that now bears his name, the merchants built Fort Orange (Albany) in 1614 to trade for furs with the Munsee and Iroquois Indians. Then, in 1621, the Dutch government chartered the West India Company, which founded the colony of New Netherland, set up New Amsterdam (on Manhattan Island) as its capital, and brought in farmers and artisans to make the enterprise self-sustaining. The new colony did not thrive. The population of the Dutch Republic was too small to support much emigration—just 1.5 million people, compared to 5 million in Britain and 20 million in France—and its migrants sought riches in Southeast Asia rather than fur-trading profits in America. To protect its colony from rival European nations, the West India Company granted huge estates along the Hudson River to wealthy Dutchmen who promised to populate them. But by 1664, New Netherland had only 5,000 residents, and fewer than half of them were Dutch.

New Amsterdam, c. 1640

As the wooden palisade suggests, New Amsterdam was a fortlike trading post at the edge of a vast land populated by alien Indian peoples feared by the Dutch. The city was also a pale miniature imitation of Amsterdam, with its many canals. The first settlers built their houses in the Dutch style, with gable ends facing the street (note the two middle houses), and excavated a canal across lower Manhattan Island (New York City's Canal Street today). Library of Congress.

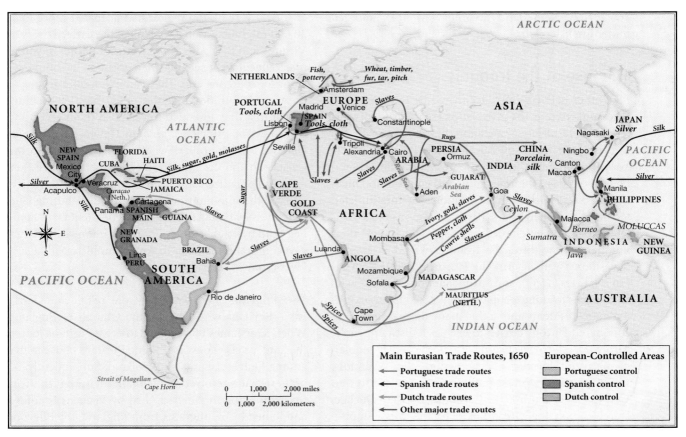

MAP 2.5

The Eurasian Trade System and European Spheres of Influence, 1650

Between 1550 and 1650, Spanish, Portuguese, and Dutch merchants took control of the maritime trade routes between Europe and India, Indonesia, and China. They also created two new trading connections. The South Atlantic System carried slaves, sugar, and manufactured goods between Europe, Africa, and the valuable plantation settlements in Brazil and the Caribbean islands. And a transpacific trade carried Spanish American silver to China in exchange for silks, ceramics, and other manufactures. (To trace long-term changes in trade and empires, see Map 1.4 on p. 24 and Map 5.1 on p. 154.)

Like New France, New Netherland flourished as a fur-trading enterprise. Trade with the powerful Iroquois, though rocky at first, gradually improved. But Dutch settlers had less respect for their Algonquian-speaking neighbors. They seized prime farming land from the Algonquian peoples and took over their trading network, which exchanged corn and wampum from Long Island for furs from Maine. In response, in 1643 the Algonquians launched attacks that nearly destroyed the colony. "Almost every place is abandoned," a settler lamented, "whilst the Indians daily threaten to overwhelm us." To defeat the Algonquians, the Dutch waged vicious warfare — maiming, burning, and killing hundreds of men, women, and children — and formed an alliance with the Mohawks, who were no less brutal. The grim progression of Euro-Indian relations — an uneasy welcome, followed by rising tensions and war — afflicted even the Dutch, who had few designs on Indian lands or on their "unregenerate" souls and were only looking to do business.

After the crippling Indian war, the West India Company ignored New Netherland and expanded its profitable trade in African slaves and Brazilian sugar. In New Amsterdam, Governor Peter Stuyvesant ruled in an authoritarian fashion, rejecting demands for a representative system of government and alienating the colony's diverse Dutch, English, and Swedish residents. Consequently, the residents of New Netherland offered little resistance when England invaded the colony in

IDENTIFY CAUSES
Why did New France and New Netherland struggle to attract colonists?

1664. New Netherland became New York and fell under English control.

The Rise of the Iroquois

Like other native groups decimated by European diseases and warfare, the Five Nations of the Iroquois suffered as a result of colonization, but they were able to capitalize on their strategic location in central New York to dominate the region between the French and Dutch colonies. Obtaining guns and goods from Dutch merchants at Fort Orange, Iroquois warriors inflicted terror on their neighbors. Partly in response to a virulent smallpox epidemic in 1633, which cut their number by one-third, the Iroquois waged a series of devastating wars against the Hurons (1649), Neutrals (1651), Eries (1657), and Susquehannocks (1660) — all Iroquoian-speaking peoples. They razed villages, killing many residents and taking many more captive. The conquered Hurons ceased to exist as a distinct people; survivors trekked westward with displaced Algonquian peoples and formed a new nation, the Wyandots. Iroquois warriors pressed still farther — eastward into New England, south to the Carolinas, north to Quebec, and west via the Great Lakes to the Mississippi — dominating Indian groups along the way. Collectively known as the Beaver Wars, these Iroquois campaigns dramatically altered the map of northeastern North America.

Many Iroquois raids came at the expense of French-allied Algonquian Indians, and in the 1660s New France committed to all-out war against the Iroquois. In 1667, the Mohawks were the last of the Five Nations to admit defeat. As part of the peace settlement, the Five Nations accepted Jesuit missionaries into their communities. A minority of Iroquois — perhaps 20 percent of the population — converted to Catholicism and moved to the St. Lawrence Valley, where they settled in mission communities near Montreal (where their descendants still live today).

The Iroquois who remained in New York did not collapse, however. Forging a new alliance with the Englishmen who had taken over New Netherland, they would continue to be a dominant force in the politics of the Northeast for generations to come.

New England

In 1620, 102 English Protestants landed at a place they called Plymouth, near Cape Cod. A decade later, a much larger group began to arrive just north of Plymouth, in the newly chartered Massachusetts Bay Colony. By 1640, the region had attracted more than 20,000 migrants (Map 2.6). Unlike the early arrivals in Virginia and Barbados, these were not parties of young male adventurers seeking their fortunes or bound to labor for someone else. They came in family groups to create communities like the ones they left behind, except that they intended to establish them according to Protestant principles, as John Calvin had done in Geneva. Their numbers were small compared to the Caribbean and the Chesapeake, but their balanced sex ratio and organized approach to community formation allowed them to multiply quickly. By distributing land broadly, they built a society of independent farm families. And by establishing a "holy commonwealth," they gave a moral dimension to American history that survives today.

The Pilgrims   The **Pilgrims** were religious separatists — Puritans who had left the Church of England. When King James I threatened to drive Puritans "out of the land, or else do worse," some Puritans chose to live among Dutch Calvinists in Holland. Subsequently, 35 of these exiles resolved to maintain their English identity by moving to America. Led by William Bradford and joined by 67 migrants from England, the Pilgrims sailed to America aboard the *Mayflower*. Because they lacked a royal charter, they combined themselves "together into a civill body politick," as their leader explained. This Mayflower Compact used the Puritans' self-governing religious congregation as the model for their political structure.

Only half of the first migrant group survived until spring, but thereafter Plymouth thrived; the cold climate inhibited the spread of mosquito-borne disease, and the Pilgrims' religious discipline encouraged a strong work ethic. Moreover, a smallpox epidemic in 1618 devastated the local Wampanoags, minimizing the danger they posed. By 1640, there were 3,000 settlers in Plymouth. To ensure political stability, they established representative self-government, broad political rights, property ownership, and religious freedom of conscience.

Meanwhile, England plunged deeper into religious turmoil. When King Charles I repudiated certain Protestant doctrines, including the role of grace in salvation, English Puritans, now powerful in Parliament, accused the king of "popery" — of holding Catholic beliefs. In 1629, Charles dissolved Parliament, claimed the authority to rule by "divine right," and raised money through royal edicts and the sale of monopolies. When Charles's Archbishop William Laud began to purge dissident ministers, thousands of

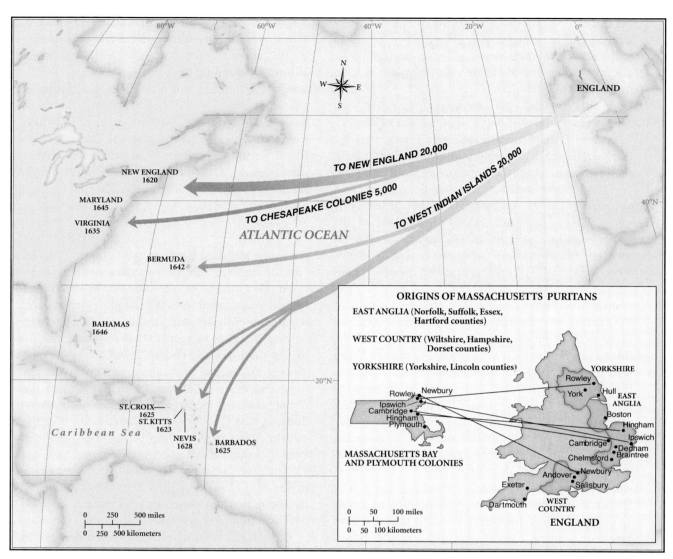

MAP 2.6
The Puritan Migration to America, 1620–1640
Forty-five thousand Puritans left England for America and the West Indies between 1620 and 1640. About half traveled to the New England colonies of Plymouth, Massachusetts Bay, and Connecticut, where they created durable societies with deep religious identities. Migrants from the three major centers of Puritanism in England—Yorkshire, East Anglia, and the West Country—commonly settled among those from their own region. Often they named American communities after their English towns of origin and tried to live as they had in Old England. For example, settlers from Rowley in Yorkshire transplanted their customary system of open-field agriculture to Rowley in Massachusetts Bay.

Puritans—Protestants who did not separate from the Church of England but hoped to purify it of its ceremony and hierarchy—fled to America.

John Winthrop and Massachusetts Bay The Puritan exodus began in 1630 with the departure of 900 migrants led by John Winthrop, a well-educated country squire who became the first governor of the Massachusetts Bay Colony. Calling England morally corrupt and "overburdened with people," Winthrop sought land for his children and a place in Christian history for his people. "We must consider that we shall be as a City upon a Hill," Winthrop told the migrants. "The eyes of all people are upon us." Like the Pilgrims,

 To see a longer excerpt of Winthrop's "City Upon a Hill" sermon, along with other primary sources from this period, see *Sources for America's History*.

the Puritans envisioned a reformed Christian society with "authority in magistrates, liberty in people, purity in the church," as minister John Cotton put it. By their example, they hoped to inspire religious reform throughout Christendom.

Winthrop and his associates governed the Massachusetts Bay Colony from the town of Boston. They transformed their **joint-stock corporation**—a commercial agreement that allows investors to pool their resources—into a representative political system with a governor, council, and assembly. To ensure rule by the godly, the Puritans limited the right to vote and hold office to men who were church members. Rejecting the Plymouth Colony's policy of religious toleration, the Massachusetts Bay Colony established Puritanism as the state-supported religion, barred other faiths from conducting services, and used the Bible as a legal guide. "Where there is no Law," they said, magistrates should rule "as near the law of God as they can." Over the next decade, about 10,000 Puritans migrated to the colony, along with 10,000 others fleeing hard times in England.

COMPARE AND CONTRAST
What made New England different from New France and New Netherland?

The New England Puritans sought to emulate the simplicity of the first Christians. Seeing bishops as "traitours unto God," they placed power in the congregation of members—hence the name *Congregationalist* for their churches. Inspired by John Calvin, many Puritans embraced **predestination**, the idea that God saved only a few chosen people. Church members often lived in great anxiety, worried that God had not placed them among the "elect." Some hoped for a conversion experience, the intense sensation of receiving God's grace and being "born again." Other Puritans relied on "preparation," the confidence in salvation that came from spiritual guidance by their ministers. Still others believed that they were God's chosen people, the new Israelites, and would be saved if they obeyed his laws.

Roger Williams and Rhode Island

To maintain God's favor, the Massachusetts Bay magistrates purged their society of religious dissidents. One target was Roger Williams, the Puritan minister in Salem, a coastal town north of Boston. Williams opposed the decision to establish an official religion and praised the Pilgrims' separation of church and state. He advocated **toleration**, arguing that political magistrates had authority over only the "bodies, goods, and outward estates of men," not their spiritual lives. Williams also

questioned the Puritans' seizure of Indian lands. The magistrates banished him from the colony in 1636.

Williams and his followers settled 50 miles south of Boston, founding the town of Providence on land purchased from the Narragansett Indians. Other religious dissidents settled nearby at Portsmouth and Newport. In 1644, these settlers obtained a corporate charter from Parliament for a new colony—Rhode Island—with full authority to rule themselves. In Rhode Island, as in Plymouth, there was no legally established church, and individuals could worship God as they pleased.

Anne Hutchinson

The Massachusetts Bay magistrates saw a second threat to their authority in Anne Hutchinson. The wife of a merchant and mother of seven, Hutchinson held weekly prayer meetings for women and accused various Boston clergymen of placing undue emphasis on good behavior. Like Martin Luther, Hutchinson denied that salvation could be earned through good deeds. There was no "**covenant of works**" that would save the well-behaved; only a "**covenant of grace**" through which God saved those he predestined for salvation. Hutchinson likewise declared that God "revealed" divine truth directly to individual believers, a controversial doctrine that the Puritan magistrates denounced as heretical.

The magistrates also resented Hutchinson because of her sex. Like other Christians, Puritans believed that both men and women could be saved. But gender equality stopped there. Women were inferior to men in earthly affairs, said leading Puritan divines, who told married women: "Thy desires shall bee subject to thy husband, and he shall rule over thee." Puritan women could not be ministers or lay preachers, nor could they vote in church affairs. In 1637, the magistrates accused Hutchinson of teaching that inward grace freed an individual from the rules of the Church and found her guilty of holding heretical views. Banished, she followed Roger Williams into exile in Rhode Island.

Other Puritan groups moved out from Massachusetts Bay in the 1630s and settled on or near the Connecticut River. For several decades, the colonies of Connecticut, New Haven, and Saybrook were independent of one another; in 1660, they secured a charter from King Charles II (r. 1660–1685) for the self-governing colony of Connecticut. Like Massachusetts Bay, Connecticut had a legally established church and an elected governor and assembly; however, it granted voting rights to most property-owning men, not just to church members as in the original Puritan colony.

The Puritan Revolution in England Meanwhile, a religious civil war engulfed England. Archbishop Laud had imposed the Church of England prayer book on Presbyterian Scotland in 1637; five years later, a rebel Scottish army invaded England. Thousands of English Puritans (and hundreds of American Puritans) joined the Scots, demanding religious reform and parliamentary power. After years of civil war, parliamentary forces led by Oliver Cromwell emerged victorious. In 1649, Parliament beheaded King Charles I, proclaimed a republican Commonwealth, and banished bishops and elaborate rituals from the Church of England.

The Protestant Almanack, 1700
The conflict between Protestants and Catholics took many forms. To reinforce the religious identity of English Protestants, a writer using the pseudonym *Philopretes* published this almanac that charted not only the passage of the seasons (and the influence of the pagan signs of the "Zodiack") but also the "Pernicious Revolutions of the Papacy against the Lord and his Anointed." Cambridge University Library.

The Puritan triumph in England was short-lived. Popular support for the Commonwealth ebbed after Cromwell took dictatorial control in 1653. Following his death in 1658, moderate Protestants and a resurgent aristocracy restored the monarchy and the hierarchy of bishops. With Charles II (r. 1660–1685) on the throne, England's experiment in radical Protestant government came to an end.

For the Puritans in America, the restoration of the monarchy began a new phase of their "errand into the wilderness." They had come to New England expecting to return to Europe in triumph. When the failure of the English Revolution dashed that sacred mission, ministers exhorted congregations to create a godly republican society in America. The Puritan colonies now stood as outposts of Calvinism and the Atlantic republican tradition.

Puritanism and Witchcraft Like Native Americans, Puritans believed that the physical world was full of supernatural forces. Devout Christians saw signs of God's (or Satan's) power in blazing stars, birth defects, and other unusual events. Noting after a storm that the houses of many ministers "had been smitten with Lightning," Cotton Mather, a prominent Puritan theologian, wondered "what the meaning of God should be in it."

Puritans were hostile toward people who they believed tried to manipulate these forces, and many were willing to condemn neighbors as Satan's "wizards" or "witches." People in the town of Andover "were much addicted to sorcery," claimed one observer, and "there were forty men in it that could raise the Devil as well as any astrologer." Between 1647 and 1662, civil authorities in New England hanged fourteen people for witchcraft, most of them older women accused of being "double-tongued" or of having "an unruly spirit."

The most dramatic episode of witch-hunting occurred in Salem in 1692. Several girls who had experienced strange seizures accused neighbors of bewitching them. When judges at the accused witches' trials allowed the use of "spectral" evidence — visions of evil beings and marks seen only by the girls — the accusations spun out of control. Eventually, Massachusetts Bay authorities tried 175 people for witchcraft and executed 19 of them. The causes of this mass hysteria were complex and are still debated. Some historians point to group rivalries: many accusers were the daughters or servants of poor farmers, whereas many of the alleged witches were wealthier church members or their friends. Because 18 of those put to death were women, other historians see the episode as part of a broader

Puritan effort to subordinate women. Still others focus on political instability in Massachusetts Bay in the early 1690s and on fears raised by recent Indian attacks in nearby Maine, which had killed the parents of some of the young accusers. It is likely that all of these causes played some role in the executions.

Whatever the cause, the Salem episode marked a major turning point. Shaken by the number of deaths, government officials now discouraged legal prosecutions for witchcraft. Moreover, many influential people embraced the outlook of the European Enlightenment, a major intellectual movement that began around 1675 and promoted a rational, scientific view of the world. Increasingly, educated men and women explained strange happenings and sudden deaths by reference to "natural causes," not witchcraft. Unlike Cotton Mather (1663–1728), who believed that lightning was a supernatural sign, Benjamin Franklin (1706–1790) and other well-read men of his generation would investigate it as a natural phenomenon.

A Yeoman Society, 1630–1700   In building their communities, New England Puritans consciously rejected the feudal practices of English society. Many Puritans came from middling families in East Anglia, a region of pasture lands and few manors, and had no desire to live as tenants of wealthy aristocrats or submit to oppressive taxation by a distant government. They

had "escaped out of the pollutions of the world," the settlers of Watertown in Massachusetts Bay declared, and vowed to live "close togither" in self-governing communities. Accordingly, the General Courts of Massachusetts Bay and Connecticut bestowed land on groups of settlers, who then distributed it among the male heads of families.

Widespread ownership of land did not mean equality of wealth or status. "God had Ordained different degrees and orders of men," proclaimed Boston merchant John Saffin, "some to be Masters and Commanders, others to be Subjects, and to be commanded." Town proprietors normally awarded the largest plots to men of high social status who often became selectmen and justices of the peace. However, all families received some land, and most adult men had a vote in the **town meeting**, the main institution of local government (Map 2.7).

In this society of independent households and self-governing communities, ordinary farmers had much more political power than Chesapeake yeomen and European peasants did. Although Nathaniel Fish was one of the poorest men in the town of Barnstable — he owned just a two-room cottage, 8 acres of land, an ox, and a cow — he was a voting member of the town meeting. Each year, Fish and other Barnstable farmers levied taxes; enacted ordinances governing fencing, roadbuilding, and the use of common fields; and chose

The Mason Children

This 1670 portrait of David, Joanna, and Abigail Mason by an unknown painter illustrates the growing prosperity of well-to-do Boston households. All three wear white linen edged with fine lace and expensive ribbons. Eight-year-old David is dressed like a gentleman; his slashed sleeves, kid gloves, and silver-tipped walking stick represent the height of English fashion. Puritans, with their plain style, were uneasy about such finery. As minister Samuel Torrey complained, "a spirit of worldliness, a spirit of sensuality" was gaining strength in the younger generation. The Fine Arts Museums of San Francisco, M. H. de Young Memorial Museum, Gift of Mr. and Mrs. John D. Rockefeller III, 1979.7.3. © Fine Arts Museums of San Francisco.

The key to the right indicates that a central purpose of this map is to show the geographic distribution of nucleated and dispersed villages. Why are there so many nucleated towns in the Connecticut River Valley and so many dispersed settlements in eastern Massachusetts?

The map of Andover shows how an originally nucleated settlement changed over time into a dispersed town. New farms tended to be located farther and farther from the meeting house and town center, represented by a triangle on the town plan.

Wethersfield in 1640 is an example of a nucleated village, with house lots clustered around the meeting house and fields arranged in geometric patterns in the surrounding countryside.

The field boundaries in Wethersfield indicate that the land is flat in the Connecticut River Valley. In contrast, the pattern of roads and paths in Andover suggests a hilly topography. These uplands gave the Merrimack River a strong current and many rapids, which were later harnessed for industrial development. (See Map 9.1 on page 288.)

MAP 2.7
Settlement Patterns in New England Towns, 1630–1700

Throughout New England, colonists pressed onto desirable Indian lands. Initially, most Puritan towns were compact: families lived close to one another in village centers and traveled daily to work in the surrounding fields. This 1640 map of Wethersfield, Connecticut, a town situated on the broad plains of the Connecticut River Valley, shows this pattern clearly. The first settlers in Andover, Massachusetts, also chose to live in the village center. However, the rugged topography of eastern Massachusetts encouraged the townspeople to disperse. By 1692 (as the varied location of new houses shows), many Andover residents were living on farms distant from the village center.

the selectmen who managed town affairs. The farmers also selected the town's representatives to the General Court, which gradually displaced the governor as the center of political authority. For Fish and thousands of other ordinary settlers, New England had proved to be a new world of opportunity.

Instability, War, and Rebellion

Everywhere in the colonies, conflicts arose over the control of resources, the legitimacy of colonial leaders' claims to power, and attempts to define social and cultural norms. Periodically, these conflicts flared spectacularly into episodes of violence. Each episode has its own story — its own unique logic and narrative — but taken together, they also illustrate the way that, in their formative stages, colonial societies pressured people to accept new patterns of authority and new claims to power. When these claims were contested, the results could quickly turn deadly.

New England's Indian Wars

Relations between colonists and Indians in early New England were bewilderingly complex. Many rival Indian groups lived there before Europeans arrived; by the 1630s, these groups were bordered by the Dutch colony of New Netherland to their west and the various English settlements to the east: Plymouth, Massachusetts Bay, Rhode Island, Connecticut, New Haven, and Saybrook. The region's Indian leaders created various alliances for the purposes of trade and defense: Wampanoags with Plymouth; Mohegans with Massachusetts and Connecticut; Pequots with New Netherland; Narragansetts with Rhode Island.

Puritan-Pequot War Because of their alliance with the Dutch, the Pequots became a thorn in the side of English traders. A series of violent encounters began in July 1636 with the killing of English trader John Oldham and escalated until May 1637, when a combined force of Massachusetts and Connecticut

The Hurons' Feast of the Dead

Hurons buried their dead in temporary raised tombs so they could easily care for their spirits. When they moved their villages in search of fertile soil and better hunting, the Hurons held a Feast of the Dead and reburied the bones of their own deceased (and often bones from other villages) in a common pit lined with beaver robes. This solemn ceremony united living as well as dead clan members, strengthening the bonds of the Huron Confederacy. It also was believed to release the spirits of the dead, allowing them to travel to the land where the first Huron, Aataentsic, fell from the sky, "made earth and man," and lived with her son and assistant, Iouskeha. Library of Congress.

militiamen, accompanied by Narragansett and Mohegan warriors, attacked a Pequot village and massacred some five hundred men, women, and children. In the months that followed, the New Englanders drove the surviving Pequots into oblivion and divided their lands.

Believing they were God's chosen people, Puritans considered their presence to be divinely ordained. Initially, they pondered the morality of acquiring Native American lands. "By what right or warrant can we enter into the land of the Savages?" they asked themselves. Responding to such concerns, John Winthrop detected God's hand in a recent smallpox epidemic: "If God were not pleased with our inheriting these parts," he asked, "why doth he still make roome for us by diminishing them as we increase?" Experiences like the Pequot War confirmed New Englanders' confidence in their enterprise. "God laughed at the Enemies of his People," one soldier boasted after the 1637 massacre, "filling the Place with Dead Bodies."

Like Catholic missionaries, Puritans believed that their church should embrace all peoples. However, their strong emphasis on predestination — the idea that God saved only a few chosen people — made it hard for them to accept that Indians could be counted among the elect. "Probably the devil" delivered these "miserable savages" to America, Cotton Mather suggested, "in hopes that the gospel of the Lord Jesus Christ would never come here." A few Puritan ministers committed themselves to the effort to convert Indians. On Martha's Vineyard, Jonathan Mayhew helped to create an Indian-led community of Wampanoag Christians. John Eliot translated the Bible into Algonquian and created fourteen Indian praying towns. By 1670, more than 1,000 Indians lived in these settlements, but relatively few Native Americans were ever permitted to become full members of Puritan congregations.

Metacom's War, 1675–1676

By the 1670s, Europeans in New England outnumbered Indians by three to one. The English population had multiplied to 55,000, while native peoples had diminished from an estimated 120,000 in 1570 to barely 16,000. To the Wampanoag leader Metacom (also known as King Philip), the prospects for coexistence looked dim. When his people copied English ways by raising hogs and selling pork in Boston, Puritan officials accused them of selling at "an under rate" and restricted their trade. When Indians killed wandering hogs that devastated their cornfields, authorities prosecuted them for violating English property rights (American Voices, p. 68).

Metacom concluded that the English colonists had to be expelled. In 1675, the Wampanoags' leader forged

Metacom (King Philip), Chief of the Wampanoags
The Indian War of 1675–1676 left an indelible mark on the history of New England. This painting from the 1850s, done on semitransparent cloth and lit from behind for effect, was used by traveling performers to tell the story of King Philip's War. Notice that Metacom is pictured not as a savage but as a dignified man. No longer in danger of Indian attack, nineteenth-century whites in New England adopted a romanticized version of their region's often brutal history.
© Shelburne Museum, Shelburne, Vermont.

a military alliance with the Narragansetts and Nipmucks and attacked white settlements throughout New England. Almost every day, settler William Harris fearfully reported, he heard new reports of the Indians' "burneing houses, takeing cattell, killing men & women & Children: & carrying others captive." Bitter fighting continued into 1676, ending only when the Indian warriors ran short of gunpowder and the Massachusetts Bay government hired Mohegan and Mohawk warriors, who killed Metacom.

Metacom's War of 1675–1676 (which English settlers called King Philip's War) was a deadly affair. Indians destroyed one-fifth of the English towns in

> **UNDERSTAND POINTS OF VIEW**
> How did New Englanders' religious ideas influence their relations with neighboring Native American peoples?

The Causes of
Metacom's War

The causes of—and responsibility for—every American war are much debated, and the war of 1675–1676 between Puritans and Native Americans is no exception. The English settlers called it King Philip's War, suggesting that the Wampanoag chief Metacom (King Philip) instigated it. Was that the case? We have no firsthand Indian accounts of its origins, but three English accounts offer different versions of events. Given the variation among the accounts and their fragmentary character, how can historians reconstruct what "really happened"?

John Easton
A Relacion of the Indyan Warre

John Easton was the deputy governor of Rhode Island and a Quaker. Like many Quakers, Easton was a pacifist and tried to prevent the war. He wrote this "Relacion" shortly after the conflict ended.

In [January 1675], an Indian was found dead; and by a coroner inquest of Plymouth Colony judged murdered. . . . The dead Indian was called Sassamon, and a Christian that could read and write. . . .

The report came that . . . three Indians had confessed and accused Philip [of employing them to kill Sassamon, and that consequently] . . . the English would hang Philip. So the Indians were afraid, and reported that . . . Philip [believed that the English] . . . might kill him to have his land. . . . So Philip kept his men in arms.

Plymouth governor [Josiah Winslow] required him to disband his men, and informed him his jealousy [his worry about land seizure] was false. Philip answered he would do no harm, and thanked the Governor for his information. The three Indians were hung [on June 8, 1675]. . . . And it was reported [that] Sassamon, before his death had informed [the English] of the Indian plot, and that if the Indians knew it they would kill him, and that the heathen might destroy the English for their wickedness as God had permitted the heathen to destroy the Israelites of old.

So the English were afraid and Philip was afraid and both increased in arms; but for forty years' time reports and jealousies of war had been very frequent that we did not think that now a war was breaking forth. But about a week before it did we had cause to think it would; then to endeavor to prevent it, we sent a man to Philip. . . .

He called his council and agreed to come to us; [Philip] came himself, unarmed, and about forty of his men, armed. Then five of us went over [to speak to the Indians]. Three were magistrates. We sat very friendly together [June 14–18]. We told him our business was to endeavor that they might not . . . do wrong. They said that was well; they had done no wrong; the English wronged them. We said we knew the English said that the Indians wronged them, and the Indians said the English wronged them, but our desire was the quarrel might rightly be decided in the best way, and not as dogs decide their quarrels.

The Indians owned that fighting was the worst way; then they propounded how right might take place; we said by arbitration. They said all English agreed against them; and so by arbitration they had had much wrong, many square miles of land so taken from them, for the English would have English arbitrators. . . .

Another grievance [of the Indians]: the English cattle and horses still increased [and that] . . . they could not keep their corn from being spoiled [by the English livestock]. . . .

So we departed without any discourtesies; and suddenly [c. June 25] had [a] letter from [the] Plymouth governor, [that] they intended in arms to [subjugate] Philip . . . and in a week's time after we had been with the Indians the war thus begun.

Source: John Easton, "A Relacion of the Indyan Warre, by Mr. Easton, of Roade Isld., 1675," in *Narratives of the Indian Wars, 1675–1699*, ed. Charles H. Lincoln (New York: Charles Scribner's Sons, 1913), 7–17.

Edward Randolph
Short Narrative of My Proceedings

Edward Randolph, an English customs official in Boston, denounced the independent policies of the Puritan colonies and tried to subject them to English control. His "Short Narrative," written in 1675, was a report to his superiors in London.

Various are the reports and conjectures of the causes of the present Indian war. Some impute it to an impudent zeal in the magistrates of Boston to Christianize those heathen before they were civilized and enjoining them the strict observation of their laws, which, to a people so rude and licentious, hath proved even intolerable. . . . While the magistrates, for their profit, put the laws severely in execution against the Indians, the people, on the other side, for lucre and gain, entice and provoke the Indians . . . to drunkenness, to which those people are so generally addicted that they will strip themselves to their skin to have their fill of rum and brandy. . . .

Some believe there have been vagrant and jesuitical [French] priests, who have made it their business, for some years past, to go from Sachem to Sachem [chief to chief], to exasperate the Indians against the English and to bring them into a confederacy, and that they were promised supplies from France and other parts to extirpate the English nation out of the continent of America. . . . Others impute the cause to some injuries offered to the Sachem Philip; for he being possessed of a tract of land called Mount Hope . . . some English had a mind to dispossess him thereof, who never wanting one pretence or other to attain their end, complained of injuries done by Philip and his Indians to their stock and cattle, whereupon Philip was often summoned before the magistrate, sometimes imprisoned, and never released but upon parting with a considerable part of his land.

But the government of the Massachusetts . . . do declare [that because of the sins of the people] . . . God hath given the heathen commission to rise against them. . . . For men wearing long hair and periwigs made of women's hair; for women . . . cutting, curling and laying out the hair. . . . For profaneness in the people not frequenting their [church] meetings.

Source: Albert B. Hart, ed., *American History Told by Contemporaries* (New York: Macmillan, 1897), 1: 458–460.

Benjamin Church
Entertaining Passages

Captain Benjamin Church fought in the war and helped end it by capturing Metacom's wife and son and leading the expedition that killed the Indian chieftain. Forty years later, in 1716, Church's son Thomas wrote an account of the war based on his father's notes and recollections.

While Mr. Church was diligently settling his new farm . . . Behold! The rumor of a war between the English and the natives gave a check to his projects. . . . Philip, according to his promise to his people, permitted them to march out of the neck [of the Mount Hope peninsula,

where they lived]. . . . They plundered the nearest houses that the inhabitants had deserted [on the rumor of a war], but as yet offered no violence to the people, at least none were killed. . . . However, the alarm was given by their numbers, and hostile equipage, and by the prey they made of what they could find in the forsaken houses.

An express came the same day to the governor [c. June 25], who immediately gave orders to the captains of the towns to march the greatest part of their companies [of militia], and to rendezvous at Taunton. . . .

The enemy, who began their hostilities with plundering and destroying cattle, did not long content themselves with that game. They thirsted for English blood, and they soon broached it; killing two men in the way not far from Mr. Miles's garrison. And soon after, eight more at Mattapoisett, upon whose bodies they exercised more than brutish barbarities. . . .

These provocations drew out the resentment of some of Capt. Prentice's troop, who desired they might have liberty to go out and seek the enemy in their own quarters [c. June 26].

Source: Benjamin Church, *Entertaining Passages Relating to Philip's War Which Began in the Month of June, 1675*, ed. Thomas Church (Boston: B. Green, 1716).

QUESTIONS FOR ANALYSIS

1. Compare what these documents say about the causes of the war. Where do the documents agree and disagree about these causes?

2. According to Randolph, what did the magistrates of Massachusetts Bay believe to be a major cause of the war? Could historians verify or disprove their explanation? How? What additional sources of evidence might be useful?

3. Drawing from these sources, who was the prime instigator of the war? Which documents provide the most compelling evidence for your conclusion? Why?

Massachusetts and Rhode Island and killed 1,000 settlers, nearly 5 percent of the adult population; for a time the Puritan experiment hung in the balance. But the natives' losses — from famine and disease, death in battle, and sale into slavery — were much larger: about 4,500 Indians died, one-quarter of an already diminished population. Many of the surviving Wampanoag, Narragansett, and Nipmuck peoples moved west, intermarrying with Algonquian tribes allied to the French. Over the next century, these displaced Indian peoples would take their revenge, joining with French Catholics to attack their Puritan enemies. Metacom's War did not eliminate the presence of Native Americans in southern New England, but it effectively destroyed their existence as independent peoples.

Bacon's Rebellion

At the same time that New England fought its war with Metacom, Virginia was wracked by a rebellion that nearly toppled its government. It, too, grew out of a conflict with neighboring Indians, but this one inspired a popular uprising against the colony's royal governor. Like Metacom's War, it highlighted the way that a land-intensive settler colony created friction with Native American populations; in addition, it dramatized the way that ordinary colonists could challenge the right of a new planter elite to rule over them.

By the 1670s, economic and political power in Virginia was in the hands of a small circle of men who amassed land, slaves, and political offices. Through headrights and royal grants, they controlled nearly half of all the settled land in Virginia; what they could not plant themselves, they leased to tenants. Freed indentured servants found it ever harder to get land of their own; many were forced to lease lands, or even sign new indentures, to make ends meet. To make matters worse, the price of tobacco fell until planters received only a penny a pound for their crops in the 1670s.

At the top of Virginia's narrow social pyramid was William Berkeley, governor between 1642 and 1652 and again after 1660. To consolidate power, Berkeley bestowed large land grants on members of his council. The councilors exempted these lands from taxation and appointed friends as justices of the peace and county judges. To win support in the House of Burgesses, Berkeley bought off legislators with land grants and lucrative appointments as sheriffs and tax collectors. But social unrest erupted when the Burgesses took the vote away from landless freemen, who by now constituted half the adult white men. Although property-holding yeomen retained their voting rights, they were angered by falling tobacco prices, political corruption, and "grievous taxations" that threatened the "utter ruin of us the poor commonalty." Berkeley and his allies were living on borrowed time.

Frontier War   An Indian conflict ignited the flame of social rebellion. In 1607, when the English intruded, 30,000 Native Americans resided in Virginia; by 1675, the native population had dwindled to only 3,500. By then, Europeans numbered some 38,000 and Africans another 2,500. Most Indians lived on treaty-guaranteed territory along the frontier, where poor freeholders and landless former servants now wanted to settle, demanding that the natives be expelled or exterminated. Their demands were ignored by wealthy planters, who wanted a ready supply of tenants and laborers, and by Governor Berkeley and the planter-merchants, who traded with the Occaneechee Indians for beaver pelts and deerskins.

Fighting broke out late in 1675, when a vigilante band of Virginia militiamen murdered thirty Indians. Defying Berkeley's orders, a larger force then surrounded a fortified Susquehannock village and killed five leaders who came out to negotiate. The Susquehannocks retaliated by attacking outlying plantations and killing three hundred whites. In response, Berkeley proposed a defensive strategy: a series of frontier forts to deter Indian intrusions. The settlers dismissed this scheme as a militarily useless plot by planter-merchants to impose high taxes and take "all our tobacco into their own hands."

Challenging the Government   Enter Nathaniel Bacon, a young, well-connected migrant from England who emerged as the leader of the rebels. Bacon held a position on the governor's council, but he was shut out of Berkeley's inner circle and differed with Berkeley on Indian policy. When the governor refused to grant him a military commission, Bacon mobilized his neighbors and attacked any Indians he could find. Condemning the frontiersmen as "rebels and mutineers," Berkeley expelled Bacon from the council and had him arrested. But Bacon's army forced the governor to release their leader and hold legislative elections. The newly elected House of Burgesses enacted far-reaching reforms that curbed the powers of the governor and council and restored voting rights to landless freemen.

These much-needed reforms came too late. Poor farmers and servants resented years of exploitation by wealthy planters, arrogant justices of the peace, and

Nathaniel Bacon

Condemned as a rebel and a traitor in his own time, Nathaniel Bacon emerged in the late nineteenth century as a southern hero, a harbinger of the Confederate rebels of 1860–1865. The Association for the Preservation of Virginia Antiquities, founded in 1888, commissioned this stained-glass window depicting Bacon in dual guises of a well-dressed gentleman and a rebel in body armor. Installing Bacon's portrait in a window of the Powder Magazine in Williamsburg (built by Governor Alexander Spotswood in 1715), explained a leading member of the association, would connect "present Virginia with her great and noble past" and commemorate those who shed their "blood for Virginia and the South." Preservation Virginia.

"wicked & pernicious Counsellors." As one yeoman rebel complained, "A poor man who has only his labour to maintain himself and his family pays as much [in taxes] as a man who has 20,000 acres." Backed by 400 armed men, Bacon issued a "Manifesto and Declaration of the People" that demanded the removal of Indians and an end to the rule of wealthy "parasites." "All the power and sway is got into the hands of the rich," Bacon proclaimed as his army burned Jamestown to the ground and plundered the plantations of Berkeley's allies. When Bacon died suddenly of dysentery in October 1676, the governor took revenge, dispersing the rebel army, seizing the estates of well-to-do rebels, and hanging 23 men.

In the wake of Bacon's Rebellion, Virginia's leaders worked harder to appease their humble neighbors. But the rebellion also coincided with the time when Virginia planters were switching from indentured servants, who became free after four years, to slaves, who labored for life. In the eighteenth century, wealthy planters would make common cause with poorer whites, while slaves became the colony's most exploited workers. That fateful change eased tensions within the free population but committed subsequent generations of Americans to a labor system based on racial exploitation. Bacon's Rebellion, like Metacom's War, reminds us that these colonies were unfinished worlds, still searching for viable foundations.

> **PLACE EVENTS IN CONTEXT**
>
> In what ways was Bacon's Rebellion symptomatic of social tensions in the colony of Virginia?

SUMMARY

During the sixteenth and seventeenth centuries, three types of colonies took shape in the Americas. In Mesoamerica and the Andes, Spanish colonists made indigenous empires their own, capitalizing on pre-existing labor systems and using tribute and the discovery of precious metals to generate enormous wealth, which Philip II used to defend the interests of the Catholic Church in Europe. In tropical and subtropical regions, colonizers transferred the plantation complex — a centuries-old form of production and labor discipline — to places suited to growing exotic crops like sugar, tobacco, and indigo. The rigors of plantation agriculture demanded a large supply of labor, which was first filled in English colonies by indentured servitude and later supplemented and eclipsed by African slavery. The third type of colony, neo-European settlement, developed in North America's temperate zone, where European migrants adapted familiar systems of social and economic organization in new settings.

Everywhere in the Americas, colonization was, first and foremost, a process of experimentation. As resources from the Americas flowed to Europe, monarchies were strengthened and the competition among them — sharpened by the schism between Protestants and Catholics — gained new force and energy. Establishing colonies demanded political, social, and cultural innovations that threw Europeans, Native Americans, and Africans together in bewildering circumstances, triggered massive ecological change through the Columbian Exchange, and demanded radical adjustments. In the Chesapeake and New England — the two earliest regions of English settlement on mainland North America — the adjustment to new circumstances sparked conflict with neighboring Indians and waves of instability within the colonies. These external and internal crises were products of the struggle to adapt to the rigors of colonization.

CHAPTER REVIEW

 MAKE IT STICK   Go to **LearningCurve** to retain what you've read.

TERMS TO KNOW   Identify and explain the significance of each term below.

Key Concepts and Events

chattel slavery (p. 40)	indentured servitude (p. 54)
neo-Europes (p. 40)	Pilgrims (p. 60)
encomienda (p. 42)	Puritans (p. 61)
Columbian Exchange (p. 43)	joint-stock corporation (p. 62)
outwork (p. 45)	predestination (p. 62)
mercantilism (p. 45)	toleration (p. 62)
House of Burgesses (p. 52)	covenant of works (p. 62)
royal colony (p. 52)	covenant of grace (p. 62)
freeholds (p. 53)	town meeting (p. 64)
headright system (p. 54)	

Key People

Philip II (p. 44)
Francis Drake (p. 45)
Opechancanough (p. 52)
Lord Baltimore (p. 52)
John Winthrop (p. 61)
Roger Williams (p. 62)
Anne Hutchinson (p. 62)
Metacom (p. 67)

REVIEW QUESTIONS   Answer these questions to demonstrate your understanding of the chapter's main ideas.

1. How did Spain's conquest of central Mexico and the Andes shape European competition in the Americas? How did the Protestant Reformation affect this competition?

2. How did environmental and ecological factors shape colonial enterprise, and how did the process of colonization impact American ecology and environments?

3. What "push factors" caused people to leave England for its colonies in the seventeenth century? What "pull factors" drew them to particular colonies or regions?

4. **THEMATIC UNDERSTANDING** Review the events listed under "Politics and Power" and "Ideas,

Beliefs, and Culture" on the thematic timeline on page 5. How did political developments in seventeenth-century England impact the development of its American colonies?

MAKING CONNECTIONS

Recognize the larger developments and continuities within and across chapters by answering these questions.

1. **ACROSS TIME AND PLACE** In Chapter 1, we saw that there were many parallels between Native American, European, and African societies on the eve of contact. Yet Europeans ended up dominating both Native American and African populations in colonial American settings. Based on what you learned in Chapter 2, what factors help to explain that dominance?

2. **VISUAL EVIDENCE** Take another look at the image of John Smith and Opechancanough on page 49. It is taken from Smith's *Generall Historie of Virginia, New-England, and the Summer Isles*, which was first published in 1624. What is the dominant theme of the image? How might recent events in Virginia have colored the emphases in the book's illustrations?

MORE TO EXPLORE   Start here to learn more about the events discussed in this chapter.

Virginia DeJohn Anderson, *Creatures of Empire* (2004). Explores the significance of animal domestication in early New England and Chesapeake colonies.

Kathleen Brown, *Good Wives, Nasty Wenches, and Anxious Patriarchs* (1996). Examines the interrelationship of gender and race in early Virginia.

Alfred W. Crosby, *Ecological Imperialism* (1986). Introduces the term *neo-Europes* and asks why there are so many of them.

Jenny Hale Pulsipher, *Subjects unto the Same King* (2005). Considers the multifaceted contest for power in seventeenth-century New England.

"The Plymouth Colony Archive Project" (**histarch .uiuc.edu/plymouth/**). A rich array of fully searchable texts and material culture resources.

"Salem Witch Trials" (**etext.virginia.edu/salem /witchcraft/home.html**). Extensive materials on the Salem witchcraft trials, including a fascinating interactive map feature.

TIMELINE   Ask yourself why this chapter begins and ends with these dates and then identify the links among related events.

1550–1630	• English crown supports mercantilism
1556–1598	• Reign of Philip II, king of Spain
1558–1603	• Reign of Elizabeth I, queen of England
1577–1580	• Francis Drake's *Golden Hind* circles the globe, captures Spanish treasure fleet
1560–1620	• Growth of English Puritan movement
1588	• Storms and English ships destroy Spanish Armada
1603–1625	• Reign of James I, king of England
1607	• English traders settle Jamestown (Virginia)
1608	• Samuel de Champlain founds Quebec
1609	• Henry Hudson explores North America for the Dutch
1614	• Dutch set up fur-trading post at Fort Orange (Albany)
1619	• First Africans arrive in Chesapeake region • House of Burgesses convenes in Virginia
1620	• Pilgrims found Plymouth Colony
1620–1660	• Chesapeake colonies enjoy tobacco boom
1621	• Dutch West India Company chartered
1622	• Opechancanough's uprising
1624	• Virginia becomes royal colony
1625–1649	• Reign of Charles I, king of England
1630	• Puritans found Massachusetts Bay Colony
1634	• Colonists arrive in Maryland
1636	• Beginning of Puritan-Pequot War • Roger Williams founds Providence
1637	• Anne Hutchinson banished from Massachusetts Bay
1640s	• Iroquois initiate wars over fur trade
1642–1659	• Puritan Revolution in England
1660	• Restoration of the English monarchy • tobacco prices fall and remain low
1664	• English conquer New Netherland
1675	• Bacon's Rebellion in Virginia
1675–1676	• Metacom's War in New England
1692	• Salem witchcraft trials

KEY TURNING POINTS: The Chesapeake tobacco boom (1620–1660), Opechancanough's uprising (1622), and the takeover of Virginia by the crown (1624). How were these events related to each other? What was their cumulative result?

2

British North America and the Atlantic World
1660–1763

By 1660, the patterns of colonial enterprise in the Americas were becoming clear. For the colonies of England — which became Britain after the 1707 Act of Union with Scotland — the period from 1660 to 1763 was one of growth and diversification. Slave imports to plantation colonies exploded, while a wide array of European peoples — coming from Ireland and continental Europe as well as England, Wales, and Scotland — jostled together in rapidly growing regions of neo-European settlement. Yet a coherent imperial vision for these American holdings emerged slowly, and the colonies remained largely independent of crown control.

After 1689, Europe plunged into a century of warfare that had an enormous impact on the Americas. As wars spilled over into North America, British, French, and Spanish colonies all engaged more deeply with neighboring Indians, whom they often sought to employ as allies in their struggles to control North American territory. Native American polities were undergoing dramatic transformations in these same years, reshaping themselves to function more effectively in relation to their European neighbors. At the same time, warfare, immigration, and trade laid the foundation for more intensive interactions across the Atlantic. These interactions, and the cultural movements they supported, helped to knit together the increasingly diverse colonies of British North America.

Part 2 addresses these developments, giving particular attention to the following three main concepts:

The Diversification of British North America

The American colonies of the various European nations gradually diverged from each other in character. The tribute-based societies at the core of Spain's empire developed into complex multiracial societies; Portuguese Brazil was dominated by its plantation and mining enterprises; the Dutch largely withdrew their energies from the Americas, except for a few plantation colonies; the French, too, developed several important plantation colonies in the West Indies but struggled to populate their vast North American holdings. The population of Britain's colonies, by contrast, grew and diversified after 1660. Britain came to dominate the Atlantic slave trade and brought more than two million slaves to its American colonies. The great majority went to Jamaica, Barbados, and the other sugar islands, but half a million found their way to the mainland, where, by 1763, they constituted nearly 20 percent of the mainland colonies' populations. Slavery was a growing and thriving institution in British North America.

Non-English Europeans also crossed the Atlantic in very large numbers. The ethnic landscape of Britain's mainland colonies was dramatically altered by 115,000 migrants from Ireland (most of them Scots-Irish Presbyterians) and 100,000 Germans. Most immigrated to Pennsylvania, which soon had the most ethnically diverse population of Europeans on the continent. Relations among these groups were often divisive, as each struggled to maintain its identity and autonomy in a rapidly changing landscape.

Rise of the British Atlantic World

These population movements were part of the larger growth and development of the Atlantic World, a phrase historians use to refer to the quickening pace of contacts and exchanges connecting Europe, Africa, and the Americas. The rise of the British Atlantic was a layered phenomenon that began with the strength of Britain's transatlantic shipping networks, which in turn laid the foundation for large-scale population flows, rising economic productivity, and dramatic cultural transformations. The growing power of its navy, merchant marine, and manufacturing sector allowed Britain to dominate the eighteenth-century Atlantic. Much of the cultural impact of its maritime power derived from two further developments: the print revolution, which brought a vast array of ideas into circulation; and the consumer revolution, which flooded the Atlantic World with a wide array of newly available merchandise.

The British Atlantic World gave rise to four critically important cultural developments. It spread Enlightenment ideas and helped to create a transatlantic community of literati interested in science and rationalism; it supported communities of Pietists who promoted the revival and expansion of Christianity; it gave well-to-do colonists access to genteel values and the finery needed to put them into action; and, by making such an abundance of consumer goods available, it encouraged colonists to go further into debt than they ever had before.

Contact and Conflict

Alongside the diversification of colonial populations and the rise of the British Atlantic, the eighteenth century was shaped by contact and conflict: between colonies and their Native American neighbors, and also among rival European empires. In Europe, the period after 1689 has sometimes been called the Second Hundred Years' War, when Britain, France, and their European allies went to war against each other repeatedly. As these conflicts came to the North American theater, they decisively influenced Indian relations. Native American populations shrank dramatically or disappeared altogether during the seventeenth century, devastated by the effects of the Columbian Exchange (Chapter 2). The rise of imperial warfare encouraged the process of "tribalization," whereby Indians regrouped into political structures—called "tribes" by Europeans—that could deal more effectively with their colonial neighbors and strike alliances in times of war. Europeans, in turn, employed Indian allies as proxy warriors in their conflicts over North American territory.

This pattern culminated in the Great War for Empire, which began in the North American backcountry, engaged thousands of provincial soldiers and Native American warriors, and reshaped the map of North America. The Treaty of Paris of 1763 gave Britain control of the entire continent east of the Mississippi. Events would soon show what a mixed blessing that outcome would turn out to be.

British North America and the Atlantic World 1660–1763

Thematic Understanding

This timeline organizes some of the important developments of this period into themes. How did the demographic changes outlined under the theme "Peopling" impact the developments that are listed under "Work, Exchange, and Technology"?   **>**

	WORK, EXCHANGE, & TECHNOLOGY	PEOPLING	POLITICS & POWER	IDEAS, BELIEFS, & CULTURE	IDENTITY
1660	• South Atlantic System links plantation and neo-European colonies • Mercantilist legislation in England: Navigation Acts (1651, 1660, 1663) • New York inherits Hudson River Valley manors from the Dutch; Carolina proprietors try but fail to institute a manorial system • Migrants to Pennsylvania seek freehold lands • Rapid expansion of African slave imports undergirds sugar, tobacco, and rice plantation systems	• The Middle Passage shapes Africans' experiences of arrival • Indian slave trade emerges in South Carolina • First Mennonites arrive in Pennsylvania (1683)	• Dominion of New England (1686–1689) • Glorious Revolution (1688–1689) • War of the League of Augsburg (1689–1697) • Founding of the Restoration Colonies: the Carolinas (1663), New York (1664), Pennsylvania (1681)	• Collapse of the Puritan Commonwealth leads to toleration in England • Isaac Newton publishes *Principia Mathematica* (1687)	• Restoration makes England a monarchy again; royalist revival • The Glorious Revolution makes England a constitutional monarchy • Massachusetts loses its charter (1684) and gains a new one (1691)
1690	• New England shipbuilding industry and merchant community come to dominate the coastal trade • Agricultural labor and artisanal skills in high demand in the Middle colonies	• Quakers emigrate to Pennsylvania and New Jersey • Second wave of Germans arrives in Pennsylvania, Shenandoah Valley	• Parliament creates Board of Trade (1696) • War of the Spanish Succession (1702–1713)	• John Locke publishes *Two Treatises on Government* (1690) • Rise of toleration among colonial Protestants • Print revolution begins	• Colonists gain autonomy in the post–Glorious Revolution era • Tribalization developing among Native American peoples
1720	• The price of wheat rises (doubles in Philadelphia, 1720–1770) • British trade dominates the Atlantic • Opportunity and inequality in the Middle colonies • Ohio Company of Virginia receives 200,000 acres (1749)	• Scots-Irish begin migrating to Pennsylvania (c. 1720) • Parliament charters Georgia (1732) • Penns make Walking Purchase from the Delawares (1737)	• Robert Walpole is prime minister (1720–1742) • Stono Rebellion (1739) • War of Jenkins's Ear (1739–1741) • War of the Austrian Succession (1740–1748)	• George Whitefield's visit to America sparks the Great Awakening (1739) • Benjamin Franklin founds American Philosophical Society (1743) • New colleges, newspapers, magazines	• African American community forms in the Chesapeake • Planter aristocracy emerges in the Chesapeake and South Carolina • Culture of gentility spreads among well-to-do
1750	• Freehold society in crisis in New England • Half of Middle colonies' white men landless • Conflicts over western lands and political power (1750–1775) • British industry being mechanized; colonial debt crisis	• 40,000 Germans and Swiss emigrate to Pennsylvania (1749–1756) • Anglo-Americans pushing onto backcountry lands	• French and Indian War/Seven Years' War (1754–1763) • The Albany Congress (1754) • The Treaty of Paris (1763) • Pontiac's Rebellion (1763)	• At least twelve religious denominations in Philadelphia • Neolin promotes nativist revival among Ohio Indians (1763)	• Victory in the Great War for Empire sparks pro-British pride in the colonies • Desire for political autonomy and economic independence strong

3

CHAPTER

The British Atlantic World
1660–1750

For two weeks in June 1744, the town of Lancaster, Pennsylvania, hosted more than 250 Iroquois men, women, and children for a diplomatic conference with representatives from Pennsylvania, Maryland, and Virginia. Crowds of curious observers thronged Lancaster's streets and courthouse. The conference grew out of a diplomatic system between the colonies and the Iroquois designed to air grievances and resolve conflict: the Covenant Chain. Participants welcomed each other, exchanged speeches, and negotiated agreements in public ceremonies whose minutes became part of the official record of the colonies.

At Lancaster, the colonies had much to ask of their Iroquois allies. For one thing, they wanted them to confirm a land agreement. The Iroquois often began such conferences by resisting land deals; as the Cayuga orator Gachradodon said, "You know very well, when the White people came first here they were poor; but now they have got our Lands, and are by them become rich, and we are now poor; what little we have had for the Land goes soon away, but the Land lasts forever." In the end, however, they had little choice but to accept merchandise in exchange for land, since colonial officials were unwilling to take no for an answer. The colonists also announced that Britain was once again going to war with France, and they requested military support from their Iroquois allies. Canassatego—a tall, commanding Onondaga orator, about sixty years old, renowned for his eloquence—replied, "We shall never forget that you and we have but one Heart, one Head, one Eye, one Ear, and one Hand. We shall have all your Country under our Eye, and take all the Care we can to prevent any Enemy from coming into it."

 To see a longer excerpt of the Canassatego document, along with other primary sources from this period, see *Sources for America's History*.

The Lancaster conference—and dozens of others like it that occurred between 1660 and 1750—demonstrates that the British colonies, like those of France and Spain, relied ever more heavily on alliances with Native Americans as they sought to extend their power in North America. Indian nations remade themselves in these same years, creating political structures—called "tribes" by Europeans—that allowed them to regroup in the face of population decline and function more effectively alongside neighboring colonies. The colonies, meanwhile, were drawn together into an integrated economic sphere—the South Atlantic System—that brought prosperity to British North America, while they achieved a measure of political autonomy that became essential to their understanding of what it meant to be British subjects.

IDENTIFY THE BIG IDEA

How did the South Atlantic System create an interconnected Atlantic World, and how did this system impact development in the British colonies?

English Tobacco Label, c. 1700 This label, which was used to advertise Virginia tobacco to London consumers, illustrates the growth of plantation economies in North America. Three well-to-do planters, bewigged and dressed in fashionable, colorful coats, take their ease with pipes of tobacco and glasses of liquor while slaves labor for them in the fields. The product's name—London's Virginia—highlights the relationship between production on colonial plantations and consumption in the English metropolis. The Granger Collection, New York.

Colonies to Empire, 1660–1713

Before 1660, England governed its New England and Chesapeake colonies haphazardly. Taking advantage of that laxness and the English civil war, local "big men" (Puritan magistrates and tobacco planters) ran their societies as they wished. Following the restoration of the monarchy in 1660, royal bureaucrats tried to impose order on the unruly settlements and, enlisting the aid of Indian allies, warred with rival European powers.

The Restoration Colonies and Imperial Expansion

Charles II (r. 1660–1685) expanded English power in Asia and America. In 1662, he married the Portuguese princess Catherine of Braganza, whose dowry included the islands of Bombay (present-day Mumbai). Then, in 1663, Charles initiated new outposts in America by authorizing eight loyal noblemen to settle Carolina, an area that had long been claimed by Spain and populated by thousands of Indians. The following year, he awarded the just-conquered Dutch colony of New Netherland to his brother James, the Duke of York, who renamed the colony New York and then re-granted a portion of it, called New Jersey, to another group of proprietors. Finally, in 1681, Charles granted a vast track to William Penn: Pennsylvania, or "Penn's Woods." In a great land grab, England had ousted the Dutch from North America, intruded into Spain's northern empire, and claimed all the land in between.

The Carolinas   In 1660, English settlement was concentrated in New England and the Chesapeake. Five corporate colonies coexisted in New England: Massachusetts Bay, Plymouth, Connecticut, New Haven, and Rhode Island. (Connecticut absorbed New Haven in 1662, while Massachusetts Bay became a royal colony and absorbed Plymouth in 1692.) In the Chesapeake, Virginia was controlled by the crown while Maryland was in the hands of a Lord Proprietor. Like Lord Baltimore's Maryland, the new settlements in Carolina, New York, New Jersey, and Pennsylvania — the Restoration Colonies, as historians call them — were **proprietorships**: the Carolina and Jersey grantees, the Duke of York, and William Penn owned all the land in their new colonies and could rule them as they wished, provided that their laws conformed broadly to those of England (Table 3.1). Indeed, in New York, James II refused to allow an elective assembly and ruled by decree. The Carolina proprietors envisioned a

traditional European society; there the Fundamental Constitutions of Carolina (1669) legally established the Church of England and prescribed a manorial system, with a mass of serfs governed by a handful of powerful nobles.

The manorial system proved a fantasy. The first North Carolina settlers were a mixture of poor families and runaway servants from Virginia and English Quakers, an equality-minded Protestant sect (also known as the Society of Friends). Quakers "think there is no difference between a Gentleman and a labourer," complained an Anglican clergyman. Refusing to work on large manors, the settlers raised corn, hogs, and tobacco on modest family farms. Inspired by Bacon's Rebellion, they rebelled in 1677 against taxes on tobacco and again in 1708 against taxes to support the Anglican Church. Through their stubborn independence, residents forced the proprietors to abandon their dreams of a feudal society.

In South Carolina, the colonists also went their own way. The leading white settlers there were migrants from overcrowded Barbados. Hoping to re-create that island's hierarchical slave society, they used enslaved workers — both Africans and Native Americans — to raise cattle and food crops for export to the West Indies. Carolina merchants opened a lucrative trade in deerskins and Indian slaves with neighboring peoples. Then, around 1700, South Carolina planters hit upon rice cultivation. The swampy estuaries of the coastal low country could be modified with sluices, floodgates, and check dams to create ideal rice-growing conditions, and slaves could do the backbreaking work. By 1708, white Carolinians relied upon a few thousand slaves to work their coastal plantations; thereafter, the African population exploded. Blacks outnumbered whites by 1710 and constituted two-thirds of the population by 1740.

William Penn and Pennsylvania   In contrast to the Carolinas, which languished for decades with proprietors and colonists at odds, William Penn's colony was marked by unity of purpose: all who came hoped to create a prosperous neo-European settlement that approximated the social and economic systems they knew at home. In 1681, Charles II bestowed Pennsylvania (which included present-day Delaware) on William Penn as payment for a large debt owed to Penn's father. The younger Penn, though born to wealth — he owned substantial estates in Ireland and England and lived lavishly — joined the **Quakers**, who condemned extravagance. Penn designed Pennsylvania as a refuge for his fellow Quakers, who were persecuted in England because they refused to serve in the military or pay taxes to support the Church of England. Penn

TABLE 3.1

English Colonies Established in North America, 1660–1750

Colony	Date	Original Colony Type	Religion	Status in 1775	Chief Export/ Economic Activity
Carolina	1663	Proprietary	Church of England	Royal	
North	1691				Farming, naval stores
South	1691				Rice, indigo
New Jersey	1664	Proprietary	Church of England	Royal	Wheat
New York	1664	Proprietary	Church of England	Royal	Wheat
Pennsylvania	1681	Proprietary	Quaker	Proprietary	Wheat
Georgia	1732	Trustees	Church of England	Royal	Rice
New Hampshire (separated from Massachusetts)	1741	Royal	Congregationalist	Royal	Mixed farming, lumber, naval stores
Nova Scotia	1749	Royal	Church of England	Royal	Fishing, mixed farming, naval stores

himself had spent more than two years in jail in England for preaching his beliefs.

Like the Puritans, the Quakers sought to restore Christianity to its early simple spirituality. But they rejected the Puritans' pessimistic Calvinist doctrines, which restricted salvation to a small elect. The Quakers followed the teachings of two English visionaries, George Fox and Margaret Fell, who argued that God had imbued all men — and women — with an "inner light" of grace or understanding. Reflecting the sect's emphasis on gender equality, 350 Quaker women would serve as ministers in the colonies.

Mindful of the catastrophic history of Indian relations in the Chesapeake and New England, Penn exhorted colonists to "sit downe Lovingly" alongside the Native American inhabitants of the Delaware and Susquehanna valleys. He wrote a letter to the leaders of the Iroquois Confederacy alerting them to his intention to settle a colony, and in 1682 he arranged a public treaty with the Delaware Indians to purchase the lands that Philadelphia and the surrounding settlements would soon occupy.

Penn's Frame of Government (1681) applied the Quakers' radical beliefs to politics. It ensured religious freedom by prohibiting a legally established church, and it promoted political equality by allowing all property-owning men to vote and hold office.

Cheered by these provisions, thousands of Quakers, mostly yeoman families from the northwest Midland region of England, flocked to Pennsylvania. To attract European Protestants, Penn published pamphlets in Germany promising cheap land and religious toleration. In 1683, migrants from Saxony founded Germantown (just outside Philadelphia), and thousands of other Germans soon followed. Ethnic diversity, pacifism, and freedom of conscience made Pennsylvania the most open and democratic of the Restoration Colonies.

From Mercantilism to Imperial Dominion

As Charles II distributed American land, his ministers devised policies to keep colonial trade in English hands. Since the 1560s, the English crown had pursued mercantilist policies, using government subsidies and charters to stimulate English manufacturing and foreign trade. Now it extended these mercantilist strategies to the American settlements through the **Navigation Acts** (Table 3.2).

The Navigation Acts   Believing they had to control trade with the colonies to reap their economic benefits, English ministers wanted agricultural goods and raw materials to be carried to English ports in English

William Penn's Treaty with the Indians, 1771
Benjamin West executed this famous picture of William Penn's 1683 meeting with the Lenni-Lenapes, who called themselves the Common People. A Quaker pacifist, Penn refused to seize Indian lands by force and negotiated their purchase. But his son, Thomas Penn, probably had a political purpose when he commissioned the painting in 1771. By evoking a peaceful past, West's work reinforced the Penn family's proprietary claims, which were under strong attack by the Pennsylvania assembly. Pennsylvania Academy of the Fine Arts, Philadelphia, USA / The Bridgeman Art Library.

vessels. In reality, Dutch and French shippers were often buying sugar and other colonial products from English colonies and carrying them directly into foreign markets. To counter this practice, the Navigation Act of 1651 required that goods be carried on ships owned by English or colonial merchants. New parliamentary acts in 1660 and 1663 strengthened the ban on foreign traders: colonists could export sugar and tobacco only to England and import European goods only through England; moreover, three-quarters of the crew on English vessels had to be English. To pay the customs officials who enforced these laws, the Revenue Act of 1673 imposed a "plantation duty" on American exports of sugar and tobacco.

PLACE EVENTS IN CONTEXT
How did the ambitions of Charles II and James II remake English North America?

The English government backed these policies with military force. In three wars between 1652 and 1674, the English navy drove the Dutch from New Netherland and contested Holland's control of the Atlantic slave trade by attacking Dutch forts and ships along the West African coast. Meanwhile, English merchants expanded their fleets, which increased in capacity from 150,000 tons in 1640 to 340,000 tons in 1690. This growth occurred on both sides of the Atlantic; by 1702, only London and Bristol had more ships registered in port than did the town of Boston.

Though colonial ports benefitted from the growth of English shipping, many colonists violated the Navigation Acts. Planters continued to trade with Dutch shippers, and New England merchants imported sugar and molasses from the French West Indies. The Massachusetts Bay assembly boldly declared: "The laws of

TABLE 3.2		
Navigation Acts, 1651–1751		
	Purpose	**Compliance**
Act of 1651	Cut Dutch trade	Mostly ignored
Act of 1660	Ban foreign shipping; enumerate goods that go only to England	Partially obeyed
Act of 1663	Allow European imports only through England	Partially obeyed
Staple Act (1673)	Ensure enumerated goods go only to England	Mostly obeyed
Act of 1696	Prevent frauds; create vice-admiralty courts	Mostly obeyed
Woolen Act (1699)	Prevent export or intercolonial sale of textiles	Partially obeyed
Hat Act (1732)	Prevent export or intercolonial sale of hats	Partially obeyed
Molasses Act (1733)	Cut American imports of molasses from French West Indies	Extensively violated
Iron Act (1750)	Prevent manufacture of finished iron products	Extensively violated
Currency Act (1751)	End use of paper currency as legal tender in New England	Mostly obeyed

England are bounded within the seas [surrounding it] and do not reach America." Outraged by this insolence, customs official Edward Randolph called for troops to "reduce Massachusetts to obedience." Instead, the Lords of Trade — the administrative body charged with colonial affairs — chose a less violent, but no less confrontational, strategy. In 1679, it denied the claim of Massachusetts Bay to New Hampshire and eventually established a separate royal colony there. Then, in 1684, the Lords of Trade persuaded an English court to annul the Massachusetts Bay charter by charging the Puritan government with violating the Navigation Acts and virtually outlawing the Church of England.

The Dominion of New England   The Puritans' troubles had only begun, thanks to the accession of King James II (r. 1685–1688), an aggressive and inflexible ruler. During the reign of Oliver Cromwell, James had grown up in exile in France, and he admired its authoritarian king, Louis XIV. James wanted stricter control over the colonies and targeted New England for his reforms. In 1686, the Lords of Trade revoked the charters of Connecticut and Rhode Island and merged them with Massachusetts Bay and Plymouth to form a new royal province, the **Dominion of New England**. As governor of the Dominion, James II appointed Sir Edmund Andros, a hard-edged former military officer. Two years later, James II added New York and New Jersey to the Dominion, creating a vast colony that stretched from Maine to Pennsylvania (Map 3.1).

MAP 3.1

The Dominion of New England, 1686–1689

In the Dominion, James II created a vast royal colony that stretched nearly 500 miles along the Atlantic coast. During the Glorious Revolution in England, politicians and ministers in Boston and New York City led revolts that ousted Dominion officials and repudiated their authority. King William and Queen Mary replaced the Dominion with governments that balanced the power held by imperial authorities and local political institutions.

The Dominion extended to America the authoritarian model of colonial rule that the English government had imposed on Catholic Ireland. James II ordered Governor Andros to abolish the existing legislative assemblies. In Massachusetts, Andros banned town meetings, angering villagers who prized local self-rule, and advocated public worship in the Church of England, offending Puritan Congregationalists. Even worse, from the colonists' perspective, the governor invalidated all land titles granted under the original Massachusetts Bay charter. Andros offered to provide new deeds, but only if the colonists would pay an annual fee.

The Glorious Revolution in England and America

Fortunately for the colonists, James II angered English political leaders as much as Andros alienated colonists. The king revoked the charters of English towns, rejected the advice of Parliament, and aroused popular opposition by openly practicing Roman Catholicism. Then, in 1688, James's Spanish Catholic wife gave birth to a son. To forestall the outcome of having a Catholic heir to the English throne, Protestant bishops and parliamentary leaders in the Whig Party invited William of Orange, a staunchly Protestant Dutch prince who was married to James's Protestant daughter, Mary Stuart, to come to England at the head of an invading army. With their support, William led a quick and nearly bloodless coup, and King James II was overthrown in an event dubbed the **Glorious Revolution** by

its supporters. Whig politicians forced King William and Queen Mary to accept the Declaration of Rights, creating a constitutional monarchy that enhanced the powers of the House of Commons at the expense of the crown. The Whigs wanted political power, especially the power to levy taxes, to reside in the hands of the gentry, merchants, and other substantial property owners.

To justify their coup, the members of Parliament relied on political philosopher John Locke. In his *Two Treatises on Government* (1690), Locke rejected the divine-right monarchy celebrated by James II, arguing that the legitimacy of government rests on the consent of the governed and that individuals have inalienable natural rights to life, liberty, and property. Locke's celebration of individual rights and representative government had a lasting influence in America, where many political leaders wanted to expand the powers of the colonial assemblies.

Rebellions in America   The Glorious Revolution sparked rebellions by Protestant colonists in Massachusetts, Maryland, and New York. When news of the coup reached Boston in April 1689, Puritan leaders and 2,000 militiamen seized Governor Andros and shipped him back to England. Heeding American complaints of authoritarian rule, the new monarchs broke up the Dominion of New England. However, they refused to restore the old Puritan-dominated government of Massachusetts Bay, instead creating in 1692 a new royal colony (which included Plymouth and Maine). The new charter empowered the king to

The Leviathan Absolutist State

This detail from the title-page engraving of Thomas Hobbes's *Leviathan* (1651) conveys Hobbes's belief that peace and security required submission to a powerful sovereign. In this image, a giant king looms over his domain, his staff and sword symbolizing his civil and religious powers. He is the head of a body made up of the multitudes of his faceless and voiceless subjects, as they carry out his commands. What Hobbes celebrated, a majority of English politicians and people rejected. Fearing the claims of absolute power by Stuart kings, they revolted twice, executing Charles I in 1649 and deposing James II in 1688. Title page from the first edition of Thomas Hobbes's *Leviathan*, published in 1651.

appoint the governor and customs officials, gave the vote to all male property owners (not just Puritan church members), and eliminated Puritan restrictions on the Church of England.

In Maryland, the uprising had economic as well as religious causes. Since 1660, falling tobacco prices had hurt poorer farmers, who were overwhelmingly Protestant, while taxes and fees paid to mostly Catholic proprietary officials continued to rise. When Parliament ousted James II, a Protestant association mustered 700 men and forcibly removed the Catholic governor. The Lords of Trade supported this Protestant initiative: they suspended Lord Baltimore's proprietorship, imposed royal government, and made the Church of England the legal religion in the colony. This arrangement lasted until 1715, when Benedict Calvert, the fourth Lord Baltimore, converted to the Anglican faith and the king restored the proprietorship to the Calvert family.

In New York, a Dutchman named Jacob Leisler led the rebellion against the Dominion of New England. Initially he enjoyed broad support, but he soon alienated many English-speaking New Yorkers and well-to-do Dutch residents. Leisler's heavy-handed tactics made him vulnerable; when William and Mary appointed Henry Sloughter as governor in 1691, Leisler was indicted for treason, hanged, and decapitated—an act of ethnic vengeance that corrupted New York politics for a generation.

The Glorious Revolution of 1688–1689 began a new era in the politics of both England and its American colonies. In England, William and Mary ruled as **constitutional monarchs**; overseas, they promoted an empire based on commerce. They accepted the overthrow of James's disastrous Dominion of New England and allowed Massachusetts (under its new charter) and New York to resume self-government. In 1696, Parliament created a new body, the Board of Trade, to oversee

> **EXPLAIN CONSEQUENCES**
> How did the Glorious Revolution affect relations between England and its colonies?

King William III and Mary II

Rejecting Hobbes's vision of Leviathan and James II's attempts to impose absolutism, a group of England's most powerful politicians invited William of Orange—a prince of the Dutch Republic—to invade England, depose James II, and occupy the throne jointly with his wife Mary. William's army quickly overthrew James in the so-called Glorious Revolution of 1688, an event that reverberated across the Atlantic in rebellions in Massachusetts, Maryland, and New York. This portrait, from the Guild Book of the Barber Surgeons of York, was probably painted to celebrate the coronation of William and Mary in 1689. HIP/Art Resource, NY.

colonial affairs. While the Board of Trade continued to pursue the mercantilist policies that made the colonies economically beneficial, otherwise it permitted local elites to maintain a strong hand in colonial affairs. As England plunged into a new era of European warfare, its leaders had little choice but to allow its colonies substantial autonomy.

Imperial Wars and Native Peoples

The price that England paid for bringing William of Orange to the throne was a new commitment to warfare on the continent. England wanted William because of his unambiguous Protestant commitments; William wanted England because of the resources it could bring to bear in European wars. Beginning with the War of the League of Augsburg in 1689, England embarked on an era sometimes called the **Second Hundred Years' War**, which lasted until the defeat of Napoleon at Waterloo in 1815. In that time, England (Britain after 1707) fought in seven major wars; the longest era of peace lasted only twenty-six years (Table 3.3).

Imperial wars transformed North America. Prior to 1689, American affairs were distant from those of Europe, but the recurrent wars of the eighteenth century spilled over repeatedly into the colonies. Governments were forced to arm themselves and create new alliances with neighboring Native Americans, who tried to turn the fighting to their own advantage. Although war brought money to the American colonies in the form of war contracts, it also placed new demands on colonial governments to support the increasingly militant British Empire. To win wars in Western Europe, the Caribbean, and far-flung oceans, British leaders created a powerful central state that spent three-quarters of its revenue on military and naval expenses.

Tribalization

For Native Americans, the rise of war intersected with a process scholars have called **tribalization**: the adaptation of stateless peoples to the demands imposed on them by neighboring states. In North America, tribalization occurred in catastrophic circumstances. Eurasian diseases rapidly killed off broad swaths of native communities, disproportionately victimizing the old and the very young. In oral cultures, old people were irreplaceable repositories of knowledge, while the young were quite literally the future. With populations in free fall, many polities disappeared altogether. By the eighteenth century, the groups that survived had all been transformed. Many were polyglot peoples: Some new tribes, like the Catawbas, had not existed before and were pieced together from remnants of formerly large groups. Other nations, like the Iroquois, declined in numbers but sustained themselves by adopting many

TABLE 3.3			
English Wars, 1650–1750			
War	**Date**	**Purpose**	**Result**
Anglo-Dutch	1652–1654	Control markets and African slave trade	Stalemate
Anglo-Dutch	1664	Markets; conquest	England takes New Amsterdam
Anglo-Dutch	1673	Commercial markets	England makes maritime gains
King William's	1689–1697	Maintain European balance of power	Stalemate in North America
Queen Anne's	1702–1713	Maintain European balance of power	British acquire Hudson Bay and Nova Scotia
Jenkins's Ear	1739–1741	Expand markets in Spanish America	English merchants expand influence
King George's	1740–1748	Maintain European balance of power	Capture and return of Louisbourg

war captives. In the Carolina borderlands, a large number of Muskogean-speaking communities came together as a nation known to the British as the "Creek" Indians, so named because some of them lived on Ochese Creek. Similarly, the Cherokees, the Delawares, and other groups that were culturally linked but politically fragmented became coherent "tribes" to deal more effectively with their European neighbors.

The rise of imperial warfare exposed Native American communities to danger, but it also gave them newfound leverage. The Iroquois were radically endangered by imperial conflict: a promised English alliance failed them, and in 1693 a combined force of French soldiers, militiamen, and their Indian allies burned all three Mohawk villages to the ground. Thereafter, the Iroquois devised a strategy for playing French and English interests off against each other. In 1701, they made alliances with both empires, declaring their intention to remain neutral in future conflicts between

them. This did not mean that the Iroquois stayed on the sideline: Iroquois warriors often participated in raids during wartime, and Iroquois spokesmen met regularly with representatives of New York and New France to affirm their alliances and receive diplomatic gifts that included guns, powder, lead, clothing, and rum (from the British) or brandy (from the French). Their neutrality, paradoxically, made them more sought after as allies. For example, their alliance with New York, known as the **Covenant Chain**, soon became a model for relations between the British Empire and other Native American peoples.

Imperial warfare also reshaped Indian relations in the Southeast. During the War of the Spanish Succession (1702–1713), which pitted Britain against France and Spain, English settlers in the Carolinas armed the Creeks, whose 15,000 members farmed the fertile lands along the present-day border of Georgia and Alabama. A joint English-Creek expedition attacked Spanish

The "Four Indian Kings" in London, 1710

After a failed invasion of Canada in 1709, a colonial delegation went to London to ask the queen to try again. They brought four Indians with them—three Mohawks and a Mahican—and presented them in London as the "Four Indian Kings" of the Iroquois. The four kings met Queen Anne, dined with nobility, attended the theater, and toured the sites. They sat for several portraits, which were engraved for prints like this one. The queen agreed to make another try for Canada, but the 1711 invasion failed again. Albany Institute of History and Art, Gift of the Estate of Cornelia Cogswell (Mrs. Henry M. Sage) 1972.65.7.

Florida, burning the town of St. Augustine but failing to capture the fort. To protect Havana in nearby Cuba, the Spanish reinforced St. Augustine and unsuccessfully attacked Charleston, South Carolina.

Indian Goals

The Creeks had their own agenda: to become the dominant tribe in the region, they needed to vanquish their longtime enemies, the pro-French Choctaws to the west and the Spanish-allied Apalachees to the south. Beginning in 1704, a force of Creek and Yamasee warriors destroyed the remaining Franciscan missions in northern Florida, attacked the Spanish settlement at Pensacola, and captured a thousand Apalachees, whom they sold to South Carolinian slave traders for sale in the West Indies. Simultaneously, a Carolina-supported Creek expedition attacked the Iroquois-speaking Tuscarora people of North Carolina, killing hundreds, executing 160 male captives, and sending 400 women and children into slavery. The surviving Tuscaroras joined the Iroquois in New York (who now became the Six Nations of the Iroquois). The Carolinians, having used the Creeks to kill Spaniards, now died at the hands of their former allies: when English traders demanded payment for trade debts in 1715, the Creeks and Yamasees revolted, killing 400 colonists before being overwhelmed by the Carolinians and their new Indian allies, the Cherokees.

Native Americans also joined in the warfare between French Catholics in Canada and English Protestants in New England. With French aid, Catholic Mohawk and Abenaki warriors took revenge on their Puritan enemies. They destroyed English settlements in Maine and, in 1704, attacked the western Massachusetts town of Deerfield, where they killed 48 residents and carried 112 into captivity. In response, New England militia attacked French settlements and, in 1710, joined with British naval forces to seize Port Royal in French Acadia (Nova Scotia). However, a major British–New England expedition against the French stronghold at Quebec, inspired in part by the visit of four Indian "kings" to London, failed miserably.

Stalemated militarily in America, Britain won major territorial and commercial concessions through its victories in Europe. In the Treaty of Utrecht (1713), Britain obtained Newfoundland, Acadia, and the Hudson Bay region of northern Canada from France, as well as access through Albany to the western Indian trade. From Spain, Britain acquired the strategic fortress of Gibraltar at the entrance to the Mediterranean and a thirty-year contract to supply slaves to Spanish America. These gains advanced Britain's quest for commercial supremacy and brought peace to eastern North America for a generation (Map 3.2).

The Imperial Slave Economy

Britain's focus on America reflected the growth of a new agricultural and commercial order — the **South Atlantic System** — that produced sugar, tobacco, rice, and other tropical and subtropical products for an international market. Its plantation societies were ruled by European planter-merchants and worked by hundreds of thousands of enslaved Africans (Figure 3.1).

The South Atlantic System

The South Atlantic System had its center in Brazil and the West Indies, and sugar was its primary product. Before 1500, there were few sweet foods in Europe — mostly honey and fruits — so when European planters developed vast sugarcane plantations in America, they found a ready market for their crop. (The craving for the potent new sweet food was so intense that, by 1900, sugar accounted for an astonishing 20 percent of the calories consumed by the world's people.)

European merchants, investors, and planters garnered the profits of the South Atlantic System. Following mercantilist principles, they provided the plantations with tools and equipment to grow and process the sugarcane and ships to carry it to Europe. But it was the Atlantic slave trade that made the system run. Between 1520 and 1650, Portuguese traders carried about 820,000 Africans across the Atlantic — about 4,000 slaves a year before 1600 and 10,000 annually thereafter. Over the next half century, the Dutch dominated the Atlantic slave trade; then, between 1700 and 1800, the British transported about 2.5 million of the total of 6.1 million Africans carried to the Americas.

England and the West Indies   England was a latecomer to the plantation economy, but from the beginning the prospect of a lucrative cash crop drew large numbers of migrants. On St. Kitts, Nevis, Montserrat, and Barbados, most early settlers were small-scale English farmers (and their indentured servants) who exported tobacco and livestock hides; on this basis, they created small but thriving colonies. In 1650, there were more English residents in the West Indies (some 44,000) than in the Chesapeake (20,000) and New England (23,000) colonies combined.

UNDERSTAND POINTS OF VIEW
What did Native Americans have to gain by participating in imperial wars?

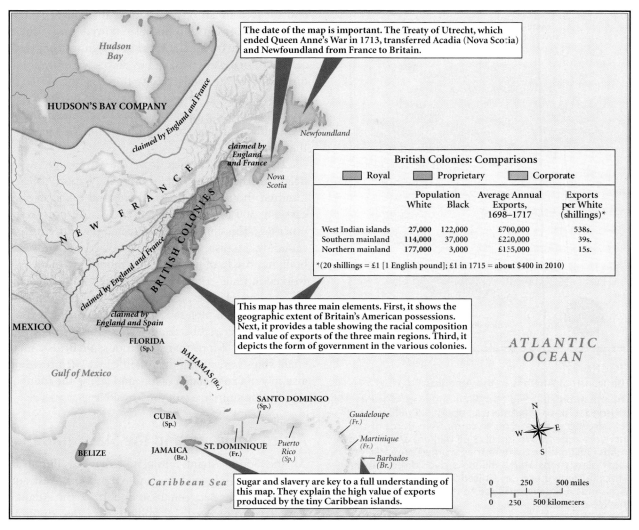

Within the map:

Hudson Bay

HUDSON'S BAY COMPANY

claimed by England and France

Newfoundland

> The date of the map is important. The Treaty of Utrecht, which ended Queen Anne's War in 1713, transferred Acadia (Nova Scotia) and Newfoundland from France to Britain.

claimed by England and France

Nova Scotia

NEW FRANCE

BRITISH COLONIES

claimed by England and France

MEXICO

claimed by England and Spain

FLORIDA (Sp.)

BAHAMAS (Br.)

Gulf of Mexico

SANTO DOMINGO (Sp.)

Guadeloupe (Fr.)

CUBA (Sp.)

Martinique (Fr.)

BELIZE

JAMAICA (Br.)

ST. DOMINIQUE (Fr.)

Puerto Rico (Sp.)

Barbados (Br.)

Caribbean Sea

ATLANTIC OCEAN

> This map has three main elements. First, it shows the geographic extent of Britain's American possessions. Next, it provides a table showing the racial composition and value of exports of the three main regions. Third, it depicts the form of government in the various colonies.

> Sugar and slavery are key to a full understanding of this map. They explain the high value of exports produced by the tiny Caribbean islands.

0   250   500 miles
0   250   500 kilometers

British Colonies: Comparisons

Royal   Proprietary   Corporate

	Population White	Black	Average Annual Exports, 1698–1717	Exports per White (shillings)*
West Indian islands	27,000	122,000	£700,000	538s.
Southern mainland	114,000	37,000	£220,000	39s.
Northern mainland	177,000	3,000	£135,000	15s.

*(20 shillings = £1 [1 English pound]; £1 in 1715 = about $400 in 2010)

MAP 3.2
Britain's American Empire, 1713

Many of Britain's possessions in the West Indies were tiny islands, mere dots on the Caribbean Sea. However, in 1713, these small pieces of land were by far the most valuable parts of the empire. Their sugar crops brought wealth to English merchants, commerce to the northern colonies, and a brutal life and early death to the hundreds of thousands of African slaves working on the plantations.

After 1650, sugar transformed Barbados and the other islands into slave-based plantation societies, a change facilitated by English capital combined with the knowledge and experience of Dutch merchants. By 1680, an elite group of 175 planters, described by one antislavery writer of the time as "inhumane and barbarous," dominated Barbados's economy; they owned more than half of the island, thousands of indentured servants, and half of its more than 50,000 slaves. In 1692, exploited Irish servants and island-born African slaves staged a major uprising, which was brutally suppressed. The "leading principle" in a slave society, declared one West Indian planter, was to instill "fear" among workers and a commitment to "absolute coercive" force among masters. As social inequality and racial conflict increased, hundreds of English farmers fled to South Carolina and the large island of Jamaica. But the days of Caribbean smallholders were numbered. English sugar merchants soon invested heavily in Jamaica; by 1750, it had seven hundred large sugar plantations, worked by more than 105,000 slaves, and had become the wealthiest British colony.

Sugar was a rich man's crop because it could be produced most efficiently on large plantations. Scores of slaves planted and cut the sugarcane, which was then processed by expensive equipment — crushing mills,

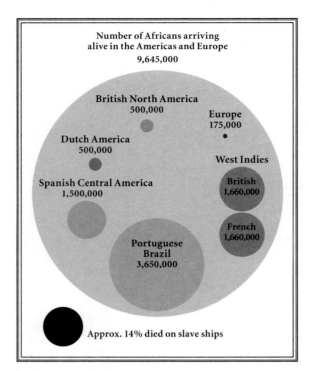

**Number of Africans arriving
alive in the Americas and Europe
9,645,000**

British North America
500,000

Europe
175,000

Dutch America
500,000

West Indies

Spanish Central America
1,500,000

British
1,660,000

French
1,660,000

Portuguese
Brazil
3,650,000

Approx. 14% died on slave ships

FIGURE 3.1
The Transit of Africans to the Americas
Though approximately 11 million enslaved Africans boarded ships to the Americas, about 1.5 million (14 percent) of them died en route. Two-thirds of the survivors ended up in Brazil (3.65 million) and the West Indies (3.32 million), where they worked primarily on sugar plantations. Half a million arrived directly from Africa in the present-day United States, while many thousands more were traded to the mainland from the West Indies.

boiling houses, distilling apparatus — into raw sugar, molasses, and rum. The affluent planter-merchants who controlled the sugar industry drew annual profits of more than 10 percent on their investment. As Scottish economist Adam Smith noted in his famous treatise *The Wealth of Nations* (1776), sugar was the most profitable crop grown in America or Europe.

The Impact on Britain   The South Atlantic System brought wealth to the entire British and European economy and helped Europeans achieve world economic leadership. Most British West Indian plantations belonged to absentee owners who lived in England, where they spent their profits and formed a powerful sugar lobby. The Navigation Acts kept the British sugar trade in the hands of British merchants, who exported it to foreign markets, and by 1750 reshipments of American sugar

EXPLAIN CONSEQUENCES
How did the South Atlantic System affect the British economy?

and tobacco to Europe accounted for half of British exports. Enormous profits also flowed into Britain from the slave trade. The value of the guns, iron, rum, and cloth that were used to buy slaves was only about one-tenth (in the 1680s) to one-third (by the 1780s) of the value of the crops those slaves produced in America, allowing English traders to sell slaves in the West Indies for three to five times what they paid for them in Africa.

These massive profits drove the slave trade. At its height in the 1790s, Britain annually exported three hundred thousand guns to Africa, and a British ship carrying 300 to 350 slaves left an African port every other day. This commerce stimulated the entire British economy. English, Scottish, and American shipyards built hundreds of vessels, and thousands of people worked in trade-related industries: building port facilities and warehouses, refining sugar and tobacco, distilling rum from molasses, and manufacturing textiles and iron products for the growing markets in Africa and America. More than one thousand British merchant ships were plying the Atlantic by 1750, providing a supply of experienced sailors and laying the foundation for the supremacy of the Royal Navy.

Africa, Africans, and the Slave Trade

As the South Atlantic System enhanced European prosperity, it imposed enormous costs on West and Central Africa. Between 1550 and 1870, the Atlantic slave trade uprooted 11 million Africans, draining lands south of the Sahara of people and wealth and changing African society (Map 3.3). By directing commerce away from the savannas and the Islamic world on the other side of the Sahara, the Atlantic slave trade changed the economic and religious dynamics of the African interior. It also fostered militaristic, centralized states in the coastal areas.

Africans and the Slave Trade   Warfare and slaving had been part of African life for centuries, but the South Atlantic System made slaving a favorite tactic of ambitious kings and plundering warlords. "Whenever the King of Barsally wants Goods or Brandy," an observer noted, "the King goes and ransacks some of his enemies' towns, seizing the people and selling them." Supplying slaves became a way of life in the West African state of Dahomey, where the royal house monopolized the sale of slaves and used European guns to create a military despotism. Dahomey's army, which included a contingent of 5,000 women, raided the interior for captives; between 1680 and 1730, Dahomey annually exported 20,000 slaves from the

MAP 3.3

Africa and the Atlantic Slave Trade, 1700–1810

The tropical rain forest of West Africa was home to scores of peoples and dozens of kingdoms. With the rise of the slave trade, some of these kingdoms became aggressive slavers. Dahomey's army, for example, seized tens of thousands of captives in wars with neighboring peoples and sold them to European traders. About 14 percent of the captives died during the grueling Middle Passage, the transatlantic voyage between Africa and the Americas. Most of the survivors labored on sugar plantations in Brazil and the British and French West Indies.

ports of Allada and Whydah. The Asante kings likewise used slaving to conquer states along the Gold Coast as well as Muslim kingdoms in the savanna. By the 1720s, they had created a prosperous empire of 3 to 5 million people. Yet participation in the transatlantic slave trade remained a choice for Africans, not a necessity. The powerful kingdom of Benin, famous for its cast bronzes and carved ivory, prohibited for decades the export of all slaves, male and female. Other Africans atoned for their guilt for selling neighbors into slavery by building hidden shrines, often in the household granary.

The trade in humans produced untold misery. Hundreds of thousands of young Africans died, and millions more endured a brutal life in the Americas. In

Africa itself, class divisions hardened as people of noble birth enslaved and sold those of lesser status. Gender relations shifted as well. Two-thirds of the slaves sent across the Atlantic were men, partly because European planters paid more for men and "stout men boys" and partly because Africans sold enslaved women locally and across the Sahara as agricultural workers, house servants, and concubines. The resulting sexual imbalance prompted African men to take several wives, changing the meaning of marriage. Finally, the expansion of the Atlantic slave trade increased the extent of slavery in Africa. Sultan Mawlay Ismail of Morocco (r. 1672–1727) owned 150,000 black slaves, obtained by trade in Timbuktu and in wars he waged in Senegal. In Africa, as in the Americas, slavery eroded the dignity of human life.

The Middle Passage and Beyond   Africans sold into the South Atlantic System suffered the bleakest fate. Torn from their villages, they were marched in chains to coastal ports, their first passage in slavery. Then they endured the perilous **Middle Passage** to the New World in hideously overcrowded ships. The captives had little to eat or drink, and some died from dehydration. The feces, urine, and vomit belowdecks prompted outbreaks of dysentery, which took more lives. "I was so overcome by the heat, stench, and foul air that I nearly fainted," reported a European doctor.

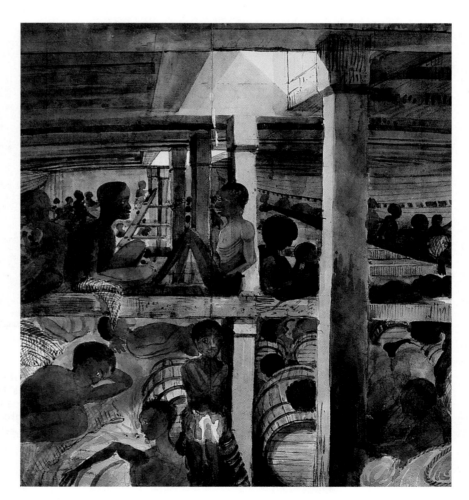

Two Views of the Middle Passage

An 1846 watercolor (on the right) shows the cargo hold of a slave ship en route to Brazil, which imported large numbers of African slaves until the 1860s. Painted by a ship's officer, the work minimizes the brutality of the Middle Passage—none of the slaves are in chains—and captures the Africans' humanity and dignity. The illustration on the left, which was printed by England's Abolitionist Society, shows the plan of a Liverpool slave ship designed to hold 482 Africans, packed in with no more respect than that given to hogsheads of sugar and tobacco. Records indicate that the ship actually carried as many as 609 Africans at once. Private Collection/© Michael Graham-Stewart/The Bridgeman Art Library / © National Maritime Museum, London.

Olaudah Equiano: The Brutal "Middle Passage"

Olaudah Equiano claimed to have been born in Igboland (present-day southern Nigeria). But Vincent Carretta of the University of Maryland has discovered strong evidence that Equiano was born in South Carolina. He suggests that Equiano drew on conversations with African-born slaves to create a fictitious account of his kidnapping at the age of eleven and a traumatic passage across the Atlantic. After being purchased by an English sea captain, Equiano bought his freedom in 1766. In London, he became an antislavery activist, and in 1789 he published the memoir from which the following selections are drawn.

My father, besides many slaves, had a numerous family. . . . I was trained up from my earliest years in the art of war, . . . and my mother adorned me with emblems after the manner of our greatest warriors. One day, when all our people were gone out to their works as usual and only I and my dear sister were left to mind the house, two men and a woman got over our walls, and in a moment seized us both. . . .

I was . . . sold and carried through a number of places till . . . at the end of six or seven months after I had been kidnapped I arrived at the sea coast.

. . . I now saw myself deprived of all chance of returning to my native country. . . . I was soon put down under the decks, and there I received such a salutation in my nostrils as I had never experienced in my life; so that with the loathsomeness of the stench and crying together, I became so sick and low that I was not able to eat, nor had I the least desire to taste anything. I now wished for the last friend, death, to relieve me; but soon, to my grief, two of the white men offered me eatables, and on my refusing to eat, one of them held me fast by the hands and . . . tied my feet while the other flogged me severely. I had never experienced anything of this kind before, and . . . could I have got over the nettings, I would have jumped over the side. . . . One day, when we had a smooth sea and moderate wind, two of my wearied countrymen who were chained together . . . , preferring death to such a life of misery, somehow made it through the nettings and jumped into the sea. . . .

At last we came in sight of the island of Barbados; the white people got some old slaves from the land to pacify us. They told us we were not to be eaten but to work, and were soon to go on land where we should see many of our country people. This report eased us much; and sure enough soon after we were landed there came to us Africans of all languages.

Source: *The Interesting Narrative of the Life of Olaudah Equiano, or Gustavus Vassa, the African, Written by Himself* (London, 1789), 15, 22–23, 28–29.

QUESTIONS FOR ANALYSIS

1. What elements of Equiano's account might explain the average slave mortality rate of about 14 percent during the Atlantic crossing?
2. Assuming that Carretta is correct, and Equiano was not born in Africa, why do you think he composed this fictitious narrative of his childhood instead of describing his own childhood in slavery?

Some slaves jumped overboard to drown rather than endure more suffering. Others staged violent shipboard revolts. Slave uprisings occurred on two thousand voyages, roughly one of every ten Atlantic passages. Nearly 100,000 slaves died in these insurrections, and nearly 1.5 million others — about 14 percent of those who were transported — died of disease or illness on the month-long journey (America Compared, above).

For those who survived the Atlantic crossing, things only got worse as they passed into endless slavery. Life on the sugar plantations of northwestern Brazil and the West Indies was one of relentless exploitation. Slaves worked ten hours a day under the hot tropical sun; slept in flimsy huts; and lived on a starchy diet of corn, yams, and dried fish. They were subjected to brutal discipline: "The fear of punishment is the principle [we use] . . . to keep them in awe and order," one planter declared. When punishments came, they were brutal. Flogging was commonplace; some planters rubbed salt, lemon juice, or urine into the resulting wounds.

Planters often took advantage of their power by raping enslaved women. Sexual exploitation was a largely unacknowledged but ubiquitous feature of master-slave relations: something that many slave masters considered to be an unquestioned privilege of their position. "It was almost a constant practice with our clerks, and other whites," Olaudah Equiano wrote, "to commit violent depredations on the chastity of the female slaves." Thomas Thistlewood was a Jamaica planter who kept an unusually detailed journal in which he noted every act of sexual exploitation he committed. In thirty-seven years as a Jamaica planter, Thistlewood recorded 3,852 sex acts with 138 enslaved women.

With sugar prices high and the cost of slaves low, many planters simply worked their slaves to death and then bought more. Between 1708 and 1735, British planters on Barbados imported about 85,000 Africans; however, in that same time the island's black population increased by only 4,000 (from 42,000 to 46,000). The constant influx of new slaves kept the population thoroughly "African" in its languages, religions, and culture. "Here," wrote a Jamaican observer, "each different nation of Africa meet and dance after the manner of their own country . . . [and] retain most of their native customs."

Slavery in the Chesapeake and South Carolina

West Indian–style slavery came to Virginia and Maryland following Bacon's Rebellion. Taking advantage of the expansion of the British slave trade (following the end of the Royal African Company's monopoly in 1698), elite planter-politicians led a "tobacco revolution" and bought more Africans, putting these slaves to work on ever-larger plantations. By 1720, Africans made up 20 percent of the Chesapeake population; by 1740, nearly 40 percent. Slavery had become a core institution, no longer just one of several forms of unfree labor. Moreover, slavery was now defined in racial terms. Virginia legislators prohibited sexual intercourse between English and Africans and defined virtually all resident Africans as slaves: "All servants imported or brought into this country by sea or land who were not Christians in their native country shall be accounted and be slaves."

On the mainland as in the islands, slavery was a system of brutal exploitation. Violence was common, and the threat of violence always hung over master-slave relationships. In 1669, Virginia's House of Burgesses decreed that a master who killed a slave in the process of "correcting" him could not be charged with a felony, since it would be irrational to destroy his own property. From that point forward, even the most extreme punishments were permitted by law. Slaves could not carry weapons or gather in large numbers. Slaveholders were especially concerned to discourage slaves from running away. Punishments for runaways commonly included not only brutal whipping but also branding or scarring to make recalcitrant slaves easier to identify. Virginia laws spelled out the procedures for capturing and returning runaway slaves in detail. If a runaway slave was killed in the process of recapturing him, the county would reimburse the slave's owner for his full value. In some cases, slave owners could choose to put runaway slaves up for trial; if they were found guilty and executed, the owner would be compensated for his loss (Thinking Like a Historian, p. 98).

Despite the inherent brutality of the institution, slaves in Virginia and Maryland worked under better conditions than those in the West Indies. Many lived relatively long lives. Unlike sugar and rice, which were "killer crops" that demanded strenuous labor in a tropical climate, tobacco cultivation required steadier and less demanding labor in a more temperate environment. Workers planted young tobacco seedlings in spring, hoed and weeded the crop in summer, and in fall picked and hung the leaves to cure over the winter. Nor did diseases spread as easily in the Chesapeake, because plantation quarters were less crowded and more dispersed than those in the West Indies. Finally, because tobacco profits were lower than those from sugar, planters treated their slaves less harshly than West Indian planters did.

Many tobacco planters increased their workforce by buying female slaves and encouraging them to have children. In 1720, women made up more than one-third of the Africans in Maryland, and the black population had begun to increase naturally. "Be kind and indulgent to the breeding wenches," one slave owner told his overseer, "[and do not] force them when with child upon any service or hardship that will be injurious to them." By midcentury, more than three-quarters of the enslaved workers in the Chesapeake were American-born.

Slaves in South Carolina labored under much more oppressive conditions. The colony grew slowly until 1700, when planters began to plant and export rice to southern Europe, where it was in great demand. Between 1720 and 1750, rice production increased fivefold. To expand production, planters imported thousands of Africans, some of them from rice-growing societies. By 1710, Africans formed a majority of the total population, eventually rising to 80 percent in rice-growing areas (Figure 3.2).

Most rice plantations lay in inland swamps, and the work was dangerous and exhausting. Slaves planted, weeded, and harvested the rice in ankle-deep mud.

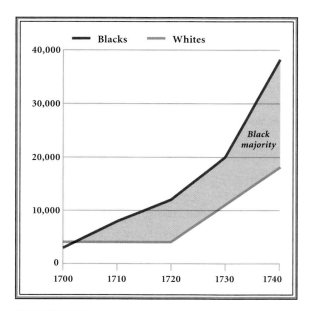

FIGURE 3.2
A Black Majority Emerges in South Carolina, 1700–1740
Between disease and the toll taken by the Indian wars, South Carolina's white population hardly grew at all between 1690 and 1720. But white planters imported thousands of enslaved Africans to grow rice, an extremely profitable plantation crop. As early as 1705, the colony had a black majority, which allowed the development among slaves of a strongly African-influenced language and culture.

Pools of stagnant water bred mosquitoes, which transmitted diseases that claimed hundreds of African lives. Other slaves, forced to move tons of dirt to build irrigation works, died from exhaustion. "The labour required [for growing rice] is only fit for slaves," a Scottish traveler remarked, "and I think the hardest work I have seen them engaged in." In South Carolina, as in the West Indies and Brazil, there were many slave deaths and few births, and the arrival of new slaves continually "re-Africanized" the black population.

An African American Community Emerges

Slaves came from many peoples in West Africa and the Central African regions of Kongo and Angola. White planters welcomed ethnic diversity to deter slave revolts. "The safety of the Plantations," declared a widely read English pamphlet, "depends upon having Negroes from all parts of Guiny, who do not understand each other's languages and Customs and cannot agree to Rebel." By accident or design, most plantations drew laborers of many languages, including Kwa, Mande, and Kikongo. Among Africans imported after

1730 into the upper James River region of Virginia, 41 percent came from ethnic groups in present-day Nigeria, and another 25 percent from West-Central Africa. The rest hailed from the Windward and Gold coasts, Senegambia, and Sierra Leone. In South Carolina, plantation owners preferred laborers from the Gold Coast and Gambia, who had a reputation as hardworking farmers. But as African sources of slaves shifted southward after 1730, more than 30 percent of the colony's workers later came from Kongo and Angola.

Initially, the slaves did not think of themselves as Africans or blacks but as members of a specific family, clan, or people — Wolof, Hausa, Ibo, Yoruba, Teke, Ngola — and they sought out those who shared their language and customs. In the upper James River region, Ibo men and women arrived in equal numbers, married each other, and maintained their Ibo culture. In most places, though, this was impossible. Slaves from varying backgrounds were thrown together and only gradually discovered common ground.

Building Community   Through painful trial and error, slaves eventually discovered what limited freedoms their owners would allow them. Those who were not too rebellious or too recalcitrant were able to carve out precarious family lives — though they were always in danger of being disrupted by sale or life-threatening punishment — and build the rudiments of a slave community.

One key to the development of families and communities was a more or less balanced sex ratio that encouraged marriage and family formation. In South Carolina, the high death rate among slaves undermined ties of family and kinship; but in the Chesapeake, after 1725 some slaves, especially on larger plantations, were able to create strong nuclear families and extended kin relations. On one of Charles Carroll's estates in Maryland, 98 of the 128 slaves were members of two extended families. These African American kin groups passed on family names, traditions, and knowledge to the next generation, and thus a distinct culture gradually developed. As one observer suggested, blacks had created a separate world, "a Nation within a Nation."

As the slaves forged a new identity, they carried on certain African practices but let others go. Many Africans arrived in America with ritual scars that white planters called "country markings"; these signs of ethnic identity fell into disuse on culturally diverse plantations. (Ironically, on some plantations these African markings were replaced by

COMPARE AND CONTRAST
How did the experiences of slaves in the Chesapeake differ from their experiences in South Carolina?

Servitude and Slavery

Britain's American colonies relied heavily on bound labor. Two forms predominated: indentured servitude and African slavery. The idea of being bound to a master is alien to most of us today; the following texts allow us to glimpse some aspects of the experience. In what ways were these two institutions similar, and how did they differ?

1. **Slave advertisement from Charlestown, Virginia, July 24, 1769.**

Charlestown, July 24th, 1769.

TO BE SOLD,

On THURSDAY the third Day of AUGUST next,

A CARGO

OF

NINETY-FOUR

PRIME, HEALTHY

NEGROES,

CONSISTING OF

Thirty-nine MEN, Fifteen BOYS, Twenty-four WOMEN, and Sixteen GIRLS.

JUST ARRIVED,

In the Brigantine DEMBIA, *Francis Bare*, Master, from SIERRA-LEON, by

DAVID & JOHN DEAS.

Source: Courtesy American Antiquarian Society.

2. **Indentured servant advertisement from the *Pennsylvania Gazette*, 1770.** *This advertisement offers to sell the remainder of a servant girl's indenture.*

TO BE SOLD, A HEALTHY servant GIRL'S Time, about 17 Years old, who has between 3 and 4 years to serve. She is sold for no other Reason, only there being more Servants than are needful in the family where she is.

N. B. She has had the Small pox, can wash, and do all Sorts of Housework. Enquire of the Printers.

3. **Poem by James Revel, c. 1680.** *James Revel was an Englishman convicted of theft and transported to Virginia, where he served fourteen years as an indentured servant. Upon returning he published*

A Poor Unhappy Transported Felon's Sorrowful Account of His Fourteen Years' Transportation at Virginia, in America *(1680).*

At last to my new master's house I came,
At the town of Wicocc[o]moco call'd by name,
Where my Europian clothes were took from me,
Which never after I again could see.

A canvas shirt and trowsers then they gave,
With a hop-sack frock in which I was to slave:
No shoes nor stockings had I for to wear,
Nor hat, nor cap, both head and feet were bare.

Thus dress'd into the Field I nex[t] must go,
Amongst tobacco plants all day to hoe,
At day break in the morn our work began,
And so held to the setting of the Sun.

My fellow slaves were just five Transports more,
With eighteen Negroes, which is twenty four . . .
We and the Negroes both alike did fare,
Of work and food we had an equal share.

4. **Mechanisms used to control slaves, from Thomas Branagan, *The Penitential Tyrant; or, slave trader reformed*, 1807.** *The shackles and spurs (lower left) were intended to prevent escape; the faceguard with spiked collar (top and lower right) kept its wearer from either eating or lying down.*

Source: Library of Congress.

5. Court deposition of Joseph Mulders, July 31, 1649. *In a court case in Lower Norfolk County, Virginia indentured servant Joseph Mulders testified that his mistress, Deborah Fernehaugh, brutally beat her maidservant, Charity Dallen.*

[Mulders testified] That Deborah Fernehaugh, the Mistress of this deponent, did beate her mayd Sarvant in the quartering house before the dresser more Liken a dogge then a Christian, and that at a Certaine time, I felt her head, which was beaten as soft as a sponge, in one place, and that as there shee was a weeding, shee complained and sayd, her backe bone as shee thought was broken with beating, and that I did see the mayds arme naked which was full of blacke and blew bruises and pinches, and her necke Likewise and that after wards, I tould my Mistress of it and said, that two or three blowes, could not make her in such a Case, and after this my speeches shee Chidge [i.e., chided] the said mayd, for shewing her body to the men, and very often afterwards she [the maid] would have shoen mee, how shee had been beaten, but I refused to have seene it, saying it concernes me not, I will doe my worke and if my Mistress abuse you; you may complaine, and about 8 dayes since, being about the time shee last went to Complaine, I knew of her goeing, but would not tell my mistress of it, although shee asked mee, and sayd I could not chuse but know of it.

6. Runaway slave advertisement, Chestertown, Maryland, March 12, 1755. *Absconding from their masters was a common method of resistance for both slaves and servants, and masters frequently posted runaway advertisements in local newspapers.*

Chestertown, Maryland, March 12, 1755. TEN PISTOLES Reward. RAN away last night, from James Ringgold, of Eastern Neck, in Kent county, in the province of Maryland, the two following servant men; one named James Francis, an indented servant for five years, a middle siz'd young fellow, about 26 years of age, of a smooth fair complexion, his hair cut off, is an Englishman, and speaks a little in the west country dialect; was brought up to farming and husbandry: Had on, a country kersey jacket and breeches, blue fearnought jacket, and an old dark colour'd coat. The other a lusty young Mulatto fellow, named Toby, a slave about the same age, he is a well set, clean limb'd, stout fellow neither a very bright or very dark Mulatto, has large nostrils, is a likely fellow, and when he talks drawls his words out in a very slow manner, is no other way remarkable; he had on the same sort of clothes with

the other servant, and one of them has a check or striped green and red everlasting jacket on or with them; and perhaps the Mulatto may set up for a cooper or carpenter, having work at both those business, and also understands plantation affairs. Whoever takes up and secures the above persons, and gives notice, so as their master gets them again, shall have Four Pistoles reward for the white servant, and Six Pistoles for the Mulatto. . . . That this slave should runaway, and attempt getting his liberty, is very alarming, as he has always been too kindly used, if any thing by his master, and one in whom his master has put great confidence, and depended on him to overlook the rest of his slaves, and he had no kind of provocation to go off. It seems to be the interest at least of every gentleman that has slaves, to be active in the beginning of these attempts . . . THOMAS RINGGOLD.

Sources: (2) *Pennsylvania Gazette*, May 3, 1770; (3) John Melville Jennings, ed., *The Virginia Magazine of History and Biography* 56 (April 1948), 187–194; (5) *Second to None: A Documentary History of American Women*, Vol. 1 (University of Nebraska Press, 1993), 67–68; (6) *Pennsylvania Gazette*, March 12, 1755.

ANALYZING THE EVIDENCE

1. What information do the traders in sources 1 and 2 want to convey to prospective buyers, and why? What similarities and differences do you see in the way sellers might choose to market servants and slaves?

2. What aspects of servitude did James Revel object to (source 3)? How did he compare the experiences of servants and slaves?

3. Source 4 appeared in an abolitionist work published in New York in 1807. How does that fact influence your interpretation of the images?

4. How does Mulders grapple with his position as a fellow servant as he testifies against his mistress (source 5)? Based on Mulders's testimony, the court removed Dallen from Fernehaugh's household. How might things have worked differently if either Mulders or Dallen had been a slave?

5. In source 6, what characteristics of each man does the ad emphasize? How does Ringgold view himself as a master, and what does his special plea to other slaveholders tell us about slaveholding culture?

PUTTING IT ALL TOGETHER

Using the sources above, along with what you learned in class and in Chapter 3, write a short essay that compares servitude and slavery. In what ways did African slavery in the British colonies grow out of servitude and bear close similarities to it, and in what ways were slaves set apart and treated fundamentally differently than their servant counterparts?

Hulling Rice in West Africa and Georgia
Cultural practices often extend over time and space. The eighteenth-century engraving on the left shows West African women using huge wooden mortars and pestles to strip the tough outer hull from rice kernels. In the photo on the right, taken a century and a half later, African American women in Georgia use similar tools to prepare rice for their families. Library of Congress. / Courtesy Georgia Vanishing Archives Collection, sap093.

brands or scars that identified them with their owners.) But other tangible markers of African heritage persisted, including hairstyles, motifs used in wood carvings and pottery, the large wooden mortars and pestles used to hull rice, and the design of houses, in which rooms were arranged from front to back in a distinctive "I" pattern, not side by side as was common in English dwellings. Musical instruments—especially drums, gourd rattles, and a stringed instrument called a "molo," forerunner to the banjo—helped Africans preserve cultural traditions and, eventually, shape American musical styles.

African values also persisted. Some slaves passed down Muslim beliefs, and many more told their children of the spiritual powers of conjurers, called *obeah* or *ifa*, who knew the ways of the African gods. Enslaved Yorubas consulted Orunmila, the god of fate, and other Africans (a Jamaican planter noted) relied on *obeah* "to revenge injuries and insults, discover and punish thieves and adulterers; [and] to predict the future."

Resistance and Accommodation   Slaves' freedom of action was always dramatically circumscribed. It became illegal to teach slaves to read and write, and most slaves owned no property of their own. Because the institution of slavery rested on fear, planters had to learn a ferocious form of cruelty. Slaves might be whipped, restrained, or maimed for any infraction, large or small. A female cook in a Virginia household "was cruelly loaded with various kinds of iron machines; she had one particularly on her head, which locked her mouth so fast that she could scarcely speak; and could not eat nor drink." Thomas Jefferson, who witnessed such punishments on his father's Virginia plantation, noted that each generation of whites was "nursed, educated, and daily exercised in tyranny," and he concluded that the relationship "between master and slave is a perpetual exercise of the most unremitting despotism on the one part, and degrading submission on the other." A fellow Virginian, planter George Mason, agreed: "Every Master is born a petty tyrant."

Virginian Luxuries, c. 1810

This painting by an unknown artist depicts the brutality and sexual exploitation inherent in a slave society. On the right, an owner chastises a male slave by beating him with a cane; on the left, a white master asserts his sexual prerogative with a female slave. Abby Aldrich Rockefeller Folk Art Museum, Williamsburg, VA.

VIRGINIAN   LUXURIES.

The extent of white violence often depended on the size and density of the slave population. As Virginia planter William Byrd II complained of his slaves in 1736, "Numbers make them insolent." In the northern colonies, where slaves were few, white violence was sporadic. But plantation owners and overseers in the sugar- and rice-growing areas, where Africans outnumbered Europeans eight or more to one, routinely whipped assertive slaves. They also prohibited their workers from leaving the plantation without special passes and called on their poor white neighbors to patrol the countryside at night.

Despite the constant threat of violence, some slaves ran away, a very small number of them successfully. In some parts of the Americas — for example, in Jamaica — runaway slaves were able to form large, independent Maroon communities. But on the mainland, planters had the resources necessary to reclaim runaways, and such communities were unusual and precarious. More often, slaves who spoke English and possessed artisanal skills fled to colonial towns, where they tried to pass as free; occasionally they succeeded. Slaves who did not run away were engaged in a constant tug-of-war with their owners over the terms of their enslavement. Some blacks bartered extra work for better food and clothes; others seized a small privilege and dared the master to revoke it. In this way, Sundays gradually became a day of rest — asserted as a right, rather than granted as a privilege. When bargaining failed, slaves protested silently by working slowly or stealing.

Slave owners' greatest fear was that their regime of terror would fail and slaves would rise up to murder them in their beds. Occasionally that fear was realized. In the 1760s, in Amherst County, Virginia, a slave killed four whites; in Elizabeth City County, eight slaves strangled their master in bed. But the circumstances of slavery made any larger-scale uprising all but impossible. To rebel against their masters, slaves would have to be able to communicate secretly but effectively across long distances; choose leaders they could trust; formulate and disseminate strategy; accumulate large numbers of weapons; and ensure that no one betrayed their plans. This was all but impossible: in plantation slavery, the preponderance of force was on the side of the slave owners, and blacks who chose to rise up did so at their peril.

TRACE CHANGE OVER TIME
How much autonomy could slaves attain, and what did slave owners do to control them?

The Stono Rebellion   The largest slave uprising in the mainland colonies, South Carolina's **Stono Rebellion** of 1739, illustrates the impossibility of success. The Catholic governor of Spanish Florida instigated the revolt by promising freedom to fugitive slaves. By February 1739, at least 69 slaves had escaped to St. Augustine, and rumors circulated "that a Conspiracy was formed by Negroes in Carolina to rise and make their way out of the province." When war between England and Spain broke out in September, 75 Africans rose in revolt and killed a number of whites near the

Stono River. According to one account, some of the rebels were Portuguese-speaking Catholics from the Kingdom of Kongo who hoped to escape to Florida. Displaying their skills as soldiers — decades of brutal slave raiding in Kongo had militarized the society there — the rebels marched toward Florida "with Colours displayed and two Drums beating."

Though their numbers and organization were impressive, the Stono rebels were soon met by a well-armed, mounted force of South Carolina militia. In the ensuing battle, 44 slaves were killed and the rebellion was suppressed, preventing any general uprising. In response, frightened South Carolinians cut slave imports and tightened plantation discipline.

The Rise of the Southern Gentry

As the southern colonies became full-fledged slave societies, life changed for whites as well as for blacks. Consider the career of William Byrd II (1674–1744). Byrd's father, a successful planter-merchant in Virginia, hoped to marry his children into the English gentry. To smooth his son's entry into landed society, Byrd sent him to England for his education. But his status-conscious classmates shunned young Byrd, calling him a "colonial," a first bitter taste of the gradations of rank in English society.

IDENTIFY CAUSES
How did the planter elite maintain alliances with their smallholder neighbors?

Other English rejections followed. Lacking aristocratic connections, Byrd was denied a post with the Board of Trade, passed over three times for the royal governorship of Virginia, and rejected as a suitor by a rich Englishwoman. In 1726, at age fifty-two, Byrd finally gave up and moved back to Virginia, where he sometimes felt he was "being buried alive." Accepting his lesser destiny as a member of the colony's elite, Byrd built an elegant brick mansion on the family's estate at Westover, sat in "the best pew in the church," and won an appointment to the governor's council.

William Byrd II's experience mirrored that of many planter-merchants, trapped in Virginia and South Carolina by their inferior colonial status. They used their wealth to rule over white yeomen families and tenant farmers and relied on violence to exploit enslaved blacks. Planters used Africans to grow food, as well as tobacco; to build houses, wagons, and tobacco casks; and to make shoes and clothes. By making their plantations self-sufficient, the Chesapeake elite survived the depressed tobacco market between 1670 and 1720.

White Identity and Equality   To prevent uprisings like Bacon's Rebellion, the Chesapeake gentry found ways to assist middling and poor whites. They gradually lowered taxes; in Virginia, for example, the annual head tax (on each adult man) fell from 45 pounds of tobacco in 1675 to just 5 pounds in 1750. They also encouraged smallholders to improve their economic lot by using slave labor, and many did so. By 1770, 60 percent of English families in the Chesapeake owned at least one slave. On the political front, planters now allowed poor yeomen and some tenants to vote. The strategy of the leading families — the Carters, Lees, Randolphs, and Robinsons — was to bribe these voters with rum, money, and the promise of minor offices in county governments. In return, they expected the yeomen and tenants to elect them to office and defer to their rule. This horse-trading solidified the authority of the planter elite, which used its control of the House of Burgesses to limit the power of the royal governor. Hundreds of yeomen farmers benefitted as well, tasting political power and garnering substantial fees and salaries as deputy sheriffs, road surveyors, estate appraisers, and grand jurymen.

Even as wealthy Chesapeake gentlemen formed political ties with smallholders, they took measures to set themselves apart culturally. As late as the 1720s, leading planters were boisterous, aggressive men who lived much like the common folk — hunting, drinking, gambling on horse races, and demonstrating their manly prowess by forcing themselves on female servants and slaves. As time passed, however, the planters began, like William Byrd II, to model themselves on the English aristocracy, remaining sexual predators but learning from advice books how to act like gentlemen in other regards: "I must not sit in others' places; Nor sneeze, nor cough in people's faces. Nor with my fingers pick my nose, Nor wipe my hands upon my clothes." Cultivating **gentility** — a refined but elaborate lifestyle — they replaced their modest wooden houses with mansions of brick and mortar. Planters educated their sons in London as lawyers and gentlemen. But unlike Byrd's father, they expected them to return to America, marry local heiresses, and assume their fathers' roles: managing plantations, socializing with fellow gentry, and running the political system.

Wealthy Chesapeake and South Carolina women likewise emulated the English elite. They read English newspapers and fashionable magazines, wore the finest English clothes, and dined in the English fashion, including an elaborate afternoon tea. To enhance their daughters' gentility (and improve their marriage prospects), parents hired English tutors. Once married, planter women deferred to their husbands, reared pious children, and maintained elaborate social networks, in time creating a new ideal: the southern gentlewoman. Using the profits generated by enslaved Africans in the South Atlantic System of commerce, wealthy planters formed an increasingly well-educated, refined, and stable ruling class.

The Northern Maritime Economy

The South Atlantic System had a broad geographical reach. As early as the 1640s, New England farmers supplied the sugar islands with bread, lumber, fish, and meat. As a West Indian explained, planters "had rather buy foode at very deare rates than produce it by labour, soe infinite is the profitt of sugar works." By 1700, the economies of the West Indies and New England were closely interwoven. Soon farmers and merchants in New York, New Jersey, and Pennsylvania were also shipping wheat, corn, and bread to the Caribbean. By the 1750s, about two-thirds of New England's exports and half of those from the Middle Atlantic colonies went to the British and French sugar islands.

The sugar economy linked Britain's entire Atlantic empire. In return for the sugar they sent to England, West Indian planters received credit, in the form of bills of exchange, from London merchants. The planters used these bills to buy slaves from Africa and to pay North American farmers and merchants for their provisions and shipping services. The mainland colonists then exchanged the bills for British manufactures, primarily textiles and iron goods.

The Urban Economy

The West Indian trade created the first American merchant fortunes and the first urban industries. Merchants in Boston, Newport, Providence, Philadelphia, and New York invested their profits in new ships; some set up manufacturing enterprises, including twenty-six refineries that processed raw sugar into finished loaves. Mainland distilleries turned West Indian molasses into rum, producing more than 2.5 million gallons in Massachusetts alone by the 1770s. Merchants in Salem, Marblehead, and smaller New England ports built a major fishing industry by selling salted mackerel and cod to the sugar islands and to southern Europe. Baltimore merchants transformed their town into a major

port by developing a bustling export business in wheat, while traders in Charleston shipped deerskins, indigo, and rice to European markets (Map 3.4).

As transatlantic commerce expanded — from five hundred voyages a year in the 1680s to fifteen hundred annually in the 1730s — American port cities grew in size and complexity. By 1750, the populations of Newport and Charleston were nearly 10,000; Boston had 15,000 residents; and New York had almost 18,000. The largest port was Philadelphia, whose population by 1776 had reached 30,000, the size of a large European provincial city. Smaller coastal towns emerged as centers of the lumber and shipbuilding industries. Seventy sawmills lined the Piscataqua River in New Hampshire, providing low-cost wood for homes, warehouses, and especially shipbuilding. Hundreds of shipwrights turned out oceangoing vessels, while other artisans made ropes, sails, and metal fittings for the new fleet. By the 1770s, colonial-built ships made up one-third of the British merchant fleet.

The South Atlantic System extended far into the interior. A fleet of small vessels sailed back and forth on the Hudson and Delaware rivers, delivering cargoes of European manufactures and picking up barrels of flour and wheat to carry to New York and Philadelphia for export to the West Indies and Europe. By the 1750s, hundreds of professional teamsters in Maryland were transporting 370,000 bushels of wheat and corn and 16,000 barrels of flour to urban markets each year — more than 10,000 wagon trips. To service this traffic, entrepreneurs and artisans set up taverns, horse stables, and barrel-making shops in towns along the wagon roads. Lancaster (the town that hosted the Iroquois conference described in the chapter opening), in a prosperous wheat-growing area of Pennsylvania, boasted more than 200 German and English artisans and a dozen merchants.

EXPLAIN CONSEQUENCES
How did the rise of the South Atlantic System impact economic development in the northern colonies?

Urban Society

Wealthy merchants dominated the social life of seaport cities. In 1750, about 40 merchants controlled more than 50 percent of Philadelphia's trade. Like the Chesapeake gentry, urban merchants imitated the British upper classes, importing architectural design books from England and building Georgian-style mansions to display their wealth. Their wives strove to create a genteel culture by buying fine furniture and entertaining guests at elegant dinners.

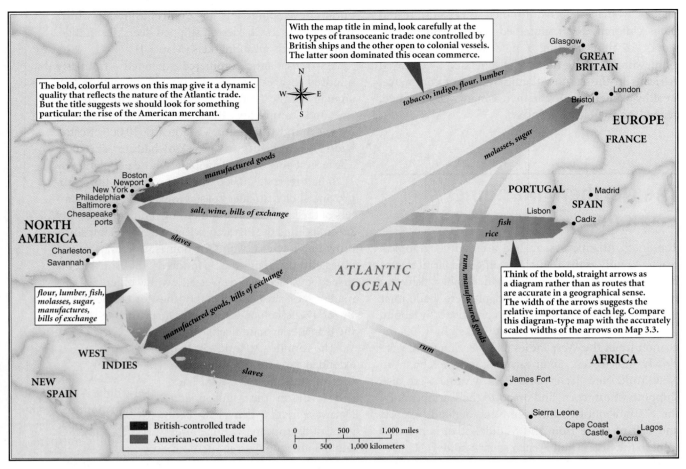

With the map title in mind, look carefully at the two types of transoceanic trade: one controlled by British ships and the other open to colonial vessels. The latter soon dominated this ocean commerce.

The bold, colorful arrows on this map give it a dynamic quality that reflects the nature of the Atlantic trade. But the title suggests we should look for something particular: the rise of the American merchant.

Think of the bold, straight arrows as a diagram rather than as routes that are accurate in a geographical sense. The width of the arrows suggests the relative importance of each leg. Compare this diagram-type map with the accurately scaled widths of the arrows on Map 3.3.

flour, lumber, fish, molasses, sugar, manufactures, bills of exchange

tobacco, indigo, flour, lumber
manufactured goods
molasses, sugar
salt, wine, bills of exchange
slaves
fish
rice
manufactured goods, bills of exchange
rum, manufactured goods
rum
slaves

■ British-controlled trade
■ American-controlled trade

0   500   1,000 miles
0   500   1,000 kilometers

MAP 3.4
The Growing Power of American Merchants, 1750
Throughout the colonial era, British merchant houses dominated the transatlantic trade in manufactures, sugar, tobacco, and slaves. However, by 1750, American-born merchants in Boston, New York, and Philadelphia had seized control of the commerce between the mainland and the West Indies. In addition, Newport traders played a small role in the slave trade from Africa, and Boston and Charleston merchants grew rich carrying fish and rice to southern Europe.

Artisan and shopkeeper families, the middle ranks of seaport society, made up nearly half the population. Innkeepers, butchers, seamstresses, shoemakers, weavers, bakers, carpenters, masons, and dozens of other skilled workers toiled to gain an income sufficient to maintain their families in modest comfort. Wives and husbands often worked as a team and taught the "mysteries of the craft" to their children. Some artisans aspired to wealth and status, an entrepreneurial ethic that prompted them to hire apprentices and expand production. However, most artisans were not well-to-do. During his working life, a tailor was lucky to accumulate £30 worth of property, far less than the £2,000 owned at death by an ordinary merchant or the £300 listed in the probate inventory of a successful blacksmith.

Laboring men and women formed the lowest ranks of urban society. Merchants needed hundreds of dockworkers to unload manufactured goods and molasses from inbound ships and reload them with barrels of wheat, fish, and rice. For these demanding jobs, merchants used enslaved blacks and indentured servants, who together made up 30 percent of the workforce in Philadelphia and New York City until the 1750s; otherwise, they hired unskilled wageworkers. Poor white and black women eked out a living by washing clothes, spinning wool, or working as servants or prostitutes. To make ends meet, laboring families sent their children out to work.

Periods of stagnant commerce threatened the financial security of merchants and artisans alike. For laborers, seamen, and seamstresses—whose

The Greenwood-Lee Family, 1747

Born in Massachusetts and apprenticed as an engraver, John Greenwood (1727–1792) painted dozens of commissioned works there before moving to Surinam in 1752. He painted this scene of his own family at the age of twenty. Group portraits with so many people were rare in the colonies, and it is a technically impressive composition. Greenwood himself is at the right rear, wigless (he wears a velvet cap to keep his head warm) and holding a palette and brushes. The table displays a basket of needlework and a volume of *The Spectator,* the popular London periodical published by Joseph Addison and Richard Steele.

Photograph © 2014 Museum of Fine Arts, Boston. Bequest of Henry Lee Shattuck in memory of the late Morris Gray, 1983.34.

household budgets left no margin for sickness or unemployment—depressed trade meant hunger, dependence on public charity, and (for the most desperate) petty thievery or prostitution. The sugar- and slave-based South Atlantic System, and cycles of imperial warfare, brought economic uncertainty as well as opportunity to the people of the northern colonies.

The New Politics of Empire, 1713–1750

The South Atlantic System also changed the politics of empire. British ministers, pleased with the wealth produced by the trade in slaves, sugar, rice, and tobacco, ruled the colonies with a gentle hand. The colonists took advantage of that leniency to strengthen their political institutions and eventually to challenge the rules of the mercantilist system.

The Rise of Colonial Assemblies

After the Glorious Revolution, representative assemblies in America copied the English Whigs and limited the powers of crown officials. In Massachusetts during the 1720s, the assembly repeatedly ignored the king's instructions to provide the royal governor with a permanent salary, and legislatures in North Carolina,

New Jersey, and Pennsylvania did the same. Using such tactics, the legislatures gradually took control of taxation and appointments, angering imperial bureaucrats and absentee proprietors. "The people in power in America," complained William Penn during a struggle with the Pennsylvania assembly, "think nothing taller than themselves but the Trees."

Leading the increasingly powerful assemblies were members of the colonial elite. Although most property-owning white men had the right to vote, only men of wealth and status stood for election. In New Jersey in 1750, 90 percent of assemblymen came from influential political families (Figure 3.3). In Virginia, seven members of the wealthy Lee family sat in the House of Burgesses and, along with other powerful families, dominated its major committees. In New England, affluent descendants of the original Puritans formed a core of political leaders. "Go into every village in New England," John Adams wrote in 1765, "and you will find that the office of justice of the peace, and even the place of representative, have generally descended from generation to generation, in three or four families at most."

However, neither elitist assemblies nor wealthy property owners could impose unpopular edicts on the people. Purposeful crowd actions were a fact of colonial life. An uprising of ordinary citizens overthrew the

> **IDENTIFY CAUSES**
> What explains the increasing political autonomy of the colonies in the eighteenth century?

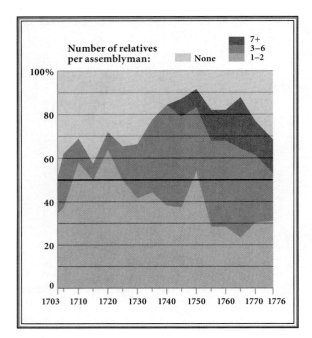

FIGURE 3.3
Family Connections and Political Power, New Jersey, 1700–1776

As early as 1700, more than 50 percent of the members of the New Jersey assembly came from families with a history of political leadership. By 1750, the percentage whose fathers or other relatives had served in the assembly reached 90 percent; indeed, some members had seven relatives who were (or had been) political leaders, clear testimony of the emergence of powerful political families and an experienced governing elite. However, as the conflict with Britain increased after 1765, voters in New Jersey and elsewhere ousted lukewarm patriots, and new families entered the political ranks.

Dominion of New England in 1689. In New York, mobs closed houses of prostitution; in Salem, Massachusetts, they ran people with infectious diseases out of town; and in New Jersey in the 1730s and 1740s, mobs of farmers battled with proprietors who were forcing tenants off disputed lands. When officials in Boston restricted the sale of farm produce to a single public market, a crowd destroyed the building, and its members defied the authorities to arrest them. "If you touch One you shall touch All," an anonymous letter warned the sheriff, "and we will show you a Hundred Men where you can show one." These expressions of popular discontent, combined with the growing authority of the assemblies, created a political system that was broadly responsive to popular pressure and increasingly resistant to British control.

Salutary Neglect

British colonial policy during the reigns of George I (r. 1714–1727) and George II (r. 1727–1760) allowed for this rise of American self-government as royal bureaucrats, pleased by growing trade and import duties, relaxed their supervision of internal colonial affairs. In 1775, British political philosopher Edmund Burke would praise this strategy as **salutary neglect**.

Salutary neglect was a by-product of the political system developed by Sir Robert Walpole, the Whig leader in the House of Commons from 1720 to 1742. By providing supporters with appointments and pensions, Walpole won parliamentary approval for his policies. However, his patronage appointments filled the British government, including the Board of Trade and the colonial bureaucracy, with do-nothing political hacks. When Governor Gabriel Johnson arrived in North Carolina in the 1730s, he vowed to curb the powers of the assembly and "make a mighty change in the face of affairs." Receiving little support from the Board of Trade, Johnson renounced reform and decided "to do nothing which can be reasonably blamed, and leave the rest to time, and a new set of inhabitants."

Walpole's tactics also weakened the empire by undermining the legitimacy of the political system. Radical Whigs protested that Walpole had betrayed the Glorious Revolution by using **patronage** — the practice of giving offices and salaries to political allies — and bribery to create a strong Court (or Kingly) Party. The Country Party, whose members were landed gentlemen, likewise warned that Walpole's policies of high taxes and a bloated royal bureaucracy threatened British liberties. Heeding these arguments, colonial legislators complained that royal governors abused their patronage powers. To preserve American liberty, the colonists strengthened the powers of the representative assemblies, unintentionally laying the foundation for the American independence movement (American Voices, p. 108).

Protecting the Mercantile System

In 1732, Walpole provided a parliamentary subsidy for the new colony of Georgia. While Georgia's reform-minded trustees envisioned the colony as a refuge for Britain's poor, Walpole had little interest in social reform; he subsidized Georgia to protect the valuable rice-growing colony of South Carolina. The subsidy, however, did exactly the opposite. Britain's expansion into Georgia outraged Spanish officials, who were

Succession (1740–1748). Massive French armies battled British-subsidized German forces in Europe, and French naval forces roamed the West Indies, vainly trying to conquer a British sugar island. Three thousand New England militiamen, supported by a British naval squadron, in 1745 captured Louisbourg, the French fort guarding the entrance to the St. Lawrence River. To the dismay of New England Puritans, who feared invasion from Catholic Quebec, the Treaty of Aix-la-Chapelle (1748) returned Louisbourg to France. The treaty made it clear to colonial leaders that England would act in its own interests, not theirs.

Mercantilism and the American Colonies

Though Parliament prohibited Americans from manufacturing textiles (Woolen Act, 1699), hats (Hat Act, 1732), and iron products such as plows, axes, and skillets (Iron Act, 1750), it could not prevent the colonies from maturing economically. American merchants soon controlled over 75 percent of the transatlantic trade in manufactures and 95 percent of the commerce between the mainland and the British West Indies (see Map 3.4, p. 104).

Moreover, by the 1720s, the British sugar islands could not absorb all the flour, fish, and meat produced by mainland settlers. So, ignoring Britain's intense rivalry with France, colonial merchants sold their produce to the French sugar islands. When American rum distillers began to buy cheap molasses from the French islands, the West Indian sugar lobby in London persuaded Parliament to pass the Molasses Act of 1733. The act placed a high tariff on French molasses, so high that it would no longer be profitable for American merchants to import it. Colonists protested that the Molasses Act would cripple the distilling industry; cut farm exports; and, by slashing colonial income, reduce the mainland's purchases of British goods. When Parliament ignored these arguments, American merchants smuggled in French molasses by bribing customs officials.

The lack of currency in the colonies prompted another conflict with British officials. To pay for British manufactures, American merchants used the bills of exchange and the gold and silver coins earned in the West Indian trade. These payments drained the colonial economy of money, making it difficult for Americans to borrow funds or to buy and sell goods among themselves. To remedy the problem, ten colonial assemblies established public **land banks**, which lent paper money

Sir Robert Walpole, the King's Minister

All eyes are on the secretary of the Treasury, Sir Robert Walpole (left), as he offers advice to the Speaker of the House of Commons. A brilliant politician, Walpole used patronage to command a majority in the Commons and also won the confidence of George I and George II, the German-speaking monarchs from the duchy of Hanover. Walpole's personal motto, "Let sleeping dogs lie," helps explain his colonial policy of salutary neglect. Clandon Park, Surrey, UK/National Trust Photographic Library/Hawksley Studios/The Bridgeman Art Library.

already angry about the rising tide of smuggled British manufactures in New Spain. To counter Britain's commercial imperialism, Spanish naval forces stepped up their seizure of illegal traders, in the process mutilating an English sea captain, Robert Jenkins.

Yielding to parliamentary pressure, Walpole declared war on Spain in 1739. The so-called War of Jenkins's Ear (1739–1741) was a fiasco for Britain. In 1740, British regulars failed to capture St. Augustine because South Carolina whites, still shaken by the Stono Rebellion, refused to commit militia units to the expedition. A year later, an assault on the prosperous seaport of Cartagena (in present-day Colombia) also failed; 20,000 British sailors and soldiers and 2,500 colonial troops died in the attack, mostly from tropical diseases.

The War of Jenkins's Ear quickly became part of a general European conflict, the War of the Austrian

The Rise of Colonial Self-Government

Between 1700 and 1760, members of the representative assemblies in British North America gradually expanded their authority and power. Their success was the result of greater popular participation in politics and their own political skills. However, the shift in power from imperial appointees to colonial legislators occurred in a piecemeal fashion, as the almost unconscious product of a series of small, seemingly inconsequential struggles. As you read the following correspondence among legislators, governors, and British officials, look closely at the character of the disputes and how they were resolved.

Alexander Spotswood
Confronting the House of Burgesses

As a reward for his military service fighting the forces of Louis XIV of France, Alexander Spotswood became governor of Virginia in 1710. A contentious man, Spotswood was a controversial governor. He told the House of Burgesses to its face that the voters had mistakenly chosen "a set of representatives whom heaven has not generally endowed with the ordinary [intellectual or social] qualifications requisite to legislators." Spotswood set out to reform the voting system that, in his judgment, produced such mediocre representatives. His efforts to oust popular members of the gentry from the House of Burgesses created few friends; in 1722, his enemies in Virginia used their influence in London to have him removed from office.

To ye Council of Trade, Virginia, October 15, 1712
MY LORDS:
. . . The Indians continue their Incursions in North Carolina, and the Death of Colo. Hyde, their Gov'r, which happened the beginning of last Month, increases the misery of that province. . . .

This Unhappy State of her Maj't's Subjects in my Neighbourhood is ye more Affecting to me because I have very little hopes of being enabled to relieve them by our Assembly, which I have called to meet next Week; for the Mob of this Country, having tried their Strength in the late Election and finding themselves able to carry whom they please, have generally chosen representatives of their own Class, who as their principal Recommendation have declared their resolution to raise no Tax on the people, let the occasion be what it will. This is owing to a defect in the Constitution, which allows to every one, tho' but just out of the Condition of a Servant, and that can but purchase half an acre of Land, an equal Vote with the Man of the best Estate in the Country.

The Militia of this Colony is perfectly useless without Arms or ammunition, and by an unaccountable infatuation, no arguments I have used can prevail on these people to make their Militia more Serviceable, or to fall into any other measures for the Defence of their Country. [From the Journal of the Virginia Council] December the 17th, 1714

The Governor this day laying before the Council a letter from the Right Honorable the Lords Commissioners for Trade dated the 23d of April 1713 directing him to advise with the Council & to recommend to the Generall Assembly to pass a law for qualifying the Electors & the persons Elected Burgesses to serve in the Generall Assembly of this Colony in a more just & equal manner than the Laws now in force do direct. . . . The Council declare that they cannot advise the Governor to move for any alteration in the present method of Electing of Burgesses, some being of opinion that this is not a proper time, & others that the present manner of electing of Burgesses & the qualifications of the elected is sufficiently provided for by the Laws now in force.

To Mr. Secretary James Stanhope, July 15, 1715

. . . I cannot forbear regretting yt I must always have to do with ye Representatives of ye Vulgar People, and mostly with such members as are of their Stamp and Understanding, for so long as half an Acre of Land (which is of small value in this Country) qualifys a man to be an Elector, the meaner sort of People will ever carry ye Elections, and the humour generally runs to choose such men as are their most familiar Companions, who very eagerly seek to be Burgesses merely for the lucre of the Salary, and who, for fear of not being chosen again, dare in Assembly do nothing that may be disrelished [disapproved] out of the House by ye Common People. Hence it often happens yt what appears prudent and feasible to his Majesty's Governors and Council here will not pass with the House of Burgesses, upon whom they must depend for the means of putting their designs in Execution.

To the Lords Commissioners of Trade, May 23, 1716

. . . The behaviour of this Gentleman [Philip Ludwell Jr., the colony's Auditor] in constantly opposing whatever I have offered for ye due collecting the Quitt rents [annual feudal dues on land] and regulating the Acc'ts; his stirring up ye humours of the people before the last election of Burgesses; tampering with the most mutinous of that house, and betraying to them the measures resolved on in Council for his Majesty's Service, would have made me likewise suspend him from ye Council, but I find by the late Instructions I have received from his Majesty that Power is taken from ye Governor and transferred upon the majority of that Board [of Councilors], and while there are no less than seven of his Relations there, it is impossible to get a Majority to consent to the Suspension of him.

Sources: R. A. Brock, ed., *The Official Letters of Alexander Spotswood* (Richmond: Virginia Historical Society, 1885), 2: 1–2, 124, 154–155; H. R. MacIlwaine, ed., *Executive Journals of the Council of Colonial Virginia* (Richmond: Virginia State Library, 1928), 3: 392.

George Clinton
A Plea for Assistance

George Clinton served as governor of New York from 1744 to 1752. Like many governors during the era of salutary neglect, Clinton owed his appointment to political connections in England. As the second son of the seventh Earl of Lincoln, he would inherit neither the family's estate nor his father's position in the House of Lords; those went to his elder brother. To provide an income for Clinton, his family traded its votes in Parliament for patronage appointments. However, once Clinton was installed as governor of New York, he found himself dependent on the assembly for the payment of his salary—and the salaries of all members of his administration.

My Lords,

I have in my former letters inform'd Your Lordships what Incroachments the Assemblys of this province have from time to time made on His Majesty's Prerogative & Authority in this Province in drawing an absolute dependence of all the Officers upon them for their Saleries & Reward of their services, & by their taking in effect the Nomination to all Officers. . . .

1stly, That the Assembly refuse to admit of any amendment to any money bill, in any part of the Bill; so that the Bill must pass as it comes from the Assembly, or all the Supplies granted for the support of Government, & the most urgent services must be lost.

2ndly, It appears that they take the Payment of the [military] Forces, passing of Muster Rolls into their own hands by naming the Commissaries for those purposes in the Act.

3rdly, They by granting the Saleries to the Officers personally by name & not to the Officer for the time being, intimate that if any person be appointed to any Office his Salary must depend upon their approbation of the Appointment. . . .

I must now refer it to Your Lordships' consideration whether it be not high time to put a stop to these usurpations of the Assembly on His Majesty's Authority in this Province and for that purpose may it not be proper that His Majesty signify his Disallowance of the Act at least for the payment of Saleries.

Source: E. B. O'Callaghan, ed., *Documents Relative to the Colonial History of the State of New York* (Albany, 1860 on), 2: 211.

QUESTIONS FOR ANALYSIS

1. What policies does Spotswood wish to pursue? Why can't he persuade the House of Burgesses to implement them? According to Spotswood, what is wrong with Virginia's political system? How does he propose to reform it?

2. Unlike the House of Burgesses, which was elected by qualified voters, the members of the Governor's Council in Virginia were appointed by the king, usually on the governor's recommendation. What is the council's response to the plan to reform the political system? Given Spotswood's description of the incident involving Philip Ludwell, where did the political sympathies of the council lie?

3. What were Clinton's complaints about the actions of the New York assembly? Did these actions represent a more or less serious threat to imperial power than the activities of the Virginia Burgesses? Based on their correspondence with the Board of Trade, which governor—Spotswood or Clinton—was the stronger representative of the interests of the crown?

The Siege and Capture of Louisbourg, 1745

In 1760, as British and colonial troops moved toward victory in the French and Indian War (1754–1763), the London artist J. Stevens sought to bolster imperial pride by celebrating an earlier Anglo-American triumph. In 1745, a British naval squadron led a flotilla of colonial ships and thousands of New England militiamen in an attack on the French fort at Louisbourg, on Cape Breton Island, near the mouth of the St. Lawrence River. After a siege of forty days, the Anglo-American force captured the fort, long considered impregnable. The victory was bittersweet because the Treaty of Aix-la-Chapelle (1748) returned the island to France. Anne S. K. Brown Military Collection, Brown University Library.

to farmers who pledged their land as collateral for the loans. Farmers used the currency to buy tools or livestock or to pay creditors, thereby stimulating trade. However, some assemblies, particularly the legislature in Rhode Island, issued huge quantities of paper money (which consequently decreased in value) and required merchants to accept it as legal tender. English merchants and other creditors rightly complained about being forced to accept devalued money. So in 1751, Parliament passed the Currency Act, which barred the New England colonies from establishing new land banks and prohibited the use of publicly issued paper money to pay private debts.

These conflicts over trade and paper money angered a new generation of English political leaders. In 1749, Charles Townshend of the Board of Trade charged that the American assemblies had assumed many of the "ancient and established prerogatives wisely preserved in the Crown," and he vowed to replace salutary neglect with more rigorous imperial control.

The wheel of empire had come full circle. In the 1650s, England had set out to create a centrally managed Atlantic empire and, over the course of a century, achieved the military and economic aspects of that goal. Mercantilist legislation, maritime warfare, commercial expansion, and the forced labor of a million African slaves brought prosperity to Britain. However, internal unrest (the Glorious Revolution) and a policy of salutary neglect had weakened Britain's political

authority over its American colonies. Recognizing the threat self-government posed to the empire, British officials in the late 1740s vowed to reassert their power in America — an initiative with disastrous results.

SUMMARY

In this chapter, we examined processes of change in politics and society. The political story began in the 1660s as Britain imposed controls on its American possessions. Parliament passed the Acts of Trade and Navigation to keep colonial products and trade in English hands. Then King James II abolished representative institutions in the northern colonies and created the authoritarian Dominion of New England. Following the Glorious Revolution, the Navigation Acts remained in place and tied the American economy to that of Britain. But the uprisings of 1688–1689 overturned James II's policy of strict imperial control, restored colonial self-government, and ushered in an era of salutary political neglect. It also initiated a long era of imperial warfare, in which Native American peoples allied themselves to the colonies and often served as proxy warriors against French- and Spanish-allied peoples, pursuing their own goals in the process.

The social story centers on the development of the South Atlantic System of production and trade, which involved an enormous expansion in African slave raiding; the Atlantic slave trade; and the cultivation of sugar, rice, and tobacco in America. This complex system created an exploited African American labor force in the southern mainland and West Indian colonies, while it allowed European American farmers, merchants, and artisans on the North American mainland to prosper. How would the two stories play out? In 1750, slavery and the South Atlantic System seemed firmly entrenched, but the days of salutary neglect appeared numbered.

C H A P T E R R E V I E W

MAKE IT STICK Go to **LearningCurve** to retain what you've read.

TERMS TO KNOW Identify and explain the significance of each term below.

Key Concepts and Events

proprietorship (p. 82)
Quakers (p. 82)
Navigation Acts (p. 83)
Dominion of New England (p. 85)
Glorious Revolution (p. 86)
constitutional monarchy (p. 87)
Second Hundred Years' War (p. 88)

tribalization (p. 88)
Covenant Chain (p. 89)
South Atlantic System (p. 90)
Middle Passage (p. 94)
Stono Rebellion (p. 101)
gentility (p. 102)
salutary neglect (p. 106)
patronage (p. 106)
land banks (p. 110)

Key People

William Penn (p. 82)
Edmund Andros (p. 85)
William of Orange (p. 86)
John Locke (p. 86)
Jacob Leisler (p. 87)
William Byrd II (p. 102)
Robert Walpole (p. 106)

REVIEW QUESTIONS Answer these questions to demonstrate your understanding of the chapter's main ideas.

1. What strategies did Charles II and James II employ to try to gain more centralized control over England's American colonies? What did James hope to accomplish by creating the Dominion of New England?

2. How did the long era of imperial warfare beginning in 1689 affect the colonies, Native Americans, and relations between them?

3. What was the South Atlantic System, and how did it shape colonial society?

4. How did the institution of slavery develop, and why did it develop differently in the Chesapeake, the Carolina low country, and the West Indies?

5. THEMATIC UNDERSTANDING Trace the developments outlined in the section entitled "Politics and Power" from 1660 to 1750 on the thematic timeline on page 79. What pattern of political evolution do you see in colonial interactions with Britain?

MAKING CONNECTIONS

Recognize the larger developments and continuities within and across chapters by answering these questions.

1. **ACROSS TIME AND PLACE**   In Chapter 2, we traced the emergence of three distinct colonial types in the Americas during the sixteenth and seventeenth centuries: tribute, plantation, and neo-European colonies. In Chapter 3, we have seen how Britain's plantation and neo-European colonies became more closely interconnected after 1700. What developments caused them to become more closely tied to each other? How did they benefit from these ties? Can you see any disadvantages to the colonies in a more fully integrated Atlantic system?

2. **VISUAL EVIDENCE**   Consider the illustrations of women hulling rice in West Africa and Georgia on page 100. Historians have long debated the role Africans played in developing rice cultivation in the South Carolina and Georgia low country. These debates have focused primarily on methods of cultivation: Did Africans who had prior experience with rice teach English planters how to grow it? How can these two images contribute to the debate and expand our perspective on the question of African influences in American rice production?

MORE TO EXPLORE

Start here to learn more about the events discussed in this chapter.

Ira Berlin, *Many Thousands Gone* (2000). Explores the varieties of slave experience in North America.

Olaudah Equiano, *The Interesting Narrative of the Life of Olaudah Equiano* (1789; reprint 2006). A compelling and influential eighteenth-century slave autobiography.

Paul Mapp, *The Elusive West and the Contest for Empire, 1713–1763* (2011). Offers a continental perspective on the contest for European control of North America.

Owen Stanwood, *The Empire Reformed* (2011). Tells the story of the Glorious Revolution in the American colonies.

Africans in America, Part 1: Terrible Transformation, 1450–1750 (PBS video, 1998) and the related Web site (**pbs.org/wgbh/aia/part1/title.html**). Treats the early African American experience.

"The Atlantic Slave Trade and Slave Life in the Americas: A Visual Record" (**hitchcock.itc.virginia.edu/Slavery**). An extensive collection of slave images.

TIMELINE

Ask yourself why this chapter begins and ends with these dates and then identify the links among related events.

1651	• First Navigation Act
1660–1685	• Reign of Charles II, king of England
1663	• Charles II grants Carolina proprietorship
1664	• English capture New Netherland, rename it New York
1669	• Virginia law declares that the murder of a slave cannot be treated as a felony
1681	• William Penn founds Pennsylvania
1685–1688	• Reign of James II, king of England
1686–1689	• Dominion of New England
1688–1689	• Glorious Revolution in England
1689	• William and Mary ascend throne in England • Revolts in Massachusetts, Maryland, and New York
1689–1713	• England, France, and Spain at war
1696	• Parliament creates Board of Trade
1714–1750	• British policy of salutary neglect • American assemblies gain power
1720–1742	• Robert Walpole leads Parliament
1720–1750	• African American communities form • Rice exports from South Carolina soar • Planter aristocracy emerges • Seaport cities expand
1732	• Parliament charters Georgia, challenging Spain • Hat Act limits colonial enterprise
1733	• Molasses Act threatens distillers
1739	• Stono Rebellion in South Carolina
1739–1748	• War with Spain in the Caribbean and France in Canada and Europe
1750	• Iron Act restricts colonial iron production
1751	• Currency Act prohibits land banks and paper money

KEY TURNING POINTS: The Glorious Revolution (1688–1689), salutary neglect and the rise of the assemblies (1714–1750), and the Hat, Molasses, Iron, and Currency Acts (1732–1751). How do these developments reflect Britain's new attitude toward its colonies? In what matters did Parliament seek to control the colonies, and in what did it grant them autonomy?

4

CHAPTER

Growth, Diversity, and Conflict
1720–1763

In 1736, Alexander MacAllister left the Highlands of Scotland for the back-country of North Carolina, where his wife and three sisters soon joined him. MacAllister prospered as a landowner and mill proprietor and had only praise for his new home. Carolina was "the best poor man's country," he wrote to his brother Hector, urging him to "advise all poor people . . . to take courage and come." In North Carolina, there were no landlords to keep "the face of the poor . . . to the grinding stone," and so many Highlanders were arriving that "it will soon be a new Scotland." Here, on the far margins of the British Empire, people could "breathe the air of liberty, and not want the necessarys of life." Some 300,000 European migrants—primarily Highland Scots, Scots-Irish, and Germans—heeded MacAllister's advice and helped swell the population of Britain's North American settlements from 400,000 in 1720 to almost 2 million by 1765.

MacAllister's "air of liberty" did not last forever, as the rapid increase in white settlers and the arrival of nearly 300,000 enslaved Africans transformed life throughout mainland British North America. Long-settled towns in New England became overcrowded, and antagonistic ethnic and religious communities jostled uneasily with one another in the Middle Atlantic colonies; in 1748, there were more than a hundred German Lutheran and Reformed congregations in Quaker-led Pennsylvania. By then, the MacAllisters and thousands of other Celtic and German migrants had altered the social landscape and introduced religious conflict into the southern backcountry.

Everywhere, two European cultural movements, the Enlightenment and Pietism, changed the tone of intellectual and spiritual life. Advocates of "rational thought" viewed human beings as agents of moral self-determination and urged Americans to fashion a better social order. Religious Pietists outnumbered them and had more influence. Convinced of the weakness of human nature, evangelical ministers told their followers to seek regeneration through divine grace. Amidst this intellectual and religious ferment, migrants and the landless children of long-settled families moved inland and sparked wars with the native peoples and with France and Spain. A generation of dynamic growth produced a decade of deadly warfare that would set the stage for a new era in American history.

IDENTIFY THE BIG IDEA

In what ways were Britain's American colonies affected by events across the Atlantic, and how were their societies taking on a life of their own?

John Collet, *George Whitefield Preaching* No painting could capture English minister George Whitefield's charismatic appeal, although this image conveys his open demeanor and religious intensity. When Whitefield spoke to a crowd near Philadelphia, an observer noted that his words were "sharper than a two-edged sword. . . . Some of the people were pale as death; others were wringing their hands . . . and most lifting their eyes to heaven and crying to God for mercy." An astute businessman as well as a charismatic preacher, Whitefield tirelessly promoted the sale of his sermons and books. © Private Collection/The Bridgeman Art Library.

New England's Freehold Society

In the 1630s, the Puritans had fled England, where a small elite of nobles and gentry owned 75 percent of the arable land, while **tenants** (renters) and property-less workers farmed it. In New England, the Puritans created a yeoman society of relatively equal landowning farm families. But by 1750, the migrants' numerous descendants had parceled out the best farmland, threatening the future of the freehold ideal.

Farm Families: Women in the Household Economy

The Puritans' vision of social equality did not extend to women, and their ideology placed the husband firmly at the head of the household. In *The Well-Ordered Family* (1712), the Reverend Benjamin Wadsworth of Boston advised women, "Since he is thy Husband, God has made him the head and set him above thee." It was a wife's duty "to love and reverence" her husband.

UNDERSTAND POINTS OF VIEW
What ideas, institutions, and responsibilities shaped New England farm women's lives?

Women learned this subordinate role throughout their lives. Small girls watched their mothers defer to their fathers, and as young women, they were told to be "silent in company." They saw the courts prosecute more women than men for the crime of fornication (sex outside of marriage), and they found that their marriage portions would be inferior to those of their brothers. Thus Ebenezer Chittendon of Guilford, Connecticut, left his land to his sons, decreeing that "Each Daughter [shall] have half so much as Each Son, one half in money and the other half in Cattle."

Throughout the colonies, women assumed the role of dutiful helpmeets (helpmates) to their husbands. In addition to tending gardens, farmwives spun thread and yarn from flax and wool and then wove it into cloth for shirts and gowns. They knitted sweaters and stockings, made candles and soap, churned milk into butter, fermented malt for beer, preserved meats, and mastered dozens of other household tasks. "Notable women"—those who excelled at domestic arts—won praise and high status (Thinking Like a Historian, p. 118).

Bearing and rearing children were equally important tasks. Most women in New England married in their early twenties and by their early forties had given birth to six or seven children, delivered with the help of a female neighbor or a midwife. One Massachusetts mother confessed that she had little time for religious activities because "the care of my Babes takes up so large a portion of my time and attention." Yet most Puritan congregations were filled with women: "In a Church of between *Three* and *Four* Hundred *Communicants*," the eminent minister Cotton Mather noted, "there are but few more than *One* Hundred *Men*; all the Rest are Women."

Women's lives remained tightly bound by a web of legal and cultural restrictions. Ministers praised women for their piety but excluded them from an equal role in the church. When Hannah Heaton, a Connecticut farmwife, grew dissatisfied with her

Prudence Punderson (1758–1784), *The First, Second and Last Scenes of Mortality*

This powerful image reveals both the artistic skills of colonial women in the traditional medium of needlework and the Puritans' continuing cultural concern with the inevitability of death. Prudence Punderson, the Connecticut woman who embroidered this scene, rejected a marriage proposal and followed her Loyalist father into exile on Long Island in 1778. Sometime later, she married a cousin, Timothy Rossiter, and bore a daughter, Sophia, who may well be the baby in the cradle being rocked by "Jenny," a slave owned by Prudence's father. Long worried by "my ill state of health" and perhaps now anticipating her own death, Prudence has inscribed her initials on the coffin—and, in creating this embroidery, transformed her personal experience into a broader meditation on the progression from birth, to motherhood, to death. Connecticut Historical Society.

Congregationalist minister, thinking him unconverted and a "blind guide," she sought out equality-minded Quaker and evangelist Baptist churches that welcomed questioning women such as herself and treated "saved" women equally with men. However, by the 1760s, many evangelical congregations had reinstituted men's dominance over women. "The government of Church and State must be . . . family government" controlled by its "king," declared the Danbury (Connecticut) Baptist Association.

Farm Property: Inheritance

By contrast, European men who migrated to the colonies escaped many traditional constraints, including the curse of landlessness. "The hope of having land of their own & becoming independent of Landlords is what chiefly induces people into America," an official noted in the 1730s. Owning property gave formerly dependent peasants a new social identity.

Unlike the adventurers seeking riches in other parts of the Americas, most New England migrants wanted farms that would provide a living for themselves and ample land for their children. In this way, they hoped to secure a **competency** for their families: the ability to keep their households solvent and independent and to pass that ability on to the next generation. Parents who could not give their offspring land placed these children as indentured servants in more prosperous households. When the indentures ended at age eighteen or twenty-one, propertyless sons faced a decades-long climb up the agricultural ladder, from laborer to tenant and finally to freeholder.

Sons and daughters in well-to-do farm families were luckier: they received a marriage portion when they were in their early twenties. That portion — land, livestock, or farm equipment — repaid them for their past labor and allowed parents to choose their marriage partners. Parents' security during old age depended on a wise choice of son- or daughter-in-law. Although the young people could refuse an unacceptable match, they did not have the luxury of falling in love with and marrying whomever they pleased.

Marriage under eighteenth-century English common law was not a contract between equals. A bride relinquished to her husband the legal ownership of all her property. After his death, she received a dower right, the right to use (though not sell) one-third of the family's property. On the widow's death or remarriage, her portion was divided among the children. Thus the widow's property rights were subordinate to those of the family line, which stretched across the generations.

A father's duty was to provide inheritances for his children so that one day they could "be for themselves." Men who failed to do so lost status in the community. Some fathers willed the family farm to a single son and provided other children with money, an apprenticeship, or uncleared frontier tracts. Other yeomen moved their families to the frontier, where life was hard but land was cheap and abundant. "The Squire's House stands on the Bank of the Susquehannah," traveler Philip Fithian reported from the Pennsylvania backcountry in the early 1760s. "He tells me that he will be able to settle all his sons and his fair Daughter Betsy on the Fat of the Earth."

Freehold Society in Crisis

Because of rapid natural increase, New England's population doubled each generation, from 100,000 in 1700, to nearly 200,000 in 1725, to almost 400,000 in 1750. Farms had been divided and then subdivided, making them so small — 50 acres or less — that parents could provide only one child with an adequate inheritance. In the 1740s, the Reverend Samuel Chandler of Andover, Massachusetts, was "much distressed for land for his children," seven of them young boys. A decade later, in nearby Concord, about 60 percent of the farmers owned less land than their fathers had.

Because parents had less to give their sons and daughters, they had less control over their children's lives. The traditional system of arranged marriages broke down, as young people engaged in premarital sex and then used the urgency of pregnancy to win permission to marry. Throughout New England, premarital conceptions rose dramatically, from about 10 percent of firstborn children in the 1710s to more than 30 percent in the 1740s. Given another chance, young people "would do the same again," an Anglican minister observed, "because otherwise they could not obtain their parents' consent to marry."

Even as New England families changed, they maintained the freeholder ideal. Some parents chose to have smaller families and used birth control to do so: abstention, coitus interruptus, or primitive condoms. Other families petitioned the provincial government for frontier land grants and hacked new farms out of the forests of central Massachusetts, western Connecticut, and eventually New Hampshire and Vermont. Still others improved their farms' productivity by replacing the traditional English crops of wheat and barley with high-yielding potatoes

IDENTIFY CAUSES
What factors threatened the freeholder ideal in midcentury New England, and what strategies did farming families use to preserve this ideal?

Women's Labor

As these documents show, women bore the responsibility for a wide variety of work, from keeping up households to supporting themselves independently.

1. Thomas Tusser, *Five Hundred Pointes of Good Husbandrie*, 1557. *Advice manuals like Tusser's circulated for generations and offered guidance on household management. In this couplet, Tusser stresses the virtues of a wife's economy and hard work.*

Wife, make thine own candle,
Spare penny to handle.
Provide for thy tallow ere frost cometh in,
And make thine own candle ere winter begin.

2. Eliza Lucas, letters, 1740–1742. *George Lucas owned three South Carolina plantations, but, as lieutenant governor of Antigua, he was frequently absent. When his daughter was sixteen, he gave her responsibility for managing them. She introduced indigo cultivation in South Carolina, and it soon became the colony's second-leading cash crop. These letters were written when she was between the ages of eighteen and twenty.*

May 2, 1740

"I have the business of 3 plantations to transact, which requires much writing and more business and fatigue of other sorts than you can imagine. But least you should imagine it too burthensom to a girl at my early time of life, give me leave to answer you: I assure you I think myself happy that I can be useful to so good a father, and by rising very early I find I can go through much business."

July 1740

"Wrote my Father a very long letter on his plantation affairs and on . . . the pains I had taken to bring the Indigo, Ginger, Cotton and Lucerne and Casada to perfection, and had greater hopes from the Indigo . . . than any of the rest of the things I tried."

February 6, 1741

". . . I have a Sister to instruct and a parcel of little Negroes whom I have undertaken to teach to read."

April 23, 1741

"Wrote to my Father informing him of the loss of a Negro man — also the boat being overset in Santilina [Saint Helena] Sound and 20 barrels of Rice lost."

[1742]

"Wont you laugh at me if I tell you I am so busey in providing for Posterity I hardly allow my self time to Eat or sleep. . . . I am making a large plantation of Oaks which I look upon as my own property, whether my father gives me the land or not; and therefore I design many years hence when oaks are more valueable than they are now — which you know they will be when we come to build fleets."

[c. June 1742]

"I am engaged with the rudiments of the law to which I am yet but a stranger. . . . If You will not laugh too immoderately at me I'll Trust you with a secrett. I have made two wills already."

3. Mary Vial Holyoke, diary excerpts, 1761. *Mary Vial Holyoke, wife of a prominent physician in Salem, Massachusetts, kept a diary that offers a glimpse of the range of household tasks women faced.*

[1761]

Jan. 16: Began upon the firkin of butter of 40 lb. . . .
22: Bo't hog, weighed 182 pounds, at 2/5. Salted hog with half Lisbon & half saltertudas [Tortugas] salt. . . .
Mar. 4: Ironing. . . .
7: Scower'd pewter. . . .
17: Made the Dr. six Cravats marked H. . . .
Apr. 17: Made soap. . . .
23: Dressed a Calves Head turtle fashion. . . .
May 20: Began to whitewash. . . .
28: Ironed. . . .
30: Scower'd pewter. . . .
July 7: Scowered rooms. . . .

4. Colonial house interiors in Germantown, Pennsylvania, and Augusta, Maine. *These images show the dining room of Benjamin Chew, a wealthy Philadelphia lawyer (below), and the kitchen of the Howards, an extended family of soldiers and merchants on the Maine frontier (opposite).*

Source: Photo by Ron Blunt, Courtesy of Cliveden, a National Trust Historic Site, Philadelphia, PA.

Source: Old Fort Western, Augusta, Maine.

5. Business advertisement in the *Pennsylvania Gazette*, 1758. *Not all women's work was done in the home. Hannah Breintnall, a Philadelphia widow, ran a tavern before opening a shop specializing in eyeglasses.*

Juft imported in the Ship Myrtilla, Capta'n Bolithr, from London, and to be fold by

HANNAH BREINTNALL,

At the Sign of the Speffacles, in Second-ftreet, near Black-Horfe Alley,

A Great Variety of the fineft Chryftal Speffacles, fet in Temple, Steel, Leather or other Frames. Likewife true Venetian green Speffac'es, for weak or watery Eyes, of various Sorts. Alfo Concave Speffacles, for fhort fighted Perfons; Magnifying and Reading Glaffes; and an Affortment of large and fmall Spy gl•ff•s and Bone Microfcopes, with magnifying and mu'tiplying Glafs, &c. &c. Pocket Compaffes, of different Sizes, &c. || 10 s. Thetf.

Source: Library Company of Philadelphia.

6. *Hilliad Magna: Being the Life and Adventures of Moll Placket-Hole*, 1765. *Moll Placket-Hole was a satirical, seven-page pamphlet that purported to describe the life of a Philadelphia prostitute. Moll was an eighteenth-century term for a loose woman or prostitute, while placket-hole referred to a slit that might be found in a woman's skirt.*

MOLL PLACKET-HOLE was born in a *Bawdy House* in a *Lane* in the City of *Brotherly Love*. . . . [A]t the Age of twelve (Shocking to consider!) . . . [her] Mother *sold* her Virginity — *sold* it for the Trifling Consideration of *Ten Pounds*. Her Purchaser was soon cloyed and abandoned her. Virtue lost and good Reputation (if ever she had it) gone, she commenced open Prostitute and dealt out her Favours to the highest Bidder. . . . [S]he understood the Trade and set up a *Bawdy-House*. . . . It was necessary, however, that a Man should live with her, that they might appear to the Publick, as *honest* Housekeepers. . . . The Trade became at last so publick, that it gave Offence to her sober Neighbours. . . . [T]he Town tired out with her Insolence, and her Escape from Justice in a regular Manner, set a Mob (many of whom had been her Beneficiaries) upon her. They pulled down her House, and destroyed her Furniture &c. She stormed and raged and swore if her Customers would not build her a better House, she would expose them. . . . They opened a Subscription, and a hundred Pounds were subscribed in one Day.

Sources: (1) Alice Morse Earle, *Home Life in the Colonial Days* (New York: The Macmillan Company, 1898), 35; (2) From *The Letterbook of Eliza Lucas Pinckney, 1739–1762*, edited by Elise Pinckney, University of North Carolina Press, 1972. Based on original documents from the South Carolina Historical Society. Courtesy of the South Carolina Historical Society; (3) George Francis Dow, ed., *The Holyoke Diaries, 1709–1856* (Salem, MA: The Essex Institute, 1911), 49–51; (6) *Hilliad Magna: Being the Life and Adventures of Moll Placket-Hole* ([Philadelphia]: Printed [by Anthony Armbruster], 1765).

ANALYZING THE EVIDENCE

1. Compare the advice manual (source 1) with Eliza Lucas's letters and Mary Vial Holyoke's diary. What themes do they share in common, and how do these women's experiences deviate from the expectations of the advice book authors?

2. Eliza Lucas supervised slave labor, and Mary Vial Holyoke very likely employed servants. How do these facts affect the way you interpret sources 2 and 3?

3. Compare the two house interiors (source 4). What work would women have done in these spaces? The Chews were a slaveholding family, and the Howards probably employed servants. With that in mind, consider the relationship between supervisory and manual labor.

4. Hannah Breintnall was a well-to-do widow, while Moll Placket-Hole was a fictional stereotype. What does Breintnall's experience tell us about the prospects of a woman living without a male protector? How does Moll Placket-Hole shed light on popular attitudes toward such women?

PUTTING IT ALL TOGETHER

With all these sources in mind, write a short essay that considers the role of hierarchy and social power in women's work. How did economic and social status affect the work that was expected of women? How did the women whose lives are documented here navigate the challenges and opportunities they faced? And how does the satire of Moll Placket-Hole illuminate popular attitudes toward women's work and its place in colonial society?

and maize (Indian corn). Corn was an especially wise choice: good for human consumption, as well as for feeding cattle and pigs, which provided milk and meat. Gradually, New England changed from a grain to a livestock economy, becoming a major exporter of salted meat to the plantations of the West Indies.

As the population swelled, New England farmers developed the full potential of what one historian has called the "**household mode of production**," in which families swapped labor and goods. Women and children worked in groups to spin yarn, sew quilts, and shuck corn. Men loaned neighbors tools, draft animals, and grazing land. Farmers plowed fields owned by artisans and shopkeepers, who repaid them with shoes, furniture, or store credit. Partly because currency was in short supply, no cash changed hands. Instead, farmers, artisans, and shopkeepers recorded debits and credits and "balanced" the books every few years. This system helped New Englanders to maximize agricultural output and preserve the freehold ideal.

Diversity in the Middle Colonies

The Middle colonies—New York, New Jersey, and Pennsylvania—became home to peoples of differing origins, languages, and religions. Scots-Irish Presbyterians, English and Welsh Quakers, German Lutherans and Moravians, Dutch Reformed Protestants, and others all sought to preserve their cultural and religious identities as they pursued economic opportunity. At the same time, rapid population growth throughout the region strained public institutions, pressured Indian lands, and created a dynamic but unstable society.

Economic Growth, Opportunity, and Conflict

Previously home to New Netherland and New Sweden, the Mid-Atlantic region was already ethnically diverse before England gained control of it. The founding of Pennsylvania and New Jersey amplified this pattern. Fertile land seemed abundant, and grain exports to Europe and the West Indies financed the colonies' rapid settlement (America Compared, p. 121). Between 1720 and 1770, a growing demand for wheat, corn, and flour doubled their prices and brought people and prosperity to the region. Yet that very growth led to conflict, both within the Middle colonies and in their relations with Native American neighbors.

Tenancy in New York   In New York's fertile Hudson River Valley, wealthy Dutch and English families presided over the huge manors created by the Dutch West India Company and English governors (Map 4.1). Like Chesapeake planters, the New York landlords aspired to live in the manner of the European gentry but found that few migrants wanted to labor as peasants. To

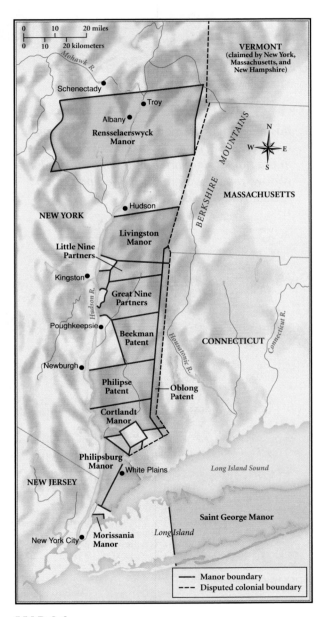

MAP 4.1
The Hudson River Manors

Dutch and English manorial lords owned much of the fertile east bank of the Hudson River, where they leased farms on perpetual contracts to German tenants and refused to sell land to freehold-seeking migrants from overcrowded New England. This powerful landed elite produced aristocratic-minded Patriot leaders such as Gouverneur Morris and Robert Livingston, as well as prominent American families such as the Roosevelts.

Transatlantic Migration, 1500–1760

The following graph compares the number of European and African migrants who arrived in the American colonies of Spain, Portugal, Britain, France, and the Netherlands. It also charts change over time: while immigrants in the sixteenth and early seventeenth centuries went predominantly to the colonies of Spain and Portugal, Britain's colonies became the principal destination for both Europeans and Africans between 1640 and 1760.

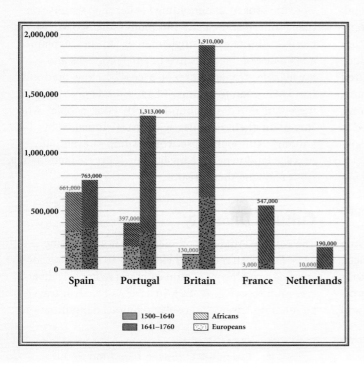

FIGURE 4.1
Transatlantic Migration

Source of data: Stanley L. Engerman and Kenneth L. Sokoloff, "Factor Endowments, Institutions, and Differential Paths of Growth Among New World Economies: A View from Economic Historians of the United States," in *How Latin America Fell Behind: Economic Histories of Brazil and Mexico, 1800–1914*, ed. Stephen Haber (Palo Alto, CA: Stanford University Press, 1997), 264.

QUESTIONS FOR ANALYSIS

1. What relationship do you see between the number of European emigrants and the importation of African slaves? Which nation's colonies had the highest percentage of Africans relative to Europeans? Which had the lowest? Which time periods had the highest and lowest percentages of Africans?

2. Compare France and the Netherlands to Spain, Portugal, and Britain. Why do you suppose that the ratio of Africans to Europeans is so much higher in French and Dutch colonies than in the other nations? Which type of colony—tribute, plantation, or neo-European—was likely to have been most important to the French and Dutch?

---

attract tenants, the manorial lords granted long leases, with the right to sell improvements such as houses and barns to the next tenant. They nevertheless struggled to populate their estates.

Most tenant families hoped that with hard work and ample sales they could eventually buy their own farmsteads. But preindustrial technology limited output. A worker with a hand sickle could reap only half an acre of wheat, rye, or oats a day. The cradle scythe, a tool introduced during the 1750s, doubled or tripled the amount of grain one worker could cut. Even so, a family with two adult workers could reap only about 12 acres of grain, or roughly 150 to 180 bushels of wheat. After saving enough grain for food and seed, the surplus might be worth £15 — enough to buy salt and sugar, tools, and cloth, but little else. The road to land-ownership was not an easy one.

Conflict in the Quaker Colonies In Quaker-dominated Pennsylvania and New Jersey, wealth was initially distributed more evenly than in New York,

but the proprietors of each colony, like the manor lords of New York, had enormous land claims. The first migrants lived simply in small, one- or two-room houses with a sleeping loft, a few benches or stools, and some wooden platters and cups. Economic growth brought greater prosperity, along with conflicts between ordinary settlers and the proprietors who tried to control their access to land, resources, and political power.

William Penn's early appeals to British Quakers and continental Protestants led to a boom in immigrants. When these first arrivals reported that Pennsylvania and New Jersey were "the best poor man's country in the world," thousands more followed. Soon the proprietors of both colonies were overwhelmed by the demand for land. By the 1720s, many new migrants were forced to become **squatters**, settling illegally on land they hoped eventually to be able to acquire on legal terms.

Frustration over the lack of land led the Penn family to perpetrate one of the most infamous land frauds of the eighteenth century, the so-called Walking Purchase of 1737, in which they exploited an old (and probably fraudulent) Indian deed to claim more than a million acres of prime farmland north of Philadelphia. This purchase, while opening new lands to settlement, poisoned Indian relations in the colony. Delaware and Shawnee migration to western Pennsylvania and the Ohio Valley, which was already under way, accelerated rapidly in response.

Immigrants flooded into Philadelphia, which grew from 2,000 people in 1700 to 25,000 by 1760. Many families came in search of land; for them, Philadelphia was only a temporary way station. Other migrants came as laborers, including a large number of indentured servants. Some were young, unskilled men, but the colony's explosive growth also created a strong demand for all kinds of skilled laborers, especially in the construction trades.

EXPLAIN CONSEQUENCES

How did rapid immigration and economic growth trigger conflict in the Middle colonies?

Pennsylvania and New Jersey grew prosperous but contentious. New Jersey was plagued by contested land titles, and ordinary settlers rioted against the proprietors in the 1740s and the 1760s. By the 1760s, eastern Pennsylvania landowners with large farms were using slaves and poor Scots-Irish migrants to grow wheat. Other ambitious men were buying up land and dividing it into small tenancies, which they lent out on profitable leases. Still others sold farming equipment and

manufactured goods or ran mills. These large-scale farmers, rural landlords, speculators, storekeepers, and gristmill operators formed a distinct class of agricultural capitalists. They built large stone houses for their families, furnishing them with four-poster beds and expensive mahogany tables, on which they laid elegant linen and imported Dutch dinnerware.

By contrast, one-half of the Middle colonies' white men owned no land and little personal property. Some were the sons of smallholding farmers and would eventually inherit some land. But many were Scots-Irish or German "inmates" — single men or families, explained a tax assessor, "such as live in small cottages and have no taxable property, except a cow." In the predominantly German township of Lancaster, Pennsylvania, a merchant noted an "abundance of Poor people" who "maintain their Families with great difficulty by day Labour." Although these workers hoped eventually to become landowners, rising land prices prevented many from realizing their dreams.

Cultural Diversity

The Middle Atlantic colonies were not a melting pot. Most European migrants held tightly to their traditions, creating a patchwork of ethnically and religiously diverse communities (Figure 4.2). In 1748, a Swedish traveler counted no fewer than twelve religious denominations

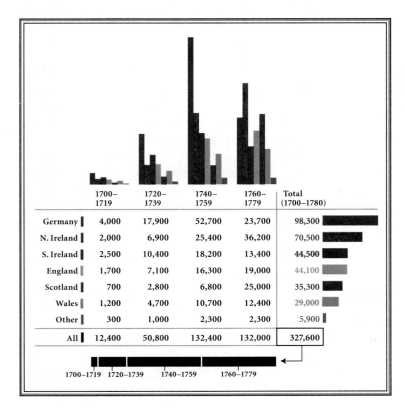

FIGURE 4.2

Estimated European Migration to the British Mainland Colonies, 1700–1780

After 1720, European migration to British North America increased dramatically, peaking between 1740 and 1780, when more than 264,000 settlers arrived in the mainland colonies. Emigration from Germany peaked in the 1740s, but the number of migrants from Ireland, Scotland, England, and Wales continued to increase during the 1760s and early 1770s. Most migrants, including those from Ireland, were Protestants.

	1700–1719	1720–1739	1740–1759	1760–1779	Total (1700–1780)
Germany	4,000	17,900	52,700	23,700	98,300
N. Ireland	2,000	6,900	25,400	36,200	70,500
S. Ireland	2,500	10,400	18,200	13,400	44,500
England	1,700	7,100	16,300	19,000	44,100
Scotland	700	2,800	6,800	25,000	35,300
Wales	1,200	4,700	10,700	12,400	29,000
Other	300	1,000	2,300	2,300	5,900
All	12,400	50,800	132,400	132,000	327,600

1700–1719   1720–1739   1740–1759   1760–1779

in Philadelphia, including Anglicans, Baptists, Quakers, Swedish and German Lutherans, Mennonites, Scots-Irish Presbyterians, and Roman Catholics.

Migrants preserved their cultural identity by marrying within their ethnic groups. A major exception was the Huguenots, Calvinists who had been expelled from Catholic France in the 1680s and resettled in Holland, England, and the British colonies. Huguenots in American port cities such as Boston, New York, and Charleston quickly lost their French identities by intermarrying with other Protestants. More typical were the Welsh Quakers in Chester County, Pennsylvania: 70 percent of the children of the original Welsh migrants married other Welsh Quakers, as did 60 percent of the third generation.

In Pennsylvania and western New Jersey, Quakers shaped the culture because of their numbers, wealth, and social cohesion. Most Quakers came from English counties with few landlords and brought with them traditions of local village governance, popular participation in politics, and social equality. But after 1720, the growth of German and Scots-Irish populations challenged their dominance.

The German Influx   The Quaker vision of a "peaceable kingdom" attracted 100,000 German migrants who had fled their homelands because of military conscription, religious persecution, and high taxes. First to arrive, in 1683, were the Mennonites, religious dissenters drawn by the promise of freedom of worship. In the 1720s, a larger wave of German migrants arrived from the overcrowded villages of southwestern Germany and Switzerland. "Wages were far better" in Pennsylvania, Heinrich Schneebeli reported to his friends in Zurich, and "one also enjoyed there a free unhindered exercise of religion." A third wave of Germans and Swiss — nearly 40,000 strong — landed in Philadelphia between 1749 and 1756. To help pay

A Quaker Meeting for Worship

Quakers dressed plainly and met for worship in unadorned buildings, sitting in silence until inspired by an "inner light." Women spoke during meetings on terms of near-equality to men, a tradition that prepared Quaker women to take a leading part in the nineteenth-century women's rights movement. In this English work, titled *Quaker Meeting*, an elder (his hat on a peg above his head) conveys his thoughts to the congregation. Museum of Fine Arts, Boston. M. and M. Karolik Collection.

The Demory House, c. 1780

The Demory House lies near the Shenandoah Valley in northwestern Virginia and was probably built by a migrant from Pennsylvania according to a German design used by both German and Scots-Irish settlers. The house is small but sturdy. It measures 20 feet by 14 feet deep and has one and a half stories. The two first-floor rooms, a kitchen and a parlor, are separated by an 18 × 18–inch square chimney set in the center of the house, as well as the stairs leading up to the sleeping chamber. Clay and small stones fill the gaps in the exterior walls, which consist of timber planking about 12 inches tall and 6 to 8 inches wide. © 2003 Copyright and All Rights Reserved by Christopher C. Fennell.

the costs of the expensive trip from the Rhine Valley, German immigrants pioneered the **redemptioner** system, a flexible form of indentured servitude that allowed families to negotiate their own terms upon arrival. Families often indentured one or more children while their parents set up a household of their own.

Germans soon dominated many districts in eastern Pennsylvania, and thousands more moved down the fertile Shenandoah Valley into the western backcountry of Maryland, Virginia, and the Carolinas (Map 4.2). Many migrants preserved their cultural identity by settling in German-speaking Lutheran and Reformed communities that endured well beyond 1800. A minister in North Carolina admonished young people "not to contract any marriages with the English or Irish," arguing that "we owe it to our native country to do our part that German blood and the German language be preserved in America."

These settlers were willing colonial subjects of Britain's German-born and German-speaking Protestant monarchs, George I (r. 1714–1727) and George II (r. 1727–1760). They generally avoided politics except to protect their cultural practices; for example, they insisted that married women have the legal right to hold property and write wills, as they did in Germany.

Scots-Irish Settlers   Migrants from Ireland, who numbered about 115,000, were the most numerous of the incoming Europeans. Some were Irish and Catholic, but most were Scots and Presbyterian, the descendants of the Calvinist Protestants sent to Ireland during the

IDENTIFY CAUSES

What attracted German and Scots-Irish migrants to Pennsylvania in such large numbers?

seventeenth century to solidify English rule there. Once in Ireland, the Scots faced hostility from both Irish Catholics and English officials and landlords. The Irish Test Act of 1704 restricted voting and office holding to members of the Church of England, English mercantilist regulations placed heavy import duties on linens made by Scots-Irish weavers, and farmers paid heavy taxes. This persecution made America seem desirable. "Read this letter, Rev. Baptist Boyd," a migrant to New York wrote back to his minister, "and tell all the poor folk of ye place that God has opened a door for their deliverance . . . all that a man works for is his own; there are no revenue hounds to take it from us here."

Lured by such reports, thousands of Scots-Irish families sailed for the colonies. By 1720, most migrated to Philadelphia, attracted by the religious tolerance there. Seeking cheap land, they moved to central Pennsylvania and to the fertile Shenandoah Valley to the south. Governor William Gooch of Virginia welcomed the Scots-Irish presence to secure "the Country against the Indians." An Anglican planter, however, thought them as dangerous as "the Goths and Vandals of old" had been to the Roman Empire. Like the Germans, the Scots-Irish retained their culture, living in ethnic communities and holding firm to the Presbyterian Church.

Religion and Politics

In Western Europe, the leaders of church and state condemned religious diversity. "To tolerate all [religions] without controul is the way to have none at all," declared an Anglican clergyman. Orthodox church

MAP 4.2

Ethnic and Racial Diversity in the British Colonies, 1775

In 1700, most colonists in British North America were of English origin; by 1775, settlers of English descent constituted only about 50 percent of the total population. African Americans now accounted for one-third of the residents of the South, while tens of thousands of German and Scots-Irish migrants added ethnic and religious diversity in the Middle colonies, the southern backcountry, and northern New England (see Figure 4.2).

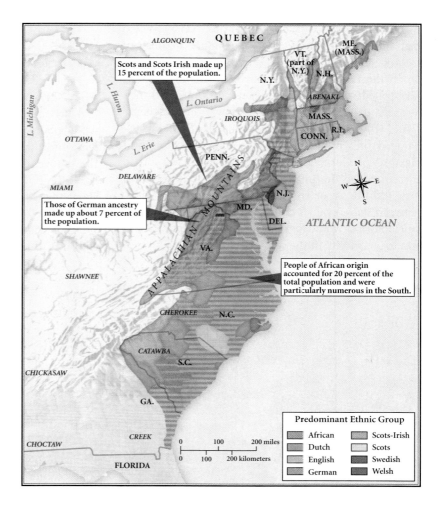

Scots and Scots Irish made up 15 percent of the population.

Those of German ancestry made up about 7 percent of the population.

People of African origin accounted for 20 percent of the total population and were particularly numerous in the South.

Predominant Ethnic Group
- African
- Dutch
- English
- German
- Scots-Irish
- Scots
- Swedish
- Welsh

officials carried such sentiments to Pennsylvania. "The preachers do not have the power to punish anyone, or to force anyone to go to church," complained Gottlieb Mittelberger, an influential German minister. As a result, "Sunday is very badly kept. Many people plough, reap, thresh, hew or split wood and the like." He concluded: "Liberty in Pennsylvania does more harm than good to many people, both in soul and body."

Mittelberger was mistaken. Although ministers in Pennsylvania could not invoke government authority to uphold religious values, the result was not social anarchy. Instead, religious sects enforced moral behavior through communal self-discipline. Quaker families attended a weekly meeting for worship and a monthly meeting for business; every three months, a committee reminded parents to provide proper religious instruction. The committee also supervised adult behavior; a Chester County meeting, for example, disciplined a member "to reclaim him from drinking to excess and keeping vain company." Significantly, Quaker meetings allowed couples to marry only if they had land and livestock sufficient to support a family. As a result, the

children of well-to-do Friends usually married within the sect, while poor Quakers remained unmarried, wed later in life, or married without permission — in which case they were often ousted from the meeting. These marriage rules helped the Quakers build a self-contained and prosperous community.

In the 1740s, the flood of new migrants reduced Quakers to a minority — a mere 30 percent of Pennsylvanians. Moreover, Scots-Irish settlers in central Pennsylvania demanded an aggressive Indian policy, challenging the pacifism of the assembly. To retain power, Quaker politicians sought an alliance with those German religious groups that also embraced pacifism and voluntary (not compulsory) militia service. In response, German leaders demanded more seats in the assembly and laws that respected their inheritance customs. Other Germans — Lutherans and Baptists — tried to gain control of the assembly by forming a "general confederacy"

UNDERSTAND POINTS OF VIEW

What issues divided the various ethnic and religious groups of the Middle colonies? What core values did they agree upon?

with Scots-Irish Presbyterians. An observer predicted that the scheme was doomed to failure because of "mutual jealousy" (Map 4.3).

By the 1750s, politics throughout the Middle colonies roiled with conflict. In New York, a Dutchman declared that he "Valued English Law no more than a Turd," while in Pennsylvania, Benjamin Franklin disparaged the "boorish" character and "swarthy complexion" of German migrants. Yet there was broad agreement on the importance of economic opportunity and liberty of conscience. The unstable balance between shared values and mutual mistrust prefigured tensions that would pervade an increasingly diverse American society in the centuries to come.

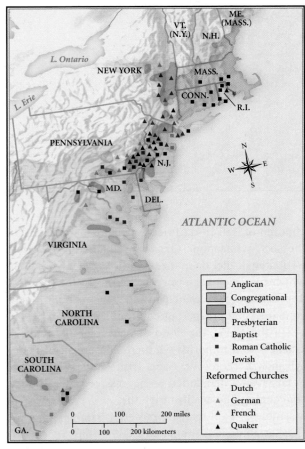

MAP 4.3
Religious Diversity in 1750

By 1750, religious diversity was on the rise, not only in the multiethnic Middle colonies but also in all of British North America. Baptists had increased their numbers in New England, long the stronghold of Congregationalists, and would soon become important in Virginia. Already there were considerable numbers of Presbyterians, Lutherans, and German Reformed in the South, where Anglicanism was the established religion.

Commerce, Culture, and Identity

After 1720, transatlantic shipping grew more frequent and Britain and its colonies more closely connected, while a burgeoning print culture flooded the colonies with information and ideas. Two great European cultural movements — the **Enlightenment**, which emphasized the power of human reason to understand and shape the world; and **Pietism**, an evangelical Christian movement that stressed the individual's personal relationship with God — reached America as a result. At the same time, an abundance of imported goods began to reshape material culture, bringing new comforts into the lives of the middling sort while allowing prosperous merchants and landowners to set themselves apart from their neighbors in new ways.

Transportation and the Print Revolution

In the eighteenth century, improved transportation networks opened Britain's colonies in new ways, and British shipping came to dominate the north Atlantic. In 1700, Britain had 40,000 sailors; by 1750, the number had grown to 60,000, while many more hailed from the colonies. An enormous number of vessels plied Atlantic waters: in the late 1730s, more than 550 ships arrived in Boston annually. About a tenth came directly from Britain or Ireland; the rest came mostly from other British colonies, either on the mainland or in the West Indies.

A road network slowly took shape as well, though roadbuilding was expensive and difficult. In 1704, Sarah Kemble Knight traveled from Boston to New York on horseback. The road was "smooth and even" in some places, treacherous in others; it took eight days of hard riding to cover 200 miles. Forty years later, a physician from Annapolis, Maryland, traveled along much better roads to Portsmouth, New Hampshire, and back — more than 1,600 miles in all. He spent four months on the road, stopping frequently to meet the locals and satisfy his curiosity. By the mid-eighteenth century, the "Great Wagon Road" carried migrating families down the Shenandoah Valley as far as the Carolina backcountry.

All of these water and land routes carried people, produce, and finished merchandise. They also carried information, as letters, newspapers, pamphlets, and crates of books began to circulate widely. The trip across the Atlantic took seven to eight weeks on average, so the news arriving in colonial ports was not fresh by our standard, but compared to earlier years, the colonies were awash in information.

Until 1695, the British government had the power to censor all printed materials. In that year, Parliament let the Licensing Act lapse, and the floodgates opened. Dozens of new printshops opened in London and Britain's provincial cities. They printed newspapers and pamphlets; poetry, ballads, and sermons; and handbills, tradesman's cards, and advertisements. Larger booksellers also printed scientific treatises, histories, travelers' accounts, and novels. The result was a print revolution. In Britain and throughout Europe, print was essential to the transmission of new ideas, and both the Enlightenment and Pietism took shape in part through its growing influence.

All this material crossed the Atlantic and filled the shops of colonial booksellers. The colonies also began printing their own newspapers. In 1704, the *Boston Newsletter* was founded; by 1720, Boston had five printing presses and three newspapers; and by 1776, the thirteen colonies that united in declaring independence had thirty-seven newspapers among them. This world of print was essential to their ability to share grievances and join in common cause.

The Enlightenment in America

To explain the workings of the natural world, some colonists relied on folk wisdom. Swedish migrants in Pennsylvania attributed magical powers to the great white mullein, a common wildflower, and treated fevers by tying the plant's leaves around their feet and arms. Traditionally, Christians believed that the earth stood at the center of the universe, and God (and Satan) intervened directly and continuously in human affairs. The scientific revolution of the sixteenth and seventeenth centuries challenged these ideas, and educated people — most of them Christians — began to modify their views accordingly.

The European Enlightenment In 1543, the Polish astronomer Copernicus published his observation that the earth traveled around the sun, not vice versa. Copernicus's discovery suggested that humans occupied a more modest place in the universe than Christian theology assumed. In the next century, Isaac Newton, in his *Principia Mathematica* (1687), used the sciences of mathematics and physics to explain the movement of the planets around the sun (and invented calculus in the process). Though Newton was himself profoundly religious, in the long run his work undermined the traditional Christian understanding of the cosmos.

In the century between the *Principia Mathematica* and the French Revolution of 1789, the philosophers of the European Enlightenment used empirical research and scientific reasoning to study all aspects of life, including social institutions and human behavior. Enlightenment thinkers advanced four fundamental principles: the lawlike order of the natural world, the power of human reason, the "natural rights" of individuals (including the right to self-government), and the progressive improvement of society.

English philosopher John Locke was a major contributor to the Enlightenment. In his *Essay Concerning Human Understanding* (1690), Locke stressed the impact of environment and experience on human behavior and beliefs, arguing that the character of individuals and societies was not fixed but could be changed through education, rational thought, and purposeful action. Locke's *Two Treatises of Government* (1690) advanced the revolutionary theory that political authority was not given by God to monarchs, as James II had insisted (see Chapter 3). Instead, it derived from social compacts that people made to preserve their **natural rights** to life, liberty, and property. In Locke's view, the people should have the power to change government policies — or even their form of government.

> **PLACE EVENTS IN CONTEXT**
> What conditions and ideas lay behind the emergence of the Enlightenment in America?

Some clergymen responded to these developments by devising a rational form of Christianity. Rejecting supernatural interventions and a vengeful Calvinist God, Congregationalist minister Andrew Eliot maintained that "there is nothing in Christianity that is contrary to reason." The Reverend John Wise of Ipswich, Massachusetts, used Locke's philosophy to defend giving power to ordinary church members. Just as the social compact formed the basis of political society, Wise argued, so the religious covenant among the lay members of a congregation made them — not the bishops of the Church of England or even ministers like himself — the proper interpreters of religious truth. The Enlightenment influenced Puritan minister Cotton Mather as well. When a measles epidemic ravaged Boston in the 1710s, Mather thought that only God could end it; but when smallpox struck a decade later, he used his newly acquired knowledge of inoculation — gained in part from a slave, who told him of the practice's success in Africa — to advocate this scientific preventive for the disease.

Enlightenment Philanthropy: Pennsylvania Hospital, Philadelphia

Using public funds and private donations, Philadelphia reformers built this imposing structure in 1753. The new hospital embodied two principles of the Enlightenment: that purposeful actions could improve society, and that the products of these actions should express reason and order, exhibited here in the building's symmetrical facade. Etchings like this one from the 1760s (*A Perspective View of the Pennsylvania Hospital*, by John Streeper and Henry Dawkins) circulated widely and bolstered Philadelphia's reputation as the center of the American Enlightenment. Historical Society of Pennsylvania.

Franklin's Contributions   Benjamin Franklin was the exemplar of the American Enlightenment. Born in Boston in 1706 to devout Calvinists, he grew to manhood during the print revolution. Apprenticed to his brother, a Boston printer, Franklin educated himself through voracious reading. At seventeen, he fled to Philadelphia, where he became a prominent printer, and in 1729 he founded the *Pennsylvania Gazette*, which became one of the colonies' most influential newspapers. Franklin also formed a "club of mutual improvement" that met weekly to discuss "Morals, Politics, or Natural Philosophy." These discussions, as well as Enlightenment literature, shaped his thinking. As Franklin explained in his *Autobiography* (1771), "From the different books I read, I began to doubt of Revelation [God-revealed truth]."

Like a small number of urban artisans, wealthy Virginia planters, and affluent seaport merchants, Franklin became a deist. **Deism** was a way of thinking, not an established religion. "My own mind is my own church," said deist Thomas Paine. "I am of a sect by myself," added Thomas Jefferson. Influenced by Enlightenment science, deists such as Jefferson believed that a Supreme Being (or Grand Architect) created the world and then allowed it to operate by natural laws but did not intervene in people's lives. Rejecting the divinity of Christ and the authority of the Bible, deists relied on "natural reason," their innate moral sense, to define right and wrong. Thus Franklin, a onetime slave owner, came to question the morality of slavery, repudiating it once he recognized the parallels between racial bondage and the colonies' political bondage to Britain.

Franklin popularized the practical outlook of the Enlightenment in *Poor Richard's Almanack* (1732–1757), an annual publication that was read by thousands. He also founded the American Philosophical Society (1743–present) to promote "useful knowledge." Adopting this goal in his own life, Franklin invented bifocal lenses for eyeglasses, the Franklin stove, and the lightning rod. His book on electricity, published in England in 1751, won praise as the greatest contribution to science since Newton's discoveries. Inspired by

Benjamin Franklin's Rise

This portrait of Benjamin Franklin, attributed to Robert Feke and executed around 1746, portrays Franklin as a successful businessman. His ruffled collar and cuffs, his fashionably curly wig, and his sober but expensive suit reveal his social ambitions. In later portraits, after he gained fame as an Enlightenment sage, he dispensed with the wig and chose more unaffected poses; but in 1746, he was still establishing his credentials as a young Philadelphia gentleman on the rise. Harvard University Art Museum, Fogg Art Museum, Bequest of Dr. John Collins Warren, 1856, H47 Photo: Imaging Department © President and Fellows of Harvard College.

Franklin, ambitious printers in America's seaport cities published newspapers and gentlemen's magazines, the first significant nonreligious periodicals to appear in the colonies. The European Enlightenment, then, added a secular dimension to colonial cultural life, foreshadowing the great contributions to republican political theory by American intellectuals of the Revolutionary era: John Adams, James Madison, and Thomas Jefferson.

American Pietism and the Great Awakening

As some colonists turned to deism, thousands of others embraced Pietism, a Christian movement originating in Germany around 1700 and emphasizing pious behavior (hence the name). In its emotional worship services and individual striving for a mystical union with God, Pietism appealed to believers' hearts rather than their minds (American Voices, p. 130). In the 1720s, German migrants carried Pietism to America, sparking a religious **revival** (or renewal of religious enthusiasm) in Pennsylvania and New Jersey, where Dutch minister Theodore Jacob Frelinghuysen preached passionate sermons to German settlers and encouraged church members to spread the message of spiritual urgency. A decade later, William Tennent and his son Gilbert copied Frelinghuysen's approach and led revivals among Scots-Irish Presbyterians throughout the Middle Atlantic region.

New England Revivalism Simultaneously, an American-born Pietist movement appeared in New England. Revivals of Christian zeal were built into the logic of Puritanism. In the 1730s, Jonathan Edwards, a minister in Northampton, Massachusetts, encouraged a revival there that spread to towns throughout the Connecticut River Valley. Edwards guided and observed the process and then published an account entitled *A Faithful Narrative of the Surprising Work of God*, printed first in London (1737), then in Boston (1738), and then in German and Dutch translations. Its publication history highlights the transatlantic network of correspondents that gave Pietism much of its vitality.

Whitefield's Great Awakening English minister George Whitefield transformed the local revivals of Edwards and the Tennents into a Great Awakening. After Whitefield had his personal awakening upon reading the German Pietists, he became a follower of John Wesley, the founder of English Methodism. In 1739, Whitefield carried Wesley's fervent message to America, where he attracted huge crowds from Georgia to Massachusetts.

Whitefield had a compelling presence. "He looked almost angelical; a young, slim, slender youth . . . cloathed with authority from the Great God," wrote a Connecticut farmer. Like most evangelical preachers, Whitefield did not read his sermons but spoke from memory. More like an actor than a theologian, he gestured eloquently, raised his voice for dramatic effect, and at times assumed a female persona — as a woman in labor struggling to deliver the word of God. When the young preacher told his spellbound listeners that they had sinned and must seek salvation, some suddenly felt a "new light" within them. As "the power of god come down," Hannah Heaton recalled, "my knees smote together . . . [and] it seemed to me I was a sinking down into hell . . . but then I resigned my distress and was perfectly easy quiet and calm . . . [and] it seemed as

Evangelical Religion and Enlightenment Rationalism

Two great historical movements, Enlightenment thought and Pietistic religion, swept across British North America in the eighteenth century and offered radically different—indeed, almost completely contradictory—worldviews. Pietism sparked religious revivals based on passion and emotion, while Enlightenment rationalism encouraged personal restraint and intellectual logic. Both movements shaped American cultural development: Pietism transformed American religious life, and Enlightenment thinking influenced the principles of the American government.

Sarah Lippet
Death as a Passage to Life

Sarah Lippet was a longtime member of the Baptist church of Middletown in eastern New Jersey. She died in October 1767 at the age of sixty-one; fellow parishioners reported her sentiments as she lay, for four days, on her deathbed.

All my lifetime I have been in fears and doubts, but now am delivered. He hath delivered them who through fear of death were all their lifetime subject to bondage. For the love I have for Christ I am willing to part with all my friends to be with Him, for I love Him above all; yet it is nothing in me, for I know if I had my desert I should be in Hell. I believe in Christ, and I know that I put my whole trust in Him, and he that believeth in Him shall not be ashamed nor be confounded. . . .

Why do you mourn when I rejoice? You should not; it is no more for me to die and leave my friends for the great love I have for Christ than for me to go to sleep. I have no fears of death in my mind. Christ has the keys of death and hell, and blessed are the dead that die in the Lord. I can't bear to see a tear shed. You should not mourn.

Source: "The Triumphant Christian," in *Historical and Genealogical Miscellany*, ed. John E. Stillwell (New York, 1964), 3: 465–466.

Nathan Cole
The Struggle for Salvation

Connecticut farmer Nathan Cole found God after listening to a sermon by George Whitefield, the great English evangelist. But Cole's spiritual quest was not easy. He struggled for two years before coming to believe that he was saved.

[After hearing Whitefield] I began to think I was not Elected, and that God made some for heaven and me for hell. And I thought God was not Just in so doing. . . . My heart then rose against God exceedingly, for his making me for hell; Now this distress lasted Almost two years —

Poor Me — Miserable me. . . . I was loaded with the guilt of Sin. . . .

Hell fire was most always in my mind; and I have hundreds of times put my fingers into my pipe when I have been smoaking to feel how fire felt: And to see how my Body could bear to lye in Hell fire for ever and ever. . . . And while these thoughts were in my mind God appeared unto me and made me Skringe: before whose face the heavens and the earth fled away; and I was Shrinked into nothing; I knew not whether I was in the body or out, I seemed to hang in open Air before God, and he seemed to Speak to me in an angry and Sovereign way[:] What? Won't you trust your Soul with God?; My heart answered O yes, yes, yes. . . .

When God disappeared or in some measure withdrew, every thing was in its place again and I was on my Bed. . . . I was set free, my distress was gone, and I was filled with a pineing desire to see Christs own words in the bible; . . . I got the bible up under my Chin and hugged it; it was sweet and lovely; the word was nigh [near] me in my hand, then I began to pray and to praise God.

Source: "The Spiritual Travels of Nathan Cole, 1741" in *The Great Awakening: Documents on the Revival of Religion, 1740–1745*, ed. Richard L. Bushman (New York: Atheneum, 1970), 68–70.

Benjamin Franklin
The Importance of a Virtuous Life

Franklin stood at the center of the American Enlightenment. In his *Autobiography*, he outlined his religious views and his human-centered moral principles.

My Parents had early given me religious Impressions, and brought me through my Childhood piously in the Dissenting Way. But I was scarce 15 when, after doubting by turns of several Points as I found them disputed in the different Books I read, I began to doubt of Revelation itself. Some Books against Deism fell into my Hands. . . . It happened that they wrought an Effect on me quite contrary to what was intended by them: For the Arguments of the Deists [that were quoted in those books] appeared to me much Stronger than the Refutations. In short I soon became a thorough Deist. . . .

I grew convinc'd that Truth, Sincerity & Integrity in Dealings between Man & Man, were of the utmost Importance to the Felicity of Life, and I form'd written Resolutions, (which still remain in my Journal Book) to practice them ever while I lived. . . .

About the Year 1734. There arrived among us from Ireland, a young Presbyterian Preacher named Hemphill, who delivered with a good Voice, & apparently extempore, most excellent Discourses, which drew together considerable Numbers of different Persuasions, who join'd in admiring them. Among the rest I became one of his constant Hearers, his Sermons pleasing me as they had little of the dogmatical kind, but inculcated strongly the Practice of Virtue, or what in the religious Stile are called Good Works. Those however, of our Congregation, who considered themselves as orthodox Presbyterians, disapprov'd his Doctrine, and were join'd by most of the old Clergy, who arraign'd him of Heterodoxy before the Synod, in order to have him silenc'd. I became his zealous Partisan. . . .

I never was without some religious Principles; I never doubted, for instance, the Existance of the Deity, that he made the World, & govern'd it by his Providence; that the most acceptable Service of God was the doing Good to Man; that our Souls are immortal; and that all Crime will be punished & Virtue rewarded either here or hereafter; these I esteem'd the Essentials of every Religion.

Source: Louis P. Masur, ed., *The Autobiography of Benjamin Franklin, with Related Documents*, 2nd ed. (Boston: Bedford/St. Martin's, 2003), 73–74, 93–94, 108.

John Wise

The Primacy of Human Reason and Natural Laws

Reverend John Wise (1652–1725) served for many years as a pastor in Ipswich, Massachusetts. A graduate of Harvard College, Wise used the Enlightenment doctrines of John Locke and Samuel von Pufendorf to justify the democratic structure of New England Congregational churches.

I Shall disclose several Principles of Natural Knowledge; plainly discovering the Law of Nature; or the true sentiments of Natural Reason, with Respect to Mans Being

and Government. . . . I shall consider Man in a state of Natural Being, as a Free-Born Subject under the Crown of Heaven, and owing Homage to none but God himself. It is certain Civil Government in General, is a very Admirable Result of Providence, and an Incomparable Benefit to Mankind, yet must needs be acknowledged to be the Effect of Humane Free-Compacts and not of Divine Institution; it is the Produce of Mans Reason, of Humane and Rational Combinations, and not from any direct Orders of Infinite Wisdom. . . .

The Prime Immunity in Mans State, is that he is most properly the Subject of the Law of Nature. He is the Favourite Animal on Earth; in that this Part of Gods Image, viz. Reason is Congenate with his Nature, wherein by a Law Immutable, Instampt upon his Frame, God has provided a Rule for Men in all their Actions; obliging each one to the performance of that which is Right, not only as to Justice, but likewise as to all other Moral Vertues, which is nothing but the Dictate of Right Reason founded in the Soul of Man. . . .

The Second Great Immunity of Man is an Original Liberty Instampt upon his Rational Nature. He that intrudes upon this Liberty, Violates the Law of Nature. . . .

The Third Capital Immunity belonging to Mans Nature, is an equality amongst Men; Which is not to be denied by the Law of Nature, till Man has Resigned himself with all his Rights for the sake of a Civil State; and then his Personal Liberty and Equality is to be cherished, and preserved to the highest degree.

Source: John Wise, *A Vindication of the Government of New England Churches* (Boston: J. Allen, for N. Boone, 1717), 32–40.

QUESTIONS FOR ANALYSIS

1. All of these writers declare a belief in God. How do their beliefs and outlooks differ?

2. These writers were variously influenced by the Great Awakening, the Enlightenment, and rational Christianity. How are these movements reflected in the passages above?

3. What roles do fear and anxiety play in the experiences of Sarah Lippet and Nathan Cole? What difference does it make that neither Franklin nor Wise expresses fear, either of God or of his own sinfulness?

4. Benjamin Franklin and John Wise stress the importance of reason and virtue as guides to human conduct. How would Nathan Cole and Sarah Lippet react to that emphasis?

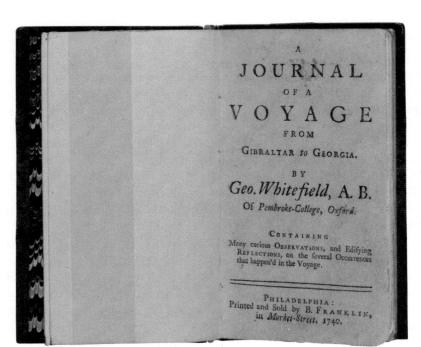

A
JOURNAL
OF A
VOYAGE
FROM
GIBRALTAR *to* GEORGIA.

BY
Geo. Whitefield, A. B.
Of Pembroke-College, Oxford.

CONTAINING
Many curious OBSERVATIONS, and Edifying
REFLECTIONS, on the several Occurrences
that happen'd in the Voyage.

PHILADELPHIA:
Printed and Sold by B. FRANKLIN,
in Market-Street, 1740.

The Print Revolution and the Great Awakening

George Whitefield made his first trip to North America in 1738, when he traveled to Savannah, Georgia. Benjamin Franklin published the first edition of this journal of his voyage in Philadelphia in 1739; the copy pictured here was printed a year later. Texts like this one highlight the importance of the print revolution to eighteenth-century culture: Whitefield was utterly unknown in North America until he began publicizing his ministry and his travels through such works. Enlightenment ideas, too, were conveyed to large and far-flung audiences in books, magazines, and newspapers. Library Company of Philadelphia.

if I had a new soul & body both." Strengthened and self-confident, these converts, the so-called New Lights, were eager to spread Whitefield's message.

The rise of print intersected with this enthusiasm. "Religion is become the Subject of most Conversations," the *Pennsylvania Gazette* reported. "No books are in Request but those of Piety and Devotion." Whitefield and his circle did their best to answer the demand for devotional reading. As he traveled, Whitefield regularly sent excerpts of his journal to be printed in newspapers. Franklin printed Whitefield's sermons and journals by subscription and found them to be among his best-selling titles. Printed accounts of Whitefield's travels, conversion narratives, sermons, and other devotional literature helped to confirm Pietists in their faith and strengthen the communication networks that sustained them.

Religious Upheaval in the North

Like all cultural explosions, the Great Awakening was controversial. Conservative ministers—passionless **Old Lights**, according to the evangelists—condemned the "cryings out, faintings and convulsions" in revivalist meetings and the New Lights' claims of "working Miracles or speaking with Tongues." Boston minister Charles Chauncy attacked the Pietist **New Lights**

COMPARE AND CONTRAST
In what ways was the spread of ideas during the Enlightenment and the Great Awakening similar, and how did it differ?

for allowing women to speak in public: it was "a plain breach of that commandment of the lord, where it is said, Let your women keep silence in the churches." In Connecticut, Old Lights persuaded the legislature to prohibit evangelists from speaking to a congregation without the minister's permission. But the New Lights refused to be silenced. Dozens of farmers, women, and artisans roamed the countryside, condemning the Old Lights as "unconverted" and willingly accepting imprisonment: "I shall bring glory to God in my bonds," a dissident preacher wrote from jail.

The Great Awakening undermined legally established churches and their tax-supported ministers. In New England, New Lights left the Congregational Church and founded 125 "separatist" churches that supported their ministers through voluntary contributions (Figure 4.3). Other religious dissidents joined Baptist congregations, which also condemned government support of churches: "God never allowed any civil state upon earth to impose religious taxes," declared Baptist preacher Isaac Backus. In New York and New Jersey, the Dutch Reformed Church split in two as New Lights refused to accept doctrines imposed by conservative church authorities in Holland.

The Great Awakening also appealed to Christians whose established churches could not serve their needs. By 1740, Pennsylvania's German Reformed and Lutheran congregations suffered from a severe lack of university-trained pastors. In the colony's Dutch Reformed, Dutch and Swedish Lutheran, and even its

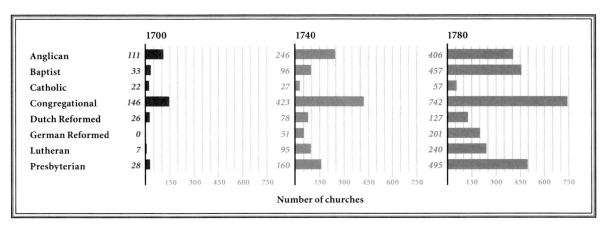

FIGURE 4.3
Church Growth by Denomination, 1700–1780
In 1700, and again in 1740, the Congregationalist and Anglican churches had the most members. By 1780, however, largely because of their enthusiastic evangelical message, Presbyterian and Baptist congregations outnumbered those of the Anglicans. The growth of immigrant denominations, such as the German Reformed and Lutheran, was equally impressive.

Anglican congregations, half the pulpits were empty. In this circumstance, itinerant preachers who stressed the power of "heart religion" and downplayed the importance of formal ministerial training found a ready audience.

The Great Awakening challenged the authority of all ministers, whose status rested on respect for their education and knowledge of the Bible. In an influential pamphlet, *The Dangers of an Unconverted Ministry* (1740), Gilbert Tennent asserted that ministers' authority should come not from theological knowledge but from the conversion experience. Reaffirming Martin Luther's belief in the priesthood of all Christians, Tennent suggested that anyone who had felt God's redeeming grace could speak with ministerial authority. Sarah Harrah Osborn, a New Light "exhorter" in Rhode Island, refused "to shut up my mouth . . . and creep into obscurity" when silenced by her minister.

As religious enthusiasm spread, churches founded new colleges to educate their young men and to train ministers. New Light Presbyterians established the College of New Jersey (Princeton) in 1746, and New York Anglicans founded King's College (Columbia) in 1754. Baptists set up the College of Rhode Island (Brown) in 1764; two years later, the Dutch Reformed Church subsidized Queen's College (Rutgers) in New Jersey. However, the main intellectual legacy of the Great Awakening was not education for the privileged few but a new sense of authority among the many. A European visitor to Philadelphia remarked in surprise, "The poorest day-laborer . . . holds it his right to advance his opinion, in religious as well as political matters, with as much freedom as the gentleman."

Social and Religious Conflict in the South

In the southern colonies, where the Church of England was legally established, religious enthusiasm triggered social conflict. Anglican ministers generally ignored the spiritual needs of African Americans and landless whites, who numbered 40 percent and 20 percent of the population, respectively. Middling white freeholders (35 percent of the residents) formed the core of most Church of England congregations. But prominent planters (just 5 percent) held the real power, using their control of parish finances to discipline ministers. One clergyman complained that dismissal awaited any minister who "had the courage to preach against any Vices taken into favor by the leading Men of his Parish."

The Presbyterian Revival   Soon, a democratization of religion challenged the dominance of both the Anglican Church and the planter elite. In 1743, bricklayer Samuel Morris, inspired by reading George Whitefield's sermons, led a group of Virginia Anglicans out of their congregation. Seeking a deeper religious experience, Morris invited New Light Presbyterian Samuel Davies to lead their prayer meetings. Davies's sermons, filled with erotic devotional imagery and urging Christians to feel "ardent Passion," sparked Presbyterian revivals across the Tidewater region, threatening the social authority of the Virginia gentry. Traditionally, planters and their well-dressed families arrived at Anglican services in fancy carriages drawn by well-bred horses and flaunted their power by sitting in the front pews. Such ritual displays of the gentry's superiority were meaningless if freeholders attended other churches. Moreover, religious pluralism threatened the tax-supported status of the Anglican Church.

To halt the spread of New Light ideas, Virginia governor William Gooch denounced them as "false teachings," and Anglican justices of the peace closed Presbyterian churches. This harassment kept most white yeomen and poor tenant families in the Church of England.

The Baptist Insurgency   During the 1760s, the vigorous preaching and democratic message of New Light Baptist ministers converted thousands of white farm families. The Baptists were radical Protestants whose central ritual was adult (rather than infant) baptism. Once men and women had experienced the infusion of grace — had been "born again" — they were baptized in an emotional public ceremony, often involving complete immersion in water.

Slaves were welcome at Baptist revivals. During the 1740s, George Whitefield had urged Carolina planters to bring their slaves into the Christian fold, but white opposition and the Africans' commitment to their ancestral religions kept the number of converts low. However, in the 1760s, native-born African Americans in Virginia welcomed the Baptists' message that all people were equal in God's eyes. Sensing a threat to the system of racial slavery, the House of Burgesses imposed heavy fines on Baptists who preached to slaves without their owners' permission.

Baptists threatened gentry authority because they repudiated social distinctions and urged followers to call one another "brother" and "sister." They also condemned the planters' decadent lifestyle. As planter Landon Carter complained, the Baptists were "destroying pleasure in the Country; for they encourage ardent Prayer . . . & an intire Banishment of *Gaming, Dancing,* & Sabbath-Day Diversions." The gentry responded with violence. In Caroline County, an Anglican posse attacked Brother John Waller at a prayer meeting. Waller "was violently jerked off the stage; they caught him by the back part of his neck, beat his head against the ground, and a gentleman gave him twenty lashes with his horsewhip."

Despite these attacks, Baptist congregations multiplied. By 1775, about 15 percent of Virginia's whites and hundreds of enslaved blacks had joined Baptist

Baptism in the Schuylkill River

The Baptist movement, which made adult baptism central to its religious practice, gained enormous influence during the Great Awakening. Baptists presented a challenge to the social order in New England, where Isaac Backus and other leaders vigorously opposed the power of established Congregationalist churches. They presented an even graver threat to established authority in Virginia, where they ministered to African American slaves and ridiculed the pretensions of the gentry. This woodcut, from an eighteenth-century history of the Baptist movement, shows a congregation gathered on the banks of the Schuylkill River in Pennsylvania to witness the baptism of a new convert. Historical Society of Pennsylvania.

churches. To signify their state of grace, some Baptist men "cut off their hair, like Cromwell's round-headed chaplains." Others forged a new evangelical masculinity, "crying, weeping, lifting up the eyes, groaning" when touched by the Holy Spirit.

The Baptist revival in the Chesapeake challenged customary authority in families and society but did not overturn it. Rejecting the pleas of evangelical women, Baptist men kept church authority in the hands of "free born male members"; and Anglican slaveholders retained control of the political system. Still, the Baptist insurgency infused the lives of poor tenant families with spiritual meaning and empowered yeomen to defend their economic interests. Moreover, as Baptist ministers spread Christianity among slaves, the cultural gulf between blacks and whites shrank, undermining one justification for slavery and giving some blacks a new religious identity. Within a generation, African Americans would develop distinctive versions of Protestant Christianity.

The Midcentury Challenge: War, Trade, and Social Conflict, 1750–1763

Between 1750 and 1763, three significant events transformed colonial life. First, Britain went to war against the French in America, sparking a worldwide conflict: the Great War for Empire. Second, a surge in trade boosted colonial consumption but caused Americans to become deeply indebted to British creditors. Third, westward migration sparked warfare with Indian peoples, violent disputes between settlers and land speculators, and backcountry rebellions against eastern-controlled governments.

The French and Indian War

In 1754, overlapping French and British claims in North America came to a head (Map 4.4). The French maintained their vast claims through a network of forts and trading posts that sustained alliances with neighboring Indians. The soft underbelly of this sprawling empire was the Ohio Valley, where French claims were tenuous. Native peoples were driven out of the valley by Iroquois attacks in the seventeenth century, but after 1720 displaced Indian populations—especially Delawares and Shawnees from Pennsylvania—resettled there in large numbers. In the 1740s, British traders from Pennsylvania began traveling down the Ohio

River. They traded with Delawares and Shawnees in the upper valley and began to draw French-allied Indians into their orbit and away from French posts. Then, in 1748, the Ohio Company of Virginia, a partnership of prominent colonial planters and London merchants, received a 200,000-acre grant from the crown to establish a new settlement on the upper Ohio, threatening French claims to the region.

Conflict in the Ohio Valley   By midcentury, Britain relied on the Iroquois Confederacy as its partner in Indian relations throughout the Northeast. By extending the Covenant Chain, the Iroquois had become a kind of Indian empire in their own right, claiming to speak for other groups throughout the region based on their seventeenth-century conquests. The Delawares, Shawnees, and other groups who repopulated the Ohio Valley did so in part to escape the Iroquois yoke. To maintain influence on the Ohio, the Iroquois sent two "half-kings," Tanaghrisson (an adopted Seneca) and Scarouady (an Oneida), to the native settlement of Logstown, a trading town on the upper Ohio, where Britain recognized them as leaders.

French authorities, alarmed by British inroads, built a string of forts from Lake Erie to the headwaters of the Ohio, culminating with Fort Duquesne on the site of present-day Pittsburgh. To reassert British claims, Governor Dinwiddie dispatched an expedition led by Colonel George Washington, a twenty-two-year-old Virginian whose half-brothers were Ohio Company stockholders. Washington discovered that most of the Ohio Indians had decided to side with the French; only the Iroquois half-kings and a few of their followers supported his efforts. After Washington's party fired on a French detachment, Tanaghrisson rushed in and killed a French officer to ensure war—a prospect that would force British arms to support Iroquois interests in the valley.

Washington's party was soon defeated by a larger French force. The result was an international incident that prompted Virginian and British expansionists to demand war. But war in North America was a worrisome prospect: the colonies were notoriously incapable of cooperating in their own defense, and the Covenant Chain was badly in need of repair.

The Albany Congress   The Iroquois Confederacy was unhappy with its British alliance and believed that the British were neglecting the Iroquois while settlers from New York pressed onto their lands. Moreover, the Ohio Indians, France, and Britain were all acting in the Ohio Valley without consulting them. To mend

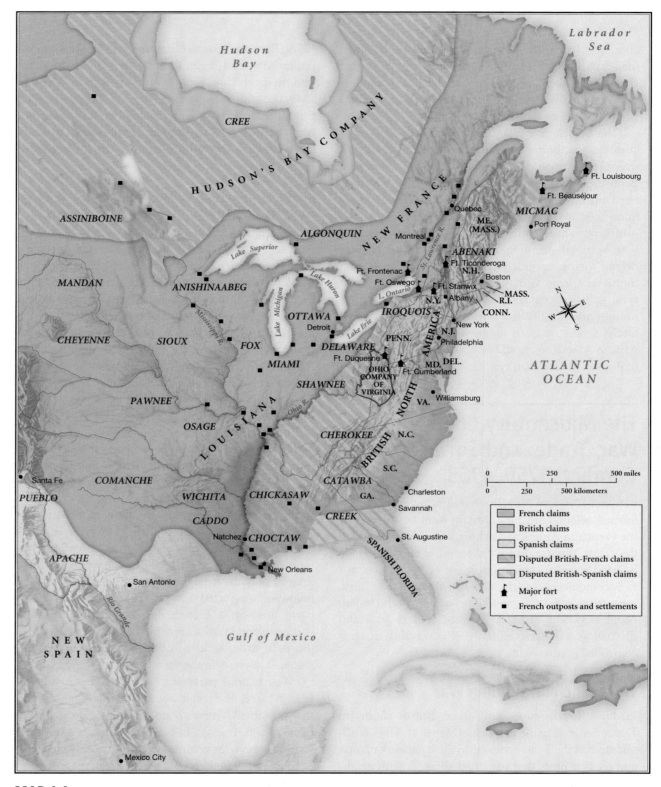

MAP 4.4

European Spheres of Influence in North America, 1754

In the mid-eighteenth century, France, Spain, and the British-owned Hudson Bay Company laid claim to the vast areas of North America still inhabited primarily by Indian peoples. British settlers had already occupied much of the land east of the Appalachian Mountains. To safeguard their lands west of the mountains, Native Americans played off one European power against another. As a British official remarked: "To preserve the Ballance between us and the French is the great ruling Principle of Modern Indian Politics." When Britain expelled France from North America in 1763, Indians had to face encroaching Anglo-American settlers on their own.

Hendrick Peters Theyanoguin, Chief of the Mohawks

Great Britain's alliance with the Iroquois Confederacy — the Covenant Chain — was central to its Indian policy in the mid-eighteenth century, and the Mohawk warrior and sachem Hendrick Peters Theyanoguin emerged as its most powerful spokesman. His speech at the Albany Congress of 1754, in which he urged Great Britain toward war, was reported in newspapers in Britain and the colonies and made him a transatlantic celebrity. This print was advertised for sale in London bookstalls just as his death at the Battle of Lake George (1755) was being reported in newspapers there. Hendrick wears a rich silk waistcoat, an overcoat trimmed with gold lace, a ruffled shirt, and a tricorn hat — gifts from his British allies — while he holds a wampum belt in one hand and a tomahawk in the other. Courtesy of the John Carter Brown Library at Brown University.

relations with the Iroquois, the British Board of Trade called a meeting at Albany in June 1754. There, a prominent Mohawk leader named Hendrick Peters Theyanoguin challenged Britain to defend its interests more vigorously, while Benjamin Franklin proposed a "Plan of Union" among the colonies to counter French expansion.

The Albany Plan of Union proposed that "one general government . . . be formed in America, including all the said colonies." It would have created a continental assembly to manage trade, Indian policy, and the colonies' defense. Though it was attractive to a few reform-minded colonists and administrators, the plan would have compromised the independence of colonial assemblies and the authority of Parliament. It never received serious consideration, but that did not stop the push toward war.

 To see a longer excerpt of the Albany Plan of Union, along with other primary sources from this period, see *Sources for America's History*.

The War Hawks Win   In Parliament, the fight for the Ohio prompted a debate over war with France. Henry Pelham, the British prime minister, urged calm: "There is such a load of debt, and such heavy taxes already laid upon the people, that nothing but an absolute necessity can justifie our engaging in a new War." But two expansionist-minded war hawks — rising British statesman William Pitt and Lord Halifax, the new head of the Board of Trade — persuaded Pelham to launch an American war. In June 1755, British and New England troops captured Fort Beauséjour in the disputed territory of Nova Scotia (which the French called Acadia). Soldiers from Puritan Massachusetts then forced nearly 10,000 French settlers from their lands, arguing they were "rebels" without property rights, and deported them to France, the West Indies, and Louisiana (where "Acadians" became "Cajuns"). English and Scottish Protestants took over the farms the French Catholics left behind.

This Anglo-American triumph was quickly offset by a stunning defeat. In July 1755, General Edward Braddock advanced on Fort Duquesne with a force of 1,500 British regulars and Virginia militiamen. Braddock alienated potential allies by treating Indians (including Tanaghrisson) dismissively and denying the privilege of rank to colonial officers like George Washington. Persuaded that British arms could easily triumph in the American backcountry, he was instead routed by a French and Indian force. Braddock was killed, and more than half his troops were killed or wounded. "We have been beaten, most shamefully beaten, by a handfull of Men," George Washington complained bitterly as he led the survivors back to Virginia.

The Great War for Empire

By 1756, the American conflict had spread to Europe, where it was known as the Seven Years' War, and pitted Britain and Prussia against France, Spain, and Austria.

Braddock's Defeat and Death, July 1755

In May 1755 General Edward Braddock led a force of 1,500 British regulars and Virginia militiamen out of Fort Cumberland in western Maryland, intending to oust the French from Fort Duquesne, 50 miles to the west. As Braddock neared the fort, the French garrison of 200 troops and about 600 Indian allies—mostly Potawatomis, Ottawas, Shawnees, and Delawares—set out to ambush his force. Instead, they unexpectedly met the British along a narrow roadway. As the French and Indians fanned out to attack from the woods, the British troops (George Washington reported) "were struck with such a panic that they behaved with more cowardice than it is possible to conceive. The officers behaved gallantly, in order to encourage their men, for which they suffered greatly." The British casualties—450 killed, 500 wounded—included General Braddock, pictured above, who later died from his wounds. © Chicago History Museum, USA/The Bridgeman Art Library.

When Britain mounted major offensives in India, West Africa, and the West Indies as well as in North America, the conflict became the Great War for Empire.

William Pitt emerged as the architect of the British war effort. Pitt was a committed expansionist with a touch of arrogance. "I know that I can save this country and that I alone can," he boasted. A master strategist, he planned to cripple France by seizing its colonies. In North America, he enjoyed a decisive demographic advantage, since George II's 2 million subjects outnumbered the French 14 to 1. To mobilize the colonists, Pitt paid half the cost of their troops and supplied them with arms and equipment, at a cost of £1 million a year. He also committed a fleet of British ships and 30,000 British soldiers to the conflict in America.

Beginning in 1758, the powerful Anglo-American forces moved from one triumph to the next, in part because they brought Indian allies back into the fold. They forced the French to abandon Fort Duquesne (renamed Fort Pitt) and then captured Fort Louisbourg, a stronghold at the mouth of the St. Lawrence. In 1759, an armada led by British general James Wolfe sailed down the St. Lawrence and took Quebec, the heart of France's American empire. The Royal Navy prevented French reinforcements from crossing the Atlantic, allowing British forces to complete the conquest of Canada in 1760 by capturing Montreal (Map 4.5).

Elsewhere, the British likewise had great success. From Spain, the British won Cuba and the Philippine Islands. Fulfilling Pitt's dream, the East India Company

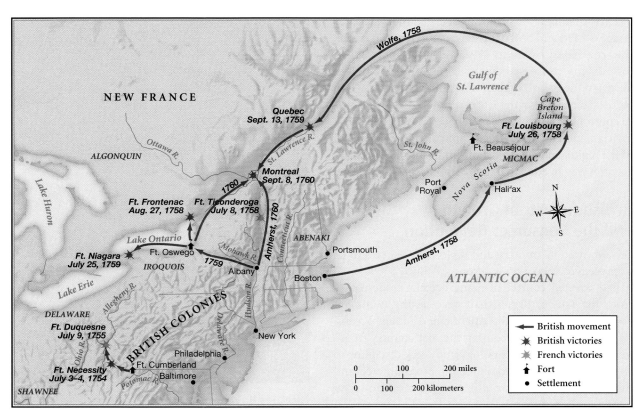

MAP 4.5

The Anglo-American Conquest of New France

After full-scale war with France began in 1756, it took almost three years for the British ministry to equip colonial forces and dispatch a sizable army to far-off America. In 1758, British and colonial troops attacked the heartland of New France, capturing Quebec in 1759 and Montreal in 1760. This conquest both united and divided the allies. Colonists celebrated the great victory: "The Illuminations and Fireworks exceeded any that had been exhibited before," reported the *Soutn Carolina Gazette*. However, British officers had little respect for colonial soldiers. Said one, "[They are] the dirtiest, most contemptible, cowardly dogs you can conceive."

ousted French traders from India, and British forces seized French Senegal in West Africa. They also captured the rich sugar islands of Martinique and Guadeloupe in the French West Indies, but at the insistence of the West Indian sugar lobby (which wanted to protect its monopoly), the ministry returned the islands to France in the Treaty of Paris of 1763. Despite that controversial decision, the treaty confirmed Britain's triumph. It granted Britain sovereignty over half of North America, including French Canada, all French territory east of the Mississippi River, Spanish Florida, and the recent conquests in Africa and India. Britain had forged a commercial and colonial empire that was nearly worldwide.

Though Britain had won cautious support from some Native American groups in the late stages of the war, its territorial acquisitions alarmed many native peoples from New York to the Mississippi, who preferred the presence of a few French traders to an influx of thousands of Anglo-American settlers. To encourage the French to return, the Ottawa chief Pontiac declared, "I am French, and I want to die French." Neolin, a Delaware prophet, went further, calling for the expulsion of all white-skinned invaders: "If you suffer the English among you, you are dead men. Sickness, smallpox, and their poison [rum] will destroy you entirely." In 1763, inspired by Neolin's nativist vision, Pontiac led a major uprising at Detroit. Following his example, Indians throughout the Great Lakes and Ohio Valley seized nearly every British military garrison west of Fort Niagara, besieged Fort Pitt, and killed or captured more than 2,000 settlers.

EXPLAIN CONSEQUENCES

How did the Seven Years' War reshape Britain's empire in North America and affect native peoples?

British military expeditions defeated the Delawares near Fort Pitt and broke the siege of Detroit, but it took the army nearly two years to reclaim all the posts it had lost. In the peace settlement, Pontiac and his allies accepted the British as their new political "fathers." The British ministry, having learned how expensive it was to control the trans-Appalachian west, issued the Royal Proclamation of 1763, which confirmed Indian control of the region and declared it off-limits to colonial settlement. It was an edict that many colonists would ignore.

British Industrial Growth and the Consumer Revolution

Britain owed its military and diplomatic success to its unprecedented economic resources. Since 1700, when it had wrested control of many oceanic trade routes from the Dutch, Britain had become the dominant commercial power in the Atlantic and Indian oceans. By 1750, it was also becoming the first country to use new manufacturing technology and work discipline to expand output. This combination of commerce and industry would soon make Britain the most powerful nation in the world.

Mechanical power was key to Britain's Industrial Revolution. British artisans designed and built water mills and steam engines that efficiently powered a wide array of machines: lathes for shaping wood, jennies and looms for spinning and weaving textiles, and hammers for forging iron. Compared with traditional manufacturing methods, the new power-driven machinery produced woolen and linen textiles, iron tools, furniture, and chinaware in greater quantities—and at lower cost. Moreover, the entrepreneurs running the new workshops drove their employees hard, forcing them to keep pace with the machines and work long hours. To market the abundant factory-produced goods, English and Scottish merchants extended credit to colonial shopkeepers for a full year instead of the traditional six months. Americans soon were purchasing 30 percent of all British exports.

To pay for British manufactures, mainland colonists increased their exports of tobacco, rice, indigo, and wheat. Using credit advanced by Scottish merchants, planters in Virginia bought land, slaves, and equipment to grow tobacco, which they exported to expanding markets in France and central Europe. In South Carolina, rice planters used British government subsidies to develop indigo and rice plantations. New York,

Nicholas Boylston, c. 1769

Merchants in the coastal and transatlantic trades gained enormous wealth in the mid-eighteenth century and displayed it in new ways. Among the most flamboyant was Nicholas Boylston. Of Boylston's home John Adams wrote, "A Seat it is for a noble Man, a Prince." In this portrait, painted by John Singleton Copley in 1769, Boylston flaunts his exotic possessions. In place of the wig he would have worn outside his home, Boylston wears a red velvet turban to keep his shaved head warm. His morning gown of heavy silk damask covers a rich waistcoat, casually unbuttoned in the middle to reveal his elegant ruffled shirt. Boylston rests his left elbow on two thick account books, an unmistakable reminder of the source of his wealth. Photograph © 2014 Museum of Fine Arts, Boston. Bequest of David P. Kimball, 23.504.

Pennsylvania, Maryland, and Virginia became the breadbasket of the Atlantic World, supplying Europe's exploding population with wheat.

Americans used their profits and the generous credit extended from overseas to buy English manufactures. When he was practicing law in Boston, John Adams visited the home of Nicholas Boylston, one of the city's wealthiest merchants, "to view the Furniture, which alone cost a thousand Pounds sterling," he wrote. "[T]he Marble Tables, the rich Beds with Crimson Damask Curtains and Counterpins, the Beautiful Chimny Clock, the Spacious Garden, are the most magnificent of any Thing I have ever seen." Through their possessions, well-to-do colonists set themselves apart from their humbler—or, as they might have said, more vulgar—neighbors.

EXPLAIN CONSEQUENCES
How did the prosperity of the British Empire improve and endanger the lives and interests of colonists?

Although Britain's **consumer revolution** raised living standards, it landed many consumers—and the colonies as a whole—in debt (Figure 4.4). Even during the wartime boom of the 1750s, exports paid for only 80 percent of British imports. Britain financed the remaining 20 percent—the Americans' trade deficit—through the extension of credit and Pitt's military expenditures. When the military subsidies ended in 1763, the colonies fell into an economic recession. Merchants looked anxiously at their overstocked warehouses and feared bankruptcy. "I think we have a gloomy prospect before us," a Philadelphia trader noted in 1765. The increase in transatlantic trade had made Americans more dependent on overseas credit and markets.

The Struggle for Land in the East

In good times and bad, the population continued to grow, intensifying the demand for arable land. Consider the experience of Kent, Connecticut. Like earlier generations, Kent's residents had moved inland to establish new farms, but Kent stood at the colony's western boundary. To provide for the next generation, many Kent families joined the Susquehanna Company (1749), which speculated in lands in the Wyoming Valley in present-day northeastern Pennsylvania. As settlers took up farmsteads there, the company urged the Connecticut legislature to claim the region on the basis of Connecticut's "sea-to-sea" royal charter of 1662. However, Charles II had also granted the Wyoming Valley to William Penn, and the Penn family had sold farms there to Pennsylvania residents. By the late 1750s, settlers from Connecticut and Pennsylvania were at war, burning down their rivals' houses and barns. Delawares with their own claim to the valley were caught in the crossfire. In April 1763, the Delaware headman Teedyuscung was burned to death in his cabin; in retaliation, Teedyuscung's son Captain Bull led a war party that destroyed a community of Connecticut settlers.

Simultaneously, three distinct but related land disputes broke out in the Hudson River Valley (Map 4.6). Dutch tenant farmers, Wappinger Indians, and migrants from Massachusetts asserted ownership rights to lands long claimed by manorial families such as the Van Rensselaers and the Livingstons. When the manor lords turned to the legal system to uphold their claims, Dutch and English farmers in Westchester, Dutchess, and Albany counties rioted to close the courts. In response, New York's royal governor ordered British troops to assist local sheriffs and manorial bailiffs: they suppressed the tenant uprisings, intimidated the Wappingers, and evicted the Massachusetts squatters.

Other land disputes erupted in New Jersey and the southern colonies, where landlords and English aristocrats had successfully revived legal claims based on long-dormant seventeenth-century charters. One

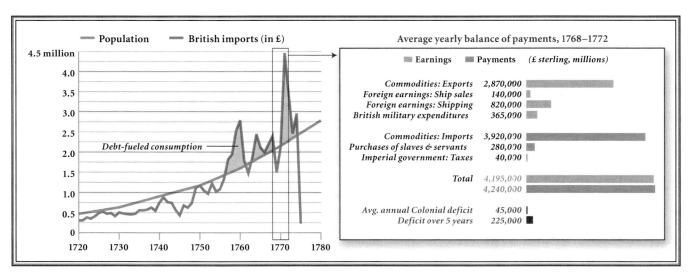

FIGURE 4.4
Mainland Population and British Imports
Around 1750, British imports were growing at a faster rate than the American population, indicating that the colonists were consuming more per capita. But Americans went into debt to pay for these goods, running an annual trade deficit with their British suppliers that by 1772 had created a cumulative debt of £2 million.

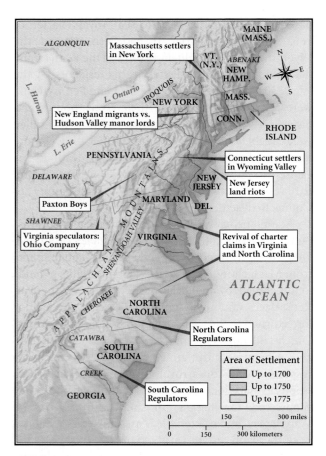

MAP 4.6
Westward Expansion and Land Conflicts, 1750–1775

Between 1750 and 1775, the mainland colonial population more than doubled—from 1.2 million to 2.5 million—triggering westward migrations and legal battles over land, which had become increasingly valuable. Violence broke out in eastern areas, where tenant farmers and smallholders contested landlords' property claims based on ancient titles; and in the backcountry, where migrating settlers fought with Indians, rival claimants, and the officials of eastern-dominated governments.

court decision allowed Lord Granville, the heir of an original Carolina proprietor, to collect an annual tax on land in North Carolina; another decision awarded ownership of the entire northern neck of Virginia (along the Potomac River) to Lord Fairfax.

The revival of these proprietary claims by manorial lords and English nobles testified to the rising value of land along the Atlantic coastal plain. It also underscored the increasing similarities between rural societies in Europe and America. To avoid the status of European peasants, native-born yeomen and tenant families joined the stream of European migrants searching for cheap land near the Appalachian Mountains.

Western Rebels and Regulators

As would-be landowners moved west, they sparked conflicts over Indian policy, political representation, and debts. During the war with France, Delaware and Shawnee warriors had exacted revenge for Thomas Penn's land swindle of 1737 by destroying frontier farms in Pennsylvania and killing hundreds of residents. Scots-Irish settlers demanded the expulsion of all Indians, but Quaker leaders refused. So in 1763, a group of Scots-Irish frontiersmen called the Paxton Boys massacred twenty Conestoga Indians, an assimilated community that had lived alongside their colonist neighbors peacefully for many years. When Governor John Penn tried to bring the murderers to justice, 250 armed Scots-Irishmen advanced on Philadelphia. Benjamin Franklin intercepted the angry mob at Lancaster and arranged a truce, averting a battle with the militia. Prosecution of the Paxton Boys failed for lack of witnesses, and the episode gave their defenders the opportunity to excoriate Pennsylvania's government for protecting Indians while it neglected the interests of backcountry colonists.

The South Carolina Regulators   Violence also broke out in the backcountry of South Carolina, where land-hungry Scottish and Anglo-American settlers clashed repeatedly with Cherokees during the war with France. After the fighting ended in 1763, a group of landowning vigilantes known as the **Regulators** demanded that the eastern-controlled government provide western districts with more courts, fairer taxation, and greater representation in the assembly. "We are *Free-Men* — British Subjects — Not Born *Slaves*," declared a Regulator manifesto. Fearing slave revolts, the lowland rice planters who ran the South Carolina assembly compromised. In 1767, the assembly created western courts and reduced the fees for legal documents; but it refused to reapportion the legislature or lower western taxes. Like the Paxton Boys in Pennsylvania, the South Carolina Regulators won attention to backcountry needs but failed to wrest power from the eastern elite.

Civil Strife in North Carolina   In 1766, a more radical Regulator movement arose in North Carolina. When the economic recession of the early 1760s brought a sharp fall in tobacco prices, many farmers could not pay their debts. When creditors sued these farmers for payment, judges directed sheriffs to seize the debtors' property. Many backcountry farmers lost their property or ended up in jail for resisting court orders.

To save their farms, North Carolina's debtors defied the government's authority. Disciplined mobs intimidated judges, closed courts, and freed their comrades from jail. The Regulators proposed a series of reforms, including lower legal fees and tax payments in the "produce of the country" rather than in cash. They also demanded greater representation in the assembly and a just revenue system that would tax each person "in proportion to the profits arising from his estate." All to no avail. In May 1771, Royal Governor William Tryon mobilized British troops and the eastern militia, which defeated a large Regulator force at the Alamance River. When the fighting ended, thirty men lay dead, and Tryon summarily executed seven insurgent leaders. Not since Bacon's Rebellion in Virginia in 1675 and the colonial uprisings during the Glorious Revolution of 1688 (see Chapter 2) had a colonial dispute caused so much political agitation.

In 1771, as in 1675 and 1688, colonial conflicts became linked with imperial politics. In Connecticut, the Reverend Ezra Stiles defended the North Carolina Regulators. "What shall an injured & oppressed people do," he asked, "[when faced with] Oppression and tyranny?" Stiles's remarks reflected growing resistance to recently imposed British policies of taxation and control. The American colonies still depended primarily on Britain for their trade and military defense. However, by the 1760s, the mainland settlements had evolved into complex societies with the potential to exist independently. British policies would play a crucial role in determining the direction the maturing colonies would take.

SUMMARY

In this chapter, we observed dramatic changes in British North America between 1720 and 1765. An astonishing surge in population — from 400,000 to almost 2 million — was the combined result of natural increase, European migration, and the African slave trade. The print revolution and the rise of the British Atlantic brought important new influences: the European Enlightenment and European Pietism transformed the world of ideas, while a flood of British consumer goods and the genteel aspirations of wealthy colonists reshaped the colonies' material culture.

Colonists confronted three major regional challenges. In New England, crowded towns and ever-smaller farms threatened the yeoman ideal of independent farming, prompting families to limit births, move to the frontier, or participate in an "exchange" economy. In the Middle Atlantic colonies, Dutch, English, German, and Scots-Irish residents maintained their religious and cultural identities while they competed for access to land and political power. Across the backcountry, new interest in western lands triggered conflicts with Indian peoples, civil unrest among whites, and, ultimately, the Great War for Empire. In the aftermath of the fighting, Britain stood triumphant in Europe and America.

C H A P T E R   R E V I E W

MAKE IT STICK Go to **LearningCurve** to retain what you've read.

TERMS TO KNOW Identify and explain the significance of each term below.

Key Concepts and Events

tenancy (p. 116)

competency (p. 117)

household mode of production (p. 120)

squatters (p. 121)

redemptioner (p. 124)

Enlightenment (p. 126)

Pietism (p. 126)

natural rights (p. 127)

deism (p. 128)

revival (p. 129)

Old Lights (p. 132)

New Lights (p. 132)

consumer revolution (p. 141)

Regulators (p. 142)

Key People

Isaac Newton (p. 127)

John Locke (p. 127)

Benjamin Franklin (p. 128)

Jonathan Edwards (p. 129)

George Whitefield (p. 129)

Tanaghrisson (p. 135)

William Pitt (p. 138)

Pontiac (p. 139)

REVIEW QUESTIONS
Answer these questions to demonstrate your understanding of the chapter's main ideas.

1. Compare colonists' "pursuits of happiness" in New England, the Middle colonies, the backcountry, and the South. How did poorer colonists in each of these regions seek to maintain their autonomy from powerful landlords and institutions, and how did this effort shape the formation of regional identities?

2. How did the print and transportation revolutions transform colonial culture and the economy in the eighteenth century?

3. The Great War for Empire delivered the eastern half of North America into British hands. How did that massive territorial acquisition affect ordinary colonists? What impact did it have on Native Americans' strategies for coexisting with their European neighbors?

4. **THEMATIC UNDERSTANDING** Review the events listed under "Work, Exchange, and Technology" and "Identity" for the period 1720–1750 on the thematic timeline on page 79. How did economic developments in the colonies influence the formation of new cultural identities in this era?

MAKING CONNECTIONS
Recognize the larger developments and continuities within and across chapters by answering these questions.

1. **ACROSS TIME AND PLACE** In Chapter 3 we saw the rise of the South Atlantic System, an engine of economic growth that tied Britain's colonies more closely together and generated prosperity throughout the British Atlantic world. What consequences of that integration and prosperity are evident in the topics discussed in this chapter? How was the Great War for Empire grounded in earlier economic developments? And how did the postwar debt crisis grow out of the South Atlantic System?

2. **VISUAL EVIDENCE** Return to the John Collet painting of George Whitefield that opened the chapter (p. 115). How does Collet portray Whitefield's audience? Consider the postures and facial expressions of individual members of the crowd and imagine what might have been running through their minds as they listened. What do the various elements of this painting (the crowd, tankard of ale, sleeping dog, setting) suggest about the Great Awakening's appeal? About Collet's attitude toward evangelical preaching?

MORE TO EXPLORE
Start here to learn more about the events discussed in this chapter.

Fred Anderson, *The War That Made America* (2005). A compelling narrative of the Seven Years' War in America. Also see *The War That Made America* (PBS video) and its Web site: **thewarthatmadeamerica.org**.

Colin G. Calloway, *White People, Indians, and Highlanders* (2008). Makes suggestive comparisons between Britain's encounters in Scotland and America.

Aaron Spencer Fogleman, *Hopeful Journeys* (1996). Covers German migrations to America.

Patrick Griffin, *The People with No Name* (2001). Treats the experience of the Scots-Irish in Ireland and America.

Susan E. Klepp and Billy G. Smith, eds., *The Infortunate* (1992). A compelling narrative of one indentured servant's experience in the Middle colonies.

Laurel Thatcher Ulrich, *A Midwife's Tale* (1990). A vivid account of one woman's experiences on the Maine frontier. See also *A Midwife's Tale* (PBS video) and two related Web sites: **pbs.org/wgbh/amex /midwife** and **DoHistory.org**.

TIMELINE

Ask yourself why this chapter begins and ends with these dates and then identify the links among related events.

1695	• Licensing Act lapses in England, triggering the print revolution
1710s–1730s	• Enlightenment ideas spread from Europe to America • Germans and Scots-Irish settle in Middle colonies • Theodore Jacob Frelinghuysen preaches Pietism to German migrants
1720s–1730s	• William and Gilbert Tennent lead Presbyterian revivals among Scots-Irish • Jonathan Edwards preaches in New England
1729	• Benjamin Franklin founds the *Pennsylvania Gazette*
1739	• George Whitefield sparks Great Awakening
1740s–1760s	• Conflict between Old Lights and New Lights • Shortage of farmland in New England threatens freehold ideal • Growing ethnic and religious pluralism in Middle Atlantic colonies • Religious denominations establish colleges
1743	• Benjamin Franklin founds American Philosophical Society • Samuel Morris starts Presbyterian revivals in Virginia
1748	• Ohio Company receives grant of 200,000 acres from the crown
1749	• Connecticut farmers form Susquehanna Company
1750s	• Industrial Revolution begins in England • British shipping dominates North Atlantic • Consumer purchases increase American imports and debt
1754	• French and Indian War begins • Iroquois and colonists meet at Albany Congress • Franklin's Plan of Union
1756	• Britain begins Great War for Empire
1759–1760	• Britain completes conquest of Canada
1760s	• Land conflict along New York and New England border • Baptist revivals win converts in Virginia
1763	• Pontiac's Rebellion leads to Proclamation of 1763 • Treaty of Paris ends Great War for Empire • Scots-Irish Paxton Boys massacre Indians in Pennsylvania
1771	• Royal governor puts down Regulator revolt in North Carolina

KEY TURNING POINTS: The Ohio Company grant (1748), the formation of the Susquehanna Company (1749), land conflict along New York and New England border (1760s), and the defeat of the North Carolina Regulators (1771). How do these events reveal tensions over the question of who would control the development of frontier lands in Britain's mainland North American colonies? What were the effects of these conflicts on Native American populations?

3
PART

Revolution and Republican Culture
1763–1820

"The American war is over," Philadelphia Patriot Benjamin Rush declared in 1787, "but this is far from being the case with the American Revolution. On the contrary, nothing but the first act of the great drama is closed. It remains yet to establish and perfect our new forms of government." The changes that had already unfolded since 1763 were revolutionary in themselves: Britain had triumphed in the Great War for Empire, only to see its American empire unravel and descend into war. Against all odds, the thirteen rebelling colonies had pulled together and won their independence; now they were forming a federal republic that would take its place among the nations of the world.

The republican revolution extended far beyond politics. It challenged many of the values and institutions that had prevailed for centuries in Europe and the Atlantic World. After 1776, Americans reconsidered basic assumptions that structured their societies, cultures, families, and communities. Here, in summary, are the three principal developments discussed in Part 3:

From British North America to the United States of America

After violently rejecting attempts to reform the British Empire, the Patriots won independence and began constructing republican governments. Their experiments extended across an entire generation, and it took still longer to decide how much power the federal republic should wield over the states. The political culture spawned by the Revolution was similarly unformed and slow to develop. Political parties, for example, were unanticipated by the founders and, at first, widely regarded as illegitimate. However, by 1820, they had become central to the adjudication of political conflict, heightening some forms of competition while blunting others. The United States also fought wars with Native Americans in the trans-Appalachian west to gain new territory, and with Great Britain to ensure its independence. Across three generations, American political culture was transformed, national borders were secured, and republican national and state governments commanded the allegiance of their citizens.

Challenges to the Social Order

As Patriots articulated values they associated with independence, they aligned their movement with currents of reform eddying through the Atlantic World: antislavery; women's rights; religious liberty; social equality. Each of these ideas was controversial, and the American Revolution endorsed none of them in an unqualified way. But its idealism—the sense that the Revolution marked "a memorable epoch in the annals of the human race," as John Adams put it—made the era malleable and full of possibility.

Legislatures abolished slavery in the North, broadened religious liberty by allowing freedom of conscience, and, except in New England, ended the system of legally established churches. Postwar evangelicalism gave enormous energy to a new wave of innovative religious developments. However, Americans continued to argue over social equality, in part because their republican creed placed family authority in the hands of men and political power in the hands of propertied individuals: this arrangement denied power and status not only to slaves but also to free blacks, women, and middling and poor white men. Though the Revolution's legacy was mixed, its meaning would be debated for decades in American public life.

Conquest, Competition, and Consolidation

One uncontested value of the Revolutionary era was a commitment to economic opportunity. To achieve this, people migrated in large numbers, and the United States dramatically expanded its boundaries: first, by conquest, pushing west to the Mississippi River; then, by purchase, all the way to the Pacific Ocean. Northern merchants created a banking system and organized rural manufacturing. State governments used charters and other privileges to assist businesses and to improve infrastructure. Southern planters used slaves to grow a new staple crop—cotton. Many yeomen farm families moved west to farm; and Eastern laborers worked in burgeoning manufacturing enterprises. By 1820, the young American republic was on the verge of achieving economic as well as political independence.

Even as the borders of the United States expanded, its diversity inhibited the effort to define an American culture and identity. Native Americans still lived in their own clans and nations; black Americans were developing a distinct African American culture; and White Americans were enmeshed in vigorous regional ethnic communities. Over time, political institutions began to unite Americans of diverse backgrounds, as did increasing participation in the market economy and in evangelical Protestant churches. By 1820, to be an American meant, for many members of the dominant white population, to be a republican, a Protestant, and an enterprising individual.

Revolution and Republican Culture 1763–1820

Thematic Understanding

This timeline arranges some of the important events of this period into themes. Consider the items listed under the theme "Ideas, Beliefs, and Culture." How did the American Revolution challenge existing social arrangements? Consider the role of religion in American life, the status of women, and the institution of slavery. What tensions developed as a result of those challenges?   **>**

	WORK, EXCHANGE, & TECHNOLOGY	PEOPLING	POLITICS & POWER	IDEAS, BELIEFS, & CULTURE	IDENTITY
1763	• Merchants defy Sugar and Stamp Acts • Patriots mount three boycotts of British goods, in 1765, 1767, and 1774 • Boycotts spur Patriot women to make textiles	• Migration into the Ohio Valley after Pontiac's Rebellion • Quebec Act (1774) allows Catholicism	• Stamp Act Congress (1765) • First Continental Congress (1774) • Second Continental Congress (1775)	• Patriots call for American unity • The idea of natural rights poses a challenge to the institution of chattel slavery	• Concept of popular sovereignty gains force in the colonies • Colonists lay claim to rights of Englishmen
1776	• Manufacturing expands during the war • Cutoff of trade and severe inflation threaten economy • War debt grows	• Declining immigration from Europe (1775–1820) enhances American identity • African American slaves seek freedom through military service	• The Declaration of Independence (1776) • States adopt republican constitutions (1776 on) • Articles of Confederation ratified (1781) • Treaty of Paris (1783)	• Judith Sargent Murray publishes "On the Equality of the Sexes" (1779) • Emancipation of slaves begins in the North • Virginia enacts religious freedom (1786)	• Thomas Paine's *Common Sense* (1776) causes colonists to rethink political loyalties • States rely on property qualifications to define citizenship rights in their new constitutions
1787	• Bank of North America founded (1781) • Land speculation increases in the West	• State cessions, land ordinances, and Indian wars create national domain in the West • The Alien Act makes it harder for immigrants to become citizens and allow for deporting aliens (1798)	• U.S. Constitution drafted (1787) • Conflict over Alexander Hamilton's economic policies • First national parties: Federalists and Republicans	• Politicians and ministers deny vote to women; praise republican motherhood • Bill of Rights ratified (1791) • Sedition Act limits freedom of the press (1798)	• Indians form Western Confederacy (1790) • Second Great Awakening (1790–1860) • Emerging political divide between South and North
1800	• Cotton output and demand for African labor expands • Farm productivity improves • Embargo encourages U.S. manufacturing • Second Bank of the United States chartered (1816–1836) • Supreme Court guards property	• Suffrage for white men expands; New Jersey retracts suffrage for propertied women (1807) • Atlantic slave trade ends (1808) • American Colonization Society founded (1817)	• Jefferson reduces activism of national government • Chief Justice Marshall asserts federal judicial powers • Triumph of Republican Party and end of Federalist Party	• Free blacks enhance sense of African American identity • Religious benevolence engenders social reform movements	• Tenskwatawa and Tecumseh revive Western Indian Confederacy • War of 1812 tests national unity • State constitutions democratized

5

The Problem of Empire
1763–1776

In June 1775, the city of New York faced a perplexing dilemma. Word arrived that George Washington, who had just been named commander in chief of the newly formed Continental army, was coming to town. But on the same day, William Tryon, the colony's crown-appointed governor, was scheduled to return from Britain. Local leaders orchestrated a delicate dance. Though the Provincial Congress was operating illegally in the eyes of the crown, it did not wish to offend Governor Tryon. It instructed the city's newly raised volunteer battalion to divide in two. One company awaited Washington's arrival, while another prepared to greet the governor. The "residue of the Battalion" was to be "ready to receive either the General or Governour *Tryon*, which ever shall first arrive." Washington arrived first. He was met by nine companies of the volunteer battalion and a throng of well-wishers, who escorted him to his rooms in a local tavern. Many of this same crowd then crossed town to join the large group assembled to greet the governor, whose ship was just landing. The crowd met him with "universal shouts of applause" and accompanied him home.

This awkward moment in the history of one American city reflects a larger crisis of loyalty that plagued colonists throughout British North America in the years between 1763 and 1776. The outcome of the Great War for Empire left Great Britain the undisputed master of eastern North America. But that success pointed the way to catastrophe. Convinced of the need to reform the empire and tighten its administration, British policymakers imposed a series of new administrative measures on the colonies. Accustomed as they were to governing their own affairs, colonists could not accept these changes. Yet the bonds of loyalty were strong, and the unraveling of British authority was tortuous and complex. Only gradually—as militancy slowly mounted on both sides—were the ties of empire broken and independence declared.

IDENTIFY THE BIG IDEA

Consider whether the collapse of British authority in the thirteen rebellious colonies might have been avoided through compromise measures and more astute leadership. Was colonial independence inevitable, and was war the only way to achieve it?

The Great New York Fire of 1776 In the wake of the Declaration of Independence, General William Howe's first objective was to capture New York, with its strategic location and excellent harbor. Patriot forces under George Washington's command attempted to defend the city but were forced into retreat and abandoned it to the British in September 1776. Early in the morning of September 21, a fire broke out near the southern tip of Manhattan and burned northwestward, driven by a strong wind. As many as a quarter of the town's buildings were destroyed; residents, already distressed by the fighting, fled into the streets with whatever possessions they could carry. Each side accused the other of arson, but that charge was never proven. Miriam and Ira D. Wallach Division of Art, Prints and Photographs, The New York Public Library. Astor, Lenox and Tilden Foundations.

An Empire Transformed

The Great War for Empire of 1756–1763 (Chapter 4) transformed the British Empire in North America. The British ministry could no longer let the colonies manage their own affairs while it contented itself with minimal oversight of the Atlantic trade. Its interests and responsibilities now extended far into the continental interior — a much more costly and complicated proposition than it had ever faced before. And neither its American colonies nor their Native American neighbors were inclined to cooperate in the transformation.

British administrators worried about their American colonists, who, according to former Georgia governor Henry Ellis, felt themselves "entitled to a greater measure of Liberty than is enjoyed by the people of England." Ireland had been closely ruled for decades, and recently the East India Company set up dominion over millions of non-British peoples (Map 5.1 and America Compared, p. 153). Britain's American possessions were likewise filled with aliens and "undesirables": "French, Dutch, Germans innumerable, Indians, Africans, and a multitude of felons from this country," as one member of Parliament put it. Consequently, declared Lord Halifax, "The people of England" considered Americans "as foreigners."

EXPLAIN CONSEQUENCES

What was the impact of the Great War for Empire on British policymakers and the colonies?

Contesting that status, wealthy Philadelphia lawyer John Dickinson argued that his fellow colonists were "not [East Indian] Sea Poys, nor Marattas, but *British subjects* who are born to liberty, who know its worth, and who prize it high." Thus was the stage set for a struggle between the conceptions of identity — and empire — held by British ministers, on the one hand, and many American colonists on the other.

The Costs of Empire

The Great War for Empire imposed enormous costs on Great Britain. The national debt soared from £75 million to £133 million and was, an observer noted, "becoming the alarming object of every British subject." By war's end, interest on the debt alone consumed 60 percent of the nation's budget, and the ministry had to raise taxes. During the eighteenth century, taxes were shifting from land — owned by the gentry and aristocracy — to consumables, and successive ministries became ever more ingenious in devising new ways to raise money. Excise (or sales) taxes were levied on all kinds of ordinary goods — salt and beer, bricks and candles, paper (in the form of a stamp tax) — that were consumed by middling and poor Britons. In the 1760s, the per capita tax burden was 20 percent of income.

To collect the taxes, the government doubled the size of the tax bureaucracy (Figure 5.1). Customs agents patrolled the coasts of southern Britain, seizing tons of contraband French wines, Dutch tea, and Flemish textiles. Convicted smugglers faced heavy penalties, including death or forced "transportation" to America as indentured servants. (Despite colonial protests, nearly fifty thousand English criminals had already been shipped to America to be sold as indentured servants.)

The price of empire abroad was thus larger government and higher taxes at home. Members of two British opposition parties, the Radical Whigs and the Country Party, complained that the huge war debt placed the nation at the mercy of the "monied interests," the banks and financiers who reaped millions of pounds' interest from government bonds. To reverse the growth of government and the threat to personal liberty and property rights, British reformers demanded that Parliament represent a broader spectrum of the property-owning classes. The Radical Whig John Wilkes condemned rotten boroughs — sparsely populated, aristocratic-controlled electoral districts — and demanded greater representation for rapidly growing commercial and manufacturing cities. The war thus transformed British politics.

The war also revealed how little power Britain wielded in its American colonies. In theory, royal governors had extensive political powers, including command of the provincial militia; in reality, they shared power with the colonial assemblies, which outraged British officials. The Board of Trade complained that in Massachusetts "almost every act of executive and legislative power is ordered and directed by votes and resolves of the General Court." To enforce the collection of trade duties, which colonial merchants had evaded for decades by bribing customs officials, Parliament passed the Revenue Act of 1762. The ministry also instructed the Royal Navy to seize American vessels carrying food crops from the mainland colonies to the French West Indies. It was absurd, declared a British politician, that French armies attempting "to Destroy one English province . . . are actually supported by Bread raised in another."

Britain's military victory brought another fundamental shift in policy: a new peacetime deployment of 15 royal battalions — some 7,500 troops — in North

Britain's Atlantic and Asian Empires

The following table enumerates the economic benefits derived by Great Britain from its various colonies, which sent a wide variety of goods to Britain and also served as markets for British exports.

TABLE 5.1

English/British Imports and Exports (annual averages in pounds sterling)

	England*		Britain*	
	1700–01	1750–51	1772–73	1789–90
Imports from Asia, Africa, and America				
North America	372,000	877,000	1,997,000	1,351,000
The Fisheries**	0	7,000	27,000	188,000
West Indies	785,000	1,484,000	3,222,000	4,045,000
Africa	24,000	43,000	80,000	87,000
East Indies	775,000	1,101,000	2,203,000	3,256,000
Total	1,956,000	3,512,000	7,529,000	8,927,000
Exports to America, Asia, and Africa				
North America	362,000	1,355,000	3,254,000	3,763,000
West Indies	336,000	589,000	1,402,000	1,892,000
Africa	145,000	188,000	777,000	799,000
East India	125,000	653,000	893,000	2,173,000
Total	968,000	2,785,000	6,326,000	8,627,000

*The "England" column shows data for England and Wales; "Britain" includes Scotland as well.
**Includes Massachusetts Bay, Maine, and Newfoundland; by the 1760s more than £500,000 worth of fish was being sent annually to the West Indies and southern Europe.
Source: Adapted from *The Oxford History of the British Empire*, vol. 2, ed. P. J. Marshall (Oxford: Oxford University Press, 1998), 101.

QUESTIONS FOR ANALYSIS

1. Compare Britain's colonies in their roles as producers of British imports to their roles as consumers of British exports. Why are the mainland colonies of North America a distant third as producers of imports, but ranked first as consumers of exports?

2. How did the American Revolution (1776–1783) impact the economic relationship between Great Britain and its mainland colonies? Is it reasonable to conclude that political independence did not bring economic independence?

America. The ministers who served under George III (r. 1760–1820) feared a possible rebellion by the 60,000 French residents of Canada, Britain's newly conquered colony (Map 5.2). Native Americans were also a concern: Pontiac's Rebellion had nearly overwhelmed Britain's frontier forts. Moreover, only a substantial military force would deter land-hungry whites from defying the Proclamation of 1763 and settling west of the Appalachian Mountains (see Chapter 4). Finally, British politicians worried about the colonists' loyalty

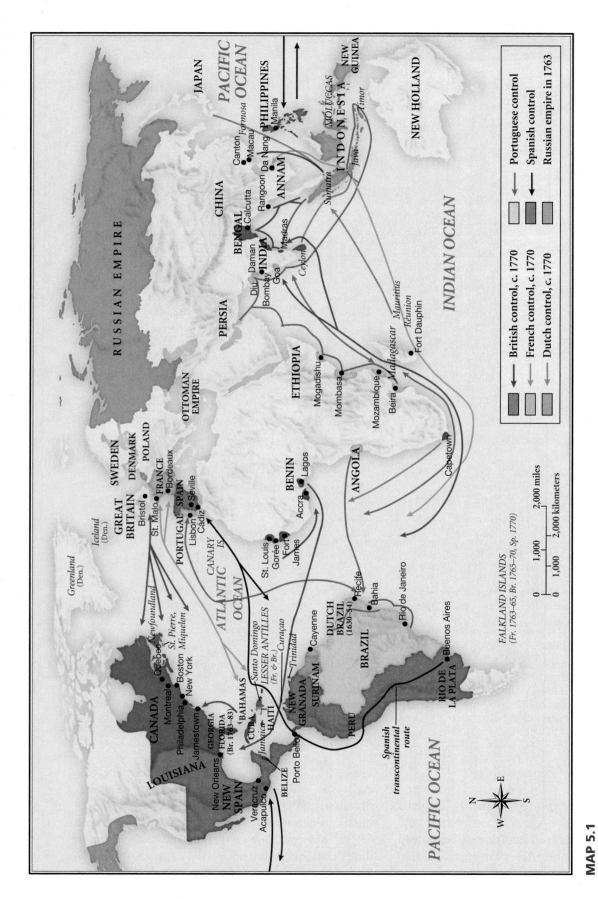

MAP 5.1
Eurasian Trade and European Colonies, c. 1770

By 1770, the Western European nations that had long dominated maritime trade had created vast colonial empires and spheres of influence. Spain controlled the western halves of North and South America, Portugal owned Brazil, and Holland ruled Indonesia. Britain, a newer imperial power, boasted settler societies in North America, rich sugar islands in the West Indies, slave ports in West Africa, and a growing presence on the Indian subcontinent. Only France had failed to acquire and hold on to a significant colonial empire. (To trace changes in empire and trade routes, see Map 1.4 on p. 24 and Map 2.2 on p. 46.)

FIGURE 5.1

The Cost of Empire, 1690–1790

It cost money to build and maintain an empire. As Britain built a great navy, subsidized the armies of European allies, and fought four wars against France and Spain between 1702 and 1783, military expenditures soared. Tax revenues did not keep pace, so the government created a large national debt by issuing bonds for millions of pounds. This policy created a class of wealthy financiers, led to political protests, and eventually prompted attempts to tax the American colonists.

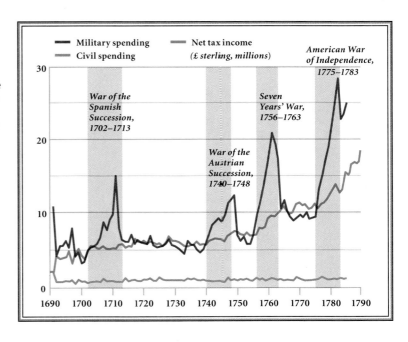

now that they no longer faced a threat from French Canada.

The cost of stationing these troops, estimated at £225,000 per year, compounded Britain's fiscal crisis, and it seemed clear that the burden had to be shared by the colonies. They had always managed their own finances, but the king's ministers agreed that Parliament could no longer let them off the hook for the costs of empire. The greatest gains from the war had come in North America, where the specter of French encirclement had finally been lifted, and the greatest new postwar expenses were being incurred in North America as well.

George Grenville and the Reform Impulse

The challenge of raising revenue from the colonies fell first to George Grenville. Widely regarded as "one of the ablest men in Great Britain," Grenville understood the need for far-reaching imperial reform. He first passed the Currency Act of 1764, which banned the American colonies from using paper money as legal tender. Colonial shopkeepers, planters, and farmers had used local currency, which was worth less than British pounds sterling, to pay their debts to British merchants. The Currency Act ensured that merchants would no longer be paid in money printed in the colonies, boosting their profits and British wealth.

The Sugar Act   Grenville also won parliamentary approval of the **Sugar Act of 1764** to replace the widely ignored Molasses Act of 1733 (see Chapter 3). The earlier act had set a tax rate of 6 pence per gallon on French molasses — a rate so high that it made the trade unprofitable. Rather than pay it, colonial merchants bribed customs officials at the going rate of 1.5 pence per gallon. Grenville settled on a duty of 3 pence per gallon, which merchants could pay and still turn a profit, and then tightened customs enforcement so that it could actually be collected.

This carefully crafted policy garnered little support in America. New England merchants, among them John Hancock of Boston, had made their fortunes smuggling French molasses. In 1754, Boston merchants paid customs duties on a mere 400 hogsheads of molasses, yet they imported 40,000 hogsheads for use by 63 Massachusetts rum distilleries. Publicly, the merchants claimed that the Sugar Act would ruin the distilling industry; privately, they vowed to evade the duty by smuggling or by bribing officials.

The End of Salutary Neglect   More important, colonists raised constitutional objections to the Sugar Act. In Massachusetts, the leader of the assembly argued that the new legislation was "contrary to a fundamental Principall of our Constitution: That all Taxes ought to originate with the people." In Rhode Island, Governor Stephen Hopkins warned: "They who are taxed at

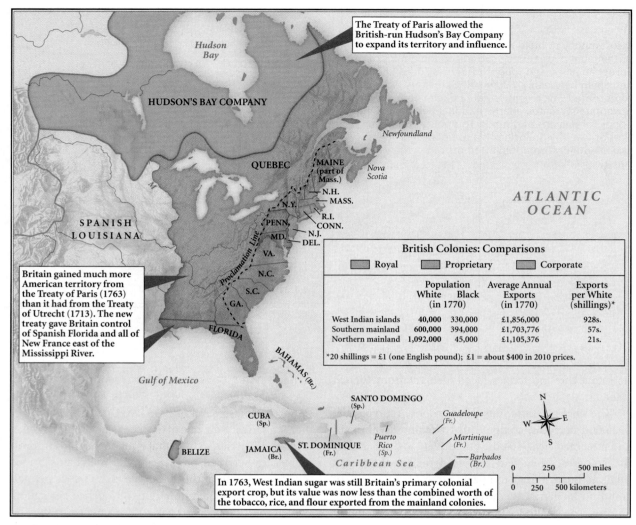

The Treaty of Paris allowed the British-run Hudson's Bay Company to expand its territory and influence.

Britain gained much more American territory from the Treaty of Paris (1763) than it had from the Treaty of Utrecht (1713). The new treaty gave Britain control of Spanish Florida and all of New France east of the Mississippi River.

British Colonies: Comparisons

Royal   Proprietary   Corporate

	Population White (in 1770)	Black	Average Annual Exports (in 1770)	Exports per White (shillings)*
West Indian islands	40,000	330,000	£1,856,000	928s.
Southern mainland	600,000	394,000	£1,703,776	57s.
Northern mainland	1,092,000	45,000	£1,105,376	21s.

*20 shillings = £1 (one English pound); £1 = about $400 in 2010 prices.

In 1763, West Indian sugar was still Britain's primary colonial export crop, but its value was now less than the combined worth of the tobacco, rice, and flour exported from the mainland colonies.

MAP 5.2
Britain's American Empire in 1763

The Treaty of Paris gave Britain control of the eastern half of North America and returned a few captured sugar islands in the West Indies to France. To protect the empire's new mainland territories, British ministers dispatched troops to Florida and Quebec. They also sent troops to uphold the terms of the Proclamation of 1763, which prohibited Anglo-American settlement west of the Appalachian Mountains.

pleasure by others cannot possibly have any property, and they who have no property, can have no freedom." The Sugar Act raised other constitutional issues as well. Merchants prosecuted under the act would be tried in **vice-admiralty courts**, tribunals governing the high seas and run by British-appointed judges. Previously, merchants accused of Navigation Acts violations were tried by local common-law courts, where friendly juries often acquitted them. The Sugar Act closed this legal loophole by extending the jurisdiction of the vice-admiralty courts to all customs offenses.

The Sugar Act revived old American fears. The influential Virginia planter Richard Bland emphasized that the American colonists "were not sent out to be the Slaves but to be the Equals of those that remained behind." John Adams, the young Massachusetts lawyer defending John Hancock on a charge of smuggling,

To see a longer excerpt of the Richard Bland document, along with other primary sources from this period, see *Sources for America's History*.

argued that the vice-admiralty courts diminished this equality by "degrad[ing] every American . . . below the rank of an Englishman."

In fact, accused smugglers in Britain were also tried in vice-admiralty courts, so there was no discrimination against Americans. The real issue was the growing power of the British state. Americans had lived for decades under an administrative policy of salutary neglect. Now they saw that the new imperial regime would deprive them "of some of their most essential Rights as British subjects," as a committee of the Massachusetts assembly put it. In response, Royal Governor Francis Bernard replied: "The rule that a British subject shall not be bound by laws or liable to taxes, but what he has consented to by his representatives must be confined to the inhabitants of Great Britain only." To Bernard, Grenville, and other imperial reformers, Americans were second-class subjects of the king, with rights limited by the Navigation Acts, parliamentary laws, and British interests.

An Open Challenge: The Stamp Act

Another new tax, the **Stamp Act of 1765**, sparked the first great imperial crisis. The new levy was to cover part of the cost of keeping British troops in America—which turned out to be £385,000 a year (about $150 million today), 70 percent more than the initial estimate. Grenville hoped the Stamp Act would raise £60,000 per year. The act would require a tax stamp on all printed items, from college diplomas, court documents, land titles, and contracts to newspapers, almanacs, and playing cards. It was ingeniously designed. Like its counterpart in England, it bore more heavily on the rich, since it charged only a penny a sheet for newspapers and other common items but up to £10 for a lawyer's license. It also required no new bureaucracy; stamped paper would be delivered to colonial ports and sold to printers in lieu of unstamped stock.

Benjamin Franklin, agent of the Pennsylvania assembly, proposed a different solution: American representation in Parliament. "If you chuse to tax us," he wrote, "give us Members in your Legislature, and let us be one People." With the exception of William Pitt, British politicians rejected Franklin's idea as too radical. They argued that the colonists already had **virtual representation** in Parliament because some of its members were transatlantic merchants and West Indian sugar planters. Colonial leaders were equally skeptical of Franklin's plan. Americans were "situate at a great Distance from their Mother Country," the Connecticut

assembly declared, and therefore "cannot participate in the general Legislature of the Nation."

Asserting "the Right of Parliament to lay an internal Tax upon the Colonies," the House of Commons ignored American opposition and passed the act by an overwhelming majority of 205 to 49. At the request of General Thomas Gage, the British military commander in America, Parliament also passed the **Quartering Act of 1765**, which required colonial governments to provide barracks and food for British troops. Finally, Parliament approved Grenville's proposal that violations of the Stamp Act be tried in vice-admiralty courts.

> ### UNDERSTAND POINTS OF VIEW
> Why did most British and colonial leaders reject the idea that the colonies should be represented in Parliament?

Using the doctrine of parliamentary supremacy, Grenville had begun to fashion a centralized imperial system in America much like that already in place in Ireland: British officials would govern the colonies with little regard for the local assemblies. Consequently, the prime minister's plan provoked a constitutional confrontation on the specific issues of taxation, jury trials, and military quartering as well as on the general question of representative self-government.

The Dynamics of Rebellion, 1765–1770

In the name of reform, Grenville had thrown down the gauntlet to the Americans. The colonists had often resisted unpopular laws and aggressive governors, but they had faced an all-out attack on their institutions only once before—in 1686, when James II had unilaterally imposed the Dominion of New England. Now the danger to colonial autonomy was even greater because both the king and Parliament backed reform. But the Patriots, as the defenders of American rights came to be called, met the challenge posed by Grenville and his successor, Charles Townshend. They organized protests—formal and informal, violent as well as peaceful—and fashioned a compelling ideology of resistance.

Formal Protests and the Politics of the Crowd

Virginia's House of Burgesses was the first formal body to complain. In May 1765, hotheaded young Patrick Henry denounced Grenville's legislation and attacked

Protesting the Stamp Act in Portsmouth, New Hampshire

Throughout the colonies, disciplined mobs protesting the Stamp Act forced stamp distributors to resign their offices. In this engraving, protesters in the small city of Portsmouth, New Hampshire, stone an effigy of the distributor as other members of the mob carry off a coffin representing the death of American "Liberty." Illustration from "Interesting Events in the History of the U.S." by J. W. Barber, 1829/Picture Research Consultants & Archives.

George III for supporting it. He compared the king to Charles I, whose tyranny had led to his overthrow and execution in the 1640s. These remarks, which bordered on treason, frightened the Burgesses; nonetheless, they condemned the Stamp Act's "manifest Tendency to Destroy American freedom." In Massachusetts, James Otis, another republican-minded firebrand, persuaded the House of Representatives to call a meeting of all the mainland colonies "to implore Relief" from the act.

The Stamp Act Congress Nine assemblies sent delegates to the **Stamp Act Congress**, which met in New York City in October 1765. The congress protested the loss of American "rights and liberties," especially the right to trial by jury. And it challenged the constitutionality of both the Stamp and Sugar Acts by declaring that only the colonists' elected representatives could tax them. Still, moderate-minded delegates wanted compromise, not confrontation. They assured Parliament that Americans "glory in being subjects of the best of Kings" and humbly petitioned for repeal of the Stamp Act. Other influential Americans favored active (but peaceful) resistance; they organized a boycott of British goods.

Crowd Actions Popular opposition also took a violent form, however. When the Stamp Act went into effect on November 1, 1765, disciplined mobs demanded the resignation of stamp-tax collectors. In Boston, a group calling itself the **Sons of Liberty** burned an effigy of collector Andrew

COMPARE AND CONTRAST
Why did the Stamp Act arouse so much more resistance than the Sugar Act?

Oliver and then destroyed Oliver's new brick warehouse. Two weeks later, Bostonians attacked the house of Lieutenant Governor Thomas Hutchinson, Oliver's brother-in-law and a prominent defender of imperial authority, breaking his furniture, looting his wine cellar, and setting fire to his library.

Wealthy merchants and Patriot lawyers, such as John Hancock and John Adams, encouraged the mobs, which were usually led by middling artisans and minor merchants. In New York City, nearly three thousand shopkeepers, artisans, laborers, and seamen marched through the streets breaking windows and crying "Liberty!" Resistance to the Stamp Act spread far beyond the port cities: in nearly every colony, angry crowds — the "rabble," their detractors called them — intimidated royal officials. Near Wethersfield, Connecticut, five hundred farmers seized tax collector Jared Ingersoll and forced him to resign his office in "the Cause of the People."

The Motives of the Crowd Such crowd actions were common in both Britain and America, and protesters had many motives. Roused by the Great Awakening, evangelical Protestants resented arrogant British military officers and corrupt royal bureaucrats. In New England, where rioters invoked the antimonarchy sentiments of their great-grandparents, an anonymous letter sent to a Boston newspaper promising to save "all the Freeborn Sons of America" was signed "Oliver Cromwell," the English republican revolutionary of the 1650s. In New York City, Sons of Liberty leaders Isaac Sears and Alexander McDougall were minor merchants and Radical Whigs who feared that imperial reform would undermine political liberty. The mobs also included apprentices, day laborers, and unemployed sailors: young men with their own notions of liberty who—especially if they had been drinking—were quick to resort to violence.

Nearly everywhere popular resistance nullified the Stamp Act. Fearing an assault on Fort George, New York lieutenant governor Cadwallader Colden called on General Gage to use his small military force to protect the stamps. Gage refused. "Fire from the Fort might disperse the Mob, but it would not quell them," he told Colden, and the result would be "an Insurrection, the Commencement of Civil War." The tax was collected in Barbados and Jamaica, but frightened collectors resigned their offices in all thirteen colonies that would eventually join in the Declaration of Independence. This popular insurrection gave a democratic cast to the emerging Patriot movement. "Nothing is wanting but your own Resolution," declared a New York rioter, "for great is the Authority and Power of the People."

The Ideological Roots of Resistance

Some Americans couched their resistance in constitutional terms. Many were lawyers or well-educated merchants and planters. Composing pamphlets of remarkable political sophistication, they gave the resistance movement its rationale, its political agenda, and its leaders.

Patriot writers drew on three intellectual traditions. The first was **English common law**, the centuries-old body of legal rules and procedures that protected the lives and property of the monarch's subjects. In the famous *Writs of Assistance* case of 1761, Boston lawyer James Otis invoked English legal precedents to challenge open-ended search warrants. In demanding a jury trial for John Hancock in the late 1760s, John Adams appealed to the Magna Carta (1215), the ancient document that, said Adams, "has for many Centuries been esteemed by Englishmen, as one of the . . . firmest Bulwarks of their Liberties." Other lawyers protested that new strictures violated specific "liberties and privileges" granted in colonial charters or embodied in Britain's "ancient constitution."

Enlightenment rationalism provided Patriots with a second important intellectual resource. Virginia planter Thomas Jefferson and other Patriots drew on the writings of John Locke, who had argued that all individuals possessed certain "**natural rights**"—life, liberty, and property—that governments must protect (see Chapter 4). And they turned to the works of

French philosopher Montesquieu, who had maintained that a "separation of powers" among government departments prevented arbitrary rule.

The republican and Whig strands of the English political tradition provided a third ideological source for American Patriots. Puritan New England had long venerated the Commonwealth era (1649–1660), when England had been a republic (see Chapter 2). After the Glorious Revolution of 1688–1689, many colonists praised the English Whigs for creating a constitutional monarchy that prevented the king from imposing taxes and other measures. Joseph Warren, a physician and a Radical Whig Patriot, suggested that the Stamp Act was part of a ministerial plot "to force the colonies into rebellion" and justify the use of "military power to reduce them to servitude." John Dickinson's *Letters from a Farmer in Pennsylvania* (1768) urged colonists to "remember your ancestors and your posterity" and oppose parliamentary taxes. The letters circulated widely and served as an early call to resistance. If Parliament could tax the colonies without their consent, he wrote, "our boasted liberty is but A sound and nothing else."

Such arguments, widely publicized in newspapers and pamphlets, gave intellectual substance to the Patriot movement and turned a series of impromptu riots, tax protests, and boycotts of British manufactures into a formidable political force.

Another Kind of Freedom

"We are taxed without our own consent," Dickinson wrote in one of his *Letters*. "We are therefore—SLAVES." As Patriot writers argued that taxation without representation made colonists the slaves of Parliament, many, including Benjamin Franklin in Philadelphia and James Otis in Massachusetts, also began to condemn the institution of chattel slavery itself as a violation of slaves' natural rights. African Americans made the connection as well. In Massachusetts, slaves submitted at least four petitions to the legislature asking that slavery be abolished. As one petition noted, slaves "have in common with other men, a natural right to be free, and without molestation, to enjoy such property, as they may acquire by their industry."

In the southern colonies, where slaves constituted half or more of the population and the economy depended on their servitude, the quest for freedom

COMPARE AND CONTRAST
Why were southerners more threatened by challenges to the institution of slavery than northerners?

Phillis Wheatley

Born in West Africa and enslaved as a child, Phillis Wheatley was purchased by Boston merchant and tailor John Wheatley when she was eight. Tutored by Wheatley's children, Phillis learned to read English, Greek, and Latin by the age of twelve. This engraving, which pictures her at a writing desk, was the frontispiece for her *Poems on Various Subjects, Religious and Moral* (1773), which was praised by George Washington and gained attention in both Britain and the colonies. Freed upon the death of her master, Wheatley married John Peters, a free black man. He was later imprisoned for debt, forcing Wheatley to take employment as a maid. She died in 1784 at age thirty-one; none of her three children survived infancy. Library of Congress.

TABLE 5.2

Ministerial Instability in Britain, 1760–1782

Leading Minister	Dates of Ministry	American Policy
Lord Bute	1760–1763	Mildly reformist
George Grenville	1763–1765	Ardently reformist
Lord Rockingham	1765–1766	Accommodationist
William Pitt / Charles Townshend	1766–1770	Ardently reformist
Lord North	1770–1782	Coercive

alarmed slaveholders. In November 1773, a group of Virginia slaves hoped to win their freedom by supporting British troops that, they heard, would soon arrive in the colony. Their plan was uncovered, and, as James Madison wrote, "proper precautions" were taken "to prevent the Infection" from spreading. He fully understood how important it was to defend the colonists' liberties without allowing the idea of natural rights to undermine the institution of slavery. "It is prudent," he wrote, "such things should be concealed as well as suppressed." Throughout the Revolution, the quest for African American rights and liberties would play out alongside that of the colonies, but unlike national independence, the liberation of African Americans would not be fulfilled for many generations.

Parliament and Patriots Square Off Again

When news of the Stamp Act riots and the boycott reached Britain, Parliament was already in turmoil. Disputes over domestic policy had led George III to dismiss Grenville as prime minister (Table 5.2). However, Grenville's allies demanded that imperial reform continue, if necessary at gunpoint. "The British legislature," declared Chief Justice Sir James Mansfield, "has authority to bind every part and every subject, whether such subjects have a right to vote or not."

Yet a majority in Parliament was persuaded that the Stamp Act was cutting deeply into British exports and thus doing more harm than good. "The Avenues of Trade are all shut up," a Bristol merchant told Parliament: "We have no Remittances and are at our Witts End for want of Money to fulfill our Engagements with our Tradesmen." Grenville's successor, the Earl of Rockingham, forged a compromise. To mollify the colonists and help British merchants, he repealed the Stamp Act and reduced the duty on molasses imposed by the Sugar Act to a penny a gallon. Then he pacified imperial reformers and hard-liners with the **Declaratory Act of 1766**, which explicitly reaffirmed Parliament's "full power and authority to make laws and statutes . . . to bind the colonies and people of America . . . in all cases whatsoever." By swiftly ending the Stamp Act crisis, Rockingham hoped it would be forgotten just as quickly.

Charles Townshend Steps In Often the course of history is changed by a small event — an illness, a personal grudge, a chance remark. That was the case in 1767, when George III named William Pitt to head a new government. Pitt, chronically ill and often absent

Celebrating Repeal

This British cartoon mocking supporters of the Stamp Act — "The Repeal, or the Funeral Procession of Miss Americ-Stamp" — was probably commissioned by merchants trading with America. Preceded by two flag bearers, George Grenville, the author of the legislation, carries a miniature coffin (representing the act) to a tomb, as a dog urinates on the leader of the procession. Two bales on the wharf, labeled "Stamps from America" and "Black cloth return'd from America," testify to the failure of the act. The Granger Collection, New York.

THE REPEAL. or the Funeral Procession, of Miss Americ-Stamp.

from parliamentary debates, left chancellor of the exchequer Charles Townshend in command. Pitt was sympathetic toward America; Townshend was not. As a member of the Board of Trade, Townshend had sought restrictions on the colonial assemblies and strongly supported the Stamp Act. In 1767, he promised to find a new source of revenue in America.

The new tax legislation, the **Townshend Act of 1767**, had both fiscal and political goals. It imposed duties on colonial imports of paper, paint, glass, and tea that were expected to raise about £40,000 a year. Though Townshend did allocate some of this revenue for American military expenses, he earmarked most of it to pay the salaries of royal governors, judges, and other imperial officials, who had always previously been paid by colonial assemblies. Now, he hoped, royal appointees could better enforce parliamentary laws and carry out the king's instructions. Townshend next devised the Revenue Act of 1767, which created a board of customs commissioners in Boston and vice-admiralty courts in Halifax, Boston, Philadelphia, and Charleston. By using parliamentary taxes to finance imperial administration, Townshend intended to undermine American political institutions.

The Townshend duties revived the constitutional debate over taxation. During the Stamp Act crisis, some Americans, including Benjamin Franklin, distinguished between external and internal taxes. They suggested that external duties on trade (such as those long mandated by the Navigation Acts) were acceptable to Americans, but that direct, or internal, taxes were not.

Townshend thought this distinction was "perfect nonsense," but he indulged the Americans and laid duties only on trade.

A Second Boycott and the Daughters of Liberty

Even so, most colonial leaders rejected the legitimacy of Townshend's measures. In February 1768, the Massachusetts assembly condemned the Townshend Act, and Boston and New York merchants began a new boycott of British goods. Throughout Puritan New England, ministers and public officials discouraged the purchase of "foreign superfluities" and promoted the domestic manufacture of cloth and other necessities.

American women, ordinarily excluded from public affairs, became crucial to the **nonimportation movement**. They reduced their households' consumption of imported goods and produced large quantities of homespun cloth. Pious farmwives spun yarn at their ministers' homes. In Berwick, Maine, "true Daughters of Liberty" celebrated American products by "drinking rye coffee and dining on bear venison." Other women's groups supported the boycott with charitable work, spinning flax and wool for the needy. Just as Patriot men followed tradition by joining crowd actions, so women's protests reflected their customary concern for the well-being of the community.

Newspapers celebrated these exploits of the Daughters of Liberty. One Massachusetts town proudly claimed an annual output of 30,000 yards of cloth; East Hartford, Connecticut, reported 17,000 yards. This

EXPLAIN CONSEQUENCES

How did the nonimportation movement bring women into the political sphere?

surge in domestic production did not offset the loss of British imports, which had averaged about 10 million yards of cloth annually, but it brought thousands of women into the public arena.

The boycott mobilized many American men as well. In the seaport cities, the Sons of Liberty published the names of merchants who imported British goods and harassed their employees and customers. By March 1769, the nonimportation movement had spread to Philadelphia; two months later, the members of the Virginia House of Burgesses vowed not to buy dutied articles, luxury goods, or imported slaves. Reflecting colonial self-confidence, Benjamin Franklin called for a return to the pre-1763 mercantilist system: "Repeal the laws, renounce the right, recall the troops, refund the money, and return to the old method of requisition."

Despite the enthusiasm of Patriots, nonimportation—accompanied by pressure on merchants and consumers who resisted it—opened fissures in colonial society. Not only royal officials, but also merchants, farmers, and ordinary folk, were subject to new forms of surveillance and coercion—a pattern that would only become more pronounced as the imperial crisis unfolded.

Troops to Boston American resistance only increased British determination. When the Massachusetts assembly's letter opposing the Townshend duties reached London, Lord Hillsborough, the secretary of state for American affairs, branded it "unjustifiable opposition to the constitutional authority of Parliament." To strengthen the "Hand of Government" in Massachusetts, Hillsborough dispatched General Thomas Gage and 2,000 British troops to Boston (Map 5.3). Once in Massachusetts, Gage accused its leaders of "Treasonable and desperate Resolves" and

Edenton Ladies' Tea Party

In October 1774, a group of fifty-one women from Edenton, North Carolina, led by Penelope Barker created a local association to support a boycott of British goods. Patriots in the colonies praised the Edenton Tea Party, which was one of the first formal female political associations in North America, but it was ridiculed in Britain, where this cartoon appeared in March 1775. The women are given a mannish appearance, and the themes of promiscuity and neglect to their female duties are suggested by the presence of a slave and an amorous man, the neglected child, and the urinating dog. Library of Congress.

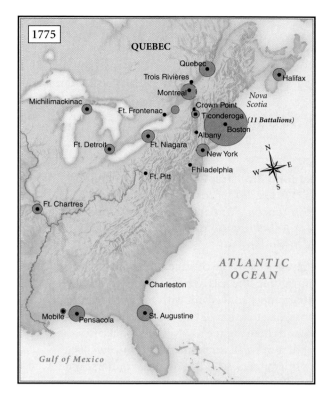

MAP 5.3
British Troop Deployments, 1763 and 1775

As the imperial crisis deepened, British military priorities changed. In 1763, most British battalions were stationed in Canada to deter Indian uprisings and French Canadian revolts. After the Stamp Act riots of 1765, the British placed large garrisons in New York and Philadelphia. By 1775, eleven battalions of British regulars occupied Boston, the center of the Patriot movement.

advised the ministry to "Quash this Spirit at a Blow." In 1765, American resistance to the Stamp Act had sparked a parliamentary debate; in 1768, it provoked a plan for military coercion.

The Problem of the West

At the same time that successive ministries addressed the problem of raising a colonial revenue, they quarreled over how to manage the vast new inland territory — about half a billion acres — acquired in the Treaty of Paris in 1763 (see Chapter 4). The Proclamation Line had drawn a boundary between the colonies and Indian country. The line was originally intended as a temporary barrier. It prohibited settlement "for the present, and until our further Pleasure be known." The Proclamation also created three new mainland colonies — Quebec, East Florida, and West Florida — and thus opened new opportunities at the northern and southern extremities of British North America.

But many colonists looked west rather than north or south. Four groups in the colonies were especially interested in westward expansion. First, gentlemen who had invested in numerous land speculation companies were petitioning the crown for large land grants in the Ohio country. Second, officers who served in the Seven Years' War were paid in land warrants — up to 5,000 acres for field officers — and some, led by George Washington, were exploring possible sites beyond the Appalachians. Third, Indian traders who had received large grants from the Ohio Indians hoped to sell land titles. And fourth, thousands of squatters were following the roads cut to the Ohio by the Braddock and Forbes campaigns during the Seven Years' War to take up lands in the hope that they could later receive a title to them. "The roads are . . . alive with Men, Women, Children, and Cattle from Jersey, Pennsylvania, and Maryland," wrote one astonished observer (Thinking Like a Historian, p. 164).

All of this activity antagonized the Ohio Indians. In 1770, Shawnees invited hundreds of Indian leaders to

IDENTIFY CAUSES
What groups were most interested in western lands, and why did Hillsborough oppose them?

Beyond the Proclamation Line

Though the Royal Proclamation of 1763 called the territory between the Appalachian Mountains and the Mississippi River "Indian country," the reality was more complex than this phrase indicates. The following documents illustrate some of the patterns that shaped life beyond the Proclamation Line between 1763 and 1776.

1. **Colonel John Bradstreet's Thoughts on Indian Affairs, 1764.** *Colonel John Bradstreet led a force of British redcoats to Fort Niagara in response to Pontiac's Rebellion. He drafted these remarks shortly afterward.*

Of all the Savages upon the continent, the most knowing, the most intriguing, the less useful, and the greatest Villains, are those most conversant with the Europeans, and deserve most the attention of Govern[men]t by way of correction, and these are the Six Nations, Shawanese and Delawares; they are well acquainted with the defenceless state of the Inhabitants, who live on the Frontiers, and think they will ever have it in their power to distress and plunder them, and never cease raising the jealousy of the Upper Nations against us, by propagating amongst them such stories, as make them believe the English have nothing so much at heart as the extirpation of all Savages. The apparent design of the Six Nations, is to keep us at war with all Savages, but themselves, that they may be employed as mediators between us and them.

2. **William Johnson to the British Lords of Trade, 1763.** *William Johnson, a New Yorker with extensive experience in Indian relations, was the crown's superintendent for Indian affairs in the northern colonies.*

[T]he Colonies, had all along neglected to cultivate a proper understanding with the Indians, and from a mistaken notion, have greatly dispised them, without considering, that it is in their power at pleasure to lay waste and destroy the Frontiers. . . . Without any exageration, I look upon the Northern Indians to be the most formidable of any uncivilized body of people in the World. Hunting and War are their sole occupations, and the one qualifies them for the other, they have few wants, and those are easily supplied, their properties of little value, consequently, expeditions against them however successful, cannot distress them, and they have courage sufficient for their manner of fighting, the nature and situation of their Countrys, require not more.

3. **"Indians Giving a Talk to Colonel Bouquet," 1766.** *Based on a painting by Benjamin West, this engraving from a book about Bouquet's campaign to the Ohio following Pontiac's Rebellion depicts a meeting with Delaware, Seneca, and Shawnee representatives in October 1764.*

Source: The Granger Collection, New York.

4. **David Jones's journal, 1773.** *David Jones was a Baptist minister who traveled down the Ohio River in 1772 and 1773. His journal offers a compelling glimpse of life in the valley's trading communities.*

FRIDAY [January] 22, in company with Mr. Irwine, set out for Chillicaathee. . . . Here Mr. Irwine kept an assortment of goods, and for that purpose rented an house from an Indian whose name is *Waappee Monneeto*, often called the White Devil. . . . Went to see Mr. Moses Henry a gunsmith and trader from Lancaster. This gentleman has lived for some years in this town, and is lawfully married to a white woman, who was captivated so young that she speaks the language as well as any Indian. . . . Mr. Henry lives in a comfortable manner, having plenty of good beef, pork, milk, &c. . . . Chillicaathee is the chief town of the Shawannee Indians — it is situated north of a large plain adjacent to a branch of Paint Creek. This plain is their corn-field, which supplies great part of their town. Their houses are made of logs. . . .

WEDNESDAY [February] 10. . . . This is a small town consisting of Delawares and Shawanees. The chief is a Shawanee woman, who is esteemed very rich — she entertains travelers — there were four of us in company, and for our use, her negro quarter was evacuated this night, which had a fire in the middle without any chimney. This woman has a large stock, and supplied us with milk. Here we also got corn for our horses at a very expensive price. . . .

FRIDAY [February] 12 . . . We passed [the Delaware chief] Captain White Eye's Town. . . . He told me that he intended to be religious, and have his children educated. He saw that their way of living would not answer much longer — game grew scarce — they could not much longer pretend to live by hunting, but must farm, &c. — But said, he could not attend to matters of religion now, for he intended to make a great *hunt* down Ohio, and take the skins himself to Philadelphia.

5. Killbuck to the governors of Pennsylvania, Maryland, and Virginia, December 1771. *John Killbuck Jr., or Gelelemend, a Delaware headman, aired grievances on behalf of Ohio Delaware, Munsie, and Mahican Indians.*

Great numbers more of your people have come over the Great Mountains and settled throughout this country, and we are sorry to tell you, that several quarrels have happened between your people and ours, in which people have been killed on both sides, and that we now see the nations round us and your people ready to embroil in a quarrel, which gives our nations great concerns, as we, on our parts, want to live in friendship with you. As you have always told us, you have laws to govern your people by, -- but we do not see that you have; therefore, brethren, unless you can fall upon some method of governing your people who live between the Great Mountains and the Ohio River and who are now very numerous, it will be out of the Indians' power to govern their young men, for we assure you the black clouds begin to gather fast in this country. . . . We find your people are very fond of our rich land. We see them quarrelling every day about land and burning one another's houses, so that we do not know how soon they may come over the river Ohio and drive us from our villages, nor do we see you, brothers, take any care to stop them.

6. Aeneas MacKay to Pennsylvania governor John Penn, April 4, 1774. *MacKay, a magistrate of Pennsylvania's Westmoreland County, reported on Virginia's effort to create a competing jurisdiction in the vicinity of Pittsburgh. Dr. John Connolly, appointed by Governor Dunmore as commander*

of the militia in Pittsburgh, was at the center of the controversy.

Since the return of the Celebrated Doctor Connelly from Virginia last to this place, which he did on the 28th of March, our village is become the scene of anarchy and Confusion. . . .

The Doctor now is in actual possession of the Fort, with a Body Guard of Militia about him, Invested, as we are told, with both Civil & military power, to put the Virginia Law in Force in these parts, and a considerable Number of the Inhabitants of these back Parts of this Country, Ready to join him on any emergency, every artifice are used to seduce the people, some by being promoted to Civil or military employments, and others with the promises of grants of Lands, on easy Terms, & the giddy headed mobs are so Infatuated as to suffer themselves to be carried away by these Insinuating Delusions. . . .

The Indians are greatly alarmed at seeing parties of armed men patrolling through our streets Daily, not knowing but there is hostility intended against them and their country.

Sources: (1, 2) E. B. O'Callaghan and Berthold Fernow, eds., *Documents Relative to the Colonial History of the State of New York*, 15 vols. (Albany, 1856–1887), 7: 690–694, 574; (4) David Jones, *A Journal of Two Visits Made to Some Nations of Indians on the West Side of the River Ohio, in the Years 1772 and 1773* (Burlington, 1774 [rep. NY, 1971]); (5) K. G. Davies, ed., *Documents of the American Revolution, 1770–1783*, 19 vols. (Shannon and Dublin, 1972–1981), 3: 254–255; (6) Samuel Hazard, ed., *Pennsylvania Archives*, series 1, 12 vols. (Philadelphia: Joseph Severns & Co., 1856), 4: 484–486.

ANALYZING THE EVIDENCE

1. John Bradstreet, a career British army officer, based his observations (source 1) on his wartime experiences in the West. William Johnson (source 2) had lived in close proximity to Iroquois Indians for many years. Compare their views: what do they agree upon, and where do they differ?

2. Charles Grignion's engraving (source 3) appeared in print a short time after Pontiac's Rebellion. How does it portray the Ohio Indians? Compare Grignion's image with the descriptions in sources 1 and 2 and John Killbuck's speech (source 5). What parallels or differences do you see?

3. What do you find most surprising about source 4? What evidence of European influence do you see in the Indian towns Jones describes?

4. Sources 5 and 6 describe the state of affairs on the upper Ohio shortly before the outbreak of Dunmore's War. What concerns does Killbuck express? Why was Virginia's willingness to organize a militia so important to the residents of the region?

PUTTING IT ALL TOGETHER

Using these documents and what you have learned in Chapter 5, write a short essay that surveys British and Anglo-American attitudes toward the Ohio Indians and explores the contradictions between these attitudes and the reality of life in the Ohio country.

gather at the town of Chillicothe on the Scioto River. There they formed the Scioto Confederacy, which pledged to oppose any further expansion into the Ohio country.

Meanwhile, in London, the idea that the Proclamation Line was only temporary gave way to the view that it should be permanent. Hillsborough, who became colonial secretary in 1768, adamantly opposed westward expansion, believing it would antagonize the Indians without benefitting the empire. Moreover, he owned vast Irish estates, and he was alarmed by the number of tenants who were leaving Ireland for America. To preserve Britain's laboring class, as well as control costs, Hillsborough wanted to make the Proclamation Line permanent.

For colonists who were already moving west to settle in large numbers, this shift in policy caused confusion and frustration. Eventually, like the Patriots along the seaboard, they would take matters into their own hands.

Parliament Wavers

In Britain, the colonies' nonimportation agreement was taking its toll. In 1768, the colonies had cut imports of British manufactures in half; by 1769, the mainland colonies had a trade surplus with Britain of £816,000. Hard-hit by these developments, British merchants and manufacturers petitioned Parliament to repeal the Townshend duties. Early in 1770, Lord North became prime minister. A witty man and a skillful politician, North designed a new compromise. Arguing that it was foolish to tax British exports to America (thereby raising their price and decreasing consumption), he persuaded Parliament to repeal most of the Townshend

duties. However, North retained the tax on tea as a symbol of Parliament's supremacy (Figure 5.2).

The Boston Massacre   Even as Parliament was debating North's repeal, events in Boston guaranteed that reconciliation between Patriots and Parliament would be hard to achieve. Between 1,200 and 2,000 troops had been stationed in Boston for a year and a half. Soldiers were also stationed in New York, Philadelphia, several towns in New Jersey, and various frontier outposts in these years, with a minimum of conflict or violence. But in Boston — a small port town on a tiny peninsula — the troops numbered 10 percent of the local population, and their presence wore on the locals. On the night of March 5, 1770, a group of nine British redcoats fired into a crowd and killed five townspeople. A subsequent trial exonerated the soldiers, but Boston's Radical Whigs, convinced of a ministerial conspiracy against liberty, labeled the incident a "massacre" and used it to rally sentiment against imperial power.

Sovereignty Debated   When news of North's compromise arrived in the colonies in the wake of the Boston Massacre, the reaction was mixed. Most of Britain's colonists remained loyal to the empire, but five years of conflict had taken their toll. In 1765, American leaders had accepted Parliament's authority; the Stamp Act Resolves had opposed only certain "unconstitutional" legislation. By 1770, the most outspoken Patriots — Benjamin Franklin in Pennsylvania, Patrick Henry in Virginia, and Samuel Adams in Massachusetts — repudiated parliamentary supremacy and claimed equality for the American assemblies within the empire. Franklin suggested that the colonies

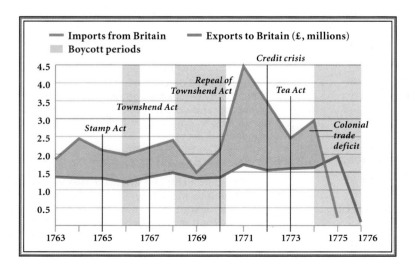

FIGURE 5.2

Trade as a Political Weapon, 1763–1776

Political upheaval did not affect the mainland colonies' exports to Britain, which rose slightly over the period, but imports fluctuated greatly. The American boycott of 1765–1766 prompted a dip in imports, but the second boycott of 1768–1770 led to a sharp drop in imports of British textiles, metal goods, and ceramics. Imports of manufactures soared after the repeal of the Townshend duties, only to plummet when the First Continental Congress proclaimed a third boycott in 1774.

Patriot Propaganda
Silversmith Paul Revere issued this engraving of the confrontation between British redcoats and snowball-throwing Bostonians in the days after it occurred. To whip up opposition to the military occupation of their town, Revere and other Patriots labeled the incident "The Boston Massacre." The shooting confirmed their Radical Whig belief that "standing armies" were instruments of tyranny. Library of Congress.

were now "distinct and separate states" with "the same Head, or Sovereign, the King."

Franklin's suggestion outraged Thomas Hutchinson, the American-born royal governor of Massachusetts. Hutchinson emphatically rejected the idea of "two independent legislatures in one and the same state." He told the Massachusetts assembly, "I know of no line that can be drawn between the supreme authority of Parliament and the total independence of the colonies."

There the matter rested. The British had twice imposed revenue acts on the colonies, and American Patriots had twice forced a retreat. If Parliament

insisted on a policy of constitutional absolutism by imposing taxes a third time, some Americans were prepared to pursue violent resistance. Nor did they flinch when reminded that George III condemned their agitation. As the Massachusetts House replied to Hutchinson, "There is more reason to dread the consequences of absolute uncontrolled supreme power, whether of a nation or a monarch, than those of total independence." Fearful of civil war, Lord North's ministry hesitated to force the issue.

TRACE CHANGE OVER TIME
What was Benjamin Franklin's position on colonial representation in 1765, and why had his view changed by 1770?

The Road to Independence, 1771–1776

Repeal of the Townshend duties in 1770 restored harmony to the British Empire, but strong feelings and mutual distrust lay just below the surface. In 1773, those emotions erupted, destroying any hope of compromise. Within two years, the Americans and the British clashed in armed conflict. Despite widespread resistance among loyal colonists, Patriot legislators created provisional governments and military forces, the two essentials for independence.

A Compromise Repudiated

Once aroused, political passions are not easily quieted. In Boston, Samuel Adams and other radical Patriots continued to warn Americans of imperial domination and, late in 1772, persuaded the town meeting to set up a committee of correspondence "to state the Rights of the Colonists of this Province." Soon, eighty Massachusetts towns had similar committees. When British officials threatened to seize the Americans responsible for the burning of the customs vessel *Gaspée* and prosecute them in Britain, the Virginia House of Burgesses and several other assemblies set up their own **committees of correspondence**. These standing committees allowed Patriots to communicate with leaders in other colonies when new threats to liberty occurred. By 1774, among the colonies that would later declare independence, only Pennsylvania was without one.

The East India Company and the Tea Act These committees sprang into action when Parliament passed the **Tea Act of May 1773**. The act provided financial relief for the East India Company, a royally chartered private corporation that served as the instrument of British imperialism. The company was deeply in debt; it also had a huge surplus of tea as a result of high import duties, which led Britons and colonists alike to drink smuggled Dutch tea instead. The Tea Act gave the company a government loan and, to boost its revenue, canceled the import duties on tea the company exported to Ireland and the American colonies. Now even with the Townshend duty of 3 pence a pound on tea, high-quality East India Company tea would cost less than the Dutch tea smuggled into the colonies by American merchants.

> **UNDERSTAND POINTS OF VIEW**
> Why did colonists react so strongly against the Tea Act, which imposed a small tax and actually lowered the price of tea?

Radical Patriots accused the British ministry of bribing Americans with the cheaper East India Company's tea so they would give up their principled opposition to the tea tax. As an anonymous woman wrote to the *Massachusetts Spy*, "The use of [British] tea is considered not as a private but as a public evil . . . a handle to introduce a variety of . . . oppressions amongst us." Merchants joined the protest because the East India Company planned to distribute its tea directly to shopkeepers, excluding American wholesalers from the trade's profits. "The fear of an Introduction of a Monopoly in this Country," British general Frederick Haldimand reported from New York, "has induced the mercantile part of the Inhabitants to be very industrious in opposing this Step and added Strength to a Spirit of Independence already too prevalent."

The Tea Party and the Coercive Acts The Sons of Liberty prevented East India Company ships from delivering their cargoes in New York, Philadelphia, and Charleston. In Massachusetts, Royal Governor Hutchinson was determined to land the tea and collect the tax. To foil the governor's plan, artisans and laborers disguised as Indians boarded three ships — the *Dartmouth*, the *Eleanor*, and the *Beaver* — on December 16, 1773, broke open 342 chests of tea (valued at about £10,000, or about $900,000 today), and threw them into the harbor. "This destruction of the Tea . . . must have so important Consequences," John Adams wrote in his diary, "that I cannot but consider it as an Epoch in History."

The king was outraged. "Concessions have made matters worse," George III declared. "The time has come for compulsion." Early in 1774, Parliament passed four **Coercive Acts** to force Massachusetts to pay for the tea and to submit to imperial authority. The Boston Port Bill closed Boston Harbor to shipping; the Massachusetts Government Act annulled the colony's charter and prohibited most town meetings; a new Quartering Act mandated new barracks for British troops; and the Justice Act allowed trials for capital crimes to be transferred to other colonies or to Britain.

Patriot leaders throughout the colonies branded the measures "Intolerable" and rallied support for Massachusetts. In Georgia, a Patriot warned the "Freemen of the Province" that "every privilege you at present claim as a birthright, may be wrested from you by the same authority that blockades the town of Boston." "The cause of Boston," George Washington declared in Virginia, "now is and ever will be considered as the cause of America." The committees of correspondence had created a firm sense of Patriot unity.

The Boston Tea Party
Led by radical Patriots disguised as Mohawk Indians, Bostonians dumped the East India Company's taxed tea into the harbor. The rioters made clear their "pure" political motives by punishing those who sought personal gain: one Son of Liberty who stole some of the tea was "stripped of his booty and his clothes together, and sent home naked." Library of Congress.

In 1774, Parliament also passed the Quebec Act, which allowed the practice of Roman Catholicism in Quebec. This concession to Quebec's predominantly Catholic population reignited religious passions in New England, where Protestants associated Catholicism with arbitrary royal government. Because the act extended Quebec's boundaries into the Ohio River Valley, it likewise angered influential land speculators in Virginia and Pennsylvania and ordinary settlers by the thousands (Map 5.4). Although the ministry did not intend the Quebec Act as a coercive measure, many colonists saw it as further proof of Parliament's intention to control American affairs.

The Continental Congress Responds

In response to the Coercive Acts, Patriot leaders convened a new continent-wide body, the **Continental Congress**. Twelve mainland colonies sent representatives. Four recently acquired colonies — Florida, Quebec, Nova Scotia, and Newfoundland — refused to send delegates, as did Georgia, where the royal governor controlled the legislature. The assemblies of Barbados, Jamaica, and the other sugar islands, although wary of British domination, were even more fearful of revolts by their predominantly African populations and therefore declined to attend.

The delegates who met in Philadelphia in September 1774 had different agendas. Southern representatives, fearing a British plot "to overturn the constitution and introduce a system of arbitrary government," advocated a new economic boycott. Independence-minded representatives from New England demanded political union and defensive military preparations. Many delegates from the Middle Atlantic colonies favored compromise.

Led by Joseph Galloway of Pennsylvania, these men of "loyal principles" proposed a new political system similar to Benjamin Franklin's proposal at the Albany Congress of 1754: each colony would retain its assembly to legislate on local matters, and a new continent-wide body would handle general American affairs. The king would appoint a president-general to preside over a legislative council selected by the colonial assemblies. Galloway's plan failed by a single vote; a bare majority thought it was too conciliatory (American Voices, p. 172).

Instead, the delegates demanded the repeal of the Coercive Acts and stipulated that British control

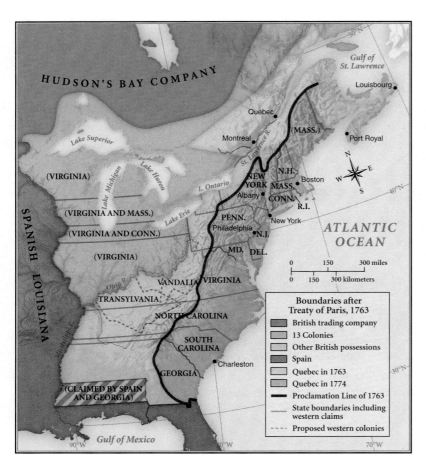

MAP 5.4

British Western Policy, 1763–1774

The Proclamation of 1763 prohibited white settlement west of the Appalachian Mountains. Nonetheless, Anglo-American settlers and land speculators proposed the new colonies of Vandalia and Transylvania to the west of Virginia and North Carolina. The Quebec Act of 1774 designated most western lands as Indian reserves and vastly enlarged the boundaries of Quebec, dashing speculators' hopes and eliminating the old sea-to-sea land claims of many seaboard colonies. The act especially angered New England Protestants, who condemned it for allowing French residents to practice Catholicism, and colonial political leaders, who protested its failure to provide Quebec with a representative assembly.

be limited to matters of trade. It also approved a program of economic retaliation: Americans would stop importing British goods in December 1774. If Parliament did not repeal the Coercive Acts by September 1775, the Congress vowed to cut off virtually all colonial exports to Britain, Ireland, and the British West Indies. Ten years of constitutional conflict had culminated in a threat of all-out commercial warfare.

> **COMPARE AND CONTRAST**
>
> Why did Parliament prefer North's solution to the Boston Tea Party to William Pitt's?

A few British leaders still hoped for compromise. In January 1775, William Pitt, now sitting in the House of Lords as the Earl of Chatham, asked Parliament to renounce its power to tax the colonies and to recognize the Continental Congress as a lawful body. In return, he suggested, the Congress should acknowledge parliamentary supremacy and provide a permanent source of revenue to help defray the national debt.

The British ministry rejected Pitt's plan. Twice it had backed down in the face of colonial resistance; a third retreat was impossible. Branding the Continental Congress an illegal assembly, the ministry rejected Lord Dartmouth's proposal to send commissioners to negotiate a settlement. Instead, Lord North set stringent terms: Americans must pay for their own defense and administration and acknowledge Parliament's authority to tax them. To put teeth in these demands, North imposed a naval blockade on American trade with foreign nations and ordered General Gage to suppress dissent in Massachusetts. "Now the case seemed desperate," the prime minister told Thomas Hutchinson, whom the Patriots had forced into exile in London. "Parliament would not — could not — concede. For aught he could see it must come to violence."

The Rising of the Countryside

The fate of the urban-led Patriot movement would depend on the colonies' large rural population. Most farmers had little interest in imperial affairs. Their lives were deeply rooted in the soil, and their prime allegiance was to family and community. But imperial policies had increasingly intruded into the lives of farm families by sending their sons to war and raising their taxes. In 1754, farmers on Long Island, New York, had paid an average tax of 10 shillings; by 1756, thanks to the Great War for Empire, their taxes had jumped to 30 shillings.

The Continental Association   The boycotts of 1765 and 1768 raised the political consciousness of rural Americans. When the First Continental Congress established the **Continental Association** in 1774 to enforce a third boycott of British goods, it quickly set up a rural network of committees to do its work. In Concord, Massachusetts, 80 percent of the male heads of families and a number of single women signed a "Solemn League and Covenant" supporting nonimportation. In other farm towns, men blacked their faces, disguised themselves in blankets "like Indians," and threatened violence against shopkeepers who traded "in rum, molasses, & Sugar, &c." in violation of the boycott.

Patriots likewise warned that British measures threatened the yeoman tradition of landownership. In Petersham, Massachusetts, the town meeting worried that new British taxes would drain "this People of the Fruits of their Toil." Arable land was now scarce and expensive in older communities, and in new settlements merchants were seizing farmsteads for delinquent debts. By the 1770s, many northern yeomen felt personally threatened by British policies, which, a Patriot pamphlet warned, were "paving the way for reducing the country to lordships" (Table 5.3).

Southern Planters Fear Dependency   Despite their higher standard of living, southern slave owners had similar fears. Many Chesapeake planters were deeply in debt to British merchants. Accustomed to being absolute masters on their slave-labor plantations and seeing themselves as guardians of English liberties, planters resented their financial dependence on British creditors and dreaded the prospect of political subservience to British officials.

That danger now seemed real. If Parliament used the Coercive Acts to subdue Massachusetts, then it might turn next to Virginia, dissolving its representative assembly and assisting British merchants to seize debt-burdened properties. Consequently, the Virginia gentry supported demands by indebted yeomen farmers to close the law courts so that they could bargain with merchants over debts without the threat of legal action. "The spark of liberty is not yet extinct among our people," declared one planter, "and if properly

TABLE 5.3		
Patriot Resistance, 1762–1776		
Date	**British Action**	**Patriot Response**
1762	Revenue Act	Merchants complain privately
1763	Proclamation Line	Land speculators voice discontent
1764	Sugar Act	Merchants and Massachusetts legislature protest
1765	Stamp Act	Sons of Liberty riot; Stamp Act Congress; first boycott of British goods
1765	Quartering Act	New York assembly refuses to fund until 1767
1767–1768	Townshend Act; military occupation of Boston	Second boycott of British goods; harassment of pro-British merchants
1772	Royal commission to investigate *Gaspée* affair	Committees of correspondence form
1773	Tea Act	Widespread resistance; Boston Tea Party
1774	Coercive Acts; Quebec Act	First Continental Congress; third boycott of British goods
1775	British raids near Boston; king's Proclamation for Suppressing Rebellion and Sedition	Armed resistance; Second Continental Congress; invasion of Canada; cutoff of colonial exports
1776	Military attacks led by royal governors in South	Paine's *Common Sense*; Declaration of Independence

The Debate over Representation and Sovereignty

Speaking before the House of Commons, Benjamin Franklin declared that before 1763 Americans had paid little attention to the question of Parliament's "right to lay taxes and duties" in the colonies. The reason was simple, Franklin said: "A right to lay internal taxes was never supposed to be in Parliament, as we are not represented there." Franklin recognized that representation was central to the imperial debate. As the following selections show, the failure to solve the problem of representation, and the closely related issue of parliamentary sovereignty, led to the American rebellion.

Jared Ingersoll
Report on the Debates in Parliament (1765)

Connecticut lawyer Jared Ingersoll (1722–1781) served as his colony's agent, or lobbyist, in Britain. In this 1765 letter to the governor of Connecticut, Ingersoll summarizes the debate then under way in Parliament over the Stamp Act. When the act passed, he returned home to become the stamp distributor in Connecticut. A mob forced him to resign that post. Ingersoll later served as a vice-admiralty judge in Philadelphia and, during the Revolution, remained loyal to Britain.

The principal Attention has been to the Stamp bill that has been preparing to Lay before Parliament for taxing America. The Point of the Authority of Parliament to impose such Tax I found on my Arrival here was so fully and Universally yielded [accepted], that there was not the least hopes of making any impressions that way. . . .

I beg leave to give you a Summary of the Arguments which are made use of in favour of such Authority. The House of Commons, say they, is a branch of the supreme legislature of the Nation, and which in its Nature is supposed to represent, or rather to stand in the place of, the Commons, that is, of the great body of the people. . . .

That this house of Commons, therefore, is now . . . a part of the Supreme unlimited power of the Nation, as in every State there must be some unlimited Power and Authority. . . .

They say a Power to tax is a necessary part of every Supreme Legislative Authority, and that if they have not that Power over America, they have none, and then America is at once a Kingdom of itself.

On the other hand those who oppose the bill say, it is true the Parliament have a supreme unlimited Authority over every Part and Branch of the Kings dominions and as well over Ireland as any other place.

Yet [they say] we believe a British parliament will never think it prudent to tax Ireland [or America]. Tis true they say, that the Commons of England and of the British Empire are all represented in and by the house of Commons, but this representation is confessedly on all hands by Construction and Virtual [because most British subjects] . . . have no hand in choosing the representatives. . . .

[They say further] that the Effects of this implied Representation here and in America must be infinitely different in the Article of Taxation. . . . By any Mistake an act of Parliament is made that prove injurious and hard the Member of Parliament here [in Britain] sees with his own Eyes and is moreover very accessible to the people. . . . [Also,] the taxes are laid equally by one Rule and fall as well on the Member himself as on the people. But as to America, from the great distance in point of Situation [they are not represented in the same way]. . . .

[Finally, the opponents of the Act say] we already by the Regulations upon their trade draw from the Americans all that they can spare. . . . This Step [of taxation] should not take place until or unless the Americans are allowed to send Members to Parliament.

Thus I have given you, I think, the Substance of the Arguments on both sides of that great and important Question of the right and also of the Expediency of taxing America by Authority of Parliament. . . . [But] upon a Division of the house upon the Question, there was about 250 to about 50 in favour of the Bill.

Source: New Haven Colony Historical Society, *Papers* (1918), 9: 306–315.

Joseph Galloway
Plan of Union (1775)

Speaker of the Pennsylvania assembly Joseph Galloway was a delegate to the First Continental Congress, where he proposed a plan that addressed the issue of representation. The colonies would remain British but operate under a continental government with the power to veto parliamentary laws that affected America. Radical Patriots in the Congress, who favored independence, prevented a vote on Galloway's plan and suppressed mention of it in the records. Galloway remained loyal to the crown, fought on the British side in the War for Independence, and moved to England in 1778.

If we sincerely mean to accommodate the difference between the two countries, . . . we must take into consideration a number of facts which led the Parliament to pass the acts complained of. . . . [You will recall] the dangerous situation of the Colonies from the intrigues of France, and the incursions of the Canadians and their Indian allies, at the commencement of the last war. . . . Great-Britain sent over her fleets and armies for their protection. . . .

In this state of the Colonies, it was not unreasonable to expect that Parliament would have levied a tax on them proportionate to their wealth, . . . Parliament was naturally led to exercise the power which had been, by its predecessors, so often exercised over the Colonies, and to pass the Stamp Act. Against this act, the Colonies petitioned Parliament, and denied its authority . . . [declaring] that the Colonies could not be represented in that body. This justly alarmed the British Senate. It was thought and called by the ablest men [in] Britain, a clear and explicit declaration of the American Independence, and compelled the Parliament to pass the Declaratory Act, in order to save its ancient and incontrovertible right of supremacy over all the parts of the empire. . . .

Having thus briefly stated the arguments in favour of parliamentary authority, . . . I am free to confess that the exercise of that authority is not perfectly constitutional in respect to the Colonies. We know that the whole landed interest of Britain is represented in that body, while neither the land nor the people of America hold the least participation in the legislative authority of the State. . . . Representation, or a participation in the supreme councils of the State, is the great principle upon which the freedom of the British Government is established and secured.

I wish to see . . . the right to participate in the supreme councils of the State extended, in some form . . . to America . . . [and therefore] have prepared the draught of a plan for uniting America more intimately, in constitutional policy, with Great-Britain. . . . I am certain when dispassionately considered, it will be found to be the most perfect union in power and liberty with the Parent State, next to a representation in Parliament, and I trust it will be approved of by both countries.

The Plan

That the several [colonial] assemblies shall [form an American union and] choose members for the grand council. . . .

That the Grand Council . . . shall hold and exercise all the like rights, liberties and privileges, as are held and exercised by and in the House of Commons of Great-Britain. . . .

That the President-General shall hold his office during the pleasure of the King, and his assent shall be requisite to all acts of the Grand Council, and it shall be his office and duty to cause them to be carried into execution. . . .

That the President-General, by and with the advice and consent of the Grand-Council, hold and exercise all the legislative rights, powers, and authorities, necessary for regulating and administering all the general police and affairs of the colonies. . . .

That the said President-General and the Grand Council, be an inferior and distinct branch of the British legislature, united and incorporated with it, . . . and that the assent of both [Parliament and the Grand Council] shall be requisite to the validity of all such general acts or statutes [that affect the colonies].

Source: Joseph Galloway, *Historical and Political Reflections on the Rise and Progress of the American Rebellion* (London, 1780), 70.

ANALYZING THE EVIDENCE

1. According to Ingersoll, what were the main arguments of those in Parliament who opposed the Stamp Act? Did those opposing the Stamp Act agree with the act's supporters that Parliament had the right to tax the colonies?

2. How did Galloway's plan solve the problem of colonial representation in Parliament? How would the British ministers who advocated parliamentary supremacy have reacted to the plan?

3. The framers of the U.S. Constitution addressed the problem of dividing authority between state governments and the national government by allowing the states to retain legal authority over most matters and delegating limited powers to the national government. Could such a solution have been implemented in the British Empire? Why or why not?

fanned by the Gentlemen of influence will, I make no doubt, burst out again into a flame."

Loyalists and Neutrals

Yet in many places, the Patriot movement was a hard sell. In Virginia, Patriot leaders were nearly all wealthy planters, and many of their poorer neighbors regarded the movement with suspicion. In regions where great landowners became Patriots — the Hudson River Valley of New York, for example — many tenant farmers supported the king because they hated their landlords. Similar social conflicts prompted some Regulators in the North Carolina backcountry and many farmers in eastern Maryland to oppose the Patriots there.

There were many reasons to resist the Patriot movement. Skeptics believed that Patriot leaders were subverting British rule only to advance their own selfish interests. Peter Oliver wrote of Samuel Adams, for example, "He was so thorough a Machiavilian, that he divested himself of every worthy Principle, & would stick at no Crime to accomplish his Ends." Some "Gentlemen of influence" worried that resistance to Britain would undermine all political institutions and "introduce Anarchy and disorder and render life and property here precarious." Their fears increased when the Sons of Liberty used intimidation and violence to uphold the boycotts. One well-to-do New Yorker complained, "No man can be in a more abject state of bondage than he whose Reputation, Property and Life are exposed to the discretionary violence . . . of the community." As the crisis deepened, such men became Loyalists — so called because they remained loyal to the British crown.

Many other colonists simply hoped to stay out of the fray. Some did so on principle: in New Jersey and Pennsylvania, thousands of pacifist Quakers and Germans resisted conscription and violence out of religious conviction. Others were ambivalent or confused about the political crisis unfolding around them. The delegate elected to New York's Provincial Congress from Queen's County, on Long Island, chose not to attend since "the people [he represented] seemed to be much inclined to remain peaceable and quiet." More than three-fourths of Queen's County voters, in fact, opposed sending any delegate at all. Many loyal or neutral colonists hoped, above all, to preserve their families' property and independence, whatever the outcome of the imperial crisis.

Historians estimate that some 15 to 20 percent of the white population — perhaps as many as 400,000 colonists — were loyal to the crown. Some managed to avoid persecution, but many were pressured by their neighbors to join the boycotts and subjected to violence and humiliation if they refused. As Patriots took over the reins of local government throughout the colonies, Loyalists were driven out of their homes or forced into silence. At this crucial juncture, Patriots commanded the allegiance, or at least the acquiescence, of the majority of white Americans.

Violence East and West

By 1774, British authority was wavering. At the headwaters of the Ohio, the abandonment of Fort Pitt left a power vacuum that was filled by opportunistic men, led by a royally appointed governor acting in defiance of his commission. In Massachusetts, the attempt to isolate and punish Boston and the surrounding countryside backfired as Patriots resisted military coercion. Violence resulted in both places, and with it the collapse of imperial control.

Lord Dunmore's War

In the years since the end of Pontiac's Rebellion, at least 10,000 people had traveled along Braddock's and Forbes's Roads to the headwaters of the Ohio River, where Fort Pitt had replaced Fort Duquesne during the Great War for Empire, and staked claims to land around Pittsburgh (Map 5.5). They relied for protection on Fort Pitt, which remained one of Britain's most important frontier outposts. But the revenue crisis forced General Gage to cut expenses, and in October 1772, the army pulled down the fort's log walls and left the site to the local population. Settler relations with the neighboring Ohio Indians were tenuous and ill-defined, and the fort's abandonment left them exposed and vulnerable.

In the ensuing power vacuum, Pennsylvania and Virginia both claimed the region. Pennsylvania had the better claim on paper. It had organized county governments, established courts, and collected taxes there. But — in keeping with its pacifist Quaker roots — it did not organize a militia. In this decision, Virginia's royal governor, the Earl of Dunmore, recognized an opportunity. Appointed to his post in 1771, Dunmore was an irascible and unscrupulous man who clashed repeatedly with the House of Burgesses. But when it suited him, he was just as willing to defy the crown. In 1773, he traveled to Pittsburgh, where, he later wrote, "the people flocked about me and beseeched me . . . to

MAP 5.5

The Ohio Country, 1774–1775

The erosion of British imperial authority caused chaos in the Ohio country. Pennsylvania and Virginia each claimed Pittsburgh and the surrounding countryside, while the Indian communities on the upper Ohio increasingly feared colonist aggression. Their fears were realized in the summer of 1774, when Lord Dunmore led a force of Virginia militia into the valley. After defeating a Shawnee force in the Battle of Point Pleasant, many Virginians began surveying and staking claims to land in the Kentucky bluegrass. In the summer of 1775, perhaps a dozen new towns were settled there, in violation of the Royal Proclamation of 1763 and the Quebec Act of 1774.

appoint magistrates and officers of militia." He organized a local militia; soon, men armed by Virginia were drilling near the ruins of Fort Pitt.

In the summer of 1774, Dunmore took the next step. In defiance of both his royal instructions and the House of Burgesses, he called out Virginia's militia and led a force of 2,400 men against the Ohio Shawnees, who had a long-standing claim to Kentucky as a hunting ground. They fought a single battle, at Point Pleasant; the Shawnees were defeated, and Dunmore and his militia forces claimed Kentucky as their own. A participant justified his actions shortly afterward: "When without a king," he wrote, "[one] doeth according to the freedom of his own will." Years of neglect left many colonists in the backcountry feeling abandoned by the crown. **Dunmore's War** was their declaration of independence.

Armed Resistance in Massachusetts

Meanwhile, as the Continental Congress gathered in Philadelphia in September 1774, Massachusetts was also defying British authority. In August, a Middlesex County Congress had urged Patriots to close the existing royal courts and to transfer their political allegiance to the popularly elected House of Representatives. Subsequently, armed crowds harassed Loyalists and ensured Patriot rule in most of New England.

In response, General Thomas Gage, now the military governor of Massachusetts, ordered British troops in Boston in September 1774 to seize Patriot armories

in nearby Charlestown and Cambridge. An army of 20,000 militiamen quickly mobilized to safeguard other Massachusetts military depots. The Concord town meeting raised a defensive force, the famous **Minutemen**, to "Stand at a minutes warning in Case of alarm." Increasingly, Gage's authority was limited to Boston, where it rested on the bayonets of his 3,500 troops. Meanwhile, the Patriot-controlled Massachusetts assembly met in nearby Salem in open defiance of Parliament, collecting taxes, bolstering the militia, and assuming the responsibilities of government.

In London, the colonial secretary, Lord Dartmouth, proclaimed Massachusetts to be in "open rebellion" and ordered Gage to march against the "rude rabble." On the night of April 18, 1775, Gage dispatched 700 soldiers to capture colonial leaders and supplies at Concord. However, Paul Revere and a series of other riders warned Patriots in many towns, and at dawn, militiamen confronted the British regulars first at Lexington and then at Concord. Those first skirmishes took a handful of lives, but as the British retreated to Boston, militia from neighboring towns repeatedly ambushed them. By the end of the day, 73 British soldiers were dead, 174 wounded, and 26 missing. British fire had killed 49 Massachusetts militiamen and wounded 39. Twelve years of economic and constitutional conflict had ended in violence.

> **PLACE EVENTS IN CONTEXT**
> What led to Dunmore's War, and why did western settlers support it?

The Second Continental Congress Organizes for War

A month later, in May 1775, Patriot leaders gathered in Philadelphia for the **Second Continental Congress**. As the Congress opened, 3,000 British troops attacked American fortifications on Breed's Hill and Bunker Hill overlooking Boston. After three assaults and 1,000 casualties, they finally dislodged the Patriot militia. Inspired by his countrymen's valor, John Adams exhorted the Congress to rise to the "defense of American liberty" by creating a continental army. He nominated George Washington to lead it. After bitter debate, the Congress approved the proposals, but, Adams lamented, only "by bare majorities."

Congress Versus King George   Despite the bloodshed in Massachusetts, a majority in the Congress still hoped for reconciliation. Led by John Dickinson of Pennsylvania, these moderates won approval of a petition expressing loyalty to George III and asking for repeal of oppressive parliamentary legislation. But Samuel Adams, Patrick Henry, and other zealous Patriots drummed up support for a Declaration of the Causes and Necessities of Taking Up Arms. Americans dreaded the "calamities of civil war," the declaration asserted, but were "resolved to die Freemen rather than to live [as] slaves." George III failed to exploit the divisions among the Patriots; instead, in August 1775, he issued a Proclamation for Suppressing Rebellion and Sedition.

Before the king's proclamation reached America, the radicals in the Congress had won support for an invasion of Canada to prevent a British attack from the north. Patriot forces easily defeated the British at Montreal; but in December 1775, they failed to capture Quebec City and withdrew. Meanwhile, American merchants waged the financial warfare promised at the First Continental Congress by cutting off exports to Britain and its West Indian sugar islands. Parliament retaliated with the Prohibitory Act, which outlawed all trade with the rebellious colonies.

EXPLAIN CONSEQUENCES
How did the violence around Boston in the spring of 1775 affect proceedings in the Second Continental Congress?

Fighting in the South   Skirmishes between Patriot and Loyalist forces now broke out in the southern colonies. In Virginia, Patriots ousted Governor Dunmore and forced him to take refuge on a British warship in Chesapeake Bay. Branding the rebels "traitors," the governor organized two military forces: one white, the

George III, 1771

King George III was a young man of twenty-seven when the American troubles began in 1765. Six years later, as this portrait by Johann Zoffany suggests, the king had aged. Initially, George had been headstrong and tried to impose his will on Parliament, but he succeeded only in generating political confusion and inept policy. He strongly supported Parliament's attempts to tax the colonies and continued the war in America long after most of his ministers agreed that it had been lost. The Royal Collection © 2011 Her Majesty Queen Elizabeth II/The Bridgeman Art Library.

Queen's Own Loyal Virginians; and one black, the Ethiopian Regiment, which enlisted 1,000 slaves who had fled their Patriot owners. In November 1775, Dunmore issued a controversial proclamation promising freedom to black slaves and white indentured servants who joined the Loyalist cause. White planters denounced this "Diabolical scheme," claiming it "point[ed] a dagger to their Throats." A new rising of the black and white underclasses, as in Bacon's Rebellion in the 1670s, seemed a possibility. In Fincastle County in southwestern Virginia, Loyalist planter John Hiell urged workers to support the king, promising "a Servant man" that soon "he and all the negroes would get their freedom." Frightened by Dunmore's aggressive tactics, Patriot yeomen and tenants called for a final break with Britain.

In North Carolina, too, military clashes prompted demands for independence. Early in 1776, Josiah Martin, the colony's royal governor, raised a Loyalist force of 1,500 Scottish Highlanders in the backcountry. In response, Patriots mobilized the lowcountry militia and, in February, defeated Martin's army at the Battle of Moore's Creek Bridge, capturing more than 800 Highlanders. Following this victory, radical Patriots in the North Carolina assembly told its representatives to the Continental Congress to join with "other Colonies in declaring Independence, and forming foreign alliances." In May, the Virginia gentry followed suit: led by James Madison, Edmund Pendleton, and Patrick Henry, the Patriots met in convention and resolved unanimously to support independence.

Occupying Kentucky   Beginning in the spring of 1775, in the wake of Dunmore's War, independent parties of adventurers began to occupy the newly won lands of Kentucky. Daniel Boone led one group to the banks of the Kentucky River, where they established the town of Boonesborough; nearby was Lexington, named in honor of the Massachusetts town that had resisted the redcoats a few months earlier. The Shawnees and other Ohio Indians opposed the settlers, and colonists built their tiny towns in the form of stations to protect themselves — groups of cabins connected by palisades to form small forts.

These western settlers had confused political loyalties. Many had marched under Dunmore and hoped to receive recognition for their claims from the crown. But as the rebellion unfolded, most recognized that the Patriots' emphasis on liberty and equality squared with their view of the world. They soon petitioned Virginia's rebel government, asking it to create a new county that would include the Kentucky settlements. They had "Fought and bled" for the land in Dunmore's War and now wanted to fight against the crown and its Indian allies in the Ohio country. Virginia agreed: in 1776, it organized six new frontier counties and sent arms and ammunition to Kentucky. In July, the Continental Congress followed suit, dispatching troops and arms to the Ohio River as well.

Thomas Paine's *Common Sense*

As military conflicts escalated, Americans were divided in their opinions of King George III. Many blamed him for supporting oppressive legislation and ordering armed retaliation, but other influential colonists held out the hope that he might mediate their conflict with Parliament. John Dickinson, whose *Letters* did so much to arouse Patriot resistance in 1768, nevertheless believed that war with Great Britain would be folly. In July 1775, he persuaded Congress to send George III the Olive Branch Petition, which pleaded with the king to negotiate. John Adams, a staunch supporter of independence, was infuriated by Dickinson's waffling. But Dickinson had many supporters, both inside and outside of Congress. For example, many of Philadelphia's Quaker and Anglican merchants were neutrals or Loyalists. In response to their passivity, Patriot artisans in the city organized a Mechanics' Association to protect America's "just Rights and Privileges."

Daniel Boone Escorting Settlers Through the Cumberland Gap

In 1775 Daniel Boone led a group of prospective settlers into Kentucky on behalf of Richard Henderson, a North Carolina judge and self-appointed proprietor of a land speculation venture called the Transylvania Colony. Henderson's venture soon collapsed, but Boonesborough was one of perhaps a dozen towns founded in Kentucky in violation of crown policy that summer. Boone became a folk hero, and in the mid-nineteenth century George Caleb Bingham painted this memorable scene. Using biblical imagery (the woman on horseback recalls Mary riding into Bethlehem on a donkey) and dramatic lighting, Bingham portrays Boone as an agent of progress bringing civilization to a howling and dangerous wilderness. George Caleb Bingham, Daniel Boone Escorting Settlers Through the Cumberland Gap, 1851–52. Oil on Canvas, 36½ x 50¼". Washington University Art Gallery, St. Louis. Gift of Nathanial Phillips, 1890.

With popular sentiment in flux, a single brief pamphlet helped tip the balance. In January 1776, Thomas Paine published *Common Sense*, a rousing call for independence and a republican form of government. Paine had served as a minor customs official in England until he was fired for joining a protest against low wages. In 1774, Paine migrated to Philadelphia, where he met Benjamin Rush and other Patriots who shared his republican sentiments.

In *Common Sense*, Paine assaulted the traditional monarchical order in stirring language. "Monarchy and hereditary succession have laid the world in blood and ashes," Paine proclaimed, leveling a personal attack at George III, "the hard hearted sullen Pharaoh of England." Mixing insults with biblical quotations, Paine blasted the British system of "mixed government" that balanced power among the three estates of king, lords, and commoners. Paine granted that the system "was noble for the dark and slavish times" of the past, but now it yielded only "monarchical tyranny in the person of the king" and "aristocratical tyranny in the persons of the peers."

Paine argued for American independence by turning the traditional metaphor of patriarchal authority on its head: "Is it the interest of a man to be a boy all his life?" he asked. Within six months, *Common Sense* had gone through twenty-five editions and reached hundreds of thousands of people. "There is great talk of independence," a worried New York Loyalist noted, "the unthinking multitude are mad for it. . . . A pamphlet called Common Sense has carried off . . .

thousands." Paine urged Americans to create independent republican states: "A government of our own is our natural right, 'tis time to part."

Independence Declared

Inspired by Paine's arguments and beset by armed Loyalists, Patriot conventions urged a break from Britain. In June 1776, Richard Henry Lee presented Virginia's resolution to the Continental Congress: "That these United Colonies are, and of right ought to be, free and independent states." Faced with certain defeat, staunch Loyalists and anti-independence moderates withdrew from the Congress, leaving committed Patriots to take the fateful step. On July 4, 1776, the Congress approved the **Declaration of Independence** (see Documents, p. D-1).

The Declaration's main author, Thomas Jefferson of Virginia, had mobilized resistance to the Coercive Acts with the pamphlet *A Summary View of the Rights of British America* (1774). Now, in the Declaration, he justified independence and republicanism to Americans and the world by vilifying George III: "He has plundered our seas, ravaged our coasts, burned our towns, and destroyed the lives of our people." Such a prince was a "tyrant," Jefferson concluded, and "is unfit to be the ruler of a free people."

Employing the ideas of the European Enlightenment, Jefferson proclaimed a series of "self-evident" truths: "that all men are created equal"; that they possess the "unalienable rights" of "Life, Liberty, and the pursuit

Independence Declared

In this painting by John Trumbull, Thomas Jefferson and the other drafters of the Declaration (John Adams of Massachusetts, Roger Sherman of Connecticut, Robert Livingston of New York, and Benjamin Franklin of Pennsylvania) present the document to John Hancock, the president of the Second Continental Congress. One Patriot observer reported that when the Declaration was read at a public meeting in New York City on July 10, a massive statue of George III was "pulled down by the Populace" and its 4,000 pounds of lead melted down to make "Musquet balls" for use against the British troops massed on Staten Island. Yale University Art Gallery/Art Resource, NY.

of Happiness"; that government derives its "just powers from the consent of the governed" and can rightly be overthrown if it "becomes destructive of these ends." By linking these doctrines of individual liberty, **popular sovereignty** (the principle that ultimate power lies in the hands of the electorate), and republican government with American independence, Jefferson established them as the defining political values of the new nation.

For Jefferson, as for Paine, the pen proved mightier than the sword. The Declaration won wide support in France and Germany; at home, it sparked celebrations in rural hamlets and seaport cities, as crowds burned effigies and toppled statues of the king. On July 8, 1776, in Easton, Pennsylvania, a "great number of spectators" heard a reading of the Declaration, "gave their hearty assent with three loud huzzahs, and cried out, 'May God long preserve and unite the Free and Independent States of America.'"

SUMMARY

Chapters 4 and 5 have focused on a short span of time—a mere two decades—and outlined the plot of a political drama. Act I of that drama, the Great War for Empire discussed in Chapter 4, prompted British political leaders to implement a program of imperial reform and taxation. Act II, discussed in this chapter, is full of dramatic action, as colonial mobs riot, colonists chafe against restrictions on western lands, Patriot pamphleteers articulate ideologies of resistance, and British ministers search for compromise between claims of parliamentary sovereignty and assertions of colonial autonomy. Act III takes the form of tragedy: the once-proud British Empire dissolves into civil war, an imminent nightmare of death and destruction.

Why did this happen? More than two centuries later, the answers still are not clear. Certainly, the lack of astute leadership in Britain was a major factor. But British leaders faced circumstances that limited their actions: a huge national debt and deep commitments to both a powerful fiscal-military state and the absolute supremacy of Parliament. Moreover, in America, decades of salutary neglect strengthened Patriots' demands for political autonomy and economic opportunity. Artisans, farmers, and aspiring western settlers all feared an oppressive new era in imperial relations. The trajectories of their conflicting intentions and ideas placed Britain and its American possessions on course for a disastrous and fatal collision.

CHAPTER REVIEW

MAKE IT STICK   Go to **LearningCurve** to retain what you've read.

TERMS TO KNOW   Identify and explain the significance of each term below.

Key Concepts and Events

Sugar Act of 1764 (p. 155)
vice-admiralty courts (p. 156)
Stamp Act of 1765 (p. 157)
virtual representation (p. 157)
Quartering Act of 1765 (p. 157)
Stamp Act Congress (p. 158)
Sons of Liberty (p. 158)
English common law (p. 159)
natural rights (p. 159)
Declaratory Act of 1766 (p. 160)
Townshend Act of 1767 (p. 161)
nonimportation movement (p. 161)

committees of correspondence (p. 168)
Tea Act of May 1773 (p. 168)
Coercive Acts (p. 168)
Continental Congress (p. 169)
Continental Association (p. 171)
Dunmore's War (p. 175)
Minutemen (p. 175)
Second Continental Congress (p. 176)
Declaration of Independence (p. 178)
popular sovereignty (p. 179)

Key People

George Grenville (p. 155)
John Dickinson (p. 159)
Charles Townshend (p. 160)
Lord North (p. 166)
Samuel Adams (p. 166)
Lord Dunmore (p. 174)
Thomas Paine (p. 178)
Thomas Jefferson (p. 178)

REVIEW QUESTIONS
Answer these questions to demonstrate your understanding of the chapter's main ideas.

1. As British administrators sought to increase colonial revenues and tighten administrative control, what might have led them to pursue a less confrontational course with the colonies? What factors do you think are most important in explaining the failure of compromise?

2. What kinds of provocation caused colonists to riot or otherwise act directly, even violently, in defense of their interests? How did common law, Enlightenment, and republican ideas shape their thinking as they took action?

3. What compromises were proposed in the colonies as alternatives to independence? Why did Patriots reject them?

4. **THEMATIC UNDERSTANDING** Consider the events listed under "Work, Exchange, and Technology" and "Politics and Power" for the period 1763–1776 on the thematic timeline on page 149. How important were the linkages between economic developments and political ones in these years?

MAKING CONNECTIONS
Recognize the larger developments and continuities within and across chapters by answering these questions.

1. **ACROSS TIME AND PLACE** Chapter 4 presented a turbulent era, marked by social and cultural conflict and imperial warfare, during which the regions of British North America were disparate and without unity. Yet by 1776 — only thirteen years after the Treaty of Paris ending the Great War for Empire — thirteen of Britain's mainland colonies were prepared to unite in a Declaration of Independence. What happened in that intervening time to strengthen and deepen colonists' sense of common cause? As they drew together to resist imperial authority, what political and cultural resources did they have in common?

2. **VISUAL EVIDENCE** Return to the Paul Revere engraving of the Boston Massacre on page 167. This image was an instrument of political propaganda. What features of the image are most important to its political purpose? Consider his depiction of both the soldiers and the townspeople. Look, too, at the buildings surrounding the crowd, especially the Custom House on the right. List the ways in which Revere invokes the idea of tyranny in this image.

MORE TO EXPLORE
Start here to learn more about the events discussed in this chapter.

David Armitage, *The Declaration of Independence: A Global History* (2007). Traces the international impact of the Declaration.

Jack P. Greene and J. R. Pole, eds., *A Companion to the American Revolution* (2000). A useful compendium of short essays on topics related to the Revolution.

Woody Holton, *Forced Founders* (1999). Considers the coming of the Revolution in Virginia.

Maya Jasanoff, *Liberty's Exiles* (2011). A compelling narrative of Loyalist experiences in the Revolution.

Andrew O'Shaughnessy, *The Men Who Lost America* (2013). A British view of the crisis.

Liberty! The American Revolution (PBS video) and its companion Web site: **pbs.org/ktca/liberty/**. A useful overview of the Revolutionary movement.

TIMELINE

Ask yourself why this chapter begins and ends with these dates and then identify the links among related events.

1763	• Proclamation Line limits white settlement
1764	• Sugar Act and Currency Act
	• Colonists oppose vice-admiralty courts
1765	• Stamp Act imposes direct tax
	• Quartering Act requires barracks for British troops
	• Stamp Act Congress meets
	• Americans boycott British goods
1766	• First compromise: Stamp Act repealed
	• Declaratory Act passed
1767	• Townshend duties
1768	• Second American boycott
1770	• Second compromise: partial repeal of Townshend Act
	• Boston Massacre
1772	• Committees of correspondence form
1773	• Tea Act leads to Boston Tea Party
1774	• Coercive Acts punish Massachusetts
	• Dunmore's War against the Shawnees
	• Continental Congress meets
	• Third American boycott
1775	• General Gage marches to Lexington and Concord
	• Second Continental Congress creates Continental army
	• Lord Dunmore recruits Loyalist slaves
	• Patriots invade Canada and skirmish with Loyalists in South
	• Western settlers occupy Kentucky
1776	• Thomas Paine's *Common Sense*
	• Declaration of Independence

KEY TURNING POINTS: The Boston Tea Party (1773), the Coercive Acts (1774), and the first Continental Congress (1774). What did Parliament hope to achieve with the Coercive Acts? How did the decision to convene a continent-wide congress demonstrate the failure of Parliament's efforts?

6

CHAPTER

Making War and Republican Governments
1776–1789

When Patriots in Frederick County, Maryland, demanded his allegiance to their cause in 1776, Robert Gassaway would have none of it. "It was better for the poor people to lay down their arms and pay the duties and taxes laid upon them by King and Parliament than to be brought into slavery and commanded and ordered about [by you]," he told them. The story was much the same in Farmington, Connecticut, where Patriot officials imprisoned Nathaniel Jones and seventeen other men for "remaining neutral." In Pennsylvania, Quakers accused of Loyalism were rounded up, jailed, and charged with treason, and some were hanged for aiding the British cause. Everywhere, the outbreak of fighting in 1776 forced families to choose the Loyalist or the Patriot side.

The Patriots' control of most local governments gave them an edge in this battle. Patriot leaders organized militia units and recruited volunteers for the Continental army, a ragtag force that surprisingly held its own on the battlefield. "I admire the American troops tremendously!" exclaimed a French officer. "It is incredible that soldiers composed of every age, even children of fifteen, of whites and blacks, almost naked, unpaid, and rather poorly fed, can march so well and withstand fire so steadfastly."

Military service created political commitment, and vice versa. Many Patriot leaders encouraged Americans not only to support the war but also to take an active role in government. As more people did so, their political identities changed. Previously, Americans had lived within a social world dominated by the links of family, kinship, and locality. Now, the abstract bonds of citizenship connected them directly to more distant institutions of government. "From subjects to citizens the difference is immense," remarked South Carolina Patriot David Ramsay. By repudiating monarchical rule and raising a democratic army, the Patriots launched the age of republican revolutions.

Soon republicanism would throw France into turmoil and inspire revolutionaries in Spain's American colonies. The independence of the Anglo-American colonies, remarked the Venezuelan political leader Francisco de Miranda, who had been in New York and Philadelphia at the end of the American Revolution, "was bound to be . . . the infallible preliminary to our own [independence movement]." The Patriot uprising of 1776 set in motion a process that gradually replaced an Atlantic colonial system that spanned the Americas with an American system of new nations.

IDENTIFY THE BIG IDEA

How revolutionary was the American Revolution? What political, social, and economic changes did it produce, and what stayed the same?

General Washington, 1780   By war's end, George Washington was a hero on both sides of the Atlantic. This engraving, printed in Paris in 1780, shows him with various British bills and declarations in tatters at his feet while he holds copies of the Declaration of Independence and the Treaty of Alliance with France. In the background of this vaguely Orientalized scene, a black slave—presumably William Lee, Washington's valet and constant companion during the Revolution—saddles his horse. Anne S. K. Brown Military Collection, Brown University Library.

The Trials of War, 1776–1778

The Declaration of Independence appeared just as the British launched a full-scale military assault. For two years, British troops manhandled the Continental army. A few inspiring American victories kept the rebellion alive, but during the winters of 1776 and 1777, the Patriot cause hung in the balance.

War in the North

Once the British resorted to military force, few Europeans gave the rebels a chance. The population of Great Britain was 11 million; the colonies, 2.5 million, 20 percent of whom were enslaved Africans. Moreover, the British government had access to the immense wealth generated by the South Atlantic System and the emerging Industrial Revolution. Britain also had the most powerful navy in the world, a standing army of 48,000 Britons plus thousands of German (Hessian) soldiers, and the support of thousands of American Loyalists and powerful Indian coalitions. In the Carolinas, the Cherokees resisted colonists' demands for their lands by allying with the British, as did four of the six Iroquois nations of New York (Map 6.1). In the Ohio country, Shawnees and their allies, armed by the British, attacked the new Kentucky settlements.

By contrast, the Americans were economically and militarily weak. They lacked a strong central government and a reliable source of tax revenue. Their new Continental army, commanded by General George Washington, consisted of 18,000 poorly trained and inexperienced recruits.

To demonstrate Britain's military superiority, the prime minister, Lord North, ordered General William Howe to capture New York City. His strategy was to seize control of the Hudson River and thereby isolate the radical Patriots in New England from the colonies to the south. As the Second Continental Congress declared independence in Philadelphia in July 1776, Howe landed 32,000 troops — British regulars and German mercenaries — outside New York City. In August 1776, Howe defeated the Americans in the **Battle of Long Island** and forced their retreat to Manhattan Island. There, Howe outflanked Washington's troops and nearly trapped them. Outgunned and outmaneuvered, the Continental army again retreated, eventually crossing the Hudson River to New Jersey.

UNDERSTAND POINTS OF VIEW
Why was control of New York City Britain's first military objective in the emerging war?

MAP 6.1
Patriot and Loyalist Strongholds

Patriots were in the majority in most of the thirteen mainland colonies and used their control of local governments to funnel men, money, and supplies to the rebel cause. Although Loyalists could be found in every colony, their strongholds were limited to Nova Scotia, eastern New York, New Jersey, and certain areas in the South. However, most Native American peoples favored the British cause and bolstered the power of Loyalist militias in central New York (see Map 6.3) and in the Carolina backcountry.

By December, the British army had pushed the rebels across New Jersey and over the Delaware River into Pennsylvania.

From the Patriots' perspective, winter came just in time. Following eighteenth-century custom, the British halted their military campaign for the cold months, allowing the Americans to catch them off guard. On Christmas night 1776, Washington crossed the Delaware River and staged a successful surprise attack on Trenton, New Jersey, where he forced the surrender of 1,000 German soldiers. In early January 1777, the Continental army won a small victory at nearby Princeton (Map 6.2). But these minor triumphs could

MAP 6.2
The War in the North, 1776–1777

In 1776, the British army drove Washington's forces across New Jersey into Pennsylvania. The Americans counterattacked successfully at Trenton and Princeton and then set up winter headquarters in Morristown. In 1777, British forces stayed on the offensive. General Howe attacked the Patriot capital, Philadelphia, from the south and captured it in early October. Meanwhile, General Burgoyne and Colonel St. Leger launched simultaneous invasions from Canada. With the help of thousands of New England militiamen, American troops commanded by General Horatio Gates defeated Burgoyne in August at Bennington, Vermont, and in October at Saratoga, New York, the military turning point in the war.

not mask British military superiority. "These are the times," wrote Thomas Paine, "that try men's souls."

Armies and Strategies

Thanks in part to General Howe, the rebellion survived. Howe had opposed the Coercive Acts of 1774 and still hoped for a political compromise. So he did not try to destroy the American army but instead tried to show its weakness and persuade the Continental

Congress to give up the struggle. Howe's restrained tactics cost Britain the opportunity to nip the rebellion in the bud. For his part, Washington acted cautiously to avoid a major defeat: "On our Side the War should be defensive," he told Congress. His strategy was to draw the British away from the seacoast, extend their lines of supply, and sap their morale.

Congress had promised Washington a regular force of 75,000 men, but the Continental army never reached even a third of that number. Yeomen, refusing to be

The Battle of Princeton

Black smoke from burning buildings partially obscures the sun as the muzzle flash from an American cannon lights up the battlefield. Pursued by Cornwallis after his surprise attack and victory at nearby Trenton, Washington (on horseback to the right of the flag) confronted three regiments of redcoats at Princeton. The Americans had an advantage in numbers and put the British to flight, but only after withstanding the bayonet charge depicted in the right-center of William Mercer's painting. Courtesy of the Historical Society of Pennsylvania Collection Atwater Kent Museum of Philadelphia.

"Haras'd with callouts" that took them away from their families and farms, would serve only in local militias. When the Virginia gentry imposed a military draft and three years of service on propertyless men — the "Lazy fellows who lurk about and are pests to Society" — they resisted so fiercely that the legislature had to pay them substantial bounties and agree to shorter terms of service. The Continental soldiers recruited in Maryland by General William Smallwood were poor American youths and older foreign-born men, often British ex-convicts and former indentured servants. Most enlisted for the $20 cash bonus (about $2,000 today) and the promise of 100 acres of land.

Molding such recruits into an effective fighting force was nearly impossible. Inexperienced soldiers panicked in the face of British attacks; thousands deserted, unwilling to submit to the discipline of military life. The soldiers who stayed resented the contempt their officers had for the "camp followers," the women who made do with the meager supplies provided to feed and care for the troops. General Philip Schuyler of New York complained that his troops were "destitute of provisions, without camp equipage, with little ammunition, and not a single piece of cannon."

The Continental army was not only poorly supplied but was also held in suspicion by Radical Whig Patriots, who believed that a standing army was a threat to liberty. Even in wartime, they preferred militias to a professional fighting force. Given these handicaps, Washington and his army were fortunate to have escaped an overwhelming defeat.

Victory at Saratoga

After Howe failed to achieve an overwhelming victory, Lord North and his colonial secretary, Lord George Germain, launched another major military campaign in 1777. Isolating New England remained the primary goal. To achieve it, Germain planned a three-pronged

IDENTIFY CAUSES

What factors made it difficult for the Continental Congress to create an effective army?

attack converging on Albany, New York. General John Burgoyne would lead a large contingent of regulars south from Quebec, Colonel Barry St. Leger and a force of Iroquois would attack from the west, and General Howe would lead troops north from New York City.

Howe instead decided to attack Philadelphia, the home of the Continental Congress, hoping to end the rebellion with a single decisive blow. But instead of marching quickly across New Jersey, Howe loaded his troops onto boats and sailed up the Chesapeake Bay to attack Philadelphia from the south. The plan worked. Howe's troops easily outflanked the American positions along Brandywine Creek in Delaware and, in late September, marched triumphantly into Philadelphia. However, the capture of the rebels' capital did not end the uprising; the Continental Congress, determined to continue the struggle, fled to the countryside.

Howe's slow campaign against Philadelphia contributed to the defeat of Burgoyne's army at **Saratoga**. Burgoyne's troops had at first advanced quickly, overwhelming the American defenses at Fort Ticonderoga in early July and driving south toward the Hudson River. Then they stalled. Burgoyne — nicknamed "Gentleman Johnny" — was used to high living and had fought in Europe in a leisurely fashion; believing his large army would easily dominate the rebels, he stopped early each day to pitch comfortable tents and eat elaborate dinners with his officers. The American troops led by General Horatio Gates also slowed Burgoyne's progress by felling huge trees in his path and raiding British supply lines to Canada.

At summer's end, Burgoyne's army of 6,000 British and German troops and 600 Loyalists and Indians was stuck near Saratoga, New York. Desperate for food and horses, in August the British raided nearby Bennington, Vermont, but were beaten back by 2,000 American militiamen. Patriot forces in the Mohawk Valley also threw St. Leger and the Iroquois into retreat. Making matters worse, the British commander in New York City recalled 4,000 troops he had sent toward Albany and ordered them to Philadelphia to bolster Howe's force. While Burgoyne waited in vain for help, thousands of Patriot militiamen from Massachusetts, New Hampshire, and New York joined Gates, blocking Burgoyne in a series of skirmishes that finally gave the British no avenue of escape. The Patriots "swarmed around the army like birds of prey," reported an English sergeant, and in October 1777, they forced Burgoyne to surrender.

The victory at Saratoga was the turning point of the war. The Patriots captured more than 5,000 British

Joseph Brant

Mohawk chief Thayendanegea, known to whites as Joseph Brant, was a devout member of the Church of England and helped to translate the Bible into the Mohawk language. Brant persuaded four of the six Iroquois nations to support Britain in the war. In 1778 and 1779, he led Iroquois warriors and Tory rangers in devastating attacks on American settlements in the Wyoming Valley of Pennsylvania and Cherry Valley in New York. In this 1797 portrait, artist Charles Willson Peale has portrayed Brant with European features. Independence National Historic Park.

troops and ensured the diplomatic success of American representatives in Paris, who won a military alliance with France.

The Perils of War

The Patriots' triumph at Saratoga was tempered by wartime difficulties. A British naval blockade cut off supplies of European manufactures and disrupted the New England fishing industry; meanwhile, the British occupation of Boston, New York, and Philadelphia reduced trade. As Patriots, along with unemployed artisans and laborers, moved to the countryside, New York City's population declined from 21,000 to 10,000. The British blockade cut tobacco exports in the Chesapeake, so planters grew grain to sell to the contending armies. All across the land, farmers and artisans adapted to a war economy.

With goods now scarce, governments requisitioned military supplies directly from the people. In 1776, Connecticut officials asked the citizens of Hartford to

American Militiamen
Beset by continuing shortages of cloth, the Patriot army dressed in a variety of uniforms and fabrics. This German engraving, taken from a drawing by a Hessian officer, shows two American militiamen (one of them barefoot) wearing hunting shirts and trousers made of ticking, the strong linen fabric often used to cover mattresses and pillows. Anne S. K. Brown Military Collection, Brown University.

provide 1,000 coats and 1,600 shirts, and soldiers echoed their pleas. After losing all his shirts "except the one on my back" in the Battle of Long Island, Captain Edward Rogers told his wife that "the making of Cloath . . . must go on." Patriot women responded; in Elizabeth, New Jersey, they promised "upwards of 100,000 yards of linnen and woolen cloth." Other women assumed the burdens of farmwork while their men were away at war and acquired a taste for decision making. "We have sow'd our oats as you desired," Sarah Cobb Paine wrote to her absent husband. "Had I been master I should have planted it to Corn." Their self-esteem boosted by wartime activities, some women expected greater legal rights in the new republican society.

Still, goods remained scarce and pricey. Hard-pressed consumers assailed shopkeepers as "enemies, extortioners, and monopolizers" and called for government regulation. But when the New England states imposed price ceilings in 1777, many farmers and artisans refused to sell their goods. Ultimately, a government official admitted, consumers had to pay the higher market prices "or submit to starving."

The fighting endangered tens of thousands of civilians. A British officer, Lord Rawdon, favored giving "free liberty to the soldiers to ravage [the country] at will, that these infatuated creatures may feel what a calamity war is." As British and American armies marched back and forth across New Jersey, they forced Patriot and Loyalist families to flee their homes to escape arrest — or worse. Soldiers and partisans looted farms, and disorderly troops harassed and raped women and girls. "An army, even a friendly one, are a dreadful scourge to any people," wrote one Connecticut soldier. "You cannot imagine what devastation and distress mark their steps."

The war divided many farm communities. Patriots formed committees of safety to collect taxes and seized the property of those who refused to pay. "Every Body submitted to our Sovereign Lord the Mob," lamented a Loyalist preacher. In parts of Maryland, the number of "nonassociators" — those who refused to join either side — was so large that they successfully defied Patriot mobs. "Stand off you dammed rebel sons of bitches," shouted Robert Davis of Anne Arundel County, "I will shoot you if you come any nearer."

Financial Crisis

Such defiance exposed the weakness of Patriot governments. Most states were afraid to raise taxes, so officials issued bonds to secure gold or silver from wealthy individuals. When those funds ran out, individual states financed the war by issuing so much paper money — some $260 million all told — that it lost worth, and most people refused to accept it at face value. In North Carolina, even tax collectors eventually rejected the state's currency.

The finances of the Continental Congress collapsed, too, despite the efforts of Philadelphia merchant Robert Morris, the government's chief treasury official. Because the Congress lacked the authority to impose taxes, Morris relied on funds requisitioned from the states, but the states paid late or not at all. So Morris secured loans from France and Holland and sold Continental loan certificates to some thirteen thousand firms and individuals. All the while, the Congress was issuing paper money — some $200 million between 1776 and 1779 — which, like state currencies, quickly fell in value. In 1778, a family needed $7 in Continental bills to buy goods worth $1 in gold or silver. As the exchange rate deteriorated — to 42 to 1 in

Paper Currency

Testifying to their independent status, the new state governments printed their own currencies. Rejecting the English system of pounds and shillings, Virginia used the Spanish gold dollar as its basic unit of currency, although the equivalent in English pounds is also shown. Initially, $1,200 was equal to £360—a ratio of 3.3 to 1. By 1781, Virginia had printed so much paper money to pay its soldiers and wartime expenses that the value of its currency had depreciated. It now took $40 in Virginia currency to buy the same amount of goods as £1 sterling. The American Numismatic Society.

1779, 100 to 1 in 1780, and 146 to 1 in 1781 — it sparked social upheaval. In Boston, a mob of women accosted merchant Thomas Boyleston, "seazd him by his Neck," and forced him to sell his wares at traditional prices. In rural Ulster County, New York, women told the committee of safety to lower food prices or "their husbands and sons shall fight no more." As morale crumbled, Patriot leaders feared the rebellion would collapse.

Valley Forge

Fears reached their peak during the winter of 1777. While Howe's army lived comfortably in Philadelphia, Washington's army retreated 20 miles to **Valley Forge**, where 12,000 soldiers and hundreds of camp followers suffered horribly. "The army . . . now begins to grow sickly," a surgeon confided to his diary. "Poor food — hard lodging — cold weather — fatigue — nasty clothes — nasty cookery. . . . Why are we sent here to starve and freeze?" Nearby farmers refused to help. Some were pacifists, Quakers and German sectarians unwilling to support either side. Others looked out for their own families, selling grain for gold from British quartermasters but refusing depreciated Continental currency. "Such a dearth of public spirit, and want of public virtue," lamented Washington. By spring, more than 200 officers had resigned, 1,000 hungry soldiers had deserted, and another 3,000 had died from malnutrition and disease. That winter at Valley Forge took as many American lives as had two years of fighting.

In this dark hour, Baron von Steuben raised the readiness of the American army. A former Prussian military officer, von Steuben was one of a handful of republican-minded foreign aristocrats who joined the American cause. Appointed as inspector general of the

Continental army, he instituted a strict drill system and encouraged officers to become more professional. Thanks to von Steuben, the smaller army that emerged from Valley Forge in the spring of 1778 was a much tougher and better-disciplined force.

The Path to Victory, 1778–1783

Wars are often won by astute diplomacy, and so it was with the War of Independence. The Patriots' prospects improved dramatically in 1778, when the Continental Congress concluded a military alliance with France, the most powerful nation in Europe. The alliance gave the Americans desperately needed money, supplies, and, eventually, troops. And it confronted Britain with an international war that challenged its domination of the Atlantic and Indian oceans.

The French Alliance

France and America were unlikely partners. France was Catholic and a monarchy; the United States was Protestant and a federation of republics. From 1689 to 1763, the two peoples had been enemies: New Englanders had brutally uprooted the French population from Acadia (Nova Scotia) in 1755, and the French and their Indian allies had raided British settlements. But the Comte de Vergennes, the French foreign minister, was determined to avenge the loss of Canada during the Great War for Empire (see Chapter 4) and persuaded King Louis XVI to provide the rebellious colonies with a secret loan and much-needed gunpowder. When news of the rebel victory at Saratoga reached Paris in December 1777, Vergennes sought a formal alliance.

Benjamin Franklin and other American diplomats craftily exploited France's rivalry with Britain to win an explicit commitment to American independence. The Treaty of Alliance of February 1778 specified that once France entered the war, neither partner would sign a separate peace without the "liberty, sovereignty, and independence" of the United States. In return, the Continental Congress agreed to recognize any French conquests in the West Indies. "France and America," warned Britain's Lord Stormont, "were indissolubly leagued for our destruction."

The alliance gave new life to the Patriots' cause. "There has been a great change in this state since the news from France," a Patriot soldier reported from Pennsylvania. Farmers — "mercenary wretches," he called them — "were as eager for Continental Money now as they were a few weeks ago for British gold." Its confidence bolstered, the Continental Congress addressed the demands of the officer corps. Most officers were gentlemen who equipped themselves and raised volunteers; in return, they insisted on lifetime military pensions at half pay. John Adams condemned the officers for "scrambling for rank and pay like apes for nuts," but General Washington urged the Congress to grant the pensions: "The salvation of the cause depends upon it." The Congress reluctantly granted the officers half pay, but only for seven years.

Meanwhile, the war had become unpopular in Britain. At first, George III was determined to crush the rebellion. If America won independence, he warned Lord North, "the West Indies must follow them. Ireland would soon follow the same plan and be a separate state, then this island would be reduced to itself, and soon would be a poor island indeed." Stunned by the defeat at Saratoga, however, the king changed his mind. To thwart an American alliance with France, he authorized North to seek a negotiated settlement. In February 1778, North persuaded Parliament to repeal the Tea and Prohibitory Acts and, amazingly, to renounce its power to tax the colonies. But the Patriots, now allied with France and committed to independence, rejected North's overture.

EXPLAIN CONSEQUENCES

What were the most important results of the Patriot victory at Saratoga?

War in the South

The French alliance did not bring a rapid end to the war. When France entered the conflict in June 1778, it hoped to seize all of Britain's sugar islands. Spain, which joined the war against Britain in 1779, aimed to regain Florida and the fortress of Gibraltar at the entrance to the Mediterranean Sea.

Britain's Southern Strategy For its part, the British government revised its military strategy to defend the West Indies and capture the rich tobacco- and rice-growing colonies: Virginia, the Carolinas, and Georgia. Once conquered, the ministry planned to use the Scottish Highlanders in the Carolinas and other Loyalists to hold them. It had already mobilized the Cherokees and Delawares against the land-hungry Americans and knew that the Patriots' fears of slave uprisings weakened them militarily (Map 6.3). As South Carolina Patriots admitted to the Continental Congress, they could raise only a few recruits "by reason of the great proportion of citizens necessary to remain at home to prevent insurrection among the Negroes."

The large number of slaves in the South made the Revolution a "triangular war," in which African Americans constituted a strategic problem for Patriots and a tempting, if dangerous, opportunity for the British. Britain actively recruited slaves to its cause. The effort began with Dunmore's controversial proclamation in November 1775 recruiting slaves to his Ethiopian Regiment (see Chapter 5). In 1779, the **Philipsburg Proclamation** declared that any slave who deserted a rebel master would receive protection, freedom, and land from Great Britain. Together, these proclamations led some 30,000 African Americans to take refuge behind British lines. George Washington initially barred blacks from the Continental army, but he relented in 1777. By war's end, African Americans could enlist in every state but South Carolina and Georgia, and some 5,000 — slave and free — fought for the Patriot cause (Thinking Like a Historian, p. 192).

It fell to Sir Henry Clinton — acutely aware of the role slaves might play — to implement Britain's southern strategy. From the British army's main base in New York City, Clinton launched a seaborne attack on Savannah, Georgia. Troops commanded by Colonel Archibald Campbell captured the town in December 1778. Mobilizing hundreds of blacks to transport supplies, Campbell moved inland and captured Augusta early in 1779. By year's end, Clinton's forces and local Loyalists controlled coastal Georgia and had 10,000 troops poised for an assault on South Carolina.

In 1780, British forces marched from victory to victory (Map 6.4). In May, Clinton forced the surrender of Charleston, South Carolina, and its garrison of 5,000 troops. Then Lord Charles Cornwallis assumed control of the British forces and, at Camden, defeated an

MAP 6.3

Native Americans and the War in the West, 1778–1779

Many Indian peoples remained neutral, but others, fearing land-hungry Patriot farmers, used British-supplied guns to raid American settlements. To thwart attacks by militant Shawnees, Cherokees, and Delawares, a Patriot militia led by George Rogers Clark captured the British fort and supply depot at Vincennes on the Wabash River in February 1779. To the north, Patriot generals John Sullivan and James Clinton defeated pro-British Indian forces near Tioga (on the New York–Pennsylvania border) in August 1779 and then systematically destroyed villages and crops throughout the lands of the Iroquois.

American force commanded by General Horatio Gates, the hero of Saratoga. Only 1,200 Patriot militiamen joined Gates at Camden, a fifth of the number at Saratoga. Cornwallis took control of South Carolina, and hundreds of African Americans fled to freedom behind British lines. The southern strategy was working.

Then the tide of battle turned. Thanks to another republican-minded European aristocrat, the Marquis de Lafayette, France finally dispatched troops to the American mainland. A longtime supporter of the American cause, Lafayette persuaded King Louis XVI to send General Comte de Rochambeau and 5,500 men

to Newport, Rhode Island, in 1780. There, they threatened the British forces holding New York City.

Guerrilla Warfare in the Carolinas Meanwhile, Washington dispatched General Nathanael Greene to recapture the Carolinas, where he found "a country that has been ravaged and plundered by both friends and enemies." Greene put local militiamen, who had been "without discipline and addicted to plundering," under strong leaders and unleashed them on less mobile British forces. In October 1780, Patriot militia defeated a regiment of Loyalists at King's Mountain, South Carolina, taking about one thousand prisoners.

The Black Soldier's Dilemma

For African American slaves, the Revolution offered no clear path to freedom. Some slaves agreed to fight for Britain because of its promise to liberate slaves who fought against their masters. While some were freed, many others died fighting, were forced into servitude in the army, or even sold into slavery in the West Indies. Patriots at first refused the service of black soldiers, then enlisted them in small numbers, but always upheld the property rights of masters.

1. **Dunmore's Proclamation, 1775.** *Virginia's Governor Dunmore issued this proclamation in response to the emerging rebellion and formed his recruits into the so-called Ethiopian Regiment.*

To defeat such unreasonable Purposes . . . that the Peace, and good Order of this Colony may be again restored . . . I have thought fit to issue this my Proclamation, hereby declaring, that until the aforesaid good Purposes can be obtained, I do in Virtue of the Power and Authority to me given, by His majesty, determine to execute Martial Law, and cause the same to be executed throughout this Colony: and to the end that Peace and good Order may the sooner be [effected], I do require every Person capable of bearing Arms, to [resort] to His majesty's standard, or be looked upon as Traitors to His [majesty] . . . I do hereby further declare all indentured Servants, Negroes, or others, (appertaining to Rebels,) free that are able and willing to bear Arms, they joining His majesty's Troops as soon as may be, for the more speedily reducing this Colony to a proper Sense of their Duty.

2. **Virginia's response to Dunmore's Proclamation, 1775.** *A month later, Virginia's General Assembly issued the following response.*

WHEREAS lord Dunmore, by his proclamation, dated on board the ship William, off Norfolk, the 7th day of November 1775, hath offered freedom to such able-bodied slaves as are willing to join him, and take up arms, against the good people of this colony, giving thereby encouragement to a general insurrection . . . it is enacted, that all negro or other slaves, conspiring to rebel or make insurrection, shall suffer death. . . . We think it proper to declare, that all slaves who have been, or shall be seduced, by his lordship's proclamation, or other arts, to desert their masters' service, and take up arms against the inhabitants of this colony, shall be liable to such punishment as shall hereafter be directed by the General Convention. . . . [A]ll such, who have taken this unlawful and wicked step, may return in safety to their duty, and escape the punishment due their crimes. . . . And we do

farther earnestly recommend it to all humane and benevolent persons in this colony to explain and make known this our offer of mercy to those unfortunate people.

3. **Runaway advertisement, 1775.** *Titus—or, as he was later known, Captain Tye of the Ethiopian Regiment—abandoned his Delaware master in response to Dunmore's Proclamation.*

THREE POUNDS Reward.

RUN away from the subscriber, living in Shrewsbury, in the county of Monmouth, New-Jersey, a NEGROE man, named TITUS, but may probably change his name; he is about 21 years of age, not very black, near 6 feet high; had on a grey homespun coat, brown breeches, blue and white stockings, and took with him a wallet, drawn up at one end with a string, in which was a quantity of clothes. Whoever takes up said Negroe, and secures him in any goal, or brings him to me, shall be entitled to the above reward of *Three Pounds* proc. and all reasonable charges, paid by

Nov. 8, 1775. § JOHN CORLIS.

Source: Courtesy American Antiquarian Society.

4. **Report of Bernardo de Gálvez, 1780.** *Fighting against the British in support of the Patriots, Louisiana governor Bernardo de Gálvez raised a mixed regiment, almost half of whom were slaves and free people of color from New Orleans. He praised their efforts in this report of his campaign.*

No less deserving of eulogy are the companies of Negroes and free Mulattoes who were continually occupied in the outposts, in false attacks, and discoveries, exchanging shots with the enemy . . . conduct[ing] themselves with as much valor and generosity as the whites.

5. **Boston King gains his freedom, 1783.** *In 1780, Boston King, like many other southern slaves, escaped to the British army. Here he describes his experiences at war's end.*

About this time, peace was restored between America and Great Britain which diffused universal joy among all parties except us, who had escaped slavery and taken refuge in the English army; for a report prevailed at New-York that all the slaves, in number two thousand, were to be delivered up to their masters, altho' some of them had been three or four years among the English. This dreadful rumour filled us with inexpressible anguish and terror, especially when we saw our old masters coming from Virginia, North-Carolina and other parts and seizing upon slaves in the streets of New-York, or even dragging them out of their beds. Many of the slaves had very cruel masters, so that the thought of returning home with them embittered life to us. For some days we lost our appetite for food, and sleep departed from our eyes. The English had compassion upon us in the day of our distress, and issued out a Proclamation importing "That all slaves should be free who had taken refuge in the British lines and claimed the sanction and privileges of the Proclamations respecting the security and protection of Negroes." In consequence of this, each of us received a certificate from the commanding officer at New-York, which dispelled our fears and filled us with joy and gratitude.

6. Jehu Grant is re-enslaved, 1778. *Jehu Grant of Narragansett, Rhode Island, was owned by a Loyalist. In August 1777 he escaped and joined the Patriot side; ten months later, his master tracked him down and reclaimed him. In 1837 Grant applied for a pension from the U.S. government and supplied the following narrative of his experience. His application was denied.*

[I] enlisted as a soldier but was put to the service of a teamster in the summer and a waiter in the winter . . . I was then grown to manhood, in the full vigor and strength of life, and heard much about the cruel and arbitrary things done by the British. Their ships lay within a few miles of my master's house, which stood near the shore, and I was confident that my master traded with them, and I suffered much from fear that I should be sent aboard a ship of war. This I disliked. But when I saw liberty poles and the people all engaged for the support of freedom, I could not but like and be pleased with such thing (God forgive me if I sinned in so feeling). And living on the borders of Rhode Island, where whole

companies of colored people enlisted, it added to my fears and dread of being sold to the British. These considerations induced me to enlist into the American army, where I served faithful about ten months, when my master found and took me home. Had I been taught to read or understand the precepts of the Gospel, "Servants obey your master," I might have done otherwise, notwithstanding the songs of liberty that saluted my ear, thrilled through my heart.

Sources: (1) Lord Dunmore's Proclamation, Learn NC, North Carolina Digital History "Revolutionary North Carolina," www.learnnc.org; (2) J. N. Brenaman, *A History of Virginia Conventions* (Richmond: J. L. Hill Printing Company, 1902), p. 30; (4) Thomas Truxtun Moebs, *Black Soldiers-Black Sailors-Black Ink: Research Guide on African-Americans in U. S. Military History, 1526–1900* (Chesapeake Bay, Paris: Moebs Publishing Company, 1994), 1125; (5) Boston King, *Book of Negroes* (New York, 1783), in Simon Schama, *Rough Crossings: Britain, the Slaves and the American Revolution* (New York: HarperCollins, 2006), 107, 150; (6) Jehu Grant, To Hon. J. L. Edwards, Commissioner of Pension, 1836, in *The Revolution Remembered: Eyewitness Accounts of the War for Independence*, ed. John C. Dann (Chicago: University of Chicago Press, 1980), 27–28.

ANALYZING THE EVIDENCE

1. Why was Dunmore willing to offer freedom to slaves (source 1) when they were a recognized form of property under the British Empire? What assumptions about the loyalties of slaves underlie the response of the Virginia assembly (source 2)?

2. Why might Louisiana governor Bernardo de Gálvez (source 4) have made a point of praising the contributions of black soldiers to the Patriot cause?

3. Compare the runaway ad for Titus (source 3) and the narratives of Boston King and Jehu Grant (sources 5 and 6). What goals did British officers hope to achieve in their relations with slaves? What Patriot values trumped slaves' individual liberties during and after the war?

PUTTING IT ALL TOGETHER

Considering these sources along with the chapter contents and what you've learned in class, write a short essay that explains how the presence of slaves created a "triangular war" in the South, assesses the choices that individual slaves had to make during the Revolution, and considers how the differences in the institution of slavery between northern and southern colonies shaped slaves' experiences in the war.

MAP 6.4
The War in the South, 1778–1781

Britain's southern military strategy started well. British forces captured Savannah in December 1778, took control of Georgia during 1779, and vanquished Charleston in May 1780. Over the next eighteen months, brutal warfare between the British troops and Loyalist units and the Continental army and militia raged in the interior of the Carolinas and ended in a stalemate. Hoping to break the deadlock, British general Charles Cornwallis carried the battle into Virginia in 1781. A Franco-American army led by Washington and Lafayette, with the help of the French fleet under Admiral de Grasse, surrounded Cornwallis's forces on the Yorktown Peninsula and forced their surrender.

American guerrillas commanded by the "Swamp Fox," General Francis Marion, also won a series of small but fierce battles. Then, in January 1781, General Daniel Morgan led an American force to a bloody victory at Cowpens, South Carolina. In March, Greene's soldiers fought Cornwallis's seasoned army to a draw at North Carolina's Guilford Court House. Weakened by this war of attrition, the British general decided to concede the Carolinas to Greene and seek a decisive victory in Virginia. There, many Patriot militiamen had refused to take up arms, claiming that "the Rich wanted the Poor to fight for them."

Exploiting these social divisions, Cornwallis moved easily through the Tidewater region of Virginia in the

Francis Marion Crossing the Pedee River

Francis Marion was a master of the ferocious guerrilla fighting that characterized the war in South Carolina. Though Patriot general Horatio Gates had little confidence in him, Marion led an irregular militia brigade in several successful attacks. After chasing Marion into a swamp, British general Banastre Tarleton declared, "As for this damned old fox, the Devil himself could not catch him." Soon Patriots began calling Marion the Swamp Fox. In 1851, William T. Ranney painted Marion (on horseback in a white shirt and blue coat) and his men crossing the Pedee River in flatboats. Ranney included an unidentified (and possibly fictionalized) black oarsman. Amon Carter Museum, Fort Worth, Texas, William T. Ranney (1813–1857). Marion Crossing the Peedee, oil on canvas, 1850.

early summer of 1781. Reinforcements sent from New York and commanded by General Benedict Arnold, the infamous Patriot traitor, bolstered his ranks. As Arnold and Cornwallis sparred with an American force led by Lafayette near the York Peninsula, Washington was informed that France had finally sent its powerful West Indian fleet to North America, and he devised an audacious plan. Feigning an assault on New York City, he secretly marched General Rochambeau's army from Rhode Island to Virginia. Simultaneously, the French fleet took control of Chesapeake Bay. By the time the British discovered Washington's scheme, Cornwallis was surrounded, his 9,500-man army outnumbered 2 to 1 on land and cut off from reinforcement or retreat by sea. In a hopeless position, Cornwallis surrendered at **Yorktown** in October 1781.

The Franco-American victory broke the resolve of the British government. "Oh God! It is all over!" Lord North exclaimed. Isolated diplomatically in Europe, stymied militarily in America, and lacking public support at home, the British ministry gave up active prosecution of the war on the American mainland.

The Patriot Advantage

How could mighty Britain, victorious in the Great War for Empire, lose to a motley rebel army? The British ministry pointed to a series of blunders by the military leadership. Why had Howe not ruthlessly pursued Washington's army in 1776? Why had Howe and Burgoyne failed to coordinate their attacks in 1777? Why had Cornwallis marched deep into the Patriot-dominated state of Virginia in 1781?

IDENTIFY CAUSES
What were the keys to the Patriot victory in the South?

Historians acknowledge British mistakes, but they also attribute the rebels' victory to French aid and the inspired leadership of George Washington. Astutely deferring to elected officials, Washington won the support of the Continental Congress and the state governments. Confident of his military abilities, he pursued a defensive strategy that minimized casualties and maintained the morale of his officers and soldiers through five difficult years of war. Moreover, the Patriots' control of local governments gave Washington a greater margin for error than the British generals had. Local militiamen provided the edge in the 1777 victory at Saratoga and forced Cornwallis from the Carolinas in 1781.

TRACE CHANGE OVER TIME

Despite being at a clear disadvantage at the start of the war, the American Patriots won. Why?

In the end, it was the American people who decided the outcome, especially the one-third of the white colonists who were zealous Patriots. Tens of thousands of these farmers and artisans accepted Continental bills in payment for supplies, and thousands of soldiers took them as pay, even as the currency literally depreciated in their pockets. Rampant inflation meant that every paper dollar held for a week lost value, imposing a hidden "**currency tax**" on those who accepted the paper currency. Each individual tax was small — a few pennies on each dollar. But as millions of dollars changed hands multiple times, the currency taxes paid by ordinary citizens financed the American military victory.

Diplomatic Triumph

After Yorktown, diplomats took two years to conclude a peace treaty. Talks began in Paris in April 1782, but the French and Spanish, still hoping to seize a West Indian island or Gibraltar, stalled for time. Their tactics infuriated American diplomats Benjamin Franklin, John Adams, and John Jay. So the Americans negotiated secretly with the British, prepared if necessary to ignore the Treaty of Alliance and sign a separate peace. British ministers were equally eager: Parliament wanted peace, and they feared the loss of a rich sugar island.

Consequently, the American diplomats secured extremely favorable terms. In the **Treaty of Paris**, signed in September 1783, Great Britain formally recognized American independence and relinquished its claims to lands south of the Great Lakes and east of the Mississippi River. The British negotiators did not insist on a separate territory for their Indian allies. "In endeavouring to assist you," a Wea Indian complained to a British general, "it seems we have wrought our own ruin." The Cherokees were forced to relinquish claims to 5 million acres — three-quarters of their territory — in treaties with Georgia, the Carolinas, and Virginia, while New York and the Continental Congress pressed the Iroquois and Ohio Indians to cede much of their land as well. British officials, like those of other early modern empires, found it easy to abandon allies they had never really understood (America Compared, p. 197).

The Paris treaty also granted Americans fishing rights off Newfoundland and Nova Scotia, prohibited the British from "carrying away any negroes or other property," and guaranteed freedom of navigation on the Mississippi to American citizens "forever." In return, the American government allowed British merchants to pursue legal claims for prewar debts and encouraged the state legislatures to return confiscated property to Loyalists and grant them citizenship.

In the Treaty of Versailles, signed simultaneously, Britain made peace with France and Spain. Neither American ally gained very much. Spain reclaimed Florida from Britain, but not the strategic fortress at Gibraltar. France received the Caribbean island of Tobago, small consolation for a war that had sharply raised taxes and quadrupled France's national debt. Just six years later, cries for tax relief and political liberty would spark the French Revolution. Only Americans profited handsomely; the treaties gave them independence and access to the trans-Appalachian west.

Creating Republican Institutions, 1776–1787

When the Patriots declared independence, they confronted the issue of political authority. "Which of us shall be the rulers?" asked a Philadelphia newspaper. The question was multifaceted. Would power reside in the national government or the states? Who would control the new republican institutions: traditional elites or average citizens? Would women have greater political and legal rights? What would be the status of slaves in the new republic?

The State Constitutions: How Much Democracy?

In May 1776, the Second Continental Congress urged Americans to reject royal authority and establish republican governments. Most states quickly complied. "Constitutions employ every pen," an observer noted. Within six months, Virginia, Maryland, North Carolina, New Jersey, Delaware, and Pennsylvania had all ratified

China's Growing Empire

As Britain was losing control of its multiethnic empire in North America, China's Qing [pronounced Ching] dynasty was consolidating its authority over borderlands peoples during the eighteenth century. And just as Europeans relied on ethnographic descriptions of Native Americans to understand the peoples and territories they hoped to control, Chinese authorities used ethnographic manuals that included prose, poetry, and illustrations to make sense of their new subjects. These excerpts from a set of "Miao albums" illustrate the cultural characteristics they observed in, or ascribed to, one such group of these non-Chinese (or non-Han) peoples.

Bulong (Basket-Repairing) Zhongjia

The Bulong Zhongjia are located in Dinfan and Guangshun Districts. Their customs are similar to those of the Kayou. For them, the New Year begins in the twelfth month. They greet it by striking a bronze drum. When they dig in the ground and find a drum, they consider it to be the legacy of Zhuge Liang [an ancient Chinese hero claimed as a forebear]. The rich must pay a high price to buy the drum. At funerals, cattle are butchered and dressed, and relatives and friends are invited. Drinking from the "ox horn of happiness," the guests often get drunk and sometimes even wind up killing each other. The host does not usually eat meat but only fish and shrimp. After burial, the grave is covered by an umbrella. By nature the Bulong are alert and fierce. When coming and going they carry sharp knives. They will avenge even an angry look.

Nong (Agricultural) Miao

The Nong Miao are located in the Zhenfeng District, which once belonged to Guangxi. . . . Men shave their heads and dress just like Han people. Women wear short tunics and long skirts, and cover their heads with colorful scarves. They still follow Miao customs. Their nature is fierce and cruel; they enjoy killing.

Gedou Miao

The Gedou Miao are found in Zhenyuan, Shibing, and Huangping. They are as good at hunting as the Turen. Women wear their hair up, inclined toward one side, with a comb inserted. Their short tunics are collarless, and their skirts do not reach beyond the knee. They embroider in five colors on the bust and the sleeves, and ornament themselves with seashells [shaped] like silkworm cocoons, stringing them together like real pearls. If a man is injured by one of their poisoned arrows he will die immediately. They are not, however, given to thievery.

Source: From *The Art of Ethnography: A Chinese "Miao Album,"* translated by David M. Deal and Laura Hostetler (Seattle: University of Washington Press, 2006). Reprinted by permission of the University of Washington Press.

QUESTIONS FOR ANALYSIS

1. What attributes seemed especially meaningful to the authors of these descriptions?
2. Why would the authors have singled out the particular qualities that are remarked upon here? How does this compare to the ways in which the British viewed their Native Americans?

---

new constitutions, and Connecticut and Rhode Island had revised their colonial charters to delete references to the king.

Republicanism meant more than ousting the king. The Declaration of Independence stated the principle of popular sovereignty: governments derive "their just powers from the consent of the governed." In the heat of revolution, many Patriots gave this clause a further democratic twist. In North Carolina, the backcountry farmers of Mecklenburg County told their delegates to the state's constitutional convention to "oppose everything that leans to aristocracy or power in the hands of the rich." In Virginia, voters elected a new assembly in 1776 that, an eyewitness remarked, "was composed of men not quite so well dressed, nor so politely educated, nor so highly born" as colonial-era legislatures (Figure 6.1).

 To see a longer excerpt of the Mecklenburg delegates' document, along with other primary sources from this period, see *Sources for America's History*.

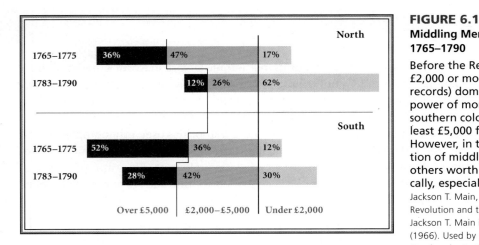

FIGURE 6.1

Middling Men Enter the Halls of Government, 1765–1790

Before the Revolution, wealthy men (with assets of £2,000 or more, as measured by tax lists and probate records) dominated most colonial assemblies. The power of money was especially apparent in the southern colonies, where representatives worth at least £5,000 formed a majority of the legislators. However, in the new American republic, the proportion of middling legislators (yeomen farmers and others worth less than £2,000) increased dramatically, especially in the northern states. Adapted from Jackson T. Main, "Government by the People: The American Revolution and the Democratization of the Legislatures," by Jackson T. Main in *William and Mary Quarterly*, series 3, 23 (1966). Used by permission of *William and Mary Quarterly*, Omohundro Institute of Early History and Culture.

Pennsylvania's Controversial Constitution This democratic impulse flowered in Pennsylvania, thanks to a coalition of Scots-Irish farmers, Philadelphia artisans, and Enlightenment-influenced intellectuals. In 1776, these insurgents ousted every officeholder of the Penn family's proprietary government, abolished property ownership as a qualification for voting, and granted all taxpaying men the right to vote and hold office. The **Pennsylvania constitution of 1776** also created a unicameral (one-house) legislature with complete power; there was no governor to exercise a veto. Other provisions mandated a system of elementary education and protected citizens from imprisonment for debt.

Pennsylvania's democratic constitution alarmed many leading Patriots. From Boston, John Adams denounced the unicameral legislature as "so democratical that it must produce confusion and every evil work." Along with other conservative Patriots, Adams wanted to restrict office holding to "men of learning, leisure and easy circumstances" and warned of oppression under majority rule: "If you give [ordinary citizens] the command or preponderance in the . . . legislature, they will vote all property out of the hands of you aristocrats."

COMPARE AND CONTRAST
What aspects of the Pennsylvania constitution were most objectionable to Adams, and what did he advocate instead?

Tempering Democracy To counter the appeal of the Pennsylvania constitution, Adams published *Thoughts on Government* (1776). In that treatise, he adapted the British Whig theory of **mixed government** (a sharing of power among the monarch, the House of Lords, and the Commons) to a republican society. To disperse authority and preserve liberty, he insisted on separate institutions: legislatures would make laws, the executive would administer them, and the judiciary would enforce them. Adams also demanded a bicameral (two-house) legislature with an upper house of substantial property owners to offset the popular majorities in the lower one. As further curbs on democracy, he proposed an elected governor with veto power and an appointed — not elected — judiciary.

Conservative Patriots endorsed Adams's governmental system. In New York's constitution of 1777, property qualifications for voting excluded 20 percent of white men from assembly elections and 60 percent from casting ballots for the governor and the upper house. In South Carolina, elite planters used property rules to disqualify about 90 percent of white men from office holding. The 1778 constitution required candidates for governor to have a debt-free estate of £10,000 (about $700,000 today), senators to be worth £2,000, and assemblymen to own property valued at £1,000. Even in traditionally democratic Massachusetts, the 1780 constitution, authored primarily by Adams, raised property qualifications for voting and office holding and skewed the lower house toward eastern, mercantile interests.

The political legacy of the Revolution was complex. Only in Pennsylvania and Vermont were radical Patriots able to create truly democratic institutions. Yet in all the new states, representative legislatures had acquired more power, and average citizens now had greater power at the polls and greater influence in the halls of government.

Women Seek a Public Voice

The extraordinary excitement of the Revolutionary era tested the dictum that only men could engage in politics. Men controlled all public institutions — legislatures, juries, government offices — but upper-class women engaged in political debate and, defying men's scorn, filled their letters, diaries, and conversations with opinions on public issues. "The men say we have no business [with politics]," Eliza Wilkinson of South Carolina complained in 1783. "They won't even allow us liberty of thought, and that is all I want."

As Wilkinson's remark suggests, most women did not insist on civic equality with men; many sought only an end to restrictive customs and laws. Abigail Adams demanded equal legal rights for married women, who under common law could not own property, enter into contracts, or initiate lawsuits. The war bonds she purchased had to be held in a trust run by a male relative. "Men would be tyrants" if they continued to hold such power over women, Adams declared to her husband, John, criticizing him and other Patriots for "emancipating all nations" from monarchical despotism while "retaining absolute power over Wives."

Most politicians ignored women's requests, and most men insisted on traditional sexual and political prerogatives. Long-married husbands remained patriarchs who dominated their households, and even young men who embraced the republican ideal of "companionate marriage" did not support legal equality for their wives and daughters. Except in New Jersey, which until 1807 allowed unmarried and widowed female property holders to vote, women remained disenfranchised. In the new American republic, only white men enjoyed full citizenship.

Nevertheless, the republican belief in an educated citizenry created opportunities for some women. In her 1779 essay "On the Equality of the Sexes," Judith Sargent Murray argued that men and women had equal capacities for memory and that women had superior imaginations. She conceded that most women were inferior to men in judgment and reasoning, but only from lack of training: "We can only reason from what we know," she argued, and most women had been denied "the opportunity of acquiring knowledge." That situation changed in the 1790s, when the attorney general of Massachusetts declared that girls had an equal right to schooling under the state constitution. By 1850, the literacy rates of women and men in the northeastern states were equal, and educated women again challenged their subordinate legal and political status.

The War's Losers: Loyalists, Native Americans, and Slaves

The success of republican institutions was assisted by the departure of as many as 100,000 Loyalists, many of whom suffered severe financial losses. Some Patriots demanded revolutionary justice: the seizure of

Judith Sargent Murray
Judith Sargent Murray was perhaps the most accomplished female essayist of the Revolutionary era. Publishing under various pen names, she advocated for economic independence and better educational opportunities for women. Two years before Mary Wollstonecraft's *A Vindication of the Rights of Woman* (1792), she published "On the Equality of the Sexes" in the *Massachusetts Magazine*. Her letter books, which run to twenty volumes, were discovered only in 1984; the Judith Sargent Murray Society (**jsmsociety.com**) is now transcribing and indexing them for publication. This striking portrait by John Singleton Copley hints at her intelligence and sardonic wit. Terra Foundation for American Art, Chicago/Art Resource, NY.

all Loyalist property and its distribution to needy Americans. But most officials were unwilling to go so far. When state governments did seize Loyalist property, they often auctioned it to the highest bidders; only rarely did small-scale farmers benefit. In the cities, Patriot merchants replaced Loyalists at the top of the economic ladder, supplanting a traditional economic elite — who often invested profits from trade in real estate — with republican entrepreneurs who tended to promote new trading ventures and domestic manufacturing. This shift facilitated America's economic development in the years to come.

> **IDENTIFY CAUSES**
> What impact did republican ideals have on gender roles and expectations during the Revolutionary era?

Though the Revolution did not result in widespread property redistribution, it did encourage yeomen, middling planters, and small-time entrepreneurs to believe that their new republican governments would protect their property and ensure widespread access to land. In western counties, former Regulators demanded that the new governments be more responsive to their needs; beyond the Appalachians, thousands of squatters who had occupied lands in Kentucky and Tennessee expected their claims to be recognized and lands to be made available on easy terms. If the United States were to secure the loyalty of westerners, it would have to meet their needs more effectively than the British Empire had.

This meant, among other things, extinguishing Native American claims to land as quickly as possible.

EXPLAIN CONSEQUENCES

How did the Revolutionary commitment to liberty and the protection of property affect enslaved African Americans and western Indians?

A Black Loyalist Pass, 1783

White Patriots claimed their freedom by fighting *against* the British; thousands of black slaves won their liberty by fighting *for* them. This pass certifies that Cato Rammsay (actually Ramsey), "a Negro, resorted to the British Lines" in search of the freedom promised by Virginia royal governor Dunmore and British commander Henry Clinton to slaves who escaped from Patriot owners. Now age forty-five and a "slim fellow," Ramsey had escaped from his owner, John Ramsey of Norfolk, Virginia, in 1776, probably fleeing to Dunmore's ships. Seven years later, he ended up in New York, reunited with his wife, China Godfrey (thirty-five), and their three children: James (twenty), Betsey (fifteen), and Nelly Ramsey (ten), who had fled subsequently from other owners. As the British evacuated New York in 1783, Ramsey and his family were free "to go to Nova-Scotia," where they worked as farmers. Nova Scotia Archives and Records Management.

At war's end, George Washington commented on the "rage for speculating" in Ohio Valley lands. "Men in these times, talk with as much facility of fifty, a hundred, and even 500,000 Acres as a Gentleman formerly would do of 1000 acres." "If we make a right use of our natural advantages," a Fourth of July orator observed, "we soon must be a truly great and happy people." Native American land claims stood as a conspicuous barrier to the "natural advantages" he imagined.

For southern slaveholders, the Revolution was fought to protect property rights, and any sentiment favoring slave emancipation met with violent objections. When Virginia Methodists called for general emancipation in 1785, slaveholders used Revolutionary principles to defend their right to human property. They "risked [their] Lives and Fortunes, and waded through Seas of Blood" to secure "the Possession of [their] Rights of Liberty and Property," only to hear of "a very subtle and daring Attempt" to "dispossess us of a very important Part of our Property." Emancipation would bring "Want, Poverty, Distress, and Ruin to the Free Citizen." The liberties coveted by ordinary white Americans bore hard on the interests of Native Americans and slaves.

The Articles of Confederation

As Patriots embraced independence in 1776, they envisioned a central government with limited powers. Carter Braxton of Virginia thought the Continental Congress should "regulate the affairs of trade, war, peace, alliances, &c." but "should by no means have authority to interfere with the internal police [governance] or domestic concerns of any Colony."

That idea informed the **Articles of Confederation**, which were approved by the Continental Congress in November 1777. The Articles provided for a loose union in which "each state retains its sovereignty, freedom, and independence." As an association of equals, each state had one vote regardless of its size, population, or wealth. Important laws needed the approval of nine of the thirteen states, and changes in the Articles required unanimous consent. Though the Confederation had significant powers on paper — it could declare war, make treaties with foreign nations, adjudicate disputes between the states, borrow and print money, and requisition funds from the states "for the common defense or general welfare" — it had major weaknesses as well. It had neither a chief executive nor a judiciary. Though it could make treaties, it could not enforce their provisions, since the states remained sovereign. Most important, it lacked the power to tax either the states or the people.

Although the Congress exercised authority from 1776 — raising the Continental army, negotiating the treaty with France, and financing the war — the Articles won formal ratification only in 1781. The delay stemmed from conflicts over western lands. The royal charters of Virginia, Massachusetts, Connecticut, and other states set boundaries stretching to the Pacific Ocean. States without western lands — Maryland and Pennsylvania — refused to accept the Articles until the land-rich states relinquished these claims to the Confederation. Threatened by Cornwallis's army in 1781, Virginia gave up its claims, and Maryland, the last holdout, finally ratified the Articles (Map 6.5).

Continuing Fiscal Crisis   By 1780, the central government was nearly bankrupt, and General Washington called urgently for a national tax system; without one, he warned, "our cause is lost." Led by Robert Morris, who became superintendent of finance in 1781, nationalist-minded Patriots tried to expand the Confederation's authority. They persuaded Congress to charter the Bank of North America, a private institution in Philadelphia, arguing that its notes would stabilize the inflated Continental currency. Morris also created a central bureaucracy to manage the Confederation's finances and urged Congress to enact a 5 percent import tax. Rhode Island and New York rejected the tax proposal. His state had opposed British import duties, New York's representative declared, and it would not accept them from Congress. To raise revenue, Congress looked to the sale of western lands. In 1783, it asserted that the recently signed Treaty of Paris had extinguished the Indians' rights to those lands and made them the property of the United States.

The Northwest Ordinance   By 1784, more than thirty thousand settlers had already moved to Kentucky and Tennessee, despite the uncertainties of frontier warfare, and after the war their numbers grew rapidly. In that year, the residents of what is now eastern Tennessee organized a new state, called it Franklin, and sought admission to the Confederation. To preserve its authority over the West, Congress refused to recognize Franklin. Subsequently, Congress created the Southwest and Mississippi Territories (the future states of Tennessee, Alabama, and Mississippi) from lands ceded by North Carolina and Georgia. Because these cessions carried the stipulation that "no regulation . . . shall tend to emancipate slaves," these states and all those south of the Ohio River allowed human bondage.

However, the Confederation Congress banned slavery north of the Ohio River. Between 1784 and 1787, it issued three important ordinances organizing the "Old Northwest." The Ordinance of 1784, written by Thomas Jefferson, established the principle that territories could become states as their populations grew. The Land Ordinance of 1785 mandated a rectangular-grid system of surveying and specified a minimum price of $1 an acre. It also required that half of the townships be sold in single blocks of 23,040 acres each, which only large-scale speculators could afford, and the rest in parcels of 640 acres each, which restricted their sale to well-to-do farmers (Map 6.6).

> **COMPARE AND CONTRAST**
> In what ways did the Confederation function effectively, and what were its greatest failings?

Finally, the **Northwest Ordinance of 1787** created the territories that would eventually become the states of Ohio, Indiana, Illinois, Michigan, and Wisconsin. The ordinance prohibited slavery and earmarked funds from land sales for the support of schools. It also specified that Congress would appoint a governor and judges to administer each new territory until the population reached 5,000 free adult men, at which point the citizens could elect a territorial legislature. When the population reached 60,000, the legislature could devise a republican constitution and apply to join the Confederation.

The land ordinances of the 1780s were a great and enduring achievement of the Confederation Congress. They provided for orderly settlement and the admission of new states on the basis of equality; there would be no politically dependent "colonies" in the West. But they also extended the geographical division between slave and free areas that would haunt the nation in the coming decades. And they implicitly invalidated Native American claims to an enormous swath of territory — a corollary that would soon lead the newly independent nation, once again, into war.

Shays's Rebellion

Though many national leaders were optimistic about the long-term prospects of the United States, postwar economic conditions were grim. The Revolution had crippled American shipping and cut exports of tobacco, rice, and wheat. The British Navigation Acts, which had nurtured colonial commerce, now barred Americans from legal trade with the British West Indies. Moreover, low-priced British manufactures (and some from India as well) were flooding American markets, driving urban artisans and wartime textile firms out of business.

MAP 6.5

The Confederation and Western Land Claims, 1781–1802

The Congress formed by the Articles of Confederation had to resolve conflicting state claims to western lands. For example, the territories claimed by New York and Virginia on the basis of their royal charters overlapped extensively. Beginning in 1781, the Confederation Congress and, after 1789, the U.S. Congress persuaded all of the states to cede their western claims, creating a "national domain" open to all citizens. In the Northwest Ordinance (1787), the Congress divided the domain north of the Ohio River into territories and set up democratic procedures by which they could eventually join the Union as states. South of the Ohio River, the Congress allowed the existing southern states to play a substantial role in settling the ceded lands.

The fiscal condition of the state governments was dire, primarily because of war debts. Well-to-do merchants and landowners (including Abigail Adams) had invested in state bonds during the war; others had speculated in debt certificates, buying them on the cheap from hard-pressed farmers and soldiers. Now creditors and speculators demanded that the state governments redeem the bonds and certificates quickly and at full value, a policy that would require tax increases and a decrease in the amount of paper currency. Most legislatures — now including substantial numbers of middling farmers and artisans — refused. Instead they

MAP 6.6
Land Division in the Northwest Territory

Throughout the Northwest Territory, government surveyors imposed a rectangular grid on the landscape, regardless of the local topography, so that farmers bought neatly defined tracts of land. The right-angled property lines in Muskingum County, Ohio (lower left), contrasted sharply with those in Baltimore County, Maryland (lower right), where—as in most of the eastern and southern states—boundaries followed the contours of the land.

authorized new issues of paper currency and allowed debtors to pay private creditors in installments. Although wealthy men deplored these measures as "intoxicating Draughts of Liberty" that destroyed "the just rights of creditors," such political intervention prevented social upheaval.

In Massachusetts, however, the new constitution placed power in the hands of a mercantile elite that owned the bulk of the state's war bonds. Ignoring the interests of ordinary citizens, the legislature increased taxes fivefold to pay off wartime debts — and it stipulated that they be paid in hard currency. Even for substantial farmers, this was a crushing burden. When cash-strapped farmers could not pay both their taxes and their debts, creditors threatened lawsuits. Debtor Ephraim Wetmore heard a rumor that merchant Stephan Salisbury "would have my Body Dead or Alive in case I did not pay." To protect their livelihoods, farmers called extralegal conventions to protest high taxes and property seizures. Then mobs of angry farmers, including men of high status, closed the courts by force. "[I] had no Intensions to Destroy the Publick Government," declared Captain Adam Wheeler, a former town selectman; his goal was simply to prevent "Valuable and Industrious members of Society [being] dragged from their families to prison" because of their debts. These crowd actions grew into a full-scale revolt led by Captain Daniel Shays, a Continental army veteran.

As a revolt against taxes imposed by an unresponsive government, **Shays's Rebellion** resembled American resistance to the British Stamp Act. Consciously linking themselves to the Patriot movement, Shays's men placed pine twigs in their hats just as Continental troops had done. "The people have turned against their teachers the doctrines which were inculcated to effect the late revolution," complained Fisher Ames, a conservative Massachusetts lawmaker. Some of the radical Patriots of 1776 likewise condemned the Shaysites: "[Men who] would lessen the Weight of Government lawfully exercised must be Enemies to our happy Revolution and Common Liberty," charged Samuel Adams. To put down the rebellion, the Massachusetts legislature passed the Riot Act, and wealthy bondholders equipped a formidable fighting force, which Governor James Bowdoin used to disperse Shays's ragtag army during the winter of 1786–1787.

Although Shays's Rebellion failed, it showed that many middling Patriot families felt that American

PLACE EVENTS IN CONTEXT
How did the Shaysites draw on the Revolution for inspiration?

oppressors had replaced British tyrants. Massachusetts voters turned Governor Bowdoin out of office, and debt-ridden farmers in New York, northern Pennsylvania, Connecticut, and New Hampshire closed courthouses and forced their governments to provide economic relief. British officials in Canada predicted the imminent demise of the United States; and American leaders urged purposeful action to save their republican experiment. Events in Massachusetts, declared nationalist Henry Knox, formed "the strongest arguments possible" for the creation of "a strong general government."

The Constitution of 1787

These issues ultimately led to the drafting of a national constitution. From its creation, the U.S. Constitution was a controversial document, both acclaimed for solving the nation's woes and condemned for perverting its republican principles. Critics charged that republican institutions worked only in small political units — the states. Advocates replied that the Constitution extended republicanism by adding another level of government elected by the people. In the new two-level political federation created by the Constitution, the national government would exercise limited, delegated powers, and the existing state governments would retain authority over all other matters.

The Rise of a Nationalist Faction

Money questions — debts, taxes, and tariffs — dominated the postwar political agenda. Americans who had served the Confederation as military officers, officials, and diplomats viewed these issues from a national perspective and advocated a stronger central government. George Washington, Robert Morris, Benjamin Franklin, John Jay, and John Adams wanted Congress to control foreign and interstate commerce and tariff policy. However, lawmakers in Massachusetts, New York, and Pennsylvania — states with strong commercial traditions — insisted on controlling their own tariffs, both to protect their artisans from low-cost imports and to assist their merchants. Most southern states opposed tariffs because planters wanted to import British textiles and ironware at the lowest possible prices.

Nonetheless, some southern leaders became nationalists because their state legislatures had cut taxes and refused to redeem state war bonds. Such policies, lamented wealthy bondholder Charles Lee of Virginia, led taxpayers to believe they would "never be compelled to pay" the public debt. Creditors also condemned state laws that "stayed" (delayed) the payment of mortgages and other private debts. "While men are madly accumulating enormous debts, their legislators are making provisions for their nonpayment," complained a South Carolina merchant. To undercut the democratic majorities in the state legislatures, creditors joined the movement for a stronger central government.

Spurred on by Shays's Rebellion, nationalists in Congress secured a resolution calling for a convention to revise the Articles of Confederation. Only an "efficient plan from the Convention," a fellow nationalist wrote to James Madison, "can prevent anarchy first & civil convulsions afterwards."

The Philadelphia Convention

In May 1787, fifty-five delegates arrived in Philadelphia. They came from every state except Rhode Island, where the legislature opposed increasing central authority. Most were strong nationalists; forty-two had served in the Confederation Congress. They were also educated and propertied: merchants, slaveholding planters, and "monied men." There were no artisans, backcountry settlers, or tenants, and only a single yeoman farmer.

Some influential Patriots missed the convention. John Adams and Thomas Jefferson were serving as American ministers to Britain and France, respectively. The Massachusetts General Court rejected Sam Adams as a delegate because he opposed a stronger national government, and his fellow firebrand from Virginia, Patrick Henry, refused to attend because he "smelt a rat."

The absence of experienced leaders and contrary-minded delegates allowed capable younger nationalists to set the agenda. Declaring that the convention would "decide for ever the fate of Republican Government," James Madison insisted on increased national authority. Alexander Hamilton of New York likewise demanded a strong central government to protect the republic from "the imprudence of democracy."

The Virginia and New Jersey Plans   The delegates elected George Washington as their presiding officer and voted to meet behind closed doors. Then — momentously — they decided not to revise the Articles of Confederation but rather to consider the so-called **Virginia Plan**, a scheme for a powerful national government devised by James Madison. Just thirty-six years old, Madison was determined to fashion national political institutions run by men of high character. A graduate of Princeton, he had read classical and

modern political theory and served in both the Confederation Congress and the Virginia assembly. Once an optimistic Patriot, Madison had grown discouraged because of the "narrow ambition" and outlook of state legislators.

Madison's Virginia Plan differed from the Articles of Confederation in three crucial respects. First, the plan rejected state sovereignty in favor of the "supremacy of national authority," including the power to overturn state laws. Second, it called for the national government to be established by the people (not the states) and for national laws to operate directly on citizens of the various states. Third, the plan proposed a three-tier election system in which ordinary voters would elect only the lower house of the national legislature. This lower house would then select the upper house, and both houses would appoint the executive and judiciary.

From a political perspective, Madison's plan had two fatal flaws. First, most state politicians and

James Madison, Statesman

Throughout his long public life, Madison kept the details of his private life to himself. His biography, he believed, should be a record of his public accomplishments, not his private affairs. Future generations celebrated him not as a great man (like Hamilton or Jefferson) or as a great president (like Washington), but as an original and incisive political thinker. The chief architect of the U.S. Constitution and the Bill of Rights, Madison was the preeminent republican political theorist of his generation. Mead Art Museum, Amherst College, Amherst, Massachusetts, Bequest of Herbert L. Pratt (Class of 1895) # 1945.82.

citizens resolutely opposed allowing the national government to veto state laws. Second, the plan based representation in the lower house on population; this provision, a Delaware delegate warned, would allow the populous states to "crush the small ones whenever they stand in the way of their ambitious or interested views."

So delegates from Delaware and other small states rallied behind a plan devised by William Paterson of New Jersey. The **New Jersey Plan** gave the Confederation the power to raise revenue, control commerce, and make binding requisitions on the states. But it preserved the states' control of their own laws and guaranteed their equality: as in the Confederation Congress, each state would have one vote in a unicameral legislature. Delegates from the more populous states vigorously opposed this provision. After a month-long debate on the two plans, a bare majority of the states agreed to use Madison's Virginia Plan as the basis of discussion.

This decision raised the odds that the convention would create a more powerful national government. Outraged by this prospect, two New York delegates, Robert Yates and John Lansing, accused their colleagues of exceeding their mandate to revise the Articles and left the convention. The remaining delegates met six days a week during the summer of 1787, debating both high principles and practical details. Experienced politicians, they looked for a plan that would be acceptable to most citizens and existing political interests. Pierce Butler of South Carolina invoked a classical Greek precedent: "We must follow the example of Solon, who gave the Athenians not the best government he could devise but the best they would receive."

The Great Compromise

As the convention grappled with the central problem of the representation of large and small states, the Connecticut delegates suggested a possible solution. They proposed that the national legislature's upper chamber (the Senate) have two members from each state, while seats in the lower chamber (the House of Representatives) be apportioned by population (determined every ten years by a national census). After bitter debate, delegates from the populous states reluctantly accepted this "Great Compromise."

Other state-related issues were quickly settled by restricting (or leaving ambiguous) the extent of central authority. Some delegates opposed a national system of courts, predicting that "the states will revolt at such encroachments" on their judicial authority.

This danger led the convention to vest the judicial power "in one supreme Court" and allow the new national legislature to decide whether to establish lower courts within the states. The convention also refused to set a property requirement for voting in national elections. "Eight or nine states have extended the right of suffrage beyond the freeholders," George Mason of Virginia pointed out. "What will people there say if they should be disfranchised?" Finally, the convention specified that state legislatures would elect members of the upper house, or Senate, and the states would select the electors who would choose the president. By allowing states to have important roles in the new constitutional system, the delegates hoped that their citizens would accept limits on state sovereignty.

Negotiations over Slavery The shadow of slavery hovered over many debates, and Gouverneur Morris of New York brought it into view. To safeguard property rights, Morris wanted life terms for senators, a property qualification for voting in national elections, and a strong president with veto power. Nonetheless, he rejected the legitimacy of two traditional types of property: the feudal dues claimed by aristocratic landowners and the ownership of slaves. An advocate of free markets and personal liberty, Morris condemned slavery as "a nefarious institution."

Many slave-owning delegates from the Chesapeake region, including Madison and George Mason, recognized that slavery contradicted republican principles and hoped for its eventual demise. They supported an end to American participation in the Atlantic slave trade, a proposal the South Carolina and Georgia delegates angrily rejected. Unless the importation of African slaves continued, these rice planters and merchants declared, their states "shall not be parties to the Union." At their insistence, the convention denied Congress the power to regulate immigration — and so the slave trade — until 1808 (American Voices, p. 208).

The delegates devised other slavery-related compromises. To mollify southern planters, they wrote a "fugitive clause" that allowed masters to reclaim enslaved blacks (or white indentured servants) who fled to other states. But in acknowledgment of the antislavery sentiments of Morris and other northerners, the delegates excluded the words *slavery* and *slave* from the Constitution; it spoke only of citizens and "all other Persons." Because slaves lacked the vote, antislavery delegates wanted their census numbers excluded when apportioning seats in Congress.

Southerners—ironically, given that they considered slaves property—demanded that slaves be counted in the census the same as full citizens, to increase the South's representation. Ultimately, the delegates agreed that each slave would count as three-fifths of a free person for purposes of representation and taxation, a compromise that helped southern planters dominate the national government until 1860.

National Authority   Having addressed the concerns of small states and slave states, the convention created a powerful national government. The Constitution declared that congressional legislation was the "supreme" law of the land. It gave the new government the power to tax, raise an army and a navy, and regulate foreign and interstate commerce, with the authority to make all laws "necessary and proper" to implement those and other provisions. To assist creditors and establish the new government's fiscal integrity, the Constitution required the United States to honor the existing national debt and prohibited the states from issuing paper money or enacting "any Law impairing the Obligation of Contracts."

The proposed constitution was not a "perfect production," Benjamin Franklin admitted, as he urged the delegates to sign it in September 1787. But the great statesman confessed his astonishment at finding "this system approaching so near to perfection." His colleagues apparently agreed; all but three signed the document.

The People Debate Ratification

The procedure for ratifying the new constitution was as controversial as its contents. Knowing that Rhode Island (and perhaps other states) would reject it, the delegates did not submit the Constitution to the state legislatures for their unanimous consent, as required by the Articles of Confederation. Instead, they arbitrarily—and cleverly—declared that it would take effect when ratified by conventions in nine of the thirteen states.

As the constitutional debate began in early 1788, the nationalists seized the initiative with two bold moves. First, they called themselves **Federalists**, suggesting that they supported a federal union—a loose, decentralized system—and obscuring their commitment to a strong national government. Second, they launched a coordinated campaign in pamphlets and newspapers to explain and justify the Philadelphia constitution.

The Antifederalists   The opponents of the Constitution, called by default the **Antifederalists**, had diverse backgrounds and motives. Some, like Governor George Clinton of New York, feared that state governments would lose power. Rural democrats protested that the proposed document, unlike most state constitutions, lacked a declaration of individual rights; they also feared that the central government would be run by wealthy men. "Lawyers and men of learning and monied men expect to be managers of this Constitution," worried a Massachusetts farmer. "[T]hey will swallow up all of us little folks . . . just as the whale swallowed up Jonah." Giving political substance to these fears, Melancton Smith of New York argued that the large electoral districts prescribed by the Constitution would restrict office holding to wealthy men, whereas the smaller districts used in state elections usually produced legislatures "composed principally of respectable yeomanry." John Quincy Adams agreed: if only "*eight* men" would represent Massachusetts, "they will infallibly be chosen from the aristocratic part of the community."

COMPARE AND CONTRAST
How did the Constitution, in its final form, differ from the plan that James Madison originally proposed?

Smith summed up the views of Americans who held traditional republican values. To keep government "close to the people," they wanted the states to remain small sovereign republics tied together only for trade and defense—not the "United States" but the "States United." Citing the French political philosopher Montesquieu, Antifederalists argued that republican institutions were best suited to small polities. "No extensive empire can be governed on republican principles," declared James Winthrop of Massachusetts. Patrick Henry worried that the Constitution would re-create British rule: high taxes, an oppressive bureaucracy, a standing army, and a "great and mighty President . . . supported in extravagant munificence." As another Antifederalist put it, "I had rather be a free citizen of the small republic of Massachusetts than an oppressed subject of the great American empire."

Federalists Respond   In New York, where ratification was hotly contested, James Madison, John Jay, and Alexander Hamilton defended the proposed constitution in a series of eighty-five essays written in 1787 and 1788, collectively titled *The Federalist*. This work influenced political leaders throughout the country and subsequently won acclaim as an important treatise of practical republicanism. Its authors denied that a

The First National Debate over Slavery

In this part of the text, we trace the impact of republican ideology on American politics and society. What happened when republicanism collided head-on with the well-established practice of slavery? After the Revolution, the Massachusetts courts abolished slavery, but in 1787, slavery was legal in the rest of the Union and was the bedrock of social order and agricultural production in the southern states. A look at the debates on the issue of the African slave trade at the Philadelphia convention and in a state ratifying convention shows that slavery was an extremely divisive issue at the birth of the nation—a dark cloud threatening the bright future of the young republic.

The Constitutional Convention

Slavery was not a major topic of discussion at the Philadelphia convention, but it surfaced a number of times, notably in the important debate over representation (which produced the three-fifths clause). A discussion of the Atlantic slave trade began when Luther Martin, a delegate from Maryland, proposed a clause allowing Congress to impose a tax on or prohibit the importation of slaves.

Mr. Martin proposed to vary article 7, sect. 4 so as to allow a prohibition or tax on the importation of slaves. . . . [He believed] it was inconsistent with the principles of the Revolution, and dishonorable to the American character, to have such a feature [promoting the slave trade] in the Constitution.

Mr. [John] Rutledge [of South Carolina declared that] religion and humanity had nothing to do with this question. Interest alone is the governing principle with nations. The true question at present is whether the Southern states shall or shall not be parties to the Union. . . .

Mr. [Oliver] Ellsworth [of Connecticut] was for leaving the clause as it stands. Let every state import what it pleases. The morality or wisdom of slavery are considerations belonging to the states themselves. . . . The old Confederation had not meddled with this point, and he did not see any greater necessity for bringing it within the policy of the new one.

Mr. [Charles C.] Pinckney [said] South Carolina can never receive the plan [for a new constitution] if it prohibits the slave trade. In every proposed extension of the powers of Congress, that state has expressly and watchfully excepted that of meddling with the importation of Negroes. . . .

Mr. [Roger] Sherman [of Connecticut] was for leaving the clause as it stands. He disapproved of the slave trade; yet, as the states were now possessed of the right to import slaves, . . . and as it was expedient to have as few objections as possible to the proposed scheme of government, he thought it best to leave the matter as we find it.

Col. [George] Mason [of Virginia stated that] this infernal trade originated in the avarice of British merchants. The British government constantly checked the attempts of Virginia to put a stop to it. The present question concerns not the importing states alone, but the whole Union. . . . Maryland and Virginia, he said, had already prohibited the importation of slaves expressly. North Carolina had done the same in substance. All this would be in vain if South Carolina and Georgia be at liberty to import. The Western people are already calling out for slaves for their new lands, and will fill that country with slaves, if they can be got through South Carolina and Georgia. Slavery discourages arts and manufactures. The poor despise labor when performed by slaves. They prevent the immigration of whites, who really enrich and strengthen a country. . . .

Every master of slaves is born a petty tyrant. They bring the judgment of Heaven on a country. As nations cannot be rewarded or punished in the next world, they must be in this. By an inevitable chain of causes and effects, Providence punishes national sins by national calamities. . . . He held it essential, in every point of view, that the general government should have power to prevent the increase of slavery.

Mr. Ellsworth, as he had never owned a slave, could not judge of the effects of slavery on character. He said, however, that if it was to be considered in a moral light, we ought to go further, and free those already in the country. . . . Let us not intermeddle. As population increases, poor laborers will be so plenty as to render slaves useless. Slavery, in time, will not be a speck in our country. . . .

Gen. [Charles C.] Pinckney [argued that] South Carolina and Georgia cannot do without slaves. As to

Virginia, she will gain by stopping the importations. Her slaves will rise in value, and she has more than she wants. It would be unequal to require South Carolina and Georgia to confederate on such unequal terms. . . . He contended that the importation of slaves would be for the interest of the whole Union. The more slaves, the more produce to employ the carrying trade; the more consumption also; and the more of this, the more revenue for the common treasury. . . . [He] should consider a rejection of the [present] clause as an exclusion of South Carolina from the Union.

Source: Max Farrand, ed., *The Records of the Federal Convention of 1787* (New Haven: Yale University Press, 1911), 2: 364–365, 369–372.

The Massachusetts Ratifying Convention

In Philadelphia, the delegates agreed on a compromise: they gave Congress the power to tax or prohibit slave imports, as Luther Martin had proposed, but withheld that power for twenty years. In the Massachusetts convention, the delegates split on this issue and on many others. They ratified the Constitution by a narrow margin, 187 to 168.

Mr. Neal (from Kittery) [an Antifederalist] went over the ground of objection to . . . the idea that slave trade was allowed to be continued for 20 years. His profession, he said, obliged him to bear witness against any thing that should favor the making merchandize of the bodies of men, and unless his objection was removed, he could not put his hand to the constitution. Other gentlemen said, in addition to this idea, that there was not even a proposition that the negroes ever shall be free: and Gen. Thompson exclaimed — "Mr. President, shall it be said, that after we have established our own independence and freedom, we make slaves of others? Oh! Washington . . . he has immortalized himself! but he holds those in slavery who have a good right to be free as he is. . . ."

On the other side, gentlemen said, that the step taken in this article, towards the abolition of slavery, was one of the beauties of the constitution. They observed, that in the confederation there was no provision whatever for its ever being abolished; but this constitution provides, that Congress may after twenty years, totally annihilate the slave trade. . . .

Mr. Heath (Federalist): . . . I apprehend that it is not in our power to do any thing for or against those who are in slavery in the southern states. No gentleman within these walls detests every idea of slavery more than I do: it is generally detested by the people of this commonwealth, and I ardently hope that the time will soon come, when our brethren in the southern states will view it as we do, and put a stop to it; but to this we have no right to compel them.

Two questions naturally arise: if we ratify the Constitution, shall we do any thing by our act to hold the blacks in slavery or shall we become the partakers of other men's sins? I think neither of them: each state is sovereign and independent to a certain degree, and they have a right, and will regulate their own internal affairs, as to themselves appears proper. . . . We are not in this case partakers of other men's sins. . . .

The federal convention went as far as they could; the migration or immigration &c. is confined to the states, now existing only, new states cannot claim it. Congress, by their ordnance for erecting new states, some time since, declared that there shall be no slavery in them. But whether those in slavery in the southern states, will be emancipated after the year 1808, I do not pretend to determine: I rather doubt it.

Source: Jonathan Elliot, ed., *The Debates . . . on the Adoption of the Federal Constitution* (Philadelphia: J. B. Lippincott, 1836), 1: 103–105, 107, 112, 117.

QUESTIONS FOR ANALYSIS

1. At the Constitutional Convention in Philadelphia, what were the main arguments for and against federal restrictions on the Atlantic slave trade? How do you explain the position taken by the Connecticut delegates in Philadelphia and Mr. Heath in the Massachusetts debate?

2. What argument does George Mason, a Virginia slave owner, make in favor of prohibiting the Atlantic slave trade?

3. What evidence of regional tensions appears in the documents? Several men from different states — Mason from Virginia, Ellsworth from Connecticut, and Heath from Massachusetts — offered predictions about the future of slavery. How accurate were they?

centralized government would lead to domestic tyranny. Drawing on Montesquieu's theories and John Adams's *Thoughts on Government*, Madison, Jay, and Hamilton pointed out that authority would be divided among the president, a bicameral legislature, and a judiciary. Each branch of government would "check and balance" the others and so preserve liberty.

In "**Federalist No. 10**," Madison challenged the view that republican governments only worked in small polities, arguing that a large state would better protect republican liberty. It was "sown in the nature of man," Madison wrote, for individuals to seek power and form factions. Indeed, "a landed interest, a manufacturing interest, a mercantile interest, a moneyed interest, with many lesser interests, grow up of necessity in civilized nations." A free society should welcome all factions but keep any one of them from becoming dominant—something best achieved in a large republic. "Extend the sphere and you take in a greater variety of parties and interests," Madison concluded, inhibiting the formation of a majority eager "to invade the rights of other citizens."

The Constitution Ratified The delegates debating these issues in the state ratification conventions included untutored farmers and middling artisans as well as educated gentlemen. Generally, backcountry delegates were Antifederalists, while those from coastal areas were Federalists. In Pennsylvania, Philadelphia merchants and artisans joined commercial farmers to ratify the Constitution. Other early Federalist successes came in four less populous states—Delaware, New Jersey, Georgia, and Connecticut—where delegates hoped that a strong national government would offset the power of large neighboring states (Map 6.7).

The Constitution's first real test came in January 1788 in Massachusetts, a hotbed of Antifederalist sentiment. Influential Patriots, including Samuel Adams and Governor John Hancock, opposed the new constitution, as did many followers of Daniel Shays. But Boston artisans, who wanted tariff protection from British imports, supported ratification. To win over other delegates, Federalist leaders assured the convention that they would recommend a national bill of

MAP 6.7
Ratifying the Constitution of 1787

In 1907, geographer Owen Libby mapped the votes of members of the state conventions that ratified the Constitution. His map showed that most delegates from seaboard or commercial farming districts (which sent many delegates to the conventions) supported the Constitution, while those from sparsely represented, subsistence-oriented backcountry areas opposed it. Subsequent research has confirmed Libby's socioeconomic interpretation of the voting patterns in North and South Carolina and in Massachusetts. However, other states' delegates were influenced by different factors. For example, in Georgia, delegates from all regions voted for ratification.

rights. By a close vote of 187 to 168, the Federalists carried the day.

Spring brought Federalist victories in Maryland, South Carolina, and New Hampshire, reaching the nine-state quota required for ratification. But it took the powerful arguments advanced in *The Federalist* and more promises of a bill of rights to secure the Constitution's adoption in the essential states of Virginia and New York. The votes were again close: 89 to 79 in Virginia and 30 to 27 in New York.

Testifying to their respect for popular sovereignty and majority rule, most Americans accepted the verdict of the ratifying conventions. "A decided majority" of the New Hampshire assembly had opposed the "new system," reported Joshua Atherton, but now they said, "It is adopted, let us try it." In Virginia, Patrick Henry vowed to "submit as a quiet citizen" and fight for amendments "in a constitutional way."

Unlike in France, where the Revolution of 1789 divided the society into irreconcilable factions for generations, the American Constitutional Revolution of 1787 created a national republic that enjoyed broad popular support. Federalists celebrated their triumph by organizing great processions in the seaport cities. By marching in an orderly fashion — in conscious contrast to the riotous Revolutionary mobs — Federalist-minded citizens affirmed their allegiance to a self-governing but elite-ruled republican nation.

SUMMARY

In this chapter, we examined the unfolding of two related sets of events. The first was the war between Britain and its rebellious colonies that began in 1776 and ended in 1783. The two great battles of Saratoga (1777) and Yorktown (1781) determined the outcome of that conflict. Surprisingly, given the military might of the British Empire, both were American victories. These triumphs testify to the determination of George Washington, the resilience of the Continental army, and support for the Patriot cause from hundreds of local militias and tens of thousands of taxpaying citizens.

This popular support reflected the Patriots' second success: building effective institutions of republican government. These elected institutions of local and state governance evolved out of colonial-era town meetings and representative assemblies. They were defined in the state constitutions written between 1776 and 1781, and their principles informed the first national constitution, the Articles of Confederation. Despite the challenges posed by conflicts over suffrage, women's rights, and fiscal policy, these self-governing political institutions carried the new republic successfully through the war-torn era and laid the foundation for the Constitution of 1787, the national charter that endures today.

CHAPTER REVIEW

MAKE IT STICK   Go to **LearningCurve** to retain what you've read.

KEY TERMS

Identify and explain the significance of each term below.

Key Concepts and Events

Battle of Long Island (1776) (p. 184)

Battle of Saratoga (1777) (p. 187)

Valley Forge (p. 189)

Philipsburg Proclamation (p. 190)

Battle of Yorktown (1781) (p. 195)

currency tax (p. 196)

Treaty of Paris of 1783 (p. 196)

Pennsylvania constitution of 1776 (p. 198)

mixed government (p. 198)

Articles of Confederation (p. 200)

Northwest Ordinance of 1787 (p. 201)

Shays's Rebellion (p. 204)

Virginia Plan (p. 205)

New Jersey Plan (p. 206)

Federalists (p. 207)

Antifederalists (p. 207)

Federalist No. 10 (p. 210)

KEY PEOPLE

General George Washington (p. 184)

General William Howe (p. 184)

General Horatio Gates (p. 187)

Robert Morris (p. 188)

Baron von Steuben (p. 189)

Judith Sargent Murray (p. 199)

James Madison (p. 205)

REVIEW QUESTIONS

Answer these questions to demonstrate your understanding of the chapter's main ideas.

1. What were the principal reasons that Great Britain, despite its enormous military advantages, lost the War for Independence?

2. The war had wrenching effects on the American economy. What economic problems became especially acute during wartime? How did the states and the Second Continental Congress attempt to address them?

3. Federalists and Antifederalists both claimed to represent the true spirit of the American Revolution. Which of these competing visions of national identity do you think was right? Why?

4. **THEMATIC UNDERSTANDING**   Consider the events listed under "Work, Exchange, and Technology" and "Politics and Power" for the period 1776–1787 on the thematic timeline on page 149. How did war debt and inflation influence the development of political institutions during these years?

MAKING CONNECTIONS

Recognize the larger developments and continuities within and across chapters by answering these questions.

1. **ACROSS TIME AND PLACE**   In Chapter 5, we saw the way that protests against imperial policy grew until colonists chose to declare their independence rather than submit to Parliament's authority. By 1787, the problems created by the Revolutionary War forced leaders of the newly independent states to consider plans for their own powerful central government. What problems led nationalists to believe such a step was necessary? How did Antifederalists draw on Revolutionary ideas to make their case against the Constitution? What claims did nationalists make in response to dampen Antifederalist fears?

2. **VISUAL EVIDENCE**   Look again at Map 6.5 on page 202 showing western land claims in the 1780s. If these claims had not been ceded to the Continental Congress, what would have been the likely result? Why was it so important to the survival of the Confederation that individual states give up their claims to these western lands?

MORE TO EXPLORE

Start here to learn more about the events discussed in this chapter.

Colin G. Calloway, *The American Revolution in Indian Country* (1995). Tracks the experiences of numerous Native American communities in the Revolution.

Saul Cornell, *The Other Founders* (1999). Explores the ideas and legacy of the Antifederalists.

John C. Dann, ed., *The Revolution Remembered* (1980). Contains vivid eyewitness accounts of the Revolution.

Pauline Maier, *Ratification* (2010). A compelling narrative of the debate over the Constitution.

Michael McDonnell, *The Politics of War* (2007). A penetrating account of Virginia's mobilization for war.

Leonard Richards, *Shays's Rebellion* (2003). A persuasive interpretation of the rebellion's participants and motives.

TIMELINE

Ask yourself why this chapter begins and ends with these dates and then identify the links among related events.

1776	• Second Continental Congress declares independence • Howe forces Washington to retreat from New York and New Jersey • Pennsylvania approves democratic state constitution • John Adams publishes *Thoughts on Government*
1777	• Articles of Confederation create central government • Howe occupies Philadelphia (September) • Gates defeats Burgoyne at Saratoga (October)
1778	• Franco-American alliance (February) • Lord North seeks political settlement • Congress rejects negotiations • British adopt southern strategy • British capture Savannah (December)
1778–1781	• Severe inflation of Continental currency
1779	• British and American forces battle in Georgia
1780	• Clinton seizes Charleston (May) • French troops land in Rhode Island
1781	• Cornwallis invades Virginia (April), surrenders at Yorktown (October) • States finally ratify Articles of Confederation
1783	• Treaty of Paris (September 3) officially ends war
1784–1785	• Congress enacts political and land ordinances for new states
1786	• Nationalists hold convention in Annapolis, Maryland • Shays's Rebellion roils Massachusetts
1787	• Congress passes Northwest Ordinance • Constitutional Convention in Philadelphia
1787–1788	• Jay, Madison, and Hamilton write *The Federalist* • Eleven states ratify U.S. Constitution

KEY TURNING POINTS: Gates defeats Burgoyne at Saratoga (1777), the Franco-American alliance (1778), and Cornwallis surrenders at Yorktown (1781). How were these three events linked? How important was the French alliance to the Patriot victory?

7
CHAPTER

Hammering Out a Federal Republic
1787–1820

Like an earthquake, the American Revolution shook the European monarchical order, and its after-shocks reverberated for decades. By "creating a new republic based on the rights of the individual, the North Americans introduced a new force into the world," the eminent German historian Leopold von Ranke warned the king of Bavaria in 1854, a force that might cost the monarch his throne. Before 1776, "a king who ruled by the grace of God had been the center around which everything turned. Now the idea emerged that power should come from below [from the people]."

Other republican-inspired upheavals—England's Puritan Revolution of the 1640s and the French Revolution of 1789—ended in political chaos and military rule. Similar fates befell many Latin American republics that won independence from Spain in the early nineteenth century. But the American states escaped both anarchy and dictatorship. Having been raised in a Radical Whig political culture that viewed standing armies and powerful generals as instruments of tyranny, General George Washington left public life in 1783 to manage his plantation, astonishing European observers but bolstering the authority of elected Patriot leaders. "'Tis a Conduct so novel," American painter John Trumbull reported from London, that it is "inconceivable to People [here]."

The great task of fashioning representative republican governments absorbed the energy and intellect of an entire generation and was rife with conflict. Seeking to perpetuate the elite-led polity of the colonial era, Federalists celebrated "natural aristocrats" such as Washington and condemned the radical republicanism of the French Revolution. In response, Jefferson and his Republican followers claimed the Fourth of July as their holiday and "we the people" as their political language. "There was a grand democrat procession in Town on the 4th of July," came a report from Baltimore: "All the farmers, tanners, black-smiths, shoemakers, etc. were there . . . and afterwards they went to a grand feast."

Many people of high status worried that the new state governments were too attentive to the demands of such ordinary workers and their families. When considering a bill, Connecticut conservative Ezra Stiles grumbled, every elected official "instantly thinks how it will affect his constituents" rather than how it would enhance the general welfare. What Stiles criticized as irresponsible, however, most Americans welcomed. The concerns of ordinary citizens were now paramount, and traditional elites trembled.

IDENTIFY THE BIG IDEA
What was required to make the United States a strong, viable, independent republic in its early years, and how did debates over the Constitution shape relations between the national government and the states?

An Emblem of America, 1800 In the first years of independence, citizens of the United States searched for a symbolic representation of their new nation. This engraving shows many of the choices: Should the symbol of "America" have an ideological meaning, as in the Goddess of Liberty? Or should it enshrine national heroes, as in the stone Memorial to Washington? Or should America's symbol be found among its unique features, such as Niagara Falls (pictured in the background) or the presence of Africans and Indians (as represented by the black youth to the right and the spear-brandishing figure in front of the falls)? Or, finally, should its symbol be the national flag? Courtesy of the John Carter Brown Library at Brown University.

The Political Crisis of the 1790s

The final decade of the eighteenth century brought fresh challenges for American politics. The Federalists split into two factions over financial policy and the French Revolution, and their leaders, Alexander Hamilton and Thomas Jefferson, offered contrasting visions of the future. Would the United States remain an agricultural nation governed by local officials, as Jefferson hoped? Or would Hamilton's vision of a strong national government and an economy based on manufacturing become reality?

The Federalists Implement the Constitution

The Constitution expanded the dimensions of political life by allowing voters to choose national leaders as well as local and state officials. The Federalists swept the election of 1788, winning forty-four seats in the House of Representatives; only eight Antifederalists won election. As expected, members of the electoral college chose George Washington as president. John Adams received the second-highest number of electoral votes and became vice president.

Devising the New Government   Once the military savior of his country, Washington now became its political father. At age fifty-seven, the first president possessed great personal dignity and a cautious personality. To maintain continuity, he adopted many of the administrative practices of the Confederation and asked Congress to reestablish the existing executive departments: Foreign Affairs (State), Finance (Treasury), and War. To head the Department of State, Washington chose Thomas Jefferson, a fellow Virginian and an experienced diplomat. For secretary of the treasury, he turned to Alexander Hamilton, a lawyer and his former military aide. The president designated Jefferson, Hamilton, and Secretary of War Henry Knox as his cabinet, or advisory body.

The Constitution mandated a supreme court, but the Philadelphia convention gave Congress the task of creating a national court system. The Federalists wanted strong national institutions, and the **Judiciary Act of 1789** reflected their vision. The act established a federal district court in each state and three circuit courts to hear appeals from the districts, with the Supreme Court having the final say. The Judiciary Act also specified that cases arising in state courts that involved federal laws could be appealed to the Supreme Court. This provision ensured that federal judges would have the final say on the meaning of the Constitution.

The Bill of Rights   The Federalists kept their promise to add a declaration of rights to the Constitution. James Madison, now a member of the House of Representatives, submitted nineteen amendments to the First Congress; by 1791, ten had been approved by Congress and ratified by the states. These ten amendments, known as the **Bill of Rights**, safeguard fundamental personal rights, including freedom of speech and religion, and mandate legal procedures, such as trial by jury. By protecting individual citizens, the amendments eased Antifederalists' fears of an oppressive national government and secured the legitimacy of the Constitution. They also addressed the issue of federalism: the proper balance between the authority of the national and state governments. But that question was constantly contested until the Civil War and remains important today.

Hamilton's Financial Program

George Washington's most important decision was choosing Alexander Hamilton as secretary of the treasury. An ambitious self-made man of great intelligence, Hamilton married into the Schuyler family, influential Hudson River Valley landowners, and was a prominent lawyer in New York City. At the Philadelphia convention, he condemned the "democratic spirit" and called for an authoritarian government and a president with near-monarchical powers.

As treasury secretary, Hamilton devised bold policies to enhance national authority and to assist financiers and merchants. He outlined his plans in three pathbreaking reports to Congress: on public credit (January 1790), on a national bank (December 1790), and on manufactures (December 1791). These reports outlined a coherent program of national mercantilism — government-assisted economic development.

Public Credit: Redemption and Assumption   The financial and social implications of Hamilton's "**Report on the Public Credit**" made it instantly controversial. Hamilton asked Congress to redeem at face value the $55 million in Confederation securities held by foreign and domestic investors (Figure 7.1). His reasons were simple: As an underdeveloped nation, the United States needed good credit to secure loans from Dutch and

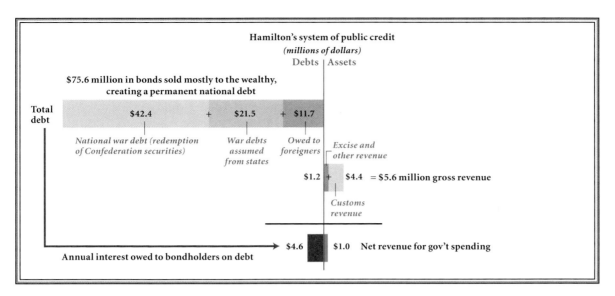

FIGURE 7.1

Hamilton's Fiscal Structure, 1792

As treasury secretary, Alexander Hamilton established a national debt by issuing government bonds and using the proceeds to redeem Confederation securities and assume the war debts of the states. To pay the annual interest due on the bonds, he used the revenue from excise taxes and customs duties. Hamilton deliberately did not attempt to redeem the bonds because he wanted to tie the interests of the wealthy Americans who owned them to the new national government.

British financiers. However, Hamilton's redemption plan would give enormous profits to speculators, who had bought up depreciated securities. For example, the Massachusetts firm of Burrell & Burrell had paid $600 for Confederation notes with a face value of $2,500; it stood to reap a profit of $1,900. Such windfall gains offended a majority of Americans, who condemned the speculative practices of capitalist financiers. Equally controversial was Hamilton's proposal to pay the Burrells and other note holders with new interest-bearing securities, thereby creating a permanent national debt.

Patrick Henry condemned this plan "to erect, and concentrate, and perpetuate a large monied interest" and warned that it would prove "fatal to the existence of American liberty." James Madison demanded that Congress recompense those who originally owned Confederation securities: the thousands of shopkeepers, farmers, and soldiers who had bought or accepted them during the dark days of the war. However, it would have been difficult to trace the original owners; moreover, nearly half the members of the House of Representatives owned Confederation securities and would profit personally from Hamilton's plan. Melding practicality with self-interest, the House rejected Madison's suggestion.

Hamilton then proposed that the national government further enhance public credit by assuming the war debts of the states. This assumption plan, costing $22 million, also favored well-to-do creditors such as Abigail Adams, who had bought depreciated Massachusetts government bonds with a face value of $2,400 for only a few hundred dollars and would reap a windfall profit. Still, Adams was a long-term investor, not a speculator like Assistant Secretary of the Treasury William Duer. Knowing Hamilton's intentions in advance, Duer and his associates secretly bought up $4.6 million of the war bonds of southern states at bargain rates. Congressional critics condemned Duer's speculation. They also pointed out that some states had already paid off their war debts; in response, Hamilton promised to reimburse those states. To win the votes of congressmen from Virginia and Maryland, the treasury chief arranged another deal: he agreed that the permanent national capital would be built along the Potomac River, where suspicious southerners could easily watch its operations. Such astute bargaining gave Hamilton the votes he needed to enact his redemption and assumption plans.

> **UNDERSTAND POINTS OF VIEW**
>
> Why did Hamilton believe a national debt would strengthen the United States and help to ensure its survival?

Creating a National Bank In December 1790, Hamilton asked Congress to charter the **Bank of the United States**, which would be jointly owned by private stockholders and the national government. Hamilton argued that the bank would provide stability to the specie-starved American economy by making loans to merchants, handling government funds, and issuing bills of credit — much as the Bank of England had done in Great Britain. These potential benefits persuaded Congress to grant Hamilton's bank a twenty-year charter and to send the legislation to the president for his approval.

At this critical juncture, Secretary of State Thomas Jefferson joined with James Madison to oppose Hamilton's financial initiatives. Jefferson charged that Hamilton's national bank was unconstitutional. "The incorporation of a Bank," Jefferson told President Washington, was not a power expressly "delegated to the United States by the Constitution." Jefferson's argument rested on a *strict* interpretation of the Constitution. Hamilton preferred a *loose* interpretation; he told Washington that Article 1, Section 8, empowered Congress to make "all Laws which shall be necessary and proper" to carry out the provisions of the Constitution. Agreeing with Hamilton, the president signed the legislation.

Raising Revenue Through Tariffs Hamilton now sought revenue to pay the annual interest on the national debt. At his insistence, Congress imposed excise taxes, including a duty on whiskey distilled in the United States. These taxes would yield $1 million a year. To raise another $4 million to $5 million, the treasury secretary proposed higher tariffs on foreign imports. Although Hamilton's "**Report on Manufactures**" (1791)

urged the expansion of American manufacturing, he did not support high protective tariffs that would exclude foreign products. Rather, he advocated moderate revenue tariffs that would pay the interest on the debt and other government expenses.

Hamilton's scheme worked brilliantly. As American trade increased, customs revenue rose steadily and paid down the national debt. Controversies notwithstanding, the treasury secretary had devised a strikingly modern and successful fiscal system; as entrepreneur Samuel Blodget Jr. declared in 1801, "the country prospered beyond all former example."

Jefferson's Agrarian Vision

Hamilton paid a high political price for his success. As Washington began his second four-year term in 1793, Hamilton's financial measures had split the Federalists into bitterly opposed factions. Most northern Federalists supported the treasury secretary, while most southern Federalists joined a group headed by Madison and Jefferson. By 1794, the two factions had acquired names. Hamiltonians remained Federalists; the allies of Madison and Jefferson called themselves Democratic Republicans or simply Republicans.

Thomas Jefferson spoke for southern planters and western farmers. Well-read in architecture, natural history, agricultural science, and political theory, Jefferson embraced the optimism of the Enlightenment. He believed in the "improvability of the human race" and deplored the corruption and social divisions that threatened its progress. Having seen the poverty of laborers in British factories, Jefferson doubted that wageworkers had the economic and political independence needed to sustain a republican polity.

Two Visions of America

Thomas Jefferson (left) and Alexander Hamilton confront each other in these portraits, as they did in the political battles of the 1790s. Jefferson was pro-French, Hamilton pro-British. Jefferson favored farmers and artisans; Hamilton supported merchants and financiers. Jefferson believed in democracy and rule by legislative majorities; Hamilton argued for strong executives and judges. Still, in the contested presidential election of 1800, Hamilton (who detested candidate Aaron Burr) threw his support to Jefferson and secured the presidency for his longtime political foe. The White House Historical Association (White House Collection). / Yale University Art Gallery/Art Resource, NY.

Jefferson therefore set his democratic vision of America in a society of independent yeomen farm families. "Those who labor in the earth are the chosen people of God," he wrote. The grain and meat from their homesteads would feed European nations, which "would manufacture and send us in exchange our clothes and other comforts." Jefferson's notion of an international division of labor resembled that proposed by Scottish economist Adam Smith in *The Wealth of Nations* (1776).

 To see a longer excerpt of Jefferson's *Notes on the State of Virginia*, along with other primary sources from this period, see *Sources for America's History*.

Turmoil in Europe brought Jefferson's vision closer to reality. The French Revolution began in 1789; four years later, the First French Republic (1792–1804) went to war against a British-led coalition of monarchies. As fighting disrupted European farming, wheat prices leaped from 5 to 8 shillings a bushel and remained high for twenty years, bringing substantial profits to Chesapeake and Middle Atlantic farmers. "Our farmers have never experienced such prosperity," remarked one observer. Simultaneously, a boom in the export of raw cotton, fueled by the invention of the cotton gin and the mechanization of cloth production in Britain, boosted the economies of Georgia and South Carolina. As Jefferson had hoped, European markets brought prosperity to American agriculture.

The French Revolution Divides Americans

American merchants profited even more handsomely from the European war. In 1793, President Washington issued a **Proclamation of Neutrality**, allowing U.S. citizens to trade with all belligerents. As neutral carriers, American merchant ships claimed a right to pass through Britain's naval blockade of French ports, and American firms quickly took over the lucrative sugar trade between France and its West Indian islands. Commercial earnings rose spectacularly, averaging $20 million annually in the 1790s — twice the value of cotton and tobacco exports. As the American merchant fleet increased from 355,000 tons in 1790 to 1.1 million tons in 1808, northern shipbuilders and merchants provided work for thousands of shipwrights, sailmakers, dockhands, and seamen. Carpenters, masons, and cabinetmakers in Boston, New York, and Philadelphia easily found work building warehouses and fashionable "Federal-style" town houses for newly affluent merchants.

Ideological Politics   As Americans profited from Europe's struggles, they argued passionately over its ideologies. Most Americans had welcomed the **French Revolution** (1789–1799) because it abolished feudalism and established a constitutional monarchy. The creation of the First French Republic was more controversial. Many applauded the end of the monarchy and embraced the democratic ideology of the radical **Jacobins**. Like the Jacobins, they formed political clubs and began to address one another as "citizen." However, Americans with strong religious beliefs condemned the new French government for closing Christian churches and promoting a rational religion based on "natural morality." Fearing social revolution at home, wealthy Americans condemned revolutionary leader Robespierre and his followers for executing King Louis XVI and three thousand aristocrats.

Their fears were well founded, because Hamilton's economic policies quickly sparked a domestic insurgency. In 1794, western Pennsylvania farmers mounted the so-called **Whiskey Rebellion** to protest Hamilton's excise tax on spirits (Thinking Like a Historian, p. 220). This tax had cut demand for the corn whiskey the farmers distilled and bartered for eastern manufactures. Like the Sons of Liberty in 1765 and the Shaysites in 1786, the Whiskey Rebels assailed the tax collectors who sent the farmers' hard-earned money to a distant government. Protesters waved banners proclaiming the French revolutionary slogan "Liberty, Equality, Fraternity!" To deter popular rebellion and uphold national authority, President Washington raised a militia force of 12,000 troops and dispersed the Whiskey Rebels.

> **COMPARE AND CONTRAST**
> How did Jefferson's idea of an agrarian republic differ from the economic vision put forward by Alexander Hamilton?

Jay's Treaty   Britain's maritime strategy intensified political divisions in America. Beginning in late 1793, the British navy seized 250 American ships carrying French sugar and other goods. Hoping to protect merchant property through diplomacy, Washington dispatched John Jay to Britain. But Jay returned with a controversial treaty that ignored the American claim that "free ships make free goods" and accepted Britain's right to stop neutral ships. The treaty also required the U.S. government to make "full and complete compensation" to British merchants for pre–Revolutionary War debts owed by American citizens. In return, the

The Social Life of Alcohol

Alcohol was ubiquitous in post-Revolutionary America. Expensive wines and distilled spirits traveled through the channels of Atlantic trade; molasses was imported from the West Indies and distilled into rum in American port towns; and cider, beer, and whiskey were produced on a small scale everywhere in the countryside. Taverns were centers of social and political activity. Alcohol both mirrored and reinforced the economic and geographical divisions in American life.

1. **James Newport's ad in the *Pennsylvania Gazette*, 1790.**

JAMES NEWPORT, At his *Wine, Spirit and Cordial Stores*, in Second street, at the upper corner of Carter's alley, has, by Wholesale and Retail,

MADEIRA, Sherry, Lisbon, Teneriffe, Malaga, Fayal, and Port Wines, Jamaica spirits, Antigua rum, Philadelphia ditto, Holland gin, Philadelphia ditto, very excellent, in cases, Coniac [sic] brandy, American ditto, good flavor, choice shrub. CORDIALS, &c. Anniseed water, clove water, all-fours, Cinnamon water, prime wine and rum colouring, wine bitters. Spirits of wine. Retail Stores and Tavern-keepers will in particular, find their interest in buying here, the articles being all the best in their kind, and selling at the most reduced prices. Philadelphia, April 30, 1790.

2. **Benjamin Chew on providing alcohol to his slaves, 1794.** *The instructions of a prominent Philadelphia lawyer and landowner to his overseer about giving rum to his slaves during the harvest.*

I have written . . . to let you have [illegible] Rum & other necessaries for the Harvest. But as these articles are so [illegible] dear I must recommend it to you to be as sparing of them as possible. . . . I must rely on you good man [to conduct] the Business. . . . I would have you let the People have a little Rum — let them be cautious in using too much Spirits during Harvest — it will be well to mix some molasses with water to drink — it is very wholesome & much recommended. . . . I need not caution you that a great deal depends upon your own proper attention to yourself and that you are careful of good Conduct during Harvest.

3. **Anonymous, *The Toast*, c. 1810–1815.**

Source: John Nugent Collection, Newburgh, Indiana.

4. **John Lewis Krimmel, *Village Tavern*, 1814.** *This painting of a postman arriving at a Pennsylvania tavern with letters and newspapers reminds us that taverns were not merely places to drink.*

Source: John Lewis Krimmel (American, 1786–1821) Village Tavern, 1813–1814, oil on canvas, 16⅞ x 22½ inches, Toledo Museum of Art (Toledo, Ohio) Purchased with funds from the Florence Scott Libbey Bequest in Memory of her Father, Maurice A. Scott. 1954.13. Photo Credit: Photography Incorporated, Toledo.

execution and obtaining a repeal of the excise law, he or they will be deemed as enemies and stand opposed to virtuous principles of republican liberty, and shall receive punishment according to the nature of the offense.

And whereas, a certain John Reed, now resident in Washington, and being at his place near Pittsburgh, called Reedsburgh, and having a set of stills employed at said Reedsburgh, entered on the excise docket, contrary to the will and good pleasure of his fellow citizens, and came not forth to assist in the suppression of the execution of said law, by aiding and assisting in the late expedition, have, by delinquency, manifested his approbation to the execution of the aforesaid law, is hereby charged forthwith to cause the contents of this paper, without adding or diminishing, to be published in the Pittsburgh Gazette, the ensuing week, under the no less penalty than the consumption of his distillery.

Given under my hand, this 19th day of July, one thousand seven hundred and ninety-four.

Sources: (1) James Newport, *Pennsylvania Gazette*, May 5, 1790; (2) Chew Family Papers, Box 773, ff. 25, 10, Historical Society of Pennsylvania; (5) *Pennsylvania Gazette*, October 1, 1794; (6) *Pennsylvania Archives*, 2nd ser., 4:61–62 (Harrisburg: E. K. Meyers, State Printer, 1890).

5. **Public notice from the *Pennsylvania Gazette*, 1794.** *Here, a tavern serves as the gathering place for citizens interested in nominating candidates for election to office.*

THE INHABITANTS of the County of Chester, are hereby requested to meet at the Centre house, kept by Abraham Marshall, in West Bradford, on FRIDAY the 10th Day of October next, at 10 o'clock, A. M. in order to form a TICKET for the ensuing Election.

6. **Tom the Tinker demands compliance, July 23, 1794.** *During the Whiskey Rebellion, "Tom the Tinker" pinned this notice to a tree near John Reed's distillery. Reed had it published in a Pittsburgh newspaper.*

In taking a survey of the troops under my direction in the late expedition against that insolent exciseman, John Neville, I find there were a great number of delinquents, even among those who carry on distilling. It will, therefore, be observed that I, Tom the Tinker, will not suffer any certain class or set of men to be excluded [from] the service of this my district, when notified to attend on any expedition carried on in order to obstruct the execution of the excise law, and obtain a repeal thereof.

And I do declare on my solemn word, that if such delinquents do not come forth on the next alarm, with equipments, and give their assistance in opposing the

ANALYZING THE EVIDENCE

1. Who is the intended audience for an advertisement like James Newport's (source 1)? How many Atlantic ports of call are represented in the products he advertises?

2. The two paintings (sources 3 and 4), set in the interiors of a private home and a tavern, depict mostly men. What have they gathered for in each case? *Village Tavern* is set during the War of 1812. How does that fact influence your interpretation of the scene? What do you think the woman and child are doing in the tavern?

3. *Village Tavern* (source 4) and the ad calling for a political gathering (source 5) both suggest the way that politics and drinking often mixed. How might the fact that taverns were gathering places for political discussion and decision making have influenced outcomes?

4. What concerns does Benjamin Chew express in his correspondence with his overseer (source 2)? Given those worries, why do you think he provides rum to his slaves at all?

5. Tom the Tinker expressed the collective will of whiskey distillers in western Pennsylvania during the Whiskey Rebellion (source 6). Why would it have been important to enforce unanimous action during the uprising?

PUTTING IT ALL TOGETHER

Considering everything you know about the trade and consumption of alcohol, social stratification in the early republic, and differences between urban and rural communities, write a short essay that considers the ways in which taverns and alcohol helped unite people in some ways while differentiating or dividing them in others.

The Whiskey Rebellion, 1794

This painting of Washington reviewing the militia forces that would march against the Whiskey Rebels in western Pennsylvania expresses a Federalist vision of hierarchy (in the form of officers on horseback) and order (represented by the ranks of troops). The reality was messier: militia was called up from four states, but when volunteers were too few the states resorted to a draft, which prompted protests and riots. In the end, the militia force of more than 12,000 men was larger than the Continental army itself through much of the Revolution. Upon its approach, the rebellion evaporated. Twenty-four men were indicted for treason; two were sentenced to hang, but Washington pardoned them to encourage peaceful reconciliation. The Granger Collection, New York.

agreement allowed Americans to submit claims for illegal seizures and required the British to remove their troops and Indian agents from the Northwest Territory. Despite Republican charges that **Jay's Treaty** was too conciliatory, the Senate ratified it in 1795, but only by the two-thirds majority required by the Constitution. As long as the Federalists were in power, the United States would have a pro-British foreign policy.

The Haitian Revolution The French Revolution inspired a revolution closer to home that would also impact the United States. The wealthy French plantation colony of Saint-Domingue in the West Indies was deeply divided: a small class of elite planters stood atop the population of 40,000 free whites and dominated the island's half million slaves. In between, some 28,000 *gens de couleur* — free men of color — were excluded from most professions, forbidden from taking the names of their white relatives, and prevented from dressing and carrying themselves like whites. The French Revolution intensified conflict between planters and free blacks, giving way to a massive slave uprising in 1791 that aimed to abolish slavery. The uprising touched off years of civil war, along with Spanish and British invasions. In 1798, black Haitians led by Toussaint L'Ouverture — himself a former slave-owning planter — seized control of the country. After five more years of fighting, in 1803 Saint-Domingue became the independent nation of Haiti: the first black republic in the Atlantic World.

The **Haitian Revolution** profoundly impacted the United States. In 1793, thousands of refugees — planters, slaves, and free blacks alike — fled the island and traveled to Charleston, Norfolk, Baltimore,

IDENTIFY CAUSES
How did events abroad during the 1790s sharpen political divisions in the United States?

horrifying paradox, a perversion of the republican ideal (America Compared, p. 224).

The Rise of Political Parties

The appearance of Federalists and Republicans marked a new stage in American politics — what historians call the First Party System. Colonial legislatures had factions based on family, ethnicity, or region, but they did not have organized political parties. Nor did the new state and national constitutions make any provision for political societies. Indeed, most Americans believed that parties were dangerous because they looked out for themselves rather than serving the public interest.

But a shared understanding of the public interest collapsed in the face of sharp conflicts over Hamilton's fiscal policies. Most merchants and creditors supported the Federalist Party, as did wheat-exporting slaveholders in the Tidewater districts of the Chesapeake. The emerging Republican coalition included southern tobacco and rice planters, debt-conscious western farmers, Germans and Scots-Irish in the southern backcountry, and subsistence farmers in the Northeast.

Party identity crystallized in 1796. To prepare for the presidential election, Federalist and Republican leaders called caucuses in Congress and conventions in the states. They also mobilized popular support by organizing public festivals and processions: the Federalists held banquets in February to celebrate Washington's birthday, and the Republicans marched through the streets on July 4 to honor the Declaration of Independence.

In the election, voters gave Federalists a majority in Congress and made John Adams president. Adams continued Hamilton's pro-British foreign policy and strongly criticized French seizures of American merchant ships. When the French foreign minister Talleyrand solicited a loan and a bribe from American diplomats to stop the seizures, Adams charged that Talleyrand's agents, whom he dubbed X, Y, and Z, had insulted America's honor. In response to the **XYZ Affair**, Congress cut off trade with France in 1798 and authorized American privateering (licensing private ships to seize French vessels). This undeclared maritime war curtailed American trade with the French West Indies and resulted in the capture of nearly two hundred French and American merchant vessels.

The Naturalization, Alien, and Sedition Acts of 1798
As Federalists became more hostile to the French Republic, they also took a harder line against their Republican critics. When Republican-minded

Toussaint L'Ouverture, Haitian Revolutionary and Statesman

The American Revolution of 1776 constituted a victory for republicanism; the Haitian revolt of the 1790s represented a triumph of liberty over slavery and a demand for racial equality. After leading the black army that ousted French planters and British invaders from Haiti, Toussaint formed a constitutional government in 1801. A year later, when French troops invaded the island, he negotiated a treaty that halted Haitian resistance in exchange for a pledge that the French would not reinstate slavery. Subsequently, the French seized Toussaint and imprisoned him in France, where he died in 1803. Snark/Art Resource, NY.

Philadelphia, and New York, while newspapers detailed the horrors of the unfolding war. Many slaveholders panicked, fearful that the "contagion" of black liberation would undermine their own slave regimes. U.S. policy toward the rebellion presented a knotty problem. The first instinct of the Washington administration was to supply aid to the island's white population. Adams — strongly antislavery and no friend of France — changed course, aiding the rebels and strengthening commercial ties. Jefferson, though sympathetic to moral arguments against slavery, was himself a southern slaveholder; he was, moreover, an ardent supporter of France. When he became president, he cut off aid to the rebels, imposed a trade embargo, and refused to recognize an independent Haiti. For many Americans, an independent nation of liberated citizen-slaves was a

The Haitian Revolution and the Problem of Race

The slave uprising on the French island of Saint-Domingue triggered international war, created a refugee crisis, and ended with the creation of a new republic. The American Revolution did all these things as well, yet the United States did not support either the rebellion or the republic of Haiti.

Savannah City Council's Resolution in Response to the Haitian Uprising, 1795

Whereas, from the mischiefs which the people of St. Domingo, and other French islands, have experienced, from the insurrection of their Negroes and People of Colour, the precautions taken by the people of South Carolina . . . to prevent the importation or landing of any such Negroes or Mulattoes amongst them, and the information the Citizens now assembled have received, that a vessel is now lying at Cockspur, recently from Kingston, with near one hundred Negroes on board, whose landing may be dangerous to the inhabitants of this state, with the daily expectation of many more; therefore, to prevent the evils that may arise from suffering people of this description, under any pretense whatever, from being introduced amongst us, the Citizens pledge themselves unanimously to support the City Council in any salutary measures they may adopt[.]

Source: Schomburg Center for Research in Black Culture, Manuscripts, Archives and Rare Books Division, Image ID 1243998, digitalgallery.nypl.org.

Excerpts from the Constitution of 1801 Established by the Central Assembly of Saint-Domingue

Article 1. – Saint-Domingue in its entire expanse, and Samana, La Tortue, La Gonave, Les Cayemites, L'Ile-a-Vache, La Saone and other adjacent islands form the territory of a single colony, which is part of the French Empire, but ruled under particular laws. . . .

Article 3. – There cannot exist slaves on this territory, servitude is therein forever abolished. All men are born, live and die free and French.

Article 4. – All men, regardless of color, are eligible to all employment.

Article 5. – There shall exist no distinction other than those based on virtue and talent, and other superiority afforded by law in the exercise of a public function.

The law is the same for all whether in punishment or in protection.

Source: *Haitian Constitution of 1801* (English), The Louverture Project, thelouvertureproject.org.

QUESTIONS FOR ANALYSIS

1. How does the first document express the fears of American slaveholders? Why do you suppose the Savannah City Council perceived Haitian refugees to be a danger?

2. How does the excerpt from the 1801 Constitution echo themes of the American Revolution? What differences do you see? Comparing the second document to the first, how would you say that the two revolutions impacted views of race in Georgia and in Haiti?

---

immigrants from Ireland vehemently attacked Adams's policies, a Federalist pamphleteer responded in kind: "Were I president, I would hang them for otherwise they would murder me." To silence the critics, the Federalists enacted three coercive laws limiting individual rights and threatening the fledgling party system. The **Naturalization Act** lengthened the residency requirement for American citizenship from five to fourteen years, the **Alien Act** authorized the deportation of foreigners, and the **Sedition Act** prohibited the publication of insults or malicious attacks on the president

or members of Congress. "He that is not for us is against us," thundered the Federalist *Gazette of the United States*. Using the Sedition Act, Federalist prosecutors arrested more than twenty Republican newspaper editors and politicians, accused them of sedition, and convicted and jailed a number of them.

This repression sparked a constitutional crisis. Republicans charged that the Sedition Act violated the First Amendment's prohibition against "abridging the freedom of speech, or of the press." However, they did not appeal to the Supreme Court because the Court's power to review congressional legislation was uncertain and because most of the justices were Federalists. Instead, Madison and Jefferson looked to the state legislatures. At their urging, the Kentucky and Virginia legislatures issued resolutions in 1798 declaring the Alien and Sedition Acts to be "unauthoritative, void, and of no force." The **Virginia and Kentucky Resolutions** set forth a states' rights interpretation of the Constitution, asserting that the states had a "right to judge" the legitimacy of national laws.

The conflict over the Sedition Act set the stage for the presidential election of 1800. Jefferson, once opposed on principle to political parties, now asserted that they could "watch and relate to the people" the activities of an oppressive government. Meanwhile, John Adams reevaluated his foreign policy. Rejecting Hamilton's advice to declare war against France (and benefit from the resulting upsurge in patriotism), Adams put country ahead of party and used diplomacy to end the maritime conflict.

The "Revolution of 1800" The campaign of 1800 degenerated into a bitter, no-holds-barred contest. The Federalists launched personal attacks on Jefferson, branding him an irresponsible pro-French radical and, because he opposed state support of religion in Virginia, "the arch-apostle of irreligion and free thought." Both parties changed state election laws to favor their candidates, and rumors circulated of a Federalist plot to stage a military coup.

The election did not end these worries. Thanks to a low Federalist turnout in Virginia and Pennsylvania and the three-fifths rule (which boosted electoral votes in the southern states), Jefferson won a narrow 73-to-65 victory over Adams in the electoral college. However, the Republican electors also gave 73 votes to Aaron Burr of New York, who was Jefferson's vice-presidential running mate (Map 7.1). The Constitution specified that in the case of a tie vote, the House of Representatives would choose between the candidates. For thirty-five rounds of balloting, Federalists in the House blocked Jefferson's election, prompting rumors that Virginia would raise a military force to put him into office.

Ironically, arch-Federalist Alexander Hamilton ushered in a more democratic era by supporting Jefferson. Calling Burr an "embryo Caesar" and the "most unfit man in the United States for the office of president," Hamilton persuaded key Federalists to allow Jefferson's election. The Federalists' concern for political stability also played a role. As Senator James Bayard of Delaware explained, "It was admitted on all

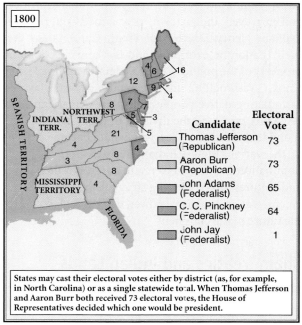

MAP 7.1

The Presidential Elections of 1796 and 1800

Both elections pitted Federalist John Adams of Massachusetts against Republican Thomas Jefferson of Virginia, and both saw voters split along regional lines. Adams carried every New England state and, reflecting Federalist strength in maritime and commercial areas, the eastern districts of the Middle Atlantic states; Jefferson won most of the agricultural-based states of the South and West (Kentucky and Tennessee). New York was the pivotal swing state. It gave its 12 electoral votes to Adams in 1796 and, thanks to the presence of Aaron Burr on the Republican ticket, bestowed them on Jefferson in 1800.

UNDERSTAND POINTS OF VIEW

Why did Jefferson consider his election in 1800 to be revolutionary?

hands that we must risk the Constitution and a Civil War or take Mr. Jefferson."

Jefferson called the election the "Revolution of 1800," and so it was. The bloodless transfer of power showed that popularly elected governments could be changed in an orderly way, even in times of bitter partisan conflict. In his inaugural address in 1801, Jefferson praised this achievement, declaring, "We are all Republicans, we are all Federalists."

A Republican Empire Is Born

In the Treaty of Paris of 1783, Great Britain gave up its claims to the trans-Appalachian region and, said one British diplomat, left the Indian nations "to the care of their [American] neighbours." *Care* was hardly the right word: many white Americans wanted to destroy native communities. "Cut up every Indian Cornfield and burn every Indian town," proclaimed Congressman William Henry Drayton of South Carolina, so that their "nation be extirpated and the lands become the property of the public." Other leaders, including Henry Knox, Washington's first secretary of war, favored assimilating native peoples into Euro-American society. Knox proposed the division of tribal lands among individual Indian families, who would become citizens of the various states. Indians resisted both forms of domination and fought to retain control of their lands and cultures. In the ensuing struggle, the United States emerged as an expansive power, determined to control the future of the continent.

Sham Treaties and Indian Lands

As in the past, the major struggle between natives and Europeans centered on land rights. Invoking the Paris treaty and regarding Britain's Indian allies as conquered peoples, the U.S. government asserted both sovereignty over and ownership of the trans-Appalachian west. Indian nations rejected both claims, pointing out they had not been conquered and had not signed the Paris treaty. "Our lands are our life and our breath," declared Creek chief Hallowing King; "if we part with them, we part with our blood." Brushing aside such objections and threatening military action, U.S. commissioners forced the pro-British Iroquois

PLACE EVENTS IN CONTEXT

Why did the United States go to war against western Indians so quickly after the Revolution?

peoples — Mohawks, Onondagas, Cayugas, and Senecas — to cede huge tracts in New York and Pennsylvania in the Treaty of Fort Stanwix (1784). New York land speculators used liquor and bribes to take a million more acres, confining the once powerful Iroquois to reservations — essentially colonies of subordinate peoples.

American negotiators used similar tactics to grab Ohio Valley lands. At the Treaties of Fort McIntosh (1785) and Fort Finney (1786), they pushed the Chippewas, Delawares, Ottawas, Wyandots, and Shawnees to cede most of the future state of Ohio. The tribes quickly repudiated the agreements, justifiably claiming they were made under duress. Recognizing the failure of these agreements, American negotiators arranged for a comprehensive agreement at Fort Harmar (1789), but it, too, failed. To defend their lands, these tribes joined with the Miami and Potawatomi Indians to form the Western Confederacy. Led by Miami chief Little Turtle, confederacy warriors crushed American expeditionary forces sent by President Washington in 1790 and 1791.

The Treaty of Greenville   Fearing an alliance between the Western Confederacy and the British in Canada, Washington doubled the size of the U.S. Army and ordered General "Mad Anthony" Wayne to lead a new expedition. In August 1794, Wayne defeated the confederacy in the Battle of Fallen Timbers (near present-day Toledo, Ohio). However, continuing Indian resistance forced a compromise. In the **Treaty of Greenville** (1795), American negotiators acknowledged Indian ownership of the land, and, in return for various payments, the Western Confederacy ceded most of Ohio (Map 7.2). The Indian peoples also agreed to accept American sovereignty, placing themselves "under the protection of the United States, and no other Power whatever." These American advances caused Britain to agree, in Jay's Treaty (1795), to reduce its trade and military aid to Indians in the trans-Appalachian region.

The Greenville treaty sparked a wave of white migration. Kentucky already had a population of 73,000 in 1790, and in 1792 it was admitted to the Union as the fifteenth state (Vermont entered a year earlier). By 1800, more than 375,000 people had moved into the Ohio and Tennessee valleys; in 1805, the new state of Ohio alone had more than 100,000 residents. Thousands more farm families moved into the future states of Indiana and Illinois, sparking new conflicts with native peoples over land and hunting rights. Between 1790 and 1810, farm families settled as much

MAP 7.2

Indian Cessions and State Formation, 1776–1840

By virtue of the Treaty of Paris (1783) with Britain, the United States claimed sovereignty over the entire trans-Appalachian west. The Western Confederacy contested this claim, but the U.S. government upheld it with military force. By 1840, armed diplomacy had forced most Native American peoples to move west of the Mississippi River. White settlers occupied their lands, formed territorial governments, and eventually entered the Union as members of separate—and equal—states. By 1860, the trans-Appalachian region constituted an important economic and political force in American national life.

land as they had during the entire colonial period. The United States "is a country in flux," a visiting French aristocrat observed in 1799, and "that which is true today as regards its population, its establishments, its prices, its commerce will not be true six months from now."

Assimilation Rejected To dampen further conflicts, the U.S. government encouraged Native Americans to assimilate into white society. The goal, as one Kentucky Protestant minister put it, was to make the Indian "a farmer, a citizen of the United States, and a Christian." Most Indians rejected wholesale assimilation; even those who joined Christian churches retained many ancestral values and religious beliefs. To think of themselves as individuals or members of a nuclear family, as white Americans were demanding, meant repudiating the clan, the very essence of Indian life. To preserve "the old Indian way," many native communities expelled white missionaries and forced Christianized Indians to participate in tribal rites. As a Munsee prophet declared, "There are two ways to God, one for the whites and one for the Indians."

A few Indian leaders sought a middle path in which new beliefs overlapped with old practices. Among the Senecas, the prophet Handsome Lake encouraged traditional animistic rituals that gave thanks to the sun, the earth, water, plants, and animals. But he included Christian elements in his teachings—the concepts of heaven and hell and an emphasis on personal morality—to deter his followers from alcohol, gambling, and witchcraft. Handsome Lake's teachings divided the Senecas into hostile factions. Led by Chief Red Jacket, traditionalists condemned European culture as evil and demanded a complete return to ancestral ways.

Most Indians also rejected the efforts of American missionaries to turn warriors into farmers and women into domestic helpmates. Among eastern woodland peoples, women grew corn, beans, and squash—the mainstays of the Indians' diet—and land cultivation rights passed through the female line. Consequently, women exercised considerable political influence, which they were eager to retain. Nor were Indian men interested in becoming farmers. When war raiding and hunting were no longer possible, many turned to grazing cattle and sheep.

Treaty Negotiations at Greenville, 1795

In 1785, Indian tribes in the Northwest Territory formed the Western Confederacy to prevent white settlement north of the Ohio River. After Indian triumphs in battles in the early 1790s, an American victory at the Battle of Fallen Timbers (1794) and the subsequent Treaty of Greenville (1795) opened up the region for white farmers. However, the treaty recognized many Indian rights because it was negotiated between relative equals on the battlefield. The artist suggests this equality: notice the height and stately bearing of the Indian leaders—ninety of whom signed the document—and their placement slightly in front of General Anthony Wayne and his officers. Chicago History Museum.

Migration and the Changing Farm Economy

Native American resistance slowed the advance of white settlers but did not stop it. Nothing "short of a Chinese Wall, or a line of Troops," Washington declared, "will restrain . . . the Incroachment of Settlers, upon the Indian Territory." During the 1790s, two great streams of migrants moved out of the southern states (Map 7.3).

Southern Migrants   One stream, composed primarily of white tenant farmers and struggling yeomen families, flocked through the Cumberland Gap into Kentucky and Tennessee. "Boundless settlements open a door for our citizens to run off and leave us," a worried Maryland landlord lamented, "depreciating all our landed property and disabling us from paying taxes." In fact, many migrants were fleeing from this planter-controlled society. They wanted more freedom and hoped to prosper by growing cotton and hemp, which were in great demand.

Many settlers in Kentucky and Tennessee lacked ready cash to buy land. Like the North Carolina Regulators in the 1770s, poorer migrants claimed a customary right to occupy "back waste vacant Lands" sufficient "to provide a subsistence to themselves and their Posterity." Virginia legislators, who administered

MAP 7.3

Regional Cultures Move West, 1790–1820

By 1790, four core cultures had developed in the long-settled states along the Atlantic seaboard. Between 1790 and 1820, migrants from these four regions carried their cultures into the trans-Appalachian west. New England customs and institutions were a dominant influence in upstate New York and along the Great Lakes, while the Lower South's hierarchical system of slavery and heavy concentration of African Americans shaped the character of the new states along the Gulf of Mexico. The pattern of cultural diffusion was more complex in the Ohio and Tennessee river valleys, which were settled by migrants from various core regions.

the Kentucky Territory, had a more elitist vision. Although they allowed poor settlers to buy up to 1,400 acres of land at reduced prices, they sold or granted huge tracts of 100,000 acres to twenty-one groups of speculators and leading men. In 1792, this landed elite owned one-fourth of the state, while half the white men owned no land and lived as quasi-legal squatters or tenant farmers.

Widespread landlessness — and opposition to slavery — prompted a new migration across the Ohio River into the future states of Ohio, Indiana, and Illinois. In a free community, thought Peter Cartwright, a Methodist lay preacher from southwestern Kentucky who moved to Illinois, "I would be entirely clear of the evil of slavery . . . [and] could raise my children to work where work was not thought a degradation." Yet land distribution in Ohio was almost exactly as unequal as in Kentucky: in 1810, a quarter of its real estate was owned by 1 percent of the population, while more than half of its white men were landless.

Meanwhile, a second stream of southern planters and slaves from the Carolinas moved along the coastal plain toward the Gulf of Mexico. Some set up new estates in the interior of Georgia and South Carolina, while others moved into the future states of Alabama, Mississippi, and Louisiana. "The Alabama Feaver rages here with great violence," a North Carolina planter remarked, "and has carried off vast numbers of our Citizens."

Cotton was the key to this migratory surge. Around 1750, the demand for raw wool and cotton increased dramatically as water-powered spinning jennies, weaving mules, and other technological innovations of the Industrial Revolution boosted textile production in England. South Carolina and Georgia planters began growing cotton, and American inventors, including Connecticut-born Eli Whitney, built machines (called gins) that efficiently extracted seeds from its strands. To grow more cotton, white planters imported about 115,000 Africans between 1776 and 1808, when Congress cut off the Atlantic slave trade. The cotton boom financed the rapid settlement of Mississippi and Alabama — in a

IDENTIFY CAUSES
Why were westward migration and agricultural improvement so widespread in the late eighteenth and early nineteenth centuries?

An Indian Log House in Georgia, 1791
The Indian peoples of the southeastern United States—the Cherokees, Creeks, Choctaws, and Chickasaws—quickly adopted European practices that fit easily into their relatively settled, agricultural-based way of life. This sturdy Creek log cabin was based on a Scots-Irish or German design and sat adjacent to the family's cornfields, visible in the background. Library of Congress.

single year, a government land office in Huntsville, Alabama, sold $7 million of uncleared land—and the two states entered the Union in 1817 and 1819, respectively.

Exodus from New England As southerners moved across the Appalachians and along the Gulf Coast, a third stream of migrants flowed out of the overcrowded communities of New England. Previous generations of Massachusetts and Connecticut farm families had moved north and east, settling New Hampshire, Vermont, and Maine. Now New England farmers moved west. Seeking land for their children, thousands of parents migrated to New York. "The town of Herkimer," noted one traveler, "is entirely populated by families come from Connecticut." By 1820, almost 800,000 New Englanders lived in a string of settlements stretching from Albany to Buffalo, and many others had traveled on to Ohio and Indiana. Soon, much of the Northwest Territory consisted of New England communities that had moved inland.

In New York, as in Kentucky and Ohio, well-connected speculators snapped up much of the best land, leasing farms to tenants for a fee. Imbued with the "homestead" ethic, many New England families preferred to buy farms. They signed contracts with the Holland Land Company, a Dutch-owned syndicate of speculators, that allowed settlers to pay for their farms as they worked them, or moved west again in an elusive search for land on easy terms.

Innovation on Eastern Farms The new farm economy in New York, Ohio, and Kentucky forced major changes in eastern agriculture. Unable to compete with lower-priced western grains, farmers in New England switched to potatoes, which were high yielding and nutritious. To make up for the labor of sons and daughters who had moved inland, Middle Atlantic farmers bought more efficient farm equipment. They replaced metal-tipped wooden plows with cast-iron models that dug deeper and required a single yoke of oxen instead of two. Such changes in crop mix and technology kept production high.

Easterners also adopted the progressive farming methods touted by British agricultural reformers. "Improvers" in Pennsylvania doubled their average yield per acre by rotating their crops. Yeomen farmers raised sheep and sold the wool to textile manufacturers. Many farmers adopted a year-round planting cycle, sowing corn in the spring for animal fodder and then planting winter wheat in September for market sale. Women and girls milked the family cows and made butter and cheese to sell in the growing towns and cities.

Whether hacking fields out of western forests or carting manure to replenish eastern soils, farmers now worked harder and longer, but their increased productivity brought them a better standard of living. European demand for American produce was high in these years, and westward migration — the settlement and exploitation of Indian lands — boosted the farming economy throughout the country.

The Jefferson Presidency

From 1801 to 1825, three Republicans from Virginia — Thomas Jefferson, James Madison, and James Monroe — each served two terms as president. Supported by farmers in the South and West and strong Republican majorities in Congress, this "Virginia Dynasty" completed what Jefferson had called the Revolution of 1800. It reversed many Federalist policies and actively supported westward expansion.

When Jefferson took office in 1801, he inherited an old international conflict. Beginning in the 1780s, the Barbary States of North Africa had raided merchant ships in the Mediterranean, and like many European nations, the United States had paid an annual bribe — massive in relation to the size of the federal budget — to protect its vessels. Initially Jefferson refused to pay this "tribute" and ordered the U.S. Navy to attack the pirates' home ports. After four years of intermittent fighting, in which the United States bombarded Tripoli and captured the city of Derna, the Jefferson administration cut its costs. It signed a peace treaty that included a ransom for returned prisoners, and Algerian ships were soon taking American sailors hostage again.

At home, Jefferson inherited a national judiciary filled with Federalist appointees, including the formidable John Marshall of Virginia, the new chief justice of the Supreme Court. To add more Federalist judges, the outgoing Federalist Congress had passed the Judiciary Act of 1801. The act created sixteen new judgeships and various other positions, which President Adams filled at the last moment with "midnight appointees." The Federalists "have retired into the judiciary as a stronghold," Jefferson complained, "and from that battery all the works of Republicanism are to be beaten down and destroyed."

Jefferson's fears were soon realized. When Republican legislatures in Kentucky and Virginia repudiated the Alien and Sedition Acts as unconstitutional,

Marshall declared that only the Supreme Court held the power of constitutional review. The Court claimed this authority for itself when James Madison, the new secretary of state, refused to deliver the commission of William Marbury, one of Adams's midnight appointees. In **Marbury v. Madison (1303)**, Marshall asserted that Marbury had the right to the appointment but that the Court did not have the constitutional power to enforce it. In defining the Court's powers, Marshall voided a section of the Judiciary Act of 1789, in effect asserting the Court's authority to review congressional legislation and interpret the Constitution. "It is emphatically the province and duty of the judicial department to say what the law is," the chief justice declared, directly challenging the Republican view that the state legislatures had that power.

Ignoring this setback, Jefferson and the Republicans reversed other Federalist policies. When the Alien and Sedition Acts expired in 1801, Congress branded them unconstitutional and refused to extend them. It also amended the Naturalization Act, restoring the original waiting period of five years for resident aliens to become citizens. Charging the Federalists with grossly expanding the national government's size and power, Jefferson had the Republican Congress shrink it. He abolished all internal taxes, including the excise tax that had sparked the Whiskey Rebellion of 1794. To quiet Republican fears of a military coup, Jefferson reduced the size of the permanent army. He also secured repeal of the Judiciary Act of 1801, ousting forty of Adams's midnight appointees. Still, Jefferson retained competent Federalist officeholders, removing only 69 of 433 properly appointed Federalists during his eight years as president.

Jefferson likewise governed tactfully in fiscal affairs. He tolerated the economically important Bank of the United States, which he had once condemned as unconstitutional. But he chose as his secretary of the treasury Albert Gallatin, a fiscal conservative who believed that the national debt was "an evil of the first magnitude." By limiting expenditures and using customs revenue to redeem government bonds, Gallatin reduced the debt from $83 million in 1801 to $45 million in 1812. With Jefferson and Gallatin at the helm, the nation's fiscal affairs were no longer run in the interests of northeastern creditors and merchants.

Jefferson and the West

Jefferson had long championed settlement of the West. He celebrated the yeoman farmer in *Notes on the State of Virginia* (1785); wrote one of the Confederation's

'AUGUST 1804.

BOMBARDMENT OF TRIPOLI.

America in the Middle East, 1804

To protect American merchants from capture and captivity in the Barbary States, President Thomas Jefferson sent in the U.S. Navy. This 1846 lithograph, created by the famous firm of Currier & Ives, depicts one of the three attacks on the North African port of Tripoli by Commodore Edward Preble in August 1804. As the USS *Constitution* and other large warships lob shells into the city, small American gunboats defend the fleet from Tripolitan gunboats. "Our loss in Killed & Wounded has been considerable," Preble reported, and "the Enemy must have suffered very much . . . among their Shipping and on shore." The Granger Collection, New York.

western land ordinances; and supported Pinckney's Treaty (1795), the agreement between the United States and Spain that reopened the Mississippi River to American trade and allowed settlers to export crops via the Spanish-held port of New Orleans.

As president, Jefferson pursued policies that made it easier for farm families to acquire land. In 1796, a Federalist-dominated Congress had set the price of land in the national domain at $2 per acre; by the 1830s, Jefferson-inspired Republican Congresses had enacted more than three hundred laws that cut the cost to $1.25, eased credit terms, and allowed illegal squatters to buy their farms. Eventually, in the Homestead Act of 1862, Congress gave farmsteads to settlers for free.

The Louisiana Purchase   International events challenged Jefferson's vision of westward expansion. In

1799, Napoleon Bonaparte seized power in France and sought to reestablish France's American empire. In 1801, he coerced Spain into signing a secret treaty that returned Louisiana to France and restricted American access to New Orleans, violating Pinckney's Treaty. Napoleon also launched an invasion to restore French rule in Saint-Domingue. It was once the richest sugar colony in the Americas, but its civil war had ruined the economy and cost France a fortune. Napoleon wanted to crush the rebellion, restore its planter class, and "destroy the new Algiers that has been growing up in the middle of America."

Napoleon's actions in Haiti and Louisiana prompted Jefferson to question his pro-French foreign policy. "The day that France takes possession of New Orleans, we must marry ourselves to the British fleet and nation," the president warned, dispatching James Monroe to

Britain to negotiate an alliance. To keep the Mississippi River open to western farmers, Jefferson told Robert Livingston, the American minister in Paris, to negotiate the purchase of New Orleans.

Jefferson's diplomacy yielded a magnificent prize: the entire territory of Louisiana. By 1802, the French invasion of Saint-Domingue was faltering in the face of disease and determined black resistance, a new war threatened in Europe, and Napoleon feared an American invasion of Louisiana. Acting with characteristic decisiveness, the French ruler offered to sell the entire territory of Louisiana for $15 million (about $500 million today). "We have lived long," Livingston remarked to Monroe as they concluded the **Louisiana Purchase** in 1803, "but this is the noblest work of our lives."

The Louisiana Purchase forced Jefferson to reconsider his strict interpretation of the Constitution. He had long believed that the national government possessed only the powers expressly delegated to it in the Constitution, but there was no provision for adding new territory. So Jefferson pragmatically accepted a loose interpretation of the Constitution and used its treaty-making powers to complete the deal with France. The new western lands, Jefferson wrote, would be "a means of tempting all our Indians on the East side of the Mississippi to remove to the West."

Secessionist Schemes The acquisition of Louisiana brought new political problems. Some New England Federalists, fearing that western expansion would hurt their region and party, talked openly of leaving the Union and forming a confederacy of northeastern states. The secessionists won the support of Aaron Burr, the ambitious vice president. After Alexander Hamilton accused Burr of planning to destroy the Union, the two fought an illegal pistol duel that led to Hamilton's death.

This tragedy propelled Burr into another secessionist scheme, this time in the Southwest. When his term as vice president ended in 1805, Burr moved west to avoid prosecution. There, he conspired with General James Wilkinson, the military governor of the Louisiana Territory, either to seize territory in New Spain or to establish Louisiana as a separate nation. But Wilkinson, himself a Spanish spy and incipient traitor, betrayed Burr and arrested him. In a highly politicized trial presided over by Chief Justice John Marshall, the jury acquitted Burr of treason.

The Louisiana Purchase had increased party conflict and generated secessionist schemes in both New England and the Southwest. Such sectional differences

would continue, challenging Madison's argument in "Federalist No. 10" that a large and diverse republic was more stable than a small one.

Lewis and Clark Meet the Mandans and Sioux A scientist as well as a statesman, Jefferson wanted information about Louisiana: its physical features, plant and animal life, and native peoples. He was also worried about intruders: the British-run Hudson's Bay Company and Northwest Company were actively trading for furs on the upper Missouri River. So in 1804, Jefferson sent his personal secretary, Meriwether Lewis, to explore the region with William Clark, an army officer. From St. Louis, Lewis, Clark, and their party of American soldiers and frontiersmen traveled up the Missouri for 1,000 miles to the fortified, earth-lodge towns of the Mandan and Hidatsa peoples (near present-day Bismarck, North Dakota), where they spent the winter.

The Mandans lived primarily by horticulture, growing corn, beans, and squash. They had acquired horses by supplying food to nomadic Plains Indians and secured guns, iron goods, and textiles by selling buffalo hides and dried meat to European traders. However, the Mandans (and neighboring Arikaras) had been hit hard by the smallpox epidemics that swept across the Great Plains in 1779–1781 and 1801–1802. Now they were threatened by Sioux peoples: Tetons, Yanktonais, and Oglalas. Originally, the Sioux had lived in the prairie and lake region of northern Minnesota. As their numbers rose and fish and game grew scarce, the Sioux moved westward, acquired horses, and hunted buffalo, living as nomads in portable skin tepees. The Sioux became ferocious fighters who tried to reduce the Mandans and other farming tribes to subject peoples. According to Lewis and Clark, they were the "pirates of the Missouri." Soon the Sioux would dominate the buffalo trade throughout the upper Missouri region.

In the spring of 1805, Lewis and Clark began an epic 1,300-mile trek into unknown country. Their party now included Toussaint Charbonneau, a French Canadian fur trader, and his Shoshone wife, Sacagawea, who served as a guide and translator. After following the Missouri River to its source on the Idaho-Montana border, they crossed the Rocky Mountains, and — venturing far beyond the Louisiana Purchase — traveled down the Columbia River to the Pacific Ocean. Nearly everywhere, Indian peoples asked for guns so they could defend themselves from other armed tribes.

EXPLAIN CONSEQUENCES
How was Jefferson's agrarian vision reflected in his policies affecting western lands?

A Mandan Village
This Mandan settlement in North Dakota, painted by George Catlin around 1837, resembled those in which the Lewis and Clark expedition spent the winter of 1804–1805. Note the palisade of logs that surrounds the village, as protection from the Sioux and other marauding Plains peoples, and the solidly built mud lodges that provided warm shelter from the bitter cold of winter. Smithsonian American Art Museum, Washington, D.C./Art Resource, NY.

In 1806, Lewis and Clark capped off their pathbreaking expedition by providing Jefferson with the first maps of the immense wilderness and a detailed account of its natural resources and inhabitants (Map 7.4). Their report prompted some Americans to envision a nation that would span the continent.

The War of 1812 and the Transformation of Politics

The Napoleonic Wars that ravaged Europe after 1802 brought new attacks on American merchant ships. American leaders struggled desperately to protect the nation's commerce while avoiding war. When this effort finally failed, it sparked dramatic political changes that destroyed the Federalist Party and split the Republicans into National and Jeffersonian factions.

Conflict in the Atlantic and the West

As Napoleon conquered European countries, he cut off their commerce with Britain and seized American merchant ships that stopped in British ports. The British ministry responded with a naval blockade and seized American vessels carrying sugar and molasses from the French West Indies. The British navy also searched American merchant ships for British deserters and used these raids to replenish its crews, a practice known as impressment. Between 1802 and 1811, British naval officers impressed nearly 8,000 sailors, including many U.S. citizens. In 1807, American anger boiled over when a British warship attacked the U.S. Navy vessel *Chesapeake*, killing three, wounding eighteen, and seizing four alleged deserters. "Never since the battle of Lexington have I seen this country in such a state of exasperation as at present," Jefferson declared.

The Embargo of 1807 To protect American interests, Jefferson pursued a policy of peaceful coercion. **The Embargo Act of 1807** prohibited American ships from leaving their home ports until Britain and France stopped restricting U.S. trade. A drastic maneuver, the embargo overestimated the reliance of Britain and France on American shipping and underestimated the resistance of merchants, who feared the embargo would ruin them. In fact, the embargo cut the American gross national product by 5 percent and weakened the entire economy. Exports plunged from $108 million in 1806 to $22 million in 1808, hurting farmers as well as merchants. "All was noise and bustle" in New York City before the embargo, one visitor remarked; afterward, everything was closed up as if "a malignant fever was raging in the place."

Despite popular discontent over the embargo, voters elected Republican James Madison to the presidency in 1808. A powerful advocate for the Constitution, the architect of the Bill of Rights, and a prominent congressman and party leader, Madison

MAP 7.4
U.S. Population Density in 1803 and the Louisiana Purchase
When the United States purchased Louisiana from France in 1803, much of the land to its east—the vast territory between the Appalachian Mountains and the Mississippi River—remained in Indian hands. The equally vast lands beyond the Mississippi were virtually unknown to Anglo-Americans, even after the epic explorations of Meriwether Lewis and William Clark. Still, President Jefferson predicted quite accurately that the huge Mississippi River Valley "from its fertility . . . will ere long yield half of our whole produce, and contain half of our whole population."

had served the nation well. But John Beckley, a loyal Republican, worried that Madison would be "too timid and indecisive as a statesman," and events proved him right. Acknowledging the embargo's failure, Madison replaced it with new economic restrictions, which also failed to protect American commerce.

Western War Hawks Republican congressmen from the West were certain that Britain was the primary offender. They pointed to its trade with Indians in the Ohio River Valley in violation of the Treaty of Paris and Jay's Treaty. Bolstered by British guns and supplies, the Shawnee war chief Tecumseh revived the Western Confederacy in 1809. His brother, the prophet Tenskwatawa, provided the confederacy with a powerful nativist ideology. He urged Indian peoples to shun

Americans, "the children of the Evil Spirit . . . who have taken away your lands"; renounce alcohol; and return to traditional ways. The Shawnee leaders found their greatest support among Kickapoo, Potawatomi, Winnebago, Ottawa, and Chippewa warriors: Indians of the western Great Lakes who had so far been largely shielded from the direct effects of U.S. westward expansion. They flocked to Tenskwatawa's holy village, Prophetstown, in the Indiana Territory.

As Tecumseh mobilized the western Indian peoples for war, William Henry Harrison, the governor of the Indiana Territory, decided on a preemptive strike. In November 1811, when Tecumseh went south to seek support from the Chickasaws, Choctaws, and Creeks, Harrison took advantage of his absence and attacked Prophetstown. The governor's 1,000 troops

Tenskwatawa, "The Prophet," 1830
Tenskwatawa added a spiritual dimension to Native American resistance by urging a holy war against the invading whites and calling for a return to sacred ancestral ways. His dress reflects his teachings: note the animal-skin shirt and the heavily ornamented ears. However, some of Tenskwatawa's religious rituals reflected the influence of French Jesuits; he urged his followers to finger a sacred string of beads (such as those in his left hand) that were similar to the Catholic rosary, thereby "shaking hands with the Prophet." Whatever its origins, Tenskwatawa's message transcended the cultural differences among Indian peoples and helped his brother Tecumseh create a formidable political and military alliance. Smithsonian American Art Museum, Washington, D.C./Art Resource.

and militiamen traded heavy casualties with the confederacy's warriors at the **Battle of Tippecanoe** and then destroyed the holy village.

With Britain assisting Indians in the western territories and seizing American ships in the Atlantic, Henry Clay of Kentucky, the new Speaker of the House of Representatives, and John C. Calhoun, a rising young congressman from South Carolina, pushed Madison toward war. Like other Republican "war hawks" from the West and South, they wanted to seize territory in British Canada and Spanish Florida. With national elections approaching, Madison issued an ultimatum to Britain. When Britain failed to respond quickly, the president asked Congress for a declaration of war. In June 1812, a sharply divided Senate voted 19 to 13 for war, and the House of Representatives concurred, 79 to 49.

The causes of the War of 1812 have been much debated. Officially, the United States went to war because Britain had violated its commercial rights as a neutral nation. But the Federalists in Congress who represented the New England and Middle Atlantic merchants voted against the war; and in the election of 1812, those regions cast their 89 electoral votes for the Federalist presidential candidate, De Witt Clinton of New York. Madison amassed most of his 128 electoral votes in the South and West, where voters and congressmen strongly supported the war. Many historians therefore argue that the conflict was actually "a western war with eastern labels" (American Voices, p. 238).

The War of 1812

The War of 1812 was a near disaster for the United States. An invasion of British Canada in 1812 quickly ended in a retreat to Detroit. Nonetheless, the United States stayed on the offensive in the West. In 1813, American raiders burned the Canadian capital of York (present-day Toronto), Commodore Oliver Hazard Perry defeated a small British flotilla on Lake Erie, and

Counting Scalps

Effective propaganda usually contains a grain of truth, in this case the Indian warriors' practice of scalping their wartime victims. Entitled "A scene on the frontiers as practiced by the humane British and their worthy allies!", this cartoon by Philadelphia artist William Charles accuses the British of paying Indians to kill—and then mutilate—American soldiers. "Bring me the scalps, and the King our master will reward you," says the British officer in the cartoon. The verse at the bottom urges "Columbia's Sons" to press forward their attacks; otherwise, "The Savage Indian with his Scalping knife, / Or Tomahawk may seek to take your life." Library of Congress.

General William Henry Harrison overcame a British and Indian force at the Battle of the Thames, taking the life of Tecumseh, now a British general.

In the East, political divisions prevented a wider war. New England Federalists opposed the war and prohibited their states' militias from attacking Canada. Boston merchants and banks refused to lend money to the federal government, making the war difficult to finance. In Congress, Daniel Webster, a dynamic young politician from New Hampshire, led Federalists opposed to higher tariffs and national conscription of state militiamen.

Gradually, the tide of battle turned in Britain's favor. When the war began, American privateers had captured scores of British merchant vessels, but by 1813 British warships were disrupting American commerce and threatening seaports along the Atlantic coast. In 1814, a British fleet sailed up the Chesapeake Bay, and troops stormed ashore to attack Washington City. Retaliating for the destruction of York, the invaders burned the U.S. Capitol and government buildings. After two years of fighting, the United States was stalemated along the Canadian frontier and on the defensive in the Atlantic, and its new capital city lay in ruins. The only U.S. victories came in the Southwest. There, a rugged slave-owning planter named Andrew Jackson and a force of Tennessee militiamen defeated British- and Spanish-supported Creek Indians in the Battle of Horseshoe Bend (1814) and forced the Indians to cede 23 million acres of land (Map 7.5).

Federalists Oppose the War   American military setbacks increased opposition to the war in New England. In 1814, Massachusetts Federalists called for a convention "to lay the foundation for a radical reform in the National Compact." When New England Federalists met in Hartford, Connecticut, some delegates proposed secession, but most wanted to revise the Constitution. To end Virginia's domination of the presidency, the Hartford Convention proposed a constitutional amendment limiting the office to a single

IDENTIFY CAUSES
What do you think is the most persuasive explanation for the United States's decision to declare war on Great Britain in 1812?

Factional Politics and the War of 1812

In the quarter-century following the ratification of the U.S. Constitution, American leaders had to deal with the wars of the French Revolution and Napoleon. These European conflicts posed two dangers to the United States. First, the naval blockades imposed by the British and the French hurt American commerce and prompted calls for a military response. Second, European ideological and political struggles intensified party conflicts in the United States. On three occasions, the American republic faced danger from the combination of an external military threat and internal political turmoil. In 1798, the Federalist administration of John Adams almost went to war with France to help American merchants and to undermine the Republican Party. In 1807, Thomas Jefferson's embargo on American commerce shocked Federalists and sharply increased political tensions. And, as the following selections show, the political divisions during the War of 1812 threatened the very existence of the American republic.

George Washington
Farewell Address, 1796

Washington's support for Alexander Hamilton's economic policies promoted political factionalism. Ignoring his own role in creating that political divide, Washington condemned factionalism and, as his presidency proceeded, tried to stand above party conflicts. In his farewell address, Washington warned Americans to stand united and avoid the "Spirit of Party."

A solicitude for your welfare [prompts me] . . . to offer . . . the disinterested warnings of a parting friend, who can possibly have no personal motive to bias his counsels. . . .

The Unity of Government which constitutes you one people . . . is a main Pillar in the Edifice of your real independence . . . your tranquility at home; your peace abroad. . . . But it is easy to foresee, that, from different causes, and from different quarters, much pains will be taken, many artifices employed, to weaken in your minds the conviction of this truth. . . .

I have already intimated to you the danger of parties in the State, with particular reference to founding them on geographical discriminations. Let me now take a more comprehensive view, and warn you, in the most solemn manner, against the baneful effects of the Spirit of Party, generally.

This spirit, unfortunately, is inseparable from our nature, having its root in the strongest passions of the human mind. It exists under different shapes, in all governments, more or less stifled, controlled or repressed; but in those of the popular form, it is seen in its greatest rankness, and is truly their worst enemy.

The alternate dominion of one faction over another, sharpened by the spirit of revenge . . . , is itself a frightful despotism; but this leads at length to a more formal and permanent despotism.

Source: James D. Richardson, ed., *A Compilation of the Messages and Papers of the Presidents, 1789–1896* (Washington, D.C.: U.S. Government Printing Office, 1896), 1: 213–215.

Josiah Quincy et al.
Federalists Protest "Mr. Madison's War"

The United States—and its two political parties— divided sharply over the War of 1812. As Congress debated the issue of going to war against Great Britain, Josiah Quincy and other antiwar Federalist congressmen published a manifesto that questioned the justifications for the war offered by President Madison and the military strategy proposed by Republican war hawks.

How will war upon the land [an invasion of British Canada] protect commerce upon the ocean? What balm has Canada for wounded honor? How are our mariners benefited by a war which exposes those who are free, without promising release to those who are impressed?

But it is said that war is demanded by honor. Is national honor a principle which thirsts after vengeance, and is appeased only by blood? . . . If honor demands a war with England, what opiate lulls that honor to sleep over the wrongs done us by France? On land, robberies, seizures, imprisonments, by French authority; at sea, pillage, sinkings, burnings, under French orders. These are notorious. Are they unfelt because they are French? . . .

There is . . . a headlong rushing into difficulties, with little calculation about the means, and little concern about the consequences. With a navy comparatively [small], we are about to enter into the lists against the greatest marine [power] on the globe. With a commerce unprotected and spread over every ocean, we propose to make a profit by privateering, and for this endanger the wealth of which we are honest proprietors. An invasion is threatened of the [British colonies in Canada, but Britain] . . . without putting a new ship into commission, or taking another soldier into pay, can spread alarm or desolation along the extensive range of our seaboard. . . .

What are the United States to gain by this war? Will the gratification of some privateersmen compensate the nation for that sweep of our legitimate commerce by the extended marine of our enemy which this desperate act invites? Will Canada compensate the Middle states for [the loss of] New York; or the Western states for [the loss of] New Orleans?

Let us not be deceived. A war of invasion may invite a retort of invasion. When we visit the peaceable, and as to us innocent, colonies of Great Britain with the horrors of war, can we be assured that our own coast will not be visited with like horrors?

Source: *Annals of Congress*, 12th Cong., 1st sess., vol. 2, cols. 2219–2221.

Hezekiah Niles
A Republican Defends the War

In 1814, what the Federalists feared had come to pass: British ships blockaded American ports, and British troops invaded American territory. In January 1815, Republican editor Hezekiah Niles used the pages of his influential Baltimore newspaper, *Niles' Weekly Register*, to explain current Republican policies and blame the Federalists for American reverses.

It is universally known that the causes for which we declared war are no obstruction to peace. The practice of blockade and impressment having ceased by the general pacification of Europe, our government is content to leave the principle as it was. . . .

We have no further business in hostility, than such as is purely defensive; while that of Great Britain is to humble or subdue us. The war, on our part, has become a contest for life, liberty and property — on the part of our enemy, of revenge or ambition. . . .

What then are we to do? Are we to encourage him by divisions among ourselves — to hold out the hope of a

separation of the states and a civil war — to refuse to bring forth the resources of the country against him? . . . I did think that in a defensive war — a struggle for all that is valuable — that all parties would have united. But it is not so — every measure calculated to replenish the treasury or raise men is opposed [by Federalists] as though it were determined to strike the "star spangled banner" and exalt the bloody cross. Look at the votes and proceedings of congress — and mark the late spirit [to secede from the Union] . . . that existed in Massachusetts, and see with what unity of action every thing has been done [by New England Federalists] to harass and embarrass the government. Our loans have failed; and our soldiers have wanted their pay, because those [New England merchants] who had the greater part of the monied capital covenanted with each other to refuse its aid to the country. They had a right, legally, to do this; and perhaps, also, by all the artifices of trade or power that money gave them, to oppress others not of their "stamp" and depress the national credit — but history will shock posterity by detailing the length to which they went to bankrupt the republic. . . .

To conclude — why does the war continue? It is not the fault of the government — we demand no extravagant thing. I answer the question, and say — *it lasts because Great Britain depends on the exertions of her "party" in this country to destroy our resources, and compel "unconditional submission."*

Thus the war began, and is continued, by our divisions.

Source: *Niles' Weekly Register*, January 28, 1815.

QUESTIONS FOR ANALYSIS

1. According to Washington, what is the ultimate cause of political factionalism? Why does Washington believe that factionalism is most dangerous in "popular" — that is, republican — governments?

2. Compare and contrast the Quincy and Niles documents. What specific dangers did Josiah Quincy and the Federalists foresee with regard to Republican war policies? According to Hezekiah Niles, what were the war goals of the Republican administration?

3. Read the section on the War of 1812 on pages 236–241, and then discuss the accuracy of the Federalists' predictions.

4. How had Republican war goals changed since the start of the war? Niles charged the Federalists and their supporters with impeding the American war effort. What were his specific charges? Did they have any merit? How might the Federalists have defended their stance with respect to the war?

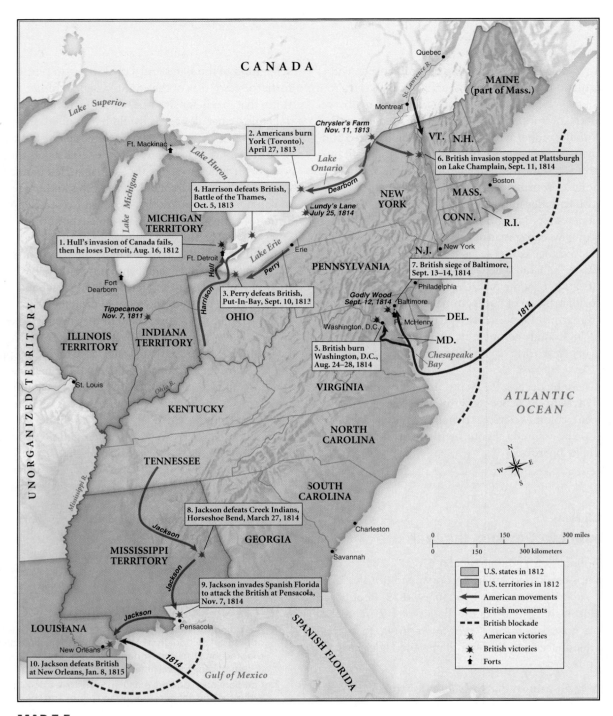

MAP 7.5

The War of 1812

Unlike the War of Independence, the War of 1812 had few large-scale military campaigns. In 1812 and 1813, most of the fighting took place along the Canadian border, as small American military forces attacked British targets with mixed success (nos. 1–4). The British took the offensive in 1814, launching a successful raid on Washington, but their attack on Baltimore failed, and they suffered heavy losses when they invaded the United States along Lake Champlain (nos. 5–7). Near the Gulf of Mexico, American forces moved from one success to another: General Andrew Jackson defeated the pro-British Creek Indians at the Battle of Horseshoe Bend, won a victory in Pensacola, and, in the single major battle of the war, routed an invading British army at New Orleans (nos. 8–10).

four-year term and rotating it among citizens from different states. The convention also suggested amendments restricting commercial embargoes to sixty days and requiring a two-thirds majority in Congress to declare war, prohibit trade, or admit a new state to the Union.

As a minority party, the Federalists could prevail only if the war continued to go badly—a very real prospect. The war had cost $88 million, raising the national debt to $127 million. And now, as Albert Gallatin warned Henry Clay in May 1814, Britain's triumph over Napoleon in Europe meant that a "well organized and large army is [now ready] . . . to act immediately against us." When an attack from Canada came in the late summer of 1814, only an American naval victory on Lake Champlain stopped the British from marching down the Hudson River Valley. A few months later, thousands of seasoned British troops landed outside New Orleans, threatening American control of the Mississippi River. With the nation politically divided and under attack from north and south, Gallatin feared that "the war might prove vitally fatal to the United States."

Peace Overtures and a Final Victory   Fortunately for the young American republic, by 1815 Britain wanted peace. The twenty-year war with France had sapped its wealth and energy, so it began negotiations with the United States in Ghent, Belgium. At first, the American commissioners—John Quincy Adams, Gallatin, and Clay—demanded territory in Canada and Florida, while British diplomats sought an Indian buffer state between the United States and Canada. Both sides quickly realized that these objectives were not worth the cost of prolonged warfare. The **Treaty of Ghent**, signed on Christmas Eve 1814, retained the prewar borders of the United States.

That result hardly justified three years of war, but before news of the treaty reached the United States, a final military victory lifted Americans' morale. On January 8, 1815, General Jackson's troops crushed the British forces attacking New Orleans. Fighting from carefully constructed breastworks, the Americans rained "grapeshot and cannister bombs" on the massed British formations. The British lost 700 men, and 2,000 more were wounded or taken prisoner; just 13 Americans died, and only 58 suffered wounds. A newspaper headline proclaimed: "Almost Incredible Victory!! Glorious News." The victory made Jackson a national hero, redeemed the nation's battered pride, and undercut the Hartford Convention's demands for constitutional revision.

The Federalist Legacy

The War of 1812 ushered in a new phase of the Republican political revolution. Before the conflict, Federalists had strongly supported Alexander Hamilton's program of national mercantilism—a funded debt, a central bank, and tariffs—while Jeffersonian Republicans had opposed it. After the war, the Republicans split into two camps. Led by Henry Clay, National Republicans pursued Federalist-like policies. In 1816, Clay pushed legislation through Congress creating the Second Bank of the United States and persuaded President Madison to sign it. In 1817, Clay won passage of the Bonus Bill, which created a national fund for roads and other internal improvements. Madison vetoed it. Reaffirming traditional Jeffersonian Republican principles, he argued that the national government lacked the constitutional authority to fund internal improvements.

Meanwhile, the Federalist Party crumbled. As one supporter explained, the National Republicans in the eastern states had "destroyed the Federalist party by the adoption of its principles" while the favorable farm policies of Jeffersonians maintained the Republican Party's dominance in the South and West. "No Federal character can run with success," Gouverneur Morris of New York lamented, and the election of 1818 proved him right: Republicans outnumbered Federalists 37 to 7 in the Senate and 156 to 27 in the House. Westward expansion and the success of Jefferson's Revolution of 1800 had shattered the First Party System.

Marshall's Federalist Law   However, Federalist policies lived on thanks to John Marshall's long tenure on the Supreme Court. Appointed chief justice by President John Adams in January 1801, Marshall had a personality and intellect that allowed him to dominate the Court until 1822 and strongly influence its decisions until his death in 1835.

Three principles informed Marshall's jurisprudence: judicial authority, the supremacy of national laws, and traditional property rights (Table 7.1). Marshall claimed the right of judicial review for the Supreme Court in *Marbury v. Madison* (1803), and the Court frequently used that power to overturn state laws that, in its judgment, violated the Constitution.

Asserting National Supremacy   The important case of ***McCulloch v. Maryland* (1819)** involved one such law. When Congress created the Second Bank of the United States in 1816, it allowed the bank to set up state branches that competed with state-chartered banks. In response, the Maryland legislature imposed a

TABLE 7.1

Major Decisions of the Marshall Court

	Date	Case	Significance of Decision
Judicial Authority	1803	*Marbury v. Madison*	Asserts principle of judicial review
Property Rights	1810	*Fletcher v. Peck*	Protects property rights through broad reading of Constitution's contract clause
	1819	*Dartmouth College v. Woodward*	Safeguards property rights, especially of chartered corporations
Supremacy of National Law	1819	*McCulloch v. Maryland*	Interprets Constitution to give broad powers to national government
	1824	*Gibbons v. Ogden*	Gives national government jurisdiction over interstate commerce

tax on notes issued by the Baltimore branch of the Second Bank. The Second Bank refused to pay, claiming that the tax infringed on national powers and was therefore unconstitutional. The state's lawyers then invoked Jefferson's argument: that Congress lacked the constitutional authority to charter a national bank. Even if a national bank was legitimate, the lawyers argued, Maryland could tax its activities within the state.

Marshall and the nationalist-minded Republicans on the Court firmly rejected both arguments. The Second Bank was constitutional, said the chief justice, because it was "necessary and proper," given the national government's control over currency and credit, and Maryland did not have the power to tax it.

The Marshall Court again asserted the dominance of national over state statutes in *Gibbons v. Ogden* (1824). The decision struck down a New York law granting a monopoly to Aaron Ogden for steamboat passenger service across the Hudson River to New Jersey. Asserting that the Constitution gave the federal government authority over interstate commerce, the chief justice sided with Thomas Gibbons, who held a federal license to run steamboats between the two states.

Upholding Vested Property Rights Finally, Marshall used the Constitution to uphold Federalist notions of property rights. During the 1790s, Jefferson Republicans had celebrated "the will of the people," prompting Federalists to worry that popular sovereignty would result in a "tyranny of the majority." If state legislatures enacted statutes infringing on the property rights of wealthy citizens, Federalist judges vowed to void them.

Marshall was no exception. Determined to protect individual property rights, he invoked the contract clause of the Constitution to do it. The contract clause (in Article I, Section 10) prohibits the states from passing any law "impairing the obligation of contracts." Economic conservatives at the Philadelphia convention had inserted the clause to prevent "stay" laws, which kept creditors from seizing the lands and goods of delinquent debtors. In *Fletcher v. Peck* (1810), Marshall greatly expanded its scope. The Georgia legislature had granted a huge tract of land to the Yazoo Land Company. When a new legislature cancelled the grant, alleging fraud and bribery, speculators who had purchased Yazoo lands appealed to the Supreme Court to uphold their titles. Marshall did so by ruling that the legislative grant was a contract that could not be revoked. His decision was controversial and far-reaching. It limited state power; bolstered vested property rights; and, by protecting out-of-state investors, promoted the development of a national capitalist economy.

The Court extended its defense of vested property rights in *Dartmouth College v. Woodward* (1819). Dartmouth College was a private institution created by a royal charter issued by King George III. In 1816, New Hampshire's Republican legislature enacted a statute converting the school into a public university. The Dartmouth trustees opposed the legislation and hired Daniel Webster to plead their case. A renowned constitutional lawyer and a leading Federalist, Webster cited the Court's decision in *Fletcher v. Peck* and argued that the royal charter was an unalterable contract. The Marshall Court agreed and upheld Dartmouth's claims.

UNDERSTAND POINTS OF VIEW

Why do historians think the decisions of the Marshall Court constitute a Federalist legacy?

***John Marshall*, by Chester Harding, c. 1830**

Even at the age of seventy-five, John Marshall (1755–1835) had a commanding personal presence. After he became chief justice of the U.S. Supreme Court in 1801, Marshall elevated the Court from a minor department of the national government to a major institution in American legal and political life. His decisions on judicial review, contract rights, the regulation of commerce, and national banking permanently shaped the character of American constitutional law. © Boston Athenaeum, USA/The Bridgeman Art Library.

The Diplomacy of John Quincy Adams Even as John Marshall incorporated important Federalist principles into the American legal system, voting citizens and political leaders embraced the outlook of the Republican Party. The political career of John Quincy Adams was a case in point. Although he was the son of Federalist president John Adams, John Quincy Adams had joined the Republican Party before the War of 1812. He came to national attention for his role in negotiating the Treaty of Ghent, which ended the war.

Adams then served brilliantly as secretary of state for two terms under James Monroe (1817–1825). Ignoring Republican antagonism toward Great Britain,

in 1817 Adams negotiated the Rush-Bagot Treaty, which limited American and British naval forces on the Great Lakes. In 1818, he concluded another agreement with Britain setting the forty-ninth parallel as the border between Canada and the lands of the Louisiana Purchase. Then, in the **Adams-Onís Treaty** of 1819, Adams persuaded Spain to cede the Florida territory to the United States (Map 7.6). In return, the American government accepted Spain's claim to Texas and agreed to a compromise on the western boundary for the state of Louisiana, which had entered the Union in 1812.

Finally, Adams persuaded President Monroe to declare American national policy with respect to the

MAP 7.6
Defining the National Boundaries, 1800–1820
After the War of 1812, American diplomats negotiated treaties with Great Britain and Spain that defined the boundaries of the Louisiana Purchase, with British Canada to the north and New Spain (which in 1821 became the independent nation of Mexico) to the south and west. These treaties eliminated the threat of border wars with neighboring states for a generation, giving the United States a much-needed period of peace and security.

Western Hemisphere. At Adams's behest, Monroe warned Spain and other European powers to keep their hands off the newly independent republics in Latin America. The American continents were not "subject for further colonization," the president declared in 1823 — a policy that thirty years later became known as the **Monroe Doctrine**. In return, Monroe pledged that the United States would not "interfere in the internal concerns" of European nations. Thanks to John Quincy Adams, the United States had successfully asserted its diplomatic leadership in the Western Hemisphere and won international acceptance of its northern and western boundaries.

The appearance of political consensus after two decades of bitter party conflict prompted observers to dub James Monroe's presidency (1817–1825) the "Era of Good Feeling." This harmony was real but transitory. The Republican Party was now split between the National faction, led by Clay and Adams, and the Jeffersonian faction, soon to be led by Martin Van Buren and Andrew Jackson. The two groups differed sharply over federal support for roads and canals and many other issues. As the aging Jefferson himself complained, "You see so many of these new [National] republicans maintaining in Congress the rankest doctrines of the old federalists." This division in the Republican Party would soon produce the Second Party System, in which national-minded Whigs and state-focused Democrats would confront each other. By the early 1820s, one cycle of American politics and economic debate had ended, and another was about to begin.

SUMMARY

In this chapter, we traced three interrelated themes: public policy, westward expansion, and party politics. We began by examining the contrasting public policies advocated by Alexander Hamilton and Thomas

Jefferson. A Federalist, Hamilton supported a strong national government and created a fiscal infrastructure (the national debt, tariffs, and a national bank) to spur trade and manufacturing. By contrast, Jefferson wanted to preserve the authority of state governments, and he envisioned an America enriched by farming rather than industry.

Jefferson and the Republicans promoted a westward movement that transformed the agricultural economy and sparked new wars with Indian peoples. Expansion westward also shaped American diplomatic and military policy, leading to the Louisiana Purchase,

the War of 1812, and the treaties negotiated by John Quincy Adams.

Finally, there was the unexpected rise of the First Party System. As Hamilton's policies split the political elite, the French Revolution divided Americans into hostile ideological groups. The result was two decades of bitter conflict and controversial measures: the Federalists' Sedition Act, the Republicans' Embargo Act, and Madison's decision to go to war with Britain. Although the Federalist Party faded away, it left as its enduring legacy Hamilton's financial innovations and John Marshall's constitutional jurisprudence.

CHAPTER REVIEW

MAKE IT STICK   Go to **LearningCurve** to retain what you've read.

TERMS TO KNOW   Identify and explain the significance of each term below.

Key Concepts and Events

Judiciary Act of 1789 (p. 216)	**Naturalization, Alien, and Sedition Acts** (p. 224)	
Bill of Rights (p. 216)	**Virginia and Kentucky Resolutions** (p. 225)	
Report on the Public Credit (p. 216)	**Treaty of Greenville** (p. 226)	
Bank of the United States (p. 218)	*Marbury v. Madison* (**1803**) (p. 231)	
Report on Manufactures (p. 218)	**Louisiana Purchase** (p. 233)	
Proclamation of Neutrality (p. 219)	**Embargo Act of 1807** (p. 234)	
French Revolution (p. 219)	**Battle of Tippecanoe** (p. 236)	
Jacobins (p. 219)	**Treaty of Ghent** (p. 241)	
Whiskey Rebellion (p. 219)	*McCulloch v. Maryland* (**1819**) (p. 241)	
Jay's Treaty (p. 222)	**Adams-Onís Treaty** (p. 243)	
Haitian Revolution (p. 222)	**Monroe Doctrine** (p. 244)	
XYZ Affair (p. 223)		

Key People

Alexander Hamilton (p. 216)
Thomas Jefferson (p. 218)
John Adams (p. 223)
Little Turtle (p. 226)
John Marshall (p. 231)
Tecumseh (p. 235)
Henry Clay (p. 241)
John Quincy Adams (p. 243)

REVIEW QUESTIONS   Answer these questions to demonstrate your understanding of the chapter's main ideas.

1. Why did Alexander Hamilton, as Washington's first secretary of the treasury, advocate the creation of a permanent national debt and a national bank? What fears did his economic plans arouse in his Republican opponents?

2. What were the principal effects of the French and Haitian Revolutions in the United States? How did they influence the development of the American economy, American politics, and westward development?

3. What forces—ideological, political, and economic—led the United States to gain dominance over eastern North America in these years?

4. Explain the rise and fall of the First Party System. How did the policies implemented by Republican presidents between 1801 and 1825 differ from those implemented during the 1790s? Why did the Federalists fall out of favor? What legacy did the Federalists leave?

5. **THEMATIC UNDERSTANDING** Look at the events listed under "Work, Exchange, and Technology" and "Politics and Power" for the period 1800–1820 on the thematic timeline on page 149. What was the relationship in these years between the activism of the national government and developments in the American economy?

MAKING CONNECTIONS

Recognize the larger developments and continuities within and across chapters by answering these questions.

1. **ACROSS TIME AND PLACE** In Chapter 6, thirteen former British colonies cooperated in war and established new republican institutions of self-government. After 1789, unforeseen divisions developed in American politics. Why did Hamiltonians and Jeffersonians disagree so sharply on key questions of national policy? Which of the factions in the First Party System—Federalists or Republicans—best embodied the principles of the Revolution? How did westward expansion and international relations force the United States to modify its Revolutionary republican ideals?

2. **VISUAL EVIDENCE** Return to the Currier & Ives print depicting the bombardment of Tripoli on page 232. What message does it convey about America's position in the world? How well does that message square with the actual outcome of the First Barbary War? What does this suggest about the artist's purpose?

MORE TO EXPLORE

Start here to learn more about the events discussed in this chapter.

Gregory Dowd, *A Spirited Resistance* (1993). A penetrating account of Indian resistance to American expansion.

Joanne B. Freeman, *Affairs of Honor* (2002). A cultural analysis of the politics of the 1790s.

Jon Kukla, *A Wilderness So Immense* (2004). A sweeping account of the contexts for the Louisiana Purchase.

Alan Taylor, *The Civil War of 1812* (2010). Presents the contest for Canada as a multiethnic civil war.

Ashli White, *Encountering Revolution* (2012). Considers the impact of the Haitian Revolution on the United States.

The War of 1812 (PBS video, 2011) and its accompanying Web site (**pbs.org/wned/war-of-1812/home/**) offer reenactments, animations, interpretive essays, and historical site analyses.

TIMELINE

Ask yourself why this chapter begins and ends with these dates and then identify the links among related events.

1784–1789	• Contested Indian treaties: Fort Stanwix (1784), Fort McIntosh (1785), Fort Finney (1786), and Fort Harmar (1789)
1789–1799	• French Revolution
1789	• Judiciary Act establishes federal courts
1790	• Hamilton's public credit system approved
1790–1791	• Western Confederacy defeats U.S. armies
1791–1803	• Haitian Revolution
1791	• Bill of Rights ratified • Bank of the United States chartered
1792	• Kentucky joins Union
1793	• War between Britain and France
1794	• Madison and Jefferson found Republican Party • Whiskey Rebellion • Battle of Fallen Timbers
1795	• Jay's Treaty with Great Britain • Pinckney's Treaty with Spain • Treaty of Greenville accepts Indian land rights
1798	• XYZ Affair • Alien, Sedition, and Naturalization Acts • Virginia and Kentucky Resolutions
1800	• Jefferson elected president
1801–1812	• Gallatin reduces national debt
1803	• Louisiana Purchase • *Marbury v. Madison* asserts judicial review
1804–1806	• Lewis and Clark explore West
1807	• Embargo Act cripples American shipping
1808	• Madison elected president
1809	• Tecumseh and Tenskwatawa revive Western Confederacy
1812–1815	• War of 1812
1817–1825	• Era of Good Feeling
1819	• Adams-Onís Treaty • *McCulloch v. Maryland; Dartmouth College v. Woodward*

KEY TURNING POINTS: The Northwest Ordinance (1787; Chapter 6), Kentucky and Tennessee join the Union (1792, 1796), and Jefferson is elected president (1800). How were developments in the West tied into national politics in the 1790s? Why did the Federalists steadily lose ground to the Republicans?

8 CHAPTER

Creating a Republican Culture
1790–1820

By the 1820s, America's white citizenry had embraced the republican political order. Their nation stood forth as a "promised land of civil liberty, and of institutions designed to liberate and exalt the human race," declared a Kentucky judge. White Americans were indeed fortunate. They lived under a representative republican government, free from arbitrary taxation and from domination by an established church. The timing of the deaths of aging political leaders John Adams and Thomas Jefferson seemed to many Americans to confirm that God looked with favor on their experiment in self-government. What other than divine intervention could explain their nearly simultaneous deaths on July 4, 1826, the fiftieth anniversary of the Declaration of Independence?

Inspired by their political freedom, many citizens sought to extend republican principles throughout their society. But what were those principles? For entrepreneurial-minded merchants, farmers, and political leaders, republicanism meant a dynamic market economy based on the private ownership of property and capital. However, they welcomed legislative policies that assisted private business and, they claimed, enhanced the "common wealth" of the society. Other Americans in the northern states championed democratic republican cultural values, such as equality in the family and in social relationships. In the southern states, sharply divided by class and race, politicians and pamphleteers endorsed aristocratic republicanism. It stressed liberty for whites rather than equality for all.

Yet another vision of American republicanism emerged from the Second Great Awakening, religious revivals that swept the nation between 1790 and 1850. As Alexis de Tocqueville reported in *Democracy in America* (1835), the Second Great Awakening gave "the Christian religion . . . a greater influence over the souls of men" than in any other country. Moreover, religious enthusiasm—what Methodist bishop McIlvaine praised as "the quickening of the people of God to a spirit and walk becoming the gospel"—prompted social reform on many fronts. For those who embraced the Awakening, the United States was both a great experiment in republican government and a Christian civilization destined to redeem the world—a moral mission that would inform American diplomacy in the centuries to come.

IDENTIFY THE BIG IDEA

In eighteenth-century Europe, the leading principles were aristocracy, patriarchy, mercantilism, arranged marriages, legal privilege, and established churches. What principles would replace those societal rules in America's new republican society?

Mrs. Hugh McCurdy and Her Daughters   This 1806 portrait of Grace Allison McCurdy and her daughters, Mary Jane and Letitia Grace, excludes her husband, the Baltimore merchant Hugh McCurdy, suggesting the increased cultural focus on mothers and children in the early republic. A few years earlier, the artist, Joshua Johnson (or Johnston, c. 1763–c. 1824), had painted a solo portrait of Letitia Grace. Here Johnson links Mrs. McCurdy and her elder daughter visually with a splash of vibrant red fruit near their laps, which probably also serves as a symbol of their fertility. Corcoran Gallery of Art, Washington D.C., USA/Museum Purchase through the gifts of William Wilson Corcoran, Elizabeth Donner Norment, Francis Biddle, Erich Cohn, Hardinge Scholle and the William A. Clark Fund/The Bridgeman Art Library.

The Capitalist Commonwealth

What did republicanism mean for economic life? In early-nineteenth-century America, it meant private property, market exchange, individual opportunity, and activist governments. Throughout the nation, and especially in the Northeast, republican state legislatures embraced a **"neomercantilist"** system of government-assisted economic development. And it worked. Beginning around 1800, the average per capita income of Americans increased by more than 1 percent a year — more than 30 percent in a single generation.

Banks, Manufacturing, and Markets

America was "a Nation of Merchants," a British visitor reported from Philadelphia in 1798, "keen in the pursuit of wealth in all the various modes of acquiring it." Acquire it they did, making spectacular profits as the wars of the French Revolution and Napoleon (1793–1815) crippled European firms. Merchants John Jacob Astor and Robert Oliver became the nation's first millionaires. After working for an Irish-owned linen firm in Baltimore, Oliver struck out on his own, achieving affluence by trading West Indian sugar and coffee. Astor, who migrated from Germany to New York in 1784, began by selling dry-goods in western New York and became wealthy by carrying furs from the Pacific Northwest to China and investing in New York City real estate (Thinking Like a Historian, p. 252).

Banking and Credit To finance their ventures, Oliver, Astor, and other merchants needed capital, from either their own savings or loans. Before the Revolution, farmers relied on government-sponsored land banks for loans, while merchants arranged partnerships or obtained credit from British suppliers. Then, in 1781, Philadelphia merchants persuaded the Confederation Congress to charter the Bank of North America, and traders in Boston and New York soon founded similar institutions that raised funds and lent them out. "Our monied capital has so much increased from the Introduction of Banks, & the Circulation of the Funds," Philadelphia merchant William Bingham boasted in 1791, "that the Necessity of Soliciting Credits from England will no longer exist."

That same year, Federalists in Congress chartered the Bank of the United States to issue notes and make commercial loans (Chapter 7, p. 218). By 1805, the bank had branches in eight seaport cities, profits that averaged a handsome 8 percent annually, and clients

A Cloth Merchant, 1789

Originally a prosperous storekeeper in New Milford, Connecticut, Elijah Boardman (1760–1832) eventually became a U.S. senator. Like other American traders during the 1780s, he imported huge quantities of cloth from Britain. When the wars of the 1790s cut off trade, some merchants financed the domestic production of textiles. Others, including Boardman, turned to land speculation. In 1795, he joined the Connecticut Land Company and bought huge tracts in Connecticut's Western Reserve, including the present towns of Medina, Palmyra, and Boardman, Ohio. Ralph Earl painted this portrait in 1789. © The Metropolitan Museum of Art. Image Source: Art Resource/NY.

with easy access to capital. As trader Jesse Atwater noted, "the foundations of our [merchant] houses are laid in bank paper."

However, Jeffersonians attacked the bank as an unconstitutional expansion of federal power. Moreover, they claimed it promoted "a consolidated, energetic government supported by public creditors, speculators, and other insidious men." When the bank's twenty-year charter expired in 1811, the Jeffersonian Republican–dominated Congress refused to renew it.

The China Trade

Following the Revolution, New England merchants traded actively with the major Asian manufacturing centers of China and India. In this painting by George Chinnery (1774–1852), the American flag flies prominently, alongside other national banners, in front of the warehouse district in Canton (modern Guangzhou). There, merchants exchanged bundles of American furs for cargoes of Chinese tea, silks, and porcelain plates, cups, and serving dishes. © Peabody Essex Museum, Salem, Massachusetts, USA/The Bridgeman Art Library.

Merchants, artisans, and farmers quickly persuaded state legislatures to charter banks—in Pennsylvania, no fewer than 41. By 1816, when Congress (now run by National Republicans) chartered a new national bank (known as the Second Bank of the United States), there were 246 state-chartered banks with tens of thousands of stockholders and $68 million in banknotes in circulation. These state banks were often shady operations that issued notes without adequate specie reserves, made loans to insiders, and lent generously to farmers buying overpriced land.

Dubious banking policies helped bring on the **Panic of 1819** (just as they caused the financial crisis of 2008), but broader forces were equally important. As the Napoleonic Wars ended in 1815, Americans sharply increased their consumption of English woolen and cotton goods. However, in 1818, farmers and planters faced an abrupt 30 percent drop in world agricultural prices. The price of raw cotton in South Carolina fell from 34 to 15 cents a pound, and as Britain closed the West Indies to American trade, wheat prices plummeted as well. As farmers' income declined, they could not pay debts owed to stores and banks, many of which went bankrupt. "A deep shadow has passed over our land," lamented one New Yorker, as land prices dropped by 50 percent. The panic gave Americans their first taste of a business cycle, the periodic boom and bust inherent to an unregulated market economy.

Rural Manufacturing   The Panic of 1819 devastated artisans and farmers who sold goods in regional or national markets. Before 1800, many artisans worked part-time and bartered their handicrafts locally. A French traveler in Massachusetts found many "men who are both cultivators and artisans," while in Lancaster, Pennsylvania, clockmaker John Hoff exchanged

The Entrepreneur and the Community

Americans of the early republic believed that with hard work and virtue, even the lowliest of white men might rise to economic and political respectability, if not prominence. In the Revolutionary generation, Benjamin Franklin, born into a large and impoverished Boston family, had become a successful businessman and an international celebrity. Franklin's success reflected the optimism that laboring men felt when contemplating the new nation's seemingly boundless opportunity.

1. **Banner of the Society of Pewterers of the City of New York, carried in the Federal Procession, July 23, 1788, celebrating the ratification of the U.S. Constitution.** *The ribbon at top right reads "The Federal Plan Most Solid & Secure/Americans Their Freedom Will Endure/All Art Shall Flourish in Columbia's Land/And All her Sons Join as One Social Band."*

Source: © Collection of the New York Historical Society, USA/The Bridgeman Art Library.

2. **John Jacob Astor quoted in Elbert Hubbard, *Little Journeys to the Homes of Great Business Men*, 1909.** *John Jacob Astor's (1763–1848) story is a parable of American entrepreneurial triumph. Arriving in America in 1783 from Germany, Astor worked in the fur industry treating pelts and, with capital borrowed from his brother, started up a musical instrument shop and fur business in 1786. Over the next three decades, Astor's American Fur Company prospered by trading furs in China, making Astor America's first millionaire. Apparently influenced by Benjamin*

Franklin's aphorism "Early to bed and early to rise, makes a man healthy wealthy and wise," Astor wrote:

The man who makes it the habit of his life to go to bed at nine o'clock, usually gets rich and is always reliable. Of course, going to bed does not make him rich — I merely mean that such a man will in all probability be up early in the morning and do a big day's work . . . good habits in America make any man rich.

3. **Anonymous, "A Working Man's Recollections of America," *Knight's Penny Magazine*, 1846.** *A cabinetmaker penned this account after returning to England following an unsuccessful stint seeking success in New York.*

I was a cabinet-maker by trade, and one of the many who, between the years 1825–35, expatriated themselves in countless thousands, drawn by the promise of fair wages for faithful work, and driven by the scanty remuneration offered to unceasing toil at home. . . . On landing in New York I made up my mind to lose none of the advantages it uttered by want of diligence on my part. During the first two years I took but one holiday. . . . In summer we began work at six; at eight took half an hour for breakfast, and then worked till twelve, when one an hour for dinner; after which we kept on till six, seven, or eight. . . . A relative who arrived from England held out to me bright prospects of advantages to be realized by the employment of a little capital, combined with a removal to some inland town. I sold off nearly the whole of our moveables . . . [and committed all my savings to this enterprise. However,] our scheme . . . completely failed, and I had no resources but my industry and chest of tools to meet the impending difficulties.

4. **Diary entry by Philip Hone, March 29, 1848.** *Philip Hone (1780–1851), a conservative Whig, was a successful merchant and entrepreneur and mayor of New York City from 1826 to 1827.*

Hone's marvelous diary (1828–1851) records the changing character of New York City, as well as his contempt for Jacksonian Democracy and its Irish immigrant supporters.

John Jacob Astor died this morning, at nine o'clock, in the eighty-fifth year of his age . . . and left reluctantly his unbounded wealth. His property is estimated at $20,000,000, some judicious persons say $30,000,000; but, at any rate, he was the richest man in the United States in productive and valuable property; and this immense, gigantic fortune was the fruit of his own labor, unerring sagacity, and far-seeing penetration. He came to this country at twenty years of age; penniless, friendless, without inheritance, without education . . . but with a determination to be rich, and ability to carry it into effect. His capital consisted of a few trifling musical instruments, which he got from his brother, George Astor, in London, a dealer in music. . . . The fur trade was the philosopher's stone of this modern Croesus; beaver-skins and musk-rats furnished the oil for the supply of Aladdin's lamp. His traffic was the shipment of furs to China, where they brought immense prices, for he monopolized the business; and the return cargoes of teas, silks, and rich productions of China brought further large profits. . . . My brother and I found in Mr. Astor a valuable customer. . . . All he touched turned to gold.

5. Editorial in the *New York Herald*, April 5, 1848.
John Jacob Astor's will included a bequest of $400,000 for the establishment of what became the New York Public Library. This editorial questioned whether this relatively meager bequest adequately repaid residents.

If we had been an associate of John Jacob Astor the first idea that we should have put into his head would have been that one-half of his immense property — ten million at least — belonged to the people of the city of New York. During the last fifty years of the life of John Jacob Astor, his property has been augmented and increased in the value by the aggregate intelligence, industry, enterprise and commerce of New York, fully to the amount of one-half its value. The farms and lots of ground which he

bought forty, twenty and ten and five years ago, have all increased in value entirely by the industry of the citizens of New York . . . half of his immense estate, in its actual value, has accrued to him by the industry of the community.

Sources: (2) Elbert Hubbard, *Little Journeys to the Homes of Great Business Men* (New York: Wm. H. Wise & Co., 1916), 201; (3) *Knight's Penny Magazine*, Vol. 1 (London: Charles Knight & Co., 1846), 97, 107, 108; (4) Philip Hone, *The Diary of Philip Hone, 1828–1851*, Vol. 2 (New York: Dodd, Mead and Company, 1889), 347–348; (5) Gustavus Myers, *History of the Great American Fortunes*, Vol. 1 (Chicago: Charles H. Kerr & Company, 1910), 199–200.

ANALYZING THE EVIDENCE

1. What does the Pewterer's Banner (source 1) suggest about personal and by extension national success in the post-Revolutionary era? What can you infer about artisan entrepreneurs in the new republic from this source?

2. According to John Jacob Astor (source 2) and the cabinetmaker (source 3), what traits are important in work? Based on the sources included here, do you agree with Astor that good habits make any man rich? Why or why not?

3. Sources 2, 4, and 5 all deal with John Jacob Astor. What do these sources suggest about the road to wealth in America?

4. Compare and contrast Hone's view of Astor (source 4) with that of the *Herald*'s editorial (source 5). Then apply the *Herald*'s critique to contemporary entrepreneurs such as Bill Gates of Microsoft or Steve Jobs of Apple. Are their fortunes also the product, in part, of "the industry of the community"?

PUTTING IT ALL TOGETHER

John Jacob Astor initially made money by trading furs in local and then in international markets. Next, he speculated in land in booming cities. Finally, he became a *rentier*, crafting long-term property leases that guaranteed wealth to future generations of his family. Using the material in Chapter 8, explain how a pewterer or a cabinetmaker might follow a somewhat similar path to wealth in the market economy of nineteenth-century America. Noting also the statement "All her Sons Join as One Social Band" (source 1), explain why other Americans were critical of the rise of such ambitious capitalist entrepreneurs.

his clocks for a dining table, a bedstead, and labor on his small farm. Then various artisans — shipbuilders in seacoast towns, ironworkers in Pennsylvania and Maryland, clockmakers in Connecticut, and shoemakers in Massachusetts — expanded their output and sold their products in wider markets.

American entrepreneurs drove this expansion of rural manufacturing. Beginning in the 1790s, enterprising merchants bought raw materials, hired farm families to process them, and distributed the finished manufactures. "Straw hats and Bonnets are manufactured by many families," a Maine census-taker noted in the 1810s. Merchants shipped rural manufactures — shoes, brooms, and palm-leaf hats as well as cups, baking pans, and other tin utensils — to stores in seaport cities. New England peddlers, who quickly acquired repute as hard-bargaining "Yankees," sold them throughout the rural South.

New technology initially played only a minor role in producing this boom in consumer goods. Take the case of textile production. During the 1780s, New England and Middle Atlantic merchants built water-powered mills to run machines that combed wool — and later cotton — into long strands. However, until the 1810s, they used the household-based outwork system for the next steps: farm women and children spun the machine-combed strands into thread and yarn on foot-driven spinning wheels, and men in other households used foot-powered looms to weave the yarn into cloth. In 1820, more than 12,000 household workers labored full-time weaving woolen cloth, which water-powered fulling mills then pounded flat, giving the cloth a smooth finish. By then, the transfer of textile production to factories was gaining speed; the number of water-driven cotton spindles soared from 8,000 in 1809 to 333,000 in 1817.

TRACE CHANGE OVER TIME

How did governments, banks, and merchants expand American commerce and manufacturing between 1780 and 1820?

The Yankee Peddler, c. 1830

Even in 1830, many Americans lived too far from a market town to go there regularly to buy goods. Instead, they purchased their tinware, clocks, textiles, and other manufactures from peddlers, often from New England, who traveled far and wide in small horse-drawn vans like the one visible through the doorway.

Collection IBM Corporation, Armonk, New York.

The growth of manufacturing offered farm families new opportunities—and new risks. Ambitious New England farmers switched from subsistence crops of wheat and potatoes to raising livestock. They sold meat, butter, and cheese to city markets and cattle hides to the booming shoe industry. "Along the whole road from Boston, we saw women engaged in making cheese," a Polish traveler reported. Other families raised sheep and sold raw wool to textile manufacturers. Processing these raw materials brought new jobs and income to stagnating farming towns. In 1792, Concord, Massachusetts, had one slaughterhouse and five small tanneries; a decade later, the town boasted eleven slaughterhouses and six large tanneries.

As the rural economy churned out more goods, it altered the environment. Foul odors from stockyards and tanning pits wafted over Concord and other leather-producing towns. Nor was that all. Tanners cut down thousands of acres of hemlock trees, using the bark to process stiff cow hides into pliable leather. More trees fell to the ax to create pasturelands for huge herds of livestock—dairy cows, cattle, and especially sheep. By 1850, most of the ancient forests in southern New England and eastern New York were gone: "The hills had been stripped of their timber," New York's *Catskill Messenger* reported, "so as to present their huge, rocky projections." Moreover, scores of textile milldams dotted New England's rivers, altering their flow and preventing fish—already severely depleted from decades of overfishing—from reaching upriver spawning grounds. Even as the income of farmers rose, the quality of their natural environment declined.

In the new capitalist-driven market economy, rural parents and their children worked longer and harder. They made yarn, hats, and brooms during the winter and returned to their regular farming chores during the warmer seasons. More important, these farm families now depended on their wage labor or market sales to purchase the textiles, shoes, and hats they had once made for themselves. The new productive system made families and communities more efficient and prosperous—and more dependent on a market they could not control.

New Transportation Systems   The expansion of the market depended on improvements in transportation, where governments also played a crucial role. Between 1793 and 1812, the Massachusetts legislature granted charters to more than one hundred private turnpike corporations. These charters gave the companies special legal status and often included monopoly rights to a transportation route. Pennsylvania issued fifty-five charters, including one to the Lancaster

Turnpike Company, which built a 65-mile graded and graveled toll road to Philadelphia. The road quickly boosted the regional economy. Although turnpike investors received only about "three percent annually," Henry Clay estimated, society as a whole "actually reap[ed] fifteen or twenty percent." A farm woman agreed: "The turnpike is finished and we can now go to town at all times and in all weather." New turnpikes soon connected dozens of inland market centers to seaport cities.

Water transport was even quicker and cheaper, so state governments and private entrepreneurs dredged shallow rivers and constructed canals to bypass waterfalls and rapids. For their part, farmers in Kentucky and Tennessee and in southern Ohio, Indiana, and Illinois settled near the Ohio River and its many tributaries, so they could easily get goods to market. Similarly, speculators hoping to capitalize on the expansion of commerce bought up property in the cities along the banks of major rivers: Cincinnati, Louisville, Chattanooga, and St. Louis. Farmers and merchants built barges to carry cotton, grain, and meat downstream to New Orleans, which by 1815 was exporting about $5 million in agricultural products yearly.

Public Enterprise: The Commonwealth System

Legislative charters for banks, turnpikes, and canal companies reflected the ideology of mercantilism: government-assisted economic development. Just as Parliament had used the Navigation Acts to spur British prosperity, so American legislatures enacted laws "of great public utility" to increase the "common wealth." These statutes generally took the form of special charters that bestowed legal privileges, such as the power of eminent domain, that allowed turnpike, bridge, and canal corporations to force the sale of privately owned land along their routes. State legislatures also aided capital-intensive flour millers and textile manufacturers, who flooded adjacent farmland as they built dams to power their water-driven machinery. In Massachusetts, the Mill Dam Act of 1795 deprived farmers of their traditional common-law right to stop the flooding and forced them to accept "fair compensation" for their lost acreage. Judges approved this state-ordered shift in property rights. "The establishment of a great mill-power for manufacturing purposes," Justice Lemuel Shaw intoned, was "one of the great industrial pursuits of the commonwealth."

UNDERSTAND POINTS OF VIEW
Did state mercantilism (the grant of privileges and charters) embody republican ideology or violate it?

View of Cincinnati, **by John Caspar Wild, c. 1835**

Thanks to its location on the Ohio River (a tributary of the Mississippi), Cincinnati quickly became one of the major processing centers for grain and hogs in the trans-Appalachian west. By the 1820s, passenger steamboats and freight barges connected the city with Pittsburgh to the north and the ocean port of New Orleans far to the south. Museum of Fine Arts, Boston, M. and M. Karolik Collection.

Critics condemned the legal privileges given to private enterprises as "Scheme[s] of an evident anti-republican tendency," as some "freeholder citizens" in Putney, Vermont, put it. Such grants to business corporations, they argued, violated the "equal rights" of citizens and infringed on the sovereignty of the governments. "Whatever power is given to a corporation, is just so much power taken from the State," argued a Pennsylvanian. Nonetheless, judges in state courts, following the lead of John Marshall's Supreme Court (Chapter 7), consistently upheld corporate charters and grants of eminent domain to private transportation companies. "The opening of good and easy internal communications is one of the highest duties of government," declared a New Jersey judge.

State mercantilism soon spread beyond transportation. Following Jefferson's embargo of 1807, which cut off goods and credit from Europe, the New England states awarded charters to two hundred iron-mining, textile-manufacturing, and banking companies, while Pennsylvania granted more than eleven hundred. By 1820, state governments had created a republican political economy: a **Commonwealth System** that funneled state aid to private businesses whose projects would improve the general welfare.

Toward a Democratic Republican Culture

After independence, many Americans in the northern states embraced a democratic republicanism that celebrated political equality and social mobility. These citizens, primarily members of the emerging middle class, redefined the nature of the family and of education by seeking egalitarian marriages and affectionate ways of rearing their children.

Opportunity and Equality— for White Men

Between 1780 and 1820, hundreds of well-educated visitors agreed that the American social order was different from that of Europe. In his famous *Letters from an American Farmer* (1782), French-born essayist J. Hector St. Jean de Crèvecoeur wrote that European society was composed "of great lords who possess everything, and of a herd of people who have nothing." By contrast, the United States had "no aristocratical families, no courts, no kings, no bishops."

The absence of a hereditary aristocracy encouraged Americans to condemn inherited social privilege and to extol legal equality. "The law is the same for everyone," noted one European traveler. Yet citizens of the new republic willingly accepted social divisions that reflected personal achievement, a phenomenon that astounded many Europeans. "In Europe to say of someone that he rose from nothing is a disgrace and a reproach," remarked a Polish aristocrat. "It is the opposite here. To be the architect of your own fortune is honorable. It is the highest recommendation."

Some Americans from long-distinguished families felt threatened by the ideology of wealth-driven social mobility. "Man is estimated by dollars," complained Nathaniel Booth, whose high-status family had once dominated the small Hudson River port town of Kingston, New York. However, for most white men, a merit-based system meant the chance to better themselves (Map 8.1).

Old cultural rules—and new laws—denied such chances to most women and African American men. When women and free blacks asked for voting rights, male legislators wrote explicit race and gender restrictions into the law. In 1802, Ohio disenfranchised African Americans, and the New York constitution of 1821 imposed a property-holding requirement on black voters. A striking case of sexual discrimination occurred in New Jersey, where the state constitution of 1776 had granted the voting franchise to all property

IDENTIFY CAUSES

What factors encouraged—and inhibited—equality and democracy in early-nineteenth-century American life?

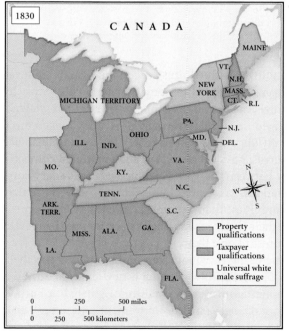

MAP 8.1

The Expansion of Voting Rights for White Men, 1800 and 1830

Between 1800 and 1830, the United States moved steadily toward political equality for white men. Many existing states revised their constitutions and replaced a property qualification for voting with less restrictive criteria, such as paying taxes or serving in the militia. Some new states in the West extended the suffrage to all adult white men. As parties sought votes from a broader electorate, the tone of politics became more open and competitive—swayed by the interests and values of ordinary people.

holders. As Federalists and Republicans competed for power, they ignored customary gender rules and urged property-owning single women and widows to vote. Sensing a threat to men's monopoly on politics, the New Jersey legislature in 1807 invoked both biology and custom to limit voting to men only: "Women, generally, are neither by nature, nor habit, nor education, nor by their necessary condition in society fitted to perform this duty with credit to themselves or advantage to the public."

Toward Republican Families

The controversy over women's political rights mirrored a debate over authority within the household. British and American husbands had long claimed patriarchal power and legal control of the family's property. However, as John Adams lamented in 1776, the republican principle of equality had "spread where it was not intended," encouraging his wife and other women to demand legal and financial rights. Patriot author and historian Mercy Otis Warren argued that patriarchy was not a "natural" rule but a social contrivance and could be justified only "for the sake of order in families."

 To see a longer excerpt of the Mercy Otis Warren document, along with other primary sources from this period, see *Sources for America's History*.

Republican Marriages Economic and cultural changes also eroded customary paternal authority. In colonial America, most property-owning parents had arranged their children's marriages. They looked for a morally upright son- or daughter-in-law with financial resources; physical attraction and emotional compatibility between the young people were secondary considerations. As landholdings shrank in long-settled communities, many yeomen fathers has less control over their children's marriages because they had fewer resources to give them.

Increasingly, young men and women chose their own partners, influenced by a new cultural attitude: **sentimentalism**. Sentimentalism originated in Europe as part of the Romantic movement and, after 1800, spread quickly through all classes of American society. Rejecting the Enlightenment's emphasis on rational thought, sentimentalism celebrated the importance of "feeling"—a physical, sensuous appreciation of God, nature, and fellow humans. This new emphasis on deeply felt emotions pervaded literary works, popular theatrical melodramas, and the passionate rhetoric of revivalist preachers.

As the passions of the heart overwhelmed the logic of the mind, magazines praised **companionate marriages**: marriages "contracted from motives of affection, rather than of interest." Many young people looked for a relationship based on intimacy and a spouse who was, as Eliza Southgate of Maine put it, "calculated to promote my happiness." As young people "fell in love" and married, many fathers changed from authoritarian patriarchs to watchful paternalists. To guard against free-spending sons-in-law, wealthy fathers often placed their daughters' inheritance in a legal trust. One Virginia planter told his lawyer "to see the property settlement properly drawn before the marriage, for I by no means consent that Polly shall be left to the Vicissitudes of Life."

As voluntary contracts between individuals, love marriages conformed more closely to republican principles than did arranged matches. In theory, such marriages would be companionate, giving wives and husbands "true equality," as one Boston man suggested. In practice, husbands dominated most marriages, because male authority was deeply ingrained in cultural mores and because American common law gave husbands control of the family's property. Moreover, the new love-based marriage system discouraged parents from protecting young wives, and governments refused to prevent domestic tyranny. The marriage contract "is so much more important in its consequences to females than to males," a young man at the Litchfield Law School in Connecticut astutely observed in 1820, for "they subject themselves to his authority. He is their all—their only relative—their only hope" (American Voices, p. 260).

Young adults who chose partners unwisely were severely disappointed when their spouses failed as providers or faithful companions. Before 1800, unhappy wives and husbands could do little; officials granted divorces infrequently and then only in cases of neglect, abandonment, or adultery—serious offenses against the moral order of society. After 1800, most divorce petitions cited emotional issues. One woman complained that her husband had "ceased to cherish her," while a man grieved that his wife had "almost broke his heart." Responding to changing cultural values, several states expanded the legal grounds for divorce to include drunkenness and personal cruelty.

Republican Motherhood Traditionally, most American women had spent their active adult years working as farmwives and bearing and nurturing children. However, after 1800, the birthrate in the northern states dropped significantly. In the farming village of

The Wedding, 1805

Bride and groom stare intently into each other's eyes as they exchange vows, suggesting that their union was a love match, not an arranged marriage based on economic calculation. The plain costumes of the guests and the sparse furnishings of the room suggest that the unknown artist may have provided us with a picture of a rural Quaker wedding. The Granger Collection, NYC.

Sturbridge in central Massachusetts, women now bore an average of six children; their grandmothers had usually given birth to eight or nine. In the growing seaport cities, native-born white women now bore an average of only four children.

The United States was among the first nations to experience this sharp decline in the birthrate — what historians call the **demographic transition**. There were several causes. Beginning in the 1790s, thousands of young men migrated to the trans-Appalachian west, which increased the number of never-married women in the East and delayed marriage for many more. Women who married in their late twenties had fewer children. In addition, white urban middle-class couples deliberately limited the size of their families. Fathers wanted to leave children an adequate inheritance, while mothers, influenced by new ideas of individualism and self-achievement, refused to spend their entire adulthood rearing children. After having four or five children, these couples used birth control or abstained from sexual intercourse.

Even as women bore fewer children, they accepted greater responsibility for the welfare of the family. In his *Thoughts on Female Education* (1787), Philadelphia physician Benjamin Rush argued that young women should ensure their husbands' "perseverance in the paths of rectitude" and called for loyal "republican mothers" who would instruct "their sons in the principles of liberty and government."

 To see a longer excerpt of *Thoughts on Female Education*, along with other primary sources from this period, see *Sources for America's History.*

Christian ministers readily embraced this idea of **republican motherhood**. "Preserving virtue and instructing the young are not the fancied, but the real 'Rights of Women,'" the Reverend Thomas Bernard told the Female Charitable Society of Salem, Massachusetts. He urged his audience to dismiss public roles for women, such as voting or serving on juries, that English feminist Mary Wollstonecraft had advocated in *A Vindication of the Rights of Woman* (1792). Instead, women should care for their children, a responsibility that gave

IDENTIFY CAUSES

How did republican ideals, new economic circumstances, and changing cultural values affect marriage practices?

The Trials of Married Life

As the text explains, the ideal American marriage of the early nineteenth century was republican (a contract between equals) and romantic (a match in which mutual love was foremost). Were these ideals attainable, given the social authority of men and the volatility of human passions? Letters, memoirs, and diaries are excellent sources for answering these questions. These selections from the personal writings of a variety of American women offer insights into the new system of marriage and how changes in cultural values intersected with individual lives.

Emma Hart Willard
The Danger of High Expectations

Born in Connecticut in 1787, Emma Hart married John Willard in 1809. An early proponent of advanced education for women, she founded female academies in Middlebury, Vermont (1814), and Waterford and Troy, New York (1821). She wrote this letter to her sister, Almira Hart, in 1815.

You think it strange that I should consider a period of happiness as more likely than any other to produce future misery. I know I did not sufficiently explain myself. Those tender and delicious sensations which accompany successful love, while they soothe and soften the mind, diminish its strength to bear or to conquer difficulties. It is the luxury of the soul; and luxury always enervates. . . . This life is a life of vicissitude. . . .

[Suppose] you are secured to each other for life. It will be natural that, at first, he should be much devoted to you; but, after a while, his business must occupy his attention. While absorbed in that he will perhaps neglect some of those little tokens of affection which have become necessary to your happiness. His affairs will sometimes go wrong, . . . and he may sometimes hastily give you a harsh word or a frown.

But where is the use, say you, of diminishing my present enjoyment by such gloomy apprehensions? Its use is this, that, if you enter the marriage state believing such things to be absolutely impossible, if you should meet them, they would come upon you with double force.

Caroline Howard Gilman
Female Submission in Marriage

Born in Boston in 1794, Caroline Howard married in 1819 and moved to Charleston, South Carolina, with her husband, Samuel Gilman, a Unitarian minister. A novelist, she published *Recollections of a Housekeeper* (1835), a portrait of domestic life in New England, and *Recollections*

of a Southern Matron (1838), a fictional account that includes this selection.

The planter's bride, who leaves a numerous and cheerful family in her paternal home, little imagines the change which awaits her in her own retired residence. She dreams of an independent sway over her household, devoted love and unbroken intercourse with her husband, and indeed longs to be released from the eyes of others, that she may dwell only beneath the sunbeam of his. And so it was with me. . . .

There we were together, asking for nothing but each other's presence and love. At length it was necessary for him to tear himself away to superintend his interests. . . . But the period of absence was gradually protracted; then a friend sometimes came home with him, and their talk was of crops and politics, draining the fields and draining the revenue. . . . A growing discomfort began to work upon my mind. I had undefined forebodings; I mused about past days; my views of life became slowly disorganized; my physical powers enfeebled; a nervous excitement followed: I nursed a moody discontent. . . .

If the reign of romance was really waning, I resolved not to chill his noble confidence, but to make a steadier light rise on his affections. . . . This task of self-government was not easy. To repress a harsh answer, to confess a fault . . . in gentle submission, sometimes requires a struggle like life and death; but these . . . efforts are the golden threads with which domestic happiness is woven. . . . How clear is it, then, that woman loses by petulance and recrimination! Her first study must be self-control, almost to hypocrisy. A good wife must smile amid a thousand perplexities.

Martha Hunter Hitchcock
Isolation, Unmentionable Sorrows, and Suffering

Martha Hunter Hitchcock married a doctor in the U.S. Army. These excerpts from letters, in the Virginia Historical

Society, to her cousins Martha and Sarah Hunter describe her emotional dependence on her husband and her unhappy life.

To Martha Hunter, 1840:

If I had never married how much of pain, and dissatisfaction, should I have escaped — at all events I should never have known what jealousy is. You must not betray me, dear cousin, for despite all my good resolutions, I find it impossible always to struggle against my nature — the school of indulgence, in which I was educated, was little calculated to teach me, those lessons of forbearance, which I have had to practice so frequently, since my marriage — it is ungrateful in me to murmur, if perchance a little bitter is mingled in my cup of life.

To Sarah Hunter, 1841:

I have lived so long among strangers since my marriage, that when I contrast it with the old warm affection, in which I was nurtured, the contrast is so terrible, that I cannot refrain from weeping at the thought of it — I hope my dear cousin, that yours, will be a happier destiny than mine, in that respect — only think of it! Nearly a year and a half have passed away, since I have seen, a single relation!

To Martha Hunter, 1845:

Uneasiness about [my daughter] Lillie, and very great sorrows of my own, which I cannot commit to paper, have almost weighed me down to the grave; and indeed, without any affectation, I look forward to that, as the only real rest, I shall ever know.

To Martha Hunter, 1846:

Lillie had the scarlet fever, during our visit to Alabama, and she has never recovered from the effects of it — My life is a constant vigil — and there is nothing which wearies mind, and body, so much, as watching a sickly child. . . . All this I have to endure, and may have to suffer more for I know not, what Fate may have in store for me.

Elizabeth Scott Neblett
My Seasons of Gloom and Despondency

Elizabeth Scott Neblett lived with her husband and children in Navarro County, Texas. In 1860, she reflected in her diary on her bouts of depression and the difficulties of

wives and husbands in understanding each other's inner lives.

It has now been almost eight years since I became a married woman. Eight years of checkered good and ill, and yet thro' all it seems the most of the ill has fallen to my lot, until now my poor weak cowardly heart sighs only for its final resting place, where sorrow grief nor pain can never reach it more.

I feel that I have faithfully discharged my duty towards you and my children, but for this I know that I deserve no credit nor aspire to none; my affection has been my prompter, and the task has proven a labor of love. You have not rightly understood me at all times, and being naturally very hopeful you could in no measure sympathize with me during my seasons of gloom and despondency. . . . But marriage is a lottery and that your draw proved an unfortunate one on your part is not less a subject of regret with me than you. . . .

It is useless to say that during these eight years I have suffered ten times more than you have and ten times more than I can begin to make you conceive of, but of course you can not help the past, nor by knowing my suffering relieve it, but it might induce you to look with more kindness upon [my] faults. . . . The 17th of this month I was 27 years old and I think my face looks older than that, perhaps I'll never see an other birth day and I don't grieve at the idea.

Source: These selections are abridged versions of materials in Anya Jabour, ed., *Major Problems in the History of American Families and Children* (Boston: Houghton Mifflin, 2005), 108–113.

QUESTIONS FOR ANALYSIS

1. What problems do these women share? How might their problems reflect larger social and economic issues in nineteenth-century America?

2. How would you characterize the unhappiness of these women? In what ways is it related to their expectations about love-based marriage?

3. What was Caroline Gilman's advice to wives? How does it apply to the other women in this section?

4. Do these selections suggest that most American women had unfulfilled marriages? Or were these isolated cases? Would you expect to find more records of happy or unhappy marriages?

them "an extensive power over the fortunes of man in every generation."

Raising Republican Children

Republican values changed assumptions about inheritance and child rearing. English common law encouraged primogeniture, the bequest of the family's property to the eldest son (Chapter 1). After the Revolution, most state legislatures enacted statutes specifying equal division of the estate among all children, when there was no will. Most American parents applauded these statutes because they were already treating their children equally and with respect.

Two Modes of Parenting   Indeed, many European visitors believed that republican parents gave their children too much respect and freedom. Because of the "general ideas of Liberty and Equality engraved on their hearts," a Polish aristocrat suggested around 1800, American children had "scant respect" for their parents. Several decades later, a British traveler stood dumbfounded when an American father excused his son's "resolute disobedience" with a smile and the remark, "A sturdy republican, sir." The traveler speculated that American parents encouraged such independence to prepare youth to "go their own way" in the world.

Permissive child rearing was not universal. Foreign visitors interacted primarily with well-to-do Episcopalians and Presbyterians who held an Enlightenment conception of children. This outlook, transmitted by religious authors influenced by John Locke, viewed children as "rational creatures" best trained by means of advice and praise. The parents' role was to develop their child's conscience, self-discipline, and sense of responsibility. Families in the rapidly expanding middle class widely adopted this rationalist method of child rearing.

By contrast, many yeomen and tenant farmers, influenced by the Second Great Awakening, raised their children in an authoritarian fashion. Evangelical Baptist and Methodist writers insisted that children were "full of the stains and pollution of sin" and needed strict rules and harsh discipline. Fear was a "useful and necessary principle in family government," minister John Abbott advised parents; a child "should submit to your authority, not to your arguments or persuasions." Abbott told parents to instill humility in children and to teach them to subordinate their personal desires to God's will.

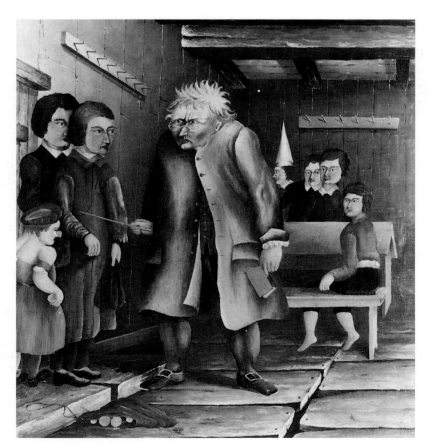

The Battle over Education

Here an unknown artist pokes fun at a tyrannical schoolmaster and, indirectly, at the strict approach to child rearing taken by evangelical authors, parents, and teachers. The students' faces reflect the artist's own rationalist outlook. One Enlightenment-minded minister suggested that we see in young children's eyes "the first dawn of reason, beaming forth its immortal rays." Copyright The Frick Collection, New York City.

Women's Education

Even in education-conscious New England, before 1800 few girls attended free public primary schools for more than a few years. Subsequently, as this detail from *Scenes from a Seminary for Young Ladies* (c. 1810–1820) indicates, some girls stayed in school into their teenage years and studied a wide variety of subjects, including geography. Many graduates of these female academies became teachers, a new field of employment for women. The St. Louis Art Museum, Missouri, USA/The Bridgeman Art Library.

Debates over Education Although families provided most moral and intellectual training, republican ideology encouraged publicly supported schooling. Bostonian Caleb Bingham, an influential textbook author, called for "an equal distribution of knowledge to make us emphatically a 'republic of letters.'" Both Thomas Jefferson and Benjamin Rush proposed ambitious schemes for a comprehensive system of primary and secondary schooling, followed by college training for bright young men. They also envisioned a university in which distinguished scholars would lecture on law, medicine, theology, and political economy.

To ordinary citizens, whose teenage children had to labor in the fields or workshops, talk of secondary and college education smacked of elitism. Farmers, artisans, and laborers wanted elementary schools that would instruct their children in the "three Rs" — reading, 'riting, and 'rithmetic — and make them literate enough to read the Bible. In New England, locally funded public schools offered basic instruction to most boys and some girls. In other regions, there were few publicly supported schools, and only 25 percent of the boys and perhaps 10 percent of the girls attended private institutions or had personal tutors. Even in New England, only a few young men and almost no young women went on to grammar school (high school), and less than 1 percent of men attended college. "Let anybody show what advantage the poor man receives from colleges," an anonymous "Old Soldier" wrote to the *Maryland Gazette*. "Why should they support them, unless it is to serve those who are in affluent circumstances, whose children can be spared from labor, and receive the benefits?"

Although many state constitutions encouraged support for education, few legislatures acted until the 1820s. Then a new generation of educational reformers, influenced by merchants and manufacturers, raised standards by certifying qualified teachers and appointing statewide superintendents of schools. To encourage students, the reformers chose textbooks such as Parson Mason Weems's *The Life of George Washington* (c. 1800), which praised honesty and hard work and condemned gambling, drinking, and laziness. To bolster patriotism and shared cultural ideals, reformers required the study of American history. As a New Hampshire schoolboy, Thomas Low recalled: "We were taught every day and in every way that ours was the freest, the happiest, and soon to be the greatest and most powerful country of the world."

UNDERSTAND POINTS OF VIEW Which form of child rearing—the rationalist or the authoritarian—was the most compatible with republican values and why?

Promoting Cultural Independence Like Caleb Bingham, writer Noah Webster wanted to raise the nation's intellectual prowess. Asserting that "America must be as independent in literature as she is in politics," he called on his fellow citizens to free themselves "from the dependence on foreign opinions and manners, which is fatal to the efforts of genius in this country." Webster's *Dissertation on the English Language* (1789) celebrated language as a marker of national identity by defining words according to American usage. With less success, it proposed that words be spelled as they were pronounced, that *labour* (British spelling), for example, be spelled *labur*. Still, Webster's famous "blue-back speller," a compact textbook first published in 1783, sold 60 million copies over the next half century and served the needs of Americans of all backgrounds. "None of us was 'lowed to see a book," an enslaved African American recalled, "but we gits hold of that Webster's old blue-back speller and we . . . studies [it]."

Despite Webster's efforts, a republican literary culture developed slowly. Ironically, the most successful writer in the new republic was Washington Irving, an elitist-minded Federalist. His whimsical essay and story collections — which included the tales of "Rip Van Winkle" and "The Legend of Sleepy Hollow" — sold well in America and won praise abroad. Frustrated by the immaturity of American cultural life, Irving lived for seventeen years in Europe, reveling in its aristocratic culture and intense intellectuality.

Apart from Irving, no American author was well known in Europe or, indeed, in the United States. "Literature is not yet a distinct profession with us," Thomas Jefferson told an English friend. "Now and then a strong mind arises, and at its intervals from business emits a flash of light. But the first object of young societies is bread and covering." Not until the 1830s and 1840s would American authors achieve a professional identity and make a significant contribution to Western literature (Chapter 11).

Aristocratic Republicanism and Slavery

Republicanism in the South differed significantly from that in the North. Enslaved Africans constituted one-third of the South's population; their bondage contradicted the new nation's professed ideology of freedom and equality. "How is it that we hear the loudest yelps for liberty among the drivers of Negroes?" British author Samuel Johnson had chided the American rebels in 1775, a point that some Patriots took to heart. "I wish most sincerely there was not a Slave in the province," Abigail Adams confessed to her husband, John. "It always appeared a most iniquitous Scheme to me — to fight ourselves for what we are daily robbing and plundering from those who have as good a right to freedom as we have."

The Revolution and Slavery, 1776–1800

In fact, the whites' struggle for independence had raised the prospect of freedom for blacks. As the Revolutionary War began, a black preacher in Georgia told his fellow slaves that King George III "came up with the Book [the Bible], and was about to alter the World, and set the Negroes free." Similar rumors, probably

prompted by Royal Governor Lord Dunmore's proclamation of 1775 (Chapter 5), circulated among slaves in Virginia and the Carolinas, prompting thousands of African Americans to flee behind British lines. Two neighbors of Virginia Patriot Richard Henry Lee lost "every slave they had in the world," as did many other planters. In 1781, when the British army evacuated Charleston, more than 6,000 former slaves went with them; another 4,000 left from Savannah. All told, 30,000 blacks may have fled their owners. Hundreds of freed black Loyalists settled permanently in Canada. More than 1,000 others, poorly treated in British Nova Scotia, sought a better life in Sierra Leone, West

Republican Families . . . and Servants
Around 1828, an unidentified artist painted this York, Pennsylvania, family with an African American servant. The artist gives equal emphasis to the wife and the husband, suggesting they enjoyed a companionate-style marriage. Reflecting the outlook of republican motherhood, the mother takes the leading role in educating the children. The family, probably of upper-middle-class status given their attire and furnishings, employs an African American woman as a domestic servant and nanny — common occupations among free black women of the time. The Saint Louis Art Museum, Missouri, USA/The Bridgeman Art Library.

Africa, a settlement founded by English antislavery organizations.

Manumission and Gradual Emancipation Yet thousands of African Americans supported the Patriot cause. Eager to raise their social status, free blacks in New England volunteered for military service in the First Rhode Island Company and the Massachusetts "Bucks." In Maryland, some slaves took up arms for the rebels in return for the promise of freedom. Enslaved Virginians struck informal bargains with their Patriot owners, trading loyalty in wartime for the hope of liberty. Following the Virginia legislature's passage of a **manumission** act in 1782, allowing owners to free their slaves, 10,000 slaves won their freedom.

Two other developments — one religious, the other intellectual — encouraged manumission. Beginning in the 1750s, Quaker evangelist John Woolman urged Friends to free their slaves, and many did so. Rapidly growing evangelical churches, especially Methodists and Baptists, initially advocated slave emancipation; in 1784, a conference of Virginia Methodists declared that slavery was "contrary to the Golden Law of God on which hang all the Law and Prophets."

Meanwhile, Enlightenment philosophy challenged the widespread belief among whites that Africans were inherently inferior to Europeans. According to John Locke, ideas were not innate but stemmed from a person's experiences in the world. Pointing out the obvious — "A state of slavery has a mighty tendency to shrink and contract the minds of men" — Enlightenment-influenced Americans suggested that the debased condition of blacks reflected their oppressive captivity. Quaker philanthropist Anthony Benezet declared that African Americans were "as capable of improvement as White People" and funded a Philadelphia school for their education.

Swept along by these religious and intellectual currents, legislators in northern states enacted gradual emancipation statutes (Map 8.2). These laws recognized white property rights by requiring slaves to buy their freedom by years — even decades — of additional

IDENTIFY CAUSES
Why did aristocratic republicanism develop in the South, and what were its defining features?

MAP 8.2

The Status of Slavery, 1800

In 1775, racial slavery was legal in all of the British colonies in North America. By the time the confederated states achieved their independence in 1783, the New England region was mostly free of slavery. By 1800, all of the states north of Maryland had provided for the gradual abolition of slavery, but the process of gradual emancipation dragged on until the 1830s. Some slave owners in the Chesapeake region manumitted a number of their slaves, leaving only the whites of the Lower South firmly committed to racial bondage.

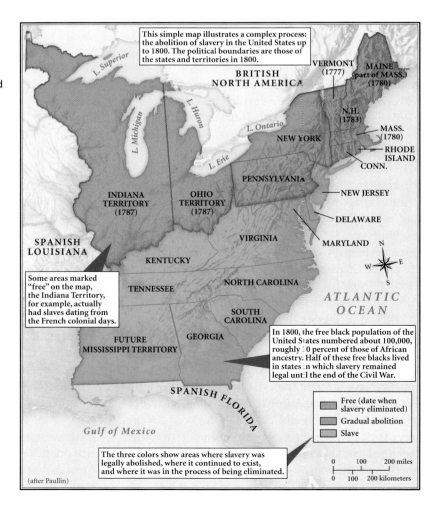

This simple map illustrates a complex process: the abolition of slavery in the United States up to 1800. The political boundaries are those of the states and territories in 1800.

Some areas marked "free" on the map, the Indiana Territory, for example, actually had slaves dating from the French colonial days.

In 1800, the free black population of the United States numbered about 100,000, roughly 10 percent of those of African ancestry. Half of these free blacks lived in states in which slavery remained legal until the end of the Civil War.

The three colors show areas where slavery was legally abolished, where it continued to exist, and where it was in the process of being eliminated.

Free (date when slavery eliminated)
Gradual abolition
Slave

(after Paullin)

0   100   200 miles
0   100   200 kilometers

labor. For example, the New York Emancipation Act of 1799 allowed slavery to continue until 1828 and freed slave children only at the age of twenty-five. Consequently, as late as 1810, almost 30,000 blacks in the northern states — nearly one-fourth of the African Americans living there — were still enslaved. Freed blacks faced severe prejudice from whites who feared job competition and racial melding. When Massachusetts judges abolished slavery through case law in 1784, the legislature reenacted an old statute that prohibited whites from marrying blacks, mulattos, or Indians. For African Americans in the North, freedom meant second-class citizenship.

Slavery Defended   The southern states faced the most glaring contradiction between liberty and property rights, because enslaved blacks represented a huge financial investment. Some Chesapeake tobacco planters, moved by evangelical religion or an oversupply of workers, manumitted their slaves or allowed them to buy their freedom by working as artisans or laborers. Such measures gradually brought freedom to one-third of the African Americans in Maryland.

Farther south, slavery remained ascendant. Fearing total emancipation, hundreds of slave owners petitioned the Virginia legislature to repeal the manumission act. Heeding this demand to protect "the most valuable and indispensible Article of our Property, our Slaves," legislators forbade further manumissions in 1792. Following the lead of Thomas Jefferson, who owned more than a hundred slaves, political leaders now argued that slavery was a "necessary evil" required to maintain white supremacy and the luxurious planter lifestyle. In North Carolina, legislators condemned private Quaker manumissions as "highly criminal and reprehensible." Moreover, the slave-hungry rice-growing states of South Carolina and Georgia reopened the Atlantic slave trade. Between 1790 and 1808, merchants in Charleston and Savannah imported about 115,000 Africans, selling thousands to French and American sugar planters in Louisiana.

Debate in the South over emancipation ended in 1800, when Virginia authorities thwarted an uprising planned by Gabriel Prosser, an enslaved artisan, and hanged him and thirty of his followers. "Liberty and equality have brought the evil upon us," a letter to the *Virginia Herald* proclaimed, denouncing such doctrines as "dangerous and extremely wicked." To preserve their privileged social position, southern leaders redefined republicanism. They restricted individual liberty and legal equality to whites, creating what historians call a **herrenvolk** ("master race") **republic**.

The North and South Grow Apart

European visitors to the United States agreed that North and South had distinct characters. A British observer labeled New England the home to religious "fanaticism" but added that "the lower orders of citizens" there had "a better education, [and were] more intelligent" than those he met in the South. "The state of poverty in which a great number of white people live in Virginia" surprised the Marquis de Chastellux. Other visitors to the South likewise commented on the rude manners, heavy drinking, and weak work ethic of its residents. White tenants and smallholding farmers seemed only to have a "passion for gaming at the billiard table, a cock-fight or cards," and rich planters squandered their wealth on extravagant lifestyles while their slaves endured bitter poverty.

Some southerners worried that human bondage had corrupted white society. "Where there are Negroes a White Man despises to work," one South Carolina merchant commented. Moreover, well-to-do planters, able to hire tutors for their own children, did little to provide other whites with elementary schooling. In 1800, elected officials in Essex County, Virginia, spent about 25 cents per person for local government, including schools, while their counterparts in Acton, Massachusetts, allocated about $1 per person. This difference in support for education mattered: by the 1820s, nearly all native-born men and women in New England could read and write, while more than one-third of white southerners could not.

Slavery and National Politics   As the northern states ended human bondage, the South's commitment to slavery became a political issue. At the Philadelphia convention in 1787, northern delegates had reluctantly accepted clauses allowing slave imports for twenty years and guaranteeing the return of fugitive slaves (Chapter 6). Seeking even more protection for their "peculiar institution," southerners in the new national legislature won approval of James Madison's resolution that "Congress have no authority to interfere in the emancipation of slaves, or in the treatment of them within any of the States."

Nonetheless, slavery remained a contested issue. The black slave revolt in Haiti brought 6,000 white and mulatto planters and their slaves to the United States in 1793, and stories of Haitian atrocities frightened American slave owners (Chapter 7). Meanwhile, northern politicians assailed the British impressment of American sailors as just "as oppressive and tyrannical as the slave trade" and demanded the end of both.

Aristocratic Republicanism in South Carolina

The money that paid for Drayton Hall came originally from raising cattle in South Carolina for sale in the West Indies. At his death in 1717, Thomas Drayton left an estate that included 1,300 cattle and 46 slaves (both Native American and African). His third son, John (1715–1779), used his inheritance to buy slaves and to create a rice-growing plantation along the Ashley River. The home he erected on the site, Drayton Hall (built 1738–1742), reflected the designs of Andrea Palladio, the Italian Renaissance architect who celebrated the concepts of classical Roman proportion and decoration in his widely read *The Four Books of Architecture* (1516). Photo courtesy of Drayton Hall.

When Congress outlawed the Atlantic slave trade in 1808, some northern representatives demanded an end to the trade in slaves between states. Southern leaders responded with a forceful defense of their labor system. "A large majority of people in the Southern states do not consider slavery as even an evil," declared one congressman. The South's political clout — its domination of the presidency and the Senate — ensured that the national government would protect slavery. American diplomats vigorously demanded compensation for slaves freed by British troops during the War of 1812, and Congress enacted legislation upholding slavery in the District of Columbia.

African Americans Speak Out Heartened by the end of the Atlantic slave trade, black abolitionists spoke out. In speeches and pamphlets, Henry Sipkins and Henry Johnson pointed out that slavery — "relentless tyranny," they called it — was a central legacy of America's colonial history. For inspiration, they looked to the Haitian Revolution; for collective support, they joined in secret societies, such as Prince Hall's African Lodge of Freemasons in Boston. Initially, black (and white) antislavery advocates hoped that slavery would die out naturally as the tobacco economy declined. However, a boom in cotton planting dramatically increased the demand for slaves, and Louisiana (1812), Mississippi (1817), and Alabama (1819) joined the Union with state constitutions permitting slavery.

As some Americans redefined slavery as a problem rather than a centuries-old social condition, a group of prominent citizens founded the **American Colonization Society** in 1817. According to Henry Clay — a society member, Speaker of the House of Representatives, and a slave owner — racial bondage hindered economic progress. It had placed his state of Kentucky "in the rear of our neighbors . . . in the state of agriculture, the progress of manufactures, the advance of improvement, and the general prosperity of society." Clay and other colonizationists argued that slaves had to be freed and then resettled, in Africa or elsewhere; emancipation without removal would lead to chaos — "a civil war that would end in the extermination or subjugation of the one race or the other." Given the cotton boom, few planters responded to the society's plea. It resettled only about 6,000 African Americans in Liberia, its colony on the west coast of Africa.

Most free blacks strongly opposed such colonization schemes because they saw themselves as Americans. As Bishop Richard Allen of the African Methodist Episcopal Church put it, "[T]his land which we have watered with our tears and our blood is now our mother country." Allen spoke from experience. Born into slavery in Philadelphia in 1760 and sold to a farmer in Delaware, Allen grew up in bondage. In 1777, Freeborn Garretson, an itinerant preacher, converted Allen to Methodism and convinced Allen's owner that on Judgment Day, slaveholders would be "weighted in the balance, and . . . found wanting." Allowed to buy his freedom, Allen enlisted in the Methodist cause, becoming a "licensed exhorter" and then a regular minister in

EXPLAIN CONSEQUENCES
Why did the colonization movement of the 1810s fail?

The Reverend Richard Allen and the African Methodist Episcopal Church
One of the best-known African Americans in the early republic, Richard Allen founded a separate congregation for Philadelphia's black Methodists, the Bethel Church. Working with other ministers in 1816, he created the first independent black religious domination in the United States—the African Methodist Episcopal (AME) Church—and became its first bishop. Library of Congress / Picture Research Consultants & Archives.

Philadelphia. In 1795, Allen formed a separate black congregation, the Bethel Church; in 1816, he became the first bishop of a new denomination: the African Methodist Episcopal Church. Two years later, 3,000 African Americans met in Allen's church to condemn colonization and to claim American citizenship. Sounding the principles of democratic republicanism, they vowed to defy racial prejudice and advance in American society using "those opportunities . . . which the Constitution and the laws allow to all."

The Missouri Crisis, 1819–1821

The abject failure of colonization set the stage for a major battle over slavery. In 1818, Congressman Nathaniel Macon of North Carolina warned that radical members of the "bible and peace societies" intended to place "the question of emancipation" on the national political agenda. When Missouri applied for admission to the Union in 1819, Congressman James Tallmadge of New York did so: he would support statehood for Missouri only if its constitution banned the entry of new slaves and provided for the emancipation of existing bonds-people. Missouri whites rejected Tallmadge's proposals, and the northern majority in the House of Representatives blocked the territory's admission.

White southerners were horrified. "It is believed by some, & feared by others," Alabama senator John

Walker reported from Washington, that Tallmadge's amendment was "merely the entering wedge and that it points already to a total emancipation of the blacks." Mississippi congressman Christopher Rankin accused his northern colleagues of brinksmanship: "You conduct us to an awful precipice, and hold us over it." Underlining their commitment to slavery, southerners used their power in the Senate—where they held half the seats—to withhold statehood from Maine, which was seeking to separate itself from Massachusetts.

Constitutional Issues In the ensuing debate, southerners advanced three constitutional arguments. First, they invoked the principle of "equal rights," arguing that Congress could not impose conditions on Missouri that it had not imposed on other territories. Second, they maintained that the Constitution guaranteed a state's sovereignty with respect to its internal affairs and domestic institutions, such as slavery and marriage. Finally, they insisted that Congress had no authority to infringe on the property rights of individual slaveholders. Beyond those arguments, southern leaders defended human bondage. Downplaying the proposition that slavery was a "necessary evil," they now justified slavery on religious grounds. "Christ himself gave a sanction to slavery," declared Senator William Smith of South Carolina. "If it be offensive and sinful to own slaves," a prominent Mississippi Methodist added, "I wish someone would just put his finger on the place in Holy Writ."

Controversy raged in Congress and the press for two years before Henry Clay devised a series of political agreements known collectively as the **Missouri Compromise**. Faced with unwavering southern opposition to Tallmadge's amendment, a group of northern congressmen deserted the antislavery coalition. They accepted a deal that allowed Maine to enter the Union as a free state in 1820 and Missouri to follow as a slave state in 1821. This bargain preserved a balance in the Senate between North and South and set a precedent for future admissions to the Union. For their part, southern senators accepted the prohibition of slavery in most of the Louisiana Purchase, all the lands north of latitude 36°30' except for the state of Missouri (Map 8.3).

As they had in the Philadelphia convention of 1787, white politicians preserved the Union by compromising over slavery. However, the delegates in Philadelphia had resolved their sectional differences in two months; it took Congress two years to work out the Missouri Compromise, which even then did not command universal support. "[B]eware," the *Richmond Enquirer* protested sharply as southern representatives agreed to exclude slavery from most of the Louisiana Purchase: "What is a territorial restriction to-day becomes a state restriction tomorrow." The fate of the western lands, enslaved blacks, and the Union itself were now intertwined, raising the specter of civil war and the end of the American republican experiment. As the aging Thomas Jefferson exclaimed during the Missouri crisis, "This momentous question, like a fire-bell in the night, awakened and filled me with terror."

PLACE EVENTS IN CONTEXT
What compromises over slavery did Congress make to settle the Missouri crisis?

Protestant Christianity as a Social Force

Throughout the colonial era, religion played a significant role in American life but not an overwhelming one. Then, beginning around 1790, religious revivals planted the values of Protestant Christianity deep in the national character and gave a spiritual dimension to American republicanism. These revivals especially changed the lives of blacks and of women. Thousands of African Americans became Baptists and Methodists and created a powerful institution: the black Christian Church. Evangelical Christianity also gave rise to new public roles for white women, especially in the North, and set in motion long-lasting movements for social reform.

MAP 8.3

The Missouri Compromise, 1820–1821

The Missouri Compromise resolved for a generation the issue of slavery in the lands of the Louisiana Purchase. The agreement prohibited slavery north of the Missouri Compromise line (36°30' north latitude), with the exception of the state of Missouri. To maintain an equal number of senators from free and slave states in the U.S. Congress, the compromise provided for the nearly simultaneous admission to the Union of Missouri and Maine.

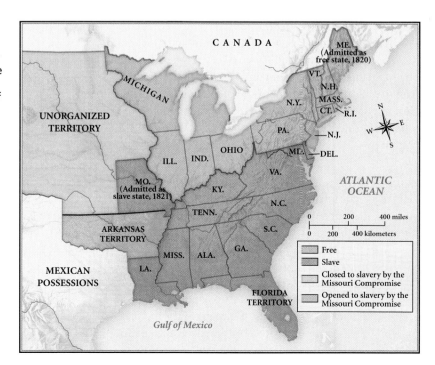

A Republican Religious Order

The republican revolution of 1776 forced American lawmakers to devise new relationships between church and state. Previously, only the Quaker- and Baptist-controlled governments of Pennsylvania and Rhode Island had rejected a legally established church that claimed everyone as a member and collected compulsory religious taxes. Then, a convergence of factors—Enlightenment principles, wartime needs, and Baptist ideology—eliminated most state support for religion and allowed voluntary church membership.

Religious Freedom   Events in Virginia revealed the dynamics of change. In 1776, James Madison and George Mason advanced Enlightenment ideas of religious toleration as they persuaded the state's constitutional convention to guarantee all Christians the "free exercise of religion." This measure, which ended the privileged legal status of the Anglican Church, won Presbyterian and Baptist support for the independence struggle. Baptists, who also opposed public support of religion, convinced lawmakers to reject a tax bill (supported by George Washington and Patrick Henry) that would have funded all Christian churches. Instead, in 1786, the Virginia legislature enacted Thomas Jefferson's bill for Establishing Religious Freedom, which made all churches equal in the eyes of the law and granted direct financial support to none.

Elsewhere, the old order of a single **established church** crumbled away. In New York and New Jersey, the sheer number of denominations—Episcopalian, Presbyterian, Dutch Reformed, Lutheran, and Quaker, among others—prevented lawmakers from agreeing on an established church or compulsory religious taxes. Congregationalism remained the official church in the New England states until the 1830s, but members of other denominations could now pay taxes to their own churches.

Church-State Relations   Few influential Americans wanted a complete separation of church and state because they believed that religious institutions promoted morality and governmental authority. "Pure religion and civil liberty are inseparable companions," a group of North Carolinians advised their minister. "It is your particular duty to enlighten mankind with the unerring principles of truth and justice, the main props of all civil government." Accepting this premise, most state governments indirectly supported churches by exempting their property and ministers from taxation.

Freedom of conscience also came with sharp cultural limits. In Virginia, Jefferson's Religious Freedom act prohibited religious requirements for holding public office, but other states discriminated against those who were not Protestant Christians. The North Carolina Constitution of 1776 disqualified from public office any citizen "who shall deny the being of God, or the Truth of the Protestant Religion, or the Divine Authority of the Old or New Testament." New Hampshire's constitution contained a similar provision until 1868.

Americans influenced by Enlightenment deism and by evangelical Protestantism condemned these religious restrictions. Jefferson, Franklin, and other American intellectuals maintained that God had given humans the power of reason so that they could determine moral truths for themselves. To protect society from "ecclesiastical tyranny," they demanded complete freedom of conscience. The "truth is great and will prevail if left to herself," Jefferson declared; "religion is a matter which lies solely between man and his God." Many evangelical Protestants likewise demanded religious liberty to protect their churches from an oppressive government. Isaac Backus, a New England minister, warned Baptists not to incorporate their churches or accept public funds because that might lead to state control. In Connecticut, a devout Congregationalist welcomed **voluntarism**, the funding of churches by their members; it allowed the laity to control the clergy, he said, while also supporting self-government and "the principles of republicanism."

Republican Church Institutions   Following independence, Americans embraced churches that preached spiritual equality and governed themselves democratically while ignoring those with hierarchical and authoritarian institutions. Preferring Luther's doctrine of the priesthood of all believers, few citizens accepted the authority claimed by Roman Catholic priests and bishops. Likewise, few Americans joined the Protestant Episcopal Church, the successor to the Church of England, because wealthy lay members dominated many congregations and it, too, had a hierarchy of bishops (Figure 8.1). The Presbyterian Church attracted more adherents, in part because its churches elected lay members to synods, the congresses that determined doctrine and practice.

Evangelical Methodist and Baptist churches were by far the most successful institutions in attracting new members, especially from the **"unchurched"**—the

UNDERSTAND POINTS OF VIEW
What were the main principles of the new republican religious regime?

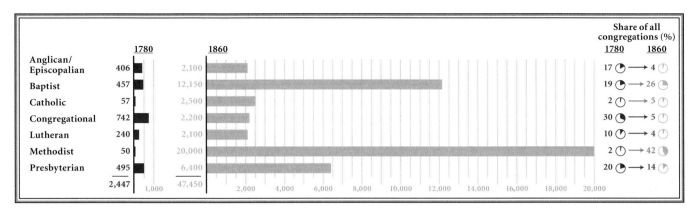

FIGURE 8.1
Number of Church Congregations by Denomination, 1780 and 1860
The growth of evangelical churches, Methodist and Baptist, transformed American Christianity during the first half of the nineteenth century. Also noteworthy was the surge in the number of Roman Catholic congregations, the result of Catholic immigration from Ireland and Germany after 1830.

great number of irreligious Americans. The Baptists boasted a thoroughly republican church organization, with self-governing congregations. Also, Baptists (and Methodists as well) developed an egalitarian religious culture marked by communal singing and emotional services. These denominations formed a dynamic new force in American religion.

The Second Great Awakening

As Americans adopted new religious principles, a decades-long series of religious revivals — the **Second Great Awakening** — made the United States a genuinely Christian society. Evangelical denominations began the revival in the 1790s, as they spread their message in seacoast cities and the backcountry of New England. A new sect of Universalists, who repudiated Calvinism and preached universal salvation, also gained tens of thousands of converts, especially in Massachusetts and northern New England. After 1800, enthusiastic camp meetings swept the frontier regions of South Carolina, Tennessee, Ohio, and Kentucky. The largest gathering, at Cane Ridge in Kentucky in 1801, lasted for nine electrifying days and nights and attracted almost 20,000 people (Map 8.4). With these revivals, Baptist and Methodist preachers reshaped the spiritual landscape throughout the South. Offering a powerful emotional message and the promise of religious fellowship, revivalists attracted both unchurched individuals and pious families searching for social ties as they migrated to new communities (America Compared, p. 272).

A New Religious Landscape The Second Great Awakening transformed the denominational makeup of American religion. The main colonial-period churches — the Congregationalists, Episcopalians, and Quakers — grew slowly through natural increase, while Methodist and Baptist churches expanded spectacularly by winning converts. In rural areas, their preachers followed a regular circuit, "riding a hardy pony or horse" with their "Bible, hymn-book, and Discipline" to visit existing congregations. They began new churches by searching out devout families, bringing them together for worship, and then appointing lay elders to lead the congregation and enforce moral discipline. Soon, Baptists and Methodists were the largest denominations.

To attract converts, evangelical ministers copied the "practical preaching" techniques of George Whitefield and other eighteenth-century revivalists (Chapter 4). They spoke from memory in plain language, raised their voice to make important points, and punctuated their words with theatrical gestures. "Preach without papers," advised one minister. "[S]eem earnest & serious; & you will be listened to with Patience, & Wonder."

In the South, evangelical religion was initially a disruptive force because many ministers spoke of spiritual equality and criticized slavery. Husbands and planters grew angry when their wives became more assertive and when blacks joined evangelical congregations. To retain white men in their churches, Methodist and Baptist preachers gradually adapted their religious

Frances Trollope

American Camp Meetings and English Church Hierarchies

Frances Trollope, a successful English author and the mother of novelist Anthony Trollope, lived for a time in Cincinnati. She won great acclaim as the author of a critical-minded study, *Domestic Manners of the Americans* (1832), a best-seller in Europe and the United States.

I found the opportunity I had long wished for, of attending a camp-meeting, . . . in a wild district on the confines of Indiana. . . .

One of the preachers began in a low nasal tone, and, like all other Methodist preachers, assured us of the enormous depravity of man as he comes from the hands of his Maker, and of his perfect sanctification after he had wrestled sufficiently with the Lord. . . . The admiration of the crowd was evinced by almost constant cries of "Amen! Amen!" "Jesus! Jesus!" "Glory! Glory!" and the like. . . . [T]he preacher told them that "this night was the time fixed upon for anxious sinners to wrestle with the Lord" . . . and that such as needed their help were to come forward. . . .

[A]bove a hundred persons, nearly all females, came forward, uttering howlings and groans, so terrible that I shall never cease to shudder when I recall them. They appeared to drag each other forward, and on the word being given, "let us pray," they all fell on their knees; but this posture was soon changed for others that permitted greater scope for the convulsive movements of their limbs. . . .

Many of these wretched creatures were beautiful young females. The preachers moved about among them, at once exciting and soothing their agonies. . . . I watched their tormentors breathing into their ears consolations that tinged the pale cheek with red. Had I been a man, I am sure I should have been guilty of some rash act of interference; nor do I believe that such a scene could have been acted in the presence of Englishmen, without instant punishment being inflicted . . . to check so turbulent and vicious a scene.

* *   **   **

The critics who have from time to time reproached me with undue severity in my strictures on the domestic manners of the Americans have said that a candid examination of matters at home would have shown me that what I reprobated might be found in England, as well as in the United States. In most cases I have felt that this might be rebutted . . . by showing that what I complained of in the Union as indicative of imperfect civilisation, [whereas] if existing at all with us, could only be met with among persons in a much lower station of life. . . .

But on the subject treated in the present chapter, justice compels me to avow that no such pleading can avail me. That such fearful profanation of the holy name of religion has rapidly increased among us since the year 1827, in which I quitted England for America, is most sadly certain. . . . [Yet, the bishops of the Church of England protect us from many excesses, while in America the lack of an established] national church, and of that guardian protection which its episcopal authority seems to promise against its desecration by the ever-varying innovations of sectarian licence, appeared to account for all the profanations I witnessed.

Source: Frances Trollope, *Domestic Manners of the Americans* (London: Whittaker, Treacher, 1832), 139, 142–144; the material following the asterisks comes from ibid., 5th ed. (London: R. Bentley, 1839), chapter 8.

QUESTIONS FOR ANALYSIS

1. According to Trollope, what accounts for the frequency of "profane" religious services in America and their relative absence in England?
2. How does Trollope use "social class" to analyze the differences between England and America?

message to justify the authority of yeomen patriarchs and slave-owning planters. Man was naturally at "the head of the woman," declared one Baptist minister, while a Methodist conference told Christian slaves to be "submissive, faithful, and obedient."

Black Christianity Other evangelists persuaded planters to spread Protestant Christianity among their African American slaves. During the eighteenth century, most blacks had maintained the religious practices of their African homelands, giving homage to

MAP 8.4

The Second Great Awakening, 1790–1860

The Second Great Awakening lasted for decades and invigorated churches in every part of the nation. The revivals in Kentucky and New York State were particularly influential. As thousands of farm families migrated to the West, they carried with them the religious excitement generated by the Cane Ridge revival in Kentucky in 1801. And, between 1825 and 1835, the area along the Erie Canal in New York witnessed such fervor that it came to be known as the Burned-over District.

In the 1820s an intense wave of revivals ignited religious fervor in communities along the Erie Canal, and this region became known as the "burned-over district."

As devout farmers moved west, they established new Protestant churches throughout the Upper South and Midwest.

Student revivals at Yale College and Andover Seminary around 1800 led to the expansion of Protestant missions in the West and also in Africa, India, and Hawaii. Societies supporting the missions combined into the American Home Missionary Society in 1826.

The Second Great Awakening started in the 1790s as Baptists, Methodists, and a new sect called Universalists proselytized in New England. After 1800 the Awakening continued in Kentucky in camp meetings of pioneer farmers, who carried evangelical religion back to their communities.

← Paths of settlement, 1790–1830
▲ Camp meeting, 1801
Kentucky revival
New York's "burned-over district"
← Paths of revival

African gods and spirits or practicing Islam. "At the time I first went to Carolina," remembered former slave Charles Ball, "there were a great many African slaves in the country. . . . Many of them believed there were several gods [and] I knew several . . . Mohamedans." Beginning in the mid-1780s, Baptist and Methodist preachers converted hundreds of African Americans along the James River in Virginia and throughout the Chesapeake and the Carolinas.

Subsequently, black Christians adapted Protestant teachings to their own needs. They generally ignored the doctrines of original sin and Calvinist predestination as well as biblical passages that prescribed unthinking obedience to authority. Some African American converts envisioned the Christian God as a warrior who had liberated the Jews. Their own "cause was similar to the Israelites," preacher Martin Prosser told his fellow slaves as he and his brother Gabriel plotted rebellion in Virginia in 1800. "I have read in my Bible where God says, if we worship him, . . . five of you shall conquer a hundred and a hundred of you a hundred thousand of our enemies." Confident of a special relationship with God, Christian slaves prepared

themselves spiritually for emancipation, the first step in their journey to the Promised Land.

Religion and Reform

Many whites also rejected the Calvinists' emphasis on human depravity and weakness; instead, they celebrated human reason and free will. In New England, educated Congregationalists discarded the mysterious concept of the Trinity — Father, Son, and Holy Spirit — and, taking the name *Unitarians*, worshipped a "united" God and promoted rational thought. "The ultimate reliance of a human being is, and must be, on his own mind," argued William Ellery Channing, a famous Unitarian minister. A children's catechism conveyed the denomination's optimistic message: "If I am good, God will love me, and make me happy."

Other New England Congregationalists softened Calvinist doctrines. Lyman Beecher, the preeminent Congregationalist clergyman, accepted the traditional Christian belief that people had a natural tendency to

COMPARE AND CONTRAST

How did evangelical and African American churches differ from other Protestant denominations?

Women in the Awakening

The Second Great Awakening was a pivotal moment in the history of American women. In this detail from *Religious Camp Meeting*, painted by J. Maze Burbank in 1839, male preachers inspire religious frenzy, mostly among young women. In fact, most women embraced evangelical Christianity in a calm and measured manner, becoming dedicated workers, teachers, and morality-minded mothers. When tens of thousands of these women also joined movements for temperance, abolition, and women's rights, they spurred a great wave of social reform. Old Dartmouth Historical Society/New Bedford Whaling Museum.

sin; but, rejecting predestination, he affirmed the capacity of all men and women to choose God. By embracing the doctrine of free will, Beecher—along with "Free Will" Baptists—testified to the growing belief that people could shape their destiny.

Reflecting this optimism, the Reverend Samuel Hopkins linked individual salvation to religious benevolence—the practice of disinterested virtue. As the Presbyterian minister John Rodgers explained, fortunate individuals who had received God's grace or bounty had a duty "to dole out charity to their poorer brothers and sisters." Heeding this message, pious

merchants in New York City founded the Humane Society and other charitable organizations. Devout women aided their ministers by holding prayer meetings and distributing charity. By the 1820s, so many Protestant men and women had embraced benevolent reform that conservative church leaders warned them not to neglect spiritual matters. Still, improving society was a key element of the new religious sensibility. The mark of a true church, declared the devout Christian social reformer Lydia Maria Child, is when members' "heads and hearts unite in working for the welfare of the human-race."

By the 1820s, many Protestant Christians had embraced that goal. Unlike the First Great Awakening, which split churches into warring factions, the Second Great Awakening fostered cooperation among denominations. Religious leaders founded five interdenominational societies: the American Education Society (1815), the Bible Society (1816), the Sunday School Union (1824), the Tract Society (1825), and the Home Missionary Society (1826). Based in eastern cities — New York, Boston, and Philadelphia — these societies dispatched hundreds of missionaries to the West and distributed thousands of religious pamphlets.

Increasingly, American Protestants saw themselves as a movement that could change the course of history. "I want to see our state evangelized," declared a churchgoer near the Erie Canal: "Suppose the great State of New York in all its physical, political, moral, commercial, and pecuniary resources should come over to the Lord's side. Why it would turn the scale and could convert the world. I shall have no rest until it is done."

Because the Second Great Awakening aroused such enthusiasm, religion became an important new force in political life. On July 4, 1827, the Reverend Ezra Stiles Ely called on the Philadelphia Presbyterians to begin a "Christian party in politics." Ely's sermon, "The Duty of Christian Freemen to Elect Christian Rulers," proclaimed a religious agenda for the American republic that Thomas Jefferson and John Adams would have found strange and troubling. The two founders had gone to their graves the previous year believing that America's mission was to spread political republicanism. In contrast, Ely urged the United States to become an evangelical Christian nation dedicated to religious conversion at home and abroad: "All our rulers ought in their official capacity to serve the Lord Jesus Christ." Evangelical Christians would issue similar calls during the Third (1880–1900) and Fourth (1970–present) Great Awakenings.

Women's New Religious Roles

The upsurge in religious enthusiasm allowed women to demonstrate their piety and even to found new sects. Mother Ann Lee organized the Shakers in Britain and in 1774 migrated to America, where she attracted numerous recruits; by the 1820s, Shaker communities dotted the American countryside from New Hampshire to Indiana. Jemima Wilkinson, a young Quaker woman in Rhode Island, found inspiration by reading George Whitefield's sermons. After experiencing a vision that she had died and been reincarnated as Christ, Wilkinson declared herself the "Publick Universal Friend," dressed in masculine attire, and preached a new gospel. Her teachings blended the Calvinist warning of "a lost and guilty, gossiping, dying World" with Quaker-inspired plain dress, pacifism, and abolitionism. Wilkinson's charisma initially won scores of converts, but her radical lifestyle and ambiguous gender aroused hostility, and her sect dwindled away.

A Growing Public Presence   Female-led sects had far less impact than thousands of women in mainstream churches. For example, women in New Hampshire churches managed more than fifty local

> **COMPARE AND CONTRAST**
> How was the Second Great Awakening similar to, and different from, the First Great Awakening of the 1740s (Chapter 4)?

Mrs. Juliann Jane Tillman, 1844

In 1837, Mrs. Tillman explained in a newspaper article that she "was strangely wrought upon" and "went to God" for help. Soon, "what seemed to be an angel made his sudden appearance, and in his hand was a roll . . . on which was written, 'Thee I have chosen to preach my gospel without delay.'" After much anguish and more supernatural visitations, Mrs. Tillman overcame strong personal doubts — and the equally strong opposition of male ministers and laity — and began to preach in the African Methodist Episcopal Church. Library of Congress.

"cent" societies to raise funds for the Society for Promoting Christian Knowledge, New York City women founded the Society for the Relief of Poor Widows, and young Quaker women in Philadelphia ran the Society for the Free Instruction of African Females.

Women took charge of religious and charitable enterprises because of their exclusion from other public roles and because of their numbers. After 1800, more than 70 percent of the members of New England Congregational churches were women. The predominance of women prompted Congregational ministers to end traditional gender-segregated prayer meetings, and evangelical Methodist and Baptist preachers actively promoted mixed-sex praying. "Our prayer meetings have been one of the greatest means of the conversion of souls," a minister in central New York reported in the 1820s, "especially those in which brothers and sisters have prayed together."

Far from leading to sexual promiscuity, as critics feared, mixing men and women in religious activities promoted greater self-discipline. Believing in female virtue, young women and the men who courted them postponed sexual intercourse until after marriage — previously a much rarer form of self-restraint. In Hingham, Massachusetts, and many other New England towns, more than 30 percent of the women who married between 1750 and 1800 bore a child within eight months of their wedding day; by the 1820s, the rate had dropped to 15 percent.

IDENTIFY CAUSES
Why did Protestant Christianity and Protestant women emerge as forces for social change?

As women claimed spiritual authority, men tried to curb their power. In both the North and the South, evangelical Baptist churches that had once advocated spiritual equality now prevented women from voting on church matters or offering public testimonies of faith. Testimonies by women, one layman declared, were "directly opposite to the apostolic command in [Corinthians] xiv, 34, 35, 'Let your women learn to keep silence in the churches.'" Another man claimed, "Women have a different calling. That they be chaste, keepers at home is the Apostle's direction." Such injunctions merely changed the focus of women's religious activism. Embracing the idea of republican motherhood, Christian women throughout the United States founded maternal associations to encourage proper child rearing. By the 1820s, *Mother's Magazine* and other newsletters, widely read in hundreds of small towns and villages, were giving women a sense of shared identity and purpose.

Religious activism also advanced female education, as churches sponsored academies where girls from the middling classes received intellectual and moral instruction. Emma Willard, the first American advocate of higher education for women, opened the Middlebury Female Seminary in Vermont in 1814 and later founded girls' academies in Waterford and Troy, New York. Beginning in the 1820s, women educated in these seminaries and academies displaced men as public-school teachers, in part because they accepted lower pay than men would. Female schoolteachers earned from $12 to $14 a month with room and board — less than a farm laborer. However, as schoolteachers, women had an acknowledged place in public life — a status that previously had been beyond their reach. Just as the ideology of democratic republicanism had expanded voting rights and the political influence of ordinary white men in the North, so the values of Christian republicanism had bolstered the public authority of middling women.

The Second Great Awakening made Americans a fervently Protestant people. Along with the values of republicanism and capitalism, this religious impulse formed the core of an emerging national identity.

SUMMARY

Like all important ideologies, republicanism has many facets. We have explored three of them in this chapter. We saw how state legislatures used government-granted charters and monopolies to support private businesses, with the goal of enhancing the commonwealth of society. This republican-inspired "commonwealth" policy of state mercantilism remained dominant until the 1840s, when classical liberal doctrines partially replaced it.

We also saw how republicanism influenced social and family values. The principle of legal equality encouraged social mobility among white men and prompted men and women to seek companionate marriages. Republicanism likewise encouraged parents to provide their children with equal inheritances and to allow them to choose their marriage partners. In the South, republican doctrines of liberty and equality coexisted uneasily with racial slavery and class divisions, and ultimately they benefitted only a minority of the white population.

Finally, we observed the complex interaction of republicanism and religion. Stirred by republican principles, many citizens joined democratic and egalitarian denominations, particularly Methodist and Baptist churches. Inspired by "benevolent" ideas and the enthusiastic preachers of the Second Great Awakening, many women devoted their energies to religious purposes and social reform organizations. The result of all these initiatives — in economic policy, social relations, and religious institutions — was the creation of a distinctive American republican culture.

C H A P T E R   R E V I E W

MAKE IT STICK   Go to **LearningCurve** to retain what you've read.

TERMS TO KNOW   Identify and explain the significance of each term below.

Key Concepts and Events

"**neomercantilist**" (p. 250)
Panic of 1819 (p. 251)
Commonwealth System (p. 256)
sentimentalism (p. 258)
companionate marriages (p. 258)
demographic transition (p. 259)
republican motherhood (p. 259)
manumission (p. 265)

herrenvolk **republic** (p. 266)
American Colonization Society (p. 267)
Missouri Compromise (p. 269)
established church (p. 270)
voluntarism (p. 270)
"**unchurched**" (p. 270)
Second Great Awakening (p. 271)

Key People

John Jacob Astor (p. 250)
Benjamin Rush (p. 259)
Henry Clay (p. 267)
Richard Allen (p. 267)
Lyman Beecher (p. 273)
Emma Willard (p. 276)

REVIEW QUESTIONS   Answer these questions to demonstrate your understanding of the chapter's main ideas.

1. How important were the regional differences in the social aspects of republicanism, given the national scope of other republican-inspired developments such as state mercantilism and religious revivalism?

2. Trace the relationship between America's republican culture and the surge of evangelism called the Second Great Awakening. In what ways are the goals of the two movements similar? How are they different?

3. In what ways did women's private and public lives change during the years between 1790 and 1820, and what were the motive forces behind those changes?

4. **THEMATIC UNDERSTANDING** Review the events listed under "Work, Exchange, and Technology," "Ideas, Beliefs, and Culture," and "Identity" on the thematic timeline on page 149. How did the emerging economic and social order of early-nineteenth-century America represent an advance upon, or a retreat from, the republican ideology articulated during the decades of the independence struggle?

MAKING CONNECTIONS

Recognize the larger developments and continuities within and across chapters by answering these questions.

1. ACROSS TIME AND PLACE The text argues that a distinct American identity had begun to emerge by 1820. How would you describe this identity, and how did it differ from the sense of identity in the American mainland colonies in 1750 (Chapter 4)? What forces might account for the changes?

2. VISUAL EVIDENCE The painting of "Republican Families . . . and Servants" (p. 264) addresses many of the themes of this chapter. What are those themes, and what position does the artist take in presenting them?

MORE TO EXPLORE

Start here to learn more about the events discussed in this chapter.

Nancy Cott, *Public Vows: A History of Marriage and the Nation* (2000). Analyzes the cultural and legal aspects of marriage.

Jan Lewis, *The Pursuit of Happiness* (1983). Discusses the paternalistic slave-owning gentry of the Upper South.

Jeffrey L. Pasley et al., eds., *Beyond the Founders* (2004). Shows how ordinary citizens promoted a democratic polity.

Randolph Ferguson Scully, *Religion and the Making of Nat Turner's Virginia* (2008). Links the rise of evangelical Christianity in the South to the slave revolt led by Nat Turner.

Bernard Weisberger, *They Gathered at the River* (1958). A classic study of the revivalists who led America's Great Awakenings.

Rosemarie Zagarri, *Revolutionary Backlash* (2007). Demonstrates the limited inclusion of women in politics.

TIMELINE

Ask yourself why this chapter begins and ends with these dates and then identify the links among related events.

1782	• St. Jean de Crèvecoeur publishes *Letters from an American Farmer* • Virginia manumission law (repealed 1792)
1783	• Noah Webster publishes his "blue-back speller"
1784	• Slavery ends in Massachusetts • Northern states begin gradual emancipation
1787	• Benjamin Rush writes *Thoughts on Female Education*
1790s	• States grant corporations charters and special privileges • Private companies build roads and canals to facilitate trade • Merchants expand rural outwork system • Chesapeake blacks adopt Protestant beliefs • Parents limit family size as farms shrink • Second Great Awakening expands church membership
1791	• Congress charters first Bank of the United States
1792	• Mary Wollstonecraft publishes *A Vindication of the Rights of Woman*
1795	• Massachusetts Mill Dam Act
1800	• Gabriel Prosser plots slave rebellion in Virginia
1800s	• Rise of sentimentalism and of companionate marriages • Women's religious activism • Founding of female academies • Religious benevolence sparks social reform
1801	• Cane Ridge revival in Kentucky
1816	• Congress charters Second Bank of the United States
1817	• Prominent whites create American Colonization Society
1819	• Plummeting agricultural prices set off financial panic
1819–1821	• Missouri Compromise
1820s	• States reform education • Women become schoolteachers

KEY TURNING POINTS: The timeline mentions books by four authors (Crèvecoeur, Webster, Rush, and Wollstonecraft) and two other entries relating to education. Based on the materials in Chapter 8, what might account for this blossoming of American literary and educational life?

Overlapping Revolutions

1800–1860

"The procession was nearly a mile long . . . [and] the democrats marched in good order to the glare of torches," a French visitor remarked in amazement during the U.S. presidential election of 1832. "These scenes belong to history . . . the wondrous epic of the coming of democracy." As Part 4 shows, Americans were making history in many ways between 1800 and 1860. Indeed, these decades constitute a distinct period precisely because the pace of historical change accelerated, especially between 1820 and 1860, as overlapping revolutions transformed American life. One revolution was political: the creation of a genuinely democratic polity. A second was economic: in 1800, the United States was predominantly an agricultural nation; by 1860, the northern states boasted one of the world's foremost industrial economies. Third, these years witnessed far-reaching cultural changes. Beginning about 1800, the Second Great Awakening swept across the nation, sparking great movements of social reform and intellectual ferment that revolutionized the culture of the North and Midwest. Finally, sectionalism increased in intensity, as the South extended its slave-labor system and the North developed a free-labor society. The overall result by 1860 was striking and alarming: now more politically democratic, economically prosperous, and deeply religious, the United States stood divided into antagonistic sections. Here, in brief, are the key aspects of those transformations.

Transforming the Economy, Society, and Culture

Impressive advances in industrial production, transportation, and commerce transformed the nation's economy. Factory owners used water- and steam-powered machines and a new system of labor discipline to boost the output of goods. Manufacturers produced 5 percent of the country's wealth in 1820 but nearly 25 percent by 1860. As enterprising merchants, entrepreneurs, and government officials developed a network of canals and markets, manufacturers sold these products throughout an expanding nation. The new economy created a class-based, urban society in the North and Midwest. A wealthy elite of merchants, manufacturers, bankers, and entrepreneurs rose to the top of the society. To preserve social stability, this elite embraced benevolent reform, preaching the gospel of temperance, Sunday observance, and universal elementary education. Simultaneously, an expanding urban middle class created a distinct material and religious culture and promoted its ideology of individual responsibility and social mobility. Some middle-class Americans advocated radical causes: joining utopian socialist communities and demanding equal rights for women and the immediate end of racial slavery. A mass of propertyless wage-earning workers, including poor immigrants from Germany and Ireland, devised a vibrant popular culture of their own. This complex story of economic change and social fragmentation is the focus of Chapter 9 and Chapter 11.

Creating a Democratic Polity

Beginning in the 1810s, the rapid expansion of white male suffrage and political parties created a competitive and responsive democratic polity. Pressure came from ordinary citizens who organized political movements, such as the Anti-Masonic, Working Men's, and Liberty parties, to advance their interests and beliefs. Farmers, workers, and entrepreneurs persuaded state legislatures to improve transportation, shorten workdays, and award valuable charters to banks and business corporations. Catholic immigrants from Ireland and Germany entered the political arena to protect their cultural habits and religious institutions from restrictive legislation advocated by Protestant nativists and reformers. Then, during the 1830s, Andrew Jackson and the Democratic Party led a political and constitutional revolution that cut federal and state government aid to financiers, merchants, and corporations. To contend with the Democrats, the Whig Party devised a competing program that stressed state-sponsored economic development, moral reform, and individual social mobility. This party competition engaged the energies of the electorate, helped to unify a fragmented social order, and, during the 1830s and 1840s, lessened sectional tensions. Chapters 10 and 12 analyze this story of political change and party politics.

Growing Sectional Divisions

However, the party system could not overcome the increasingly sharp sectional divisions. As the North developed into an urban industrial society based on free labor, the South increasingly defended white supremacy and slavery as a "positive good" and expanded its plantation-based agricultural society. Beginning in the 1820s, the two sections had differed over economic issues and Indian policy. Georgia and other southeastern states demanded and won—over the objections of northeastern reformers—the Indian Removal Act of 1830, which resettled native peoples west of the Mississippi River. Concurrently, between 1816 and 1832, northern manufacturers, workers, and farmers won high protective tariffs, which southern planters bitterly opposed. Eventually, party politicians negotiated a compromise, with the North accepting tariff reductions. The sections had clashed again over the expansion of slavery, into Missouri and the Louisiana Purchase in the 1820s and into Texas and the Southwest in the 1840s, and political leaders again devised compromises. However, by the 1850s, slavery—and the social system it symbolized—increasingly divided the nation. Moreover, because the democratic political revolution had engaged the passions of millions of ordinary Americans, the political system had become more volatile and resistant to compromise. Chapters 10 and 12 explain how national expansion led to increasing sectional struggle.

Overlapping Revolutions 1800–1860

Thematic Understanding

This timeline arranges some of the important events of this period into themes. Look at the entries under "Identity": what identities emerged in this period, and which issues shaped these developments? In the "Work, Exchange, and Technology" theme, how did industrial output and the transportation system change over time?   **>**

	WORK, EXCHANGE, & TECHNOLOGY	PEOPLING	POLITICS & POWER	IDEAS, BELIEFS, & CULTURE	IDENTITY
1810	• Congress approves funds for a National Road (1806) • First American textile factory opens in Waltham, Massachusetts (1814)	• Congress outlaws Atlantic slave trade (1776–1809) • Andrew Jackson forces Creeks to relinquish millions of acres during War of 1812	• Struggle to expand the suffrage begins with Maryland reformers • Martin Van Buren creates first statewide political machine (1817–1821) • Missouri crisis (1819–1821) over slavery	• In rural areas, people of different ranks share a common culture • Upper-class women sponsor charitable organizations	• American Colonization Society (1817) • Benjamin Franklin's *Autobiography* (1818) spreads notion of the self-made man
1820	• New England shoe industry expands • Erie Canal completed (1825) • Henry Clay's "American System" of government-assisted development • Market economy expands nationwide	• Slave trade moves African Americans west • Rural women take factory work, alter gender roles	• Rise of Andrew Jackson and Democratic Party • Anti-Masonic Party and Working Men's Party rise and decline	• Benevolent reform movements • Emerson champions transcendentalism • Charles Finney and others advance revivalist religion • Industrialism fragments society into more distinct classes and cultures	• David Walker's *Appeal . . . to the Colored Citizens* (1829) attacks slavery • Rise of southern sectionalism
1830	• U.S. textiles compete with British goods • Canal systems expand trade in eastern U.S. • Financial panic of 1837 begins six-year depression • Boom in cotton output • Increase in waged work sparks conflict between labor and capital	• Indian Removal Act (1830) forces native peoples west • Cherokees' "Trail of Tears" (1838)	• Tariff battles (1828, 1832) and nullification • Whig Party forms (1834) • Jackson destroys Second Bank, expands executive power	• Temperance crusade expands • Joseph Smith and Mormonism • Middle-class culture spreads • Slavery defended as a "positive good" • Urban popular culture (sex trade and minstrelsy)	• W. L. Garrison's American Anti-Slavery Society (1833) • Female Moral Reform Society (1834) defines gender identity • Texas gains independence (1836)
1840	• American machine tool industry expands • Walker Tariff moves U.S. toward "free trade" system and principles of "classical liberalism"	• Working-class districts emerge in cities • German and Irish immigrants spark nativist movement • Mormons resettle in Utah	• Log cabin campaign (1840) • Second Party System flourishes • Lawyers emerge as political leaders	• Fourierist and other communal settlements • Seneca Falls Convention (1848) calls for women's rights	• Antislavery Liberty Party (1840) • New African American culture develops in Mississippi Valley
1850	• Severe recession cuts industrial jobs (1858) • Railroads connect Midwest and eastern ports • Cotton production and prices rise, as does the cost of enslaved laborers	• Immigrants replace native-born women in textile mills • White farm families settle trans-Mississippi west	• Reform becomes political: states enact Maine-style temperance laws (1851 on) • "Mormon War" over polygamy (1858)	• American Renaissance: Melville, Whitman, and Hawthorne • Harriet Beecher Stowe's *Uncle Tom's Cabin* (1852)	• Black and white preachers promote Christianity among slaves • Free blacks in North become politically active

9

CHAPTER

Transforming the Economy
1800–1860

I n 1804, life turned grim for eleven-year-old Chauncey Jerome. His father died suddenly, and Jerome became an indentured servant on a Connecticut farm. Quickly learning that few farmers "would treat a poor boy like a human being," Jerome bought out his indenture by making dials for clocks and then found a job with clockmaker Eli Terry. A manufacturing wizard, Terry used water power to drive precision saws and woodworking lathes. Soon his shop, and dozens of outworkers, were turning out thousands of tall clocks with wooden works. Then, in 1816, Terry patented an enormously popular desk clock with brass parts, an innovation that turned Waterbury, Connecticut, into the clockmaking center of the United States.

In 1822, Chauncey Jerome set up his own clock factory. By organizing work more efficiently and using new machines that stamped out interchangeable metal parts, he drove down the price of a simple clock from $20 to $5 and then to less than $2. By the 1840s, Jerome was selling his clocks in England, the hub of the Industrial Revolution; a decade later, his workers were turning out 400,000 clocks a year, clear testimony to American industrial enterprise. By 1860, the United States was not only the world's leading exporter of cotton and wheat but also the third-ranked manufacturing nation behind Britain and France.

"Business is the very soul of an American: the fountain of all human felicity," author Francis Grund observed shortly after arriving from Europe. "It is as if all America were but one gigantic workshop, over the entrance of which there is the blazing inscription, 'No admission here, except on business.'" Stimulated by the entrepreneurial culture of early-nineteenth-century America, thousands of artisan-inventors like Chauncey Jerome propelled the country into the Industrial Revolution, a new system of production based on water and steam power and machine technology. Simultaneously, thousands of traders fashioned a second great economic advance, a Market Revolution that exploited advances in transportation and business organization to expand trade in farm products and manufactured goods.

Not all Americans embraced the new business-dominated society, and many failed to share in the new prosperity. Moreover, the increase in manufacturing, commerce, and finance created class divisions that challenged the founders' vision of an agricultural republic with few distinctions of wealth. As the philosopher Ralph Waldo Emerson warned in 1839: "The invasion of Nature by Trade with its Money, its Credit, its Steam, [and] its Railroad threatens to . . . establish a new, universal Monarchy."

IDENTIFY THE BIG IDEA

What were the causes and consequences of the Industrial and Market revolutions, and how did they change the way ordinary Americans lived?

Women Weavers from Maine, c. 1860 Nineteenth-century workers were proud of their skills and, like these textiles operatives from Winthrop, Maine, often posed for photographs with the tools of their craft. This small tintype, 3 by 4 inches and printed on thin metal, dates from the mid-nineteenth century. Beginning in the 1830s, cotton textile entrepreneurs built factories in rural Maine, attracted by its abundant water power and the inexpensive labor of young farm women. The women wear striped dresses of cotton fabric, which they probably helped to manufacture. American Textile History Museum.

The American Industrial Revolution

The **Industrial Revolution** came to the United States between 1790 and 1860, as merchants and manufacturers reorganized work routines, built factories, and exploited a wide range of natural resources. As output increased, goods that once had been luxury items became part of everyday life (Figure 9.1). The rapid construction of turnpikes, canals, and railroads by state governments and private entrepreneurs, working together in the Commonwealth System (Chapter 8), distributed manufactures throughout the nation.

The Division of Labor and the Factory

Increased output stemmed initially from changes in the organization of work that turned independent artisans into wage laborers. Traditionally, New England shoemakers had turned leather hides into finished shoes and boots in small wooden shacks called "ten-footers," where they worked at their own pace. During the 1820s and 1830s, merchants in Lynn, Massachusetts, destroyed the businesses of these artisans by introducing an outwork system and a **division of labor**. The merchants

IDENTIFY CAUSES

How did the division of labor increase output, and what was its impact on workers?

hired semiskilled journeymen and set them up in large shops cutting leather into soles and uppers. They sent out the upper sections to rural Massachusetts towns, where women binders sewed in fabric linings. The manufacturers then had other journeymen attach the uppers to the soles and return the shoes to the central shop for inspection, packing, and sale. This more efficient system increased output and cut the price of shoes and boots, even as it turned employers into powerful "shoe bosses" and eroded workers' wages and independence.

For products not suited to the outwork system, manufacturers created the modern factory, which concentrated production under one roof. For example, in the 1830s, Cincinnati merchants built large slaughterhouses that processed thousands of hogs every month. The technology remained simple, but a division of labor increased output. As a system of overhead rails moved the hog carcasses along a "disassembly" line, one worker split the animals, another removed the organs, and others trimmed the carcasses into pieces. Packers then stuffed the pork into barrels and salted it to prevent spoilage. Reported landscape architect and journalist Frederick Law Olmsted:

> We entered an immense low-ceiling room and followed a vista of dead swine, upon their backs, their paws stretching mutely toward heaven. Walking down to the vanishing point, we found there a sort of human chopping-machine where the hogs were

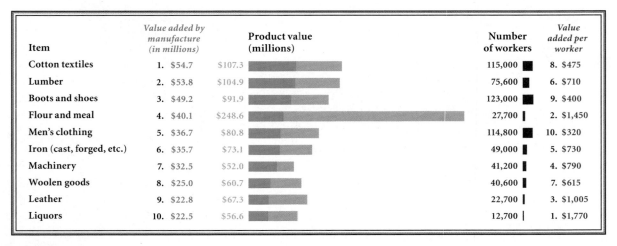

Item	Value added by manufacture (in millions)	Product value (millions)		Number of workers	Value added per worker
Cotton textiles	1. $54.7	$107.3		115,000	8. $475
Lumber	2. $53.8	$104.9		75,600	6. $710
Boots and shoes	3. $49.2	$91.9		123,000	9. $400
Flour and meal	4. $40.1	$248.6		27,700	2. $1,450
Men's clothing	5. $36.7	$80.8		114,800	10. $320
Iron (cast, forged, etc.)	6. $35.7	$73.1		49,000	5. $730
Machinery	7. $32.5	$52.0		41,200	4. $790
Woolen goods	8. $25.0	$60.7		40,600	7. $615
Leather	9. $22.8	$67.3		22,700	3. $1,005
Liquors	10. $22.5	$56.6		12,700	1. $1,770

FIGURE 9.1

Leading Branches of Manufacture, 1860

This chart shows clearly that in 1860, three industries—boots and shoes, cotton textiles, and men's clothing—each employed more than 100,000 workers. However, the workers in three other industries had the highest productivity, with each worker adding more than $1,000 in value to the finished goods. What were these industries? Why were their workers more productive? Adapted from Douglass C. North, *Growth and Welfare in the American Past*, Second Edition. Copyright © 1974. Reprinted with permission of the author.

converted into commercial pork. . . . Plump falls the hog upon the table, chop, chop; chop, chop; chop, chop, fall the cleavers. . . . We took out our watches and counted thirty-five seconds, from the moment when one hog touched the table until the next occupied its place.

The Cincinnati system was so efficient — processing sixty hogs an hour — that by the 1840s the city was known as "Porkopolis." By 1850, factories were slaughtering 334,000 hogs a year, and 400,000 by 1860.

Other factories boasted impressive new technology. In 1782, Oliver Evans, a prolific Delaware inventor, built a highly automated flour mill driven by water power. His machinery lifted the wheat to the top of the mill, cleaned the grain as it fell into hoppers, ground it into flour, and then cooled the flour as it was funneled into barrels. Evans's factory, remarked one observer, "was as full of machinery as the case of a watch." It needed only six men to mill 100,000 bushels of wheat a year — perhaps ten times as much as they could grind in a traditional mill.

By the 1830s, a new "**mineral-based economy**" of coal and metal began to emerge. Manufacturers increasingly ran their machinery with coal-burning stationary steam engines rather than with water power. And they now fabricated metal products — iron, brass, copper, and tinplate (tin-coated rolled iron) — as well as pork, leather, wool, cotton, and other agricultural goods. In Chicago, Cyrus McCormick used steam-driven machines to make parts for farm reapers, which workers assembled on a conveyor belt. In Hartford, Connecticut, Samuel Colt built an assembly line to produce his invention, the six-shooter revolver. Other New England artisans designed machines that fabricated tinplate into pails, pans, pots, and dozens of other inexpensive and useful household items. These advances in technology and factory organization alarmed British observers: "The contriving and making of machinery has become so common in this country . . . [that] it is to be feared that American manufacturers will become exporters not only to foreign countries, but even to England."

The Textile Industry and British Competition

To protect the British textile industry from American competition, the British government prohibited the export of textile machinery and the emigration of **mechanics** (skilled craftsmen who invented and improved tools for industry). Lured by the prospect of higher wages, though, thousands of British mechanics

disguised themselves as laborers and sailed to the United States. By 1812, at least three hundred British mechanics worked in the Philadelphia area alone.

Samuel Slater, the most important émigré mechanic, came to America in 1789 after working for Richard Arkwright, who had invented the most advanced British machinery for spinning cotton. A year later, Slater reproduced Arkwright's innovations in merchant Moses Brown's cotton mill in Providence, Rhode Island.

In competing with British mills, American manufacturers had the advantage of an abundance of natural resources. The nation's farmers produced huge amounts of cotton and wool, and the fast-flowing rivers that cascaded down from the Appalachian foothills to the Atlantic coastal plain provided a cheap source of energy. From Massachusetts to Delaware, these waterways were soon lined with industrial villages and textile mills as large as 150 feet long, 40 feet wide, and four stories high (Map 9.1).

American and British Advantages   Still, British producers easily undersold their American competitors. Thanks to cheap transatlantic shipping and low interest rates in Britain, they could import raw cotton from the United States, manufacture it into cloth, and sell it in America at a bargain price. (As they did in India; see America Compared p. 289.) The most important British advantage was cheap labor: Britain had a larger population — about 12.6 million in 1810 compared to 7.3 million Americans — and thousands of landless laborers prepared to accept low-paying factory jobs. To offset these advantages, American entrepreneurs relied on help from the federal government: in 1816, 1824, and 1828, Congress passed tariff bills that taxed imported cotton and woolen cloth. However, in the 1830s, Congress reduced tariffs because southern planters, western farmers, and urban consumers demanded inexpensive imports.

Better Machines, Cheaper Workers   American producers used two other strategies to compete with their British rivals. First, they improved on British technology. In 1811, Francis Cabot Lowell, a wealthy Boston merchant, toured British textile mills, secretly making detailed drawings of their power machinery. Paul Moody, an experienced American mechanic, then copied the machines and improved their design. In 1814, Lowell joined with merchants Nathan Appleton and Patrick

COMPARE AND CONTRAST
What were the advantages and strategies of British and American textile manufacturers?

MAP 9.1

New England's Dominance in Cotton Spinning, 1840

Although the South grew the nation's cotton, it did not process it. Prior to the Civil War, entrepreneurs in Massachusetts and Rhode Island built most of the factories that spun and wove raw cotton into cloth. Their factories made use of the abundant water power available in New England and the region's surplus labor force. Initially, factory managers hired young farm women to work the machines; later, they relied on immigrants from Ireland and the French-speaking Canadian province of Quebec.

Number of Spindles in Operation, 1840
- Under 5,000
- 5,000–25,000
- 25,000–100,000
- 100,000–250,000
- 250,000–500,000

Tracy Jackson to form the Boston Manufacturing Company. Having raised the staggering sum of $400,000, they built a textile plant in Waltham, Massachusetts — the first American factory to perform all clothmaking operations under one roof. Thanks to Moody's improvements, Waltham's power looms operated at higher speeds than British looms and needed fewer workers.

The second strategy was to tap a cheaper source of labor. In the 1820s, the Boston Manufacturing Company recruited thousands of young women from farm families, providing them with rooms in boardinghouses and with evening lectures and other cultural activities. To reassure parents about their daughters' moral welfare, the mill owners enforced strict curfews, prohibited alcoholic beverages, and required regular church attendance. At Lowell (1822), Chicopee (1823), and other sites in Massachusetts and New Hampshire, the company built new factories that used this labor system, known as the **Waltham-Lowell System**.

By the early 1830s, more than 40,000 New England women were working in textile mills. As an observer noted, the wages were "more than could be obtained by the hitherto ordinary occupation of housework," the living conditions were better than those in crowded farmhouses, and the women had greater independence.

Lucy Larcom became a Lowell textile operative at age eleven to avoid being "a trouble or burden or expense" to her widowed mother. Other women operatives used wages to pay off their father's farm mortgages, send brothers to school, or accumulate a marriage dowry for themselves.

 To see a longer excerpt of the Lucy Larcom document, along with other primary sources from this period, see *Sources for America's History*.

Some operatives just had a good time. Susan Brown, who worked as a Lowell weaver for eight months, spent half her earnings on food and lodging and the rest on plays, concerts, lectures, and a two-day excursion to Boston. Like most textile workers, Brown soon tired of the rigors of factory work and the never-ceasing clatter of the machinery, which ran twelve hours a day, six days a week. After she quit, she lived at home for a time and then moved to another mill. Whatever the hardships, waged work gave young women a sense of freedom. "Don't I feel independent!" a woman mill worker wrote to her sister. "The thought that I am living on no one is a happy one indeed to me." The owners of the Boston Manufacturing Company were even happier. By combining tariff protection with improved technology

The Fate of the American and Indian Textile Industries

In 1776, the United States declared its independence from the British Empire. About the same time, Britain began to create in India what historians call the Second British Empire. By 1860, Britain had become the world's leading industrial economy and dominated the princely states and peoples of the Indian subcontinent. The following tables trace the impact of political decisions on the American and Indian textile industries. As the legislature of an independent republic, the U.S. Congress could impose tariffs (taxes on imported goods) on British textiles; as colonies, Indian governments could not do so.

TABLE 9.1

Cotton Textile Production and Consumption in India

Year	Population (millions)	Imports from Britain (mill. yds.)	Production for Domestic Consumption (mill. yds.)	Exports to Britain (pieces, ave./year)
1751	190	0	1,598	632,000 (1750–1754)
1801	207	0	1,741	1,355,304 (1800–1804)
1821	205	20	1,704	542,117 (1820–1824)
1841	212	141	1,642	192,965 (1830–1834)
1861	242	514	1,538	Data not available

TABLE 9.2

Textile Production in the United States

Year	Number of Cotton Mill Workers	Number of Spindles (ave./decade)[1]	Imports from Britain (mill. yds.)	Average U.S. Tariff (as % of item's value)
1810		215,000		
1815			70.81	25.0%
1820	12,000	936,000		
1827			52.86	53.8%
1830	55,000	1,038,000		
1835			74.96	40.4%
1840	72,000	1,243,000		
1850	92,000	1,709,000	104.23	27.1%
1859			225.15	19.6%
1860	122,000			

[1]Entries in Spindle column are the average per year across the decade; i.e., there were perhaps 100,000 spindles in 1810 and 350,000 in 1820, yielding an average of 215,000 between 1810 and 1819.

QUESTIONS FOR ANALYSIS

1. Compare changes in Indian production ("Production for Domestic Consumption" and "Exports to Britain") with changes in American production ("Number of Cotton Mill Workers" and "Number of Spindles") between 1800 and 1861. Which country is "industrializing," and which is "deindustrializing"?

2. How do American tariffs change over time? (Chapter 10 will explain the reasons for these changes.) What is the impact of American tariff rates on the import of British textiles?

3. What insights does this material provide into the political and economic aspects of American industrialization?

and cheap female labor, they could undersell their British rivals. Their textiles were also cheaper than those made in New York and Pennsylvania, where farmworkers were paid more than in New England and textile wages consequently were higher. Manufacturers in those states garnered profits by using advanced technology to produce higher-quality cloth. Even Thomas Jefferson, the great champion of yeoman farming, was impressed. "Our manufacturers are now very nearly on a footing with those of England," he boasted in 1825.

American Mechanics and Technological Innovation

By the 1820s, American-born artisans had replaced British immigrants at the cutting edge of technological innovation. Though few mechanics had a formal education, they commanded respect as "men professing an ingenious art." In the Philadelphia region, the remarkable Sellars family produced the most important inventors. Samuel Sellars Jr. invented a machine for twisting worsted woolen yarn to give it an especially smooth surface. His son John improved the efficiency of the waterwheels powering the family's sawmills and built a machine to weave wire sieves. John's sons and grandsons ran machine shops that turned out riveted leather fire hoses, papermaking equipment, and eventually locomotives. In 1824, the Sellars and other mechanics founded the Franklin Institute in Philadelphia. Named after Benjamin Franklin, whom the mechanics admired for his work ethic and scientific accomplishments, the institute published a journal; provided high-school-level instruction in chemistry, mathematics, and mechanical design; and organized exhibits of new products. Craftsmen in Ohio and other states established similar institutes to disseminate technical knowledge and encourage innovation. Between 1820 and 1860, the number of patents issued by the U.S. Patent Office rose from two hundred to four thousand a year.

American craftsmen pioneered the development of **machine tools** — machines that made parts for other machines. A key innovator was Eli Whitney (1765–1825), the son of a middling New England farm family. At the age of fourteen, Whitney began fashioning nails and knife blades; later, he made women's hatpins.

Aspiring to wealth and status, Whitney won admission to Yale College and subsequently worked as a tutor on a Georgia cotton plantation. Using his expertise in making hatpins, he built a simple machine in 1793 that separated

Eli Whitney

Eli Whitney posed for this portrait in the 1820s, when he had achieved prosperity and social standing as the inventor of the cotton gin and other machines. Whitney's success prompted the artist—his young New Haven, Connecticut, neighbor Samuel F. B. Morse—to turn his creative energies from painting to industrial technology. By the 1840s, Morse had devised the hardware for the first successful commercial telegraph and the software—the "Morse Code"—that it transmitted. Yale University Art Gallery/Art Resource, NY.

the seeds in a cotton boll from the delicate fibers, work previously done slowly by hand. Although Whitney patented his cotton engine (or "gin," as it became known), other manufacturers improved on his design and captured the market.

Still seeking his fortune, Whitney decided in 1798 to manufacture military weapons. He eventually designed and built machine tools that could rapidly produce interchangeable musket parts, bringing him the wealth and fame he had long craved. After Whitney's death in 1825, his partner John H. Hall built an array of metalworking machine tools, such as turret lathes, milling machines, and precision grinders.

Technological innovation now swept through American manufacturing. Mechanics in the textile industry invented lathes, planers, and boring machines that turned out standardized parts for new spinning jennies and weaving looms. Despite being mass-produced, these jennies and looms were precisely made and operated at higher speeds than British equipment.

TRACE CHANGE OVER TIME
What new types of products came out of American factories by the 1840s and 1850s?

The leading inventor was Richard Garsed: he nearly doubled the speed of the power looms in his father's Delaware factory and patented a cam-and-harness device that allowed damask and other elaborately designed fabrics to be machine-woven. Meanwhile, the mechanics employed by Samuel W. Collins built a machine for pressing and hammering hot metal into dies (cutting forms). Using this machine, a worker could make three hundred ax heads a day — compared to twelve using traditional methods. In Richmond, Virginia, Welsh- and American-born mechanics at the Tredegar Iron Works produced great quantities of low-cost parts for complicated manufacturing equipment. As a group of British observers noted admiringly, many American products were made "with machinery applied to almost every process . . . all reduced to an almost perfect system of manufacture."

As mass production spread, the American Industrial Revolution came of age. Reasonably priced products such as Remington rifles, Singer sewing machines, and Yale locks became household names in the United States and abroad. After winning praise at the Crystal Palace Exhibition in London in 1851 — the first major international display of industrial goods — Remington, Singer, and other American firms became multinational businesses, building factories in Great Britain and selling goods throughout Europe. By 1877, the Singer Manufacturing Company controlled 75 percent of the world market for sewing machines.

Wageworkers and the Labor Movement

As the Industrial Revolution gathered momentum, it changed the nature of workers' lives. Following the American Revolution, many craft workers espoused **artisan republicanism**, an ideology of production based on liberty and equality. They saw themselves as small-scale producers, equal to one another and free to work for themselves. The poet Walt Whitman summed up their outlook: "Men must be masters, under themselves."

Free Workers Form Unions However, as the outwork and factory systems spread, more and more workers became wage earners who labored under the control of an employer. Unlike young women, who embraced factory work because it freed them from parental control and domestic service, men bridled at their status as supervised wageworkers. To assert their independent status, male wageworkers rejected the traditional terms of *master* and *servant* and used the Dutch word *boss* to refer to their employer. Likewise, lowly apprentices refused to allow masters to control their private (nonwork) lives and joined their mates in building a robust plebeian culture. Still, as hired hands, they received meager wages and had little job security. The artisan-republican ideal of "self-ownership" confronted the harsh reality of waged work in an industrializing capitalist society. Labor had become a commodity, to be bought and sold.

> ### UNDERSTAND POINTS OF VIEW
> How did the capitalist-run industrial economy conflict with artisan republicanism, and how did workers respond?

Some wage earners worked in carpentry, stonecutting, masonry, and cabinetmaking — traditional crafts that required specialized skills. Their strong sense of identity, or trade consciousness, enabled these workers to form **unions** and bargain with their master-artisan employers. They resented low wages and long hours, which restricted their family life and educational opportunities. In Boston, six hundred carpenters went on strike in 1825. That protest failed, but in 1840, craft

Diagram of McCormick's Reaper

The economic revolution was the result, in part, of increased output created by power-driven machinery used in factories. However, machines also increased farm productivity. Using McCormick's Reaper and a horse, a farmer and his son could cut as much grain in a day as seven men with scythes. They could now plant more acres and not worry about the wheat sprouting (and becoming worthless) before it could be harvested. Moreover, as this advertisement from the May 1846 issue of the *Cultivator* indicates, farmers could easily repair their new reapers by providing McCormick with the letter denoting a broken part. Wisconsin Historical Society.

M'CORMICK'S REAPER.

Woodworker, c. 1850

Skilled makers took great pride in their furniture, which was often intricately designed and beautifully executed. To underline the dignity of his occupation, this woodworker poses in formal dress and proudly displays the tools of his craft. A belief in the value of their labor was an important ingredient of the artisan-republican ideology held by many workers. Library of Congress.

workers in St. Louis secured a ten-hour day, and President Van Buren issued an executive order setting a similar workday for federal workers.

Artisans in other occupations were less successful in preserving their pay and working conditions. As aggressive entrepreneurs and machine technology took command, shoemakers, hatters, printers, furniture makers, and weavers faced the regimentation of low-paid factory work. In response, some artisans in these trades moved to small towns, while in New York City, 800 highly skilled cabinetmakers made fashionable furniture. In status and income, these cabinetmakers outranked a group of 3,200 semitrained, wage-earning workers — disparagingly called "botches" — who made cheaper tables and chairs in factories. Thus the new industrial system split the traditional artisan class into self-employed craftsmen and wage-earning workers.

When wage earners banded together to form unions, they faced a legal hurdle: English and American common law branded such groups as illegal "combinations." As a Philadelphia judge put it, unions were "a government unto themselves" and unlawfully interfered with a "master's" authority over his "servant." Other lawsuits accused unions of "conspiring" to raise wages and thereby injure employers. "It is important to the best interests of society that the price of labor be left to regulate itself," the New York Supreme Court declared in 1835, while excluding employers from this rule. Clothing manufacturers in New York City collectively agreed to set wage rates and to dismiss members of the Society of Journeymen Tailors.

Labor Ideology   Despite such obstacles, during the 1830s journeymen shoemakers founded mutual benefit societies in Lynn, Massachusetts, and other shoemaking centers. As the workers explained, "The capitalist has no other interest in us, than to get as much labor out of us as possible. We are hired men, and hired men, like hired horses, have no souls." To exert more pressure on their employers, in 1834 local unions from Boston to Philadelphia formed the National Trades Union, the first regional union of different trades.

Workers found considerable popular support for their cause. When a New York City court upheld a conspiracy verdict against their union, tailors warned that the "Freemen of the North are now on a level with the slaves of the South," and organized a mass meeting of 27,000 people to denounce the decision. In 1836, local juries hearing conspiracy cases acquitted shoemakers in Hudson, New York; carpet makers in Thompsonville, Connecticut; and plasterers in Philadelphia. Even when juries convicted workers, judges imposed only light fines, so labor organizers were not deterred. Then, in *Commonwealth v. Hunt* (1842), Chief Justice Lemuel Shaw of the Massachusetts Supreme Judicial Court overturned common-law precedents and upheld the right of workers to form unions and call strikes to enforce closed-shop agreements that limited employment to union members. But many judges continued to resist unions by issuing injunctions forbidding strikes.

Union leaders expanded artisan republicanism to include wageworkers. Arguing that wage earners were becoming "slaves to a monied aristocracy," they condemned the new factory system in which "capital and labor stand opposed." To create a just society in which workers could "live as comfortably as others," they advanced a **labor theory of value**. Under this theory, the price of goods should reflect the labor required to make them, and the income from their sale should go primarily to the producers, not to factory owners, middlemen, or storekeepers. "The poor who perform the work, ought to receive at least half of that sum which is charged" to the consumer, declared minister

Ezra Stiles Ely. Union activists agreed, organizing nearly fifty strikes for higher wages in 1836. Appealing to the spirit of the American Revolution, which had destroyed the aristocracy of birth, they called for a new revolution to demolish the aristocracy of capital.

Women textile operatives were equally active. Competition in the woolen and cotton textile industries was fierce because mechanization caused output to grow faster than consumer demand. As textile prices fell, manufacturers' revenues declined. To maintain profits, employers reduced workers' wages and imposed tougher work rules. In 1828 and again in 1834, women mill workers in Dover, New Hampshire, went on strike and won some relief. In Lowell, two thousand women operatives backed a strike by withdrawing their savings from an employer-owned bank. "One of the leaders mounted a pump," the *Boston Transcript* reported, "and made a flaming . . . speech on the rights of women and the iniquities of the 'monied aristocracy.'" Increasingly, young New England women refused to enter the mills, and impoverished Irish (and later French Canadian) immigrants took their places.

In 1857, the new economic system faltered, as overproduction and a financial panic sparked by the bankruptcies of several railroads pushed the economy into a recession. Urban unemployment soared to 10 percent and reminded Americans of the social costs of industrial production.

The Market Revolution

As American factories and farms churned out more goods, legislators and businessmen created faster and cheaper ways to get those products to consumers. Around 1820, they began constructing a massive system of canals and roads linking states along the Atlantic coast with new states in the trans-Appalachian west. This transportation system set in motion both a crucial **Market Revolution** and a massive migration of people to the Greater Mississippi River basin. This huge area, drained by six river systems (the Missouri, Arkansas, Red, Ohio, Tennessee, and Mississippi), contains the largest and most productive contiguous acreage of arable land in the world. By 1860, nearly one-third of the nation's citizens lived in eight of its states — the "Midwest," consisting of the five states carved out of the Northwest Territory (Ohio, Indiana, Illinois, Michigan, and Wisconsin) along with Missouri, Iowa, and Minnesota. There they created a rich agricultural economy and an industrializing society similar to that of the Northeast.

The Transportation Revolution Forges Regional Ties

With the Indian peoples in retreat, slave-owning planters from the Lower South settled in Missouri (admitted to the Union in 1821) and pushed on to Arkansas (admitted in 1836). Simultaneously, yeomen families from the Upper South joined migrants from New England and New York in farming the fertile lands near the Great Lakes. Once Indiana and Illinois were settled, land-hungry farmers poured into Michigan (1837), Iowa (1846), and Wisconsin (1848) — where they resided among tens of thousands of hardworking immigrants from Germany. To meet the demand for cheap farmsteads, Congress in 1820 reduced the price of federal land from $2.00 an acre to $1.25. For $100, a farmer could buy 80 acres, the minimum required under federal law. By the 1840s, this generous policy had enticed about 5 million people to states and territories west of the Appalachians (Map 9.2).

To link the midwestern settlers to the seaboard states, Congress approved funds for a National Road constructed of compacted gravel. The project began in 1811 at Cumberland in western Maryland, at the head of navigation of the Potomac River; reached Wheeling, Virginia (now West Virginia), on the Ohio River in 1818; and ended in Vandalia, Illinois, in 1839. The National Road and other interregional highways carried migrants and their heavily loaded wagons westward; these migrants passed livestock herds heading in the opposite direction, destined for eastern markets. To link the settler communities with each other, state legislatures chartered private companies to build toll roads, or turnpikes.

Canals and Steamboats Shrink Distance
Even on well-built gravel roads, overland travel was slow and expensive. To carry people, crops, and manufactures to and from the great Mississippi River basin, public money and private businesses developed a water-borne transportation system of unprecedented size, complexity, and cost. The key event was the New York legislature's 1817 financing of the **Erie Canal**, a 364-mile waterway connecting the Hudson River and Lake Erie. Previously, the longest canal in the United States was just 28 miles long — reflecting the huge capital cost of canals and the lack of American engineering expertise. New York's ambitious project had three things working in its favor: the vigorous support of New York City's merchants, who wanted access to western markets; the backing of New York's governor, De Witt Clinton, who proposed to finance the waterway from tax revenues,

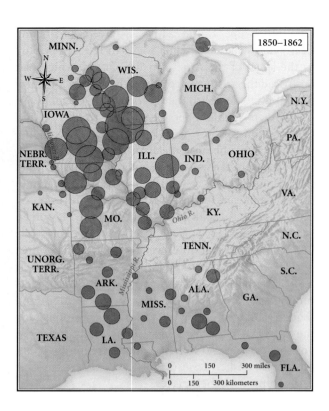

MAP 9.2

Western Land Sales, 1830–1839 and 1850–1862

The federal government set up local offices to sell land in the national domain to settlers. During the 1830s, the offices sold huge amounts of land in the corn and wheat belt of the Midwest (Ohio, Indiana, Illinois, and Michigan) and the cotton belt to the south (especially Alabama and Mississippi). As settlers moved westward in the 1850s, most sales were in the Upper Mississippi River Valley (particularly Iowa and Wisconsin). Each circle indicates the relative amount of land sold at a local office.

tolls, and bond sales to foreign investors; and the relatively gentle terrain west of Albany. Even so, the task was enormous. Workers—many of them Irish immigrants—dug out millions of cubic yards of soil, quarried thousands of tons of rock for the huge locks that raised and lowered the boats, and constructed vast reservoirs to ensure a steady supply of water.

The first great engineering project in American history, the Erie Canal altered the ecology of an entire region. As farming communities and market towns sprang up along the waterway, settlers cut down millions of trees to provide wood for houses and barns and to open the land for growing crops and grazing animals. Cows and sheep foraged in pastures that had recently been forests occupied by deer and bears, and spring rains caused massive erosion of the denuded landscape.

Whatever its environmental consequences, the Erie Canal

was an instant economic success. The first 75-mile section opened in 1819 and quickly yielded enough revenue to repay its construction cost. When workers finished the canal in 1825, a 40-foot-wide ribbon of water stretched from Buffalo, on the eastern shore of Lake Erie, to Albany, where it joined the Hudson River for the 150-mile trip to New York City. The canal's water "must be the most fertilizing of all fluids," suggested novelist Nathaniel Hawthorne, "for it causes towns with their masses of brick and stone, their churches and theaters, their business and hubbub, their luxury and refinement, their gay dames and polished citizens, to spring up."

The Erie Canal brought prosperity to the farmers of central and western New York and the entire Great Lakes region. Northeastern manufacturers shipped clothing, boots, and agricultural equipment to farm families; in return, farmers sent grain, cattle, and hogs as well as raw materials (leather, wool, and hemp, for example) to eastern cities and foreign markets. One-hundred-ton freight barges, each pulled by two horses,

IDENTIFY CAUSES

Which was more important in the Market Revolution, government support for transportation or technological innovations, and why was that the case?

View of the Erie Canal

This pastoral view of the Erie Canal near Lockport, New York, painted by artist John William Hill, hints at this waterway's profound impact on American life. Without the canal, the town in the background would not exist and farmers such as the man in the foreground would not have a regional market for their cattle and grain. The success of the Erie Canal had led to the construction of a vast system of canals by 1860. This infrastructure was as important to the nation as the railroad network of the late nineteenth century and the interstate highway and airport transportation systems of the late twentieth century. © Bettmann/ Corbis.

moved along the canal at a steady 30 miles a day, cutting transportation costs and accelerating the flow of goods. In 1818, the mills in Rochester, New York, processed 26,000 barrels of flour for export east (and north to Montreal, for sale as "Canadian" produce to the West Indies); ten years later, their output soared to 200,000 barrels; and by 1840, it was at 500,000 barrels.

The spectacular benefits of the Erie Canal prompted a national canal boom. Civic and business leaders in Philadelphia and Baltimore proposed waterways to link their cities to the Midwest. Copying New York's fiscal innovations, they persuaded their state legislatures to invest directly in canal companies or to force state-chartered banks to do so. They also won state guarantees that encouraged British and Dutch investors; as one observer noted in 1844, "The prosperity of America, her railroads, canals, steam navigation, and banks, are the fruit of English capital." Soon, artificial waterways connected Philadelphia and Baltimore, via the Pennsylvania Canal and the Chesapeake and Ohio Canal, to the Great Lakes region.

Equally important was the vast network of navigable rivers that drained into the Mississippi. Every year, 25,000 farmer-built flatboats used these waterways to carry produce to New Orleans. In 1848, the completion of the Michigan and Illinois Canal, which linked Chicago to the Mississippi River, completed an inland all-water route from New York City to New Orleans, the two most important port cities in North America (Map 9.3).

The steamboat, another product of the industrial age, added crucial flexibility to the Mississippi basin's river-based transportation system. In 1807, engineer-inventor Robert Fulton built the first American steamboat, the *Clermont*, which he piloted up the Hudson River. To navigate shallow western rivers, engineers broadened steamboats' hulls to reduce their draft and enlarge their cargo capacity. These improved vessels halved the cost of upstream river transport along the Mississippi River and its tributaries and dramatically increased the flow of goods, people, and news. In 1830, a traveler or a letter from New York could reach Buffalo or Pittsburgh by water in less than a week and Detroit, Chicago, or St. Louis in two weeks. In 1800, the same journeys had taken twice as long.

The state and national governments played key roles in developing this interregional network of trade and travel. State legislatures subsidized canals, while the national government created a vast postal system, the first network for the exchange of information. Thanks to the Post Office Act of 1792, there were more than eight thousand post offices by 1830, and they safely delivered thousands of letters and banknotes worth millions of dollars. The U.S. Supreme Court, headed by John Marshall, likewise encouraged interstate trade by firmly establishing federal authority over

MAP 9.3

The Transportation Revolution: Roads and Canals, 1820–1850

By 1850, the United States had an efficient system of water-borne transportation with three distinct parts. Short canals and navigable rivers carried cotton, tobacco, and other products from the countryside of the southern seaboard states into the Atlantic commercial system. A second system, centered on the Erie, Chesapeake and Ohio, and Pennsylvania Mainline canals, linked northeastern seaports to the vast trans-Appalachian region. Finally, a set of regional canals in the Midwest connected most of the Great Lakes region to the Ohio and Mississippi rivers and the port of New Orleans.

interstate commerce (Chapter 7). In *Gibbons v. Ogden* (1824), the Court voided a New York law that created a monopoly on steamboat travel into New York City. That decision prevented local or state monopolies — or tariffs — from impeding the flow of goods, people, and news across the nation.

Railroads Link the North and Midwest   In the 1850s, railroads, another technological innovation, joined canals as the core of the national transportation system (Map 9.4). In 1852, canals carried twice the tonnage transported by railroads. Then, capitalists in Boston, New York, and London secured state charters for railroads and invested heavily in new lines, which by 1860 had become the main carriers of wheat and freight from the Midwest to the Northeast. Serviced by a vast network of locomotive and freight-car repair shops, the Erie, Pennsylvania, New York Central, and the Baltimore and Ohio railroads connected the Atlantic ports — New York, Philadelphia, and Baltimore — with the rapidly expanding Great Lakes cities of Cleveland and Chicago (Thinking Like a Historian, p. 298).

The railroad boom also linked these western cities to adjacent states. Chicago-based railroads carried huge quantities of lumber from Michigan to the treeless prairies of Indiana, Illinois, Iowa, and Missouri, where settlers built 250,000 new farms (covering 19 million acres) and hundreds of small towns. On their

return journey, the trains moved millions of bushels of wheat to Chicago for transport to eastern markets. Increasingly, they also carried livestock to Chicago's slaughterhouses. In Jacksonville, Illinois, a farmer decided to feed his entire corn crop of 1,500 bushels "to hogs & cattle, as we think it is more profitable than to sell the corn." A Chicago newspaper boasted, "In ancient times all roads led to Rome; in modern times all roads lead to Chicago."

Initially, midwestern settlers relied on manufactured goods imported from the Northeast. They bought high-quality shovels and spades fabricated at the Delaware Iron Works and the Oliver Ames Company in Easton, Massachusetts; axes forged in Connecticut factories; and steel horseshoes manufactured in Troy, New York. However, by the 1840s, midwestern entrepreneurs were also producing machine tools, hardware, furniture, and especially agricultural implements. Working as a blacksmith in Grand Detour, Illinois, John Deere made his first steel plow out of old saws in 1837; ten years later, he opened a factory in Moline, Illinois, that mass-produced the plows. Stronger than the existing cast-iron models built in New York, Deere's steel plows allowed farmers to cut through the thick sod of the prairies. Other midwestern companies — such as McCormick and Hussey — mass-produced self-raking reapers that harvested 12 acres of grain a day (rather than the 2 acres that an adult worker could

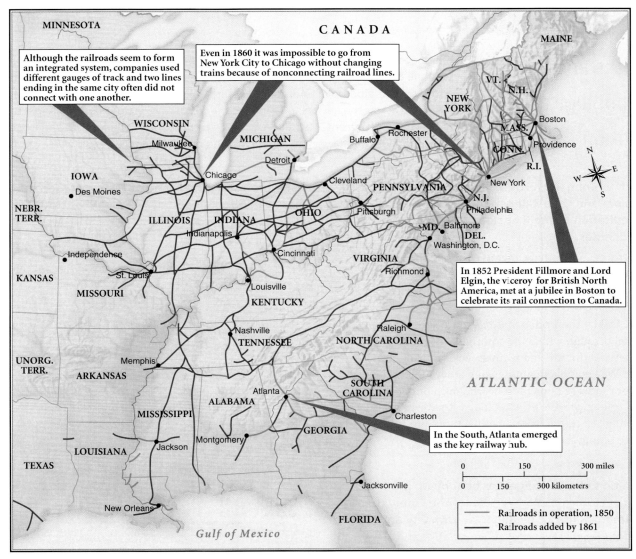

MAP 9.4

Railroads of the North and South, 1850 and 1861

In the decade before the Civil War, entrepreneurs in the Northeast and the Midwest financed thousands of miles of new railroad lines, creating an extensive and dense transportation system that stimulated economic development. The South built a more limited railroad system. In all regions, railroad companies used different track gauges, which prevented the efficient flow of traffic.

cut by hand). With the harvest bottleneck removed, farmers planted more acres and grew even more wheat. Flour soon accounted for 10 percent of all American exports to foreign markets.

Interregional trade also linked southern cotton planters to northeastern textile plants and foreign markets. This commerce in raw cotton bolstered the wealth of white southerners but did not transform their economic and social order as it did in the Midwest. With the exception of Richmond, Virginia, and a few other places, southern planters did not invest their profits in manufacturing. Lacking cities, factories, and highly trained workers, the South remained tied to agriculture, even as the commerce in wheat, corn, and livestock promoted diversified economies in the Northeast and Midwest.

The Growth of Cities and Towns

The expansion of industry and trade dramatically increased America's urban population. In 1820, there were 58 towns with more than 2,500 inhabitants; by

The Risks and Rewards of Technological Innovation

The nineteenth century was the Age of Progress, and improved transportation was one of its hallmarks. Between the 1830s and the 1860s, American capitalists and workers, aided by state governments, built steam-powered railroads that stretched across the nation and reduced the cost of moving goods and people by more than 90 percent. Yet, like all major technological changes, the railroad revolution was controversial, expensive, and politically explosive.

1. **Speech by John B. Morris, a director of the Baltimore and Ohio Railroad, July 4, 1828, at the dedication of the first steam railway in the United States.**

Fellow-Citizens. . . . We have met to celebrate the laying of the first stone of the Baltimore and Ohio Railroad. . . . The result of our labors will be felt, not only by ourselves, but also by posterity, — not only by Baltimore, but also by Maryland and by the United States. We are about opening the channel through which the commerce of the mighty country beyond the Alleghany must seek the [Atlantic] ocean. . . . We are in fact commencing a new era in our history; for there are none present who even doubt the beneficial influence which the intended Road will have in promoting the Agriculture, Manufactures and Inland Commerce of our country.

2. **Illustration of a passenger car built by M. P. & M. E. Green of Hoboken, New Jersey, for the Camden and Amboy Railway, linking New York City and Philadelphia, 1831.**

Source: Division of Work & Industry, National Museum of American History, Smithsonian Institution.

3. **Poster protesting the laying of tracks through the "most Beautiful Streets" of Philadelphia, 1839.**

Source: National Archives.

4. **Opposition to the state financing of railroads from the *Republican Compiler*, Gettysburg, Pennsylvania, October 6, 1851.** *As American track mileage grew from 3,000 miles in 1840 to 30,000 miles by 1860, entrepreneurs in Pennsylvania, assisted by the state legislature, led the nation in laying rail.*

The Governor's organ [newspaper] is still harping about the Governor having paid off the State debt, and reducing the taxes. If the taxes have been reduced, why is it that every farmer finds that he has paid MORE TAXES the last year than he has ever paid in a single year before? . . . The true issue is that Gov. Johnston and his friends created the [huge state] debt. . . .

The people remember that Gov. Johnston voted $405,000 to the Gettysburg railroad. . . .

They remember that he voted $150,000 to the Danville and Pottsville railroad.

They remember that he voted $140,000 to the Laughlintown and Pittsburg railroad, that never was incorporated.

They remember that he voted $120,000 to the Norristown railroad.

They remember that he voted for a bill appropriating over THREE MILLIONS OF DOLLARS to State and company improvements in one year, and that Gov. Ritner said that such appropriations would increase the State debt, in four years, to $45,000,000.

5. Lyrics to "The Waggoner's Curse," c. 1850.

Come all ye bold wagoners turn out man by man
That's opposed to the railroad or any such a plan;
'Tis once I made money by driving my team
But the goods are now hauled on the railroad by steam. . . .

If we go to Philadelphia, inquiring for a load,
They'll tell us quite directly it's gone out on the railroad.
The rich folks, the plan they may justly admire,
But it ruins us poor wag'ners and it makes our taxes
    higher . . .

It ruins wheelwrights, blacksmiths, and every other trade,
So damned be all the railroads that ever was made.
It ruins our mechanics, what think you of it, then?
And it fills our country full of just a lot of great rich men.

The ships they will be coming with Irishmen by loads,
All with their picks and shovels, to work on the railroads;
When they get on the railroad, it is then that they are fixed
They'll fight just like the devil with their cudgels and their
    sticks.

The American with safety can scarcely ever pass,
For they will blacken both his eyes for one word of his sass
If it wasn't for the torment I as life would be in hell,
As upon the cursed railroad, or upon the canal.

6. Henry David Thoreau, *Walden, or, Life in the Woods*, 1854. *The workers who built and ran the railroads suffered high rates of injury and death—facts noted by Henry David Thoreau, a critic of the market, transportation, and industrial revolutions of his day.*

We do not ride on the railroad; it rides upon us. Did you ever think what those sleepers are that underlie the railroad? Each one is a man. . . . The rails are laid

on them, and they are covered with sand, and the cars run smoothly over them . . . ; so that, if some have the pleasure of riding on a rail, others have the misfortune to be ridden upon.

7. Senator L. J. Rose, from *Testimony Taken by the United States Pacific Railway Commission*, 1887.

The railroads have made Southern California what it is to-day. Before the completion of the . . . Union and Central Pacific roads the southern half of California, which is now famous the world over as the most favored quarter in America in point of climate and soil conditions, was no more nor less than a barren sheep pasture. . . . Our redemption came in 1869, when the railroad people completed that gigantic and wonderful work . . . , giving California a direct rail connection with the East. The effect was marvelous and immediate. . . . We beheld ourselves in a day, as it were, surrounded by possibilities which made us a new and different people, in a new and completely changed land.

Sources: (1) Eli Bowen, *Rambles in the Path of the Steam-Horse* (Philadelphia: Wm. Bromwell and Wm. White Smith, 1855), 37; (4) Adapted from ExplorePAhistory.com; (5) George Korson, ed., *Pennsylvania Songs and Legends* (Philadelphia: University of Pennsylvania Press, 1949), 255–257; (6) Henry David Thoreau, *Walden, or, Life in the Woods*, 1854 (Boston, 1910), 102; (7) *Testimony Taken by the United States Pacific Railway Commission*, Vol. 5 (Washington, D.C.: Government Printing Office, 1887), 2505.

ANALYZING THE EVIDENCE

1. What does source 1 tell us about the hopes of steam railroad pioneers? Do the other sources suggest their hopes were achieved?

2. What does source 2 suggest about early railroad design and marketing? How does this image contrast with source 3? What threats does source 3 highlight? What audiences were the targets of these illustrations, and how successful are their respective messages?

3. According to source 4, how did Pennsylvania raise the money for these subsidies? Who was left holding the bag? Why would governments fund such private enterprises?

4. What social tensions do the lyrics to source 5 reveal? What other conflicts are manifest in the documents presented here?

5. Who are the "sleepers" in source 6? How does Thoreau calculate the cost of progress? How are these costs similar to or different from the ones described by the author of source 5?

PUTTING IT ALL TOGETHER

After re-reading the section in this chapter on the transportation revolution, answer the following questions: Why did the transportation revolution take place? What roles in the spread of the railway, canals, and turnpikes were played by entrepreneurs and capitalists? By governments, taxpayers, and various groups of workers? What were some of the unintended consequences? Who won? Lost? Using these documents and your answers, write an essay assessing the benefits and costs of the transition to new transportation technologies.

1840, there were 126 such towns, located mostly in the Northeast and Midwest. During those two decades, the total number of city dwellers grew more than fourfold, from 443,000 to 1,844,000.

The fastest growth occurred in the new industrial towns that sprouted along the "fall line," where rivers descended rapidly from the Appalachian Mountains to the coastal plain. In 1822, the Boston Manufacturing Company built a complex of mills in a sleepy Merrimack River village that quickly became the bustling textile factory town of Lowell, Massachusetts. The towns of Hartford, Connecticut; Trenton, New Jersey; and Wilmington, Delaware, also became urban centers as mill owners exploited the water power of their rivers and recruited workers from the countryside.

COMPARE AND CONTRAST

What different types of cities emerged between 1820 and 1860, and what caused their growth?

Western commercial cities such as Pittsburgh, Cincinnati, and New Orleans grew almost as rapidly. These cities expanded initially as transit centers, where workers transferred goods from farmers' rafts and wagons to steamboats or railroads. As the midwestern population grew during the 1830s and 1840s, St. Louis, Detroit, and especially Buffalo and Chicago also emerged as dynamic centers of commerce. "There can

be no two places in the world," journalist Margaret Fuller wrote from Chicago in 1843, "more completely thoroughfares than this place and Buffalo. . . . The life-blood [of commerce] rushes from east to west, and back again from west to east." To a German visitor, Chicago seemed "for the most part to consist of shops . . . [as if] people came here merely to trade, to make money, and not to live." Chicago's merchants and bankers developed the marketing, provisioning, and financial services essential to farmers and small-town shopkeepers in its vast hinterland. "There can be no better [market] any where in the Union," declared a farmer in Paw Paw, Illinois.

These midwestern hubs quickly became manufacturing centers. Capitalizing on the cities' links to rivers, canals, and railroads, entrepreneurs built warehouses, flour mills, packing plants, and machine shops, creating work for hundreds of artisans and factory laborers. In 1846, Cyrus McCormick moved his reaper factory from western Virginia to Chicago to be closer to his midwestern customers. By 1860, St. Louis and Chicago had become the nation's eighth- and ninth-largest cities; by 1870, they were the fourth and fifth, behind New York, Philadelphia, and Brooklyn (Map 9.5).

The old Atlantic seaports — Boston, Philadelphia, Baltimore, Charleston, and especially New York City —

MAP 9.5

The Nation's Major Cities, 1840

By 1840, the United States boasted three major conglomerations of cities. The long-settled ports on the Atlantic — from Boston to Baltimore — served as centers for import merchants, banks, insurance companies, and manufacturers of ready-made clothing, and their financial reach extended far into the interior — nationwide in the case of New York City. A second group of cities stretched along the Great Lakes and included the commercial hubs of Buffalo, Detroit, and Chicago, as well as the manufacturing center of Cleveland. A third urban system extended along the Ohio River, comprising the industrial cities of Pittsburgh and Cincinnati and the wholesale centers of Louisville and St. Louis.

remained important for their foreign commerce and, increasingly, as centers of finance and small-scale manufacturing. New York City and nearby Brooklyn grew at a phenomenal rate: between 1820 and 1860, their combined populations increased nearly tenfold to 1 million people, thanks to the arrival of hundreds of thousands of German and Irish immigrants. Drawing on these workers, New York became a center of the ready-made clothing industry, which relied on thousands of low-paid seamstresses. "The wholesale clothing establishments are . . . absorbing the business of the country," a "Country Tailor" complained to the *New York Tribune*, "casting many an honest and hardworking man out of employment [and helping] . . . the large cities to swallow up the small towns."

New York City's growth stemmed primarily from its dominant position in foreign and domestic trade. It had the best harbor in the United States and, thanks to the Erie Canal, was the best gateway to the Midwest and the best outlet for western grain. Recognizing the city's advantages, in 1818 four English Quaker merchants founded the Black Ball Line to carry cargo, people, and mail between New York and London, Liverpool, and Le Havre, establishing the first regularly scheduled transatlantic shipping service. By 1840, its port handled almost two-thirds of foreign imports into the United States, almost half of all foreign trade, and much of the immigrant traffic. New York likewise monopolized trade with the newly independent South American nations of Brazil, Peru, and Venezuela, and its merchants took over the trade in cotton by offering finance, insurance, and shipping to southern planters and merchants.

New Social Classes and Cultures

The Industrial Revolution and the Market Revolution improved the lives of many Americans, who now lived in larger houses, cooked on iron stoves, and wore better-made clothes. Yet in the booming cities, the new economic order spawned distinct social classes: a small but wealthy business elite, a substantial middle class, and a mass of propertyless wage earners. By creating a class-divided society, industrialization posed a momentous challenge to America's republican ideals.

The Business Elite

Before industrialization, white Americans thought of their society in terms of rank: "notable" families had higher status than those from the "lower orders." Yet in

rural areas, people of different ranks often shared a common culture. Gentlemen farmers talked easily with yeomen about crop yields, while their wives conversed about the art of quilting. In the South, humble tenants and aristocratic slave owners enjoyed the same amusements: gambling, cockfighting, and horse racing. Rich and poor attended the same Quaker meetinghouse or Presbyterian church. "Almost everyone eats, drinks, and dresses in the same way," a European visitor to Hartford, Connecticut, reported in 1798, "and one can see the most obvious inequality only in the dwellings."

The Industrial Revolution shattered this agrarian social order and fragmented society into distinct classes and cultures. The urban economy made a few city residents — the merchants, manufacturers, bankers, and landlords who made up the business elite — very rich. In 1800, the richest 10 percent of the nation's families owned about 40 percent of the wealth; by 1860, they held nearly 70 percent. In New York, Chicago, Baltimore, and New Orleans, the super-rich — the top 1 percent — owned more than 40 percent of the land, buildings, and other tangible property and an even higher share of intangible property, such as stocks and bonds.

Government tax policies facilitated the accumulation of wealth. There were no federal taxes on individual and corporate income. Rather, the U.S. Treasury raised most of its revenue from tariffs: regressive taxes on textiles and other imported goods purchased mostly by ordinary citizens. State and local governments also favored the wealthy. They taxed real estate (farms, city lots, and buildings) and tangible personal property (furniture, tools, and machinery), but almost never taxed stocks and bonds or the inheritances the rich passed on to their children.

As cities expanded in size and wealth, affluent families consciously set themselves apart. They dressed in well-tailored clothes, rode in fancy carriages, and bought expensively furnished houses tended by butlers, cooks, and other servants. The women no longer socialized with those of lesser wealth, and the men no longer labored side by side with their employees. Instead, they became managers and directors and relied on trusted subordinates to supervise hundreds of factory operatives. Increasingly, merchants, manufacturers, and bankers placed a premium on privacy and lived in separate neighborhoods, often in exclusive central areas or at the city's edge. The geographic isolation of privileged families and the massive flow of immigrants into separate districts

TRACE CHANGE OVER TIME
How and why did elite families change between 1800 and 1860?

Hartford Family

Completely at home in their elegant drawing room, this elite family in Hartford, Connecticut, enjoys the fruits of the father's business success. As the father lounges in his silk robe, his eldest son (and presumptive heir) adopts an air of studied nonchalance, and his daughter fingers a piano, signaling her musical accomplishments and the family's gentility. A diminutive African American servant (her size suggesting her status) serves fruit to the lavishly attired woman of the house. The sumptuously appointed drawing room reflects the owners' prosperity and their aesthetic and cultural interests. © White House Historical Association/Photo by National Geographic Society.

divided cities spatially along lines of class, race, and ethnicity.

The Middle Class

Standing between wealthy owners and propertyless wage earners was a growing **middle class** — the social product of increased commerce. The "middling class," a Boston printer explained, was made up of "the farmers, the mechanics, the manufacturers, the traders, who carry on professionally the ordinary operations of buying, selling, and exchanging merchandize." Professionals with other skills — building contractors, lawyers, surveyors, and so on — were suddenly in great demand and well compensated, as were middling business owners and white-collar clerks. In the Northeast, men with these qualifications numbered about 30 percent of the population in the 1840s. But they also could be found in small towns of the agrarian Midwest and South. In 1854, the cotton boomtown of Oglethorpe, Georgia (population 2,500), boasted eighty "business houses" and eight hotels.

The emergence of the middle class reflected a dramatic rise in prosperity. Between 1830 and 1857, the per capita income of Americans increased by about 2.5 percent a year, a remarkable rate that has never since

The Social Dimensions of Whaling
Whale oil fueled the lamps that illuminated the houses of well-to-do Americans in the early nineteenth century, and bright spermaceti candles made from the waxy substance in the heads of sperm whales graced their dining tables. To provide these luxuries, five hundred ships from New Bedford, Massachusetts, and the nearby island of Nantucket roamed the world on voyages lasting up to three years. Ten thousand workers—young men seeking adventure and veteran white and black sailors—manned the ships. As this painting, *Capturing a Sperm Whale* by William Page (1835, from a sketch by whaler C. B. Hulsart), suggests, whaling was a dangerous trade that took the lives of many men. © Peabody Essex Museum, Salem, Massachusetts, USA/The Bridgeman Art Library.

been matched. This surge in income, along with an abundance of inexpensive mass-produced goods, fostered a distinct middle-class urban culture. Middle-class husbands earned enough to save about 15 percent of their income, which they used to buy well-built houses in a "respectable part of town." They purchased handsome clothes and drove to work and play in smart carriages. Middle-class wives became purveyors of genteel culture, buying books, pianos, lithographs, and comfortable furniture for their front parlors. Upper-middle-class families hired Irish or African American domestic servants, while less prosperous folk enjoyed the comforts provided by new industrial goods. The middle class outfitted their residences with furnaces (to warm the entire house and heat water for bathing), cooking stoves with ovens, and Singer's treadle-operated sewing machines. Some urban families now kept their perishable food in iceboxes, which

ice-company wagons periodically refilled, and bought many varieties of packaged goods. As early as 1825, the Underwood Company of Boston was marketing jars of well-preserved Atlantic salmon.

If material comfort was one distinguishing mark of the middle class, moral and mental discipline was another. Middle-class writers denounced raucous carnivals and festivals as a "chaos of sin and folly, of misery and fun" and, by the 1830s, had largely suppressed them. Ambitious parents were equally concerned with their children's moral and intellectual development. To help their offspring succeed in life, middle-class parents often provided them with a high school education (in an era when most white children received only five years of schooling) and stressed the importance of discipline and hard work. American Protestants had long

UNDERSTAND POINTS OF VIEW
What were the moral values and material culture of the urban middle class?

[Fig. 130. Plain Timber Cottage-Villa.]

[Fig. 131. Principal Floor.]

Architecture for the Emergent Middle Class
This dwelling was well suited for a "farmer of wealth" or a middle-class suburbanite, according to Andrew Downing, author of *The Architecture of Country Houses* (1850). The exterior of the house exhibited "a considerable degree of elegance," while the interior boasted a substantial drawing room and dining room, for the entertainment of guests, and a parlor for more intimate conversations among family and friends. Downing's books helped to define the culture of the growing middle class and diffuse it across the nation.
Andrew J. Downing, *The Architecture of Country Houses*, 1850.

believed that diligent work in an earthly "calling" was a duty owed to God. Now the business elite and the middle class gave this idea a secular twist by celebrating work as the key to individual social mobility and national prosperity.

Benjamin Franklin gave the classic expression of this secular work ethic in his *Autobiography*, which was published in full in 1818 (thirty years after his death) and immediately found a huge audience. Heeding Franklin's

PLACE EVENTS IN CONTEXT
How did the increasingly urban, capitalist economy of the northeastern states affect the lives of poor workers?

suggestion that an industrious man would become a rich one, tens of thousands of young American men saved their money, adopted temperate habits, and aimed to rise in the world. There was an "almost universal ambition to get forward," observed Hezekiah Niles, editor of *Niles' Weekly Register*. Warner Myers, a Philadelphia housepainter, rose from poverty by saving his wages, borrowing from his family and friends, and becoming a builder, eventually constructing and selling sixty houses. Countless children's books, magazine stories, self-help manuals, and novels recounted the tales of similar individuals. The **self-made man** became a central theme of American popular culture and inspired many men (and a few women) to seek success. Just as the yeoman ethic had served as a unifying ideal in pre-1800 agrarian America, so the gospel of personal achievement linked the middle and business classes of the new industrializing society.

Urban Workers and the Poor

As thoughtful business leaders surveyed their society, they concluded that the yeoman farmer and artisan-republican ideal — a social order of independent producers — was no longer possible. "Entire independence ought not to be wished for," Ithamar A. Beard, the paymaster of the Hamilton Manufacturing Company (in Lowell, Massachusetts), told a mechanics' association in 1827. "In large manufacturing towns, many more must fill subordinate stations and must be under the immediate direction and control of a master or superintendent, than in the farming towns."

Beard had a point. In 1840, all of the nation's slaves, some 2.5 million people, and about half of its adult white workers, another 3 million, were laboring for others. The bottom 10 percent of white wage earners consisted of casual workers hired on a short-term basis for arduous jobs. Poor women washed clothes; their husbands and sons carried lumber and bricks for construction projects, loaded ships, and dug out dirt and stones to build canals. When they could find jobs, these men earned "their dollar per diem," a longtime resident told readers of the *Baltimore American*, but they could never save enough "to pay rent, buy fire wood and eatables" when the job market or the harbor froze up. During business depressions, casual laborers suffered and died; in good times, their jobs were temporary and dangerous.

Other laborers had greater security of employment, but few were prospering. In Massachusetts in 1825, an unskilled worker earned about two-thirds as much as a mechanic did; two decades later, it was less than half as much. A journeyman carpenter in Philadelphia reported that he was about "even with the World" after several years of work but that many of his coworkers were in debt. The 18,000 women who sewed men's ready-made clothing in New York City in the 1850s earned just a few pennies a day, less than $100 a year (about $3,000 today). Such meager wages barely paid for food and rent, so poorer workers could not take advantage of the rapidly falling prices of manufactured goods. Only the most fortunate working-class families could afford to educate their children, buy apprentice-ships for their sons, or accumulate small dowries for their daughters. Most families sent ten-year-old children out to work, and the death of a parent often threw the survivors into dire poverty. As a charity worker noted, "What can a bereaved widow do, with 5 or 6 little children, destitute of every means of support but what her own hands can furnish (which in a general way does not amount to more than 25 cents a day)?"

Impoverished workers congregated in dilapidated housing in bad neighborhoods. Single men and women lived in crowded boardinghouses, while families jammed themselves into tiny apartments in the basements and attics of small houses. As immigrants poured in after 1840, urban populations soared, and developers squeezed more and more dwellings and foul-smelling outhouses onto a single lot. Venturing into the New York City slums in the 1850s, shocked state legislators found gaunt, shivering people with "wild ghastly faces" living amid "hideous squalor and deadly effluvia, the dim, undrained courts oozing with pollution, the dark, narrow stairways, decayed with age, reeking with filth, overrun with vermin." Many wage earners sought solace in alcohol, leading to fist-fights, brawls, and robberies. The urban police, mostly low-paid watchmen and untrained constables, were unable to contain the lawlessness.

The Benevolent Empire

The disorder among wage earners alarmed the rising middle classes, who wanted safe cities and a disciplined workforce. To improve the world around them, many upwardly mobile men and women embraced religious benevolence. Led by Congregational and Presbyterian ministers, they created organizations of conservative social reform that historians call the **Benevolent Empire**, which became prominent in the 1820s. The reformers' goal was to restore "the moral government of God" by reducing the consumption of alcohol and other vices that resulted in poverty, explained Presbyterian minister Lyman Beecher. Reform-minded

individuals had regulated their own behavior; now they tried to control the lives of working people — by persuasion if possible, by law if necessary.

The Benevolent Empire targeted age-old evils such as drunkenness, adultery, prostitution, and crime, but its methods were new. Instead of relying on church sermons and admonitions from community leaders to combat evil, the reform-ers created large-scale organiza-tions: the Prison Discipline Society and the American Society for the Promotion of Temperance, among many others. Each organization had a managing staff, a network of hundreds of chapters, thousands of volunteer members, and a newspaper.

IDENTIFY CAUSES
What was the Benevolent Empire, and why did it emerge at this specific historical moment?

Often acting in concert, these benevolent groups worked to improve society. First, they encouraged people to lead disciplined lives and acquire "regular habits." They persuaded local governments to ban car-nivals of drink and dancing, such as Negro Election Day (festivities in which African Americans symboli-cally took control of the government), which had been enjoyed by whites as well as blacks. Second, they devised new institutions to help the needy and control the unruly. Reformers provided homes of refuge for abandoned children and asylums for the insane, who previously had been confined by their families in attics and cellars. They campaigned to end corporal punish-ment of criminals and to rehabilitate them in specially designed penitentiaries.

Women formed a crucial part of the Benevolent Empire. Since the 1790s, upper-class women had spon-sored charitable organizations such as the Society for the Relief of Poor Widows with Small Children, founded in 1797 in New York by Isabella Graham, a devout Presbyterian widow. Her daughter Joanna Bethune set up other charitable institutions, including the Orphan Asylum Society and the Society for the Promotion of Industry, which found jobs for hundreds of poor women as spinners and seamstresses.

Some reformers believed that declining observance by Christians of the Sabbath (Sunday) as a day devoted to religion was the greatest threat to the "moral gov-ernment of God." As the Market Revolution spread, merchants and storekeepers conducted business on Sundays, and urban saloons provided drink and enter-tainment. To halt these profane activities, Lyman Beecher and other ministers founded the General Union for Promoting the Observance of the Christian Sabbath in 1828. General Union chapters, replete with women's auxiliaries, sprang up from Maine to

Cincinnati and beyond. The General Union demanded that Congress repeal an 1810 law allowing mail to be transported — though not delivered — on Sundays. Members boycotted shipping companies that did business on the Sabbath and campaigned for municipal laws forbidding games and festivals on the Lord's day.

The Benevolent Empire's efforts to impose its **Sabbatarian values** provoked opposition from workers and freethinkers. Men who labored twelve to fourteen hours a day, six days a week, wanted the freedom to spend their one day of leisure as they wished. To keep goods moving, shipping company managers demanded that the Erie Canal provide lockkeepers on Sundays; using laws to enforce a particular set of moral beliefs was "contrary to the free spirit of our institutions," they said. When evangelical reformers proposed teaching Christianity to slaves, they aroused hostility among white southerners. This popular resistance by workers and planters limited the success of the Benevolent Empire.

IDENTIFY CAUSES
Who opposed the work of the Benevolent Empire and why?

Charles Grandison Finney: Revivalism and Reform

Presbyterian minister Charles Grandison Finney found a new way to propagate religious values. Finney was not part of the traditional religious elite. Born into a poor farming family in Connecticut, he had planned to become a lawyer and rise into the middle class. But in 1823, Finney underwent an intense religious experience and chose the ministry as his career. Beginning in towns along the Erie Canal, the young minister conducted emotional revival meetings that stressed conversion rather than doctrine. Repudiating Calvinist beliefs, he preached that God would welcome any sinner who submitted to the Holy Spirit. Finney's ministry drew on — and greatly accelerated — the Second Great Awakening, the wave of Protestant revivalism that had begun after the Revolution (Chapter 8).

Evangelical Beliefs Finney's central message was that "God has made man a **moral free agent**" who could choose salvation. This doctrine of free will was particularly attractive to members of the new middle class, who had accepted personal responsibility for their lives, improved their material condition, and welcomed Finney's assurance that heaven was also within their grasp. But Finney also had great success in converting people at both ends of the social spectrum, from the haughty rich who had placed themselves

Charles Grandison Finney, Evangelist (1792–1875)
When an unknown artist painted this flattering portrait in 1834, Finney was forty-two years old and at the height of his career as an evangelist. Handsome and charismatic, Finney had just led a series of enormously successful revivals in Rochester, New York, and other cities along the Erie Canal. In 1835, he established a theology department at newly founded Oberlin College in Ohio, where he trained a generation of ministers and served as president from 1851 to 1866. Oberlin College Archives.

above God, to the abject poor who seemed lost to drink and sloth. Finney celebrated their common fellowship in Christ and identified them spiritually with pious middle-class respectability.

Finney's most spectacular triumph came in 1830, when he moved his revivals from small towns to Rochester, New York, now a major milling and commercial city on the Erie Canal. Preaching every day for six months and promoting group prayer meetings in family homes, Finney won over the influential merchants and manufacturers of Rochester. They promised to attend church, give up intoxicating beverages, and work hard. To encourage their employees to do the same, wealthy businessmen founded a Free Presbyterian Church — "free" because members did not have to pay for pew space. Other evangelical Protestants founded churches to serve transient canal laborers, and pious businessmen set up a savings bank to encourage thrift among the working classes. Meanwhile, Finney's wife,

Lydia, and other middle-class women carried the Christian message to the wives of the unconverted, set up Sunday schools for poor children, and formed the Female Charitable Society to assist the unemployed.

Finney's efforts to create a spiritual Christian community were not completely successful. Skilled workers in strong craft organizations—boot makers, carpenters, stonemasons, and boatbuilders—protested that they needed higher wages and better schools more urgently than sermons and prayers. Poor people ignored Finney's revival, as did Irish Catholic immigrants, many of whom hated Protestants as religious heretics and political oppressors.

Nonetheless, revivalists from New England to the Midwest copied Finney's evangelical message and techniques. In New York City, wealthy silk merchants Arthur and Lewis Tappan founded a magazine, *The Christian Evangelist*, that promoted Finney's ideas. The revivals swept through Pennsylvania, North Carolina, Tennessee, and Indiana, where, a convert reported, "you could not go upon the street and hear any conversation,

except upon religion." The success of the revivals "has been so general and thorough," concluded a Presbyterian general assembly, "that the whole customs of society have changed."

Temperance The temperance movement was the most successful social reform. Beer and rum had long been standard fare in American rituals: patriotic ceremonies, work breaks, barn raisings, and games. Long before the arrival of spirit-drinking Irish and beer-drinking German immigrants, grogshops dotted almost every block in working-class districts and were centers of disorder. During the 1820s and 1830s, alcohol consumption reached new heights, even among the elite; alcoholism killed Daniel Tompkins, vice president under James Monroe, and undermined Henry Clay's bid for the presidency. Heavy drinking was especially devastating for wage earners, who could ill afford its costs. Although Methodist artisans and ambitious

EXPLAIN CONSEQUENCES
What was Finney's central message, and how did it influence the work of reform movements?

The Drunkard's Progress: From the First Glass to the Grave
This 1846 lithograph, published by N. Currier, suggests the inevitable fate of those who drink. The drunkard's descent into "Poverty and Disease" ends with "Death by suicide," leaving a grieving and destitute wife and child. Temperance reformers urged Americans to take "The Cold Water Cure" by drinking water instead of alcoholic beverages. To promote abstinence among the young, in 1836 revivalist preacher Reverend Thomas Poage Hunt founded the Cold Water Army, an organization that grew to embrace several hundred thousand children, all of whom pledged "perpetual hate to all that can Intoxicate." Library of Congress.

A Debate over Catholic Immigration

Between 1776 and 1830, few immigrants came to the United States. Then, increasing population and poverty in Europe prompted the migration of hundreds of thousands of Germans (both Catholics and Protestants) and Irish Catholics. The sudden arrival of foreign Catholics amidst the intense Protestantism of the Second Great Awakening led to religious riots, the formation of the nativist American Party, and sharp debates in the public press. Contemporary pamphlets and books offer historians access to the public rhetoric (and the private passions) of the time.

Lyman Beecher

Catholicism Is Incompatible with Republicanism

Lyman Beecher (1775–1863) was a leading Protestant minister and the father of a remarkable family: the influential minister Henry Ward Beecher and authors Harriet Beecher Stowe (*Uncle Tom's Cabin*) and Catharine Beecher (*A Treatise on Domestic Economy*). In *A Plea for the West* (1835), Lyman Beecher warned Protestants of the powerful priestly hierarchy of the Roman Catholic Church and its opposition to republicanism. Papal encyclicals issued by Pope Gregory XVI (*Mirari Vos*, 1832) and Pope Pius IX (*Quanta Cura*, 1864) condemned republicanism, freedom of conscience, and the separation of church and state as false political ideologies.

Since the irruption of the northern barbarians, the world has never witnessed such a rush of dark-minded population from one country to another, as is now leaving Europe, and dashing upon our shores. . . . They come, also, not undirected. . . . [They] are led or followed quickly by a Catholic priesthood, who maintain over them in the land of strangers and unknown tongues an [absolute] ascendancy. . . .

The ministers of no Protestant sect could or would dare to attempt to regulate the votes of their people as the Catholic priests can do, who . . . have almost unlimited power over the conscience as it respects the performance of every civil or social duty.

There is another point of dissimilarity. . . . The opinions of the Protestant clergy are congenial with liberty — they are chosen by the people who have been educated as freemen, and they are dependent on them for patronage and support. The Catholic system is adverse to liberty, and the clergy to a great extent are dependent on foreigners [the pope and European bishops] opposed to the principles of our government.

Nor is this all. . . . How many mechanics, merchants, lawyers, physicians, in any political crisis, might [the priests] reach and render timid . . . ? A tenth part of the suffrage of the nation, thus condensed and wielded by the Catholic powers of Europe, might decide our elections, perplex our policy, inflame and divide the nation, break the bond of our union, and throw down our free institutions. . . .

[Catholicism is] a religion which never prospered but in alliance with despotic governments, has always been and still is the inflexible enemy of Liberty of conscience and free inquiry, and at this moment is the main stay of the battle against republican institutions.

Source: Lyman Beecher, *A Plea for the West* (Cincinnati: Truman & Smith, 1835), 72–73, 126, 59–63, 85–86, 59.

Orestes Brownson

Catholicism as a Necessity for Popular Government

Like Lyman Beecher, Orestes Brownson was born into the Presbyterian Church, but he quickly grew dissatisfied with its doctrines. After experimenting with Unitarianism, communalism, socialism, and transcendentalism, Brownson converted to Catholicism in 1844. A zealous convert, Brownson defended Catholicism with rigorous, provocative arguments in this article, "Catholicity Necessary to Sustain Popular Liberty" (1845).

Without the Roman Catholic religion it is impossible to preserve a democratic government, and secure its free, orderly, and wholesome action. . . . The theory of democracy is, Construct your government and commit it to the people to be taken care of . . . as they shall think proper.

It is a beautiful theory, and would work admirably, if it were not for one little difficulty, namely, the people are fallible, both individually and collectively, and governed by their passions and interests, which not unfrequently lead them far astray, and produce much mischief.

We know of but one solution of the difficulty, and that is in RELIGION. There is no foundation for virtue but in religion, and it is only religion that can command the degree of popular virtue and intelligence requisite to insure to popular government the right direction. . . . But what religion? It must be a religion which is above the people and controls them, or it will not answer the purpose. It cannot be Protestantism, [because] . . . the faith and discipline of a [Protestant] sect take any and every direction the public opinion of that sect demands. All is loose, floating, — is here to-day, is there tomorrow, and, next day, may be nowhere . . . according to the prejudices, interests, or habits of the people. . . .

Here, then, is the reason why Protestantism, though it may institute, cannot sustain popular liberty. It is itself subject to popular control, and must follow in all things the popular will, passion, interest, ignorance, prejudice, or caprice.

If Protestantism will not answer the purpose, what religion will? The Roman Catholic, or none. The Roman Catholic religion assumes, as its point of departure, that it is instituted not to be taken care of by the people, but to take care of the people; not to be governed by them, but to govern them. The word is harsh in democratic ears, we admit; but it is not the office of religion to say soft or pleasing words. . . . The people need governing, and must be governed, or nothing but anarchy and destruction await them. They must have a master. . . .

Quote our expression, THE PEOPLE MUST HAVE A MASTER, as you doubtless will; hold it up in glaring capitals, to excite the unthinking and unreasoning multitude, and to doubly fortify their prejudices against Catholicity . . . [even as you] seek to bring the people into subjection to your banks or moneyed corporations. . . .

The Roman Catholic religion, then, is necessary to sustain popular liberty, because popular liberty can be sustained only by a religion free from popular control, above the people, speaking from above and able to command them.

Source: Orestes A. Brownson, *Essays and Reviews, Chiefly on Theology, Politics, and Socialism* (New York: D. & J. Sadlier, 1852), 368–370, 372–373, 376, 379–381.

QUESTIONS FOR ANALYSIS

1. According to Beecher, what specific dangers does Catholicism pose to American republican institutions? Why do Protestant churches not pose the same dangers?

2. Compare and contrast Brownson's and Beecher's views of the social and political impact of Catholicism. How does Brownson defend the values and practices of the Catholic Church?

3. Given Brownson's statement that "the people must have a master," what would be his view of popular democratic government? Would the leaders of the Protestant Benevolent Empire agree with any aspects of Brownson's social and political philosophy?

craft workers swore off liquor to protect their work skills, health, and finances, other workers drank heavily on the job — and not just during the traditional 11 A.M. and 4 P.M. "refreshers." A baker recalled how "one man was stationed at the window to watch, while the rest drank."

The evangelical Protestants who took over the **American Temperance Society** in 1832 set out to curb the consumption of alcoholic beverages. The society grew quickly to two thousand chapters and more than 200,000 members. Its nationwide campaign employed revivalist methods — group confession and prayer, using women as spiritual guides, and sudden emotional conversion — and was a stunning success. On one day in New York City in 1841, more than 4,000 people took the temperance "pledge." The annual consumption of spirits fell dramatically, from an average of 5 gallons per person in 1830 to 2 gallons in 1845.

Evangelical reformers celebrated religion as the key to moral improvement. Laziness and drinking might be cured by self-discipline, as Benjamin Franklin had argued, but religious conversion would ensure a profound change of heart. Religious discipline and the ideology of social mobility thus served as powerful cements, bonding middle-class Americans and wage-earning citizens as they grappled with the economic divisions created by industrialization, market expansion, and increasing cultural diversity.

Immigration and Cultural Conflict

Cultural diversity was the result of a vast wave of immigration. Between 1840 and 1860, about 2 million Irish, 1.5 million Germans, and 750,000 Britons poured into the United States. The British migrants were primarily Protestants and relatively prosperous — trained professionals, propertied farmers, and skilled workers. Many German immigrants also came from propertied farming and artisan families and had sufficient resources to move to the midwestern states of Wisconsin, Iowa, and Missouri. Poorer Germans and most of the Irish settled in the Northeast, where by 1860 they numbered nearly one-third of white adults. Most immigrants avoided the South because they feared competition from enslaved workers.

Irish Poverty The poorest migrants, Irish peasants and laborers, were fleeing a famine caused by severe overpopulation and a devastating blight that destroyed much of the Irish potato crop. They settled mostly in the cities of New England and New York. The men took low-paying jobs as factory hands, construction workers, and canal diggers, while the women became washerwomen and domestic servants. Irish families crowded into cheap tenement buildings with primitive sanitation systems and were the first to die when disease struck a city. In the summer of 1849, cholera epidemics took the lives of thousands of poor immigrants in St. Louis and New York City.

In times of hardship and sorrow, immigrants turned to their churches. Many Germans and virtually all the Irish were Catholics, and they fueled the growth of the American Catholic Church. In 1840, there were 16 Catholic dioceses and 700 churches; by 1860, there were 45 dioceses and 2,500 churches. Guided by their priests and bishops, Catholics built an impressive network of institutions — charitable societies, orphanages, militia companies, parochial schools, and political organizations — that maintained both their religion and their German or Irish identity.

Nativism Confronted by Catholic and German-speaking immigrants, some American-born citizens formed **nativist movements** that condemned immigration and asserted the superiority of Protestant religious and cultural values. In 1834, artist and inventor Samuel F. B. Morse published *Foreign Conspiracy Against the Liberties of the United States*, which warned of a Catholic threat to American republican institutions. Morse argued that Catholic immigrants would obey the dictates of Pope Gregory XVI (1831–1846), who urged Catholics to repudiate republicanism and acknowledge the "submission due to princes" and to the papacy. Republican-minded Protestants of many denominations shared Morse's fears of papal interference in American life and politics, and *Foreign Conspiracy* became their handbook (American Voices, p. 308).

The social tensions stemming from industrialization intensified nativist and anti-Catholic attitudes. Unemployed Protestant mechanics and factory workers joined mobs that attacked Catholic immigrants, accusing them of taking jobs and driving down wages. These cultural conflicts undercut trade unionism, because many Protestant wage earners sided more with their Protestant employers than with their Catholic coworkers. Benevolent-minded Protestants supported the anti-Catholic movement for reasons of public policy. As crusaders for public education, they opposed the use of tax resources for Catholic schools; as advocates of temperance and civilized manners, they condemned the rowdyism of drunken Irish men.

UNDERSTAND POINTS OF VIEW
Why did the Catholic hierarchy consider republicanism a threat? Why did Morse think the same of Catholicism?

Religious and cultural tensions led to violence. In 1834, in Charlestown, Massachusetts, a quarrel between Catholic laborers repairing a convent and Protestant workers in a neighboring brickyard led to a full-scale riot and the convent's destruction. In 1844, in Philadelphia, riots erupted when the Catholic bishop persuaded public-school officials to use both Catholic and Protestant versions of the Bible. Anti-Irish violence incited by the city's nativist clubs eventually escalated into open warfare between Protestants and the Pennsylvania militia. Thus even as the American economic revolution attracted millions of European immigrants, it divided society along lines of ethnicity and religion as well as class.

SUMMARY

This chapter examined the causes of the economic transformation of the first half of the nineteenth century. That transformation had two facets: a major increase in production—the Industrial Revolution—and the expansion of commerce—the Market Revolution. Water, steam, and minerals such as coal and iron were crucial ingredients in both revolutions—driving factory machinery, carrying goods to market on canals and rivers, and propelling steamboats and railroad engines.

We also explored the consequences of that transformation: the rise of an urban society, the increasing similarity between the Northeast and Midwest and their growing difference from the South, and the creation of a society divided by class and ethnicity. To shape this emerging society, benevolent reformers and evangelical revivalists worked to instill moral discipline and Christian values. However, artisan republicans, unionized workers, and Irish and German immigrants had their own cultural values and economic interests. The result was a fragmented society. As the next chapter suggests, Americans looked to their political system, which was becoming increasingly democratic, to address these social divisions. In fact, the tensions among economic inequality, cultural diversity, and political democracy became a troubling—and enduring—part of American life.

CHAPTER REVIEW

MAKE IT STICK   Go to **LearningCurve** to retain what you've read.

TERMS TO KNOW   Identify and explain the significance of each term below.

Key Concepts & Events

Industrial Revolution (p. 286)
division of labor (p. 286)
mineral-based economy (p. 287)
mechanics (p. 287)
Waltham-Lowell System (p. 288)
machine tools (p. 290)
artisan republicanism (p. 291)
unions (p. 291)
labor theory of value (p. 292)
Market Revolution (p. 293)

Erie Canal (p. 293)
middle class (p. 302)
self-made man (p. 304)
Benevolent Empire (p. 305)
Sabbatarian values (p. 306)
moral free agency (p. 306)
American Temperance Society (p. 310)
nativist movements (p. 310)

Key People

Samuel Slater (p. 287)
Francis Cabot Lowell (p. 287)
Sellars Family (p. 290)
Eli Whitney (p. 290)
Cyrus McCormick (p. 300)
Lyman Beecher (p. 305)
Charles Grandison Finney and Lydia Finney (p. 305)

REVIEW QUESTIONS
Answer these questions to demonstrate your understanding of the chapter's main ideas.

1. What was the impact of the economic revolution on the various social groups and classes?

2. What different types of reform movements arose during this period, and what types of change did they advocate? What strategies did they use, and how successful were they in their efforts?

3. Did the Industrial and Market revolutions make America a more "republican" society? Or did they undermine republicanism? Defend your interpretation by reference to specific events and developments.

4. **THEMATIC UNDERSTANDING** Review the events listed under "Work, Exchange, and Technology" on the thematic timeline on page 283. In what ways was the economy different in 1860 from what it had been in 1800? Which factors listed in the thematic timeline best explain the changes?

MAKING CONNECTIONS
Recognize the larger developments and continuities within and across chapters by answering these questions.

1. **ACROSS TIME AND PLACE** How did the economic revolution described in Chapter 9 affect the lives of women in various social groups, and how did it make their experiences different from those of their mothers, whose political and social lives were explored in Chapter 6 on the American Revolution, and their grandmothers, whose work lives and cultural experiences were considered in Chapter 4?

2. **VISUAL EVIDENCE** Look again at three images, the women weavers from Maine (p. 285), the woodworker (p. 292), and the Hartford family (p. 302). Taken together, what insights do they provide into the different aspects and social consequences of the Economic Revolution?

MORE TO EXPLORE
Start here to learn more about the events discussed in this chapter.

Stuart M. Blumin, *The Emergence of the Middle Class* (1989). Discusses urban class formation during the nineteenth century.

Stephen P. Rice, *Minding the Machine* (2004). Analyzes the ways in which language reflects and undergirds changing social and cultural relationships.

Scott A. Sandage, *Born Losers: A History of Failure in America* (2005). Focuses on failed entrepreneurs and the changing cultural meaning of failure.

Charles G. Sellers, *The Market Revolution: Jacksonian America, 1815–1846* (1991). Explores the social impact of economic change.

Laurel Thatcher Ulrich, *The Age of Homespun* (2001). Uses objects of early craft production to tell absorbing stories that reveal broad historical developments.

For a textile operative's account of mill life, see **fordham.edu/halsall/mod/robinson-lowell.html**.

For religion and benevolent societies, consult **loc.gov/exhibits/religion/rel07.html**.

TIMELINE   Ask yourself why this chapter begins and ends with these dates and then identify the links among related events.

1782	• Oliver Evans builds automated flour mill
1790	• Samuel Slater opens spinning mill in Providence, Rhode Island
1792	• Congress passes Post Office Act
1793	• Eli Whitney devises cotton gin
1814	• Boston Manufacturing Company opens factory in Waltham, Massachusetts
1816–1828	• Congress levies protective tariffs
1817	• Erie Canal begun (completed in 1825)
1820–1840	• Urban population surges in Northeast and Midwest; shoe entrepreneurs adopt division of labor
1820s	• New England women take textile jobs • Rise of Benevolent Empire spurs conservative social reforms
1824	• *Gibbons v. Ogden* promotes interstate trade
1830s	• Emergence of western commercial cities • Labor movement gains strength • Middle-class culture emerges • Growth of temperance movement
1830	• Charles G. Finney begins Rochester revivals
1840s	• Irish and German immigration sparks ethnic riots • Maturation of machine-tool industry
1842	• *Commonwealth v. Hunt* legitimizes trade unions
1850s	• Expansion of railroads in Northeast and Midwest
1857	• Overproduction and speculation trigger a business recession

KEY TURNING POINT: Many of the early timeline entries concern economic matters, while later entries refer to other subjects. Based on your reading of the chapter, when and why does this change in emphasis occur?

A Democratic Revolution
1800–1844

Europeans who visited the United States in the 1830s mostly praised its republican society but not its political parties and politicians. "The gentlemen spit, talk of elections and the price of produce, and spit again," Frances Trollope reported in *Domestic Manners of the Americans* (1832). In her view, American politics was the sport of self-serving party politicians who reeked of "whiskey and onions." Other Europeans lamented the low intellectual level of American political debate. The "clap-trap of praise and pathos" from a Massachusetts politician "deeply disgusted" Harriet Martineau, while the shallow arguments advanced by the inept "farmers, shopkeepers, and country lawyers" who sat in the New York assembly astonished Basil Hall.

The negative verdict was nearly unanimous. "The most able men in the United States are very rarely placed at the head of affairs," French aristocrat Alexis de Tocqueville concluded in *Democracy in America* (1835). The reason, said Tocqueville, lay in the character of democracy itself. Most citizens ignored important policy issues, jealously refused to elect their intellectual superiors, and listened in awe to "the clamor of a mountebank [a charismatic fraud] who knows the secret of stimulating their tastes."

These Europeans were witnessing the American Democratic Revolution. Before 1815, men of ability had sat in the seats of government, and the prevailing ideology had been republicanism, or rule by "men of TALENTS and VIRTUE," as a newspaper put it. Many of those leaders feared popular rule, so they wrote constitutions with Bills of Rights, bicameral legislatures, and independent judiciaries, and they censured overambitious men who campaigned for public office. But history took a different course. By the 1820s and 1830s, the watchwords were *democracy* and *party politics*, a system run by men who avidly sought office and rallied supporters through newspapers, broadsides, and great public processions. Politics became a sport—a competitive contest for the votes of ordinary men. "That the majority should govern was a fundamental maxim in all free governments," declared Martin Van Buren, the most talented of the new breed of professional politicians. A republican-minded Virginian condemned Van Buren as "too great an intriguer," but by encouraging ordinary Americans to burn with "election fever" and support party principles, he and other politicians redefined the meaning of democratic government and made it work.

IDENTIFY THE BIG IDEA

What were the main features of the Democratic Revolution, and what role did Andrew Jackson play in its outcome?

The Politics of Democracy   As ordinary American men asserted a claim to a voice in government affairs, politicians catered to their preferences and prejudices. Aspiring candidates took their messages to voters, in rural hamlets as well as large towns. This detail from George Caleb Bingham's *Stump Speaking* (1855) shows a swanky, tail-coated politician on an improvised stage seeking the votes of an audience of well-dressed gentlemen and local farmers—identified by their broad-brimmed hats and casual attire.

The Rise of Popular Politics, 1810–1828

Expansion of the **franchise** (the right to vote) dramatically symbolized the Democratic Revolution. By the 1830s, most states allowed nearly all white men to vote. Nowhere else in the world did ordinary farmers and wage earners exercise such political influence; in England, the Reform Bill of 1832 extended the vote to only 600,000 out of 6 million men — a mere 10 percent. Equally important, political parties provided voters with the means to express their preferences.

The Decline of the Notables and the Rise of Parties

The American Revolution weakened the elite-run society of the colonial era but did not overthrow it. Only two states — Pennsylvania and Vermont — gave the vote to all male taxpayers, and many families of low rank continued to defer to their social "betters." Consequently, wealthy **notables** — northern landlords, slave-owning planters, and seaport merchants — dominated the political system in the new republic. And rightly so, said John Jay, the first chief justice of the Supreme Court: "Those who own the country are the most fit persons to participate in the government of it." Jay and other notables managed local elections by building up an "interest": lending money to small farmers, giving business to storekeepers, and treating their tenants to rum. An outlay of $20 for refreshments, remarked one poll watcher, "may produce about 100 votes." This gentry-dominated system kept men who lacked wealth and powerful family connections from seeking office.

The Rise of Democracy To expand the suffrage, Maryland reformers in the 1810s invoked the equal-rights rhetoric of republicanism. They charged that property qualifications for voting were a "tyranny" because they endowed "one class of men with privileges which are denied to another." To defuse such arguments and deter migration to the West, legislators in Maryland and other seaboard states grudgingly accepted a broader franchise and its democratic results. The new voters often rejected candidates who wore "top boots, breeches, and shoe buckles," their hair in "powder and queues." Instead, they elected men who dressed simply and endorsed popular rule.

Smallholding farmers and ambitious laborers in the Midwest and Southwest likewise challenged the old hierarchical order. In Ohio, a traveler reported, "no white man or woman will bear being called a servant." The constitutions of the new states of Indiana (1816), Illinois (1818), and Alabama (1819) prescribed a broad male franchise, and voters usually elected middling men to local and state offices. A well-to-do migrant in Illinois was surprised to learn that the man who plowed his fields "was a colonel of militia, and a member of the legislature." Once in public office, men from modest backgrounds restricted imprisonment for debt, kept taxes low, and allowed farmers to claim squatters' rights to unoccupied land.

By the mid-1820s, many state legislatures had given the vote to all white men or to all men who paid taxes or served in the militia. Only a few — North Carolina, Virginia, and Rhode Island — still required the possession of freehold property. Equally significant, between 1818 and 1821, Connecticut, Massachusetts, and New York wrote more democratic constitutions that reapportioned legislative districts on the basis of population and mandated the popular election (rather than the appointment) of judges and justices of the peace.

Democratic politics was contentious and, because it attracted ambitious men, often corrupt. Powerful entrepreneurs and speculators — both notables and self-made men — demanded government assistance and paid bribes to get it. Speculators won land grants by paying off the members of important committees, and bankers distributed shares of stock to key legislators. When the Seventh Ward Bank of New York City received a legislative charter in 1833, the bank's officials set aside one-third of the 3,700 shares of stock for themselves and their friends and almost two-thirds for state legislators and bureaucrats, leaving just 40 shares for public sale (America Compared, p. 317).

More political disputes broke out when religious reformers sought laws to enforce the cultural agenda of the Benevolent Empire. In Utica, New York, evangelical Presbyterians insisted upon a town ordinance restricting Sunday entertainment. In response, a member of the local Universalist church — a freethinking Protestant denomination — denounced the measure as coercive and called for "Religious Liberty."

Parties Take Command The appearance of political parties encouraged such debates over government policy. Revolutionary-era Americans had condemned political "factions" as antirepublican, and the new state

IDENTIFY CAUSES
What was the relationship between the growth of democracy and the emergence of political parties?

Alexis de Tocqueville

Letter to Louis de Kergorlay, June 29, 1831

In 1831, the French aristocrat Alexis de Tocqueville (1805–1859) came to the United States to report on its innovative penal system. Instead, he produced a brilliant analysis of the new republican society and politics, *Democracy in America* (1835, 1840). This letter to a French friend reveals his thinking and insights.

Do you know what, in this country's political realm, makes the most vivid impression on me? The effect of laws governing inheritance. . . . The English had exported their laws of primogeniture, according to which the eldest acquired three-quarters of the father's fortune. This resulted in a host of vast territorial domains passing from father to son and wealth remaining in families. My American informants tell me that there was no aristocracy but, instead, a class of great landowners leading a simple, rather intellectual life characterized by its air of good breeding, its manners, and a strong sense of family pride. . . . Since then, inheritance laws have been revised.

Primogeniture gave way to equal division, with almost magical results. Domains split up, passing into other hands. Family spirit disappeared. The aristocratic bias that marked the republic's early years was replaced by a democratic thrust of irresistible force. . . . I've seen several members of these old families. . . . They regret the loss of everything aristocratic: patronage, family pride, high tone. . . .

There can be no doubt that the inheritance law is responsible in some considerable measure for this complete triumph of democratic principles. The Americans . . . agree that "it has made us what we are, it is the foundation of our republic." . . .

When I apply these ideas to France, I cannot resist the thought that Louis XVIII's charter [of 1814 sought to restore the pre-Revolutionary regime by creating] . . . aristocratic institutions in political law, but [by mandating equality before the law and retaining the Revolutionary-era inheritance laws giving all children, irrespective of sex, an equal share of the parental estate] within the domain of civil law gave shelter to a democratic principle

so vigorous that it was bound before long to destroy the foundations of the edifice it raised. . . . We are moving toward an unrestricted democracy . . . that . . . would not suit France at all. . . . [However,] there is no human power capable of changing the law of inheritance, and with this change our families will disappear, possessions will pass into other hands, wealth will be increasingly equalized, the upper class will melt into the middle, the latter will become immense and shape everything to its level. . . .

What I see in America leaves me doubting that government by the multitude, even under the most favorable circumstances — and they exist here — is a good thing. There is general agreement that in the early days of the republic, statesmen and members of the two legislative houses were much more distinguished than they are today. They almost all belonged to that class of landowners I mentioned above. The populace no longer chooses with such a sure hand. It generally favors those who flatter its passions and descend to its level.

Source: From *Letters from America: Alexis de Tocqueville*, edited, translated, and with an introduction by Frederick Brown, Yale University Press, 2010. Copyright © 2010 by Frederick Brown. Used by permission of Yale University Press.

QUESTIONS FOR ANALYSIS

1. According to Tocqueville, what is the legal basis of American social equality and political democracy? What is the comparable situation in France?
2. Why does Tocqueville doubt that democratic rule is a good thing, even in the United States, and "would not suit France at all"?

and national constitutions made no mention of political parties. However, as the power of notables waned in the 1820s, disciplined political parties appeared in a number of states. Usually they were run by professional politicians, often middle-class lawyers and journalists. One observer called the new parties **political machines** because, like the new power-driven textile looms, they

efficiently wove together the interests of diverse social and economic groups.

Martin Van Buren of New York was the chief architect of the emerging system of party government. The ambitious son of a Jeffersonian tavern keeper, Van Buren grew up in the landlord-dominated society of the Hudson River Valley. To get training as a lawyer, he

Martin Van Buren

Martin Van Buren's skills as a lawyer and a politician won him many admirers, as did his personal charm, sharp intellect, and imperturbable composure. "Little Van"—a mere 5 feet 6 inches in height—had almost as many detractors. Davy Crockett, Kentucky frontiersman, land speculator, and congressman, labeled him "an artful, cunning, intriguing, selfish lawyer," concerned only with "office and money." In truth, Van Buren was a complex man, a middle-class lawyer with republican values and aristocratic tastes who nonetheless created a democratic political party. National Portrait Gallery, Smithsonian Institution/Art Resource, NY.

 To see a longer excerpt of Martin Van Buren's autobiography, along with other primary sources from this period, see *Sources for America's History.*

relied on the Van Ness clan, a powerful local gentry family. Then, determined not to become their dependent "tool," Van Buren repudiated their tutelage and set out to create a political order based on party identity, not family connections. In justifying party governments, Van Buren rejected the traditional republican belief that political factions were dangerous and claimed that the opposite was true: "All men of sense know that political parties are inseparable from free government," because they checked an elected official's inherent "disposition to abuse power."

Between 1817 and 1821 in New York, Van Buren turned his "Bucktail" supporters (who wore a deer's tail on their hats) into the first statewide political machine. He purchased a newspaper, the *Albany Argus*, and used it to promote his policies and get out the vote. Patronage was an even more important tool. When Van Buren's Bucktails won control of the New York legislature in 1821, they acquired the power to appoint some six thousand of their friends to positions in New York's legal bureaucracy of judges, justices of the peace, sheriffs, deed commissioners, and coroners. Critics called this ruthless distribution of offices a **spoils system**, but Van Buren argued it was fair, operating "sometimes in favour of one party, and sometimes of another." Party government was thoroughly republican, he added, because it reflected the preferences of a majority of the citizenry. To ensure the passage of the party's legislative program, Van Buren insisted on disciplined voting as determined by a **caucus**, a meeting of party leaders. On one crucial occasion, the "Little Magician"—a nickname reflecting Van Buren's short stature and political dexterity—honored seventeen New York legislators for sacrificing "individual preferences for the general good" of the party.

The Election of 1824

The advance of political democracy in the states undermined the traditional notable-dominated system of national politics. After the War of 1812, the aristocratic Federalist Party virtually disappeared, and the Republican Party splintered into competing factions (Chapter 7). As the election of 1824 approached, five Republican candidates campaigned for the presidency. Three were veterans of President James Monroe's cabinet: Secretary of State John Quincy Adams, the son of former president John Adams; Secretary of War John C. Calhoun; and Secretary of the Treasury William H. Crawford. The other candidates were Henry Clay of Kentucky, the hard-drinking, dynamic Speaker of the House of Representatives; and General Andrew Jackson, now a senator from Tennessee. When the Republican caucus in Congress selected Crawford as the party's official nominee, the other candidates took their case to the voters. Thanks to democratic reforms, eighteen of the twenty-four states required popular elections (rather than a vote of the state legislature) to choose their representatives to the electoral college.

Each candidate had strengths. Thanks to his diplomatic successes as secretary of state, John Quincy

Adams enjoyed national recognition; and his family's prestige in Massachusetts ensured him the electoral votes of New England. Henry Clay based his candidacy on the **American System**, his integrated mercantilist program of national economic development similar to the Commonwealth System of the state governments. Clay wanted to strengthen the Second Bank of the United States, raise tariffs, and use tariff revenues to finance **internal improvements**, that is, public works such as roads and canals. His nationalistic program won praise in the West, which needed better transportation, but elicited sharp criticism in the South, which relied on rivers to market its cotton and had few manufacturing industries to protect. William Crawford of Georgia, an ideological heir of Thomas Jefferson, denounced Clay's American System as a scheme to "consolidate" political power in Washington. Recognizing Crawford's appeal in the South, John C. Calhoun of South Carolina withdrew from the race and endorsed Andrew Jackson.

As the hero of the Battle of New Orleans, Jackson benefitted from the surge of patriotism after the War of 1812. Born in the Carolina backcountry, Jackson settled in Nashville, Tennessee, where he formed ties to influential families through marriage and a career as an attorney and a slave-owning cotton planter. His rise from common origins symbolized the new democratic age, and his reputation as a "plain solid republican" attracted voters in all regions. Still, Jackson's strong showing in the electoral college surprised most political leaders. The Tennessee senator received 99 electoral votes; Adams garnered 84 votes; Crawford, struck down by a stroke during the campaign, won 41; and Clay finished with 37 (Map 10.1).

Because no candidate received an absolute majority, the Twelfth Amendment to the Constitution (ratified in 1804) set the rules: the House of Representatives would choose the president from among the three highest vote-getters. This procedure hurt Jackson because many congressmen feared that the rough-hewn "military chieftain" might become a tyrant. Excluded from the race, Henry Clay used his influence as Speaker to thwart Jackson's election. Clay assembled a coalition of representatives from New England and the Ohio River Valley that voted Adams into the presidency in 1825. Adams showed his gratitude by appointing Clay his secretary of state, the traditional stepping-stone to the presidency. Clay's appointment was politically fatal for both men: Jackson's supporters accused Clay and Adams of making a **corrupt bargain**, and they vowed to oppose Adams's policies and to prevent Clay's rise to the presidency.

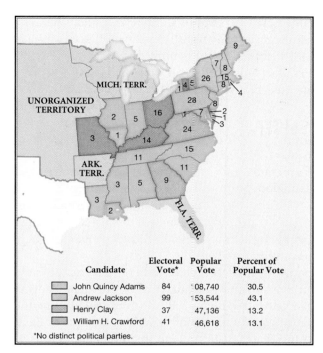

Candidate	Electoral Vote*	Popular Vote	Percent of Popular Vote
John Quincy Adams	84	108,740	30.5
Andrew Jackson	99	153,544	43.1
Henry Clay	37	47,136	13.2
William H. Crawford	41	46,618	13.1

*No distinct political parties.

MAP 10.1
The Presidential Election of 1824
Regional voting was the dominant pattern in 1824. John Quincy Adams captured every electoral vote in New England and most of those in New York; Henry Clay carried Ohio and Kentucky, the most populous trans-Appalachian states; and William Crawford took the southern states of Virginia and Georgia. Only Andrew Jackson claimed a national constituency, winning Pennsylvania and New Jersey in the East, Indiana and most of Illinois in the Midwest, and much of the South. Only 356,000 Americans voted, about 27 percent of the eligible electorate.

The Last Notable President: John Quincy Adams

As president, Adams called for bold national action. "The moral purpose of the Creator," he told Congress, was to use the president to "improve the conditions of himself and his fellow men." Adams called for the establishment of a national university in Washington, scientific explorations in the Far West, and a uniform standard of weights and measures. Most important, he endorsed Henry Clay's American System and its three key elements: protective tariffs to stimulate manufacturing, federally subsidized roads and canals to facilitate commerce, and a national bank to control credit and provide a uniform currency.

UNDERSTAND POINTS OF VIEW
Why did Jacksonians consider the political deal between Adams and Clay "corrupt"?

The Fate of Adams's Policies Manufacturers, entrepreneurs, and farmers in the Northeast and Midwest welcomed Adams's proposals. However, his policies won little support in the South, where planters opposed protective tariffs because these taxes raised the price of manufactures. Southern smallholders also feared powerful banks that could force them into bankruptcy. From his deathbed, Thomas Jefferson condemned Adams for promoting "a single and splendid government of [a monied] aristocracy . . . riding and ruling over the plundered ploughman and beggared yeomanry."

EXPLAIN CAUSES
What were the successes and failures of John Adams's presidency, and what accounted for those outcomes?

Other politicians objected to the American System on constitutional grounds. In 1817, President Madison had vetoed the Bonus Bill, which proposed using the national government's income from the Second Bank of the United States to fund improvement projects in the states. Such projects, Madison argued, were the sole responsibility of the states, a sentiment shared by the Republican followers of Thomas Jefferson. In 1824, Martin Van Buren likewise declared his allegiance to the constitutional "doctrines of the Jefferson School" and his opposition to **"consolidated government,"** a powerful and potentially oppressive national administration. Now a member of the U.S. Senate, Van Buren helped to defeat most of Adams's proposed subsidies for roads and canals.

The Tariff Battle The major battle of the Adams administration came over tariffs. The Tariff of 1816 had placed relatively high duties on imports of cheap English cotton cloth, allowing New England textile producers to control that segment of the market. In 1824, Adams and Clay secured a new tariff that protected New England and Pennsylvania manufacturers from more expensive woolen and cotton textiles and also English iron goods. Without these tariffs, British imports would have dominated the market and significantly inhibited American industrial development (Chapter 9, America Compared, p. 289).

Recognizing the appeal of tariffs, Van Buren and his Jacksonian allies hopped on the bandwagon. By increasing duties on wool, hemp, and other imported raw materials, they hoped to win the support of farmers in New York, Ohio, and Kentucky for Jackson's presidential candidacy in 1828. The tariff had become a political weapon. "I fear this tariff thing," remarked Thomas Cooper, the president of the College of South Carolina and an advocate of free trade. "[B]y some strange mechanical contrivance [it has become] . . . a machine for manufacturing Presidents, instead of broadcloths, and bed blankets." Disregarding southern protests, northern Jacksonians joined with supporters of Adams and Clay to enact the Tariff of 1828, which raised duties significantly on raw materials, textiles, and iron goods.

The new tariff enraged the South, which produced the world's cheapest raw cotton and did not need to protect its main industry. Moreover, the tariff cost southern planters about $100 million a year. Planters had to buy either higher-cost American textiles and iron goods, thus enriching northeastern businesses and workers, or highly dutied British imports, thus paying the expenses of the national government. The new tariff was "little less than legalized pillage," an Alabama legislator declared, calling it a **Tariff of Abominations**. Ignoring the Jacksonians' support for the Tariff of 1828, most southerners heaped blame on President Adams.

Southern governments also criticized Adams's Indian policy. A deeply moral man, the president supported the treaty-guaranteed land rights of Native

A CARTOON COMPARING CONDITIONS UNDER FREE TRADE AND PROTECTIVE TARIFF
From "The United States Weekly Telegram," November 5, 1832.

The "Tariff of Abominations"
Political cartoons enjoyed wide use in eighteenth-century England and became popular in the United States during the political battles of the First Party System (1794–1815). By the 1820s, American newspapers, the mouthpiece of political parties, published cartoons daily. This cartoon attacks the tariffs of 1828 and 1832 as hostile to the prosperity of the South. The gaunt figure on the left represents a southern planter, starved by high tariff duties, while the northern textile manufacturer has grown stout feasting on the bounty of protectionism. © Bettmann/Corbis.

Americans against expansion-minded whites. In 1825, U.S. commissioners had secured a treaty from one faction of Creeks ceding its lands in Georgia to the United States for eventual sale to the state's citizens. When the Creek National Council repudiated the treaty, claiming that it was fraudulent, Adams called for new negotiations. In response, Georgia governor George M. Troup attacked the president as a "public enemy . . . the unblushing ally of the savages." Mobilizing Georgia's congressional delegation, Troup persuaded Congress to extinguish the Creeks' land titles, forcing most Creeks to leave the state.

Elsewhere, Adams's primary weakness was his out-of-date political style. The last notable to serve in the White House, he acted the part: aloof, inflexible, and paternalistic. When Congress rejected his activist economic policies, Adams accused its members of following the whims of public opinion and told them not to be enfeebled "by the will of our constituents." Ignoring his waning popularity, the president refused to dismiss hostile federal bureaucrats or to award offices to his supporters. Rather than "run" for reelection in 1828, Adams "stood" for it, telling friends, "If my country wants my services, she must ask for them."

"The Democracy" and the Election of 1828

Martin Van Buren and the politicians handling Andrew Jackson's campaign for the presidency had no reservations about running for office. To put Jackson in the White House, Van Buren revived the political coalition created by Thomas Jefferson, championing policies that appealed to both southern planters and northern farmers and artisans, the "plain Republicans of the North." John C. Calhoun, Jackson's running mate, brought his South Carolina allies into Van Buren's party, and Jackson's close friends in Tennessee rallied voters throughout the Old Southwest. The Little Magician hoped that a national party would reconcile the diverse "interests" that, as James Madison suggested in "Federalist No. 10" (Chapter 6), inevitably existed in a large republic. Equally important, added Jackson's ally Duff Green, it would put the "anti-slave party in the North . . . to sleep for twenty years to come."

At Van Buren's direction, the Jacksonians orchestrated a massive publicity campaign. In New York, fifty Democrat-funded newspapers declared their support for Jackson. Elsewhere, Jacksonians used mass meetings, torchlight parades, and barbecues to celebrate the candidate's frontier origin and rise to fame. They praised "Old Hickory" as a "natural" aristocrat, a self-made man.

The Jacksonians called themselves Democrats or "the Democracy" to convey their egalitarian message. As Thomas Morris told the Ohio legislature, Democrats were fighting for equality: the republic had been corrupted by legislative charters that gave "a few individuals rights and privileges not enjoyed by the citizens at large." Morris promised that the Democracy would destroy such "artificial distinction." Jackson himself declared that "equality among the people in the rights conferred by government" was the "great radical principle of freedom."

Jackson's message appealed to many social groups. His hostility to corporations and to Clay's American System won support from northeastern artisans and workers who felt threatened by industrialization. Jackson also captured the votes of Pennsylvania ironworkers and New York farmers who had benefitted from the controversial Tariff of Abominations. Yet, by astutely declaring his support for a "judicious" tariff that would balance regional interests, Jackson remained popular in the South. Old Hickory likewise garnered votes in the Southeast and Midwest, where his well-known hostility toward Native Americans reassured white farmers seeking Indian removal.

> **TRACE CHANGE OVER TIME**
>
> Jackson lost the presidential election of 1824 and won in 1828: what changes explain these different outcomes?

The Democrats' celebration of popular rule carried Jackson into office. In 1824, about one-quarter of the electorate had voted; in 1828, more than one-half went to the polls, and 56 percent voted for the Tennessee senator (Figure 10.1 and Map 10.2). The first president from a trans-Appalachian state, Jackson cut a dignified figure as he traveled to Washington. He "wore his hair carelessly but not ungracefully arranged," an English observer noted, "and in spite of his harsh, gaunt features looked like a gentleman and a soldier." Still, Jackson's popularity and sharp temper frightened men of wealth. Senator Daniel Webster of Massachusetts, a former Federalist and now a corporate lawyer, warned his clients that the new president would "bring a breeze with him. Which way it will blow, I cannot tell [but] . . . my fear is stronger than my hope." Supreme Court justice Joseph Story shared Webster's apprehensions. Watching an unruly Inauguration Day crowd climb over the elegant White House furniture to congratulate Jackson, Story lamented that "the reign of King 'Mob' seemed triumphant."

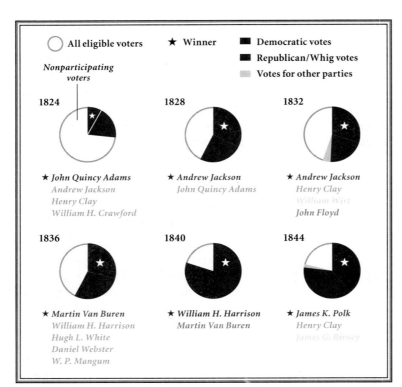

FIGURE 10.1

The Rise of Voter Turnout, 1824–1844

As the shrinking white sections of these pie graphs indicate, the proportion of eligible voters who cast ballots in presidential elections increased dramatically over time. In 1824, 27 percent voted; in 1840 and thereafter, about 80 percent went to the polls. Voter participation soared first in 1828, when Andrew Jackson and John Quincy Adams contested for the White House, and again in 1840, as competition heated up between Democrats and Whigs, who advocated different policies and philosophies of government. Democrats won most of these contests because their policies had greater appeal to ordinary citizens.

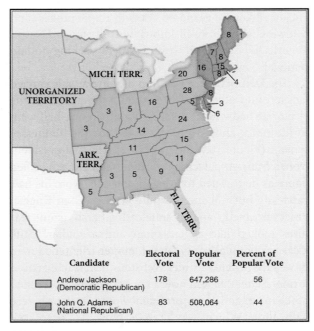

MAP 10.2

The Presidential Election of 1828

As in 1824, John Quincy Adams carried all of New England and some of the Mid-Atlantic states. However, Andrew Jackson swept the rest of the nation and won a resounding victory in the electoral college. Over 1.1 million American men cast ballots in 1828, more than three times the number who voted in 1824.

The Jacksonian Presidency, 1829–1837

American-style political democracy—a broad franchise, a disciplined political party, and policies favoring specific interests—ushered Andrew Jackson into office. Jackson used his popular mandate to transform the policies of the national government and the definition of the presidency. During his two terms, he enhanced presidential authority, destroyed the mercantilist and nationalist American System, and established a new ideology of limited government. An Ohio supporter summed up Jackson's vision: "the Sovereignty of the People, the Rights of the States, and a Light and Simple Government."

Jackson's Agenda: Rotation and Decentralization

To make policy, Jackson relied primarily on his so-called Kitchen Cabinet. Its most influential members were two Kentuckians, Francis Preston Blair, who edited the *Washington Globe*, and Amos Kendall, who wrote Jackson's speeches; Roger B. Taney of Maryland, who became attorney general, treasury secretary, and

President Andrew Jackson, 1830

The new president came to Washington with a well-deserved reputation as an aggressive Indian fighter and unpredictable military leader. In this official portrait, Jackson looks "presidential"—his dress and posture, and the artist's composition, conveyed an image of a calm, deliberate statesman. Subsequent events would show that Jackson had not lost his hard-edged authoritarian personality. Library of Congress.

then chief justice of the Supreme Court; and Martin Van Buren, whom Jackson named secretary of state.

Following Van Buren's example in New York, Jackson used patronage to create a disciplined national party. He rejected the idea of "property in office" (that a qualified official held a position permanently) and insisted on a rotation of officeholders when a new administration took power. Rotation would not lessen expertise, Jackson insisted, because public duties were "so plain and simple that men of intelligence may readily qualify themselves for their performance." William L. Marcy, a New York Jacksonian, offered a more realistic explanation for rotation: government jobs were like the spoils of war, and "to the victor belong the spoils of the enemy." Jackson used those spoils to reward his allies and win backing for his policies.

Jackson's highest priority was to destroy the American System. He believed that Henry Clay's system—and all government-sponsored plans for national economic development—were contrary to the Constitution, encouraged "consolidated government," and, through higher tariffs, increased the burden of taxation. As Clay noted apprehensively, the new president wanted "to cry down old [expansive, Hamiltonian] constructions of the Constitution . . . to make all Jefferson's opinions the articles of faith of the new Church." Declaring that the "voice of the people" called for "economy in the expenditures of the Government," Jackson rejected national subsidies for transportation projects. Invoking constitutional arguments, he vetoed four internal improvement bills in 1830, including an extension of the National Road, arguing that they infringed on "the reserved powers of states." By eliminating potential expenditures by the federal government, these vetoes also undermined the case for protective tariffs. As Jacksonian senator William Smith of South Carolina pointed out, "[D]estroy internal improvements and you leave no motive for the tariff."

> **IDENTIFY CAUSES**
> Jackson cut the national budget and the national debt but increased the number of federal employees. How do you explain this paradox?

The Tariff and Nullification

The Tariff of 1828 had helped Jackson win the presidency, but it saddled him with a major political crisis. There was fierce opposition to high tariffs throughout the South and especially in South Carolina. That state was the only one with an African American majority—56 percent of the population in 1830—and its slave owners, like the white sugar planters in the West Indies, feared a black rebellion. Even more, they worried about the legal abolition of slavery. The British Parliament had declared that slavery in its West Indian colonies would end in 1833; South Carolina planters, vividly recalling northern efforts to end slavery in Missouri (Chapter 8), worried that the U.S. Congress would follow the British lead. So they attacked the tariff, both to lower rates and to discourage the use of federal power to attack slavery.

The crisis began in 1832, when high-tariff congressmen ignored southern warnings that they were "endangering the Union" and reenacted the Tariff of Abominations. In response, leading South Carolinians called a state convention, which in November boldly adopted an Ordinance of Nullification declaring the tariffs of 1828 and 1832 to be null and void. The ordinance

The rejected Minister,
*We never can make him President,
without first making him Vice-president.*
Vide webb.
Pub by H Anthon Nº 214 Broadway. N.Y.

UNDERSTAND POINTS OF VIEW
How did South Carolina justify nullification on constitutional grounds?

prohibited the collection of those duties in South Carolina after February 1, 1833, and threatened secession if federal officials tried to collect them.

South Carolina's act of **nullification**—the argument that a state has the right to void, within its borders, a law passed by Congress—rested on the constitutional arguments developed in *The South Carolina Exposition and Protest* (1828). Written anonymously by Vice President John C. Calhoun, the *Exposition* gave a localist (or sectional) interpretation to the federal union. Because each state or geographic region had distinct interests, localists argued, protective tariffs and other national legislation that operated unequally on the various states lacked fairness and legitimacy—in fact, they were unconstitutional. An obsessive defender of the interests of southern slave owners, Calhoun exaggerated the frequency and severity of such legislation, declaring, "Constitutional government and the government of a majority are utterly incompatible."

Calhoun's constitutional doctrines reflected the arguments advanced by Jefferson and Madison in the Kentucky and Virginia Resolutions of 1798. Those resolutions asserted that, because state-based conventions had ratified the Constitution, sovereignty lay in the states, not in the people. Beginning from this premise, Calhoun argued that a state convention could declare a congressional law to be void within the state's borders. Replying to this **states' rights** interpretation of the Constitution, which had little support in the text of the document, Senator Daniel Webster of Massachusetts presented a nationalist interpretation that celebrated popular sovereignty and Congress's responsibility to secure the "general welfare."

Jackson hoped to find a middle path between Webster's strident nationalism and Calhoun's radical doctrine of localist federalism. The Constitution clearly gave the federal government the authority to establish tariffs, and Jackson vowed to enforce it. He declared that South Carolina's Ordinance of Nullification violated the letter of the Constitution and was "destructive of the great object for which it was formed." More pointedly, he warned, "Disunion by armed force is treason." At Jackson's request, Congress in early 1833 passed a military Force Bill, authorizing the president to compel South Carolina's obedience to national laws. Simultaneously, Jackson addressed the South's objections to high import duties with a new tariff act that,

The Great Webster-Hayne Debate, 1830

The "Tariff of Abominations" sparked one of the great debates in American history. When Senator Robert Y. Hayne of South Carolina (seated in the middle of the picture, with his legs crossed) opposed the federal tariffs by invoking the doctrines of states' rights and nullification, Daniel Webster rose to the defense of the Union. Speaking for two days to a spellbound Senate, Webster delivered an impassioned oration that celebrated the unity of the American people as the key to their freedom. His parting words— "Liberty and Union, now and forever, one and inseparable!" —quickly became part of the national memory. "Webster's Reply to Haynes," by G.P.A. Healy, City of Boston Art Commission.

over the course of a decade, reduced rates to the modest levels of 1816. Subsequently, export-hungry midwestern wheat farmers joined southern planters in advocating low duties to avoid retaliatory tariffs by foreign nations. "Illinois wants a market for her agricultural products," declared Senator Sidney Breese in 1846. "[S]he wants the market of the world."

Having won the political battle by securing a tariff reduction, the South Carolina convention did not press its constitutional stance on nullification. Jackson was satisfied. He had assisted the South economically while upholding the constitutional principle of national authority—a principle that Abraham Lincoln would embrace to defend the Union during the secession crisis of 1861.

The Bank War

In the midst of the tariff crisis, Jackson faced a major challenge from politicians who supported the **Second Bank of the United States**. Founded in Philadelphia in

1816 (Chapter 7), the bank was privately managed and operated under a twenty-year charter from the federal government, which owned 20 percent of its stock. The bank's most important role was to stabilize the nation's money supply, which consisted primarily of notes and bills of credit—in effect, paper money—issued by state-chartered banks. Those banks promised to redeem the notes on demand with "hard" money (or "specie")—that is, gold or silver coins minted by the U.S. or foreign governments—but there were few coins in circulation. By collecting those notes and regularly demanding specie, the Second Bank kept the state banks from issuing too much paper money and depreciating its value.

This cautious monetary policy pleased creditors—the bankers and entrepreneurs in Boston, New York, and Philadelphia, whose capital investments were underwriting economic development. However, expansion-minded bankers, including friends of Jackson's in Nashville, demanded an end to central oversight. Moreover, many ordinary Americans worried that the

Second Bank would force weak banks to close, leaving them holding worthless paper notes. Many politicians resented the arrogance of the bank's president, Nicholas Biddle. "As to mere power," Biddle boasted, "I have been for years in the daily exercise of more personal authority than any President habitually enjoys."

Jackson's Bank Veto Although the Second Bank had many enemies, a political miscalculation by its friends brought its downfall. In 1832, Henry Clay and Daniel Webster persuaded Biddle to seek an early extension of the bank's charter (which still had four years to run). They had the votes in Congress to enact the required legislation and hoped to lure Jackson into a veto that would split the Democrats just before the 1832 elections.

Jackson turned the tables on Clay and Webster. He vetoed the rechartering bill with a masterful message that blended constitutional arguments with class rhetoric and patriotic fervor. Adopting the position taken by Thomas Jefferson in 1793, Jackson declared that Congress had no constitutional authority to charter a national bank. He condemned the bank as "subversive of the rights of the States," "dangerous to the liberties of the people," and a privileged monopoly that promoted "the advancement of the few at the expense of . . . farmers, mechanics, and laborers." Finally, the president noted that British aristocrats owned much of the bank's stock. Such a powerful institution should be "purely American," Jackson declared with patriotic zeal.

Jackson's attack on the bank carried him to victory in 1832. Old Hickory and Martin Van Buren, his new running mate, overwhelmed Henry Clay, who headed the National Republican ticket, by 219 to 49 electoral votes. Jackson's most fervent supporters were eastern workers and western farmers, who blamed the Second Bank for high urban prices and stagnant farm income. "All the flourishing cities of the West are mortgaged to this money power," charged Senator Thomas Hart Benton, a Jacksonian from Missouri. Still, many of Jackson's supporters had prospered during a decade of strong economic growth. Thousands of middle-class Americans — lawyers, clerks, shopkeepers, and artisans — had used the opportunity to rise in the world and cheered Jackson's attack on privileged corporations.

PLACE EVENTS IN CONTEXT
Why — and how — did Jackson destroy the Second National Bank?

The Bank Destroyed Early in 1833, Jackson met their wishes by appointing Roger B. Taney, a strong opponent of corporate privilege, as head of the Treasury Department. Taney promptly transferred the federal government's gold and silver from the Second Bank to various state banks, which critics labeled Jackson's "pet banks." To justify this abrupt (and probably illegal) transfer, Jackson declared that his reelection represented "the decision of the people against the bank" and gave him a mandate to destroy it. This sweeping claim of presidential power was new and radical. Never before had a president claimed that victory at the polls allowed him to pursue a controversial policy or to act independently of Congress (American Voices, p. 328).

The "bank war" escalated into an all-out political battle. In March 1834, Jackson's opponents in the Senate passed a resolution composed by Henry Clay that censured the president and warned of executive tyranny: "We are in the midst of a revolution, hitherto bloodless, but rapidly descending towards a total change of the pure republican character of the Government, and the concentration of all power in the hands of one man." Clay's charges and Congress's censure did not deter Jackson. "The Bank is trying to kill me but I will kill it," he vowed to Van Buren. And so he did. When the Second Bank's national charter expired in 1836, Jackson prevented its renewal.

Jackson had destroyed both national banking — the handiwork of Alexander Hamilton — and the American System of protective tariffs and public works created by Henry Clay and John Quincy Adams. The result was a profound check on economic activism and innovative policymaking by the national government. "All is gone," observed a Washington newspaper correspondent. "All is gone, which the General Government was instituted to create and preserve."

Indian Removal

The status of Native American peoples posed an equally complex political problem. By the late 1820s, white voices throughout the South and Midwest demanded the resettlement of Indian peoples west of the Mississippi River. Many whites who were sympathetic to Native Americans also favored resettlement. Removal to the West seemed the only way to protect Indians from alcoholism, financial exploitation, and cultural decline.

However, most Indians did not want to leave their ancestral lands. For centuries, Cherokees and Creeks had lived in Georgia, Tennessee, and Alabama; Chickasaws and Choctaws in Mississippi and Alabama; and Seminoles in Florida. During the War of 1812, Andrew Jackson had forced the Creeks to relinquish millions of acres, but Indian tribes still controlled vast tracts and wanted to keep them.

Cherokee Resistance   But on what terms? Some Indians had adopted white ways. An 1825 census revealed that various Cherokees owned 33 gristmills, 13 sawmills, 2,400 spinning wheels, 760 looms, and 2,900 plows. Many of these owners were mixed-race, the offspring of white traders and Indian women. They had grown up in a bicultural world, knew the political and economic ways of whites, and often favored assimilation into white society. Indeed, some of these mixed-race people were indistinguishable from southern planters. At his death in 1809, Georgia Cherokee James Vann owned one hundred black slaves, two trading posts, and a gristmill. Three decades later, forty other mixed-blood Cherokee families each owned ten or more African American workers.

Prominent mixed-race Cherokees believed that integration into American life was the best way to protect their property and the lands of their people. In 1821, Sequoyah, a part-Cherokee silversmith, perfected a system of writing for the Cherokee language; six years later, mixed-race Cherokees devised a new charter of Cherokee government modeled directly on the U.S. Constitution. "You asked us to throw off the hunter and warrior state," Cherokee John Ridge told a Philadelphia audience in 1832. "We did so. You asked us to form a republican government: We did so. . . . You asked us to learn to read: We did so. You asked us to cast away our idols, and worship your God: We did so." Full-blood Cherokees, who made up 90 percent of the population, resisted many of these cultural and political innovations but were equally determined to retain their ancestral lands. "We would not receive money for land in which our fathers and friends are buried," one full-blood chief declared. "We love our land; it is our mother."

What the Cherokees did or wanted carried no weight with the Georgia legislature. In 1802, Georgia had given up its western land claims in return for a federal promise to extinguish Indian landholdings in the state. Now it demanded fulfillment of that pledge. Having spent his military career fighting Indians and seizing their lands, Andrew Jackson gave full support to Georgia. On assuming the presidency, he withdrew the federal troops that had protected Indian enclaves there and in Alabama and Mississippi. The states, he declared, were sovereign within their borders.

The Removal Act and Its Aftermath   Jackson then pushed the **Indian Removal Act of 1830** through Congress over the determined opposition of evangelical Protestant men — and women. To block removal, Catharine Beecher and Lydia Sigourney composed a Ladies Circular, which urged "benevolent ladies" to use "prayers and exertions to avert the calamity of removal." Women from across the nation flooded Congress with petitions. Nonetheless, Jackson's bill squeaked through the House of Representatives by a vote of 102 to 97.

The Removal Act created the Indian Territory on national lands acquired in the Louisiana Purchase and located in present-day Oklahoma and Kansas. It promised money and reserved land to Native American peoples who would give up their ancestral holdings east of the Mississippi River. Government officials promised the Indians that they could live on their new land, "they and all their children, as long as grass grows and water runs." However, as one Indian leader noted, on the Great Plains "water and timber are scarcely to be seen." When Chief Black Hawk and his Sauk and Fox

Blackhawk

This portrait of Black Hawk (1767–1838), by George Catlin, shows the Indian leader holding his namesake, a black hawk and its feathers. When Congress approved Andrew Jackson's Indian Removal Act in 1830, Black Hawk mobilized Sauk and Fox warriors to protect their ancestral lands in Illinois. "It was here, that I was born — and here lie the bones of many friends and relatives," the aging chief declared. "I . . . never could consent to leave it." Courtesy Warner Collection of Gulf States Paper Corporation, Tuscaloosa, AL.

The Character and Goals of Andrew Jackson

From the start of his career, Andrew Jackson was a controversial figure. "Hot-tempered," "Indian-hater," "military despot," said his critics, while his friends praised him as a forthright statesman. His contemporary biographer, the journalist James Parton, found him a man of many faces, an enigma. Others thought they understood his personality and policies: James Hamilton, a loyal Jacksonian congressman, recalled Jackson's volatile temper. Henry Clay, his archrival, warned that Jackson's quest for power threatened American republicanism, while wealthy New York Whig Philip Hone accused him of inciting class warfare. After talking with dozens of Americans, Frenchman Alexis de Tocqueville offered a balanced interpretation of the man and his goals.

James Parton
Preface to *The Life of Andrew Jackson* (1860)

If any one . . . had asked what I had yet discovered respecting General Jackson, I might have answered thus: "Andrew Jackson, I am given to understand, was a patriot and a traitor. He was one of the greatest of generals, and wholly ignorant of the art of war. . . . The first of statesmen, he never devised, he never framed a measure. He was the most candid of men, and was capable of the profoundest dissimulation. A most law-defying, law-obeying citizen. A stickler for discipline, he never hesitated to disobey his superior. A democratic autocrat. An urbane savage. An atrocious saint."

James Hamilton Jr.
Recalling an Event in 1827, as Jackson Campaigns for the Presidency

The steamer Pocahontas was chartered by citizens of New Orleans to convey the General and his party from Nashville to that city. She was fitted out in the most sumptuous manner. The party was General and Mrs. Jackson, . . . Governor Samuel Houston, Wm. B. Lewis, Robert Armstrong, and others. . . . The only freight was the General's cotton-crop. . . .

In the course of the voyage an event occurred, which I repeat, as it is suggestive of [his] character. A steamer of greater speed than ours, going in the same direction, passed us, crossed our bow; then stopped and let us pass her and then passed us again in triumph. This was repeated again and again, until the General, being excited by the offensive course, ordered a rifle to be brought to him; hailed the pilot of the other steamer, and swore that if he did the same thing again he would shoot him.

Philip Hone
Ruminating in His Diary on the Jacksonians' Victory in the New York Elections of 1834

I apprehend that Mr. Van Buren [Jackson's vice president] and his friends have no permanent cause of triumph in their victory. They . . . have mounted a vicious horse, who, taking the bit in his mouth, will run away with [them]. . . . This battle had been fought upon the ground of the poor against the rich, and this unworthy prejudice, this dangerous delusion, has been encouraged by the leaders of the triumphant party, and fanned into a flame by the polluted breath of the hireling press in their employ. . . .

The cry of "Down with the aristocracy!" mingled with the shouts of victory. . . . They have succeeded in raising this dangerous spirit [of the mob], and have gladly availed themselves of its support to accomplish a temporary object; but can they allay it at pleasure? . . . Eighteen thousand men in New York have voted for the high-priest of the party whose professed design is to bring down the property, the talents, the industry, the steady habits of that class which constituted the real strength of the Commonwealth, to the common level of the idle, the worthless, and the unenlightened. Look to it, ye men of respectability in the Jackson party, are ye not afraid of the weapons ye have used in this warfare?

Henry Clay
Introducing a Senate Resolution Censuring Jackson, December 26, 1833

We are in the midst of a revolution, hitherto bloodless, but rapidly tending toward a total change of the pure republican character of the government, and to the concentration of all power in the hands of one man. The powers of Congress are paralyzed, except when exerted in conformity with his will, by frequent and an extraordinary exercise of the executive veto, not anticipated by the founders of our Constitution, and not practiced by any of the predecessors of the present chief magistrate. . . .

The judiciary has not been exempt from the prevailing rage for innovation. Decisions of the tribunals, deliberately pronounced, have been contemptuously disregarded. . . . Our Indian relations, coeval with the existence of the government, and recognized and established by numerous laws and treaties, have been subverted. . . . The system of protection of improvement lies crushed beneath the veto. The system of protection of American industry [will soon meet a similar fate]. . . . In a term of eight years, a little more than equal to that which was required to establish our liberties [as an independent republic between 1776 and 1783], the government will have been transformed into an elective monarchy — the worst of all forms of government.

Alexis de Tocqueville

Analysis of Jackson in *Democracy in America* (1835)

We have been told that General Jackson has won battles; that he is an energetic man, prone by nature and habit to the use of force, covetous of power and a despot by inclination.

All this may be true; but the inferences which have been drawn from these truths are very erroneous. It has been imagined that General Jackson is bent on establishing a dictatorship in America, introducing a military spirit, and giving a degree of influence to the central authority that cannot but be dangerous to provincial [state] liberties. . . .

Far from wishing to extend the Federal power, the President belongs to the party which is desirous of limiting that power to the clear and precise letter of the Constitution and which never puts a construction upon that act favorable to the government of the Union; far from standing forth as the champion of centralization, General Jackson is the agent of the state jealousies; and he was placed in his lofty station by the passions that are most opposed to the central government.

Sources: James Parton, *The Life of Andrew Jackson. In Three Volumes* (New York: Mason Brothers, 1860), vol. 1, vii–viii; Sean Wilentz, ed., *Major Problems in the Early Republic, 1787–1848* (Lexington, MA: D. C. Heath, 1991), 374 (Hamilton) and 392–393 (Hone); Calvin Colton, ed., *The Life . . . of Henry Clay*, 6 vols. (New York: A. Barnes, 1857), 576–580; Alexis de Tocqueville, *Democracy in America*, abr. by Thomas Bender (New York: Modern Library, 1981), 271–273.

QUESTIONS FOR ANALYSIS

1. Was Jackson a "democratic autocrat," as Parton puts it? Would the authors of the other excerpts agree? Did Jackson instigate class warfare, as Hone suggests?

2. In your judgment, which writer, Clay or Tocqueville, offers the more accurate assessment of Jackson and his policies?

3. Do you agree with Philip Hone's view that the Jacksonian Democrats mobilized "poor against the rich"? What evidence would support or contradict Hone's assertion?

COMPARE AND CONTRAST
How did the views of Jackson and John Marshall differ regarding the status and rights of Indian peoples?

followers refused to leave rich, well-watered farmland in western Illinois in 1832, Jackson sent troops to expel them by force. Eventually, the U.S. Army pursued Black Hawk into the Wisconsin Territory and, in the brutal eight-hour Bad Axe Massacre, killed 850 of his 1,000 warriors. Over the next five years, American diplomatic pressure and military power forced seventy Indian peoples to sign treaties and move west of the Mississippi (Map 10.3).

In the meantime, the Cherokees had carried the defense of their lands to the Supreme Court, where they claimed the status of a "foreign nation." In *Cherokee Nation v. Georgia* (1831), Chief Justice John Marshall denied that claim and declared that Indian peoples were "domestic dependent nations." However, in *Worcester v. Georgia* (1832), Marshall and the Court sided with the Cherokees against Georgia. Voiding Georgia's extension of state law over the Cherokees, the Court held that Indian nations were "distinct political communities, having territorial boundaries, within which their authority is exclusive [and is] guaranteed by the United States."

Instead of guaranteeing the Cherokees' territory, the U.S. government took it from them. In 1835, American officials and a minority Cherokee faction

MAP 10.3

The Removal of Native Americans, 1820–1846

As white settlers moved west, the U.S. government forced scores of Native American peoples to leave their ancestral lands. Andrew Jackson's Indian Removal Act of 1830 formalized this policy. Subsequently, scores of Indian peoples signed treaties that exchanged their lands in the East, Midwest, and Southeast for money and designated reservations in an Indian Territory west of the Mississippi River. When the Sauk, Fox, Cherokees, and Seminoles resisted resettlement, the government used the U.S. Army to enforce the removal policy.

Raising Public Opinion Against the Seminoles
During the eighteenth century, hundreds of enslaved Africans fled South Carolina and Georgia and found refuge in Spanish Florida, where they lived among and intermarried with the Seminole people. This color engraving from the 1830s—showing red and black Seminoles butchering respectable white families—sought to bolster political support for the removal of the Seminoles to Indian Territory. By the mid-1840s, after a decade of warfare, the U.S. Army had forced 2,500 Seminoles to migrate to Oklahoma. However, another 2,500 Seminoles continued to fight and eventually won a new treaty allowing them to live in Florida. The Granger Collection, New York.

negotiated the Treaty of New Echota, which specified that Cherokees would resettle in Indian Territory. When only 2,000 of 17,000 Cherokees had moved by the May 1838 deadline, President Martin Van Buren ordered General Winfield Scott to enforce the treaty. Scott's army rounded up 14,000 Cherokees (including mixed-race African Cherokees) and marched them 1,200 miles, an arduous journey that became known as the **Trail of Tears**. Along the way, 3,000 Indians died of starvation and exposure. Once in Oklahoma, the Cherokees excluded anyone of "negro or mulatto parentage" from governmental office, thereby affirming that full citizenship in their nation was racially defined. Just as the United States was a "white man's country," so Indian Territory would be defined as a "red man's country."

Encouraged by generous gifts of land, the Creeks, Chickasaws, and Choctaws moved west of the Mississippi, leaving the Seminoles in Florida as the only numerically significant Indian people remaining in the Southeast. Government pressure persuaded about half of the Seminoles to migrate to Indian Territory, but families whose ancestors had intermarried with runaway slaves feared the emphasis on "blood purity" there. During the 1840s, they fought a successful guerrilla war against the U.S. Army and retained their lands in central Florida. These Seminoles were the exception: the Jacksonians had forced the removal of most eastern Indian peoples.

The Jacksonian Impact

Jackson's legacy, like that of every other great president, is complex and rich. On the institutional level, he expanded the authority of the nation's chief executive. As Jackson put it, "The President is the direct representative of the American people." Assuming that role during the nullification crisis, he upheld national authority by threatening the use of military force, laying the foundation for Lincoln's defense of the Union a generation later. At the same time (and somewhat contradictorily), Jackson curbed the reach of the national government. By undermining Henry Clay's American System of national banking, protective tariffs, and internal improvements, Jackson reinvigorated the Jeffersonian tradition of a limited and frugal central government.

The Taney Court   Jackson also undermined the constitutional jurisprudence of John Marshall by appointing Roger B. Taney as his successor in 1835. During his long tenure as chief justice (1835–1864), Taney partially reversed the nationalist and vested-property-rights decisions of the Marshall Court and gave constitutional legitimacy to Jackson's policies of states' rights and free enterprise. In the landmark case *Charles River Bridge Co. v. Warren Bridge Co.* (1837), Taney declared that a legislative charter—in this case, to build and operate a toll bridge—did not necessarily bestow a monopoly, and that a legislature could charter a competing bridge to promote the general welfare: "While the rights of private property are sacredly guarded, we must not forget that the community also has rights." This decision directly challenged Marshall's interpretation of the contract clause of the Constitution in *Dartmouth College v. Woodward* (1819), which had stressed the binding nature of public charters and the sanctity of "vested rights" (Chapter 7). By limiting the property claims of existing canal and turnpike companies, Taney's decision allowed legislatures to charter competing railroads that would provide cheaper and more efficient transportation.

The Taney Court also limited Marshall's nationalistic interpretation of the commerce clause by enhancing the regulatory role of state governments. For example, in *Mayor of New York v. Miln* (1837), the Taney Court ruled that New York State could use its "police power" to inspect the health of arriving immigrants. The Court also restored to the states some of the economic powers they had exercised prior to the Constitution of 1787. In *Briscoe v. Bank of Kentucky* (1837), the justices allowed a bank owned by the state of Kentucky to issue currency, despite the wording of Article 1, Section 10 of the Constitution, which prohibits states from issuing "bills of credit."

EXPLAIN CONSEQUENCES
How did the Taney Court and the Jacksonian state constitutions alter the American legal and constitutional system?

States Revise Their Constitutions   Inspired by Jackson and Taney, Democrats in the various states mounted their own constitutional revolutions. Between 1830 and 1860, twenty states called conventions that furthered democratic principles by reapportioning state legislatures on the basis of population and giving the vote to all white men. Voters also had more power because the new documents mandated the election, rather than the appointment, of most public officials, including sheriffs, justices of the peace, and judges.

The new constitutions also embodied the principles of **classical liberalism**, or **laissez-faire**, by limiting the government's role in the economy. (Twentieth-century social-welfare liberalism endorses the opposite principle: that government should intervene in economic and social life.) As president, Jackson had destroyed the American System, and his disciples now attacked the state-based Commonwealth System, which used chartered corporations and state funds to promote economic development. Most Jackson-era constitutions prohibited states from granting special charters to corporations and extending loans and credit guarantees to private businesses. "If there is any danger to be feared in . . . government," declared a New Jersey Democrat, "it is the danger of associated wealth, with special privileges." The revised constitutions also protected taxpayers by setting strict limits on state debt and encouraging judges to enforce them. Said New York reformer Michael Hoffman, "We will not trust the legislature with the power of creating indefinite mortgages on the people's property."

"The world is governed too much," the Jacksonians proclaimed as they embraced a small-government, laissez-faire outlook and celebrated the power of ordinary people to make decisions in the voting booth and the marketplace.

Class, Culture, and the Second Party System

The rise of the Democracy and Jackson's tumultuous presidency sparked the creation in the mid-1830s of a second national party: the **Whigs**. For the next two decades, Whigs and Democrats competed fiercely for votes and appealed to different cultural groups. Many evangelical Protestants became Whigs, while most Catholic immigrants and traditional Protestants joined the Democrats. By debating issues of economic policy, class power, and moral reform, party politicians offered Americans a choice between competing programs and political leaders. "Of the two great parties," remarked philosopher Ralph Waldo Emerson, "[the Democracy] has the best cause . . . for free trade, for wide suffrage, [but the Whig Party] has the best men."

The Whig Worldview

The Whig Party arose in 1834, when a group of congressmen contested Andrew Jackson's policies and his high-handed, "kinglike" conduct. They took the name *Whigs* to identify themselves with the pre-Revolutionary American and British parties—also called Whigs—that had opposed the arbitrary actions of British monarchs. The Whigs accused "King Andrew I" of violating the Constitution by creating a spoils system and undermining elected legislators, whom they saw as the true representatives of the sovereign people. One Whig accused Jackson of ruling in a manner "more absolute than that of any absolute monarchy of Europe."

Initially, the Whigs consisted of political factions with distinct points of view. However, guided by Senators Webster of Massachusetts, Clay of Kentucky, and Calhoun of South Carolina, they gradually coalesced into a party with a distinctive stance and coherent ideology. Like the Federalists of the 1790s, the Whigs wanted a political world dominated by men of ability and wealth; unlike the Federalists, they advocated an elite based on talent, not birth.

The Whigs celebrated the entrepreneur and the enterprising individual: "This is a country of self-made men," they boasted, pointing to the relative absence of permanent distinctions of class and status among white citizens. Embracing the Industrial Revolution, northern Whigs welcomed the investments of "moneyed capitalists," which provided workers with jobs and "bread, clothing and homes." Indeed, Whig congressman Edward Everett championed a "holy alliance" among laborers, owners, and governments and called for a return to Henry Clay's American System. Many New England and Pennsylvania textile and iron workers shared Everett's vision because they benefitted directly from protective tariffs.

Calhoun's Dissent   Support for the Whigs in the South — less widespread than that in the North — rested on the appeal of specific policies and politicians. Some southern Whigs were wealthy planters who invested in railroads and banks or sold their cotton to New York merchants. But the majority were yeomen whites who resented the power and policies of low-country planters, most of whom were Democrats. In addition, some Virginia and South Carolina Democrats, such as John Taylor, became Whigs because they condemned Andrew Jackson's crusade against nullification.

Southern Whigs rejected their party's enthusiasm for high tariffs and social mobility, and John C. Calhoun was their spokesman. Extremely conscious of class divisions in society, Calhoun believed that northern Whigs' rhetoric of equal opportunity was contradicted not only by slavery, which he considered a fundamental American institution, but also by the wage-labor system of industrial capitalism. "There is and always has been in an advanced state of wealth and civilization a conflict between labor and capital," Calhoun declared in 1837. He urged slave owners and factory owners to unite against their common foe: the working class of enslaved blacks and propertyless whites.

Most northern Whigs rejected Calhoun's class-conscious social ideology. "A clear and well-defined line between capital and labor" might fit the slave South or class-ridden Europe, Daniel Webster conceded, but in the North "this distinction grows less and less definite as commerce advances." Ignoring the ever-increasing numbers of propertyless immigrants and native-born wageworkers, Webster focused on the growing size of the middle class, whose members generally favored Whig candidates. In the election of 1834, the Whigs

John C. Calhoun (1782–1850)
This daguerreotype, made close to the time of Calhoun's death, suggests his emotional intensity and thwarted ambition. The prime advocate of the doctrines of nullification and states' rights, a founder of the Whig Party, and a steadfast defender of slavery, Calhoun found his lifelong pursuit of the presidency frustrated by Martin Van Buren's political skills and sectional divisions over tariffs and slavery. © Image courtesy of the Gibbes Museum of Art/Carolina Art Association.

took control of the House of Representatives by appealing to evangelical Protestants and upwardly mobile families — prosperous farmers, small-town merchants, and skilled industrial workers in New England, New York, and the new communities along the Great Lakes.

> **COMPARE AND CONTRAST**
> How did the ideology of the Whigs differ from that of the Jacksonian Democrats?

Anti-Masons Become Whigs   Many Whig voters in 1834 had previously supported the Anti-Masons, a powerful but short-lived party that formed in the late 1820s. As its name implies, Anti-Masons opposed the Order of Freemasonry. Freemasonry began in Europe as an organization of men seeking moral improvement by promoting the welfare and unity of humanity. Many Masons espoused republicanism, and the Order spread rapidly in America after the Revolution. Its ideology, mysterious symbols, and semisecret character gave the Order an air of exclusivity that attracted ambitious businessmen and political leaders, including George Washington, Henry Clay, and Andrew Jackson. In New

York State alone by the mid-1820s, there were more than 20,000 Masons, organized into 450 local lodges. However, after the kidnapping and murder in 1826 of William Morgan, a New York Mason who had threatened to reveal the Order's secrets, the Freemasons fell into disrepute. Thurlow Weed, a newspaper editor in Rochester, New York, spearheaded an Anti-Masonic Party, which condemned the Order as a secret aristocratic fraternity. The new party quickly ousted Freemasons from local and state offices, and just as quickly ran out of political steam.

Because many Anti-Masons espoused temperance, equality of opportunity, and evangelical morality, they gravitated to the Whig Party. Throughout the Northeast and Midwest, Whig politicians won election by proposing legal curbs on the sale of alcohol and local ordinances that preserved Sunday as a day of worship. The Whigs also secured the votes of farmers, bankers, and shopkeepers, who favored Henry Clay's American System. For these citizens of the growing Midwest, the Whigs' program of government subsidies for roads, canals, and bridges was as important as their moral agenda.

In the election of 1836, the Whig Party faced Martin Van Buren, the architect of the Democratic Party and Jackson's handpicked successor. Like Jackson, Van Buren denounced the American System and warned that its revival would create a "consolidated government." Positioning himself as a defender of individual rights, Van Buren also condemned the efforts of Whigs and moral reformers to enact state laws imposing temperance and national laws abolishing slavery. "The government is best which governs least" became his motto in economic, cultural, and racial matters.

To oppose Van Buren, the Whigs ran four candidates, each with a strong regional reputation. They hoped to garner enough electoral votes to throw the contest into the House of Representatives. However, the Whig tally — 73 electoral votes collected by William Henry Harrison of Ohio, 26 by Hugh L. White of Tennessee, 14 by Daniel Webster of Massachusetts, and 11 by W. P. Mangum of Georgia — fell far short of Van Buren's 170 votes. Still, the four Whigs won 49 percent of the popular vote, showing that the party's message of economic and moral improvement had broad appeal.

Labor Politics and the Depression of 1837–1843

As the Democrats battled Whigs on the national level, they faced challenges from urban artisans and workers. Between 1828 and 1833, artisans and laborers in fifteen

states formed Working Men's Parties. "Past experience teaches us that we have nothing to hope from the aristocratic orders of society," declared the New York Working Men's Party. It vowed "to send men of our own description, if we can, to the Legislature at Albany."

The new parties' agenda reflected the values and interests of ordinary urban workers. The Philadelphia Working Men's Party set out to secure "a just balance of power . . . between all the various classes." It called for the abolition of private banks, chartered monopolies, and debtors' prisons, and it demanded universal public education and a fair system of taxation (Thinking Like a Historian, p. 336). It won some victories, electing a number of assemblymen and persuading the Pennsylvania legislature in 1834 to authorize tax-supported schools. Elsewhere, Working Men's candidates won office in many cities, but their parties' weakness in statewide contests soon took a toll. By the mid-1830s, most politically active workers had joined the Democratic Party.

The Working Men's Parties left a mixed legacy. They mobilized craft workers and gave political expression to their ideology of artisan republicanism. As labor intellectual Orestes Brownson defined their distinctive vision, "All men will be independent proprietors, working on their own capitals, on their own farms, or in their own shops." However, this emphasis on proprietorship inhibited alliances between the artisan-based Working Men's Parties and the rapidly increasing class of dependent wage earners. As Joseph Weydemeyer, a close friend of Karl Marx, reported from New York in the early 1850s, many American craft workers "are incipient bourgeois, and feel themselves to be such."

Moreover, the **Panic of 1837** threw the American economy — and the workers' movement — into disarray. The panic began when the Bank of England tried to boost the faltering British economy by sharply curtailing the flow of money and credit to the United States. Since 1822, British manufacturers had extended credit to southern planters to expand cotton production, and British investors had purchased millions of dollars of the canal bonds from the northern states. Suddenly deprived of British funds, American planters, merchants, and canal corporations had to withdraw gold from domestic banks to pay their foreign debts. Moreover, British textile mills drastically reduced their purchases of raw cotton, causing its price to plummet from 20 cents a pound to 10 cents or less.

Falling cotton prices and the drain of specie to Britain set off a financial panic. On May 8, the Dry Dock Bank of New York City ran out of specie, prompting worried depositors to withdraw gold and silver coins from other banks. Within two weeks, every American bank had stopped trading specie and called in its loans, turning a financial panic into an economic crisis. "This sudden overthrow of the commercial credit" had a "stunning effect," observed Henry Fox, the British minister in Washington. "The conquest of the land by a foreign power could hardly have produced a more general sense of humiliation and grief."

To stimulate the economy, state governments increased their investments in canals and railroads. However, as governments issued (or guaranteed) more and more bonds to finance these ventures, they were unable to pay the interest charges, sparking a severe financial crisis on both sides of the Atlantic in 1839. Nine state governments defaulted on their debts, and hard-pressed European lenders cut the flow of new capital to the United States.

The American economy fell into a deep depression. By 1843, canal construction had dropped by 90 percent, prices and wages had fallen by 50 percent, and unemployment in seaports and industrial centers had reached 20 percent. Bumper crops drove down cotton prices,

pushing hundreds of planters and merchants into bankruptcy. Minister Henry Ward Beecher described a land "filled with lamentation . . . its inhabitants wandering like bereaved citizens among the ruins of an earthquake, mourning for children, for houses crushed, and property buried forever."

By creating a surplus of unemployed workers, the depression completed the decline of the union movement and the Working Men's Parties. In 1837, six thousand masons, carpenters, and other building-trades workers lost their jobs in New York City, destroying their unions' bargaining power. By 1843, most local unions, all the national labor organizations, and all the workers' parties had disappeared.

"Tippecanoe and Tyler Too!"

Many Americans blamed the Democrats for the depression of 1837–1843. They criticized Jackson for destroying the Second Bank and directing the Treasury

> **IDENTIFY CAUSES**
> What factors led to the demise of the Anti-Masonic and Working Men's political parties?

Hard Times

The Panic of 1837 struck hard at Americans of all social ranks. This anti-Democratic cartoon shows unemployed workers turning to drink; women and children begging in the streets; and fearful depositors withdrawing funds as their banks collapse. As the plummeting hot-air balloon in the background symbolizes, the rising "Glory" of an independent America was crashing to earth. © Museum of the City of New York, USA/The Bridgeman Art Library.

Becoming Literate: Public Education and Democracy

The struggle for a genuinely *democratic* polity — "government of the people, by the people, and for the people," as Lincoln put it — played out at the local and state level in battles over who should participate in the political arena. As legislators argued over extending the franchise, they considered the knowledge that citizens needed to participate responsibly in politics. Although primary education was publicly supported in most New England towns (giving that region nearly universal literacy), it received only spotty funding in the other northern states and almost none in the South (restricting literacy there to one-third of the white population). The following documents address the resulting debate over publicly supported education and citizenship.

1. Editorial from the *Philadelphia National Gazette*, 1830. *Pennsylvania was one of the first states to debate legislation regarding universal free public education.*

The scheme of Universal Equal Education . . . is virtually "Agrarianism" [redistribution of land from rich to poor]. It would be a compulsory application of the means of the richer, for the direct use of the poorer classes. . . . One of the chief excitements to industry . . . is the hope of earning the means of educating their children respectably . . . that incentive would be removed, and the scheme of state and equal education be a premium for comparative idleness, to be taken out of the pockets of the laborious and conscientious.

2. Thaddeus Stevens, speech before the Pennsylvania General Assembly, February 1835. *Pennsylvania's Free Public School Act of 1834 was the handiwork of the Working Men's Party of Philadelphia (see p. 334). When over half of Pennsylvania's school districts refused to implement the law, the legislature threatened to repeal it. Thaddeus Stevens, later a leading antislavery advocate, turned back that threat through this speech to the Pennsylvania General Assembly.*

It would seem to be humiliating to be under the necessity, in the nineteenth century, of entering into a formal argument to prove the utility, and to free governments, the absolute necessity of education. . . . Such necessity would be degrading to a Christian age and a free republic. If an elective republic is to endure for any great length of time, every elector must have sufficient information, not only to accumulate wealth and take care of his pecuniary concerns, but to direct wisely the Legislatures, the Ambassadors, and the Executive of the nation; for some part of all these things, some agency in approving or disapproving of them, falls to every freeman. If,

then, the permanency of our government depends upon such knowledge, it is the duty of government to see that the means of information be diffused to every citizen. This is a sufficient answer to those who deem education a private and not a public duty — who argue that they are willing to educate their own children, but not their neighbor's children.

3. "Letter from a Teacher" in Catharine E. Beecher, *The True Remedy for the Wrongs of Women*, 1851. *The public school movement created new opportunities not just for children of middle and lower classes but also for the young Protestant women who contributed to the "Benevolent Empire" as professional educators. Beecher's academy (see p. 369) in Hartford, Connecticut, sent out dozens of young women to establish schools.*

I am now located in this place, which is the county-town of a newly organized county [in a midwestern state]. . . . The Sabbath is little regarded, and is more a day for diversion than devotion. . . . My school embraces both sexes and all ages from five to seventeen, and not one can read intelligibly.

4. "Popular Education," 1833. *This piece appeared in the* North American Review, *the nation's first literary and cultural journal and the mouthpiece of New England's intellectual elite.*

[T]he mind of a people, in proportion as it is educated, will not only feel its own value, but will also perceive its rights. We speak now of those palpable rights which are recognised by all free states. . . . [T]he palpable rights of men, those of personal security, of property and of the free and unembarrassed pursuit of individual welfare, it is obviously impossible to conceal from an educated and reading people. Such a people rises at once above the condition of feudal tenants. . . . It directs its attention to the laws and institutions that govern it. It compels public office to give an account of itself. It strips off the veil of secrecy from the machinery of power. . . . And when all this is spread abroad in newspaper details . . . of a people that can read; when the estimate is freely made, of what the government tax levies upon the daily hoard, and upon apparel, and upon every comfort of life, can it be doubted that such a people will demand and obtain an influence in affairs that so vitally concern it? This would be freedom.

5. **Judge Baker, sentencing hearing in the court case against Mrs. Margaret Douglass of Norfolk, Virginia, January 10, 1854.** *Southern whites considered the acquisition of literacy by blacks, whether slave or free, as a public danger, especially after the Nat Turner uprising in Southampton County, Virginia, in 1831 (Chapter 11, p. 362). A Virginia court sent Mrs. Margaret Douglass to jail for a month "as an example to all others" for teaching free black children to read so they might have access to books on religion and morality.*

There are persons, I believe, in our community, opposed to the policy of the law in question. They profess to believe that universal intellectual culture is necessary to religious instruction and education, and that such culture is suitable to a state of slavery. . . .

Such opinions in the present state of our society I regard as manifestly mischievous. It is not true that our slaves cannot be taught religious and moral duty, without being able to read the Bible and use the pen. Intellectual and religious instruction often go hand in hand, but the latter may well be exist without the former; . . . among the whites one-fou[r]th or more are entirely without a knowledge of letters, [nonetheless,] respect for the law, and for moral and religious conduct and behavior, are justly and prope[r]ly appreciated and practiced. . . .

The first legislative provision upon this subject was introduced in the year 1831, immediately succeeding the bloody scenes of the memorable Southampton insurrection; and . . . was re-enacted with additional penalties in the year 1848. . . . After these several and repeated recognitions of the wisdom and propriety of the said act, it may well be said that bold and open opposition to it [must be condemned] . . . as a measure of self-preservation and protection.

Sources: (1) "Religion and Social Reform," the Gilder Lehrman Institute of American History, gilderlehrman.org; (2) *New York Legislature Documents*, Vol. 34, No. 65, Part 1 (Albany, NY: J. B. Lyon Company, 1919), 60; (3) Catharine E. Beecher, *Educational Reminiscences and Suggestions* (New York: J. D. Ford & Company, 1874), 127; (4) *The North American Review* 36, no. 58 (January 1833); (5) "The Case of Mrs. Margaret Douglass," *Africans in America*, pbs.org.

6. **Working Men's Party poster for immigrant voters, New York, 1830.**

Source: Joshua R. Greenberg, Advocating the Man.

ANALYZING THE EVIDENCE

1. What arguments does the editorial in the *Philadelphia National Gazette* (source 1) advance? How does Stevens (source 2) reframe this argument?

2. What does the letter from a former student of Beecher's (source 3) tell us about the links between educational reform and other social movements, such as Sabbatarianism (p. 305)? How does it help us to understand the fate of the "notables" and the "log cabin campaign" of 1840?

3. What is the larger agenda of the author of source 4? How is the argument here similar to, or different from, that in sources 1 and 2?

4. How does Judge Baker (source 5) justify the denial of education to African Americans?

5. What do the occupations of the Working Men's Party candidates suggest about its definition of "worker" (source 6)? How does the political agenda of the party relate to the arguments advanced in sources 2 and 4? To present-day debates regarding the education of illegal immigrants?

PUTTING IT ALL TOGETHER

As these selections indicate, the debate over education had many facets. Did the power traditionally held by "notables" rest on their access to private schooling? Should a democratic society ensure the literacy of citizen voters? Was religious instruction a telling argument for slave literacy? Using these documents, your answers to the questions above, and materials in Chapters 8 and 10, write an essay that discusses public education, responsible citizenship, and social reform in America between 1820 and 1860.

Department in 1836 to issue the **Specie Circular**, an executive order that required the Treasury Department to accept only gold and silver in payment for lands in the national domain. Critics charged—mistakenly—that the Circular drained so much specie from the economy that it sparked the Panic of 1837. In fact (as noted above), the curtailing of credit by the Bank of England was the main cause of the panic.

Nonetheless, the public turned its anger on Van Buren, who took office just before the panic struck. Ignoring the pleas of influential bankers, the new president refused to revoke the Specie Circular or take actions to stimulate the economy. Holding to his philosophy of limited government, Van Buren advised Congress that "the less government interferes with private pursuits the better for the general prosperity." As the depression deepened in 1839, this laissez-faire outlook commanded less and less political support. Worse, Van Buren's major piece of fiscal legislation, the Independent Treasury Act of 1840, delayed recovery by pulling federal specie out of Jackson's pet banks (where it had backed loans) and placing it in government vaults, where it had little economic impact.

The Log Cabin Campaign   The Whigs exploited Van Buren's weakness. In 1840, they organized their first national convention and nominated William Henry Harrison of Ohio for president and John Tyler of Virginia for vice president. A military hero of the Battle of Tippecanoe and the War of 1812, Harrison was well advanced in age (sixty-eight) and had little political experience. However, the Whig leaders in Congress, Henry Clay and Daniel Webster, wanted a president who would rubber-stamp their program for protective tariffs and a national bank. An unpretentious, amiable man, Harrison told voters that Whig policies were "the only means, under Heaven, by which a poor industrious man may become a rich man without bowing to colossal wealth."

The depression stacked the political cards against Van Buren, but the election turned as much on style as on substance. It became the great "log cabin campaign"—the first time two well-organized parties competed for votes through a new style of campaigning. Whig songfests, parades, and well-orchestrated mass meetings drew new voters into politics. Whig speakers assailed "Martin Van Ruin" as a manipulative politician with aristocratic tastes—a devotee of fancy wines, elegant clothes, and polite refinement, as indeed he was. Less truthfully, they portrayed Harrison as a self-made man who lived contentedly in a log cabin and quaffed hard cider, a drink of the common people. In fact, Harrison's father was a wealthy Virginia planter who

The Whigs Boost Harrison and Tyler for the White House

In their quest for victory in 1840, Whig political strategists advanced a wide-ranging (and misleading) set of policies. This poster celebrates William Henry Harrison and John Tyler as candidates who would secure protective tariffs for American manufacturers—a policy that appealed to northern voters but one that Tyler opposed. It also promises to cut the size of the U.S. Army, which General Harrison did not favor. However, denouncing a large "Standing Army" would win votes in Virginia, where it recalled the fears of Radical Whig Patriots of 1776 and remained central to the states' rights ideology espoused by Senator Tyler and other "Old Republicans." Grouseland Foundation, Inc./Photo courtesy of "Fords the Art of Photography," Vincennes, IN.

President John Tyler (1790–1862)
Both as an "accidental" president and as a man, John Tyler left his mark on the world. His initiative to annex Texas made the election of 1844 into a pivotal contest and led to the war with Mexico in 1846. Tyler's first wife, Letitia, give birth to eight children before dying in the White House in 1842. Two years later, he married twenty-four-year-old Julia Gardiner, who bore him seven more children. White House Historical Association (White House Collection).

had signed the Declaration of Independence, and Harrison himself lived in a series of elegant mansions.

The Whigs boosted their electoral hopes by welcoming women to campaign festivities — a "first" for American politics. Many Jacksonian Democrats had long embraced an ideology of aggressive manhood, likening politically minded females to "public" women, prostitutes who plied their trade in theaters and other public places. Whigs took a more restrained view of masculinity and recognized that Christian women had already entered American public life through the temperance movement and other benevolent activities. In October 1840, Daniel Webster celebrated moral reform to an audience of twelve hundred women and urged them to back Whig candidates. "This way of making politicians of their women is something new under the sun," exclaimed one Democrat, worried that it would bring more Whig men to the polls. And it did: more than 80 percent of the eligible male voters cast ballots in 1840, up from fewer than 60 percent in 1832 and 1836 (see Figure 10.1). Heeding the Whigs' campaign slogan "Tippecanoe and Tyler Too," they voted Harrison into the White House with 53 percent of the popular vote and gave the party a majority in Congress.

Tyler Subverts the Whig Agenda   Led by Clay and Webster, the Whigs in Congress prepared to reverse the Jacksonian revolution. Their hopes were short-lived; barely a month after his inauguration in 1841, Harrison died of pneumonia, and the nation got "Tyler Too." But in what capacity: as acting president or as president? The Constitution was vague on the issue. Ignoring his Whig associates in Congress, who wanted a weak chief executive, Tyler took the presidential oath of office and declared his intention to govern as he pleased. As it turned out, that would not be like a Whig.

Tyler had served in the House and the Senate as a Jeffersonian Democrat, firmly committed to slavery and states' rights. He had joined the Whigs only to protest Jackson's stance against nullification. On economic issues, Tyler shared Jackson's hostility to the Second Bank and the American System. He therefore vetoed Whig bills that would have raised tariffs and created a new national bank. Outraged by this betrayal, most of Tyler's cabinet resigned in 1842, and the Whigs expelled Tyler from their party. "His Accidency," as he

UNDERSTAND POINTS OF VIEW
How did Whigs and Democrats view women in politics, and why did they hold those views?

was called by his critics, was now a president without a party.

The split between Tyler and the Whigs allowed the Democrats to regroup. The party vigorously recruited subsistence farmers in the North, smallholding planters in the South, and former members of the Working Men's Parties in the cities. It also won support among Irish and German Catholic immigrants — whose numbers had increased during the 1830s — by backing their demands for religious and cultural liberty, such as the freedom to drink beer and whiskey. A pattern of **ethnocultural politics**, as historians refer to the practice of voting along ethnic and religious lines, now became a prominent feature of American life. Thanks to these urban and rural recruits, the Democrats remained the majority party in most parts of the nation. Their program of equal rights, states' rights, and cultural liberty was attractive to more white Americans than the Whig platform of economic nationalism, moral reform, temperance laws, and individual mobility.

SUMMARY

In this chapter, we examined the causes and the consequences of the democratic political revolution. We saw that the expansion of the franchise weakened the political system run by notables of high status and encouraged the transfer of power to professional politicians — men like Martin Van Buren, who were mostly of middle-class origin.

We also witnessed a revolution in government policy, as Andrew Jackson and his Democratic Party dismantled the mercantilist economic system of government-supported economic development. On the national level, Jackson destroyed Henry Clay's American System; on the state level, Democrats wrote new constitutions that ended the Commonwealth System of government charters and subsidies to private businesses. Jackson's treatment of Native Americans was equally revolutionary; the Removal Act of 1830 forcefully resettled eastern Indian peoples west of the Mississippi River, opening their ancestral lands to white settlement.

Finally, we watched the emergence of the Second Party System. Following the split in the Republican Party during the election of 1824, two new parties — the Democrats and the Whigs — developed on the national level and eventually absorbed the members of the Anti-Masonic and Working Men's parties. The new party system established universal suffrage for white men and a mode of representative government that was responsive to ordinary citizens. In their scope and significance, these political innovations matched the economic advances of both the Industrial Revolution and the Market Revolution.

CHAPTER REVIEW

MAKE IT STICK Go to **LearningCurve** to retain what you've read.

TERMS TO KNOW Identify and explain the significance of each term below.

Key Concepts and Events

franchise (p. 316)

notables (p. 316)

political machine (p. 317)

spoils system (p. 318)

caucus (p. 318)

American System (p. 319)

internal improvements (p. 319)

corrupt bargain (p. 319)

"consolidated government"
(p. 320)

Tariff of Abominations (p. 320)

nullification (p. 324)

states' rights (p. 324)

Second Bank of the United States
(p. 325)

Indian Removal Act of 1830
(p. 327)

Trail of Tears (p. 331)

classical liberalism, or laissez-
faire (p. 332)

Whigs (p. 332)

Panic of 1837 (p. 334)

Specie Circular (p. 338)

ethnocultural politics (p. 340)

Key People

Martin Van Buren (p. 317)

John Quincy Adams (p. 318)

Henry Clay (p. 319)

Andrew Jackson (p. 319)

John C. Calhoun (p. 324)

Daniel Webster (p. 324)

Nicholas Biddle (p. 326)

Roger B. Taney (p. 331)

John Tyler (p. 339)

REVIEW QUESTIONS Answer these questions to demonstrate your understanding of the chapter's main ideas.

1. How did Andrew Jackson and the Democratic Party fundamentally change public policy? Illustrate your argument with specific examples.

2. What were the various constitutional arguments underlying the debates over internal improvements, the tariff, and nullification?

3. How and why did the policies of the federal and state governments toward Native Americans change between the 1790s (Chapter 7) and the 1850s, and what were the reactions of Indian peoples to those policies?

4. **THEMATIC UNDERSTANDING** Review the events listed under "Politics and Power" on the thematic timeline on page 283. As the timeline indicates, the Working Men's and Anti-Masonic parties rose and declined between 1827 and 1834, and then the Whig Party emerged. How do you explain the timing of these events?

MAKING CONNECTIONS

Recognize the larger developments and continuities within and across chapters by answering these questions.

1. **ACROSS TIME AND PLACE** The chapter argues that a democratic revolution swept America in the decades after 1820 and uprooted the old system of politics. After reviewing the discussions of politics in Chapters 6 and 7, explain how party systems and political alignments changed over time and then assess the strength of this argument.

2. **VISUAL EVIDENCE** Look again at the political cartoons on the tariff (p. 320) and the vice-presidency (p. 324). What point of view does the cartoonist support, and how effective are the cartoons in championing that view? How are today's negative political advertisements on television similar or different?

MORE TO EXPLORE   Start here to learn more about the events discussed in this chapter.

Robert J. Conley, *Mountain Windsongs: A Novel of the Trail of Tears* (1992). Captures the human impact of Jackson's removal policy.

Richard Hofstadter, *The Idea of a Party System* (1969). Lucidly explains the triumph of party politics.

Thomas N. Ingersoll, *To Intermix with Our White Brothers* (2005). Argues that fear of racial intermixture shaped popular thought and government policy toward Indians.

Robert V. Remini, *The Life of Andrew Jackson* (1988). Highlights Jackson's triumphs and shortcomings.

Alexis de Tocqueville, *Democracy in America* (1835). A classic that is still worth dipping into; also available at **xroads.virginia.edu/~hyper/detoc/home.html**.

Sean Wilentz, *Chants Democratic* (1986). Covers the ideology of working men.

TIMELINE
Ask yourself why this chapter begins and ends with these dates and then identify the links among related events.

1810s	• States expand white male voting rights • Martin Van Buren creates disciplined party in New York
1825	• House of Representatives selects John Quincy Adams as president • Adams endorses Henry Clay's American System
1828	• Working Men's Parties win support • Tariff of Abominations raises duties • Andrew Jackson elected president • John C. Calhoun's *South Carolina Exposition and Protest*
1830	• Jackson vetoes National Road bill • Congress enacts Jackson's Indian Removal Act
1831	• *Cherokee Nation v. Georgia* denies Indians' independence, but *Worcester v. Georgia* (1832) upholds their political autonomy
1832	• Massacre of 850 Sauk and Fox warriors at Bad Axe • Jackson vetoes renewal of Second Bank • South Carolina adopts Ordinance of Nullification
1833	• Congress enacts compromise tariff
1834	• Whig Party formed by Clay, Calhoun, and Daniel Webster
1835	• Roger Taney named Supreme Court chief justice
1836	• Van Buren elected president
1837	• *Charles River Bridge* case weakens chartered monopolies • Panic of 1837 derails economy and labor movement
1838	• Many Cherokees die in Trail of Tears march to Indian Territory
1839–1843	• Defaults on bonds by state governments spark international financial crisis and depression
1840	• Whigs win "log cabin campaign"
1841	• John Tyler succeeds William Henry Harrison as president

KEY TURNING POINTS: Based on the events in the timeline (and your reading in Chapter 10), which five-year period brought more significant changes to American political and economic life: 1829–1833, Andrew Jackson's first term as president, or 1837–1842, the years of panic and depression? Explain and defend your choice.

11

CHAPTER

Religion and Reform
1800–1860

"The spirit of reform is in every place," declared the children of legal reformer David Dudley Field in their handwritten monthly *Gazette* in 1842:

> The labourer with a family says "reform the common schools," the merchant and the planter say, "reform the tariff," the lawyer "reform the laws," the politician "reform the government," the abolitionist "reform the slave laws," the moralist "reform intemperance," . . . the ladies wish their legal privileges extended, and in short, the whole country is wanting reform.

IDENTIFY THE BIG IDEA
To what extent did individualism, new religious sects, abolitionism, and women's rights (as the movement was called in the nineteenth century) change American culture between 1820 and 1860?

Like many Americans, the Field children sensed that the political whirlwind of the 1830s had transformed the way people thought about themselves and about society. Suddenly, thousands of men and women took inspiration from the economic progress and democratic spirit of the age. Drawing on the religious optimism of the Second Great Awakening, they felt that they could improve their personal lives and society as a whole. Some activists dedicated themselves to the cause of reform. William Lloyd Garrison began as an antislavery advocate and foe of Indian removal and then went on to campaign for women's rights, pacifism, and the abolition of prisons. Susan B. Anthony embraced antislavery, temperance, and female suffrage. Such obsessively reform-minded individuals, warned Unitarian minister Henry W. Bellows, were pursuing "an object, which in its very nature is unattainable — the perpetual improvement of [people's] outward condition." In Bellows's view, human progress depended on inner character, the "regeneration of man" through Christian precepts.

Such debates reveal the multifaceted character of the reform impulse. Like Bellows, the first wave of American reformers, the benevolent religious improvers of the 1820s, hoped to promote morality and enforce social discipline. They championed regular church attendance, temperance, and a strict moral code. Their zeal offended many upright citizens: "A peaceable man can hardly venture to eat or drink, . . . to correct his child or kiss his wife, without obtaining the permission . . . of some moral or other reform society," said one.

A second wave of reformers — Garrison, Anthony, and other activists of the 1830s and 1840s — undertook to liberate people from archaic customs and traditional lifestyles. Mostly middle-class northerners and midwesterners, these activists promoted a bewildering assortment of radical ideals: extreme individualism, common ownership of property, the immediate emancipation of slaves, and sexual equality. Although their numbers were small, second-wave reformers challenged deeply rooted cultural practices and elicited horrified opposition among the majority of Americans. As one fearful southerner saw it, radical reformers favored a chaotic world with "No-Marriage, No-Religion, No-Private Property, No-Law and No-Government."

A Middle-Class Marriage   During the 1830s, Joseph H. Davis used bright watercolors to paint scores of family portraits—150 still survive—that capture the comfortable lives of New England's middle classes. This double portrait commemorates the marriage of Hannah Roberts and Lewis Tebbets of Berwick, Maine. To emphasize their romantic love, Davis shows them gazing into each other's eyes, their hands linked by a prayer book, a symbol of their education and piety. Such respectable couples—Lewis Tebbets became a minister of the Methodist Episcopal Church—flocked to hear Ralph Waldo Emerson and other lecturers on the lyceum circuit. Terra Foundation for American Art, Chicago/Art Resource, NY.

Individualism: The Ethic of the Middle Class

Those fears were not exaggerated. Rapid economic growth and geographical expansion had weakened traditional institutions, forcing individuals to fend for themselves. In 1835, Alexis de Tocqueville coined the word *individualism* to describe the result. Native-born white Americans were "no longer attached to each other by any tie of caste, class, association, or family," the French aristocrat lamented, and so lived in social isolation. As Tocqueville mourned the loss of social ties, the New England essayist and philosopher Ralph Waldo Emerson (1803–1882) celebrated the liberation of the individual. Emerson's vision influenced thousands of ordinary Americans and a generation of important artists, who, in the **American Renaissance**, a mid-nineteenth-century flourishing of literature and philosophy, wrote a remarkable number of first-class novels, poems, and essays.

Ralph Waldo Emerson and Transcendentalism

Emerson was the leading voice of **transcendentalism**, an intellectual movement rooted in the religious soil of New England. Its first advocates were Unitarian ministers from well-to-do New England families who questioned the constraints of their Puritan heritage (Chapter 8). For inspiration, they turned to European romanticism, a new conception of self and society. Romantic thinkers, such as German philosopher Immanuel Kant and English poet Samuel Taylor Coleridge, rejected the ordered, rational world of the eighteenth-century Enlightenment. They embraced human passion and sought deeper insight into the mysteries of existence. By tapping their intuitive powers, the young Unitarians believed, people could come to know the infinite and the eternal.

As a Unitarian, Emerson stood outside the mainstream of American Protestantism. Unlike most Christians, Unitarians believed that God was a single being, not a trinity of Father, Son, and Holy Spirit. In 1832, Emerson took a more radical step by resigning his Boston pulpit and rejecting all organized religion. He moved to Concord, Massachusetts, and wrote influential essays probing what he called "the infinitude of the private man," the radically free person.

The young philosopher argued that people were trapped by inherited customs and institutions. They

The Founder of Transcendentalism

As this painting of Ralph Waldo Emerson by an unknown artist indicates, the young philosopher was an attractive man, his face brimming with confidence and optimism. With his radiant personality and incisive intellect, Emerson deeply influenced dozens of influential writers, artists, and scholars and enjoyed great success as a lecturer to the emerging middle class. © The Metropolitan Museum of Art. Image source: Art Resource, NY.

wore the ideas of earlier times — New England Calvinism, for example — as a kind of "faded masquerade," and they needed to shed those values. "What is a man born for but to be a Reformer, a Remaker of what man has made?" Emerson asked. In his view, individuals could be remade only by discovering their "original relation with Nature" and entering into a mystical union with the "currents of Universal Being." The ideal setting for this transcendent discovery was under an open sky, in solitary communion with nature. The revivalist Charles Grandison Finney described his religious conversion in Emersonian terms: an individual in the woods, alone, joining with God in a mystical union.

The transcendentalist message of individual self-realization reached hundreds of thousands of people through Emerson's writings and lectures. Public lectures had become a spectacularly successful way of spreading information and fostering discussion among the middle classes. Beginning in 1826, the lyceum movement — modeled on the public forum of the ancient Greek philosopher Aristotle — arranged lecture tours by hundreds of poets, preachers, scientists, and reformers. The lyceum became an important cultural institution in the North and Midwest, but not in the South, where the middle class was smaller and popular education had a lower priority. In 1839, nearly 150 lyceums in Massachusetts invited lecturers to address more than 33,000 subscribers. Emerson was the most popular speaker, eventually delivering fifteen hundred lectures in more than three hundred towns in twenty states.

Emerson celebrated those who rejected tradition and practiced self-discipline and civic responsibility. His individualistic ethos spoke directly to the experiences of many middle-class Americans, who had left family farms to make their way in the urban world. His pantheistic view of nature — that it was saturated with the presence of God — encouraged Unitarians in Boston to create the Mount Auburn Cemetery, a beautiful planned landscape of trees and bushes and burial markers for the dead of all faiths; soon there were similar rural cemeteries in many American cities. Emerson's optimism also inspired many religious preachers of the Second Great Awakening, such as Finney, who told believers to transcend old doctrines and constraints. "God has made man a moral free agent," Finney declared.

Emerson worried that the new market society — the focus on work, profits, and consumption — was debasing Americans' spiritual lives. "Things are in the saddle," he wrote, "and ride mankind." Seeking to revive intellectual life, transcendentalists created communal experiments. The most important was Brook Farm, just outside Boston, where Emerson, Henry David Thoreau, and Margaret Fuller were residents or frequent visitors. Members recalled that they "inspired the young with a passion for study, and the middle-aged with deference and admiration." Whatever its intellectual excitement and spiritual rewards, Brook Farm was an economic failure. The residents planned to produce their own food and exchange their surplus milk, vegetables, and hay for manufactures. However, most members were ministers, teachers, writers, and students who had few farming skills; only the cash of affluent residents kept the enterprise afloat for five years. After a devastating fire in 1846, the organizers disbanded the community and sold the farm.

With the failure of Brook Farm, the Emersonians abandoned their quest for new social institutions. They accepted the brute reality of the emergent commercial and industrial order and tried to reform it, especially through the education of workers and the movement to abolish slavery.

> **UNDERSTAND POINTS OF VIEW**
> What were the main principles of transcendentalism, and how did they differ from the beliefs of most Protestant Christians?

Emerson's Literary Influence

Even as Emerson urged his fellow citizens to break free from tradition and expand their spiritual awareness, he issued a declaration of literary independence. In "The American Scholar" (1837), Emerson urged American authors to free themselves from the "courtly muse" of Old Europe and find inspiration in the experiences of ordinary Americans: "the ballad in the street; the news of the boat; the glance of the eye; the form and gait of the body."

Thoreau, Fuller, and Whitman One young New England intellectual, Henry David Thoreau (1817–1862), heeded Emerson's call and sought inspiration from the natural world. In 1845, depressed by his beloved brother's death, Thoreau built a cabin near Walden Pond in Concord, Massachusetts, and lived alone there for two years. In 1854, he published *Walden, or Life in the Woods*, an account of his search for meaning beyond the artificiality of civilized society:

> I went to the woods because I wished to live deliberately, to front only the essential facts of life, and see if I could not learn what it had to teach, and not, when I came to die, discover that I had not lived.

Walden's most famous metaphor provides an enduring justification for independent thinking: "If a man does not keep pace with his companions, perhaps it is because he hears a different drummer." Beginning from this premise, Thoreau advocated a thoroughgoing individuality, urging readers to avoid unthinking conformity to social norms and peacefully to resist unjust laws.

As Thoreau was seeking self-realization for men, Margaret Fuller (1810–1850) was exploring the possibilities of freedom for women. Born into a wealthy Boston family, Fuller mastered six languages and read broadly in classic literature. Embracing Emerson's ideas, she started a transcendental "conversation," or discussion group, for educated Boston women in 1839. While editing *The Dial*, the leading transcendentalist journal, Fuller published *Woman in the Nineteenth Century* (1844).

Margaret Fuller, 1848
At the age of thirty-eight, the American transcendentalist author Margaret Fuller moved to Italy, where she reported on the Revolution of 1848 for the *New York Tribune*. There she fell in love with Thomas Hicks (1823–1890), a much younger American artist. Hicks rebuffed Fuller's romantic advances but painted this flattering portrait, softening her features and giving her a pensive look. Fuller took as a lover a petty noble and republican revolutionary, Giovanni Angelo, Marchese d'Ossoli, and gave birth to a son in September 1848. Two years later, the entire family died in a shipwreck while en route to the United States. Constance Fuller Threinen.

To see a longer excerpt of *Woman in the Nineteenth Century*, along with other primary sources from this period, see *Sources for America's History.*

The poet Walt Whitman (1819–1892) also responded to Emerson's call. He had been "simmering, simmering," he recalled, and then Emerson "brought me to a boil." Whitman worked as a printer, a teacher, a journalist, an editor of the *Brooklyn Eagle*, and an influential publicist for the Democratic Party. However, poetry was the "direction of his dreams." In *Leaves of Grass*, a collection of wild, exuberant poems first published in 1855 and constantly revised and expanded, Whitman recorded in verse his efforts to transcend various "invisible boundaries": between solitude and community, between prose and poetry, even between the living and the dead. At the center of *Leaves of Grass* is the individual — "I, Walt." He begins alone: "I celebrate myself, and sing myself." Because he has an Emersonian "original relation" with nature, Whitman claims perfect communion with others: "For every atom belonging to me as good belongs to you." For Emerson, Thoreau, and Fuller, the individual had a divine spark; for Whitman, the collective democracy assumed a sacred character.

The transcendentalists were optimistic but not naive. Whitman wrote about human suffering with passion, and Emerson laced his accounts of transcendence with twinges of anxiety. "I am glad," he once said, "to the brink of fear." Thoreau was gloomy about everyday life: "The mass of men lead lives of quiet desperation." Nonetheless, dark murmurings remain muted in their work, overshadowed by assertions that nothing was impossible for the individual who could break free from tradition.

Darker Visions Emerson's writings also influenced two great novelists, Nathaniel Hawthorne and Herman Melville, who had more pessimistic worldviews. Both sounded powerful warnings that unfettered egoism could destroy individuals and those around them. Hawthorne brilliantly explored the theme of excessive individualism in his novel *The Scarlet Letter* (1850). The two main characters, Hester Prynne and Arthur Dimmesdale, blatantly challenge their seventeenth-century New England community by committing adultery and producing a child. Their decision to ignore social restraints results not in liberation but in degradation: a profound sense of guilt and condemnation by the community.

Herman Melville explored the limits of individualism in even more extreme and tragic terms and emerged

Fuller embraced the transcendental principle that all people could develop a life-affirming mystical relationship with God. Every woman therefore deserved psychological and social independence: the ability "to grow, as an intellect to discern, as a soul to live freely and unimpeded." She wrote: "We would have every arbitrary barrier thrown down [and] every path laid open to Woman as freely as to Man." Fuller became the literary critic of the *New York Tribune* and traveled to Italy to report on the Revolution of 1848, only to drown in a shipwreck en route home to the United States. Fuller's life and writings inspired a rising generation of women writers and reformers.

EXPLAIN CONSEQUENCES
How did authors of the American Renaissance incorporate transcendentalist ideas into their work?

as a scathing critic of transcendentalism. His most powerful statement was *Moby Dick* (1851), the story of Captain Ahab's obsessive hunt for a mysterious white whale that ends in death for Ahab and all but one member of his crew. Here, the quest for spiritual meaning in nature brings death, not transcendence, because Ahab, the liberated individual, lacks inner discipline and self-restraint.

Moby Dick was a commercial failure. The middle-class audience that devoured sentimental American fiction refused to follow Melville into the dark, dangerous realm of individualism gone mad. What middle-class readers emphatically preferred were the more modest examples of individualism offered by Emerson and Finney: personal improvement and religious piety through spiritual awareness and self-discipline.

Rural Communalism and Urban Popular Culture

Between 1820 and 1860, thousands of Americans grew dissatisfied with life in America's emerging market society and retreated into rural areas of the Northeast and Midwest (Map 11.1). There they sought to create ideal communities, or **utopias**, that would allow people to live differently and realize their spiritual potential.

Simultaneously, tens of thousands of rural Americans and European immigrants poured into the larger cities of the United States. There, they created a popular culture that challenged some sexual norms, reinforced traditional racist feelings, and encouraged new styles of dress and behavior.

The Utopian Impulse

Many rural communalists were farmers and artisans seeking refuge from the economic depression of 1837–1843. Others were religious idealists. Whatever their origins, these rural utopias were symbols of social protest and experimentation. By advocating the common ownership of property (socialism) and unconventional forms of marriage and family life, the communalists challenged traditional property rights and gender roles.

Mother Ann and the Shakers   The United Society of Believers in Christ's Second Appearing, known as the Shakers because of the ecstatic dances that were part of their worship, was the first successful American communal movement. In 1770, Ann Lee Stanley (Mother Ann), a young cook in Manchester, England, had a vision that she was an incarnation of Christ. Four years later, she led a few followers to America and established a church near Albany, New York.

After Mother Ann's death in 1784, the Shakers honored her as the Second Coming of Christ, withdrew from the profane world, and formed disciplined

MAP 11.1

Major Communal Experiments Before 1860
Some experimental communities settled along the frontier, but the vast majority chose rural areas in settled regions of the North and Midwest. Because they opposed slavery, communalists usually avoided the South. Most secular experiments failed within a few decades, as the founders lost their reformist enthusiasm or died off; tightly knit religious communities, such as the Shakers and the Mormons, were longer-lived.

Shakers at Prayer

Most Americans viewed the Shakers with a mixture of fascination and suspicion. They feared the sect's radical aspects, such as a commitment to celibacy and communal property, and considered the Shakers' dancing more an invitation to debauchery than a form of prayer. Those apprehensions surfaced in this engraving, *The Shakers of New Lebanon* (New York), which expresses both the powerful intensity and the menacing character of this Shaker spiritual ritual. The work of the journalist-engraver Joseph Becker, the picture appeared in Frank Leslie's *Illustrated Newspaper* in 1873. © Bettmann.

religious communities. Members embraced the common ownership of property; accepted strict oversight by church leaders; and pledged to abstain from alcohol, tobacco, politics, and war. Shakers also repudiated sexual pleasure and marriage. Their commitment to celibacy followed Mother Ann's testimony against "the lustful gratifications of the flesh as the source and foundation of human corruption." The Shakers' theology was as radical as their social thought. They held that God was "a dual person, male and female." This doctrine prompted Shakers to repudiate male leadership and to place community governance in the hands of both women and men — the Eldresses and the Elders.

IDENTIFY CAUSES

What factors led to the proliferation of rural utopian communities in nineteenth-century America?

Shakers founded twenty communities, mostly in New England, New York, and Ohio. Their agriculture and crafts, especially furniture making, acquired a reputation for quality that made most Shaker communities self-sustaining and even comfortable. Because the Shakers disdained sexual intercourse, they relied on conversions and the adoption of thousands of young orphans to increase their numbers. During the 1830s, three thousand adults, mostly women, joined the Shakers, attracted by their communal intimacy and sexual equality. To Rebecca Cox Jackson, an African American seamstress from Philadelphia, the Shakers seemed to be "loving to live forever." However, with the proliferation of public and private orphanages during the 1840s and 1850s, Shaker communities began to decline and, by 1900, had virtually disappeared. They left as a material legacy a plain but elegant style of wood furniture.

Albert Brisbane and Fourierism

As the Shakers' growth slowed during the 1840s, the American Fourierist movement mushroomed. Charles Fourier (1777–1837) was a French reformer who devised an eight-stage theory of social evolution that predicted the imminent decline of individual property rights and capitalist values. Fourier's leading disciple in America was Albert Brisbane. Just as republicanism had freed Americans from slavish monarchical government, Brisbane argued, so Fourierist **socialism** would liberate workers from capitalist employers and the "menial and slavish system of Hired Labor or Labor for Wages." Members would work for the community, in cooperative groups called phalanxes; they would own its property in common, including stores and a bank, a school, and a library.

Fourier and Brisbane saw the phalanx as a humane system that would liberate women as well as men. "In society as it is now constituted," Brisbane wrote, individual freedom was possible only for men, while "woman is subjected to unremitting and slavish domestic duties." In the "new Social Order . . . based upon Associated households," men would share women's domestic labor and thereby increase sexual equality.

Brisbane skillfully promoted Fourier's ideas in his influential book *The Social Destiny of Man* (1840), a regular column in Horace Greeley's *New York Tribune*, and hundreds of lectures. Fourierist ideas found a receptive audience among educated farmers and craftsmen, who yearned for economic stability and communal solidarity following the Panic of 1837. During the 1840s, Fourierists started nearly one hundred cooperative communities, mostly in western New York and the Midwest. Most communities quickly collapsed as members fought over work responsibilities and social policies. Fourierism's rapid decline revealed the difficulty of maintaining a utopian community in the absence of a charismatic leader or a compelling religious vision.

John Humphrey Noyes and Oneida

John Humphrey Noyes (1811–1886) was both charismatic and religious. He ascribed the Fourierists' failure to their secular outlook and embraced the pious Shakers as the true "pioneers of modern Socialism." The Shakers' marriageless society also inspired Noyes to create a community that defined sexuality and gender roles in radically new ways.

Attacking the Women's Rights Movement

Amelia Jenks Bloomer (1818–1894) wrote for her husband's newspaper, the *County Courier* of Seneca Falls, New York. In 1848 she attended the women's convention there and began her own biweekly newspaper, *The Lily*, focusing on temperance and women's rights. In 1851, Bloomer enthusiastically promoted—and serendipitously gave her name to—the comfortable women's costume devised by another temperance activist: loose trousers gathered at the ankles topped by a short skirt. Fearing women's quest for equal dress and equal rights, humorists such as John Leech ridiculed the new female attire. Here, bloomer-attired women smoke away and belittle the male proprietor as "one of the 'inferior animals,' " a thinly veiled effort by Leech to reassert men's "natural" claim as the dominant sex. From *Punch* 1851, John Leech Archive.

No. VI.—*SOMETHING MORE OF BLOOMERISM.*
(BEHIND THE COUNTER THERE IS ONE OF THE "INFERIOR ANIMALS.")

Noyes was a well-to-do graduate of Dartmouth College who joined the ministry after hearing a sermon by Charles Grandison Finney. Dismissed as the pastor of a Congregational church for holding unorthodox beliefs, Noyes turned to **perfectionism**, an evangelical Protestant movement of the 1830s that attracted thousands of New Englanders who had migrated to New York and Ohio. Perfectionists believed that Christ had already returned to earth (the Second Coming) and therefore people could aspire to sinless perfection in their earthly lives. Unlike most perfectionists, who lived conventional personal lives, Noyes rejected marriage, calling it a major barrier to perfection. "Exclusiveness, jealousy, quarreling have no place at the marriage supper of the Lamb," Noyes wrote. Instead of the Shakers' celibacy, Noyes embraced "complex marriage," in which all members of the community were married to one another. He rejected monogamy partly to free women from their status as the property of their husbands, as they were by custom and by common law. Symbolizing the quest for equality, Noyes's women followers cut their hair short and wore pantaloons under calf-length skirts.

In 1839, Noyes set up a perfectionist community near his hometown of Putney, Vermont. However, local outrage over the practice of complex marriage forced Noyes to relocate the community in 1848 to an isolated area near Oneida, New York, where the members could follow his precepts. To give women the time and energy to participate fully in community affairs, Noyes urged them to avoid multiple pregnancies. He asked men to help by avoiding orgasm during intercourse. Less positively, he encouraged sexual relations at a very early age and used his position of power to manipulate the sexual lives of his followers.

By the mid-1850s, the Oneida settlement had two hundred residents and became self-sustaining when the inventor of a highly successful steel animal trap joined the community. With the profits from trap making, the Oneidians diversified into the production of silverware. When Noyes fled to Canada in 1879 to avoid prosecution for adultery, the community abandoned complex marriage but retained its cooperative spirit. The Oneida Community, Ltd., a jointly owned silverware-manufacturing company, remained a successful communal venture until the middle of the twentieth century.

The historical significance of the Oneidians, Shakers, and Fourierists does not lie in their numbers, which were small, or in their fine crafts. Rather, it stems from their radical questioning of traditional sexual norms and of the capitalist values and class divisions of the emerging market society. Their utopian communities stood as countercultural blueprints of a more egalitarian social and economic order.

Joseph Smith and the Mormon Experience

The Mormons, members of the Church of Jesus Christ of Latter-day Saints, were religious utopians with a conservative social agenda: to perpetuate close-knit communities and patriarchal power. Because of their cohesiveness, authoritarian leadership, and size, the Mormons provoked more animosity than the radical utopians did.

Joseph Smith   Like many social movements of the era, **Mormonism** emerged from religious ferment among families of Puritan descent who lived along the

A Mormon Man and His Wives

The practice of polygamy split the Mormon community and, because it deviated from Christian religious principles, enraged Protestant denominations. This Mormon household, pictured in the late 1840s, was unusually prosperous, partly because of the labor of the husband's multiple wives. Although the cabin provides cramped quarters for a large polygamous family, it boasts a brick chimney and—a luxury for any pioneer home—a glass window. Library of Congress.

Erie Canal and who were heirs to a religious tradition that believed in a world of wonders, supernatural powers, and visions of the divine.

The founder of the Latter-day Church, Joseph Smith Jr. (1805–1844), was born in Vermont to a poor farming and shop-keeping family that migrated to Palmyra in central New York. In 1820, Smith began to have religious experiences similar to those described in conversion narratives: "[A] pillar of light above the brightness of the sun at noonday came down from above and rested upon me and I was filled with the spirit of God." Smith came to believe that God had singled him out to receive a special revelation of divine truth. In 1830, he published *The Book of Mormon*, which he claimed to have translated from ancient hieroglyphics on gold plates shown to him by an angel named Moroni. *The Book of Mormon* told the story of an ancient Jewish civilization from the Middle East that had migrated to the Western Hemisphere and of the visit of Jesus Christ, soon after his Resurrection, to those descendants of Israel. Smith's account explained the presence of native peoples in the Americas and integrated them into the Judeo-Christian tradition.

Smith proceeded to organize the Church of Jesus Christ of Latter-day Saints. Seeing himself as a prophet in a sinful, excessively individualistic society, Smith revived traditional social doctrines, including patriarchal authority. Like many Protestant ministers, he encouraged practices that led to individual success in the age of capitalist markets and factories: frugality, hard work, and enterprise. Smith also stressed communal discipline to safeguard the Mormon "New Jerusalem." His goal was a church-directed society that would restore primitive Christianity and encourage moral perfection.

Constantly harassed by anti-Mormons, Smith struggled to find a secure home for his new religion. At one point, he identified Jackson County in Missouri as the site of the sacred "City of Zion," and his followers began to settle there. Agitation led by Protestant ministers quickly forced them out: "Mormons were the common enemies of mankind and ought to be destroyed," said one cleric. Smith and his growing congregation eventually settled in Nauvoo, Illinois, a town they founded on the Mississippi River (Map 11.2). By the early 1840s, Nauvoo had 30,000 residents. The Mormons' rigid discipline and secret rituals — along with their prosperity, hostility toward other sects, and bloc voting in Illinois elections — fueled resentment among their neighbors. That resentment increased when Smith refused to accept Illinois laws of which he disapproved, asked Congress to make Nauvoo a separate federal territory, and declared himself a candidate for president of the United States.

Moreover, Smith claimed to have received a new revelation justifying polygamy, the practice of a man having multiple wives. When leading Mormon men took several wives — "plural celestial marriage" — they threw the Mormon community into turmoil and enraged nearby Christians. In 1844, Illinois officials arrested Smith and charged him with treason for allegedly conspiring to create a Mormon colony in Mexican territory. An anti-Mormon mob stormed the jail in Carthage, Illinois, where Smith and his brother were being held and murdered them.

Brigham Young and Utah   Led by Brigham Young, Smith's leading disciple and now the sect's "prophet, seer and revelator," about 6,500 Mormons fled the United States. Beginning in 1846, they crossed the

> **COMPARE AND CONTRAST**
>
> In what ways were Mormons similar to, and different from, other communal movements of the era?

MAP 11.2

The Mormon Trek, 1830–1848

Because of their unorthodox religious views and communal solidarity, Mormons faced hostility first in New York and then in Missouri and Illinois. After founder Joseph Smith Jr. was murdered, Brigham Young led the polygamist faction of Mormons into lands claimed by Mexico and thinly populated by Native Americans. From Omaha, the migrants followed the path of the Oregon Trail to Fort Bridger and then struck off to the southwest. They settled along the Wasatch Range in the basin of the Great Salt Lake in present-day Utah.

Great Plains into Mexican territory and settled in the Great Salt Lake Valley in present-day Utah. Using cooperative labor and an irrigation system based on communal water rights, the Mormon pioneers quickly spread agricultural communities along the base of the Wasatch Range. Many Mormons who rejected polygamy remained in the United States. Led by Smith's son, Joseph Smith III, they formed the Reorganized Church of Jesus Christ of Latter-day Saints and settled throughout the Midwest.

When the United States acquired Mexico's northern territories in 1848, the Salt Lake Mormons petitioned Congress to create a vast new state, Deseret, stretching from Utah to the Pacific coast. Instead, Congress set up the much smaller Utah Territory in 1850 and named Brigham Young its governor. Young and his associates ruled in an authoritarian fashion, determined to ensure the ascendancy of the Mormon Church and its practices. By 1856, Young and the Utah territorial legislature were openly vowing to resist federal laws. Pressed by Protestant church leaders to end polygamy and considering the Mormons' threat of nullification "a declaration of war," President James Buchanan dispatched a small army to Utah. As the "Nauvoo Legion" resisted the army's advance, aggressive Mormon militia massacred a party of 120 California-bound emigrants and murdered suspicious travelers and Mormons seeking to flee Young's regime. Despite this bloodshed, the "Mormon War" ended quietly in June 1858. President Buchanan, a longtime supporter of the white South, feared that the forced abolition of polygamy would serve as a precedent for ending slavery and offered a pardon to Utah citizens who would acknowledge federal authority. (To enable Utah to win admission to the Union in 1896, its citizens ratified a constitution that "forever" banned the practice of polygamy. However, the state government has never strictly enforced that ban.)

The Salt Lake Mormons had succeeded even as other social experiments had failed. Reaffirming traditional values, their leaders resolutely used strict religious controls to perpetuate patriarchy and communal discipline. However, by endorsing private property and individual enterprise, Mormons became prosperous contributors to the new market society. This blend of economic innovation, social conservatism, and hierarchical leadership, in combination with a strong missionary impulse, created a wealthy and expansive church that now claims a worldwide membership of about 12 million people.

Urban Popular Culture

As utopians organized communities in the countryside, rural migrants and foreign immigrants created a new urban culture. In 1800, American cities were overgrown towns with rising death rates: New York had only 60,000 residents, Philadelphia had 41,000, and life expectancy at birth was a mere twenty-five years. Then urban growth accelerated as a huge in-migration outweighed the high death rates. By 1840, New York's population had ballooned to 312,000; Philadelphia and its suburbs had 150,000 residents; and three other cities — New Orleans, Boston, and Baltimore — each had about 100,000. By 1860, New York had become a metropolis with more than 1 million residents: 813,000 in Manhattan and another 266,000 in the adjacent community of Brooklyn.

Sex in the City   These newly populous cities, particularly New York, generated a new urban culture. Thousands of young men and women flocked to the city searching for adventure and fortune, but many found only a hard life. Young men labored for meager wages building thousands of tenements, warehouses, and workshops. Others worked as low-paid clerks or operatives in hundreds of mercantile and manufacturing firms. The young women had an even harder time. Thousands toiled as live-in domestic servants, ordered about by the mistress of the household and often sexually exploited by the master. Thousands more scraped out a bare living as needlewomen in New York City's booming ready-made clothes industry. Unwilling to endure domestic service or subsistence wages, many young girls turned to prostitution. Dr. William Sanger's careful survey, commissioned in 1855 by worried city officials, found six thousand women engaged in commercial sex. Three-fifths were native-born whites, and the rest were foreign immigrants; most were between fifteen and twenty years old. Half were or had been domestic servants, half had children, and half were infected with syphilis.

Commercialized sex — and sex in general — formed one facet of the new urban culture. "Sporting men" engaged freely in sexual conquests; otherwise respectable married men kept mistresses in handy apartments; and working men frequented bawdy houses. New York City had two hundred brothels in the 1820s and five hundred by the 1850s. Prostitutes — so-called "public" women — openly advertised their wares on Broadway,

COMPARE AND CONTRAST
How were the cultures of utopian communalists and urban residents similar to and different from the mainstream culture described in Chapters 8 and 9?

Night Life in Philadelphia

This watercolor by Russian painter Pavel Svinin (1787–1839) captures the social diversity and allure of urban America. A respectable gentleman relishes the delicacies sold by a black oysterman. Meanwhile, a young woman—probably a prostitute but perhaps an adventurous working girl—engages the attention of two well-dressed young "swells" outside the Chestnut Street Theatre. Such scenes were new to Americans and marked the beginning of a profound split between the nation's rural and urban cultures. © The Metropolitan Museum of Art. Image source: Art Resource, NY.

the city's most fashionable thoroughfare, and welcomed clients on the infamous "Third Tier" of the theaters. Many men considered illicit sex as a right. "Man is endowed by nature with passions that must be gratified," declared the *Sporting Whip*, a working-class magazine. Even the Reverend William Berrian, pastor of the ultra-respectable Trinity Episcopal Church, remarked from the pulpit that he had resorted ten times to "a house of ill-fame."

Prostitution formed only the tip of the urban sexual volcano. Freed from family oversight, men formed homoerotic friendships and relationships; as early as 1800, the homosexual "Fop" was an acknowledged character in Philadelphia. Young people moved from partner to partner until they chanced on an ideal mate. Middle-class youth strolled along Broadway in the latest fashions: elaborate bonnets and silk dresses for young women; flowing capes, leather boots, and

silver-plated walking sticks for young men. Rivaling the elegance on Broadway was the colorful dress on the Bowery, the broad avenue that ran along the east side of lower Manhattan. By day, the "Bowery Boy" worked as an apprentice or journeyman. By night, he prowled the streets as a "consummate dandy," his hair cropped at the back of his head "as close as scissors could cut," with long front locks "matted by a lavish application of *bear's grease*, the ends tucked under so as to form a roll and brushed until they shone like glass bottles." The "B'hoy," as he was called, cut a dashing figure as he walked along with a "Bowery Gal" in a striking dress and shawl: "a light pink contrasting with a deep blue" or "a bright yellow with a brighter red."

Minstrelsy   Popular entertainment was a central facet of the new urban culture. In New York, working-men could partake of traditional rural blood sports—rat and terrier fights as well as boxing matches—at Sportsmen Hall, or they could seek drink and fun in billiard and bowling saloons. Other workers crowded into the pit of the Bowery Theatre to see the "Mad Tragedian," Junius Brutus Booth, deliver a stirring (abridged) performance of Shakespeare's *Richard III*. Reform-minded couples enjoyed evenings at the huge Broadway Tabernacle, where they could hear an abolitionist lecture, see the renowned Hutchinson Family Singers lead a roof-raising rendition of their antislavery anthem, "Get Off the Track," and sentimentally lament the separation of a slave couple in Stephen Foster's "Oh Susanna," a popular song of the late 1840s. Families could visit the museum of oddities (and hoaxes) created by P. T. Barnum, the great cultural entrepreneur and founder of the Barnum & Bailey Circus.

However, the most popular theatrical entertainments were the minstrel shows, in which white actors in blackface presented comic routines that combined racist caricature and social criticism. **Minstrelsy** began around 1830, when a few actors put on blackface and performed song-and-dance routines (Thinking Like a Historian, p. 358). The most famous was John Dartmouth Rice, whose "Jim Crow" blended a weird shuffle-dance-and-jump with unintelligible lyrics delivered in "Negro dialect." By the 1840s, there were hundreds of minstrel troupes, including a group of black entertainers, Gavitt's Original Ethiopian Serenaders. The actor-singers' rambling lyrics poked racist fun at African Americans, portraying them as lazy, sensual, and irresponsible while simultaneously using them to criticize white society. Minstrels ridiculed the drunkenness of Irish immigrants, parodied the halting English of German immigrants, denounced women's demands for political rights, and mocked the arrogance of upper-class men. Still, by caricaturing blacks, the minstrels declared the importance of being white and spread racist sentiments among Irish and German immigrants.

Immigrant Masses and Nativist Reaction   By 1850, immigrants were a major presence throughout the Northeast. Irish men and women in New York City numbered 200,000, and Germans 110,000 (Figure 11.1). German-language shop signs filled entire neighborhoods, and German foods (sausages, hamburgers, sauerkraut) and food customs (such as drinking beer in family *biergärten*) became part of the city's culture. The mass of impoverished Irish migrants found allies in the American Catholic Church, which soon became an Irish-dominated institution, and the Democratic Party, which gave them a foothold in the political process.

Native-born New Yorkers took alarm as hordes of ethnically diverse migrants altered the city's culture. They organized a nativist movement—a final aspect of the new urban world. Beginning in the mid-1830s, nativists called for a halt to immigration and mounted a cultural and political assault on foreign-born residents (Chapter 9). Gangs of B'hoys assaulted Irish youths in the streets, employers restricted Irish workers to the most menial jobs, and temperance reformers denounced the German fondness for beer. In 1844, the American Republican Party, with the endorsement of the Whigs, swept the city elections by focusing on

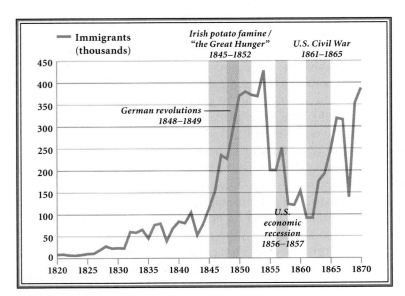

FIGURE 11.1

The Surge in Imigration, 1854–1855

In 1845, the failure of the potato crop in Ireland prompted the wholesale migration to the United States of peasants from the overcrowded farms of its western counties. Population growth and limited economic prospects likewise spurred the migration of tens of thousands of German peasants, while the failure of the liberal republican political revolution of 1848 prompted hundreds of prominent German politicians and intellectuals to follow them. An American economic recession cut the flow of immigrants, but the booming northern economy during the Civil War again persuaded Europeans to set sail for the United States.

the culturally emotional issues of temperance, anti-Catholicism, and nativism.

In the city, as in the countryside, new values were challenging old beliefs. The sexual freedom celebrated by Noyes at Oneida had its counterpart in commercialized sex and male promiscuity in New York City, where it came under attack from the Female Moral Reform Society. Similarly, the disciplined rejection of tobacco and alcohol by the Shakers and the Mormons found a parallel in the Washington Temperance Society and other urban reform organizations. American society was in ferment, and the outcome was far from clear.

Abolitionism

Like other reform movements, the **abolitionist** crusade of the 1830s drew on the religious enthusiasm of the Second Great Awakening. Around 1800, antislavery activists had assailed human bondage as contrary to republicanism and liberty. Three decades later, white abolitionists condemned slavery as a sin and demanded immediate, uncompensated emancipation. Their uncompromising stance led to fierce political debates, urban riots, and sectional conflict.

Rampant Racism

Minstrel shows and their music were just two facets of the racist culture of mid-nineteenth-century America. Exploiting the market for almanacs among farmers and city-folk alike, the publishing firm of Fisher and Brother produced the *Black Joke Al-Ma-Nig* for 1852. Like other almanacs, it provided astrological charts, weather predictions, and a detailed calendar of events. To boost sales, the almanac included "new an' original nigga' stories, black jokes, puns, parodies" that would "magnetize bofe white an' black." Such racist caricatures of black faces and language influenced white views of African Americans well into the twentieth century. Courtesy: The Library Company of Philadelphia.

Dance and Social Identity in Antebellum America

Styles of dance and attitudes toward them tell us a great deal about cultural and social norms. When nineteenth-century Americans took to partying, their dances—regardless of the class or ethnic identity of the dancers—focused more on individual couples and allowed more room for improvisation and intimacy than the dance forms of the previous century.

1. **William Sidney Mount, *Rustic Dance After a Sleigh Ride*, 1830.** *In the eighteenth century, wealthy, fashionable Americans danced the French minuet, a ceremonious and graceful dance in which couples executed prescribed steps while barely touching. Ordinary white folks preferred the country dances brought by their ancestors from Europe, which also involved intricate steps, line formations, and limited physical contact. Mount (1807–1868) was self-taught, lived in rural Long Island, and depicted scenes of everyday life. This painting, replete with amorous pursuits, depicts a traditional contra dance in which the lead couple advances a few steps and then sashays to the back of the line, as another couple takes its place.*

was the most widely circulated American periodical prior to the Civil War and an arbiter of good taste among the aspiring middle classes. Each issue contained a sheet of music for the latest dance craze. The Lady's Book cautiously endorsed the waltz, a sensuous dance that required a close embrace, but enthusiastically welcomed its cousin, the polka, whose lively tempo and rapid spinning had a wholesome and joyful quality. Introduced from Bohemia, the polka dominated the ballrooms of America's upper and middle classes in the 1840s and 1850s.

Private Collection/The Bridgeman Art Library.

Museum of Fine Arts, Boston, Massachusetts, USA/Bequest of Martha C. Karolik for the M. and M. Karolik/Collection of American Paintings, 1815–65/The Bridgeman Art Library.

2. **"The Polka Fashions," from *Godey's Lady's Book*, 1845.** *"A magazine of elegant literature," according to its publisher, Louis A. Godey, the* Lady's Book

3. **George Templeton Strong, diary entry, December 23, 1845.**

Well, last night I spent at Mrs. Mary Jones's great ball. Very splendid affair — "the Ball of the Season." . . . Two houses open, standing supper table, "dazzling array of beauty and fashion." "Polka" for the first time brought under my inspection. It's a kind of insane Tartar jig performed to disagreeable music of an uncivilized character.

4. **Description of juba dancing from Charles Dickens, *American Notes for General Circulation*, 1842.** *In New York's Five Points slum in 1842, Charles Dickens described a challenge dance featuring William Henry Lane, or Master Juba, a young African American who created juba dancing, a blend of Irish jig and African dance moves.*

The corpulent black fiddler, and his friend who plays the tambourine, stamp upon the boarding of the small raised orchestra in which they sit, and play a lively measure. Five or six couples come upon the floor, marshalled by a lively young negro, who is the wit of the assembly, and the greatest dancer known. . . . Instantly the fiddler grins, and goes at it tooth and nail; there is new energy in the tambourine. . . . Single shuffle, double shuffle, cut and cross-cut; snapping his fingers, rolling his eyes, turning in his knees, presenting the backs of his legs in front, spinning about on his toes and heels like nothing but the man's fingers on the tambourine; dancing with two left legs, two right legs, two wooden legs, two wire legs, two spring legs — all sorts of legs and no legs — . . . having danced his partner off her feet, and himself too, he finishes by leaping gloriously on the bar-counter, and calling for something to drink.

5. **Poster advertising Barlow, Wilson, Primrose, and West's "Mammoth Minstrels' Colored Masquerade."** *Unlike slavery, minstrelsy survived the Civil War and remained popular until the early twentieth century, when it evolved into vaudeville. Barlow, Wilson, Primrose, and West's Mammoth*

Minstrels toured the United States, Europe, and Australia between 1877 and 1882, thrilling audiences with the clog dances that had devolved out of juba.

Sources: (3) Luther S. Harris, *Around Washington Square: An Illustrated History of Greenwich Village* (Baltimore, 2003), 41; (4) Charles Dickens, *American Notes and Pictures from Italy* (C. Scribner: New York, 1868), 107.

ANALYZING THE EVIDENCE

1. What do sources 1 and 2 suggest about sexual manners among rural folk and genteel urbanites?
2. What does the polka (sources 3 and 4) reveal about changing cultural practices among the social elite?
3. Compare the juba and minstrelsy dances described above (sources 4 and 5) with the polka and contra dance forms (sources 1 and 2). How were dance forms and popular entertainment evolving? How did those changes relate to broader social developments?
4. The waltz, polka, and juba dances were popular during the Second Great Awakening, when (and long afterward) preachers often complained that "dance is destructive to Christian life." Why might ministers (and priests) take such a view? Would any form of dance be acceptable to them?

PUTTING IT ALL TOGETHER

Using the material on class, religion, and culture in Chapters 9 and 11, the description of the Quarterons Ball in Chapter 12 (p. 387), and the insights you have gathered by a careful inspection of these sources, write an essay showing how dance and other entertainments reflect or reveal differences among American social groups.

Private Collection/Photo © Barbara Singer/The Bridgeman Art Library.

Black Social Thought: Uplift, Race Equality, and Rebellion

Beginning in the 1790s, leading African Americans in the North advocated a strategy of social uplift, encouraging free blacks to "elevate" themselves through education, temperance, and hard work. By securing "respectability," they argued, blacks could become the social equals of whites. To promote that goal, black leaders — men such as James Forten, a Philadelphia sailmaker; Prince Hall, a Boston barber; and ministers Hosea Easton and Richard Allen (Chapter 8) — founded an array of churches, schools, and self-help associations. Capping this effort, John Russwurm and Samuel D. Cornish of New York published the first African American newspaper, *Freedom's Journal*, in 1827.

The black quest for respectability elicited a violent response in Boston, Pittsburgh, and other northern cities among whites who refused to accept African Americans as their social equals. "I am Mr. _____'s help," a white maid informed a British visitor. "I am no sarvant; none but negers are sarvants." Motivated by racial contempt, white mobs terrorized black communities. The attacks in Cincinnati were so violent and destructive that several hundred African Americans fled to Canada for safety.

David Walker's *Appeal*   Responding to the attacks, David Walker published a stirring pamphlet, *An Appeal . . . to the Colored Citizens of the World* (1829), protesting black "wretchedness in this Republican Land of Liberty!!!!!" Walker was a free black from North Carolina who had moved to Boston, where he sold secondhand clothes and copies of *Freedom's Journal*. A self-educated author, Walker ridiculed the religious pretensions of slaveholders, justified slave rebellion, and in biblical language warned of a slave revolt if justice were delayed. "We must and shall be free," he told white Americans. "And woe, woe, will be it to you if we have to obtain our freedom by fighting. . . . Your destruction is at hand, and will be speedily consummated unless you repent." Walker's pamphlet quickly went through three printings and, carried by black merchant seamen, reached free African Americans in the South.

In 1830, Walker and other African American activists called a national convention in Philadelphia. The delegates refused to endorse either Walker's radical call for a slave revolt or the traditional program of uplift for free blacks. Instead, this new generation of activists demanded freedom and "race equality" for those of African descent. They urged free blacks to use every legal means, including petitions and other forms of political protest, to break "the shackles of slavery."

Nat Turner's Revolt   As Walker threatened violence in Boston, Nat Turner, a slave in Southampton County,

A Call for Revolution

David Walker (1785–1830), who ran a used clothing shop in Boston, spent his hard-earned savings to publish *An Appeal . . . to the Colored Citizens of the World* (1829), a learned and passionate attack on racial slavery. Walker depicted Christ as an avenging "God of justice and of armies" and raised the banner of slave rebellion. A year later, a passerby found Walker in the doorway of his shop, dead from unknown causes. Library of Congress.

Virginia, staged a bloody revolt — a chronological coincidence that had far-reaching consequences. As a child, Turner had taught himself to read and had hoped for emancipation, but one new master forced him into the fields, and another separated him from his wife. Becoming deeply spiritual, Turner had a religious vision in which "the Spirit" explained that "Christ had laid down the yoke he had borne for the sins of men, and that I should take it on and fight against the Serpent, for the time was fast approaching when the first should be last and the last should be first." Taking an eclipse of the sun in August 1831 as an omen, Turner and a handful of relatives and friends rose in rebellion and killed at least 55 white men, women, and children. Turner hoped that hundreds of slaves would rally to his cause, but he mustered only 60 men. The white militia quickly dispersed his poorly armed force and took their revenge. One company of cavalry killed 40 blacks in two days and put 15 of their heads on poles to warn "all those who should undertake a similar plot." Turner died by hanging, still identifying his mission with that of his Savior. "Was not Christ crucified?" he asked.

Deeply shaken by Turner's Rebellion, the Virginia assembly debated a law providing for gradual emancipation and colonization abroad. When the bill failed by a vote of 73 to 58, the possibility that southern planters would voluntarily end slavery was gone forever. Instead, the southern states toughened their slave codes, limited black movement, and prohibited anyone from teaching slaves to read. They would meet Walker's radical *Appeal* with radical measures of their own.

Evangelical Abolitionism

Rejecting Walker's and Turner's resort to violence, a cadre of northern evangelical Christians launched a moral crusade to abolish the slave regime. If planters did not allow blacks their God-given status as free

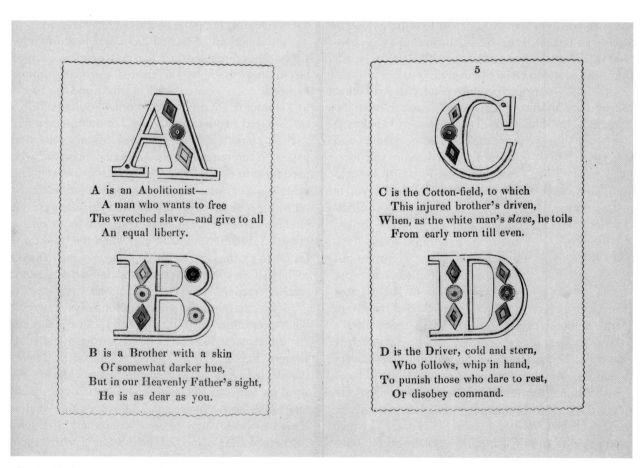

The Anti-Slavery Alphabet

Girding themselves for a long fight, abolitionists conveyed their beliefs to the next generation. This primer, written by Quakers Hannah and Mary Townsend and published in Philadelphia in 1846, taught young children the alphabet by spreading the antislavery message. "A" was for "Abolitionist," and "B" was for a "Brother," an enslaved black who, though of a "darker hue," was considered by God "as dear as you." The Huntington Library & Art Collections, San Marino, CA.

moral agents, these radical Christians warned, they faced eternal damnation at the hands of a just God.

William Lloyd Garrison, Theodore Weld, and Angelina and Sarah Grimké

The most determined abolitionist was William Lloyd Garrison (1805–1879). A Massachusetts-born printer, Garrison had worked during the 1820s in Baltimore on an antislavery newspaper, the *Genius of Universal Emancipation*. In 1830, Garrison went to jail, convicted of libeling a New England merchant engaged in the domestic slave trade. In 1831, Garrison moved to Boston, where he immediately started his own weekly, *The Liberator* (1831–1865), and founded the New England Anti-Slavery Society.

Influenced by a bold pamphlet, *Immediate, Not Gradual Abolition* (1824), by an English Quaker, Elizabeth Coltman Heyrick, Garrison demanded immediate abolition without compensation to slaveholders. "I will not retreat a single inch," he declared, "AND I WILL BE HEARD." Garrison accused the American Colonization Society (Chapter 8) of perpetuating slavery and assailed the U.S. Constitution as "a covenant with death and an agreement with Hell" because it implicitly accepted racial bondage.

In 1833, Garrison, Theodore Weld, and sixty other religious abolitionists, black and white, established the American Anti-Slavery Society. The society won financial support from Arthur and Lewis Tappan, wealthy silk merchants in New York City. Women abolitionists established separate groups, including the Philadelphia Female Anti-Slavery Society, founded by Lucretia Mott in 1833, and the Anti-Slavery Conventions of American Women, a network of local societies. The women raised money for *The Liberator* and carried the movement to the farm villages and small towns of the Midwest, where they distributed abolitionist literature and collected thousands of signatures on antislavery petitions.

Abolitionist leaders launched a three-pronged plan of attack. To win the support of religious Americans, Weld published *The Bible Against Slavery* (1837), which used passages from Christianity's holiest book to discredit slavery. Two years later, Weld teamed up with the Grimké sisters — Angelina, whom he married, and Sarah. The Grimkés had left their father's plantation in South Carolina, converted to Quakerism, and taken up the abolitionist cause in Philadelphia. In *American*

COMPARE AND CONTRAST
How did the ideology and tactics of the Garrisonian abolitionists differ from those of the antislavery movements discussed in Chapters 6 and 8?

Slavery as It Is: Testimony of a Thousand Witnesses (1839), Weld and the Grimkés addressed a simple question: "What is the actual condition of the slaves in the United States?" Using reports from southern newspapers and firsthand testimony, they presented incriminating evidence of the inherent violence of slavery. Angelina Grimké told of a treadmill that South Carolina slave owners used for punishment: "One poor girl, [who was] sent there to be flogged, and who was accordingly stripped naked and whipped, showed me the deep gashes on her back — I might have laid my whole finger in them — large pieces of flesh had actually been cut out by the torturing lash." Filled with such images of pain and suffering, the book sold more than 100,000 copies in a single year.

The American Anti-Slavery Society

To spread their message, the abolitionists turned to mass communication. Using new steam-powered presses to print a million pamphlets, the American Anti-Slavery Society carried out a "great postal campaign" in 1835, flooding the nation, including the South, with its literature.

The abolitionists' second tactic was to aid fugitive slaves. They provided lodging and jobs for escaped blacks in free states and created the **Underground Railroad**, an informal network of whites and free blacks in Richmond, Charleston, and other southern towns that assisted fugitives (Map 11.3). In Baltimore, a free African American sailor loaned his identification papers to future abolitionist Frederick Douglass, who used them to escape to New York. Harriet Tubman and other runaways risked re-enslavement or death by returning repeatedly to the South to help others escape. "I should fight for . . . liberty as long as my strength lasted," Tubman explained, "and when the time came for me to go, the Lord would let them take me." Thanks to the Railroad, about one thousand African Americans reached freedom in the North each year.

There, they faced an uncertain future because most whites continued to reject civic or social equality for African Americans. Voters in six northern and midwestern states adopted constitutional amendments that denied or limited the franchise for free blacks. "We want no masters," declared a New York artisan, "and least of all no negro masters." Moreover, the Fugitive Slave Law (1793) allowed owners and their hired slave catchers to seize suspected runaways and return them to bondage. To thwart these efforts, white abolitionists and free blacks formed mobs that attacked slave catchers, released their captives, and often spirited them off to British-ruled Canada, which refused to extradite fugitive slaves.

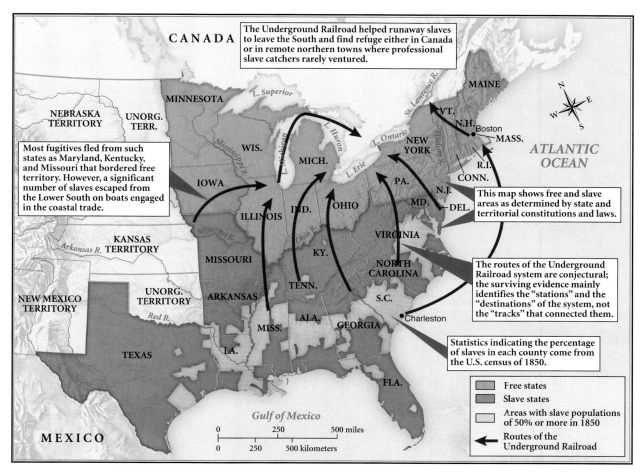

The Underground Railroad helped runaway slaves to leave the South and find refuge either in Canada or in remote northern towns where professional slave catchers rarely ventured.

Most fugitives fled from such states as Maryland, Kentucky, and Missouri that bordered free territory. However, a significant number of slaves escaped from the Lower South on boats engaged in the coastal trade.

This map shows free and slave areas as determined by state and territorial constitutions and laws.

The routes of the Underground Railroad system are conjectural; the surviving evidence mainly identifies the "stations" and the "destinations" of the system, not the "tracks" that connected them.

Statistics indicating the percentage of slaves in each county come from the U.S. census of 1850.

Free states
Slave states
Areas with slave populations of 50% or more in 1850
Routes of the Underground Railroad

MAP 11.3
The Underground Railroad in the 1850s
Before 1840, most African Americans who fled slavery did so on their own or with the help of family and friends. Thereafter, they could count on support from members of the Underground Railroad. Provided with food and directions by free blacks in the South, fugitive slaves crossed into free states. There, they received protection and shelter from abolitionists who arranged for their transportation to Canada or to "safe" American cities and towns.

A political campaign was the final element of the abolitionists' program. Between 1835 and 1838, the American Anti-Slavery Society bombarded Congress with petitions containing nearly 500,000 signatures. They demanded the abolition of slavery in the District of Columbia, an end to the interstate slave trade, and a ban on admission of new slave states.

Thousands of deeply religious farmers and small-town proprietors supported these efforts. The number of local abolitionist societies grew from two hundred in 1835 to two thousand by 1840, with nearly 200,000 members, including many transcendentalists. Emerson condemned Americans for supporting slavery, and Thoreau, viewing the Mexican War as a naked scheme to extend slavery, refused to pay taxes and submitted to arrest. In 1848, he published "Resistance to Civil Government," an essay urging individuals to follow a higher moral law. The black abolitionist Henry Highland Garnet went further; his *Address to the Slaves of the United States of America* (1841) called for "Liberty or Death" and urged slave "Resistance! Resistance! Resistance!"

Opposition and Internal Conflict

Still, abolitionists remained a minority, even among churchgoers. Perhaps 10 percent of northerners and midwesterners strongly supported the movement, and only another 20 percent were sympathetic to its goals.

Attacks on Abolitionism Slavery's proponents were more numerous and equally aggressive. The

THE NEGRO IN HIS OWN COUNTRY.

THE NEGRO IN AMERICA.

"The Negro in His Own Country" Versus "The Negro in America"

Slave owners and their intellectual and religious allies responded to abolitionists' attacks by defending slavery as a "positive good." These two images, from Josiah Priest's *Bible Defence of Slavery* (1852), support the argument that enslavement saved Africans from a savage, war-ridden life (note the skeleton in the top image) and exposed them to the civilized world. Such publications achieved wide circulation and popularity among the planter classes. Chicago History Museum.

abolitionists' agitation, ministers warned, risked "embroiling neighborhoods and families — setting friend against friend, overthrowing churches and institutions of learning, embittering one portion of the land against the other." Wealthy men feared that the attack on slave property might become an assault on all property rights, conservative clergymen condemned the public roles assumed by abolitionist women, and northern wage earners feared that freed blacks would work for lower wages and take their jobs.

Underlining the national "reach" of slavery, northern merchants and textile manufacturers supported the southern planters who supplied them with cotton, as did hog farmers in Ohio, Indiana, and Illinois and pork packers in Cincinnati and

UNDERSTAND POINTS OF VIEW

Which groups of Americans opposed the abolitionists, and why did they do so?

Chicago who profited from lucrative sales to slave plantations. Finally, whites almost universally opposed "**amalgamation**," the racial mixing and intermarriage that Garrison seemed to support by holding meetings of blacks and whites of both sexes.

Racial fears and hatreds led to violent mob actions. White workers in northern towns laid waste to taverns and brothels where blacks and whites mixed, and they vandalized "respectable" African American churches, temperance halls, and orphanages. In 1833, a mob of 1,500 New Yorkers stormed a church in search of Garrison and Arthur Tappan. Another white mob swept through Philadelphia's African American neighborhoods, clubbing and stoning residents and destroying homes and churches. In 1835, "gentlemen of property and standing" — lawyers, merchants, and bankers — broke up an abolitionist convention in Utica, New

York. Two years later, a mob in Alton, Illinois, shot and killed Elijah P. Lovejoy, editor of the abolitionist *Alton Observer*. By pressing for emancipation and equality, the abolitionists had revealed the extent of racial prejudice and had heightened race consciousness, as both whites and blacks identified across class lines with members of their own race.

Racial solidarity was especially strong in the South, where whites banned abolitionists. The Georgia legislature offered a $5,000 reward for kidnapping Garrison and bringing him to the South to be tried (or lynched) for inciting rebellion. In Nashville, vigilantes whipped a northern college student for distributing abolitionist pamphlets; in Charleston, a mob attacked the post office and destroyed sacks of abolitionist mail. After

1835, southern postmasters simply refused to deliver mail suspected to be of abolitionist origin.

Politicians joined the fray. President Andrew Jackson, a longtime slave owner, asked Congress in 1835 to restrict the use of the mails by abolitionist groups. Congress refused, but in 1836, the House of Representatives adopted the so-called **gag rule**. Under this informal agreement, which remained in force until 1844, the House automatically tabled antislavery petitions, keeping the explosive issue of slavery off the congressional stage.

Internal Divisions Assailed by racists from the outside, evangelical abolitionists fought among themselves over gender issues. Many antislavery clergymen

AN AFFECTING SCENE IN KENTUCKY.

The Complexities of Race

This cartoon takes aim at Richard Mentor Johnson of Kentucky, the distraught man being comforted by abolitionists Frederick Douglass and William Lloyd Garrison. A longtime congressman and senator, Johnson was the Democrats' vice-presidential candidate in 1836. Although the party stood for the South and slavery—and condemned mixed-race unions—Johnson lived openly with an African American woman, Julia Chinn, whose daughters hold her portrait. Future Supreme Court justice John Catron noted with disgust that Johnson tried "to force his daughters into society" and that they and their mother "claimed equality." Racial prejudice cost Johnson some votes, but he won a plurality in the electoral college, and, on a party-line vote, Democrats in the Senate elected him Martin Van Buren's vice president. Library of Congress.

opposed an activist role for women, but Garrison had broadened his reform agenda to include pacifism, the abolition of prisons, and women's rights: "Our object is universal emancipation, to redeem women as well as men from a servile to an equal condition." In 1840, Garrison's demand that the American Anti-Slavery Society support women's rights split the abolitionist movement. Abby Kelley, Lucretia Mott, and Elizabeth Cady Stanton, among others, remained with Garrison in the American Anti-Slavery Society and assailed both the institutions that bound blacks and the customs that constrained free women.

Garrison's opponents founded a new organization, the American and Foreign Anti-Slavery Society, which turned to politics. Its members mobilized their churches to oppose racial bondage and organized the Liberty Party, the first antislavery political party. In 1840, the new party nominated James G. Birney, a former Alabama slave owner, for president. Birney and the Liberty Party argued that the Constitution did not recognize slavery and, consequently, that slaves became free when they entered areas of federal authority, such as the District of Columbia and the national territories. However, Birney won few votes, and the future of political abolitionism appeared dim.

Popular violence in the North, government-aided suppression in the South, and internal schisms stunned the abolitionist movement. By melding the energies and ideas of evangelical Protestants, moral reformers, and transcendentalists, it had raised the banner of antislavery to new heights, only to face a hostile backlash. "When we first unfurled the banner of *The Liberator*,"

Garrison admitted, "it did not occur to us that nearly every religious sect, and every political party would side with the oppressor."

The Women's Rights Movement

The prominence of women among the abolitionists reflected a broad shift in American culture. By joining religious revivals and reform movements, women entered public life. Their activism caused many gender issues — sexual behavior, marriage, family authority — to become subjects of debate. The debate entered a new phase in 1848, when some reformers focused on women's rights and demanded complete equality with men.

Origins of the Women's Movement

"Don't be afraid, not afraid, fight Satan; stand up for Christ; don't be afraid." So spoke Mary Walker Ostram on her deathbed in 1859. Her religious convictions were as firm at the age of fifty-eight as they had been in 1816, when she joined the first Sunday school in Utica, New York. Married to a lawyer-politician and childless, Ostram had devoted her life to evangelical Presbyterianism and its program of benevolent social reform. At her funeral, minister Philemon Fowler celebrated Ostram as a "living fountain" of faith, an exemplar of "Women's Sphere of Influence" in the world.

A Nineteenth-Century Middle-Class Family

Whereas colonial-era families were large, often with six to eight children, nineteenth-century middle-class couples, such as Azariah and Eliza Caverly, pictured here in 1836 by Joseph H. Davis (1811–1865), consciously limited their fertility, treated their spouses with affection, and carefully supervised the education of their children. The Caverlys' daughter fingers a Bible, suggesting her future moral responsibilities as a mother, while their son holds a square ruler, either indicating Azariah's profession or foreshadowing the son's career as a prosperous architect or engineer. Fenimore Art Museum, Cooperstown, New York.

Although Reverend Fowler heaped praise on Ostram, he rejected a public presence for women. Like men of the Revolutionary era, Fowler thought women should limit their political role to that of "republican mother," instructing "their sons in the principles of liberty and government." Women inhabited a "**separate sphere**" of domestic life, he said, and had no place in "the markets of trade, the scenes of politics and popular agitation, the courts of justice and the halls of legislation. Home is her peculiar sphere."

However, Ostram and many other middle-class women were redefining the notion of the domestic sphere by becoming active in their churches. Their spiritual activism bolstered their authority within the household and gave them new influence over many areas of family life, including the timing of pregnancies. Publications such as *Godey's Lady's Book*, a popular monthly periodical, and Catharine Beecher's *Treatise on Domestic Economy* (1841) taught women how to make their homes examples of middle-class efficiency and domesticity. Women in propertied farm families were equally vigilant and carried domestic issues into the public sphere. To protect their homes and husbands from alcoholic excess, they joined the Independent Order of Good Templars, a temperance group which made women full members (American Voices, p. 368).

Moral Reform   Some religious women developed a sharp consciousness of gender and became public actors. In 1834, middle-class women in New York City founded the Female Moral Reform Society and elected Lydia Finney, the wife of revivalist Charles Grandison Finney, as its president. The society tried to curb prostitution and to protect single women from moral corruption. Rejecting the sexual double standard, its members demanded chaste behavior by men. By 1840, the Female Moral Reform Society had blossomed into a national association, with 555 chapters and 40,000 members throughout the North and Midwest. Employing only women as agents, the society provided moral guidance for young women who were working as factory operatives, seamstresses, or servants. Society members visited brothels, where they sang hymns, offered prayers, searched for runaway girls, and noted the names of clients. They also founded homes of refuge for prostitutes and won the passage of laws in Massachusetts and New York that made seduction a crime.

Improving Prisons, Creating Asylums, Expanding Education   Other women set out to improve public institutions, and Dorothea Dix (1801–1887) was their model. Dix's paternal grandparents were prominent Bostonians, but her father, a Methodist minister, ended

up an impoverished alcoholic. Emotionally abused as a child, Dix grew into a compassionate young woman with a strong sense of moral purpose. She used money from her grandparents to set up charity schools to "rescue some of America's miserable children from vice" and became a successful author. By 1832, she had published seven books, including *Conversations on Common Things* (1824), an enormously successful treatise on natural science and moral improvement.

In 1841, Dix took up a new cause. Discovering that insane women were jailed alongside male criminals, she persuaded Massachusetts lawmakers to enlarge the state hospital to house indigent mental patients. Exhilarated by that success, Dix began a national movement to establish state asylums for the mentally ill. By 1854, she had traveled more than 30,000 miles and had visited eighteen state penitentiaries, three hundred county jails, and more than five hundred almshouses and hospitals. Dix's reports and agitation prompted many states to improve their prisons and public hospitals.

Both as reformers and teachers, other northern women transformed public education. From Maine to Wisconsin, women vigorously supported the movement led by Horace Mann to increase elementary schooling and improve the quality of instruction. As secretary of the Massachusetts Board of Education from 1837 to 1848, Mann lengthened the school year; established teaching standards in reading, writing, and arithmetic; and recruited well-educated women as teachers. The intellectual leader of the new women educators was Catharine Beecher, who founded academies for young women in Hartford, Connecticut, and Cincinnati, Ohio. In widely read publications, Beecher argued that "energetic and benevolent women" were better qualified than men were to impart moral and intellectual instruction to the young. By the 1850s, most teachers were women, both because local school boards heeded Beecher's arguments and because they could hire women at lower salaries than men. As secular educators as well as moral reformers, women were now part of American public life.

From Black Rights to Women's Rights

As women addressed controversial issues such as moral reform and emancipation, they faced censure over their public presence. Offended by this criticism, which revealed their own social and legal inferiority, some women sought full freedom for their sex.

> **TRACE CHANGE OVER TIME**
>
> Using the material on women's lives in Chapters 4, 8, and 11, analyze and explain the changing nature of their "private" and "public" lives.

Saving the Nation from Drink

The temperance crusade was the most successful antebellum reform movement. It mobilized more than a million supporters in all sections of the nation and significantly lowered the consumption of alcoholic beverages. Nonetheless, like other reform efforts, the antidrinking crusade divided over questions of strategy and tactics. The following passages, taken from the writings of leading temperance advocates, show that some reformers favored legal regulation while others preferred persuasion and voluntary abstinence.

Lyman Beecher

"Intemperance Is the Sin of Our Land"

A leading Protestant minister and spokesman for the Benevolent Empire, Lyman Beecher regarded drunkenness as a sin. His *Six Sermons on . . . Intemperance* (1829) condemned the recklessness of working-class drunkards and called on responsible members of the middle class to lead the way to a temperate society.

Intemperance is the sin of our land, and, with our boundless prosperity, is coming in upon us like a flood; and if anything shall defeat the hopes of the world, which hang upon our experiment of civil liberty, it is that river of fire. . . .

In every city and town the poor-tax, created chiefly by intemperance, is [increasing the burden on taxpaying citizens]. . . . The frequency of going upon the town [relying on public welfare] has taken away the reluctance of pride, and destroyed the motives to providence which the fear of poverty and suffering once supplied. The prospect of a destitute old age, or of a suffering family, no longer troubles the vicious portion of our community. They drink up their daily earnings, and bless God for the poor-house, and begin to look upon it as, of right, the drunkard's home. . . . Every intemperate and idle man, whom you behold tottering about the streets and steeping himself at the stores, regards your houses and lands as pledged to take care of him, puts his hands deep, annually, into your pockets. . . .

What then is this universal, natural, and national remedy for intemperance? IT IS THE BANISHMENT OF ARDENT SPIRITS FROM THE LIST OF LAWFUL ARTICLES OF COMMERCE, BY A CORRECT AND EFFICIENT PUBLIC SENTIMENT; SUCH AS HAS TURNED SLAVERY OUT OF HALF OUR LAND, AND WILL YET EXPEL IT FROM THE WORLD.

We are not therefore to come down in wrath upon the distillers, and importers, and venders of ardent spirits. None of us are enough without sin to cast the first stone. . . . It is the buyers who have created the demand for ardent spirits, and made distillation and importation a gainful traffic. . . . Let the temperate cease to buy — and the demand for ardent spirits will fall in the market three fourths, and ultimately will fail wholly. . . .

This however cannot be done effectually so long as the traffic in ardent spirits is regarded as lawful, and is patronized by men of reputation and moral worth in every part of the land. Like slavery, it must be regarded as sinful, impolitic, and dishonorable. That no measures will avail short of rendering ardent spirits a contraband of trade, is nearly self-evident.

Abraham Lincoln

"A New Class of Champions"

In Baltimore in 1840, a group of reformed alcoholics formed the Washington Temperance Society, which turned the antidrinking movement in a new direction. By talking publicly about their personal experiences of alcoholic decline and spiritual recovery, they inspired thousands to "sign the pledge" of total abstinence. (Its philosophy exists today in the organization Alcoholics Anonymous.) In 1842, Lincoln, an ambitious lawyer and Illinois legislator who did not drink, praised such "moral suasion" in an address to the Washingtonians of Springfield, Illinois.

Although the temperance cause has been in progress for near twenty years, it is apparent to all that it is just now being crowned with a degree of success hitherto unparalleled. The list of its friends is daily swelled by the additions of fifties, of hundreds, and of thousands.

The warfare heretofore waged against the demon intemperance has somehow or other been erroneous. . . . [Its] champions for the most part have been preachers [such as Beecher], lawyers, and hired agents. Between these and the mass of mankind there is a want of approachability. . . .

But when one who has long been known as a victim of intemperance bursts the fetters that have bound him, and appears before his neighbors "clothed and in his right mind," . . . to tell of the miseries once endured, now to be endured no more . . . there is a logic and an eloquence in it that few with human feelings can resist. . . .

In my judgment, it is to the battles of this new class of champions that our late success is greatly, perhaps chiefly, owing. . . . [Previously,] too much denunciation against dram-sellers and dram-drinkers was indulged in. This I think was both impolitic and unjust. . . . When the dram-seller and drinker were incessantly [condemned] . . . as moral pestilences . . . they were slow [to] . . . join the ranks of their denouncers in a hue and cry against themselves.

By the Washingtonians this system of consigning the habitual drunkard to hopeless ruin is repudiated. . . . They teach hope to all—despair to none. As applying to their cause, they deny the doctrine of unpardonable sin. . . .

If the relative grandeur of revolutions shall be estimated by the great amount of human misery they alleviate, and the small amount they inflict, then indeed will this be the grandest the world shall ever have seen. Of our political revolution of '76 we are all justly proud. It has given us a degree of political freedom far exceeding that of any other nation of the earth. . . . But, with all these glorious results, past, present, and to come, [this freedom] had its evils too. It [was abused by drunken husbands and thereby] breathed forth famine, swam in blood, and rode in fire; and long, long after, the orphan's cry and the widow's wail continued to break the sad silence that ensued. These were the price, the inevitable price, paid for the blessings it brought. . . .

Turn now to the temperance revolution. In it we shall find a stronger bondage broken, a viler slavery manumitted, a greater tyrant deposed; in it, more of want supplied, more disease healed, more sorrow assuaged. By it no orphans starving, no widows weeping.

Glorious consummation! Hail, fall of fury! Reign of reason, all hail!

American Temperance Magazine
"You Shall Not Sell"

In 1851, the Maine legislature passed a statute prohibiting the sale of alcoholic beverages in the state. The Maine Supreme Court upheld the statute, arguing that the legislature had the "right to regulate by law the sale of any article, the use of which would be detrimental of the morals of the people." Subsequently, the *American Temperance Magazine* became a strong advocate of legal prohibition and by 1856 had won passage of "Maine Laws" in twelve other states (Chapter 9).

This is a utilitarian age. The speculative has in all things yielded to the practical. Words are mere noise unless they are things [and result in action].

In this sense, moral suasion is moral balderdash. "Words, my lord, words" . . . are a delusion. . . . The drunkard's mental and physical condition pronounces them an absurdity. He is ever in one or other extreme—under the excitement of drink, or in a state of morbid collapse. . . . Reason with a man when all reason has fled, and it is doubtful whether he or you is the greater fool. . . . Moral suasion! Bah!

Place this man we have been describing out of the reach of temptation. He will have time to ponder. His mind and frame recover their native vigor. The public-house does not beset his path. . . . Thus, and thus only, will reformation and temperance be secured. And how is this accomplished? Never except through the instrumentality of the law. If it were possible to reason the drunkard into sobriety, it would not be possible to make the rum-seller forego his filthy gains. Try your moral suasion on him. . . . The only logic he will comprehend, is some such ordinance as this, coming to him in the shape and with the voice of law—you shall not sell.

Source: David Brion Davis, *Antebellum American Culture: An Interpretive Anthology* (University Park: Pennsylvania State University Press, 1997), 395–398, 403–409.

QUESTIONS FOR ANALYSIS

1. What does Lincoln's address suggest about his general political philosophy?

2. Compare Beecher's position to Lincoln's. In what ways are they similar? How are they different? Then compare Beecher's solution to that of the *American Temperance Magazine*. Are they the same? Whose view of personal responsibility versus institutional coercion is closest to the position of Orestes Brownson (Chapter 9, pp. 308–309)?

3. In which of these selections do you see the influence of the Second Great Awakening, especially the evangelical message of Charles Grandison Finney? Where do you see the influence of the Market Revolution and the cultural values of the rising middle class? What positions do these selections take with respect to the appropriate role of government in regulating morality and personal behavior?

Abolitionist Women   Women were central to the antislavery movement because they understood the special horrors of slavery for women. In her autobiography, *Incidents in the Life of a Slave Girl*, black abolitionist Harriet Jacobs described forced sexual intercourse with her white owner. "I cannot tell how much I suffered in the presence of these wrongs," she wrote. According to Jacobs and other enslaved women, such sexual assaults incited additional cruelty by their owners' wives, who were enraged by their husbands' promiscuity. In her best-selling novel, *Uncle Tom's Cabin* (1852), Harriet Beecher Stowe pinpointed the sexual abuse of women as a profound moral failing of the slave regime.

As Garrisonian women attacked slavery, they frequently violated social taboos by speaking to mixed audiences of men and women. Maria W. Stewart, an African American, spoke to mixed crowds in Boston in the early 1830s. As abolitionism blossomed, scores of white women delivered lectures condemning slavery, and thousands more made home "visitations" to win converts to their cause (Map 11.4). When Congregationalist clergymen in New England assailed Angelina and Sarah Grimké for such activism in a Pastoral Letter in 1837, Sarah Grimké turned to the Bible for justification: "The Lord Jesus defines the duties of his followers in his Sermon on the Mount . . . without any reference to sex or condition," she replied: "Men and women were CREATED EQUAL; both are moral and accountable beings and whatever is right for man to do, is right for woman." In a pamphlet debate with Catharine Beecher (who believed that women should exercise authority primarily as wives, mothers, and schoolteachers), Angelina Grimké pushed the argument beyond religion by invoking Enlightenment principles to claim equal civic rights:

> It is a woman's right to have a voice in all the laws and regulations by which she is governed, whether in Church or State. . . . The present arrangements of society on these points are a violation of human rights, a rank usurpation of power, a violent seizure and confiscation of what is sacredly and inalienably hers.

By 1840, female abolitionists were asserting that traditional gender roles resulted in the **domestic slavery** of women. "How can we endure our present marriage relations," asked Elizabeth Cady Stanton, "[which give a woman] no charter of rights, no individuality of her own?" As reformer Ernestine Rose put it: "The radical difficulty . . . is that women are considered as belonging to men." Having acquired a public voice and

MAP 11.4

Women and Antislavery, 1837–1838

Beginning in the 1830s, abolitionists and antislavery advocates dispatched dozens of petitions to Congress demanding an end to forced labor. Women accounted for two-thirds of the 67,000 signatures on the petitions submitted in 1837–1838, a fact that suggests not only the influence of women in the antislavery movement but also the extent of female organizations and social networks. Lawmakers, eager to avoid sectional conflict, devised an informal agreement (the "gag rule") to table the petitions without discussion.

Antislavery Petitions to Congress, 1837–38

Female signers | Male signers

Total signers	67,202	100%
Female signers	44,929	67%
Male signers	22,273	33%

political skills in the crusade for African American freedom, thousands of northern women now advocated greater rights for themselves.

Seneca Falls and Beyond   During the 1840s, women's rights activists devised a pragmatic program of reform. Unlike radical utopians, they did not challenge the institution of marriage or the conventional division of labor within the family. Instead, they tried to strengthen the legal rights of married women by seeking legislation that permitted them to own property (America Compared, p. 372). This initiative won crucial support from affluent men, who feared bankruptcy in the volatile market economy and wanted to put

Crusading Reformers

Elizabeth Cady Stanton (1815–1902) and Susan B. Anthony (1820–1906) were a dynamic duo. Stanton, the well-educated daughter of a prominent New York judge, was an early abolitionist and the mother of seven children. Anthony came from a Quaker family and became a teacher and a temperance activist. Meeting in 1851, Stanton and Anthony became friends and co-organizers. From 1854 to 1860, they led a successful struggle to expand New York's Married Women's Property Law of 1848. During the Civil War, they formed the Women's Loyal National League, which helped win passage of the Thirteenth Amendment, ending slavery. In 1866, they joined the American Equal Rights Association, which demanded the vote for women and African Americans. © Bettmann/Corbis.

some family assets in their wives' names. Fathers also desired their married daughters to have property rights to protect them (and their paternal inheritances) from financially irresponsible husbands. Such motives prompted legislatures in three states — Mississippi, Maine, and Massachusetts — to enact **married women's property laws** between 1839 and 1845. Then, women activists in New York won a comprehensive statute that became the model for fourteen other states. The New York statute of 1848 gave women full legal control over the property they brought to a marriage.

Also in 1848, Elizabeth Cady Stanton and Lucretia Mott organized a gathering of women's rights activists in the small New York town of Seneca Falls. Seventy women and thirty men attended the **Seneca Falls Convention**, which issued a rousing manifesto extending to women the egalitarian republican ideology of the Declaration of Independence. "All men and women are created equal," the Declaration of Sentiments declared, "[yet] the history of mankind is a history of repeated injuries and usurpations on the part of man toward woman [and] the establishment of an absolute tyranny over her." To persuade Americans to right this long-standing wrong, the activists resolved to "employ agents, circulate tracts, petition the State and National legislatures, and endeavor to enlist the pulpit and the press on our behalf." By staking out claims for equality for women in public life, the Seneca Falls reformers repudiated both the natural inferiority of women and the ideology of separate spheres.

Most men dismissed the Seneca Falls declaration as nonsense, and many women also rejected the activists and their message. In her diary, one small-town mother and housewife lashed out at the female reformer who "aping mannish manners . . . wears absurd and barbarous attire, who talks of her wrongs in harsh tone, who struts and strides, and thinks that she proves herself superior to the rest of her sex."

Still, the women's rights movement grew in strength and purpose. In 1850, delegates to the first national women's rights convention in Worcester, Massachusetts, hammered out a program of action. The women called on churches to eliminate notions of female inferiority in their theology. Addressing state legislatures, they proposed laws to allow married women to institute lawsuits, testify in court, and assume custody of their children in the event of divorce or a husband's death. Finally, they began a concerted campaign to win the vote for women. As delegates to the 1851 convention

PLACE EVENTS IN CONTEXT

What was the relationship between the abolitionist and women's rights movements?

Women's Rights in France and the United States, 1848

During the political uprising in France in 1848, Pauline Roland and Jeanne Deroine unsuccessfully sought voting rights and an equal civil status for French women. However, the two women won election to the Central Committee of the Associative Unions, the umbrella organization of French trade unions. Imprisoned for their activism, they dispatched a letter to the Second Woman's Rights Convention, which met in Worcester, Massachusetts, in 1851.

When their letter was read to the Convention, Ernestine Potowsky Rose (1810–1892) offered the following response, which indicated the different perspective and political strategy of the American women's movement.

Pauline Roland and Jeanne Deroine
Letter to the Convention of the Women of America

Dear Sisters: Your courageous declaration of Woman's Rights has resounded even to our prison and has filled our souls with inexpressible joy. In France the [conservative] reaction [to the uprising of 1848] has suppressed the cry of liberty of the women of the future. . . . The Assembly kept silence in regard to the right of one half of humanity. . . . No mention was made of the right of woman in a Constitution framed in the name of Liberty, Equality, and Fraternity. . . .

[However,] the right of woman has been recognized by the laborers and they have consecrated that right by the election of those who had claimed it in vain for both sexes. . . . It is by labor; it is by entering resolutely into the ranks of the working people that women will conquer the civil and political equality on which depends the happiness of the world. . . . Sisters of America! your socialist sisters of France are united with you in the vindication of the right of woman to civil and political equality. . . . [Only] by the union of the working classes of both sexes [can we achieve] . . . the civil and political equality of woman.

Ernestine Rose
Speech to the Second Woman's Rights Convention

After having heard the letter read from our poor incarcerated sisters of France, well might we exclaim, Alas poor France! Where is thy glory?

. . . But need we wonder that France, governed as she is by Russian and Austrian despotism, does not recognize . . . the Rights of Woman, when even here, in this far-famed land of freedom . . . woman, the mockingly so-called "better half" of man, has yet to plead for her rights. . . . In the laws of the land, she has no rights; in government she has no voice. . . . From the cradle to the grave she is subject to the power and control of man. Father, guardian, or husband, one conveys her like some piece of merchandise over to the other.

. . . Carry out the republican principle of universal suffrage, or strike it from your banners and substitute "Freedom and Power to one half of society, and Submission and Slavery to the other." Give women the elective franchise. Let married women have the same right to property that their husbands have. . . .

There is no reason against woman's elevation, but . . . prejudices. The main cause is a pernicious falsehood propagated against her being, namely that she is inferior by her nature. Inferior in what? What has man ever done that woman, under the same advantages could not do?

Source: *History of Woman Suffrage*, ed. Elizabeth Cady Stanton, Susan B. Anthony, and Matilda Joslyn Gage (New York: Fowler & Wells, 1887), 1: 234–242.

QUESTIONS FOR ANALYSIS

1. What strategy to achieve women's rights do Roland and Deroine advocate? What strategy can be detected in Rose's remarks? How are their perspectives similar to, or different from, one another?

2. What does this French-American comparison (and your reading in Chapter 11) suggest about the nature and values of the American women's rights movement?

proclaimed, suffrage was "the corner-stone of this enterprise, since we do not seek to protect woman, but rather to place her in a position to protect herself."

The activists' legislative campaign required talented organizers and lobbyists. The most prominent political operative was Susan B. Anthony (1820–1906), a Quaker who had acquired political skills in the temperance and antislavery movements. Those experiences, Anthony reflected, taught her "the great evil of woman's utter dependence on man." Joining the women's rights movement, she worked closely with Elizabeth Cady Stanton. Anthony created an activist network of political "captains," all women, who relentlessly lobbied state legislatures. In 1860, her efforts secured a New York law granting women the right to control their own wages (which fathers or husbands had previously managed); to own property acquired by "trade, business, labors, or services"; and, if widowed, to assume sole guardianship of their children. Genuine individualism for women, the dream of transcendentalist Margaret Fuller, had advanced a tiny step closer to reality. In such small and much larger ways, the mid-century reform movements had altered the character of American culture.

SUMMARY

In this chapter, we examined four major cultural movements of the mid-nineteenth century — transcendentalist reform, communalism, abolitionism, and women's rights — as well as the new popular culture in New York City. Our discussion of the transcendentalists highlighted the influence of Ralph Waldo Emerson

on the great literary figures of the era and linked transcendentalism to the rise of individualism and the character of middle-class American culture.

Our analysis of communal experiments probed their members' efforts to devise new rules for sexual behavior, gender relationships, and property ownership. We saw that successful communal experiments, such as Mormonism, required a charismatic leader or a religious foundation and endured if they developed strong, even authoritarian, institutions.

We also traced the personal and ideological factors that linked the abolitionist and women's rights movements. Lucretia Mott, Elizabeth Cady Stanton, and the Grimké sisters began as antislavery advocates, but, denied access to lecture platforms by male abolitionists and conservative clergy, they became staunch advocates of women's rights. This transition was a logical one: both enslaved blacks and married women were "owned" by men, either as property or as their legal dependents. Consequently, the efforts to abolish the legal prerogatives of husbands were as controversial as those to end the legal property rights of slave owners. As reformers took aim at such deeply rooted institutions and customs, many Americans feared that their activism would not perfect society but destroy it.

CHAPTER REVIEW

MAKE IT STICK   Go to **LearningCurve** to retain what you've read.

TERMS TO KNOW   Identify and explain the significance of each term below.

Key Concepts and Events

individualism (p. 346)

American Renaissance (p. 346)

transcendentalism (p. 346)

utopias (p. 349)

socialism (p. 351)

perfectionism (p. 352)

Mormonism (p. 352)

minstrelsy (p. 356)

abolitionism (p. 357)

Underground Railroad (p. 362)

amalgamation (p. 364)

gag rule (p. 365)

separate sphere (p. 367)

domestic slavery (p. 370)

married women's property laws (p. 371)

Seneca Falls Convention (p. 371)

Key People

Ralph Waldo Emerson (p. 346)

Henry David Thoreau (p. 347)

Margaret Fuller (p. 347)

Walt Whitman (p. 348)

Herman Melville (p. 349)

Nat Turner (p. 360)

William Lloyd Garrison (p. 362)

Dorothea Dix (p. 367)

Elizabeth Cady Stanton (p. 371)

Susan B. Anthony (p. 371)

REVIEW QUESTIONS
Answer these questions to demonstrate your understanding of the chapter's main ideas.

1. Analyze the relationship between religion and reform in the decades from 1800 to 1860. Why did many religious people feel compelled to remake society? How successful were they? Do you see any parallels with social movements today?

2. The word *reform* has a positive connotation, as an effort to make things better. Yet many mid-nineteenth-century Americans viewed some "reforms," such as abolitionism and women's rights, as destructive to the social order, and other "reforms," such as Sabbatarianism and temperance, as threats to individual freedom. What was the apparent conflict among reform, social order, and liberty?

3. THEMATIC UNDERSTANDING Review the events listed under "Ideas, Beliefs, and Culture" on the thematic timeline on page 283, paying particular attention to the entries related to individualism and rights on the one hand and to various communal and religious movements on the other. What was the relationship between these somewhat contradictory cultural impulses? How were these two movements related to the social and economic changes in America in the decades after 1800?

MAKING CONNECTIONS
Recognize the larger developments and continuities within and across chapters by answering these questions.

1. ACROSS TIME AND PLACE Did the era of reform (1820–1860) increase or diminish the extent of social and cultural freedom that existed during the Revolutionary era (1770–1820)?

2. VISUAL EVIDENCE Compare the cheerful depiction of the young woman in the watercolor depicting "night life in Philadelphia" on page 355 with the thoughtful or intense expression on the faces of the social reformers depicted in this chapter (Emerson, p. 346; Fuller, p. 348; and Stanton and Anthony, p. 371). Given their beliefs, would those reformers have approved or disapproved of the conduct of the young Philadelphia woman? Explain your reasoning.

MORE TO EXPLORE
Start here to learn more about the events discussed in this chapter.

Patricia Cline Cohen, *The Murder of Helen Jewett: The Life and Death of a Prostitute in New York City* (1998). A gripping murder mystery that probes the nature of the new plebeian culture.

Daniel Walker Howe, *What Hath God Wrought: The Transformation of America, 1815–1848* (2007). A comprehensive history from a cultural perspective.

Paul E. Johnson and Sean Wilentz, *The Kingdom of Matthias* (1995). A compelling story of religious utopianism gone mad.

Stephen B. Oates, *The Fires of Jubilee* (1975). Explores the life and rebellion of Nat Turner.

Mark Perry, *Lift Up Thy Voice* (2001). Offers a study of the Grimké family.

David Roediger, *The Wages of Whiteness* (1995). Shows how racism shaped white working-class culture.

TIMELINE

Ask yourself why this chapter begins and ends with these dates and then identify the links among related events.

1826	• Lyceum movement begins
1829	• David Walker's *Appeal . . . to the Colored Citizens of the World*
1830	• Joseph Smith publishes *The Book of Mormon*
1830s	• Emergence of minstrelsy shows
1831	• William Lloyd Garrison founds *The Liberator* • Nat Turner's uprising in Virginia
1832	• Ralph Waldo Emerson turns to transcendentalism
1833	• Garrison organizes American Anti-Slavery Society
1834	• New York activists create Female Moral Reform Society
1835	• Abolitionists launch great postal campaign, sparking series of antiabolitionist riots
1836	• House of Representatives adopts gag rule
1837	• Grimké sisters defend public roles for women
1840	• Liberty Party runs James G. Birney for president
1840s	• Fourierist communities arise in Midwest
1841	• Dorothea Dix promotes hospitals for mentally ill
1844	• Margaret Fuller publishes *Woman in the Nineteenth Century*
1845	• Henry David Thoreau goes to Walden Pond
1846	• Brigham Young leads Mormons to Salt Lake
1848	• Seneca Falls Convention proposes women's equality
1850	• Nathaniel Hawthorne's *The Scarlet Letter*
1851	• Herman Melville publishes *Moby Dick*
1852	• Harriet Beecher Stowe writes *Uncle Tom's Cabin*
1855	• Dr. Sanger surveys sex trade in New York City • Walt Whitman's *Leaves of Grass*
1858	• "Mormon War" over polygamy

KEY TURNING POINTS: Most of the entries here relate to events in the 1830s, 1840s, and 1850s. In your judgment, which is the most important event in each decade? Over all three decades? Write a coherent essay that justifies your choices and, if possible, relates those events to each other.

12 CHAPTER

The South Expands: Slavery and Society
1800–1860

L ife in South Carolina had been good to James Lide. A slave-owning planter along the Pee Dee River, Lide and his wife raised twelve children and long resisted the "Alabama Fever" that prompted thousands of Carolinians to move west. Finally, at age sixty-five, probably seeking land for his many offspring, he moved his slaves and family—including six children and six grandchildren—to a plantation near Montgomery, Alabama. There, the family lived initially in a squalid log cabin with air holes but no windows. Even after building a new house, the Lides' life remained unsettled. "Pa is quite in the notion of moving somewhere," his daughter Maria reported. Although James Lide died in Alabama, many of his children moved on. In 1854, at the age of fifty-eight, Eli Lide migrated to Texas, telling his father, "Something within me whispers onward and onward."

The Lides' story was that of southern society. Between 1800 and 1860, white planters moved west and, using the muscles and sweat of a million enslaved African Americans, brought millions of acres into cultivation. By 1840, the South was at the cutting edge of the American Market Revolution (Figure 12.1). It annually produced and exported 1.5 million bales of raw cotton—over two-thirds of the world's supply—and its economy was larger and richer than that of most nations. "Cotton is King," boasted the *Southern Cultivator*.

No matter how rich they were, few cotton planters in Alabama, Mississippi, and Texas lived in elegant houses or led cultured lives. They had forsaken the aristocratic gentility of the Chesapeake and the Carolinas to make money. "To sell cotton in order to buy negroes—to make more cotton to buy more negroes, 'ad infinitum,' is the aim . . . of the thorough-going cotton planter," a traveler reported from Mississippi in 1835. "His whole soul is wrapped up in the pursuit." Plantation women lamented the loss of genteel surroundings and polite society. Raised in North Carolina, where she was "blest with every comfort, & even luxury," Mary Drake found Mississippi and Alabama "a dreary waste."

Enslaved African Americans knew what "dreary waste" really meant: unremitting toil, unrelieved poverty, and profound sadness. Sold south from Maryland, where his family had lived for generations, Charles Ball's father became "gloomy and morose" and ran off and disappeared. With good reason: on new cotton plantations, slaves labored from "sunup to sundown" and from one end of the year to the other, forced to work by the threat of the lash. Always wanting more, southern planters and politicians plotted to extend their plantation economy across the continent.

IDENTIFY THE BIG IDEA

How did the creation of a cotton-based economy change the lives of whites and blacks in all regions of the South?

A Slave Family Picking Cotton Picking cotton—thousands of small bolls attached to 3-foot-high woody and often prickly stalks—was a tedious and time-consuming task, taking up to four months on many plantations. However, workers of both sexes and all ages could pick cotton, and masters could measure output by weighing the baskets of each picker or family, chastising those who failed to meet their quotas. What does this early photograph of a family of pickers, taken on a plantation near Savannah, Georgia, suggest about women's and children's lives, family relations, and living conditions?

The Domestic Slave Trade

In 1817, when the American Colonization Society began to transport a few freed blacks to Africa (Chapter 8), the southern plantation system was expanding rapidly. In 1790, its western boundary ran through the middle of Georgia; by 1830, it stretched through western Louisiana; by 1860, the slave frontier extended far into Texas (Map 12.1). That advance of 900 miles more than doubled the geographical area cultivated by slave labor and increased the number of slave states from eight in 1800 to fifteen by 1850. The federal government played a key role in this expansion. It acquired Louisiana from the French in 1803, welcomed the slave states of Mississippi and Alabama into the Union in 1817 and 1819, removed Native Americans from the southeastern states in the 1830s, and annexed Texas and Mexican lands in the 1840s.

To cultivate this vast area, white planters imported enslaved laborers first from Africa and then from the Chesapeake region. Between 1776 and 1809, when Congress outlawed the Atlantic slave trade, planters purchased about 115,000 Africans. "The Planter will . . . Sacrifice every thing to attain Negroes," declared one slave trader. Despite the influx, the demand for labor far exceeded the supply. Consequently, planters imported new African workers illegally, through the Spanish colony of Florida until 1819 and then through the Mexican province of Texas. Yet these Africans — about 50,000 between 1810 and 1865 — did not satisfy the demand.

The Upper South Exports Slaves

Planters seeking labor looked to the Chesapeake region, home in 1800 to nearly half of the nation's black population. There, the African American population

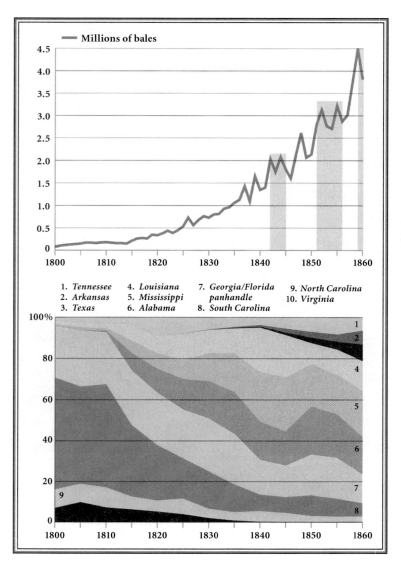

FIGURE 12.1

Cotton Production and Producers, 1800–1860

Until 1820, Georgia and South Carolina plantations (marked #7 and #8 on the right side of the lower graph) grew more than one-half of American cotton. As output increased significantly between 1820 and 1840 (see the upper graph), the locus of production shifted. By the early 1840s, planters had moved hundreds of thousands of slaves to the Mississippi Valley, and Louisiana, Mississippi, and Alabama (#4, #5, and #6) grew nearly 70 percent of a much larger cotton crop. Simultaneously, production leapt dramatically, reaching (as the red bars show) 2 million bales a year by the mid-1840s, 3 million by the mid-1850s, and 4 million on the eve of the Civil War.

Source: From *Time on the Cross: The Economics of American Negro Slavery*, by Robert W. Fogel and Stanley L. Engerman. Copyright © 1974 Little Brown.

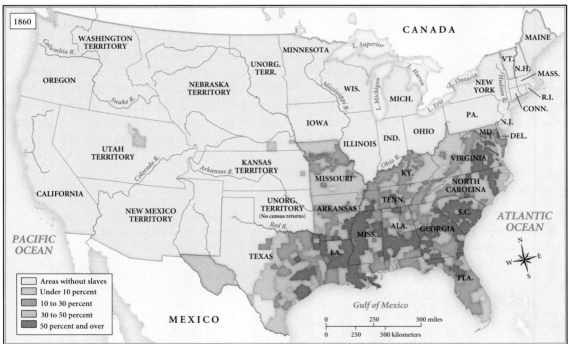

MAP 12.1

Distribution of the Slave Population in 1790, 1830, and 1860

The cotton boom shifted the African American population to the South and West. In 1790, most slaves lived and worked on Chesapeake tobacco and Carolina rice and indigo plantations. By 1830, those areas were still heavily populated by black families, but hundreds of thousands of slaves also labored on the cotton and sugar lands of the Lower Mississippi Valley and on cotton plantations in Georgia and northern Florida. Three decades later, the majority of blacks lived and worked along the Mississippi River and in an arc of fertile cotton lands—the "black belt"—sweeping from Mississippi through South Carolina.

was growing rapidly from natural increase — an average of 27 percent a decade by the 1810s — and creating a surplus of enslaved workers on many plantations. The result was a growing domestic trade in slaves. Between 1818 and 1829, planters in just one Maryland tobacco-growing county — Frederick — sold at least 952 slaves to traders or cotton planters. Plantation owners in Virginia disposed of 75,000 slaves during the 1810s and again during the 1820s. The number of forced Virginia migrants jumped to nearly 120,000 during the 1830s and then averaged 85,000 during the 1840s and 1850s. In Virginia alone, then, slave owners ripped 440,000 African Americans from communities where their families had lived for three or four generations. By 1860, the "mania for buying negroes" from the Upper South had resulted in a massive transplantation of more than 1 million slaves (Figure 12.2). A majority of African Americans now lived and worked in the Deep South, the lands that stretched from Georgia to Texas.

This African American migration took two forms: transfer and sale. Looking for new opportunities, thousands of Chesapeake and Carolina planters — men like James Lide — sold their existing plantations and moved their slaves to the Southwest. Many other planters gave slaves to sons and daughters who moved west. Such transfers accounted for about 40 percent of the African American migrants. The rest — about 60 percent of the 1 million migrants — were "sold south" through traders.

Just as the Atlantic slave trade enriched English merchants in the eighteenth century, so the domestic market brought wealth to American traders between 1800 and 1860. One set of routes ran to the Atlantic coast and sent thousands of slaves to sugar plantations in Louisiana, the former French territory that entered the Union in 1812. As sugar output soared, slave traders scoured the countryside near the port cities of Baltimore, Alexandria, Richmond, and Charleston — searching, as one of them put it, for "likely young men such as I think would suit the New Orleans market." Each year, hundreds of muscular young slaves passed through auction houses in the port cities bound for the massive trade mart in New Orleans. Because this **coastal trade** in laborers was highly visible, it elicited widespread condemnation by northern abolitionists.

Sugar was a "killer" crop, and Louisiana (like the eighteenth-century West Indies) soon had a well-deserved reputation among African Americans "as a place of slaughter." Hundreds died each year from disease, overwork, and brutal treatment. Maryland farmer John Anthony Munnikhuysen refused to allow his daughter Priscilla to marry a Louisiana sugar planter, declaring: "Mit has never been used to see negroes flayed alive and it would kill her."

The **inland system** that fed slaves to the Cotton South was less visible than the coastal trade but more extensive. Professional slave traders went from one rural village to another buying "young and likely Negroes." The traders marched their purchases in coffles — columns of slaves bound to one another — to Alabama, Mississippi, and Missouri in the 1830s and to Arkansas and Texas in the 1850s. One slave described the arduous journey: "Dem Speculators would put the chilluns in a wagon usually pulled by oxens and de

IDENTIFY CAUSES

What factors drove the expansion of the domestic slave trade, and how did it work?

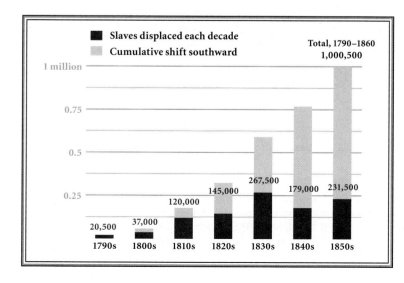

FIGURE 12.2

Forced Slave Migration to the Lower South, 1790–1860

The cotton boom set in motion a vast redistribution of the African American population. Between 1790 and 1860, white planters moved or sold more than a million enslaved people from the Upper to the Lower South, a process that broke up families and long-established black communities. Based on data in Robert William Fogel and Stanley L. Engerman, *Time on the Cross: The Economics of American Negro Slavery*, by Robert W. Fogel and Stanley L. Engerman. Copyright © 1974 Little Brown and in *Speculators and Slaves: Masters, Traders, and Slaves in the Old South*, by Michael Tadman, University of Wisconsin Press, 1996.

The Inland Slave Trade

Mounted whites escort a convoy of slaves from Virginia to Tennessee in Lewis Miller's *Slave Trader, Sold to Tennessee* (1853). For white planters, the interstate trade in slaves was lucrative; it pumped money into the declining Chesapeake economy and provided young workers for the expanding plantations of the cotton belt. For blacks, it was a traumatic journey, a new Middle Passage that broke up their families and communities. "Arise! Arise! and weep no more, dry up your tears, we shall part no more," the slaves sing sorrowfully as they journey to new lives in Tennessee. Abby Aldrich Rockefeller Folk Art Museum, Williamsburg, VA.

older folks was chained or tied together sos dey could not run off." Once a coffle reached its destination, the trader would sell slaves "at every village in the county."

Chesapeake and Carolina planters provided the human cargo. Some planters sold slaves when poor management or their "own extravagances" threw them into debt. "Trouble gathers thicker and thicker around me," Thomas B. Chaplin of South Carolina lamented in his diary. "I will be compelled to send about ten prime Negroes to Town on next Monday, to be sold." Many more planters doubled as slave traders, earning substantial profits by traveling south to sell some of their slaves and those of their neighbors. Thomas Weatherly of South Carolina drove his surplus slaves to Hayneville, Alabama, where he "sold ten negroes." Colonel E. S. Irvine, a member of the South Carolina legislature and "a highly respected gentleman" in white circles, likewise traveled frequently "to sell a drove of Negroes." Prices marched in step with those for cotton; during a boom year in the 1850s, a planter noted that a slave "will fetch $1000, cash, quick."

The domestic slave trade was crucial to the prosperity of the migrating white planters because it provided workers to fell the forests and plant cotton in the Gulf states. Equally important, it sustained the wealth of slave owners in the Upper South. By selling surplus black workers, tobacco, rice, and grain producers in the Chesapeake and Carolinas added about 20 percent to their income. As a Maryland newspaper remarked in 1858, "[The trade serves as] an almost universal resource to raise money. A prime able-bodied slave is worth three times as much to the cotton or sugar planter as to the Maryland agriculturalist."

The Impact on Blacks

For African American families, the domestic slave trade was a personal disaster that underlined their status — and vulnerability — as chattel slaves. In law, they were the movable personal property of the whites who owned them. As Lewis Clark, a fugitive from slavery, noted: "Many a time i've had 'em say to me, 'You're my property.'" "The being of slavery, its soul and its body, lives and moves in the **chattel principle**, the property principle, the bill of sale principle," declared former slave James W. C. Pennington. As a South Carolina master put it, "[The slave's earnings] belong to me because I bought him."

Slave property underpinned the entire southern economic system. Whig politician Henry Clay noted that the "immense amount of capital which is invested in slave property . . . is owned by widows and orphans, by the aged and infirm, as well as the sound and vigorous. It is the subject of mortgages, deeds of trust, and family settlements." Clay concluded: "I know that there is a visionary dogma, which holds that negro slaves cannot be the subject of property [but] . . . that is property which the law declares to be property."

As a slave owner, Clay also knew that property rights were key to slave discipline. "I govern them . . . without the whip," another master explained, "by stating . . . that I should sell them if they do not conduct themselves as I wish." The threat was effective. "The Negroes here dread nothing on earth so much as this," a Maryland observer noted. "They regard the south with perfect horror, and to be sent there is considered as the worst punishment." Thousands of slaves suffered

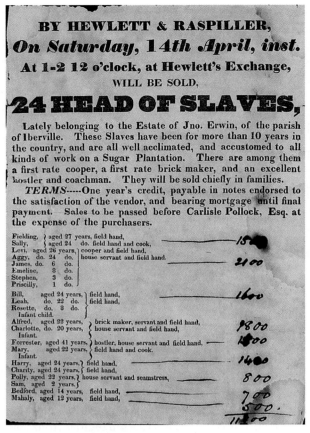

Slave Auction Notice

This public notice for a slave auction to be held in Iberville, Louisiana, advertises "24 Head of Slaves" as if they were cattle—a striking commentary on the "chattel principle" and business of slavery. Library of Congress.

that fate, which destroyed about one in every four slave marriages. "Why does the slave ever love?" asked black abolitionist Harriet Jacobs in her autobiography, *Incidents in the Life of a Slave Girl*, when her partner "may at any moment be wrenched away by the hand of violence?" After being sold, one Georgia slave lamented, "My Dear wife for you and my Children my pen cannot Express the griffe I feel to be parted from you all."

The interstate slave trade often focused on young adults. In northern Maryland, planters sold away boys and girls at an average age of seventeen years. "Dey sole my sister Kate," Anna Harris remembered decades later, "and I ain't seed or heard of her since." The trade also separated almost a third of all slave children under the age of fourteen from one or both of their parents. Sarah Grant remembered,

EXPLAIN CONSEQUENCES
What were the effects of the slave trade on black families?

"Mamma used to cry when she had to go back to work because she was always scared some of us kids would be sold while she was away." Well might she worry, for slave traders worked quickly. "One night I lay down on de straw mattress wid my mammy," Vinny Baker recalled, "an' de nex' mo'nin I woke up an' she wuz gone." When their owner sold seven-year-old Laura Clark and ten other children from their plantation in North Carolina, Clark sensed that she would see her mother "no mo' in dis life."

Despite these sales, 75 percent of slave marriages remained unbroken, and the majority of children lived with one or both parents until puberty. Consequently, the sense of family among African Americans remained strong. Sold from Virginia to Texas in 1843, Hawkins Wilson carried with him a mental picture of his family. Twenty-five years later and now a freedman, Wilson set out to find his "dearest relatives" in Virginia. "My sister belonged to Peter Coleman in Caroline County and her name was Jane. . . . She had three children, Robert, Charles and Julia, when I left — Sister Martha belonged to Dr. Jefferson. . . . Sister Matilda belonged to Mrs. Botts."

During the decades between sale and freedom, Hawkins Wilson and thousands of other African Americans constructed new lives for themselves in the Mississippi Valley. Undoubtedly, many did so with a sense of foreboding, knowing from personal experience that their owners could disrupt their lives at any moment. Like Charles Ball, some "longed to die, and escape from the bonds of my tormentors." The darkness of slavery shadowed even moments of joy. Knowing that sales often ended slave marriages, a white minister blessed one couple "for so long as God keeps them together."

Many white planters "saw" only the African American marriages that endured and ignored those they had broken. Accordingly, many owners considered themselves **benevolent masters**, committed to the welfare of "my family, black and white." Some masters gave substance to this paternalist ideal by treating kindly "loyal and worthy" slaves — black overseers, the mammy who raised their children, and trusted house servants. By preserving the families of these slaves, many planters could believe that they "sold south" only "coarse" troublemakers and uncivilized slaves who had "little sense of family." Other owners were more honest about the human cost of their pursuit of wealth. "Tomorrow the negroes are to get off [to Kentucky]," a slave-owning woman in Virginia wrote to a friend, "and I expect there will be great crying and moaning, with children Leaving there mothers, mothers there children, and women there husbands."

Whether or not they acknowledged the slaves' pain, few southern whites questioned the morality of the slave trade. Responding to abolitionists' criticism, the city council of Charleston, South Carolina, declared that "the removal of slaves from place to place, and their transfer from master to master, by gift, purchase, or otherwise" was completely consistent "with moral principle and with the highest order of civilization" (American Voices, p. 384).

 To see a longer excerpt of the city council of Charleston, South Carolina, document, along with other primary sources from this period, see *Sources for America's History*.

The World of Southern Whites

American slavery took root in the early eighteenth century on the tobacco plantations of the Chesapeake and in the rice fields of the Carolina low country. However, it grew to maturity during the first half of the nineteenth century on the cotton fields and sugar plantations of the Mississippi Valley. By then, a small elite of extraordinarily wealthy planter families stood at the top of southern society. These families — about three thousand in number — each owned more than one hundred slaves and huge tracts of the most fertile lands. Their ranks included many of the richest families in the United States. On the eve of the Civil War, southern slave owners accounted for nearly two-thirds of all American men with wealth of $100,000 or more. Other white southerners — backcountry yeomen farmers and cotton-planting tenants in particular — occupied some of the lowest rungs of the nation's social order. The expansion of southern slavery, like the flowering of northern capitalism, increased inequalities of wealth and status.

The Dual Cultures of the Planter Elite

The westward movement split the plantation elite into two distinct groups: the traditional aristocrats of the Old South, whose families had gained their wealth from tobacco and rice, and the upstart capitalist-inclined planters of the cotton states.

The Traditional Southern Gentry   The Old South gentry dominated the Tidewater region of the Chesapeake and the low country of South Carolina and Georgia. During the eighteenth century, these planters built impressive mansions and adopted the manners and values of the English landed gentry (Chapter 3). Their aristocratic-oriented culture survived the Revolution of 1776 and soon took on a republican glaze

Redcliffe Plantation

In 1857, James Henry Hammond began construction of this house on a 400-acre site in Aiken County, South Carolina. It originally had a double-decked porch in the Greek Revival style, which gave it an even more imposing presence. Fifty enslaved African Americans worked at Redcliffe, and nearly three hundred more on Hammond's other properties, providing the wealth that allowed his family to live in comfort. Hammond lived at Redcliffe until he died in 1864 at the age of fifty-seven, his health undermined by his struggles with Confederate leaders over wartime policies and by mercury poisoning from the laxatives he had taken for nearly forty years. Michael A. Stroud.

The Debate over Free and Slave Labor

As the abolitionist assault on slavery mounted, its rhetoric shaped the debate over the emergent system of wage labor in the northern states. By the 1850s, New York senator William Seward starkly contrasted the political systems of the South and the North in terms of their labor systems: "the one resting on the basis of servile or slave labor, the other on voluntary labor of freemen." Seward strongly favored the "free-labor system," crediting to it "the strength, wealth, greatness, intelligence, and freedom, which the whole American people now enjoy." As the following documents show, some Americans agreed with Seward, while others, such as *New York Tribune* editor Horace Greeley and South Carolina senator James Henry Hammond (who is quoted often in this chapter and whose house appears on page 383), contested his premises and conclusions.

South Carolina Senator James Henry Hammond
Speech to the Senate, March 4, 1858

In response to New York senator Seward, Senator Hammond urged admission of Kansas under the proslavery Lecompton Constitution and, by way of argument, celebrated the success of the South's cotton economy and its political and social institutions.

In all social systems there must be a class to do the menial duties, to perform the drudgery of life. . . . Such a class you must have, or you would not have that other class which leads progress, civilization, and refinement. It constitutes the very mud-sill of society and of political government. . . . Fortunately for the South, she found a race adapted to that purpose to her hand. A race inferior to her own, but eminently qualified in temper, in vigor, in docility, in capacity to stand the climate, to answer all her purposes. We use them for our purpose, and call them slaves. . . .

The Senator from New York said yesterday that the whole world had abolished slavery. Aye, the name, but not the thing; . . . for the man who lives by daily labor, and scarcely lives at that, and who has to put out his labor in the market, and take the best he can get for it; in short, your whole hireling class of manual laborers and "operatives," as you call them, are essentially slaves. The difference between us is, that our slaves are hired for life and well compensated; there is no starvation, no begging, no want of employment among our people, and not too much employment either. Yours are hired by the day, not cared for, and scantily compensated, which may be proved in the most painful manner, at any hour in any street in any of your large towns.

Source: *The Congressional Globe* (Washington, DC, March 6, 1858), 962.

New York Protestant Episcopal Church Mission Society
Sixth Annual Report, 1837

This excerpt demonstrates the society's belief that a class-bound social order could be avoided by encouraging "a spirit of independence and self-estimation" among the poor.

In the older countries of Europe, there is a CLASS OF POOR: families born to poverty, living in poverty, dying in poverty. With us there are none such. In our bounteous land individuals alone are poor; but they form no poor class, because with them poverty is but a transient evil . . . save [except] paupers and vagabonds . . . all else form one common class of citizens; some more, others less advanced in the career of honorable independence.

Source: New York Protestant Episcopal Church Mission Society, Sixth Annual Report (New York, 1837), 15–16.

Horace Greeley
Public Letter Declining an Invitation to Attend an Antislavery Convention in Cincinnati, Ohio, June 3, 1845

This letter from the editor of the *New York Tribune* explains his broad definition of slavery.

Dear Sir: — I received, weeks since, your letter inviting me to be present at a general convention of opponents of Human Slavery. . . . What is Slavery? You will probably answer; "The legal subjection of one human being to the will and power of another." But this definition appears to me inaccurate. . . .

I understand by Slavery, that condition in which one human being exists mainly as a convenience for other human beings. . . . In short, . . . where the relation [is one] of authority, social ascendency and power over subsistence on the one hand, and of necessity, servility, and degradation on the other — there, in my view, is Slavery. . . . If I am less troubled concerning the Slavery prevalent in Charleston or New-Orleans, it is because I see so much Slavery in New-York. . . .

Wherever Opportunity to Labor is obtained with difficulty, and is so deficient that the Employing class may virtually prescribe their own terms and pay the Laborer only such share as they choose of the produce, there is a strong tendency to Slavery.

Source: Horace Greeley, *Hints Toward Reform in Lectures, Addresses, and Other Writings* (New York: Harper & Brothers, 1850), 352–355.

Editorial in the *Staunton Spectator*, 1859

Entitled "Freedom and Slavery," this editorial argues that "the black man's lot as a slave, is vastly preferable to that of his free brethren at the North."

The intelligent, christian slave-holder at the South is the best friend of the negro. He does not regard his bondsmen as mere chattel property, but as human beings to whom he owes duties. While the Northern Pharisee will not permit a negro to ride on the city railroads, Southern gentlemen and ladies are seen every day, side by side, in cars and coaches, with their faithful servants. Here the honest black man is not only protected by the laws and public sentiment, but he is respected by the community as truly as if his skin were white. Here there are ties of genuine friendship and affection between whites and blacks, leading to an interchange of all the comities of life. The slave nurses his master in sickness, and sheds tears of genuine sorrow at his grave.

Source: *Staunton Spectator*, December 6, 1859, p. 2, c. 1.

James Henry Hammond
Private Letter to His Son Harry Hammond, 1856

This letter regards the future of Hammond's slave mistress, Sally Johnson, her son Henderson, and her daughter Louisa, who was the common mistress of father and son, and Louisa's children whom they sired.

In the last will I made I left to you . . . Sally Johnson the mother of Louisa & all the children of both. Sally says Henderson is my child. It is possible, but I do not believe it Yet act on her's rather than my opinion. Louisa's first child may be mine. I think not. Her second I believe is mine. Take care of her & her children who are both of your blood if not of mine. . . . The services of the rest will compensate for indulgence to these. I cannot free these people & send them North. It would be cruelty to them. Nor would I like that any but my own blood should own as slaves my own blood or Louisa. I leave them to your charge, believing that you will best appreciate & most independently carry out my wishes in regard to them. Do not let Louisa or any of my children or possible children be the Slaves of Strangers. Slavery in the family will be their happiest earthly condition.

Source: James Hammond to Harry Hammond, February 19, 1856, in JHH Papers, SCL, quoted in Drew Gilpin Faust, *James Henry Hammond and the Old South: A Design for Mastery* (Baton Rouge: Louisiana State University Press, 1982), 87.

QUESTIONS FOR ANALYSIS

1. Which of these documents argue for slave owners as benevolent paternalists and the institution of slavery as a "positive good"? What other points of view are represented?

2. Given the discussion of "class" and "honorable independence" in the Mission Society statement, how would an Episcopalian reply to Hammond's critique of the northern labor system?

3. How can we understand Hammond's treatment of Sally Johnson and her daughter, as well as his refusal to free his and his son's children, in the context of his 1858 speech and the *Staunton Spectator*'s editorial?

4. Using the principles asserted in his letter, how would Horace Greeley analyze the southern labor system, as described by Hammond and the *Staunton Spectator*? Why does Greeley suggest that the northern system has only "a strong tendency to Slavery"?

5. Consider the sources above in the light of this Abraham Lincoln comment: "although volume upon volume is written to prove slavery a very good thing, we never hear of the man who wishes to take the good of it, by being a slave himself."

(Chapter 8). Classical republican theory, which had long identified political tyranny as the major threat to liberty, had its roots in the societies of Greece and Rome, where slavery was part of the natural order of society. That variety of republicanism appealed to wealthy southerners, who feared federal government interference with their slave property. On the state level, planters worried about populist politicians who would mobilize poorer whites, and so they demanded that authority rest in the hands of incorruptible men of "virtue."

Indeed, affluent planters cast themselves as a **republican aristocracy**. "The planters here are essentially what the nobility are in other countries," declared James Henry Hammond of South Carolina. "They stand at the head of society & politics . . . [and form] an aristocracy of talents, of virtue, of generosity and courage." Wealthy planters criticized the democratic polity and middle-class society that was developing in the Northeast and Midwest. "Inequality is the fundamental law of the universe," declared one planter. Others condemned professional politicians as "a set of demagogues" and questioned the legitimacy of universal suffrage. "Times are sadly different now to what they were when I was a boy," lamented David Gavin, a prosperous South Carolinian. Then, the "Sovereign people, alias mob" had little influence; now they vied for power with the elite. "[How can] I rejoice for a freedom," Gavin thundered, "which allows every bankrupt, swindler, thief, and scoundrel, traitor and seller of his vote to be placed on an equality with myself?"

To maintain their privileged identity, aristocratic planters married their sons and daughters to one another and expected them to follow in their footsteps — the men working as planters, merchants, lawyers, newspaper editors, and ministers and the women hosting plantation balls and church bazaars. To confirm their social preeminence, they lived extravagantly and entertained graciously. James Henry Hammond built a Greek Revival mansion with a center hall 53 feet by 20 feet, its floor embellished with stylish Belgian tiles and expensive Brussels carpets. "Once a year, like a great feudal landlord," Hammond's neighbor recounted, "[he] gave a fete or grand dinner to all the country people."

Rice planters remained at the apex of the plantation aristocracy. In 1860, the fifteen proprietors of the vast plantations in All Saints Parish in South Carolina

TRACE CHANGE OVER TIME
Between 1800 and 1860, what changes occurred in the South's plantation crops, labor system, defense of slavery, and elite planter lifestyle?

owned 4,383 slaves — nearly 300 apiece — who annually grew and processed 14 million pounds of rice. As inexpensive Asian rice entered the world market in the 1820s and cut their profits, the Carolina rice aristocrats sold some slaves and worked the others harder, sustaining their luxurious lifestyle. The "hospitality and elegance" of Charleston and Savannah impressed savvy English traveler John Silk Buckingham. Buckingham likewise found "polished" families among long-established French Catholic planters in New Orleans and along the Mississippi River: There, the "sugar and cotton planters live in splendid edifices, and enjoy all the luxury that wealth can impart" (America Compared, p. 387).

In tobacco-growing regions, the lives of the planter aristocracy followed a different trajectory, in part because slave ownership was widely diffused. In the 1770s, about 60 percent of white families in the Chesapeake region owned at least one African American. As wealthy tobacco planters moved their estates and slaves to the Cotton South, middling whites (who owned between five and twenty slaves) came to dominate the Chesapeake economy. The descendants of the old tobacco aristocracy remained influential, but increasingly as slave-owning grain farmers, lawyers, merchants, industrialists, and politicians. They hired out surplus slaves, sold them south, or allowed them to purchase their freedom.

The Ideology and Reality of "Benevolence"   The planter aristocracy flourished around the periphery of the South's booming Cotton Belt — in Virginia, South Carolina, and Louisiana — but it took the lead in defending slavery. Ignoring the Jeffersonian response to slavery as a "misfortune" or a "necessary evil" (Chapter 8), southern apologists in the 1830s argued that the institution was a **"positive good"** because it subsidized an elegant lifestyle for a white elite and provided tutelage for genetically inferior Africans. "As a race, the African is inferior to the white man," declared Alexander Stephens, the future vice president of the Confederacy. "Subordination to the white man, is his normal condition." Apologists depicted planters and their wives as aristocratic models of "disinterested benevolence," who provided food and housing for their workers and cared for them in old age. One wealthy Georgian declared, "Plantation government should be eminently patriarchal. . . . The pater-familias, or head of the family, should, in one sense, be the father of the whole concern, negroes and all."

Those planters who embraced Christian stewardship tried to shape the religious lives of their chattel.

Bernhard, Duke of Saxe-Weimar-Eisenach

The Racial Complexities of Southern Society

In 1825 and 1826, Bernhard, heir to the German principality of Saxe-Weimar-Eisenach, traveled throughout the United States, and in 1828 he published an account of his adventures. After a military career, the duke ruled his principality from 1853 until his death in 1862.

In New Orleans we were invited to a subscription ball. . . . Only good society is invited to these balls. The first to which we came was not very well attended; but most of the ladies were very nice looking and well turned out in the French manner. Their clothing was elegant after the latest Paris fashions. They danced very well and did credit to their French dancing masters. Dancing and some music are the main branches of the education of a Creole [an American-born white] woman. . . .

The native men are far from matching the women in elegance. And they stayed only a short time, preferring to escape to a so-called "Quarterons Ball" which they find more amusing and where they do not have to stand on ceremony. . . .

A "quarteron" [actually an octoroon, a person of one-eighth African ancestry] is the offspring of a mestizo mother and a white father, just as the mestizo is the child of a mulatto and a white man. The "quarterons" are almost completely white. There would be no way of recognizing them by their complexion, for they are often fairer than the Creoles. Black hair and eyes are generally the signs of their status, although some are quite blond. The ball is attended by the free "quarterons." Yet the deepest prejudice reigns against them on account of their colored origin; the white women particularly feel or affect to feel a strong repugnance to them.

Marriage between colored and white people is forbidden by the laws of the state. Yet the "quarterons," for their part, look upon the Negroes and mulattoes as inferiors and are unwilling to mix with them. The girls therefore have no other recourse than to become the mistresses of white men. The "quarterons" regard such attachment as the equivalent of marriage. They would not think of entering upon it other than with a formal contract in which the man engages to pay a stipulated sum to the mother or father of the girl. . . .

Some of these women have inherited from their fathers and lovers, and possess considerable fortunes. Their status is nevertheless always very depressed. They must not ride in the street in coaches, and their lovers can bring them to the balls in their own conveyances only after nightfall. . . . But many of these girls are much more carefully educated than the whites, behave with more polish and more politeness, and make their lovers happier than white wives their husbands. And yet the white ladies speak of these unfortunate depressed creatures with great disdain, even bitterness. Because of the depth of these prejudices, many fathers send their daughters, conceived after this manner, to France where good education and wealth are no impediments to the attainment of a respectable place.

Source: From *Travels by His Highness Duke Bernhard of Saxe-Weimar-Eisenach Through North America in the Years 1825 and 1826*, edited by C. J. Jeronimus and translated by William Jeronimus. Copyright © 2001 University Press of America. Used by permission of the Rowan & Littlefield Publishing Company.

QUESTIONS FOR ANALYSIS

1. What does this passage suggest about the effect of slavery and the meaning of racial identity on sexual relationships and marriages in America and in France?
2. How does Bernhard's account help to explain the values and outlook of the free black population in the South?

They built churches on their plantations, welcomed evangelical preachers, and required their slaves to attend services. A few encouraged African Americans with spiritual "gifts" to serve as exhorters and deacons. Most of these planters acted from sincere Christian belief, but they also hoped to counter abolitionist criticism and to use religious teachings to control their workers.

Indeed, slavery's defenders increasingly used religious justifications for human bondage. Protestant ministers in the South pointed out that the Hebrews, God's chosen people, had owned slaves and that Jesus Christ had never condemned slavery. As James Henry Hammond told a British abolitionist in 1845: "What God ordains and Christ sanctifies should surely command the respect and toleration of man." However, many aristocratic defenders of slavery were absentee owners or delegated authority to overseers, and they rarely glimpsed the day-to-day brutality of their regime of forced labor. "I was at the plantation last Saturday and the crop was in fine order," an absentee's son wrote to his father, "but the negroes are most brutally scarred & several have run off."

Cotton Entrepreneurs   There was much less hypocrisy and far less elegance among the entrepreneurial planters of the Cotton South. "The glare of expensive luxury vanishes" in the black soil regions of Alabama and Mississippi, John Silk Buckingham remarked as he traveled through the Cotton South. Frederick Law Olmsted — the future architect of New York's Central Park, who during the mid-1850s traveled through the South for the *New York Times* — found that the plantations in Mississippi mostly had "but small and mean residences." Aristocratic paternalism vanished as well. A Mississippi planter put it plainly: "Everything has to give way to large crops of cotton, land has to be cultivated wet or dry, negroes [must] work, hot or cold."

Angry at being sold south and pressed to hard labor, many slaves grew "mean" and stubborn. Those who would not labor were subject to the lash. "Whiped all the hoe hands," Alabama planter James Torbert wrote matter-of-factly in his journal. Overseers pushed workers hard because their salaries often depended on the amount of cotton they were able "to make for the market." A Mississippi slave recalled, "When I wuz so tired I cu'dnt hardly stan', I had to spin my cut of cotton befor' I cu'd go to sleep. We had to card, spin, an' reel at nite."

Cotton was a demanding crop because of its long growing season. Slaves plowed the land in March; dropped seeds into the ground in early April; and, once the plants began to grow, continually chopped away the surrounding grasses. In between these tasks, they planted the corn and peas that would provide food for them and the plantation's hogs and chickens. When the cotton bolls ripened in late August, the long four-month picking season began. Slaves in the Cotton South, concluded Olmsted, worked "much harder and more unremittingly" than those in the tobacco regions. Moreover, fewer of them acquired craft skills than in tobacco, sugar, and rice areas, where slave coopers and

engineers made casks, processed sugar, and built irrigation systems.

To increase output, profit-seeking cotton planters began during the 1820s to use a rigorous **gang-labor system**. Previously, many planters had supervised their workers sporadically or assigned them specific tasks to complete at their own pace. Now masters with twenty or more slaves organized disciplined teams, or "gangs," supervised by black drivers and white overseers. They instructed the supervisors to work the gangs at a steady pace, clearing and plowing land or hoeing and picking cotton. A traveler in Mississippi described two gangs returning from work:

> First came, led by an old driver carrying a whip, forty of the largest and strongest women I ever saw together; they were all in a simple uniform dress of a bluish check stuff, the skirts reaching little below the knee.... They carried themselves loftily, each having a hoe over the shoulder, and walking with a free, powerful swing.

Next marched the plow hands with their mules, "the cavalry, thirty strong, mostly men, but a few of them women." Finally, "a lean and vigilant white overseer, on a brisk pony, brought up the rear."

The gang-labor system enhanced profits by increasing productivity. Because slaves in gangs finished tasks in thirty-five minutes that took a white yeoman planter an hour to complete, gang labor became ever more prevalent. In one Georgia county, the percentage of blacks working in gangs doubled between 1830 and 1850. As the price of raw cotton surged after 1846, the wealth of the planter class skyrocketed. And no wonder: nearly 2 million enslaved African Americans now labored on the plantations of the Cotton South and annually produced 4 million bales of the valuable fiber.

Planters, Smallholding Yeomen, and Tenants

Although the South was a **slave society** — that is, a society in which the institution of slavery affected all aspects of life — most white southerners did not own slaves. The percentage of white families who held blacks in bondage steadily decreased — from 36 percent in 1830, to 31 percent in 1850, to about 25 percent a decade later. However, slave ownership varied by region. In some cotton-rich counties, 40 percent of the white families owned slaves; in the hill country near the Appalachian Mountains, the proportion dropped to 10 percent.

The Inherent Brutality of Slavery

Like all systems of forced labor, American racial slavery relied ultimately on physical coercion. Slave owners and overseers routinely whipped slaves who worked slowly or defied their orders. On occasion, they applied the whip with such ferocity that the slave was permanently injured or killed. This photograph of a Mississippi slave named Gordon, taken after he fled to the Union army in Louisiana in 1863 and published in *Harper's Weekly*, stands as graphic testimony to the inherent brutality of the system. Library of Congress.

Planter Elites   A privileged minority of 395,000 southern families owned slaves in 1860, their ranks divided into a strict hierarchy. The top one-fifth of these families owned twenty or more slaves. This elite — just 5 percent of the South's white population — dominated the economy, owning over 50 percent of the entire slave population of 4 million and growing 50 percent of the South's cotton crop. The average wealth of these planters was $56,000 (about $1.6 million in purchasing power today); by contrast, a prosperous southern yeoman or northern farmer owned property worth a mere $3,200.

Substantial proprietors, another fifth of the slave-owning population, held title to six to twenty bondsmen

and -women. These middling planters owned almost 40 percent of the enslaved laborers and produced more than 30 percent of the cotton. Often they pursued dual careers as skilled artisans or professional men. Thus some of the fifteen slaves owned by Georgian Samuel L. Moore worked in his brick factory, while others labored on his farm. Dr. Thomas Gale used the income from his medical practice to buy a Mississippi plantation that annually produced 150 bales of cotton. In Alabama, lawyer Benjamin Fitzpatrick used his legal fees to buy ten slaves.

Like Fitzpatrick, lawyers acquired wealth by managing the affairs of the slave-owning elite, representing planters and merchants in suits for debt, and helping smallholders and tenants register their deeds and contracts. Standing at the legal crossroads of their small towns, they rose to prominence and regularly won election to public office. Less than 1 percent of the male population, in 1828 lawyers made up 16 percent of the Alabama legislature and an astounding 26 percent in 1849.

Smallholding Planters and Yeomen   Smallholding slave owners were much less visible than the wealthy grandees and the middling lawyer-planters. These planters held from one to five black laborers in bondage and owned a few hundred acres of land. Some smallholders were well-connected young men who would rise to wealth when their father's death blessed them with more land and slaves. Others were poor but ambitious men trying to pull themselves up by their bootstraps, often encouraged by elite planters and proslavery advocates. "Ours is a proslavery form of Government, and the proslavery element should be increased," declared a Georgia newspaper. "We would like to see every white man at the South the owner of a family of negroes." Some aspiring planters achieved modest prosperity. A German settler reported from Alabama in 1855 that "nearly all his countrymen" who emigrated with him were slaveholders. "They were poor on their arrival in the country; but no sooner did they realize a little money than they invested it in slaves."

Bolstered by the patriarchal ideology of the planter class, yeomen farmers ruled their smallholdings with a firm hand. The male head of the household had legal authority over all the dependents — wives, children, and slaves — and, according to one South Carolina judge, the right on his property "to be as churlish as he pleases." Yeomen wives had little power; like women

UNDERSTAND POINTS OF VIEW

By 1860, what different groups made up the South's increasingly complex society? How did these groups interact?

in the North, they lost their legal identity when they married. To express their concerns, many southern women joined churches, where they usually outnumbered men by a margin of two to one. Women especially welcomed the message of spiritual equality preached in evangelical Baptist and Methodist churches, and they hoped that the church community would hold their husbands to the same standards of Christian behavior to which they conformed. However, most churches supported patriarchal rule and told female members to remain in "wifely obedience," whatever the actions of their husbands.

Whatever their authority within the household, most southern yeomen lived and died as hardscrabble farmers. They worked alongside their slaves in the fields, struggled to make ends meet as their families grew, and moved regularly in search of opportunity. Thus, in 1847, James Buckner Barry left North Carolina with his new wife and two slaves to settle in Bosque County, Texas. There he worked part-time as an Indian fighter while his slaves toiled on a drought-ridden farm that barely kept the family in food. In South Carolina, W. J. Simpson struggled for years as a smallholding cotton planter and then gave up. He hired out one of his two slaves and went to work as an overseer on his father's farm.

Less fortunate smallholders fell from the privileged ranks of the slave-owning classes. Selling their land and slaves to pay off debts, they joined the mass of propertyless tenants who farmed the estates of wealthy landlords. In 1860, in Hancock County, Georgia, there were 56 slave-owning planters and 300 propertyless white farm laborers and factory workers; in nearby Hart County, 25 percent of the white farmers were tenants. Across the South, about 40 percent of the white population worked as tenants or farm laborers; as the *Southern Cultivator* observed, they had "no legal right nor interest in the soil [and] no homes of their own."

Poor Freemen   Propertyless whites suffered the ill consequences of living in a slave society that accorded little respect to hardworking white laborers. Nor could

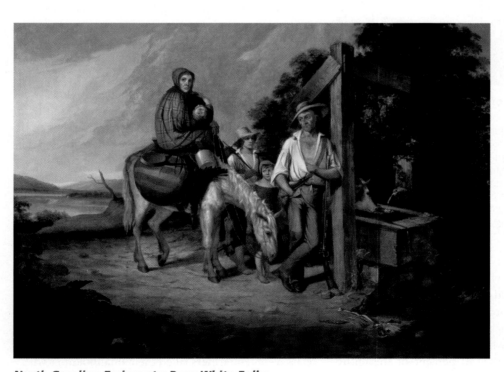

North Carolina Emigrants: Poor White Folks

Completed in 1845, James Henry Beard's (1811–1893) painting depicts a family moving north to Ohio. Unlike many optimistic scenes of emigration, the picture conveys a sense of resigned despair. The family members, led by a sullen, disheveled father, pause at a water trough while their cow drinks and their dog chews a bone. The mother looks apprehensively toward the future as she cradles a child; two barefoot older children listlessly await their father's command. New York writer Charles Briggs interpreted the painting as an "eloquent sermon on Anti-Slavery . . . , the blight of Slavery has paralyzed the strong arm of the man and destroyed the spirit of the woman." Although primarily a portrait painter, Beard questioned the ethics and optimism of American culture in *Ohio Land Speculator* (1840) and *The Last Victim of the Deluge* (1849), as well as in *Poor White Folks*. Cincinnati Art Museum, Ohio, USA/Gift of the Proctor & Gamble Company/The Bridgeman Art Library.

they hope for a better life for their children, because slave owners refused to pay taxes to fund public schools. Moreover, wealthy planters bid up the price of African Americans, depriving white laborers and tenants of easy access to the slave labor required to accumulate wealth. Finally, planter-dominated legislatures forced all white men, whether they owned slaves or not, to serve in the patrols and militias that deterred black uprisings. The majority of white southerners, Frederick Law Olmsted concluded, "are poor. They . . . have little — very little — of the common comforts and consolations of civilized life. Their destitution is not material only; it is intellectual and it is moral."

Marking this moral destitution, poor whites enjoyed the psychological satisfaction that they ranked above blacks. As Alfred Iverson, a U.S. senator from Georgia (1855–1861), explained: a white man "walks erect in the dignity of his color and race, and feels that he is a superior being, with the more exalted powers and privileges than others." To reinforce that sense of racial superiority, planter James Henry Hammond told his poor white neighbors, "In a slave country every freeman is an aristocrat."

Rejecting that half-truth, many southern whites fled planter-dominated counties in the 1830s and sought farms in the Appalachian hill country and beyond — in western Virginia, Kentucky, Tennessee, the southern regions of Illinois and Indiana, and Missouri. Living as yeomen farmers, they used family labor to grow foodstuffs for sustenance. To obtain cash or store credit to buy agricultural implements, cloth, shoes, salt, and other necessities, yeomen families sold their surplus crops, raised hogs for market sale, and — when the price of cotton rose sharply — grew a few bales. Their goals were modest: on the family level, they wanted to preserve their holdings and buy enough land to set up their children as small-scale farmers. As citizens, smallholders wanted to control their local government and elect men of their own kind to public office. However, thoughtful yeomen understood that the slave-based cotton economy sentenced family farmers to a subordinate place in the social order. They could hope for a life of independence and dignity only by moving north or farther west, where labor was "free" and hard work was respected.

Expanding and Governing the South

By the 1830s, settlers from the South had carried both yeoman farming and plantation slavery into Arkansas and Missouri. Between those states and the Rocky Mountains stretched great grasslands. An army explorer, Major Stephen H. Long, thought the plains region "almost wholly unfit for cultivation" and in 1820 labeled it the Great American Desert. The label stuck. Americans looking for land turned south, to Mexican territory. At the same time, elite planters struggled to control state governments in the Cotton South.

The Settlement of Texas

After winning independence from Spain in 1821, the Mexican government pursued an activist settlement policy. To encourage migration to the refigured state of Coahuila y Tejas, it offered sizable land grants to its citizens and to American emigrants. Moses Austin, an American land speculator, settled smallholding farmers on his large grant, and his son, Stephen F. Austin, acquired even more land — some 180,000 acres — which he sold to newcomers. By 1835, about 27,000 white Americans and their 3,000 African American slaves were raising cotton and cattle in the well-watered plains and hills of eastern and central Texas. They far outnumbered the 3,000 Mexican residents, who lived primarily near the southwestern Texas towns of Goliad and San Antonio.

When Mexico in 1835 adopted a new constitution creating a stronger central government and dissolving state legislatures, the Americans split into two groups. The "war party," led by Sam Houston and recent migrants from Georgia, demanded independence for Texas. Members of the "peace party," led by Stephen Austin, negotiated with the central government in Mexico City for greater political autonomy. They believed Texas could flourish within a decentralized Mexican republic, a "federal" constitutional system favored by the Liberal Party in Mexico (and advocated in the United States by Jacksonian Democrats). Austin won significant concessions for the Texans, including an exemption from a law ending slavery, but in 1835 Mexico's president, General Antonio López de Santa Anna, nullified them. Santa Anna wanted to impose national authority throughout Mexico. Fearing central control, the war party provoked a rebellion that most of the American settlers ultimately supported. On March 2, 1836, the American rebels proclaimed the independence of Texas and adopted a constitution legalizing slavery.

To put down the rebellion, President Santa Anna led an army that wiped out the Texan garrison defending the **Alamo** in San Antonio and then captured Goliad,

> **UNDERSTAND POINTS OF VIEW**
> What issues divided the Mexican government and the Americans in Texas, and what proposals sought to resolve them?

Starting Out in Texas

Thousands of white farmers, some owning a few slaves, moved onto small farms in Texas and Arkansas during the 1840s and 1850s. They lived in crudely built log huts; owned a few cows, horses, and oxen; and eked out a meager living by planting a few acres of cotton in addition to their crops of corn. Their aspirations were simple: to achieve modest prosperity during their lives and to assist their children to own farms of their own. Daughters of the Republic of Texas Library.

executing about 350 prisoners of war (Map 12.2). Santa Anna thought that he had crushed the rebellion, but New Orleans and New York newspapers romanticized the deaths at the Alamo of folk heroes Davy Crockett and Jim Bowie. Drawing on anti-Catholic sentiment aroused by Irish immigration and the massacre at Goliad, they urged Americans to "Remember the Alamo" and depicted the Mexicans as tyrannical butchers in the service of the pope. American adventurers, lured by offers of land grants, flocked to Texas to join the rebel forces. Commanded by General Sam Houston, the Texans routed Santa Anna's overconfident army in the Battle of San Jacinto in April 1836, winning de facto independence. The Mexican government refused to recognize the Texas Republic but, for the moment, did not seek to conquer it.

The Texans voted for annexation by the United States, but President Martin Van Buren refused to bring the issue before Congress. As a Texas diplomat reported, the cautious Van Buren and other party politicians feared that annexation would spark a war with Mexico and, beyond that, a "desperate death-struggle . . . between the North and the South [over the extension of slavery]; a struggle involving the probability of a dissolution of the Union."

The Politics of Democracy

As national leaders refused admission to Texas, elite planters faced political challenges in the Cotton South. Unlike the planter-aristocrats who ruled the colonial world, they lived in a republican society with a

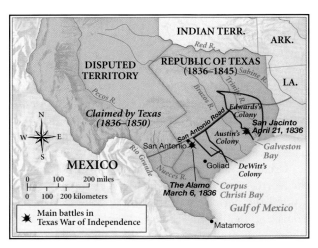

MAP 12.2
American Settlements, the Texas-Mexican War, and Boundary Disputes

During the 1820s the Mexican government encouraged Americans to settle in the sparsely populated state of Coahuila y Tejas. By 1835 the nearly 30,000 Americans far outnumbered Mexican residents. To put down an American-led revolt, General Santa Anna led 6,000 soldiers into Tejas in 1836. After overwhelming the rebels at the Alamo in March, Santa Anna set out to capture the Texas Provisional Government, which had fled to Galveston. But the Texans' victory at San Jacinto in April ended the war and secured de facto independence for the Republic of Texas (1836–1845). However, the annexation of Texas to the United States sparked a war with Mexico in 1846, and the state's boundaries remained in dispute until the Compromise of 1850.

democratic ethos. The Alabama Constitution of 1819 granted suffrage to all white men; it also provided for a **secret ballot** (rather than voice-voting); apportionment of legislative seats based on population; and the election of county supervisors, sheriffs, and clerks of court. Given these democratic provisions, political factions in Alabama had to compete for votes. When a Whig newspaper sarcastically asked whether the state's policies should "be governed and controlled by the whim and caprice of the majority of the people," Democrats hailed the power of the common folk. They called on "Farmers, Mechanics, laboring men" to repudiate Whig "aristocrats . . . the soft handed and soft headed gentry."

Taxation Policy   Whatever the electioneering rhetoric, most Whig and Democrat political candidates were men of substance. In the early 1840s, nearly 90 percent of Alabama's legislators owned slaves, testimony to the political power of the slave-owning minority. Still, relatively few lawmakers — only about 10 percent — were

rich planters, a group voters by and large distrusted. "A rich man cannot sympathize with the poor," declared one candidate. Consequently, the majority of elected state officials, and most county officials, in the Cotton South came from the ranks of middle-level planters and planter-lawyers. Astute politicians, they refrained from laying "oppressive" taxes on the people, particularly the white majority who owned no slaves. Between 1830 and 1860, the Alabama legislature obtained about 70 percent of the state's revenue from taxes on slaves and land. Another 10 to 15 percent came from levies on carriages, gold watches, and other luxury goods and on the capital invested in banks, transportation companies, and manufacturing enterprises.

To win the votes of taxpaying slave owners, Alabama Democrats advocated limited government and low taxes. They attacked their Whig opponents for favoring higher taxes and for providing government subsidies for banks, canals, railroads, and other internal improvements. "Voting against appropriations is the safe and popular side," one Democratic legislator declared, and his colleagues agreed; until the 1850s, they rejected most of the bills that would have granted subsidies to transportation companies or banks.

If tax policy in Alabama had a democratic thrust, elsewhere in the South it did not. In some states, wealthy planters used their political muscle to exempt slave property from taxation. Or they shifted the burden to backcountry yeomen, who owned low-quality pasturelands, by taxing farms according to acreage rather than value. Planter-legislators also spared themselves the cost of building fences around their fields by enacting laws that required yeomen to "fence in" their livestock. And, during the 1850s, wealthy legislators throughout the South used public funds to subsidize the canals and railroads in which they had invested, ignoring the protests of yeoman-backed legislators.

The Paradox of Southern Prosperity   Even without these internal improvements, the South had a strong economy. Indeed, it ranked fourth in the world in 1860, with a per capita income among whites higher than that of France and Germany. As a contributor to a Georgia newspaper argued in the 1850s, planters and yeomen should not complain about "tariffs, and merchants, and manufacturers" because "the most highly prosperous people now on earth, are to be found in these very [slave] States." Such arguments tell only part of the story. Nearly all African Americans — 40 percent of the population — lived in dire and permanent poverty. And, although the average southern white man was 80 percent richer than the average northerner in

EXPLAIN CONSEQUENCES

How did the political power of slave owners affect tax policy and the character of economic development in the south-ern states?

1860, the southerner's *non-slave* wealth was only 60 percent of the northern average. Moreover, the wealth of the industrializing Northeast was increasing at a faster pace than that of the South. Between 1820 and 1860, slave-related trade across the Atlantic declined from 12.6 percent of world trade to 5.3 percent.

Influential southerners blamed the shortcomings of their plantation-based economy on outsiders: "Purely agricultural people," intoned slave-owning planter-politician James Henry Hammond, "have been in all ages the victims of rapacious tyrants grinding them down." And they steadfastly defended their way of life. "We have no cities — we don't want them," boasted U.S. senator Louis Wigfall of Texas in 1861. "We want no manufactures: we desire no trading, no

mechanical or manufacturing classes. . . . As long as we have our rice, our sugar, our tobacco, and our cotton, we can command wealth to purchase all we want." So wealthy southerners continued to buy land and slaves, a strategy that neglected investments in the great technological innovations of the nineteenth century — water- and steam-powered factories, machine tools, steel plows, and crushed-gravel roads — that would have raised the South's productivity and wealth.

Urban growth, the key to prosperity in Europe and the North, occurred primarily in the commercial cities around the periphery of the South: New Orleans, St. Louis, and Baltimore. Factories — often staffed by slave labor — appeared primarily in the Chesapeake region, which had a diverse agricultural economy and a surplus of bound workers. Within the Cotton South, wealthy planters invested in railroads primarily to grow more cotton; when the Western & Atlantic Railroad reached the Georgia upcountry, the cotton

Colonel and Mrs. James A. Whiteside, Son Charles and Servants

James A. Whiteside (1803–1861) was a Tennessee lawyer, politician, land speculator, and entrepreneur, with investments in iron manufacturing, banking, steamboats, and railroads. In 1857, he became vice president of the Nashville, Chattanooga, and St. Louis Railroad. The following year, Whiteside persuaded the Scottish-born painter James Cameron (1817–1882) to move to Chattanooga, where Cameron completed this ambitious portrait of the colonel; his second wife, Harriet; their youngest child, Charles; and two enslaved "servants." The painting shows the family at home, with a view of Chattanooga and of Lookout Mountain, where the colonel had built a hotel. Whiteside died from pneumonia in 1861 after returning home from Virginia with his son James, who had fallen ill while serving in the Confederate army. Hunter Museum of American Art, Chattanooga, Tennessee. Gift of Mr. & Mrs. Thomas B. Whiteside, 1975.7.

crop there quickly doubled. Cotton and agriculture remained King.

Slavery also deterred Europeans from migrating to the South, because they feared competition from bound labor. Their absence deprived the region of skilled artisans and of hardworking laborers to drain swamps, dig canals, smelt iron, and work on railroads. When entrepreneurs tried to hire slaves for these dangerous tasks, planters replied that "a negro's life is too valuable to be risked." Slave owners also feared that hiring out would make their slaves too independent. As a planter told Frederick Law Olmsted, such workers "had too much liberty . . . and got a habit of roaming about and taking care of themselves."

Thus, despite its increasing size and booming exports, the South remained an economic colony: Great Britain and the North bought its staple crops and provided its manufactures, financial services, and shipping facilities. In 1860, some 84 percent of southerners — more than double the percentage in the northern states — still worked in agriculture, and southern factories turned out only 10 percent of the nation's manufactures. The South's fixation on an "exclusive and exhausting" system of cotton monoculture and slave labor filled South Carolina textile entrepreneur William Gregg with "dark forebodings": "It has produced us such an abundant supply of all the luxuries and elegances of life, with so little exertion on our part, that we have become enervated, unfitted for other and more laborious pursuits."

The African American World

By the 1820s, the cultural life of most slaves reflected both the values and customs of their West African ancestors and the language, laws, and religious beliefs of the South's white population. This mix of African- and European-derived cultural values persisted for decades because whites discouraged blacks from assimilating and because slaves prized their diverse African heritages.

Evangelical Black Protestantism

The emergence of black Christianity illustrated the synthesis of African and European cultures. From the 1790s to the 1840s, the Second Great Awakening swept over the South, and evangelical Baptist and Methodist preachers converted thousands of white families and hundreds of enslaved blacks (see Chapter 8). Until that time, African-born blacks, often identifiable by their ritual scars, had maintained the religious practices of their homelands.

African Religions and Christian Conversion Africans carried their traditional religious practices to the United States. Some practiced Islam, but the majority relied on African gods and spirits. As late as 1842, Charles C. Jones, a Presbyterian minister, noted that the blacks on his family's plantation in Georgia believed "in second-sight, in apparitions, charms, witchcraft . . . [and other] superstitions brought from Africa." Fearing for their own souls if they withheld "the means of salvation" from African Americans, Jones and other zealous Protestant preachers and planters set out to convert slaves.

Other Protestant crusaders came from the ranks of pious black men and women who had become Christians in the Chesapeake. Swept to the Cotton South by the domestic slave trade, they carried with them the evangelical message of emotional conversion, ritual baptism, and communal spirituality. Equally important, these crusaders adapted Protestant doctrines to black needs. Enslaved Christians pointed out that blacks as well as whites were "children of God" and should be treated accordingly. **Black Protestantism** generally ignored the doctrines of original sin and predestination, and preachers didn't use biblical passages that encouraged unthinking obedience to authority. A white minister in Liberty County, Georgia, reported that when he urged slaves to obey their masters, "one half of my audience deliberately rose up and walked off."

> **PLACE EVENTS IN CONTEXT**
> How did the Second Great Awakening affect the development of black religion?

Black Worship Indeed, some African American converts envisioned the deity as the Old Testament warrior who had liberated the Jews and so would liberate them. Inspired by a vision of Christ, Nat Turner led his bloody rebellion against slavery in Virginia (see Chapter 11). Other black Christians saw themselves as Chosen People: "de people dat is born of God." Charles Davenport, a Mississippi slave, recalled black preachers "exhort[ing] us dat us was de chillun o' Israel in de wilderness an' de Lawd done sont us to take dis lan' o' milk an' honey."

Still, African Americans expressed their Christianity in distinctive ways. The thousands of blacks who joined the Methodist Church respected its ban on profane dancing but praised the Lord in what minister Henry George Spaulding called the "religious dance of the Negroes." Spaulding described the African-derived

Black Kitchen Ball

From time to time, festive celebrations punctuated the demanding work routine of slaves' lives. In this 1838 painting, *Kitchen Ball at White Sulphur Springs Virginia*, African Americans dance to the music of a fiddle and a fife (on the right). Note the light complexions and Europeanized features of the most prominent figures, the result of either racial mixing or the cultural perspective of the artist. The painter, Christian Mayr, was born in Germany in 1805 and migrated to the United States in 1833. After working for years as a traveling portrait painter, Mayr settled in New York City in 1845 and died there in 1850.
North Carolina Museum of Art, Raleigh. Purchased with funds from the State of North Carolina.

"ring shout" this way: "Three or four, standing still, clapping their hands and beating time with their feet, commence singing in unison one of the peculiar shout melodies, while the others walk around in a ring, in single file, joining also in the song." The songs themselves were usually collective creations, devised spontaneously from bits of old hymns and tunes. Recalled an ex-slave:

> We'd all be at the "prayer house" de Lord's day, and de white preacher he'd splain de word and read whar Esekial done say — Dry bones gwine ter lib ergin. And, honey, de Lord would come a-shinin' thoo dem pages and revive dis ole nigger's heart, and I'd jump up dar and den and holler and shout and sing and pat, and dey would all cotch de words and I'd sing it to some ole shout song I'd heard 'em sing from

> Africa, and dey'd all take it up and keep at it, and keep a-addin' to it, and den it would be a spiritual.

By such African-influenced means, black congregations devised a distinctive and joyous brand of Protestant worship to sustain them on the long journey to emancipation and the Promised Land. "O my Lord delivered Daniel," the slaves sang, "O why not deliver me too?"

Forging Families and Communities

Black Protestantism was one facet of an increasingly homogeneous African American culture in the rural South. Even in South Carolina — a major point of entry for imported slaves — only 20 percent of the black residents in 1820 had been born in Africa. The domestic slave trade mingled blacks from many states, erased regional differences, and prompted the emergence of a core culture in the Lower Mississippi Valley. A prime example was the fate of the Gullah dialect, which combined words from English and a variety of African languages in an African grammatical structure. Spoken by blacks in the Carolina low country well into the twentieth century, Gullah did not take root on the cotton plantations of Alabama and Mississippi. There, slaves from Carolina were far outnumbered by migrants from the Chesapeake, who spoke black English. Like Gullah, black English used double negatives and other African grammatical forms, but it consisted primarily of English words rendered with West African pronunciation (for example, with *th* pronounced as *d* — "de preacher").

Nonetheless, African influences remained significant. At least one-third of the slaves who entered the United States between 1776 and 1809 came from the Congo region of West-Central Africa, and they brought their cultures with them. As traveler Isaac Holmes reported in 1821: "In Louisiana, and the state of Mississippi, the slaves . . . dance for several hours during Sunday afternoon. The general movement is in what they call the Congo dance." Similar descriptions of blacks who "danced the Congo and sang a purely African song to the accompaniment of . . . a drum" appeared as late as 1890.

African Americans also continued to respect African incest taboos by shunning marriages between cousins. On the Good Hope Plantation in South Carolina, nearly half of the slave children born between 1800 and 1857 were related by blood to one another; yet when they married, only one of every forty-one unions took place between cousins. White planters were not the source of this taboo: cousin marriages were frequent among the 440 South Carolina men and women who owned at least one hundred slaves in 1860, in part because such unions kept wealth within an extended family (Thinking Like a Historian, p. 398).

Unlike white marriages, slave unions were not legally binding. According to a Louisiana judge, "slaves have no legal capacity to assent to any contract . . . because slaves are deprived of all civil rights." Nonetheless, many African Americans took marriage vows before Christian ministers or publicly marked their union in ceremonies that included the West African custom of jumping over a broomstick together. Once married, newly arrived young people in the Cotton South often chose older people in their new communities as fictive "aunts" and "uncles." The slave trade had destroyed their family, but not their family values.

The creation of fictive kinship ties was part of a community-building process, a partial substitute for the family ties that sustained whites during periods of crisis. Naming children was another. Recently imported slaves frequently gave their children African names. Males born on Friday, for example, were often called Cuffee — the name of that day in several West African languages. Many American-born parents chose names of British origin, but they usually named sons after fathers, uncles, or grandfathers and daughters after grandmothers. Those transported to the Cotton South often named their children for relatives left behind. Like incest rules and marriage rituals, this intergenerational sharing of names evoked memories of a lost world and bolstered kin ties in the new one.

> **UNDERSTAND POINTS OF VIEW**
> In what respects did African cultural practices affect the lives of enslaved African Americans?

Negotiating Rights

By forming stable families and communities, African Americans gradually created a sense of order in the harsh and arbitrary world of slavery. In a few regions, slaves won substantial control over their lives.

Working Lives   During the Revolutionary era, blacks in the rice-growing lowlands of South Carolina successfully asserted the right to labor by the "task." Under the **task system**, workers had to complete a precisely defined job each day — for example, digging up a quarter-acre of land, hoeing half an acre, or pounding seven mortars of rice. By working hard, many finished their tasks by early afternoon, a Methodist preacher reported, and had "the rest of the day for themselves, which they spend in working their own private fields . . . planting rice, corn, potatoes, tobacco &c. for their own use and profit."

Slaves on sugar and cotton plantations led more regimented lives, thanks to the gang-labor system. As one field hand put it, there was "no time off [between] de change of de seasons. . . . Dey was allus clearin' mo' lan' or sump'." Many slaves faced bans on growing crops on their own. "It gives an excuse for trading," explained one owner, and that encouraged roaming and independence. Still, many masters hired out surplus workers as teamsters, drovers, steamboat workers, turpentine gatherers, and railroad builders; in 1856, no fewer than 435 hired slaves laid track for the Virginia & Tennessee Railroad. Many owners regretted the result. As an overseer remarked about a slave named John, "He is not as good a hand as he was before he went to Alabamy."

Childhood in Black and White

A major theme of Harriet Beecher Stowe's powerful antislavery novel *Uncle Tom's Cabin* is the sin of separating black families and denying parental rights to enslaved mothers and fathers. The following documents reveal the dynamics of plantation family life, and particularly mother-child relations.

1. **Ex-slave Josephine Smith, interviewed at age ninety-four by Mary A. Hicks, Raleigh, North Carolina, 1930s.** *Slave children had loving but limited relationships with their mothers, who worked long hours in the fields and were sometimes sold away from their children.*

I 'members seein' a heap o' slave sales, wid de niggers in chains, an' de spec'ulators sellin' an' buyin' dem off. I also 'members seein' a drove of slaves wid nothin' on but a rag 'twixt dere legs bein' galloped roun' 'fore de buyers. 'Bout de wust thing dat eber I seed do' wuz a slave 'woman at Louisburg who had been sold off from her three weeks old baby, an wuz bein' marched ter New Orleans.

She had walked till she quz give out, an' she wuz weak enough ter fall in de middle o' de road. . . . As I pass by dis 'oman begs me in God's name fer a drink o' water, an' I gives it ter her. I ain't neber be so sorry fer nobody. . . . Dey walk fer a little piece an' dis 'oman fall out. She dies dar side o' de road, an' right dar dey buries her, cussin', dey tells me, 'bout losin' money on her.

2. **"Narrative of James Curry, a Fugitive Slave," The Liberator, January 10, 1840.** *The abolitionist newspaper* The Liberator *published heartrending accounts of death and separation in slave families and how "fictive kinship" assisted the survivors.*

My mother's labor was very hard. She would go to the house in the morning, take her pail upon her head, and go away to the cow-pen, and milk fourteen cows. She then put on the bread for the family breakfast, and got the cream ready for churning, and set a little child to churn it, she having the care of from ten to fifteen children, whose mothers worked in the field. . . . Among the slave children, were three little orphans, whose mothers, at their death, committed them to the care of my mother. One of them was a babe. She took them and treated them as her own. The master took no care about them. She always took a share of the cloth she had provided for her own children, to cover these little friendless ones.

3. **Former slave Barney Alford, interview for the Works Progress Administration in Mississippi, 1930s.**

Ole mammy 'Lit' wus mity ole en she lived in one corner of de big yard en she keered fur all de black chilluns while de old folks wurk in de field. Mammy Lit wus good to all de chilluns en I had ter help her wid dem chilluns en keep dem babies on de pallet. Mammy Lit smoked a pipe, en sum times I wuld hide dat pipe, en she wuld slap me fur it, den sum times I wuld run way en go ter de kitchen whar my mammy wus at wurk en mammy Lit wuld hafter cum fur me en den she wuld whip me er gin. She sed I wus bad.

4. **"Mrs. Meriwether Administering Bitters," illustration from John Pendleton Kennedy, Swallow Barn, Or, A Sojourn in the Old Dominion, 1851.** *Bitters—strong alcoholic beverages flavored with bitter herbs—were administered as medicine in the nineteenth century, as in this depiction of a planter's wife tending to enslaved children. Kennedy's cheerful depictions of Virginia plantation life in this popular book, first published in 1832, reinforced the notion of slavery as a "positive good."*

Source: Picture Research Consultants & Archives.

5. G. M. J., "Early Culture of Children," 1855. *This excerpt from a Christian advice manual for mothers reflects the values of the mid-nineteenth-century white Protestant middle class.*

"Train up a child in the way he should go," is a law as imperative in the 19th century, as when first uttered by the lips of the wise man. Mothers are the natural executors of this law to their daughters. Nothing but the most unavoidable and pressing force of circumstances, should wrench this power from their hands. Who will guard with a mother's jealous eye the health, habits, morals, and religion of this most delicate part of creation. . . . How often I have been pained to see mothers place those delicate plants in the nursery with servants, whose tastes, feelings, morals, manners, and language are but a little removed from the lower animals of creation; there to receive impressions, and imbibe habits, which will grow with their growth, and strengthen with their strength, until like the branches of the giant oak, they shall expand and deepen into a shade that will forever conceal the parent stock.

6. Visiting Cards Created by Philadelphia Portrait Painter and Photographer Peregrine F. Cooper, As We Found Them (left), As They Are Now (right), 1864. *One of the ways to "train up a child in the way he should go" was to inculcate abolitionist sentiments early and often.*

AS WE FOUND THEM.

These children were owned by Thomas White, of Mathews Co., Va., until Feb. 20th, when Capt. Riley, 6th U. S. C. I., took them and gave them to the Society of Friends to educate at the Orphan's Shelter, Philadelphia.

Profits from sale, for the benefit of the children.

AS THEY ARE NOW

The Mother of these children was beaten, branded and sold at auction because she was kind to Union Soldiers. As she left for Richmond, Va., Feb. 13th, 1864, bound down in a cart, she prayed "O! God send the Yankees to take my children away."

Profits from sale, for the benefit of the children.

Source: George Eastman House.

Sources: (1) WPA Slave Narrative Project, 1936–38, learnnc.org; (2) "Narrative of James Curry, a Fugitive Slave," *The Liberator*, January 10, 1840, learnnc.org; (3) The MS Gen Web Project, msgw.org/slaves/alford-xslave.htm; (5) *Home Garner; or the Intellectual and Moral Store House*, ed. Mary G. Clarke (Philadelphia: J. P. Lippincott & Co., 1855), 115.

ANALYZING THE EVIDENCE

1. What do these sources reveal about slave communities? About the extent to which the ideology of "benevolent paternalism" governed the behavior of slave owners?

2. How does the engraving (source 4) compare to the descriptions of the care of slave children (sources 1–3)? What biases, if any, can you detect in these sources?

3. How would a person holding the beliefs described in source 5 react to the engraving of Mrs. Meriwether? To images showing slave "mammies" raising the master's children?

4. How do the images of enslaved children in source 6 pertain to "train[ing] up a child in the way he should go"? How effective are they? What emotions do they play upon?

PUTTING IT ALL TOGETHER

In the political system, debate over "the peculiar institution" of slavery often focused on property rights and constitutional principles. In the actual world of the plantation, human bondage evoked a range of human emotions—jealousy, resentment, anger, love, fear, tenderness—and human pain. Write an essay that assesses the economic, legal, and political arguments over slavery in light of the experiences of enslaved mothers and children.

Antebellum Slave Quarters
During the colonial period, owners often housed their slaves by gender in communal barracks. In the nineteenth century, slaves usually lived in family units in separate cabins. The slave huts on this South Carolina plantation were sturdily built but had few windows. Inside, they were sparsely furnished. Library of Congress.

The planters' greatest fear was that enslaved African Americans — a majority of the population in most cotton-growing counties — would rise in rebellion. Legally speaking, owners had virtually unlimited power over their slaves. "The power of the master must be absolute," intoned Justice Thomas Ruffin of the North Carolina Supreme Court in 1829. But absolute power required brutal coercion, and only hardened or sadistic masters had the stomach for such violence. "These poor negroes, receiving none of the fruits of their labor, do not love work," explained one woman who worked her own farm; "if we had slaves, we should have to . . . beat them to make use of them."

Moreover, passive resistance by African Americans seriously limited their owners' power. Slaves slowed the pace of work by feigning illness and losing or breaking tools. One Maryland slave, faced with transport to Mississippi and separation from his wife, flatly refused "to accompany my people, or to be exchanged or sold," his owner reported. Masters ignored such feelings at their peril. A slave (or a relative) might retaliate by setting fire to the master's house and barns, poisoning his food, or destroying his crops. Fear of resistance, as well as critical scrutiny by abolitionists, prompted many masters to reduce their reliance on the lash and use positive incentives such as food and special privileges. Noted Frederick Law Olmsted: "Men of sense have discovered that it was better to offer them rewards than to whip them." Nonetheless, owners could always resort to violence, and countless masters regularly asserted their power by demanding sex from their female slaves. As ex-slave Bethany Veney lamented in her autobiography, from "the unbridled lust of the slave-owner . . . the law holds . . . no protecting arm" over black women.

Survival Strategies   Slavery remained an exploitative system grounded in fear and coercion. Over the decades, hundreds of individual slaves responded by attacking their masters and overseers. But only a few blacks — among them Gabriel and Martin Prosser (1800) and Nat Turner (1831) — plotted mass uprisings. Most slaves recognized that revolt would be futile; they lacked the autonomous institutions such as the communes of European peasants, for example, needed to organize a successful rebellion. Moreover, whites

PLACE EVENTS IN CONTEXT
How successful were slaves in securing significant control over their lives?

were numerous, well armed, and determined to maintain their position of racial superiority.

Escape was equally problematic. Blacks in the Upper South could flee to the North, but only by leaving their family and kin. Slaves in the Lower South escaped to sparsely settled regions of Florida, where some intermarried with the Seminole Indians. Elsewhere in the South, escaped slaves eked out a meager existence in inhospitable marshy areas or mountain valleys. Consequently, most African Americans remained on plantations; as Frederick Douglass put it, they were

CLASS No. 1.

Comprises those prisoners who were found guilty and executed.

Prisoners Names.	Owners' Names.	Time of Commit.	How Disposed of.
Peter	James Poyas	June 18	Hanged on Tuesday the 2d July, 1822, on Blake's lands, near Charleston.
Ned	Gov. T. Bennett,	do.	
Rolla	do.	do	
Batteau	do.	do.	
Denmark Vesey	A free black man	22	
Jessy	Thos. Blackwood	23	
John	Elias Horry	July 5	Do on the Lines near Ch.; Friday July 12.
Gullah Jack	Paul Pritchard	do.	
Mingo	Wm. Harth	June 21	
Lot	Forrester	27	
Joe	P. L. Jore	July 6	
Julius	Thos. Forrest	8	
Tom	Mrs. Russell	10	
Smart	Robt. Anderson	do.	
John	John Robertson	11	
Robert	do.	do.	
Adam	do.	do.	
Polydore	Mrs. Faber	do.	Hanged on the Lines near Charleston, on Friday, 26th July.
Bacchus	Benj. Hammet	do.	
Dick	Wm. Sims	13	
Pharaoh	— Thompson	do.	
Jemmy	Mrs. Clement	18	
Mauidore	Mordecai Cohen	19	
Dean	— Mitchell	do.	
Jack	Mrs. Purcell	12	
Bellisle	Est. of Jos. Yates	18	
Naphur	do.	do.	
Adam	do.	do.	
Jacob	John S. Glen	16	
Charles	John Billings	18	
Jack	N. McNeill	22	
Cæsar	Miss Smith	do.	
Jacob Stagg	Jacob Lankester	23	Do. Tues. July 30.
Tom	Wm. M. Scott	24	
William	Mrs. Garner	Aug. 2	Do. Friday, Aug. 9.

"An Account of the Late Intended Insurrection, Charleston, South Carolina"

In 1820, Charleston had a free black population of 1,500 and an array of African American institutions, including the Brown Fellowship Society (for those of mixed racial ancestry) and an African Methodist Episcopal (AME) church. In 1822, Charleston authorities accused a free black, Denmark Vesey, of organizing a revolt to free the city's slaves. Although historians long accepted the truth of that charge, recent scholarship suggests that Vesey's only offense was antagonizing some whites by claiming his rights as a free man and that fearful slave owners conjured up the plot. Regardless, South Carolina officials hanged Vesey and thirty-four alleged co-conspirators and tore down the AME church where they allegedly plotted the uprising. David M. Rubenstein Rare Book & Manuscript Library, Duke University.

"pegged down to one single spot, and must take root there or die."

"Taking root" meant building the best possible lives for themselves. Over time, enslaved African Americans pressed their owners for a greater share of the product of their labor, much like unionized workers in the North were doing. Thus slaves insisted on getting paid for "overwork" and on the right to cultivate a garden and sell its produce. "De menfolks tend to de gardens round dey own house," recalled a Louisiana slave. "Dey raise some cotton and sell it to massa and git li'l money dat way." Enslaved women raised poultry and sold chickens and eggs. An Alabama slave remembered buying "Sunday clothes with dat money, sech as hats and pants and shoes and dresses." By the 1850s, thousands of African Americans were reaping the small rewards of this underground economy, and some accumulated sizable property. Enslaved Georgia carpenter Alexander Steele owned four horses, a mule, a silver watch, two cows, a wagon, and large quantities of fodder, hay, and corn.

Whatever their material circumstances, few slaves accepted the legitimacy of their status. Although he was fed well and never whipped, a former slave told an English traveler, "I was cruelly treated because I was kept in slavery."

The Free Black Population

Some African Americans escaped slavery through flight or a grant of freedom by their owners and, if they lived in the North, through gradual emancipation laws that, by 1840, had virtually ended bound labor. The proportion of free blacks rose from 8 percent of the African American population in 1790 to about 13 percent between 1820 and 1840, and then (because of high birthrates among enslaved blacks) fell to 11 percent. Still, the number of free blacks continued to grow. In the slave state of Maryland in 1860, half of all African Americans were free, and many more were "term" slaves, guaranteed their freedom in exchange for a few more years of work.

Northern Blacks   Almost half of free blacks in the United States in 1840 (some 170,000) and again in 1860 (250,000) lived in the free states of the North. However, few of them enjoyed unfettered freedom. Most whites regarded African Americans as their social inferiors and confined them to low-paying jobs. In rural areas, blacks worked as farm laborers or tenant farmers; in

COMPARE AND CONTRAST

How were the lives of free African Americans different in the northern and southern states?

A Master Bridge Builder

Horace King (1807–1885) was a self-made man of color, a rarity in the nineteenth-century South. Born a slave of mixed European, African, and Native American (Catawba) ancestry, King built major bridges in Georgia, Alabama, and Mississippi during the early 1840s. After winning his freedom in 1846, he built and ran a toll bridge across the Chattahoochee River in Alabama. During the Civil War, King worked as a contractor for the Confederacy; during Reconstruction, he served two terms as a Republican in the Alabama House of Representatives. Collection of the Columbus Museum, Columbus, Georgia; Museum Purchase.

towns and cities, they toiled as domestic servants, laundresses, or day laborers. Only a small number of African Americans owned land. "You do not see one out of a hundred . . . that can make a comfortable living, own a cow, or a horse," a traveler in New Jersey noted. In most states, law or custom prohibited northern blacks from voting, attending public schools, or sitting next to whites in churches. They could testify in court against whites only in Massachusetts. The federal government did not allow African Americans to work for the postal service, claim public lands, or hold a U.S. passport. As black activist Martin Delaney remarked in 1852: "We are slaves in the midst of freedom."

Of the few African Americans able to make full use of their talents, several achieved great distinction. Mathematician and surveyor Benjamin Banneker (1731–1806) published an almanac and helped lay out the new capital in the District of Columbia; Joshua Johnston (1765–1832) won praise for his portraiture;

and merchant Paul Cuffee (1759–1817) acquired a small fortune from his business enterprises. More impressive and enduring were the community institutions created by free African Americans. Throughout the North, these largely unknown men and women founded schools, mutual-benefit organizations, and fellowship groups, often called Free African Societies. Discriminated against by white Protestants, they formed their own congregations and a new religious denomination — the African Methodist Episcopal Church, headed by Bishop Richard Allen (see Chapter 8).

These institutions gave African Americans a measure of cultural autonomy, even as they marked sharp social divisions among blacks. "Respectable" blacks tried through their dress, conduct, and attitude to win the "esteem and patronage" of prominent whites — first Federalists and then Whigs and abolitionists — who were sympathetic to their cause. Those efforts separated them from impoverished blacks, who distrusted not only whites but also blacks who "acted white."

Standing for Freedom in the South   The free black population in the slave states numbered approximately 94,000 in 1810 and 225,000 in 1860. Most of these men and women lived in coastal cities — Mobile, Memphis, New Orleans — and in the Upper South. Partly because skilled Europeans avoided the South, free blacks formed the backbone of the urban artisan workforce. African American carpenters, blacksmiths, barbers, butchers, and shopkeepers played prominent roles in the economies of Baltimore, Richmond, Charleston, and New Orleans. But whatever their skills, free blacks faced many dangers. White officials often denied jury trials to free blacks accused of crimes, and sometimes they forced those charged with vagrancy back into slavery. Some free blacks were simply kidnapped and sold.

As a privileged minority among African Americans in the South, free blacks had divided loyalties. To advance the welfare of their families, some distanced themselves from plantation slaves and assimilated white culture and values. Indeed, mixed-race individuals sometimes joined the ranks of the planter class. David Barland, one of twelve children born to a white Mississippi planter and his black slave Elizabeth, himself owned no fewer than eighteen slaves. In neighboring Louisiana, some free blacks supported secession because they owned slaves and were "dearly attached to their native land."

Such individuals were exceptions. Most free African Americans acknowledged their ties to the great mass of slaves, some of whom were their relatives. "We's different [from whites] in color, in talk and in 'ligion and

An African American Clergyman

This flattering portrait is one of two paintings of African Americans by black artist Joshua Johnson (who also went by the surname Johnston). The son of an enslaved black woman and a white man, who bought his son's freedom in 1782, Johnson described himself in an advertisement in the *Baltimore Intelligence* in 1798 as a "Portrait Painter . . . a self-taught genius deriving from nature and industry his knowledge of the Art." White merchant families in Maryland and Virginia held Johnson's work in high regard and commissioned most of his thirty or so extant works. Bowdoin College Museum of Art, Brunswick, Maine. Museum Purchase, George Otis Hamlin Fund.

beliefs," said one. Calls by white planters in the 1840s to re-enslave free African Americans reinforced black unity. Knowing their own liberty was not secure so long as slavery existed, free blacks celebrated on August 1, the day slaves in the British West Indies won emancipation, and sought a similar goal for enslaved African Americans. As a delegate to the National Convention of Colored People in 1848 put it, "Our souls are yet dark under the pall of slavery." In the rigid American caste system, free blacks stood as symbols of hope to enslaved African Americans and as symbols of danger to most whites.

SUMMARY

In this chapter, we focused on the theme of an expanding South. Beginning about 1800, planters carried the system of plantation slavery from its traditional home in the Upper South to the Mississippi Valley and beyond. Powered by cotton, this movement westward involved the forced migration of more than 1 million enslaved African Americans and divided the planter elite into aristocratic paternalists and entrepreneurial capitalists.

We also examined the character of white and black societies in the Cotton South. After 1820, less than a third of white families owned slaves, and another third were yeomen farmers; propertyless tenant farmers and laborers made up the rest. Many whites joined evangelical Protestant churches, as did blacks, who infused their churches with African modes of expression. Indeed, church and family became core institutions of African American society, providing strength and solace amid the tribulations of slavery. Finally, we explored the initiatives taken by the free black population, in both the northern and southern states, to achieve individual mobility and to build community institutions. These efforts resulted in a church-based leadership class and a black abolitionist movement.

C H A P T E R   R E V I E W

 MAKE IT STICK   Go to **LearningCurve** to retain what you've read.

TERMS TO KNOW   Identify and explain the significance of each term below.

Key Concepts and Events

coastal trade (p. 380)

inland system (p. 380)

chattel principle (p. 381)

benevolent masters (p. 382)

republican aristocracy (p. 386)

"positive good" argument (p. 386)

gang-labor system (p. 388)

slave society (p. 388)

Alamo (p. 391)

secret ballot (p. 393)

black Protestantism (p. 395)

task system (p. 397)

Key People

Harriet Jacobs (p. 382)

James Henry Hammond (p. 384)

Stephen Austin (p. 391)

Antonio López de Santa Anna (p. 391)

Sam Houston (p. 391)

REVIEW QUESTIONS   Answer these questions to demonstrate your understanding of the chapter's main ideas.

1. Why in 1860 did white southerners remain committed to the institution of slavery and its expansion?

2. Based on what you have learned in Part 4, compare and contrast society in the American South with that in the North. Was America, in fact, two distinct societies by 1860? If not, what bonds, beliefs, and cultural practices united Americans across regional boundaries? If so, what factors contributed to the development of separate regional identities?

3. **THEMATIC UNDERSTANDING** Review the events listed under "Identity" on the thematic time-line on page 283, and then discuss how the end of the Atlantic slave trade in 1807 and the subsequent rise of the domestic slave trade affected the identity of the African American population.

MAKING CONNECTIONS   Recognize the larger developments and continuities within and across chapters by answering these questions.

1. **ACROSS TIME AND PLACE** After reviewing the relevant materials in Chapters 3, 8, and 12, explain how the plantation economy and the system of slavery changed between 1720 and 1860.

2. **VISUAL EVIDENCE** Chapter 12 contains a number of paintings or photographs of enslaved African Americans. In your judgment, do those images, either individually or as a group, capture the reality of slave life? Explain your position while evaluating the strengths and weaknesses of paintings and photographs as historical evidence.

MORE TO EXPLORE   Start here to learn more about the events discussed in this chapter.

Edward Ball, *Slaves in the Family* (1998). Recounts Ball's ancestors' ownership of slaves, their illicit sexual unions, and the family's diverse racial identity.

Ira Berlin, *Generations of Captivity* (2003). Traces the history of slavery in the United States.

Charlene M. Boyer Lewis, *Ladies and Gentlemen on Display* (2001). Explores the lives of the planter class.

Stephanie McCurry, *Masters of Small Worlds* (1995). Evokes the patriarchal lives of yeomen families.

Adam Rothman, *Slave Country: American Expansion and the Origins of the Deep South* (2005). Analyzes the changing character of slavery and African American society.

For primary documents on the black Christian church, consult **docsouth.unc.edu/church/index .html**.

TIMELINE   Ask yourself why this chapter begins and ends with these dates and then identify the links among related events.

1810s	• Africans from Congo region influence black culture for decades
	• Natural increase produces surplus of slaves in Old South
	• Domestic slave trade expands, disrupting black family life
1812	• Louisiana becomes a state, and its sugar output increases
1817	• Mississippi becomes a state; Alabama follows (1819)
1820s	• Free black population increases in North and South
	• Entrepreneurial planters in Cotton South turn to gang labor
	• Southern Methodists and Baptists become socially conservative
	• African Americans increasingly adopt Christian beliefs
1830s	• Gentry in Old South adopt paternalistic ideology and argue that slavery is a "positive good"
	• Boom in cotton production
	• Percentage of slave-owning white families falls
	• Yeomen farm families retreat to hill country
	• Lawyers become influential in southern politics
1840s	• Southern Whigs advocate economic diversification
	• Gradual emancipation completed in North
1850s	• Cotton prices and production increase
	• Slave prices rise
	• Southern states subsidize railroads, but industry remains limited

KEY TURNING POINTS: Using the five entries in the timeline for the 1830s, write an essay that describes the economy, society, and polity of the South in that decade and that analyzes the significance of the decade's developments in the evolution of the region between 1800 and 1860.

5 PART

Creating and Preserving a Continental Nation
1844–1877

Between 1844 and 1877, the United States became a continental nation by winning three wars and creating a stronger central government. This energetic process of national expansion and purposeful state building spanned three decades and three periods often treated as distinct: antebellum America, the Civil War, and Reconstruction. In fact, these decades constitute a single, distinct period of American political and constitutional development that produced a consolidated national republic.

This era of state building began in the 1840s as the United States expanded to the Pacific through a diplomatic deal with Great Britain and a war of conquest against Mexico. However, geographic expansion sharpened the conflict between free and slave states and led eventually to the secession of the South in 1861. The Union government defeated the secessionists in a bloody Civil War and reconstructed the Union under the ideals of the Republican Party. Freed from slavery, millions of African Americans fought for better pay and equal citizenship rights. Under pressure to assimilate, most Native Americans adapted selectively while maintaining tribal ties and traditional lifeways. Subsequently, the national government promoted Euro-American settlement of the West by conquering Indian peoples and confining them to reservations.

The story of these transforming events focuses on three sets of historical issues:

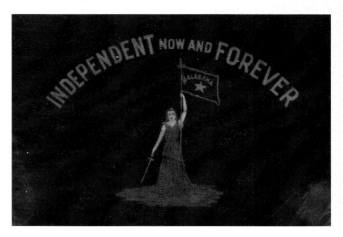

Continental Empire and Cultural Conflict

A romantic spirit of geographic expansion grew during the 1840s, prompting southerners to demand the annexation of Texas and midwesterners to favor the acquisition of Oregon. Northeastern railroad entrepreneurs championed western settlement, as did merchants eager to trade across the Pacific. The quest for western lands sparked seizure of the Mexican provinces of New Mexico and California and purchase of Russian claims to Alaska. We analyze these events in Chapter 13.

This process of expansion and state building, combined with the arrival of millions of immigrants, created new systems of racial and ethnic conflict. In the East, Irish Catholics and German-speaking migrants organized politically to protect their churches, saloons, and cultural identity, prompting a sharp reaction among native-born Protestants. In the West, the U.S. government fought wars against Cheyennes, Sioux, and Comanches on the Great Plains as it sought to integrate the region into the national economy. In the conquered Mexican territories, newly arriving whites jostled uneasily with Hispanic residents and despised Chinese immigrants. In an era of rapid economic development, western disputes often centered on access to land, jobs, and natural resources. For these conflicts, see Chapters 13 and 16.

Sectional Tensions, Political Divisions, and Civil War

The Mexican War prompted a decade-long debate over the expansion of slavery into the newly acquired lands. This bitter struggle led to the Compromise of 1850, a complex legislative agreement that won little support either in the North or in the South and divided the Whig Party. As southern Whigs became Democrats and northern Whigs turned into Republicans or Know-Nothings, the parties split along sectional lines. The Kansas-Nebraska Act of 1854 began a downward spiral of political conflict that ended in the election of Republican Abraham Lincoln in 1860 and the secession of thirteen southern states. Chapter 13 details this breakdown of the political system.

In the long Civil War that followed, the military forces of the North and South were at first evenly matched. However, the North's superior financial and industrial resources gradually gave it the advantage, as did Lincoln's proclamation of freedom for slaves in 1863. Emancipation undermined European support for the secessionists and added thousands of African Americans to the northern armies. Union forces swept across the South and ended the war, which left a legacy of half-won freedom for blacks and decades of bitter animosity between northern and southern whites. The Civil War is the focus of Chapter 14.

National Power and Consolidation

The Civil War increased national authority. Three Republican-sponsored constitutional amendments limited the powers of the states and imposed definitions of citizenship—prohibiting slavery, mandating suffrage for black men, and forbidding state action that denied people equal protection under the law. The U.S. Army remained a significant force, enforcing Reconstruction in the South as late as 1877, while suppressing Indian uprisings and extending national control in the West.

The Civil War created a powerful American state, as the Union government mobilized millions of men and billions of dollars. It created a modern fiscal system, an elaborate network of national banks, and—for the first time in American history—a significant national bureaucracy. Inspired by Whig ideology, Republican-run Congresses intervened forcefully to integrate the national economy and promote industrialization, granting subsidies to railroad companies, protecting industries and workers through protective tariffs, and distributing western lands to farmers and cattlemen. In the 1850s and 1860s, U.S. officials also intervened aggressively in Japan and then built coaling stations that enabled U.S. steamships to carry products to Asia and bring Chinese workers to the United States. The nation's dynamic postwar economy had set the nation on a course toward global power. Chapters 15 and 16 discuss all of these events.

Creating and Preserving a Continental Nation 1844–1877

Thematic Understanding

This timeline arranges some of the important events of this period into themes. Consider the events listed under each of the five themes. Which set of events seems the most important? The least important? The theme of "Politics and Power" begins with a reference to sectional conflict and concludes with the section-driven Compromise of 1877. Based on other entries in this theme and your reading in Chapters 13, 14, and 15, explain how the nature of sectionalism and the power of the various sections changed between 1844 and 1877. **>**

	POLITICS & POWER	AMERICA IN THE WORLD	IDEAS, BELIEFS, & CULTURE	WORK, EXCHANGE, & TECHNOLOGY	IDENTITY
1840	• Mexican War and Wilmot Proviso (1846) increase sectional conflict • Gold rush makes California eligible for statehood—free or slave?	• U.S. confronts Mexico and Britain: annexes Texas (1845), acquires Oregon (1846), fights Mexican War (1846–1848) extending U.S. borders to Pacific	• Ideology of Manifest Destiny prompts U.S. expansionism • Free-Soil Party (1848) advocates white smallholder farm society • Women seek legal rights at Seneca Falls (1848)	• Irish immigrants build northern canal system • Some states default on canal bonds • Walker Tariff (1846) lowers rates, increases foreign imports	• Whites migrate to Oregon and California • Arrival of millions of Germans and Irish causes social conflicts • Wars against Seminole peoples in Florida (1835–1842, 1855–1858)
1850	• Compromise of 1850 • Whig Party disintegrates; Know-Nothing Party attacks immigrants • Kansas-Nebraska Act (1854) sparks creation of Republican Party	• President Pierce opens Japan to trade; seeks to expand American territory and slavery into Caribbean by diplomacy and filibustering actions	• Harriet Beecher Stowe's *Uncle Tom's Cabin* (1852) attacks slavery • *Dred Scott* decision (1857) opens way to legalize slavery nationwide • Southern secessionists agitate for independence	• Enslaved blacks expand cotton output in South • White settlers expand farm society to trans-Mississippi west • Entrepreneurs promote railroad building and manufacturing in North and Midwest	• Conflict of Hispanics and Anglos in the Southwest • White diseases and brutality kill most California Indians • Comanches and Sioux dominate Great Plains peoples and control trade in horses and buffalo hides
1860	• Eleven southern states secede from Union, sparking Civil War (1861–1865); the Union's triumph preserves a continental nation • Fourteenth Amendment (1868) extends legal and political rights	• U.S. diplomacy and Union army victories in 1863 cause British government to stop sale of ironclad ships to the Confederacy • Secretary of State Seward buys Alaska from Russia (1867) • Burlingame Treaty (1868) protects missionaries in China and limits Chinese immigration	• Confederate States of America (1861–1865) vow to continue slavery • Republicans seek to impose equal rights ideology on South • Black families accept ideal of domesticity	• Republicans enact Whigs' economic policies: Homestead Act (1862), railroad aid, high tariffs, and national banking • Women assume new tasks in war economies	• Emancipation Proclamation (1863) and Thirteenth Amendment (1865) free blacks from slavery • Aided by Freedmen's Bureau, African Americans struggle for freedom, land, and education
1870	• Fifteenth Amendment (1870) extends vote to black men • Compromise of 1877 ends Reconstruction	• Britain pays the U.S. $15.5 million for the depredations of the *Alabama* during the war • Anti-Chinese riots in San Francisco in late 1870s prompt Chinese Exclusion Act (1882)	• Ku Klux Klan attacks Reconstruction governments • Republicans embrace classical liberalism • White elites challenge ideal of universal suffrage and deny women's suffrage	• Sharecropping spreads in South • Ranchers create cattle empire on Great Plains • Depression of 1873 halts railway expansion	• U.S. wars against Plains Indians (Cheyennes, Sioux, Apaches, and Nez Perce) open their lands to white miners, ranchers, and farmers • Dawes Act (1887) seeks Indian assimilation

13

CHAPTER

Expansion, War, and Sectional Crisis
1844–1860

The expansionist surge of the 1840s had deep roots. Since the nation's founding in 1776, visionaries conceived its future both as a republic and as an empire, and they predicted a glorious expansion across the continent. "It belongs of right to the United States to regulate the future destiny of North America," declared the *New-York Evening Post* in 1803. Politicians soon took up the refrain. "Our natural boundary is the Pacific Ocean," asserted Massachusetts congressman Francis Baylies in 1823. "The swelling tide of our population must and will roll on until that mighty ocean interposes its waters." However, the creation of a continental republic was far from inevitable. It would require a revolution in transportation—canals and railways—to access the nation's fertile core in the vast Mississippi River basin and a growing population and dynamic economy to exploit its riches. By the 1840s, all those prerequisites were in place.

Other obstacles remained. Well-armed Indian peoples controlled the Great Plains, Mexico held sovereignty over Texas and the lands west of the Rocky Mountains, and Great Britain laid claim to the Oregon Country. To extend the American republic would involve new Indian wars and possibly armed conflict with Great Britain and with Mexico (and perhaps France, its main creditor). An ardent imperialist, President James Polk willingly assumed those risks. "I would meet the war which either England or France . . . might wage and fight until the last man," he told Secretary of State James Buchanan in 1846.

Polk's aggressive expansionism sparked fighting abroad and conflict at home. A war with Mexico intended to be "brief, cheap, and bloodless" became "long, costly, and sanguinary," complained Senator Thomas Hart Benton of Missouri. Even Polk's great territorial acquisitions—New Mexico, California, the Oregon Country—proved double-edged by reigniting a bitter debate over slavery. Northerners vowed to prevent the expansion of bound labor into the newly acquired territories, prompting southerners to threaten secession from the Union. Rhetoric spiraled downward into violence, as white and black abolitionists attacked slave catchers in the North and secessionists harassed Union supporters in the South. When Massachusetts senator Charles Sumner accused his South Carolina colleague Andrew P. Butler of taking "the harlot slavery" as his mistress, a southern congressman beat Sumner unconscious with a walking cane. As this violence shook Washington in 1856, proslavery migrants fought armed New England abolitionists in the Kansas Territory. Passion had replaced compromise as the hallmark of American political life.

IDENTIFY THE BIG IDEA

What were the causes of the Mexican War, and in what ways did it bring about a growing sectional crisis during the 1850s?

John Gast, *American Progress* In 1845, journalist John O'Sullivan coined the term *Manifest Destiny* to describe Americans' suddenly urgent longing to extend the boundaries of the republic to the Pacific Ocean. More than a quarter century later, John Gast's *American Progress* (1872) gave visual form to that aspiration in an allegorical painting that was widely distributed through color lithographs. The goddess Liberty floats westward, holding a "School Book" in one hand and telegraph lines trailing from the other as symbols of the advance of Anglo-American civilization across the continent. Library of Congress

Manifest Destiny: South and North

The upsurge in violence reflected a generational shift in culture and politics. The Missouri crisis of 1819–1822 (Chapter 8) had frightened the nation's leaders. For the next two decades, the professional politicians who ran the Second Party System avoided policies, such as the annexation of the slaveholding Republic of Texas, that would prompt regional strife. Then, during the 1840s, many citizens embraced an ideology of expansion and proclaimed a God-given duty to extend American republicanism to the Pacific Ocean. But whose republican institutions: the hierarchical slave system of the South, or the more egalitarian, reform-minded, capitalist-managed society of the North and Midwest? Or both? Ultimately, the failure to find a political solution to this question would rip the nation apart.

The Push to the Pacific

As expansionists developed continental ambitions, the term **Manifest Destiny** captured those dreams. John L. O'Sullivan, editor of the *Democratic Review*, coined the phrase in 1845: "Our manifest destiny is to overspread the continent allotted by Providence for the free development of our yearly multiplying millions." Underlying the rhetoric of Manifest Destiny was a

sense of Anglo-American cultural and racial superiority: the "inferior" peoples who lived in the Far West — Native Americans and Mexicans — would be subjected to American dominion, taught republicanism, and converted to Protestantism.

Oregon Land-hungry farmers of the Ohio River Valley had already cast their eyes toward the fertile lands of the Oregon Country, a region that stretched along the Pacific coast between the Mexican province of California and Russian settlements in Alaska. Since 1818, a British-American agreement had allowed settlement by people from both nations. The British-run Hudson's Bay Company developed a lucrative fur business north of the Columbia River, while Methodist missionaries and a few hundred American farmers settled to the south, in the Willamette Valley (Map 13.1).

In 1842, American interest in Oregon increased dramatically. The U.S. Navy published a glowing report of fine harbors in the Puget Sound, which New England merchants trading with China were already using. Simultaneously, a party of one hundred farmers journeyed along the Oregon Trail, which fur traders and explorers had blazed from Independence, Missouri, across the Great Plains and the Rocky Mountains (Map 13.2). Their letters from Oregon told of a mild climate and rich soil.

"Oregon fever" suddenly raged. A thousand men, women, and children — with a hundred wagons and

MAP 13.1

Territorial Conflict in Oregon, 1819–1846

As thousands of American settlers poured into the Oregon Country in the early 1840s, British authorities tried to keep them south of the Columbia River. However, the migrants—and fervent expansionists—asserted that Americans could settle anywhere in the territory, raising the prospect of armed conflict. In 1846, British and American diplomats resolved the dispute by dividing most of the region at the forty-ninth parallel while giving both nations access to fine harbors (Vancouver and Seattle) through the Strait of Juan de Fuca.

Settling Oregon
Americans quickly populated the Far West and re-created there the small-town life of the eastern states. As early as 1845, as this drawing by a British military officer shows, Oregon City boasted a steepled church, several large merchandise warehouses, and several dozen houses. On the riverbank opposite the town stand several Native Americans, who had a very different way of life and would be steadily pushed off the lands of their ancestors. Library of Congress.

five thousand oxen and cattle — gathered in Independence in April 1843. As the spring mud dried, they began their six-month trek, hoping to miss the winter snows. Another 5,000 settlers, mostly yeomen farm families from the southern border states (Missouri, Kentucky, and Tennessee), set out over the next two years. These pioneers overcame floods, dust storms, livestock deaths, and a few armed encounters with native peoples before reaching Oregon, a journey of 2,000 miles.

By 1860, about 250,000 Americans had braved the Oregon Trail, with 65,000 heading for Oregon, 185,000 to California, and others staying in Wyoming, Idaho, and Montana. More than 34,000 migrants died, mostly from disease and exposure; fewer than 500 deaths resulted from Indian attacks. The walking migrants wore paths 3 feet deep, and their wagons carved 5-foot ruts across sandstone formations in southern Wyoming — tracks that are visible today. Women found the trail especially difficult; in addition to their usual chores and the new work of driving wagons and animals, they lacked the support of female kin and the

security of their domestic space. About 2,500 women endured pregnancy or gave birth during the long journey, and some did not survive. "There was a woman died in this train yesterday," Jane Gould Tortillott noted in her diary. "She left six children, one of them only two days old."

The 10,000 migrants who made it to Oregon in the 1840s mostly settled in the Willamette Valley. Many families squatted on 640 acres and hoped Congress would legalize their claims so that they could sell surplus acreage to new migrants. The settlers quickly created a race- and gender-defined polity by restricting voting to a "free male descendant of a white man."

California   About 3,000 other early pioneers ended up in the Mexican province of California. They left the Oregon Trail along the Snake River, trudged down the California Trail, and mostly settled in the interior along the Sacramento River, where there were few Mexicans.

IDENTIFY CAUSES
Did the idea of Manifest Destiny actually cause events, such as the political support for territorial expansion, or simply justify actions taken for other reasons?

MAP 13.2

The Great Plains: Settler Trails, Indian Raiders, and Traders

By the 1850s, the Mormon, Oregon, and Santa Fe trails ran across "Indian Country," the semiarid, buffalo-filled Great Plains west of the 95th meridian, and then through the Rocky Mountains. Tens of thousands of Americans set out on these trails to found new communities in Utah, Oregon, New Mexico, and California. This mass migration exposed sedentary Indian peoples to American diseases, guns, and manufactures. However, raids by Comanches and Sioux affected their lives even more significantly, as did the Euro-American traders who provided a ready market for Indian horses and mules, dried meat, and buffalo skins.

A remote outpost of Spain's American empire, California had few nonnative residents until the 1770s, when Spanish authorities built a chain of forts and religious missions along the Pacific coast. When Mexico achieved independence in 1821, its government took over the Franciscan-run missions and freed the 20,000 Indians whom the monks had persuaded or coerced into working on them. Some mission Indians rejoined their tribes, but many intermarried with mestizos (Mexicans of mixed Spanish and Indian ancestry).

William Henry Jackson, *California Crossing, South Platte River*, detail, 1867

The South Platte River was wide (stretching from the foreground to the low bluff in the middle of the picture) but shallow, allowing relatively easy passage for the migrants' cattle and covered wagons. Wagon trains followed the course of the various branches of the Platte River for more than 300 miles across the Great Plains. During the late spring and early summer, wagons often stretched as far as the eye could see. National Park Service/Picture Research Consultants & Archives.

They worked on huge ranches — the 450 estates created by Mexican officials and bestowed primarily on their families and political allies. The owners of these vast properties (averaging 19,000 acres) mostly raised Spanish cattle, prized for their hides and tallow.

The ranches soon linked California to the American economy. New England merchants dispatched dozens of agents to buy leather for the booming Massachusetts boot and shoe industry and tallow to make soap and candles. Many agents married the daughters of the elite Mexican ranchers — the **Californios** — and adopted their manners, attitudes, and Catholic religion. A crucial exception was Thomas Oliver Larkin, a successful merchant in the coastal town of Monterey. Although Larkin worked closely with Mexican politicians and landowners, he remained strongly American in outlook.

Like Larkin, the American migrants in the Sacramento River Valley did not assimilate into Mexican society. Some hoped to emulate the Americans in Texas by colonizing the country and then seeking annexation. However, in the early 1840s, these settlers numbered only about 1,000, far outnumbered by the 7,000 Mexicans who lived along the coast.

The Plains Indians

As the Pacific-bound wagon trains rumbled across Nebraska along the broad Platte River, the migrants encountered the unique ecology of the Great Plains. A vast sea of wild grasses stretched from Texas to Saskatchewan in Canada, and west from the Missouri River to the Rocky Mountains. Tall grasses flourished in the eastern regions of the future states of Kansas, Nebraska, and the Dakotas, where there was ample rainfall. To the west, in the semiarid region beyond the 100th meridian, the migrants found short grasses that sustained a rich wildlife dominated by buffalo and grazing antelopes. Nomadic buffalo-hunting Indian peoples roamed the western plains, while the eastern river valleys were home to semisedentary tribes and, since the 1830s, the Indian peoples whom Andrew Jackson had "removed" to the west. A line of military forts — stretching from Fort Jesup in Louisiana to Fort Snelling, then in the Wisconsin Territory — policed the boundary between white settlements and what Congress in 1834 designated as Permanent Indian Territory.

For centuries, the Indians who lived on the eastern edge of the plains, such as the Pawnees and the Mandans on the Upper Missouri River, subsisted primarily on corn and beans, supplemented by buffalo meat. They hunted buffalo on foot, driving them over cliffs or into canyons for the kill. To the south, the nomadic Apaches acquired horses from Spanish settlers in New Mexico and ranged widely across the plains. The Comanches, who migrated down the Arkansas River from the Rocky Mountains around 1750, developed both a horse-based culture and imperial ambitions. Skilled buffalo hunters and fierce warriors, the Comanches slowly pushed the Apaches to the southern edge of the plains. They also raided Spanish settlements in New Mexico, incorporating captured women and children into their society.

After 1800, the Comanches gradually built up a pastoral economy, raising horses and mules and selling them to northern Indian peoples and to Euro-American farmers in Missouri and Arkansas. Many Comanche families owned thirty to thirty-five horses or mules, far more than the five or six required for hunting buffalo and fighting neighboring peoples. The Comanches also exchanged goods with merchants and travelers along the Santa Fe Trail, which cut through their territory as it connected Missouri and New Mexico. By the early 1840s, goods worth nearly $1 million moved along the trail each year.

By the 1830s, the Kiowas, Cheyennes, and Arapahos had also adopted this horse culture and, allied with the Comanches, dominated the plains between the Arkansas and Red rivers. The new culture brought sharper social divisions. Some Kiowa men owned hundreds of horses and had several "chore wives" and captive children who worked for them. Poor men, who owned only a few horses, had difficulty finding marriage partners and often had to work for their wealthy kinsmen.

While European horses made Plains Indians wealthier and more mobile, European diseases and

Comanches Meeting the Dragoons, 1830s

In the 1830s, when artist George Catlin accompanied the dragoons of the U.S. Army into Indian Territory, the Comanches were masters of the southern plains. They hunted buffalo, raised horses and mules for sale, and used their skills as horsemen to dominate other Indian peoples and control the passage of Americans along the Santa Fe Trail. Smithsonian American Art Museum, Washington, DC/Art Resource, NY.

guns thinned their ranks. A devastating smallpox epidemic spread northward from New Spain in 1779–1781 and killed half of the Plains peoples. Twenty years later, another smallpox outbreak left dozens of deserted villages along the Missouri River. Smallpox struck the northern plains again from 1837 to 1840, killing half of the Assiniboines and Blackfeet and nearly a third of the Crows, Pawnees, and Cheyennes. "If I could see this thing, if I knew where it came from, I would go there and fight it," exclaimed a distressed Cheyenne warrior.

European weapons also altered the geography of native peoples. Around 1750, the Crees and Assiniboines, who lived on the far northern plains, acquired guns by trading wolf pelts and beaver skins to the British-run Hudson's Bay Company. Once armed, they drove the Blackfoot peoples westward into the Rocky Mountains and took control of the Saskatchewan and Upper Missouri River basins. When the Blackfeet obtained guns and horses around 1800, they emerged from the mountains and pushed the Shoshones and Crows to the south. Because horses could not easily find winter forage in the snow-filled plains north of the Platte River, Blackfoot families kept only five to ten horses and remained hunters rather than pastoralists.

The powerful Lakota Sioux, who acquired guns and ammunition from French, Spanish, and American traders along the Missouri River, also remained buffalo hunters. A nomadic war-prone people who lived in small groups, the Lakotas largely avoided major epidemics. They kept some sedentary peoples, such as the Arikaras, in subjection and raided others for their crops and horses. By the 1830s, the Lakotas were the dominant tribe on the central as well as the northern plains. "Those lands once belonged to the Kiowas and the Crows," boasted the Oglala Sioux chief Black Hawk, "but we whipped those nations out of them, and in this we did what the white men do when they want the lands of the Indians."

The Sioux's prosperity also came at the expense of the buffalo, which provided them with a diet rich in protein and with hides and robes to sell. The number of hides and robes shipped down the Missouri River each year by the American Fur Company and the Missouri Fur Company increased from 3,000 in the 1820s, to 45,000 in the 1830s, and to 90,000 annually after 1840. North of the Missouri, the story was much the same. The 24,000 Indians of that region — Blackfeet, Crees, and Assiniboines — annually killed about 160,000 buffalo. The women dried the meat to feed their people and to sell to white traders and soldiers. The women also undertook the arduous work of skinning and tanning the hides, which they fashioned into tepees,

buffalo robes, and sleeping covers. Over time, Indian hunters increased the kill and traded surplus hides and robes — about 40,000 annually by the 1840s — for pots, knives, guns, and other Euro-American manufactures. As among the Kiowas, trade increased social divisions. "It is a fine sight," a traveler noted around 1850, "to see one of those big men among the Blackfeet, who has two or three lodges, five or six wives, twenty or thirty children, fifty to a hundred head of horses; for his trade amounts to upward of $2,000 per year."

Although the Blackfeet, Kiowas, and Lakotas contributed buffalo hides to the national economy, they did not fully grasp their market value as winter clothes, leather accessories, and industrial drive belts. Consequently, they could not demand the best price. Moreover, the increasing size of the kill diminished the buffalo herds. Between 1820 and 1870, the northern herd shrank from 5 million to less than 2 million. When the Assiniboines' cultural hero Inkton'mi had taught his people how to kill the buffalo, he told them, "The buffalo will live as long as your people. There will be no end of them until the end of time." Meant as a perpetual guarantee, by the 1860s Inkton'mi's words prefigured the end of time — the demise of traditional buffalo hunting and, perhaps, of the Assiniboines as well.

> **TRACE CHANGE OVER TIME**
>
> Why did some Great Plains peoples flourish between 1750 and 1860 while others did not?

The Fateful Election of 1844

The election of 1844 changed the American government's policy toward the Great Plains, the Far West, and Texas. Since 1836, southern leaders had supported the annexation of Texas, but cautious party politicians, pressured by northerners who opposed the expansion of slavery, had rebuffed them (Chapter 12). Now rumors swirled that Great Britain was encouraging Texas to remain independent; wanted California as payment for the Mexican debts owed to British investors; and had designs on Spanish Cuba, which some slave owners wanted to add to the United States. To thwart such imagined schemes, southern expansionists demanded the immediate annexation of Texas.

At this crucial juncture, Oregon fever altered the political landscape in the North. In 1843, Americans in the Ohio River Valley and the Great Lakes states organized "Oregon conventions," and Democratic and Whig politicians alike called for American sovereignty over the entire Oregon Country, from Spanish California to Russian Alaska (which began at 54°40' north latitude). With northerners demanding Oregon,

President John Tyler, a proslavery zealot, called for the annexation of Texas. Disowned by the Whigs because he thwarted Henry Clay's nationalist economic program, Tyler hoped to win reelection in 1844 as a Democrat. To curry favor among northern expansionists, Tyler supported claims to all of Oregon.

In April 1844, Tyler and John C. Calhoun, his proslavery, expansionist-minded secretary of state, sent the Senate a treaty to bring Texas into the Union. However, the two major presidential hopefuls, Democrat Martin Van Buren and Whig Henry Clay, opposed Tyler's initiative. Fearful of raising the issue of slavery, they persuaded the Senate to reject the treaty.

UNDERSTAND POINTS OF VIEW
Why did party politicians initially oppose the annexation of Texas, and how did this view change during the election of 1844?

Nonetheless, expansion into Texas and Oregon became the central issue in the election of 1844. Most southern Democrats favored Texas annexation and refused to support Van Buren's candidacy. The party also passed over Tyler, whom they did not trust. Instead, the Democrats selected Governor James K. Polk of Tennessee, a slave owner and an avowed expansionist. Known as "Young Hickory" because he was a protégé of Andrew Jackson, Polk shared his mentor's iron will, boundless ambition, and determination to open up lands for American settlement. Accepting the false claim in the Democratic Party platform that both areas already belonged to the United States, Polk campaigned for the "Re-occupation of Oregon and the Re-annexation of Texas." He insisted that the United States defy British claims and occupy "the whole of the territory of Oregon" to the Alaskan border. **"Fifty-four forty or fight!"** became his jingoistic cry.

The Whigs nominated Henry Clay, who again advocated his American System of high tariffs, internal improvements, and national banking. Clay initially dodged the issue of Texas but, seeking southern votes, ultimately supported annexation. Northern Whigs who opposed the admission of a new slave state refused to vote for Clay and cast their ballots for James G. Birney of the Liberty Party (Chapter 11). Birney garnered less than 3 percent of the national vote but took enough Whig votes in New York to cost Clay that state — and the presidency.

Following Polk's narrow victory, congressional Democrats called for immediate Texas statehood. However, they lacked the two-thirds majority in the Senate needed to ratify a treaty of annexation. So the Democrats admitted Texas using a joint resolution of Congress, which required just a majority vote in each

house, and Texas became the twenty-eighth state in December 1845. Polk's strategy of linking Texas and Oregon had put him in the White House and Texas in the Union. Shortly, it would make the expansion of the South — and its system of slavery — the central topic of American politics.

War, Expansion, and Slavery, 1846–1850

The acquisition of Texas whetted Polk's appetite for the Mexican lands between Texas and the Pacific Ocean. If necessary, he was ready to go to war for them. What he and many Democrats consciously ignored was the domestic crisis that a war of conquest to expand slavery would unleash.

The War with Mexico, 1846–1848

Since gaining independence in 1821, Mexico had not prospered. Its civil wars and political instability produced a stagnant economy, a weak government, and modest tax revenues, which a bloated bureaucracy and debt payments to European bankers quickly devoured. Although the distant northern provinces of California and New Mexico remained undeveloped and sparsely settled, with a Spanish-speaking population of only 75,000 in 1840, Mexican officials vowed to preserve their nation's historic boundaries. When its breakaway province of Texas prepared to join the American Union, Mexico suspended diplomatic relations with the United States.

Polk's Expansionist Program   President Polk now moved quickly to acquire Mexico's other northern provinces. He hoped to foment a revolution in California that, like the 1836 rebellion in Texas, would lead to annexation. In October 1845, Secretary of State James Buchanan told merchant Thomas Oliver Larkin, now the U.S. consul for the Mexican province, to encourage influential Californios to seek independence and union with the United States. To add military muscle to this scheme, Polk ordered American naval commanders to seize San Francisco Bay and California's coastal towns in case of war with Mexico. The president also instructed the War Department to dispatch Captain John C. Frémont and an "exploring" party of soldiers into Mexican territory. By December 1845, Frémont's force had reached California's Sacramento River Valley.

With these preparations in place, Polk launched a secret diplomatic initiative: he sent Louisiana congressman John Slidell to Mexico, telling him to secure the Rio Grande boundary for Texas and to buy the provinces of California and New Mexico for $30 million. However, Mexican officials refused to meet with Slidell.

Events now moved quickly toward war. Polk ordered General Zachary Taylor and an American army of 2,000 soldiers to occupy disputed lands between the Nueces River (the historic southern boundary of Spanish Texas) and the Rio Grande, which the Republic of Texas had claimed as its border with Mexico. "We were sent to provoke a fight," recalled Ulysses S. Grant, then a young officer serving with Taylor, "but it was essential that Mexico should commence it." When the armies clashed near the Rio Grande in May 1846, Polk delivered the war message he had drafted long before. Taking liberties with the truth, the president declared that Mexico "has passed the boundary of the United States, has invaded our territory, and shed American blood upon the American soil." Ignoring pleas by some Whigs for a negotiated settlement, an overwhelming majority in Congress voted for war—a decision greeted with great popular acclaim. To avoid a simultaneous war with Britain, Polk retreated from his demand for "fifty-four forty or fight" and in June 1846 accepted British terms that divided the Oregon Country at the forty-ninth parallel.

American Military Successes American forces in Texas quickly established their military superiority. Zachary Taylor's army crossed the Rio Grande; occupied the Mexican city of Matamoros; and, after a fierce six-day battle in September 1846, took the interior Mexican town of Monterrey. Two months later, a U.S. naval squadron in the Gulf of Mexico seized Tampico, Mexico's second most important port. By the end of 1846, the United States controlled much of northeastern Mexico (Map 13.3).

Fighting also broke out in California. In June 1846, naval commander John Sloat landed 250 marines in Monterey and declared that California "henceforward will be a portion of the United States." Simultaneously,

MAP 13.3

The Mexican War, 1846–1848

After moving west from Fort Leavenworth in present-day Kansas, American forces commanded by Captain John C. Frémont and General Stephen Kearny defeated Mexican armies in California in 1846 and early 1847. Simultaneously, U.S. troops under General Zachary Taylor and Colonel Alfred A. Doniphan won victories over General Santa Anna's forces south of the Rio Grande. In mid-1847, General Winfield Scott mounted a successful seaborne attack on Veracruz and Mexico City, ending the war.

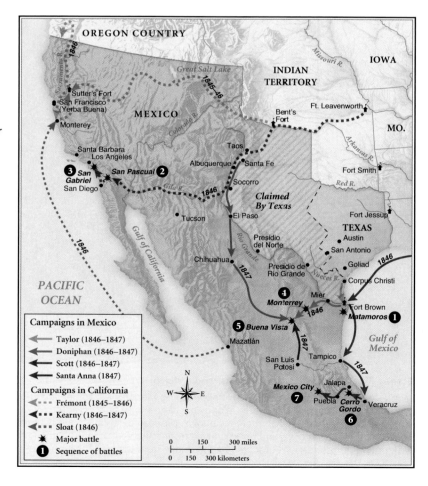

COMPARE AND CONTRAST

How was the American acquisition of California similar to, and different from, the American-led creation of the Texas Republic (discussed in Chapter 12)?

American settlers in the Sacramento River Valley staged a revolt and, supported by Frémont's force, captured the town of Sonoma, where they proclaimed the independence of the "Bear Flag Republic." To cement these victories, Polk ordered army units to capture Santa Fe in New Mexico and then march to southern California. Despite stiff Mexican resistance, American forces secured control of California early in 1847.

Polk expected these victories to end the war, but he underestimated the Mexicans' national pride and the determination of President Santa Anna. In February 1847 in the Battle of Buena Vista, Santa Anna nearly defeated Taylor's army in northeastern Mexico. With most Mexican troops deployed in the north, Polk approved General Winfield Scott's plan to capture the port of Veracruz and march 260 miles to Mexico City. An American army of 14,000 seized the Mexican capital in September 1847. That American victory cost Santa Anna his presidency, and a new Mexican government made a forced peace with the United States.

Street Fighting in the Calle de Iturbide, 1846

Monterrey, which had resisted Spanish troops during Mexico's war for independence (1820–1821), was captured by the Americans only after bloody house-to-house fighting in the Mexican War (1846–1848). Protected by thick walls and shuttered windows, Mexican defenders pour a withering fire on the dark-uniformed American troops and buckskin-clad frontier fighters. A large Catholic cathedral looms in the background, its foundations obscured by the smoke from the Mexicans' cannons. West Point Museum, United States Military Academy, West Point, NY.

A Divisive Victory

Initially, the war with Mexico sparked an explosion of patriotic expansionism. The *Nashville Union* hailed it as a noble struggle to extend "the principles of free government." However, the war soon divided the nation (American Voices, p. 422). Some northern Whigs — among them Charles Francis Adams of Massachusetts (the son of John Quincy Adams) and Chancellor James Kent of New York — opposed the war on moral grounds, calling it "causeless & wicked & unjust." Adams, Kent, and other **conscience Whigs** accused Polk of waging a war of conquest to add new slave states and give slave-owning Democrats permanent control of the federal government. Swayed by such arguments, troops deserted in droves (creating the highest desertion rate of any American war), and antiwar activists denounced enlistees as "murderers and robbers." "The United States will conquer Mexico," Ralph Waldo Emerson had predicted as the war began, but "Mexico will poison us."

When voters repudiated Polk's war policy in the elections of 1846, the Whig Party took control of Congress. Whig leaders called for "No Territory" — a congressional pledge that the United States would not seek any land from the Mexican republic. "Away with this wretched cant about a 'manifest destiny,' a 'divine mission' . . . to civilize, and Christianize, and democratize our sister republics at the mouth of a cannon," declared New York senator William Duer.

The Wilmot Proviso

Polk's expansionist policies also split the Democrats. As early as 1839, Ohio Democrat Thomas Morris had warned that "the power of slavery is aiming to govern the country, its Constitutions and laws." In 1846, David Wilmot, an antislavery Democratic congressman from Pennsylvania, took up that refrain and proposed the so-called **Wilmot Proviso**, a ban on slavery in any territories gained from the war. Whigs and antislavery Democrats in the House of Representatives quickly passed the bill, dividing Congress along sectional lines. "The madmen of the North . . . ," grumbled the *Richmond Enquirer*, "have, we fear, cast the die and numbered the days of this glorious Union." Fearing that outcome, a few proslavery northern senators joined their southern colleagues to kill the proviso.

Fervent Democratic expansionists now became even more aggressive. President Polk, Secretary of State Buchanan, and Senators Stephen A. Douglas of Illinois and Jefferson Davis of Mississippi called for the annexation of a huge swath of Mexican territory south of the Rio Grande. However, John C. Calhoun and other southern whites feared this demand would extend the costly war and require the assimilation of many dark-skinned mestizos. They favored only the annexation of sparsely settled New Mexico and California. "Ours is a government of the white man," proclaimed Calhoun, which should never welcome "into the Union any but the Caucasian race." To unify the Democratic Party, Polk and Buchanan accepted Calhoun's policy. In 1848, Polk signed, and the Senate ratified, the Treaty of Guadalupe Hidalgo, in which the United States agreed to pay Mexico $15 million in return for more than one-third of its territory (Map 13.4).

Congress also created the Oregon Territory in 1848 and, two years later, passed the Oregon Donation Land Claim Act, which granted farm-sized plots of "free land" to settlers who took up residence before 1854. Soon, treaties with native peoples extinguished Indian titles to much of the new territory. With the settlement of Oregon and the acquisition of New Mexico and California, the American conquest of the Far West was far advanced.

Free Soil

However, the political debate over expansion was far from over and dominated the election of 1848. The Senate's rejection of the Wilmot Proviso revived Thomas Morris's charge that leading southerners were part of a "Slave Power" conspiracy to dominate national life. To thwart any such plan, thousands of ordinary northerners, including farmer Abijah Beckwith of Herkimer County, New York, joined the **free-soil movement**. Slavery, Beckwith wrote in his diary, was an institution of "aristocratic men" and a danger to "the great mass of the people [because it] . . . threatens the general and equal distribution of our lands into convenient family farms."

The free-soilers quickly organized the Free-Soil Party in 1848. The new party abandoned the Garrisonians' and Liberty Party's emphasis on the sinfulness of slavery and the natural rights of African Americans. Instead, like Beckwith, it depicted slavery as a threat to republicanism and to the Jeffersonian ideal of a freeholder society, arguments that won broad support among aspiring white farmers. Hundreds of men and women in the Great Lakes states joined the free-soil organizations formed by the American and Foreign Anti-Slavery Society. So, too, did Frederick Douglass, the foremost black abolitionist, who attended the first Free-Soil Party convention in the summer of 1848 and endorsed its strategy. However, William Lloyd Garrison and other radical abolitionists condemned the Free-Soilers' stress on white freehold farming as racist "whitemanism."

The Mexican War: Expansion and Slavery

Conflict with Mexico prompted debates over the Polk administration's aggressive efforts to acquire territory and spread slavery. Here, Polk's critics face off against the expansionists.

John L. O'Sullivan, Editor
"Manifest Destiny," from *United States Magazine and Democratic Review*, July 1845

Texas is now ours . . . [Britain and France tried] to intrude themselves [into Texas affairs] . . . for the avowed object of thwarting our policy and hampering our power, limiting our greatness and checking the fulfillment of our manifest destiny to overspread the continent allotted by Providence for the free development of our yearly multiplying millions. . . .

The independence of Texas was complete and absolute. It was an independence, not only in fact, but of right. . . . What then can be more preposterous than all this clamor by Mexico and the Mexican interest, against Annexation, as a violation of any rights of hers . . . ?

Nor is there any just foundation for the charge that Annexation is a great pro-slavery measure — calculated to increase and perpetuate that institution. Slavery had nothing to do with it. . . . That it will tend to facilitate and hasten the disappearance of Slavery from all the northern tier of the present Slave States, cannot surely admit of serious question. The greater value in Texas of the slave labor now employed in those States, must soon produce the effect of draining off that labor southwardly. . . .

California will, probably, next fall away. . . . Already the advance guard of the irresistible army of Anglo-Saxon emigration has begun to pour down upon it, armed with the plough and the rifle, and marking its trail with schools and colleges, courts and representative halls, mills and meeting-houses. A population will soon be in actual occupation of California. . . . And they will have a right to independence — to self-government . . . a better and a truer right than the artificial title of sovereignty in Mexico, a thousand miles distant, inheriting from Spain a title good only against those who have none better.

Source: Sean Wilentz, ed., *Major Problems in the Early Republic, 1787–1848* (Lexington, MA: D. C. Heath, 1991), 525–528.

James Buchanan, U.S. Secretary of State
Letter to John Slidell, Minister Plenipotentiary to Mexico, November 1845

In your negotiations with Mexico, the independence of Texas must be considered a settled fact, and is not to be called in question. . . .

It may, however, be contended on the part of Mexico, that the Nueces and not the Rio del Norte [Rio Grande], is the true western boundary of Texas. I need not furnish you arguments to controvert this position. . . . The jurisdiction of Texas has been extended beyond that river [the Nueces] and . . . representatives from the country between it and the Del Norte have participated in the deliberations both of her Congress and her Convention. . . .

The case is different in regard to New Mexico. Santa Fe, its capital, was settled by the Spaniards more than two centuries ago; and that province has been ever since in their possession and that of the Republic of Mexico. The Texans never have conquered or taken possession of it. . . . [However,] a great portion of New Mexico being on this side of the Rio Grande and included within the limits already claimed by Texas, it may hereafter, should it remain a Mexican province, become a subject of dispute. . . . It would seem to be equally the interest of both Powers, that New Mexico should belong to the United States. . . .

It is to be seriously apprehended that both Great Britain and France have designs upon California. . . . This Government . . . would vigorously interpose to prevent the latter from becoming either a British or a French Colony. . . . The possession of the Bay and harbor of San Francisco, is all important to the United States. . . . Money would be no object.

Source: Victoria Bissell Brown and Timothy J. Shannon, eds., *Going to the Source: The Bedford Reader in American History* (Boston: Bedford/St. Martin's, 2004), 1: 260–262.

Charles Sumner, Conscience Whig and Future Republican Senator from Massachusetts

Letter to Robert Winthrop, Whig Congressman from Massachusetts, October 25, 1846

If we regard Texas as a province of Mexico, its boundaries must be sought in the geography of that republic. If we regard it as an independent State, they must be determined by the extent of jurisdiction which the State was able to maintain. Now it seems clear that the river Nueces was always recognized by Mexico as the western boundary; and it is undisputed that the State of Texas, since its Declaration of Independence, never exercised any jurisdiction beyond the Nueces. . . .

In the month of January, 1846, the President of the United States directed the troops under General Taylor, called the Army of Occupation, to take possession of this region [west of the Nueces River]. Here was an act of aggression. As might have been expected, it produced collision. The Mexicans, aroused in self-defence, sought to repel the invaders. . . .

Here the question occurs, What was the duty of Congress in this emergency? Clearly to withhold all sanction to unjust war, — to aggression upon a neighboring Republic. . . . The American forces should have been directed to retreat, not from any human force, but from wrongdoing; and this would have been a true victory.

Alas! This was not the mood of Congress. With wicked speed a bill was introduced, furnishing large and unusual supplies of men and money. . . . This was adopted by a vote of 123 to 67; and the bill then leaped forth, fully armed, as a measure of open and active hostility against Mexico.

Source: Sean Wilentz, ed., *Major Problems in the Early Republic, 1787–1848* (Lexington, MA: D. C. Heath, 1991), 541.

Walt Whitman, Poet and Editor of the *Brooklyn Eagle*

Editorial, September 1, 1847

The question whether or no there shall be slavery in the new territories . . . is a question between the grand body of white workingmen, the millions of mechanics, farmers, and operatives of our country, with their interests on the one side — and the interests of the few thousand rich, "polished," and aristocratic owners of slaves at the South, on the other side.

Experience has proved . . . that a stalwart mass of respectable workingmen, cannot exist, much less flourish, in a thorough slave State. Let any one think for a moment what a different appearance New York, Pennsylvania, or Ohio, would present — how much less sturdy independence and family happiness there would be — were slaves the workmen there, instead of each man as a general thing being his own workman. . . .

Slavery is a good thing enough . . . to the rich — the one out of thousands; but it is destructive to the dignity and independence of all who work, and to labor itself. . . . All practice and theory . . . are strongly arrayed in favor of limiting slavery to where it already exists.

Source: Sean Wilentz, ed., *Major Problems in the Early Republic, 1787–1848* (Lexington, MA: D. C. Heath, 1991), 543.

QUESTIONS FOR ANALYSIS

1. What arguments do Buchanan and Sumner make about the boundaries of Texas, the issue that sparked the fighting? Whose argument is more persuasive and why?

2. Do O'Sullivan's and Buchanan's assertions support or undercut the claim that the Mexican War was an aggressive act of imperialism?

3. Why does Whitman oppose the expansion of slavery? Given Whitman's views, who might have gotten his vote in the election of 1848? Why?

4. Two of the sources are newspaper editorials; two are letters written by or addressed to public officials. How does the nature of each of these sources influence its content?

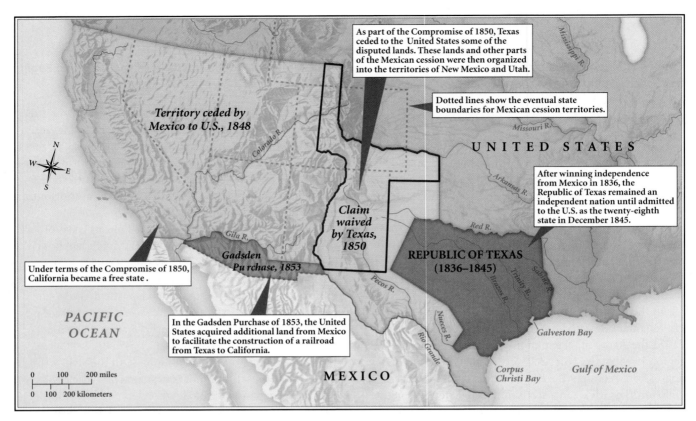

As part of the Compromise of 1850, Texas ceded to the United States some of the disputed lands. These lands and other parts of the Mexican cession were then organized into the territories of New Mexico and Utah.

Dotted lines show the eventual state boundaries for Mexican cession territories.

Territory ceded by Mexico to U.S., 1848

UNITED STATES

After winning independence from Mexico in 1836, the Republic of Texas remained an independent nation until admitted to the U.S. as the twenty-eighth state in December 1845.

Claim waived by Texas, 1850

REPUBLIC OF TEXAS (1836–1845)

Under terms of the Compromise of 1850, California became a free state.

Gadsden Purchase, 1853

In the Gadsden Purchase of 1853, the United States acquired additional land from Mexico to facilitate the construction of a railroad from Texas to California.

PACIFIC OCEAN

0 100 200 miles
0 100 200 kilometers

MEXICO

Galveston Bay

Corpus Christi Bay *Gulf of Mexico*

MAP 13.4

The Mexican Cession, 1848

In the Treaty of Guadalupe Hidalgo (1848), Mexico ceded to the United States its vast northern territories—the present-day states of California, Nevada, Utah, Arizona, New Mexico, and half of Colorado. These new territories, President Polk boasted to Congress, "constitute of themselves a country large enough for a great empire, and the acquisition is second in importance only to that of Louisiana in 1803."

The Election of 1848 The conflict over slavery took a toll on Polk and the Democratic Party. Scorned by Whigs and Free-Soilers and exhausted by his rigorous dawn-to-midnight work regime, Polk declined to run for a second term and died just three months after leaving office. In his place, the Democrats nominated Senator Lewis Cass of Michigan, an avid expansionist who had advocated buying Cuba, annexing Mexico's Yucatán Peninsula, and taking all of Oregon. To maintain party unity on the slavery issue, Cass promoted a new idea, **squatter sovereignty**. Under this plan, Congress would allow settlers in each territory to determine its status as free or slave.

Cass's doctrine of squatter sovereignty failed to persuade those northern Democrats who opposed any expansion of slavery. They joined the Free-Soil Party, as did former Democratic president Martin Van Buren, who became its candidate for president. To attract Whig votes, the Free-Soilers chose conscience Whig Charles Francis Adams for vice president.

The Whigs nominated General Zachary Taylor. Taylor was a Louisiana slave owner firmly committed to the defense of slavery in the South but not in the territories, a position that won him support in the North. Moreover, the general's military exploits had made him a popular hero, known affectionately among his troops as "Old Rough and Ready." In 1848, as in 1840 with the candidacy of William Henry Harrison, running a military hero worked for the Whigs. Taylor took 47 percent of the popular vote to Cass's 42 percent. However, Taylor won a majority in the electoral college (163 to 127) only because Van Buren and the Free-Soil ticket

PLACE EVENTS IN CONTEXT

What did conscience Whigs, David Wilmot, and free-soilers have in common, and why did they all rise to prominence between 1846 and 1848?

"This Is the House That Polk Built"

President James Polk's administration started off with a bang—a long-sought Democratic free-trade tariff, a compromise settlement of the Oregon boundary dispute with Great Britain, and a war to seize California and other Mexican provinces. This ambitious agenda promised fame for the president, but the cartoonist pictures Polk as a worried man, afraid that he has built a house of cards that might collapse at any time. © Bettmann/Corbis.

took enough votes in New York to deny Cass a victory there. Although their numbers were small, antislavery voters in New York had denied the presidency to Clay in 1844 and to Cass in 1848. The bitter debate over slavery had changed the dynamics of national politics.

California Gold and Racial Warfare

Even before Taylor took office, events in sparsely settled California took center stage. In January 1848, workers building a milldam for John A. Sutter in the Sierra Nevada foothills came across flakes of gold. Sutter was a Swiss immigrant who came to California in 1839, became a Mexican citizen, and accumulated

land in the Sacramento River Valley. He tried to hide the discovery, but by mid-1848 Americans from Monterey and San Francisco were pouring into the foothills, along with hundreds of Indians and Californios and scores of Australians, Mexicans, and Chileans. The gold rush was on (America Compared, p. 426). By January 1849, sixty-one crowded ships had left New York and other northeastern ports to sail around Cape Horn to San Francisco; by May, twelve thousand wagons had crossed the Missouri River bound for the goldfields (Map 13.5). For Bernard Reid, the overland trip on the Pioneer Line was "a long dreadful dream," beset by cholera, scurvy, and near starvation. Still, by the end of 1849, more than 80,000 people, mostly men — the so-called **forty-niners** — had arrived in California.

The Forty-Niners The forty-niners lived in crowded, chaotic towns and mining camps amid gamblers, saloon keepers, and prostitutes. They set up "claims clubs" to settle mining disputes and cobbled together a system of legal rules based on practice "back East." The American miners usually treated alien whites fairly but ruthlessly expelled Indians, Mexicans, and Chileans from the goldfields or confined them to marginal diggings. When substantial numbers of Chinese miners arrived in 1850, often in the employ of Chinese companies, whites called for laws to expel them from California.

The first miners to exploit a site often struck it rich. They scooped up the easily reached deposits, leaving small pickings for later arrivals. His "high hopes" wrecked, one latecomer saw himself and most other forty-niners as little better than "convicts condemned to exile and hard labor." They faced disease and death as well: "Diarrhea was so general during the fall and winter months" and so often fatal, a Sacramento doctor remarked, that it was called "the disease of California." Like many migrants, William Swain gave up the search for gold in 1850 and borrowed funds to return to his wife, infant daughter, and aged mother on a New York farm. "O William," his wife Sabrina had written, "I wish you had been content to stay at home, for there is no real home for me without you."

Thousands of disillusioned forty-niners were either too ashamed or too tired or too ambitious to go home. Some became wageworkers for companies that engaged in hydraulic or underground mining; others turned to farming. "Instead of going to the mines where fortune hangs upon the merest chance," a frustrated miner advised emigrants, "[you] should at once commence the cultivation of the soil."

The Gold Rush: California and Australia

In 1849, hundreds of Australian men booked passage for San Francisco, hoping to make their fortune in the California goldfields. A mere two years later, thousands more Australian "diggers" flocked to the colony of Victoria in Australia itself, drawn by a gold strike that yielded one-third of the world's gold output during the 1850s.

In California and Victoria, miners lived mostly in canvas tents and flimsy wood shanties and found gold initially in stream beds. In both territories, the huge migration virtually wiped out the aboriginal peoples. Similarly, both rushes attracted about 40,000 Chinese miners, an influx that, in the race-conscious, English-speaking world of the nineteenth century, prompted riots and legislation in both regions to restrict Asian migrants. Finally, only a few California "forty-niners" or Australian "diggers" made a fortune, perhaps 5 of every 100.

There were differences as well. Upon a gold strike in California, the prospectors would stake their claims and collectively protect those claims—a rough system of democratic self-rule. In Victoria, the British crown owned much of the land and gold commissioners and police administered the diggings, selling licenses to dig for 30 shillings a month (about $200 in present-day U.S. dollars). Distressed by license fees and corrupt local officials, 10,000 miners at Ballarat voted to create a Reform League, which demanded abolition of fees and universal male suffrage. When authorities ignored their demands, 500 miners seized a rich mine at Eureka. In the ensuing struggle, British troops killed 22 miners, ending the armed uprising.

Despite these differences—as well as a significant disparity in the proportion of women—California and Victoria were both transformed by the nearly simultaneous discovery of gold. Within a few decades a mining boom vastly increased their wealth and boasted their populations, as the following chart indicates:

TABLE 13.1

Nonnative Population Increases from Gold Rush in United States and Australia

	California, United States				Victoria, Australia		
	Total	Women	Nonwhite		Total	Women	Nonwhite
1845	11,000						
1850	93,000	7,000	7%	1%	1851	97,000	39,000	40%	0%
1860	380,000	120,000	31%	15%	1861	540,000	219,000	40%	5%
1870	560,000	211,000	37%	11%	1871	746,000	339,000	45%	4%

QUESTIONS FOR ANALYSIS

1. How would you account for the relative numbers of women in Victoria and California and how those proportions changed over time? How might the percentage of women affect the character of the two societies?

2. Why were there no equivalents of the Ballarat Reform League and the Eureka Stockade in California, given that the two rushes were similar in so many ways and fostered similar anti-Chinese violence and legislation?

Racial Warfare and Land Rights Farming required arable land, and Mexican grantees and native peoples owned or claimed much of it. The American migrants brushed aside both groups, brutally eliminating the Indians and wearing down Mexican claimants with legal tactics and political pressure. The subjugation of the native peoples came first. When the gold rush began in 1848, there were about 150,000 Indians in California; by 1861, there were only 30,000. As elsewhere in the Americas, European diseases took the lives of thousands. In California, white settlers also undertook systematic campaigns of extermination,

MAP 13.5

The California Gold Rush, 1849–1857

Traveling from all parts of the world—South America, Europe, China, and Australia, as well as the eastern United States—tens of thousands of bonanza-seekers converged on the California gold-fields. Miners traveling by sea landed at San Francisco, which mushroomed into a substantial city; many other prospectors trekked overland to the goldfields on the California Trail. By the mid-1850s, the gold rush was over: almost as many people were sailing from San Francisco each year as were arriving to seek their fortune.

and local political leaders did little to stop them: "A war of extermination will continue to be waged . . . until the Indian race becomes extinct," predicted Governor Peter Burnett in 1851. Congress abetted these assaults. At the bidding of white Californians, it repudiated treaties that federal agents had negotiated with 119 tribes and that had provided the Indians with 7 million acres of land. Instead, in 1853, Congress authorized five reservations of only 25,000 acres each and refused to provide the Indians with military protection.

Consequently, some settlers simply murdered Indians to push them off nonreservation lands. The Yuki people, who lived in the Round Valley in northern California, were one target. As the *Petaluma Journal* reported in April 1857: "Within the past three weeks, from 300 to 400 bucks, squaws and children have been killed by whites." Other white Californians turned to slave trading: "Hundreds of Indians have been stolen and carried into the settlements and sold," the state's Indian Affairs superintendent reported in 1856. Labor-hungry farmers quickly put them to work. Indians were "all among us, around us, with no house and kitchen without them," recalled one farmer. Expelled from their lands and widely dispersed, many Indian peoples simply vanished as distinct communities. Those tribal communities that survived were a shadow of their former selves. In 1854, at least 5,000 Yukis lived

in the Round Valley; a decade later, only 85 men and 215 women remained.

The Mexicans and Californios who held grants to thousands of acres were harder to dislodge. The Treaty of Guadalupe Hidalgo guaranteed that the property owned by Mexicans would be "inviolably respected." Although many of the 800 grants made by Spanish and Mexican authorities in California were either fraudulent or poorly documented, the Land Claims Commission created by Congress eventually upheld the validity of 75 percent of them. In the meantime, hundreds of Americans had set up farms on the sparsely settled grants. Having come of age in the antimonopoly Jacksonian era, these American squatters rejected the legitimacy of the Californios' claims to unoccupied and unimproved land and successfully pressured local land commissioners and judges to void or reduce the size of many grants. Indeed, the Americans' clamor for land was so intense and their numbers so large that many Californio claimants sold off their properties at bargain prices.

In northern California, farmers found that they could grow most eastern crops: corn and oats to feed work horses, pigs, and chickens; potatoes, beans, and

EXPLAIN CONSEQUENCES
What were the main changes caused by the huge increase in California's population and its composition between 1849 and 1870?

A Californio Patriarch

The descendant of a Spanish family that had lived—and prospered—in Mexico since the Spanish Conquest, Mariano Guadalupe Vallejo served in Mexican California as a military officer. In the 1830s and 1840s, he received land grants totaling 270,000 acres in the Sonoma Valley north of San Francisco. Vallejo, the father of seventeen children (eleven of whom survived childhood), presents himself in this photograph as a proud patriarch, surrounded by two daughters and three granddaughters. Although he favored the American conquest of 1846, Vallejo was imprisoned for a short period and subsequently suffered severe financial setbacks, losing most of his vast landholdings to squatters and rival claimants. University of California at Berkeley, Bancroft Library.

peas for the farm table; and refreshing grapes, apples, and peaches. Ranchers gradually replaced Spanish cattle with American breeds that yielded more milk and meat, which found a ready market as California's population shot up to 380,000 by 1860 and 560,000 by 1870. Most important, using the latest agricultural machinery and scores of hired workers, California farmers produced huge crops of wheat and barley, which San Francisco merchants exported to Europe at high prices. The gold rush turned into a wheat boom.

1850: Crisis and Compromise

The rapid settlement of California qualified it for admission to the Union. Hoping to avoid an extended debate over slavery, President Taylor advised the settlers to skip the territorial phase and immediately apply for statehood. In November 1849, Californians ratified a state constitution prohibiting slavery, and the president urged Congress to admit California as a free state.

Constitutional Conflict   California's bid for admission produced passionate debates in Congress and four distinct positions regarding the expansion of slavery. First, John C. Calhoun took his usual extreme stance. On the verge of death, Calhoun reiterated his deep resentment of the North's "long-continued agitation of the slavery question." To uphold southern honor (and political power), he proposed a constitutional amendment to create a dual presidency, permanently dividing executive power between the North and the South. Calhoun also advanced the radical argument that Congress had no constitutional authority to regulate slavery in the territories. Slaves were property, Calhoun insisted, and the Constitution restricted Congress's power to abrogate or limit property rights. That argument ran counter to a half century of practice: Congress had prohibited slavery in the Northwest Territory in 1787 and had extended that ban to most of the Louisiana Purchase in the Missouri Compromise of 1820. But Calhoun's assertion that **"slavery follows the flag"** — that planters could by right take their slave property into new territories — won support in the Deep South.

However, many southerners favored a second, more moderate proposal to extend the Missouri Compromise line to the Pacific Ocean. This plan won the backing of Pennsylvanian James Buchanan and other influential northern Democrats. It would guarantee slave owners access to some western territory, including a separate state in southern California.

A third alternative was squatter sovereignty— allowing settlers in a territory to decide the status of slavery. Lewis Cass had advanced this idea in 1848, and Democratic senator Stephen Douglas of Illinois now became its champion. Douglas called his plan "popular sovereignty" to link it to republican ideology, which placed ultimate power in the hands of the people (Chapter 5), and it had considerable appeal. Politicians hoped it would remove the explosive issue of slavery from Congress, and settlers welcomed the power it would give them. However, popular sovereignty was a slippery concept. Could residents accept or ban slavery when a territory was first organized? Or must they delay that decision until a territory had enough people to frame a constitution and apply for statehood? No one knew.

For their part, antislavery advocates refused to accept any plan for California or the territories that would allow slavery. Senator Salmon P. Chase of Ohio, elected by a Democratic–Free-Soil coalition, and Senator William H. Seward, a New York Whig, urged a fourth position: that federal legislation restrict slavery within its existing boundaries and eventually extinguish it completely. Condemning slavery as "morally unjust, politically unwise, and socially pernicious" and invoking "a higher law than the Constitution," Seward demanded bold action to protect freedom, "the common heritage of mankind."

A Complex Compromise Standing on the brink of disaster, senior Whig and Democratic politicians worked desperately to preserve the Union. Aided by Millard Fillmore, who became president in 1850 after Zachary Taylor's sudden death, Whig leaders Henry Clay and Daniel Webster and Democrat Stephen A. Douglas won the passage of five separate laws known collectively as the **Compromise of 1850**. To mollify the South, the compromise included a new Fugitive Slave Act giving federal support to slave catchers. To satisfy the North, the legislation admitted California as a free state, resolved a boundary dispute between New Mexico and Texas in favor of New Mexico, and abolished the slave trade (but not slavery) in the District of Columbia. Finally, the compromise organized the rest of the conquered Mexican lands into the territories of New Mexico and Utah and, invoking popular sovereignty, left the issue of slavery in the hands of their residents (Map 13.6).

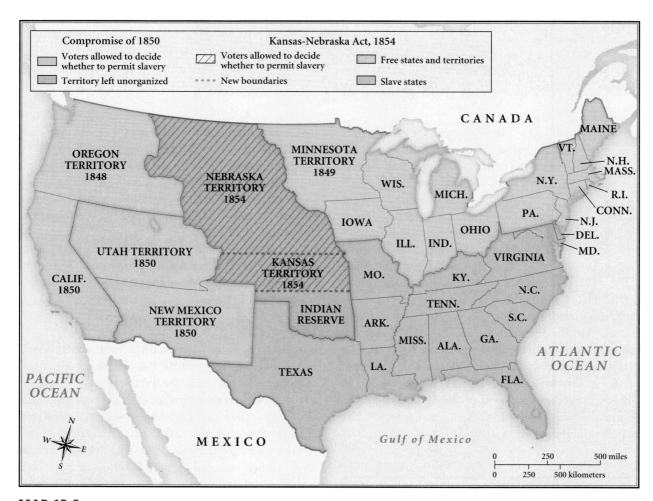

MAP 13.6
The Compromise of 1850 and the Kansas-Nebraska Act of 1854
The contest over the expansion of slavery involved vast territories. The Compromise of 1850 peacefully resolved the status of the Far West: California would be a free state, and settlers in the Utah and New Mexico territories would vote for or against slavery (the doctrine of popular sovereignty). However, the Kansas-Nebraska Act of 1854 voided the Missouri Compromise (1820) and instituted popular sovereignty in those territories. That decision sparked a bitter local war and revealed a fatal flaw in the doctrine.

Resolving the Crisis of 1850

By 1850, Whig Henry Clay had been in Congress for nearly four decades. Now in partnership with fellow Whig Daniel Webster and Democrat Stephen Douglas, Clay fashioned a complex—and controversial—compromise that preserved the Union. In this engraving, he addresses a crowded Senate chamber, with Webster sitting immediately to his left. Clay addresses his remarks to his prime antagonist, southern advocate John C. Calhoun, the man with the long white hair at the far right of the picture. Library of Congress.

PLACE EVENTS IN CONTEXT
How did the Compromise of 1850 resolve the various disputes over slavery, and who benefitted more from its terms?

The Compromise of 1850 preserved national unity by accepting once again the stipulation advanced by the South since 1787: no Union without slavery. Still, southerners feared for the future and threatened secession. Militant activists (or "fire-eaters") in South Carolina, Georgia, Mississippi, and Alabama organized special conventions to safeguard "southern rights." Georgia congressman Alexander H. Stephens called on convention delegates to prepare "men and money, arms and munitions, etc. to meet the emergency." A majority of delegates remained committed to the Union, but only on the condition that Congress protect slavery where it existed and grant statehood to any territory that ratified a proslavery constitution. Political wizardry had solved the immediate crisis, but not the underlying issues.

The End of the Second Party System, 1850–1858

The Missouri Compromise had endured for a generation, and the architects of the Compromise of 1850 hoped their agreement would have an even longer life.

Religious leaders, conservative businessmen, and leading judges called upon citizens to support the compromise to preserve "government and civil society." Their hopes quickly faded. Demanding freedom for fugitive slaves and free soil in the West, antislavery northerners refused to accept the legitimacy of the compromise. For their part, proslavery southerners plotted to extend slavery into the West, the Caribbean, and Central America. The resulting disputes destroyed the Second Party System and deepened the crisis of the Union.

Resistance to the Fugitive Slave Act

The Fugitive Slave Act proved the most controversial element of the compromise. The act required federal magistrates to determine the status of alleged runaways and denied them a jury trial or even the right to testify. Using its provisions, southern owners re-enslaved about 200 fugitives (as well as some free blacks).

The plight of the runaways and the presence of slave catchers aroused popular hostility in the North and Midwest. Ignoring the threat of substantial fines and prison sentences, free blacks and white abolitionists protected fugitives. In October 1850, Boston abolitionists helped two slaves escape from Georgia slave catchers. Rioters in Syracuse, New York, broke into a courthouse, freed a fugitive, and accused the U.S. marshal of kidnapping. Abandoning nonviolence,

Frederick Douglass declared, "The only way to make a Fugitive Slave Law a dead letter is to make half a dozen or more dead kidnappers." Precisely such a deadly result occurred in Christiana, Pennsylvania, in September 1851, when twenty African Americans exchanged gunfire with Maryland slave catchers, killing two of them. Federal authorities indicted thirty-six blacks and four whites for treason and other crimes, but a Pennsylvania jury acquitted one defendant, and the government dropped charges against the rest.

Harriet Beecher Stowe's novel *Uncle Tom's Cabin* (1852) boosted opposition to the Fugitive Slave Act. Conveying the moral principles of abolitionism in heartrending personal situations — using the now familiar literary trope of sentimental domesticity — Stowe's book quickly sold 310,000 copies in the United States and double that number in Britain, where it prompted an antislavery petition signed by 560,000 English women. As *Uncle Tom's Cabin* sparked an unprecedented discussion of race and slavery, state legislators in the North protested that the Fugitive Slave Act violated state sovereignty, and they passed **personal-liberty laws** that guaranteed to all residents, including alleged fugitives, the right to a jury trial. In 1857, the Wisconsin Supreme Court went further, ruling in *Ableman v. Booth* that the Fugitive Slave Act was unconstitutional because it violated the rights of Wisconsin's citizens. Taking a states' rights stance — traditionally a southern position — the Wisconsin court denied the authority of the federal judiciary to review its decision. In 1859, Chief Justice Roger B. Taney led a unanimous Supreme Court in affirming the supremacy of federal courts — a position that has withstood the test of time — and upholding the constitutionality of the Fugitive Slave Act. By then, as Frederick Douglass had hoped, popular opposition had made the law a "dead letter."

The Whigs Disintegrate and New Parties Rise

The conflict over slavery split both major political parties along sectional lines. Hoping to unify their party, the Whigs ran another war hero, General Winfield Scott, as their presidential candidate in 1852. Among the Democrats, southerners demanded a candidate who embraced Calhoun's constitutional argument that all territories were open to slavery. However, northern and midwestern Democrats stood behind the three leading candidates — Lewis Cass of Michigan, Stephen Douglas of Illinois, and James Buchanan of Pennsylvania — who advocated popular sovereignty.

Ultimately, the party settled on Franklin Pierce of New Hampshire, a congenial man who was sympathetic to the South. As the Whig Party fragmented over slavery, Pierce swept to victory.

IDENTIFY CAUSES
Why did the Fugitive Slave Act fail?

Proslavery Initiatives   As president, Pierce pursued an expansionist foreign policy. To assist northern merchants, who wanted a commercial empire, he negotiated a trade-opening treaty with Japan. To mollify southern expansionists, who desired a plantation empire, he sought extensive Mexican lands south of the Rio Grande. Ultimately, Pierce settled for a smaller slice of land — the **Gadsden Purchase** of 1853, now part of Arizona and New Mexico — that opened the way for his negotiator, James Gadsden, to build a transcontinental rail line from New Orleans to Los Angeles.

Pierce's most controversial initiatives came in the Caribbean and Central America. Southern expansionists had long urged Cuban slave owners to declare independence from Spain and join the United States. To assist the expansionists and the American traders who still supplied enslaved Africans to Cuba, Pierce threatened war with Spain and covertly supported filibustering (private military) expeditions to Cuba. When Secretary of State William L. Marcy arranged in 1854 for American diplomats in Europe to compose the **Ostend Manifesto**, which urged Pierce to seize Cuba, northern Democrats denounced these aggressive initiatives and scuttled the planters' dreams of American expansion into the Caribbean.

The Kansas-Nebraska Act   The Caribbean was a sideshow. The main stage was the trans-Mississippi west, where a major controversy in 1854 destroyed the Whig Party and sent the Union spinning toward disaster. The Missouri Compromise prohibited new slave states in the Louisiana Purchase north of 36°30′, so southern senators had long prevented the creation of new territories there. It remained Permanent Indian Territory. Now Senator Stephen A. Douglas of Illinois wanted to open it up, allowing a transcontinental railroad to link Chicago to California. Douglas proposed to extinguish Native American rights on the Great Plains and create a large free territory called Nebraska.

Southern politicians opposed Douglas's initiative. They hoped to extend slavery throughout the Louisiana Purchase and to have a southern city — New Orleans, Memphis, or St. Louis — as the eastern terminus of a transcontinental railroad. To win their support, Douglas amended his bill so that it explicitly repealed the Missouri Compromise and organized the region on the basis of popular sovereignty. He also agreed to the formation of two territories, Nebraska and Kansas, raising the prospect that settlers in the southern one, Kansas, would choose slavery. Knowing the revised bill would "raise a hell of a storm" in the North, Douglas argued that Kansas was not suited to plantation agriculture and would become a free state. After weeks of bitter debate, the Senate passed the **Kansas-Nebraska Act**. As 1,600 petitions opposing the bill flooded the House of Representatives, the measure barely squeaked through.

The Republican and American Parties

The Kansas-Nebraska Act of 1854 was a disaster for the American political system. It finished off the Whig Party: "We went to bed one night old fashioned, conservative Union Whigs & and waked up stark mad abolitionists," cotton textile magnate Amos Lawrence lamented. And it crippled the Democracy, because "anti-Nebraska Democrats" denounced the act as "part of a great scheme for extending and perpetuating supremacy of the slave power." In 1854, they joined ex-Whigs, Free-Soilers, and abolitionists to form a new Republican Party.

The new party was a coalition of "strange, discordant and even hostile elements," one Republican observed. However, all its members opposed slavery, which, they argued, drove down the wages of free workers and degraded the dignity of manual labor. Like Thomas Jefferson, Republicans praised a society based on "the middling classes who own the soil and work it with their own hands." Abraham Lincoln, an ex-Whig from Illinois, conveyed the new party's vision of social mobility. "There is no permanent class of hired laborers among us," he declared, ignoring the growing social divisions in the industrializing North and Midwest. Lincoln and his fellow Republicans envisioned a society of independent farmers, artisans, and proprietors, and they celebrated middle-class values: domesticity and respectability, religious commitment, and capitalist enterprise.

The Republicans faced strong competition from the **American, or Know-Nothing, Party**, which had its origins in the anti-immigrant and anti-Catholic movements of the 1840s (Chapter 9). In 1850, these nativist societies banded together as the Order of the Star-Spangled Banner; the following year, they formed the American Party. When questioned, the party's secrecy-conscious members often replied, "I know nothing," hence the nickname. The American (or Know-Nothing) Party program was far from secret, however: party supporters wanted to mobilize native-born Protestants against the "alien menace" of Irish and German Catholics, prohibit further immigration, and institute literacy tests for voting. Northern members of the party had a strong antislavery outlook. In 1854, voters elected dozens of American Party candidates to the House of Representatives and gave the party control of the state governments of Massachusetts and Pennsylvania. The emergence of a Protestant-based nativist party to replace the Whigs became a real possibility.

Bleeding Kansas

Meanwhile, thousands of settlers rushed into the Kansas Territory, putting Douglas's

> **COMPARE AND CONTRAST**
> What were the main policy objectives of the Republican and American parties?

Armed Abolitionists in Kansas, 1859

The confrontation between North and South in Kansas took many forms. In the spring of 1859, Dr. John Doy (seated) slipped across the border into Missouri and tried to lead thirteen escaped slaves to freedom in Kansas, only to be captured and jailed in St. Joseph, Missouri. The serious-looking men standing behind Doy, well armed with guns and Bowie knives, attacked the jail and carried Doy back to Kansas. The photograph celebrated and memorialized their successful exploit. Kansas State Historical Society.

concept of popular sovereignty to the test. On the side of slavery, Missouri senator David R. Atchison encouraged residents of his state to cross temporarily into Kansas to vote in crucial elections there. Opposing Atchison was the abolitionist New England Emigrant Aid Society, which dispatched free-soilers to Kansas. In 1855, the Pierce administration accepted the legitimacy of a proslavery legislature in Lecompton, Kansas, which had been elected with aid from border-crossing Missourians. However, the majority of Kansas residents favored free soil and refused allegiance to the Lecompton government.

In 1856, both sides turned to violence, prompting Horace Greeley of the *New York Tribune* to label the territory **"Bleeding Kansas."** A proslavery force, seven hundred strong, looted and burned the free-soil town of Lawrence. The attack enraged John Brown, a fifty-six-year-old abolitionist from New York and Ohio, who commanded a free-state militia. Brown was a complex man with a record of failed businesses, but he had an intellectual and moral intensity that won the trust of influential people. Avenging the sack of Lawrence, Brown and his followers murdered five proslavery settlers at Pottawatomie. Abolitionists must "fight fire with fire" and "strike terror in the hearts of the proslavery people," Brown declared. The attack on Lawrence and the Pottawatomie killings started a guerrilla war in Kansas that took nearly two hundred lives.

Buchanan's Failed Presidency

The violence in Kansas dominated the presidential election of 1856. The new Republican Party counted on anger over Bleeding Kansas to boost the party's fortunes. Its platform denounced the Kansas-Nebraska Act and demanded that the federal government prohibit slavery in all the territories. Republicans also called for federal subsidies for transcontinental railroads, reviving a Whig economic proposal popular among midwestern Democrats. For president, the Republicans nominated Colonel John C. Frémont, a free-soiler who had won fame in the conquest of Mexican California.

The Election of 1856   The American Party entered the election with equally high hopes, but like the Whigs and Democrats, it split along sectional lines over slavery. The southern faction of the American Party nominated former Whig president Millard Fillmore, while the northern contingent endorsed Frémont. During the campaign, the Republicans won the votes

of many northern Know-Nothings by demanding legislation banning foreign immigrants and imposing high tariffs on foreign manufactures. As a Pennsylvania Republican put it, "Let our motto be, protection to everything American, against everything foreign." In New York, Republicans campaigned on a reform platform designed to unite "all of the Anti-Slavery, Anti-Popery and Anti-Whiskey" voters.

The Democrats reaffirmed their support for popular sovereignty and the Kansas-Nebraska Act, and they nominated James Buchanan of Pennsylvania. A tall, dignified, and experienced politician, Buchanan was staunchly prosouthern. He won the three-way race with 1.8 million popular votes (45.3 percent) and 174 electoral votes; Frémont polled 1.3 million popular votes (33.2 percent) and 114 electoral votes; Fillmore won 873,000 popular votes (21.5 percent) but captured only 8 electoral votes.

The dramatic restructuring of the political system was now apparent (Map 13.7). With the splintering of the American Party, the Republicans had replaced the Whigs as the second major party. However, Frémont had not won a single vote in the South; had he triumphed, a North Carolina newspaper warned, the result would have been "a separation of the states." The fate of the republic hinged on President Buchanan's ability to quiet the passions of the past decade and to hold the Democratic Party—the only national party—together.

Dred Scott: Petitioner for Freedom   Events—and his own values and weaknesses—conspired against Buchanan. Early in 1857, the Supreme Court decided the case of **Dred Scott v. Sandford**, which raised the controversial issue of Congress's constitutional authority over slavery. Dred Scott was an enslaved African American who had lived for a time with his owner, an army surgeon, in the free state of Illinois and at Fort Snelling in the northern part of the Louisiana Purchase (then part of the Wisconsin Territory), where the Missouri Compromise (1820) prohibited slavery. Scott claimed that residence in a free state and a free territory had made him free. Buchanan opposed Scott's appeal and pressured the two justices from Pennsylvania to side with their southern colleagues. Seven of the nine justices declared that Scott was still a slave, but they disagreed on the legal rationale (Thinking Like a Historian, p. 434).

PLACE EVENTS IN CONTEXT
Why did northern Democratic presidents, such as Pierce and Buchanan, adopt prosouthern policies?

Biography as History

Sometimes the life of one individual can exemplify an era, and Bridget "Biddy" Mason was such a person. Mason was born into slavery in Georgia in 1818, of mixed African American and Native American descent. In 1836, her owner gave Biddy, age eighteen, to his recently married cousins, Robert and Rebecca Smith, who owned a Mississippi plantation. Trained as a midwife, Biddy delivered all six of Rebecca's babies as well as working in the fields. Biddy herself gave birth to three daughters, probably fathered by Smith, as were at least two of her sister Hannah's eight children. In the mid-1840s, the Smiths converted to Mormonism and, in 1847, along with other Mississippi converts and their slaves, journeyed 1,700 miles to the Utah Territory.

1. **Joseph Smith's Plan to End Slavery, February 7, 1844.** *Like many Americans, members of the Church of Jesus Christ of Latter-day Saints struggled with the question of slavery. Running for president in 1844, its founder, Joseph Smith, decried the institution.*

Petition, also, ye goodly inhabitants of the slave States, your legislators to abolish slavery by the year 1850, or now. . . . Pray Congress to pay every man a reasonable price for his slaves out of the surplus revenue arising from the sale of public lands, and from the deduction of pay from the members of Congress. Break off the shackles from the poor black man, and hire him to labor like other human beings; for "an hour of virtuous liberty on earth is worth a whole eternity of bondage."

2. **Orson Hyde on slavery, the *Millennial Star*, February 15, 1851.** *Orson Hyde was an important Mormon missionary who, like most Mormons, refused to baptize slaves without their owner's permission.*

The laws of the land recognize slavery, we do not wish to oppose the laws of the country. . . . Our counsel to all our ministers in the North and South is, to avoid contention upon the subject, and to oppose no institution which the laws of the country authorize; but to labor to bring men into the Church and Kingdom of God, and teach them to do right, and honor their God in His creatures.

3. **Mormon apostle Amasa Mason Lyman and his wives.** *In 1851, at the behest of Brigham Young, five hundred Mormons—including the Robert Smiths and their slaves—moved to San Bernardino, California. They settled on land purchased from Antonio Maria Lugo, who held the 35,000 acres of the Rancho Bernardino under a Mexican grant, a claim protected by the Treaty of Guadalupe Hidalgo (1848) that ended the Mexican War. The settlement's leader was Amasa Mason Lyman, whom Biddy knew through the Smith family and whose middle name she eventually took for her surname.*

Source: George and Sadie Frey Family.

4. ***Mason v. Smith*, 1856 (the Bridget "Biddy" Mason case).** *Most Mormon migrants to California heeded Brigham Young's advice to free their slaves, as California was a free state. Robert Smith refused to do so and, in 1855, prepared to move to Texas. However, in 1856, members of the free black community assisted Biddy to file a habeas corpus petition and obtain freedom for herself and her extended family of thirteen women and children. In a later interview, Mason stated: "I feared this trip to Texas since I first heard of it."*

And it further appearing by satisfactory proof to the judge here, that all of the said persons of color are entitled to their freedom, and are free and cannot be held in slavery or involuntary servitude . . . And it further appearing to the satisfaction of the judge here that the said Robert Smith intended to and is about to remove from the State of California where slavery does not exist, to the State of Texas, where slavery of Negroes and persons of color does exist, and is established by the municipal laws, and intends to remove the said before-mentioned persons of color, to his own use without the free will and consent of all or any of the said persons of color, whereby their liberty will be greatly jeopardized, and there is good reason to apprehend and believe that they may be sold into slavery or involuntary servitude . . . and it further appearing that none of the said persons of color can read and write, and are almost entirely ignorant of the laws of the state of California as well as those of the State of Texas, and of their rights and that the said Robert Smith, from his past relations to them as members of his family does possess and exercise over them an undue influence in respect to the matter of their said removal insofar that they have been in duress and not in possession and exercise of their free will so as to give a binding consent to any engagement or arrangement with him.

5. **Photograph of Biddy Mason and the deed of her first land purchase, 1866.** *Once free, Biddy prospered as a midwife and an investor in Los Angeles real estate. When she died in 1891, Biddy had accumulated a fortune of $300,000 (about $7.6 million today). Despite her contact with Mormonism, Biddy Mason never joined the Mormon church. Instead, in 1872 she was a founding member of the first African Methodist Episcopal (AME) Church in Los Angeles. An active philanthropist of charitable causes, she funded a traveler's aid society and an elementary school for black children.*

Source: Los Angeles Public Library.

Sources: (1) *History of the Church of Jesus Christ of Latter-Day Saints*, Vol. VI (Salt Lake City, UT: Mormon Church, 1912), 205; (2) *The Latter-Day Saints' Millennial Star*, Vol. XIII (Liverpool: Franklin D. Richards, 1851), 63; (4) Golden State Insurance Company Records, UCLA, Dept. of Special Collections, Charles E. Young Research Library.

ANALYZING THE EVIDENCE

1. Were Smith's and Hyde's positions on slavery and property rights (sources 1 and 2) similar or different?

2. How might the set of photographs of Amasa Mason Lyman and his wives (source 3) suggest that Mormon family life resembled Biddy's experience in growing up on a southern plantation? How might it mirror her own sexual experience, and that of her sister Hannah, as Robert Smith's slaves?

3. As a slave, Biddy did not have a surname. Why might have she taken Lyman's middle name as her surname when she became free in 1856?

4. How does the ruling in Biddy's case (source 4) by Judge Benjamin Ignatius Hayes, in a California state court, reflect the political and constitutional turmoil that westward expansion created with regard to slavery? How is this ruling similar to, and different from, the famous case brought by Dred Scott in Missouri and decided eventually by the U.S. Supreme Court in *Dred Scott v. Sandford* (1857)?

5. What do you think explains Biddy Mason's religious choices and charitable activities as described in the headnote to source 5?

PUTTING IT ALL TOGETHER

List the main themes and arguments presented in Chapters 12 and 13. Then, write an essay that explores the ways in which Biddy Mason's experiences—plantation labor in Georgia and Mississippi, coerced miscegenation, exposure to the new religion of Mormonism, a trek by foot across a continent, legally won emancipation, and entrepreneurial success in formerly Mexican California—either exemplify or are inconsistent with those themes and arguments.

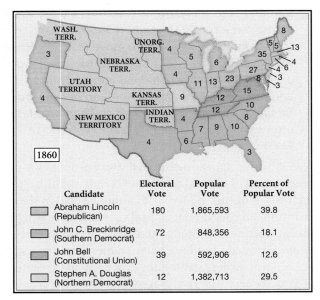

Candidate	Electoral Vote	Popular Vote	Percent of Popular Vote
Zachary Taylor (Whig)	163	1,360,967	47.4
Lewis Cass (Democrat)	127	1,222,342	42.5
Martin Van Buren (Free-Soil)	—	291,263	10.1

Candidate	Electoral Vote	Popular Vote	Percent of Popular Vote
Abraham Lincoln (Republican)	180	1,865,593	39.8
John C. Breckinridge (Southern Democrat)	72	848,356	18.1
John Bell (Constitutional Union)	39	592,906	12.6
Stephen A. Douglas (Northern Democrat)	12	1,382,713	29.5

MAP 13.7
Political Realignment, 1848 and 1860

In the presidential election of 1848, both the Whig and Democratic candidates won electoral votes throughout the nation. Subsequently, the political conflict over slavery and the Compromise of 1850 destroyed the Whig Party in the South. As the only nationwide party, the Democrats won easily over the Whigs in 1852 and, with the opposition split between the Republican and American parties, triumphed in 1856 as well. However, a new region-based party system appeared by 1860 and persisted for the next seventy years—with Democrats dominant in the South and Republicans usually controlling the Northeast, Midwest, and Far West.

Chief Justice Roger B. Taney of Maryland, a slave owner himself, wrote the most influential opinion. He declared that Negroes, whether enslaved or free, could not be citizens of the United States and that Scott therefore had no right to sue in federal court. That argument was controversial, given that free blacks were citizens in many states and therefore had access to the federal courts. Taney then made two even more controversial claims. First, he endorsed John C. Calhoun's argument that the Fifth Amendment, which prohibited "taking" of property without due process of law, meant that Congress could not prevent southern citizens from moving their slave property into the territories and owning it there. Consequently, the chief justice concluded, the provisions of the Northwest Ordinance and the Missouri Compromise that prohibited slavery had never been constitutional. Second, Taney declared that Congress could not give to territorial governments any powers that it did not possess, such as the authority to prohibit slavery. Taney thereby endorsed Calhoun's interpretation of popular sovereignty: only when settlers wrote a constitution and requested statehood could they prohibit slavery.

In a single stroke, Taney had declared the Republican proposals to restrict the expansion of slavery through legislation to be unconstitutional. The Republicans could never accept the legitimacy of Taney's constitutional arguments, which indeed had significant flaws. Led by Senator Seward of New York, they accused the chief justice and President Buchanan of participating in the Slave Power conspiracy.

Buchanan then added fuel to the raging constitutional fire. Ignoring reports that antislavery residents held a clear majority in Kansas, he refused to allow a popular vote on the proslavery Lecompton constitution and in 1858 strongly urged Congress to admit Kansas as a slave state. Angered by Buchanan's machinations, Stephen Douglas, the most influential Democratic senator and architect of the Kansas-Nebraska Act, broke with the president and persuaded Congress to deny statehood to Kansas. (Kansas would enter the Union as a free state in 1861.) Still determined to aid the South, Buchanan resumed negotiations to buy Cuba in December 1858. By pursuing a proslavery agenda—first in *Dred Scott* and then in Kansas and Cuba—Buchanan widened the split in his party and the nation.

Abraham Lincoln and the Republican Triumph, 1858–1860

As the Democratic Party split along sectional lines, the Republicans gained support in the North and Midwest. Abraham Lincoln of Illinois emerged as the only Republican leader whose policies and temperament might have saved the Union. However, few southerners trusted Lincoln, and his presidential candidacy revived secessionist agitation.

Lincoln's Political Career

The middle-class world of storekeepers, lawyers, and entrepreneurs in the small towns of the Ohio River Valley shaped Lincoln's early career. He came from a hardscrabble yeoman farm family that was continually on the move — from Kentucky, where Lincoln was born in 1809, to Indiana, and then to Illinois. In 1831, Lincoln rejected his father's life as a subsistence farmer and became a store clerk in New Salem, Illinois. Socially ambitious, Lincoln won entry to the middle class by mastering its culture; he joined the New Salem Debating Society, read Shakespeare, and studied law.

Admitted to the bar in 1837, Lincoln moved to Springfield, the new state capital. There, he met Mary Todd, the cultured daughter of a Kentucky banker; they married in 1842. Her tastes were aristocratic; his were humble. She was volatile; he was easygoing but suffered bouts of depression that tried her patience and tested his character.

An Ambitious Politician   Lincoln's ambition was "a little engine that knew no rest," a close associate remarked, and it propelled him into politics. An admirer of Henry Clay, Lincoln joined the Whig Party and won election to four terms in the Illinois legislature, where he promoted education, banks, canals, and railroads. He became a dexterous party politician, adept in the use of patronage and the passage of legislation.

In 1846, the rising lawyer-politician won election to a Congress that was bitterly divided over the Wilmot Proviso. Lincoln believed that human bondage was unjust but doubted that the federal government had the constitutional authority to tamper with slavery. With respect to the Mexican War, he took a middle ground by voting for military appropriations but also for the Wilmot Proviso's ban on slavery in any acquired territories. Lincoln also introduced legislation that

Abraham Lincoln, 1859

Lincoln was not a handsome man, and he photographed poorly. His campaign managers had this photo — and many others — retouched to soften Lincoln's features. However, no photograph, no matter how realistic, captured Lincoln's complex personality and wit or the intensity of his spirit and intellect. To grasp Lincoln, it is necessary to read his words. Chicago History Museum.

would require the gradual (and thus compensated) emancipation of slaves in the District of Columbia. To avoid future racial strife, he favored the colonization of freed blacks in Africa or South America. Both abolitionists and proslavery activists heaped scorn on Lincoln's middle-of-the-road policies, and he lost his bid for reelection. Dismayed by the rancor of ideological debate, he withdrew from politics and prospered as a lawyer by representing railroads and manufacturers.

Lincoln returned to the political fray because of the Kansas-Nebraska Act. Shocked by the act's repeal of the Missouri Compromise and Senator Douglas's advocacy of popular sovereignty, Lincoln reaffirmed his opposition to slavery in the territories. He now likened slavery to a cancer that had to be cut out if the nation's republican ideals and moral principles were to endure.

The Lincoln-Douglas Debates   Abandoning the Whigs, Lincoln quickly emerged as the leading Republican in Illinois, and in 1858 he ran for the U.S. Senate seat held by Douglas. Lincoln pointed out that the proslavery Supreme Court might soon declare that the Constitution "does not permit a state to exclude slavery," just as it had decided in *Dred Scott* that "neither Congress nor the territorial legislature" could ban slavery in a territory. In that event, he warned, "we shall awake to the reality . . . that the Supreme Court has made Illinois a slave state." This prospect informed Lincoln's famous "House Divided" speech. Quoting the biblical adage "A house divided against itself cannot stand," he predicted that American society "cannot endure permanently half slave and half free. . . . It will become all one thing, or all the other."

The Senate race in Illinois attracted national interest because of Douglas's prominence and Lincoln's reputation as a formidable speaker. During a series of seven debates, Douglas declared his support for white supremacy: "This government was made by our fathers, by white men for the benefit of white men," he said, attacking Lincoln for supporting "negro equality." Lincoln parried Douglas's racist attacks by arguing that free blacks should have equal economic opportunities but not equal political rights. Taking the offensive, he asked how Douglas could accept the *Dred Scott* decision (which protected slave property in the territories) yet advocate popular sovereignty (which allowed settlers to exclude slavery). Douglas responded with the so-called **Freeport Doctrine**: that a territory's residents could exclude slavery by not adopting laws to protect it. That position pleased neither proslavery nor antislavery advocates. Nonetheless, when Democrats won a narrow majority in the state legislature, they reelected Douglas to the U.S. Senate.

> **UNDERSTAND POINTS OF VIEW**
> What was Lincoln's position on slavery and people of African descent during the 1840s and 1850s?

The Union Under Siege

The debates with Douglas gave Lincoln a national reputation, and in the election of 1858 the Republican Party won control of the U.S. House of Representatives.

The Rise of Radicalism   Shaken by the Republicans' advance, southern Democrats divided again into moderates and fire-eaters. The moderates, who included Senator Jefferson Davis of Mississippi, strongly defended "southern rights" and demanded ironclad political or constitutional protections for slavery. The fire-eaters — men such as Robert Barnwell Rhett of South Carolina and William Lowndes Yancey of Alabama — repudiated the Union and actively promoted secession. Radical antislavery northerners likewise took a strong stance.

Senator Seward of New York declared that freedom and slavery were locked in "an irrepressible conflict," and ruthless abolitionist John Brown, who had perpetrated the Pottawatomie massacre, showed what that might mean. In October 1859, Brown led eighteen heavily armed black and white men in a raid on the federal arsenal at Harpers Ferry, Virginia. Brown hoped to arm slaves with the arsenal's weapons and mount a major rebellion to end slavery.

Republican leaders condemned Brown's unsuccessful raid, but Democrats called his plot "a natural, logical, inevitable result of the doctrines and teachings of the Republican party." When the state of Virginia sentenced Brown to be hanged, transcendentalist reformers Henry David Thoreau and Ralph Waldo Emerson (Chapter 11) proclaimed him a "saint awaiting his martyrdom." The slaveholding states looked to the future with terror. "The aim of the present black republican organization is the destruction of the social system of the Southern States," warned one newspaper. Once Republicans came to power, another cautioned, they "would create insurrection and servile war in the South — they would put the torch to our dwellings and the knife to our throats."

Nor could the South count any longer on the Democratic Party to protect its interests. At the party's convention in April 1860, northern Democrats rejected Jefferson Davis's proposal to protect slavery in the territories, and delegates from eight southern states quit the meeting. At a second Democratic convention, northern and midwestern delegates nominated Stephen Douglas for president; meeting separately, southern Democrats nominated the sitting vice president, John C. Breckinridge of Kentucky.

The Election of 1860   With the Democrats divided, the Republicans sensed victory. They courted white voters with a free-soil platform that opposed both slavery and racial equality: "Missouri for white men and white men for Missouri," declared that state's Republican platform. The national Republican convention chose Lincoln as its presidential candidate because he was more moderate on slavery than the best-known Republicans, Senators William Seward of New York and Salmon Chase of Ohio. Lincoln also conveyed a compelling egalitarian image that appealed to small-holding farmers, wage earners, and midwestern voters.

The Republican strategy worked. Although Lincoln received less than 1 percent of the popular vote in the South and only 40 percent of the national poll, he won every northern and western state except New Jersey, giving him 180 (of 303) electoral votes and an absolute

THE NATIONAL GAME. THREE "OUTS" AND ONE "RUN".
ABRAHAM WINNING THE BALL.

Lincoln on Home Base

Beginning in the 1820s, the language and imagery of sports penetrated politics, cutting across the lines of class and party. Wielding a long, bat-like rail labeled "EQUAL RIGHTS AND FREE TERRITORY," Abraham Lincoln holds a baseball and appears ready to score a victory in the election. His three opponents—from left to right, John Bell (the candidate of a new Constitutional Union Party), Stephen A. Douglas, and John C. Breckinridge—will soon be "out." Indeed, according to the pro-Lincoln cartoonist, they were about to be "skunk'd." As Douglas laments, their attempt to put a "short stop" to Lincoln's presidential ambitions had failed. Museum of American Political Life.

majority in the electoral college. Breckinridge took 72 electoral votes by sweeping the Deep South and picking up Delaware, Maryland, and North Carolina. Douglas won 30 percent of the popular ballot but secured only 51 electoral votes in Missouri and New Jersey. The Republicans had united voters in the Northeast, Midwest, and Pacific coast behind free soil.

A revolution was in the making. "Oh My God!!! This morning heard that Lincoln was elected," Keziah Brevard, a widowed South Carolina plantation mistress and owner of two hundred slaves, scribbled in her diary. "Lord save us." Slavery had permeated the American federal republic so thoroughly that southerners saw it as a natural part of the constitutional order—an order that was now under siege. Fearful of a massive black uprising, Chief Justice Taney recalled "the horrors of St. Domingo [Haiti]." At the very least, warned John Townsend of South Carolina, a Republican administration in Washington would suppress "the inter-State slave trade" and thereby "cripple this vital Southern institution of slavery." To

PLACE EVENTS IN CONTEXT

What was the relationship between the collapse of the Second Party System and the Republican victory in the election of 1860?

many southerners, it seemed time to think carefully about Lincoln's 1858 statement that the Union must "become all one thing, or all the other."

 To see a longer excerpt of Keziah Brevard's diary, along with other primary sources from this period, see *Sources for America's History*.

SUMMARY

In this chapter, we examined four related themes: the ideology of Manifest Destiny and the westward movement of Americans in the 1840s, the impact of American traders and settlers on the Indian peoples of the Great Plains and California, the causes and consequences of the Mexican War (1846–1848), and the disintegration of the Second Party System during the 1850s.

We saw that the determination of Presidents John Tyler and James Polk to add territory and slave states to the Union pushed the United States into the Mexican War and into a new debate over the expansion of slavery. To resolve the resulting crisis, Henry Clay, Daniel Webster, and Stephen Douglas devised the Compromise of 1850. Their efforts were in vain: antislavery northerners defied the Fugitive Slave Act, and expansionist-minded southerners sought new slave states in the Caribbean. Ideology (the pursuit of absolutes) replaced politics (the art of compromise) as the ruling principle of American political life.

The Second Party System rapidly disintegrated. The Whig Party vanished, and two issue-oriented parties, the nativist American Party and the antislavery Republican Party, competed for its members. As the Republicans gained strength, the Democratic Party splintered into sectional factions over Bleeding Kansas and other slavery-related issues. The stage was set for Lincoln's victory in the climactic election of 1860.

C H A P T E R   R E V I E W

 MAKE IT STICK Go to **LearningCurve** to retain what you've read.

TERMS TO KNOW   Identify and explain the significance of each term below.

Key Concepts and Events

Manifest Destiny (p. 412)

Californios (p. 415)

"Fifty-four forty or fight!" (p. 418)

conscience Whigs (p. 421)

Wilmot Proviso (p. 421)

free-soil movement (p. 421)

squatter sovereignty (p. 424)

forty-niners (p. 425)

"slavery follows the flag" (p. 428)

Compromise of 1850 (p. 429)

personal-liberty laws (p. 431)

Gadsden Purchase (p. 431)

Ostend Manifesto (p. 431)

Kansas-Nebraska Act (p. 432)

American, or Know-Nothing, Party (p. 432)

"Bleeding Kansas" (p. 433)

Dred Scott v. Sandford (p. 433)

Freeport Doctrine (p. 438)

Key People

James K. Polk (p. 418)

Frederick Douglass (p. 421)

Zachary Taylor (p. 424)

Lewis Cass (p. 424)

Stephen Douglas (p. 431)

Harriet Beecher Stowe (p. 431)

John Brown (p. 433)

Abraham Lincoln (p. 437)

REVIEW QUESTIONS
Answer these questions to demonstrate your understanding of the chapter's main ideas.

1. In what specific ways did the ideology of Manifest Destiny influence events during the 1840s and 1850s?

2. What were the main constitutional arguments presented during the debate over slavery in the territories? Which of those arguments influenced Chief Justice Taney's opinion in *Dred Scott*?

3. How did the Compromise of 1850, the Kansas-Nebraska Act, and the *Dred Scott* decision seek to address the issue of slavery, and what was the effect of each of them on sectional conflicts?

4. **THEMATIC UNDERSTANDING** Some historians claim that the mistakes of a "blundering generation" of political leaders led, by 1860, to the imminent breakup of the Union. Using the events from "Politics and Power" on the thematic timeline on page 409, explain why you agree or disagree.

MAKING CONNECTIONS
Recognize the larger developments and continuities within and across chapters by answering these questions.

1. **ACROSS TIME AND PLACE** How were the American territorial acquisitions of the 1840s similar to, and/or different from, those of the Louisiana Purchase and the Paris Treaty of 1783 (discussed in Chapters 6 and 7)?

2. **VISUAL EVIDENCE** In *American Progress* (p. 411), why does John Gast choose Liberty to lead the republic westward? How does he interpret the American experience, and what stories does he tell in the image's foreground, middle ground, and background? How does the evidence in the chapter challenge Gast's interpretation of westward expansion?

MORE TO EXPLORE
Start here to learn more about the events discussed in this chapter.

Eric Foner, *Free Soil, Free Labor, Free Men* (1970). Still offers the best analysis of the ideology of the Republican Party.

Patricia Nelson Limerick, *The Legacy of Conquest* (1989). Highlights social conflicts in the West.

William A. Link, *Roots of Secession* (2003). A good state-focused study about the causes of secession.

Stephen Oates, *With Malice Toward None* (1977). A classic biography about Lincoln.

Leonard L. Richards, *The Slave Power: The Free North and Southern Domination, 1780–1860* (2000). Offers a broad cultural analysis.

The PBS documentary *The West* and its Web site (**pbs .org/weta/thewest**) offer a comprehensive history of the West, and the PBS Web site on the *U.S.-Mexican War: 1846–1848* (**pbs.org/usmexicanwar**) covers both American and Mexican perspectives of this pivotal event.

TIMELINE

Ask yourself why this chapter begins and ends with these dates and then identify the links among related events.

1844	• James Polk elected president
1845	• Texas admitted into Union
1846	• United States declares war on Mexico • Treaty with Britain divides Oregon Country • Wilmot Proviso approved by House but not by Senate
1847	• American troops capture Mexico City
1848	• Gold found in California • Treaty of Guadalupe Hidalgo transfers Mexican lands to United States • Free-Soil Party forms
1850	• President Taylor dies • Millard Fillmore assumes presidency • Compromise of 1850 preserves Union • Northern abolitionists reject Fugitive Slave Act
1851	• American (Know-Nothing) Party forms
1852	• Harriet Beecher Stowe publishes *Uncle Tom's Cabin*
1854	• Ostend Manifesto urges seizure of Cuba • Kansas-Nebraska Act tests policy of popular sovereignty • Republican Party forms
1856	• Turmoil in Kansas undermines popular sovereignty • James Buchanan elected president
1857	• *Dred Scott v. Sandford* allows slavery in U.S. territories
1858	• President Buchanan urges Congress to admit Kansas under the proslavery Lecompton constitution and seeks to buy and annex Cuba as a slave state • Abraham Lincoln debates Stephen Douglas for U.S. Senate seat
1859	• John Brown raids federal arsenal at Harpers Ferry
1860	• Abraham Lincoln elected president in four-way contest

KEY TURNING POINT: Three new political parties appeared in the six years from 1848 to 1854: Free-Soil, American (Know-Nothing), and Republican. What accounts for this upsurge in political activity, and what was its result?

14

Two Societies at War
1861–1865

What a scene it was," Union soldier Elisha Hunt Rhodes wrote in his diary at Gettysburg in July 1863. "Oh the dead and the dying on this bloody field." Thousands of men had already died, and the slaughter would continue for two more years. "Why is it that 200,000 men of one blood and tongue . . . [are] seeking one another's lives?" asked Confederate lieutenant R. M. Collins as another gruesome battle ended. "We could settle our differences by compromising and all be at home in ten days." But there was no compromise. "God wills this contest, and wills that it shall not yet end," President Abraham Lincoln reflected. "The Almighty has His own purposes."

While the reasons for the war are complex, racial slavery played a primary role. To southern whites, the Republican victory in 1860 presented an immediate danger to the slave-owning republic that had existed since 1776. "[O]ur struggle is for inherited rights," declared one southern leader. Southerners did not believe Lincoln when he promised not "directly or indirectly, to interfere with the institution of slavery in the States where it exists." Soon, a southern senator warned, "cohorts of Federal office-holders, Abolitionists, may be sent into [our] midst" to encourage slave revolts and, even worse, racial mixture. By *racial mixture*, white southerners meant sexual relations between black men and white women, given that white masters had already fathered untold thousands of children by their enslaved black women. "Better, far better! [to] endure all horrors of civil war," insisted a Confederate recruit, "than to see the dusky sons of Ham leading the fair daughters of the South to the altar." To preserve black subordination and white supremacy, radical southerners chose the dangerous enterprise of secession.

Lincoln and the North would not let them go in peace. Living in a world still ruled by monarchies, northern leaders believed that the collapse of the American Union might forever destroy the possibility of democratic republican governments. "We cannot escape history," Lincoln eloquently declared. "We shall nobly save, or meanly lose, the last best hope of earth."

And so came the conflict. Called the War Between the States by southerners and the War of the Rebellion by northerners, the struggle finally resolved the great issues of the Union and slavery. The costs were terrible: more American lives lost than the combined total for all the nation's other wars, and a century-long legacy of bitterness between the triumphant North and the vanquished white South.

IDENTIFY THE BIG IDEA

How did the military and political goals of the war bring significant changes to social, economic, and cultural life?

Fields of Death   Fought with mass armies and new weapons, the Civil War took a huge toll in human lives, as evidenced by this grisly photograph of a small section of the battlefield at Antietam, Maryland. The most costly single-day battle in American history, it left 22,700 dead, wounded, and missing Confederate and Union soldiers. After the equally bloody three-day battle at Shiloh, Tennessee, in April 1862, General Ulysses Grant surveyed a field "so covered with dead that it would have been possible to walk . . . in any direction, stepping on dead bodies, without a foot touching the ground." Library of Congress.

Secession and Military Stalemate, 1861–1862

Following Lincoln's election in November 1860, secessionist fervor swept through the Deep South. Veteran party leaders in Washington still hoped to save the Union. In the four months between Lincoln's election and his inauguration on March 4, 1861, they sought a new compromise.

The Secession Crisis

The Union collapsed first in South Carolina, the home of John C. Calhoun, nullification, and southern rights. Robert Barnwell Rhett and other fire-eaters had demanded secession since the Compromise of 1850, and their goal was now within reach. "Our enemies are about to take possession of the Government," warned one South Carolinian. Frightened by that prospect, a state convention voted unanimously on December 20, 1860, to dissolve "the union now subsisting between South Carolina and other States."

The Lower South Secedes Fire-eaters elsewhere in the Deep South quickly called similar conventions and organized mobs to attack local Union supporters. In early January, white Mississippians joyously enacted a secession ordinance, and Florida, Alabama, Georgia, and Louisiana quickly followed. Texans soon joined them, ousting Unionist governor Sam Houston and ignoring his warning that "the North . . . will overwhelm the South" (Map 14.1). In February, the jubilant secessionists met in Montgomery, Alabama, to proclaim a new nation: the Confederate States of America. Adopting a provisional constitution, the delegates named Mississippian Jefferson Davis, a former U.S. senator and secretary of war, as the Confederacy's president and Georgia congressman Alexander Stephens as vice president.

Secessionist fervor was less intense in the four states of the Middle South (Virginia, North Carolina, Tennessee, and Arkansas), where there were fewer slaves. White opinion was especially divided in the four border slave states (Maryland, Delaware, Kentucky, and Missouri), where yeomen farmers held greater political power and, from bitter experience as well as the writings of journalist Hilton Helper, knew that all too often "the slaveholders . . . have hoodwinked you." Reflecting such sentiments, the legislatures of Virginia and Tennessee refused to join the secessionist movement and urged a compromise.

Alabama Secession Flag

In January 1861, a Secession Convention in Alabama voted to leave the Union and marked their decision for independence by designating this pennant—created by a group of Montgomery women—as their official flag. Like John Gast's *American Progress* (p. 411), the Goddess of Liberty forms the central image. Here she holds a sword and a flag with a single star, symbolizing Alabama's new status as an independent republic. Alabama Department of Archives and History.

Meanwhile, the Union government floundered. President Buchanan declared secession illegal but—in line with his states' rights outlook—claimed that the federal government lacked authority to restore the Union by force. Buchanan's timidity prompted South Carolina's new government to demand the surrender of Fort Sumter (a federal garrison in Charleston Harbor) and to cut off its supplies. The president again backed down, refusing to use the navy to supply the fort.

The Crittenden Compromise Instead, the outgoing president urged Congress to find a compromise. The plan proposed by Senator John J. Crittenden of Kentucky received the most support. The **Crittenden Compromise** had two parts. The first, which Congress approved, called for a constitutional amendment to protect slavery from federal interference in any state where it already existed. Crittenden's second provision called for the westward extension of the Missouri Compromise line (36°30' north latitude) to the California border. The provision would ban slavery north of the line and allow bound labor to the south, including any territories "hereafter acquired," raising the prospect of expansion into Cuba or Central America. Congressional Republicans rejected Crittenden's second proposal on strict instructions from president-elect Lincoln. With good reason, Lincoln feared it

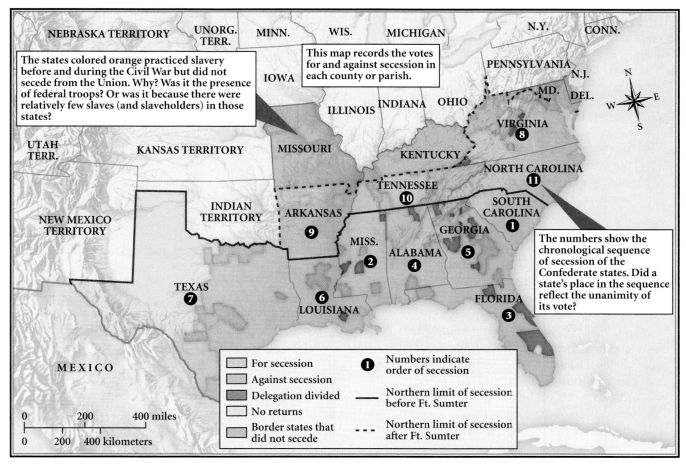

This map records the votes for and against secession in each county or parish.

The states colored orange practiced slavery before and during the Civil War but did not secede from the Union. Why? Was it the presence of federal troops? Or was it because there were relatively few slaves (and slaveholders) in those states?

The numbers show the chronological sequence of secession of the Confederate states. Did a state's place in the sequence reflect the unanimity of its vote?

For secession
Against secession
Delegation divided
No returns
Border states that did not secede

Numbers indicate order of secession
Northern limit of secession before Ft. Sumter
Northern limit of secession after Ft. Sumter

MAP 14.1
The Process of Secession, 1860–1861
The states of the Lower South had the highest concentration of slaves, and they led the secessionist movement. After the attack on Fort Sumter in April 1861, the states of the Upper South joined the Confederacy. Yeomen farmers in Tennessee and the backcountry of Alabama, Georgia, and Virginia opposed secession but, except in the future state of West Virginia, initially rallied to the Confederate cause. Consequently, the South entered the Civil War with its white population relatively united.

would unleash new imperialist adventures. "I want Cuba," Senator Albert G. Brown of Mississippi had candidly stated in 1858. "I want Tamaulipas, Potosi, and one or two other Mexican States . . . for the planting or spreading of slavery." In 1787, 1821, and 1850, the North and South had resolved their differences over slavery. In 1861, there would be no compromise.

In his March 1861 inaugural address, Lincoln carefully outlined his positions. He promised to safeguard slavery where it existed but vowed to prevent its expansion. Equally important, the Republican president declared that the Union was "perpetual"; consequently, the secession of the Confederate states was illegal. Lincoln asserted his intention to "hold, occupy, and possess" federal property in the seceded states and "to

collect duties and imposts" there. If military force was necessary to preserve the Union, Lincoln — like Democrat Andrew Jackson during the nullification crisis — would use it. The choice was the South's: Return to the Union, or face war.

The Upper South Chooses Sides

The South's decision came quickly. When Lincoln dispatched an unarmed ship to resupply Fort Sumter, Jefferson Davis and his associates in the Provisional Government of the Confederate States decided to seize the fort. The Confederate forces opened fire on April 12, with ardent fire-eater Edmund Ruffin supposedly firing the first cannon. Two days later, the Union

PLACE EVENTS IN CONTEXT
How important was the conflict at Fort Sumter, and would the Confederacy—or the Union—have gone to war without it?

defenders capitulated. On April 15, Lincoln called 75,000 state militiamen into federal service for ninety days to put down an insurrection "too powerful to be suppressed by the ordinary course of judicial proceedings."

Northerners responded to Lincoln's call to arms with wild enthusiasm. Asked to provide thirteen regiments of volunteers, Republican governor William Dennison of Ohio sent twenty. Many northern Democrats also lent their support. "Every man must be for the United States or against it," Democratic leader Stephen Douglas declared. "There can be no neutrals in this war, only patriots — or traitors." How then could the Democratic Party function as a "loyal opposition," supporting the Union while challenging certain Republican policies? It would not be an easy task.

Whites in the Middle and Border South now had to choose between the Union and the Confederacy, and their decision was crucial. Those eight states accounted for two-thirds of the whites in the slaveholding states, three-fourths of their industrial production, and well over half of their food. They were home to many of the nation's best military leaders, including Colonel Robert E. Lee of Virginia, a career officer whom veteran General Winfield Scott recommended to Lincoln to lead the new Union army. Those states were also geographically strategic. Kentucky, with its 500-mile border on the Ohio River, was essential to the movement of troops and supplies. Maryland was vital to the Union's security because it bordered the nation's capital on three sides.

The weight of its history as a slave-owning society decided the outcome in Virginia. On April 17, 1861, a convention approved secession by a vote of 88 to 55, with the dissenters concentrated in the state's yeomen-dominated northwestern counties. Elsewhere, Virginia whites embraced the Confederate cause. "The North was the aggressor," declared Richmond lawyer William Poague as he enlisted. "The South resisted her invaders." Refusing General Scott's offer of the Union command, Robert E. Lee resigned from the U.S. Army. "Save in defense of my native state," Lee told Scott, "I never desire again to draw my sword." Arkansas, Tennessee, and North Carolina quickly joined Virginia in the Confederacy.

Lincoln moved aggressively to hold strategic areas where

IDENTIFY CAUSES
Per Figure 14.1, was slave ownership in a state the main cause of early secession? What other factors drove the secession movement?

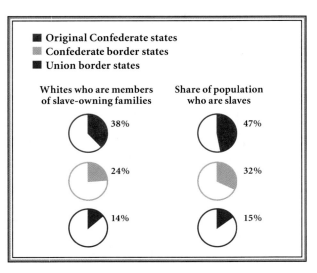

FIGURE 14.1
Slavery and Secession
As the pie charts indicate, slave labor dominated the economies of the Confederate states that initially seceded from the Union, but it was much less important in Confederate states further to the north that seceded later.

relatively few whites owned slaves (Figure 14.1). To secure the railway line connecting Washington to the Ohio River Valley, the president ordered General George B. McClellan to take control of northwestern Virginia. In October 1861, yeomen there voted overwhelmingly to create a breakaway territory, West Virginia. Unwilling to "act like madmen and cut our own throats merely to sustain . . . a most unwarrantable rebellion," West Virginia joined the Union in 1863. Unionists also carried the day in Delaware. In Maryland, where slavery was still entrenched, a pro-Confederate mob attacked Massachusetts troops traveling through Baltimore, causing the war's first combat deaths: four soldiers and twelve civilians. When Maryland secessionists destroyed railroad bridges and telegraph lines, Lincoln ordered Union troops to occupy the state and arrest Confederate sympathizers, including legislators. He released them only in November 1861, after Unionists had secured control of Maryland's government.

Lincoln was equally energetic in the Mississippi River Valley. To win control of Missouri (and the adjacent Missouri and Upper Mississippi rivers), Lincoln mobilized the state's German American militia, which strongly opposed slavery. In July, the German Americans defeated a force of Confederate sympathizers commanded by the state's governor. Despite continuing raids by Confederate guerrilla bands, which included the notorious outlaws Jesse and Frank James, the Union retained control of Missouri.

In Kentucky, where secessionist and Unionist sentiment was evenly balanced, Lincoln moved cautiously. He allowed Kentucky's thriving trade with the Confederacy to continue until August 1861, when Unionists took over the state government. When the Confederacy responded to the trade cutoff by invading Kentucky in September, Illinois volunteers commanded by Ulysses S. Grant drove them out. Mixing military force with political persuasion, Lincoln had kept four border states (Delaware, Maryland, Missouri, and Kentucky) and the northwestern portion of Virginia in the Union.

Setting War Objectives and Devising Strategies

Speaking as provisional president of the Confederacy in April 1861, Jefferson Davis identified the Confederates' cause with that of the Patriots of 1776: like their grandfathers, he said, white southerners were fighting for the "sacred right of self-government." The Confederacy sought "no conquest, no aggrandizement . . . ; all we ask is to be let alone." Davis's renunciation of expansion was probably a calculated short-run policy; after all, the quest to extend slavery into Kansas and Cuba had sparked Lincoln's election. Still, this decision simplified the Confederacy's military strategy; it needed only to defend its boundaries to achieve independence. Ignoring strong antislavery sentiment among potential European allies, the Confederate constitution explicitly ruled out gradual emancipation or any other law "denying or impairing the right of property in negro slaves." Indeed, Confederate vice president Alexander Stephens insisted that his nation's "cornerstone rests upon the great truth that the Negro is not equal to the white man, that slavery — subordination to the superior race — is his natural or normal condition."

Lincoln responded to Davis in a speech to Congress on July 4, 1861. He portrayed secession as an attack on representative government, America's great contribution to world history. The issue, Lincoln declared, was "whether a constitutional republic" had the will and the means to "maintain its territorial integrity against a domestic foe." Determined to crush the rebellion, Lincoln rejected General Winfield Scott's strategy of peaceful persuasion through economic sanctions and a naval blockade. Instead, he insisted on an aggressive military campaign to restore the Union.

Union Thrusts Toward Richmond Lincoln hoped that a quick strike against the Confederate capital of Richmond, Virginia, would end the rebellion. Many northerners were equally optimistic. "What a picnic," thought one New York volunteer, "to go down South for three months and clean up the whole business." So in July 1861, Lincoln ordered General Irvin McDowell's army of 30,000 men to attack General P. G. T. Beauregard's force of 20,000 troops at Manassas, a Virginia rail junction 30 miles southwest of Washington. McDowell launched a strong assault near Bull Run, but panic swept his troops when the Confederate soldiers counterattacked, shouting the hair-raising "rebel yell." "The peculiar corkscrew sensation that it sends down your backbone . . . can never be told," one Union veteran wrote. "You have to feel it." McDowell's troops — and the many civilians who had come to observe the battle — retreated in disarray to Washington.

The Confederate victory at Bull Run showed the strength of the rebellion. Lincoln replaced McDowell with General George McClellan and enlisted a million men to serve for three years in the new Army of the Potomac. A cautious military engineer, McClellan spent the winter of 1861–1862 training the recruits and launched a major offensive in March 1862. With great logistical skill, the Union general ferried 100,000 troops down the Potomac River to the Chesapeake Bay and landed them on the peninsula between the York and James rivers (Map 14.2). Ignoring Lincoln's advice to "strike a blow" quickly, McClellan advanced slowly toward Richmond, allowing the Confederates to mount a counterstrike. Thomas J. "Stonewall" Jackson marched a Confederate force rapidly northward through the Shenandoah Valley in western Virginia and threatened Washington. When Lincoln recalled 30,000 troops from McClellan's army to protect the Union capital, Jackson returned quickly to Richmond to bolster General Robert E. Lee's army. In late June, Lee launched a ferocious six-day attack that cost 20,000 casualties to the Union's 10,000. When McClellan failed to exploit the Confederates' losses, Lincoln ordered a withdrawal and Richmond remained secure.

> **COMPARE AND CONTRAST**
> In 1861 and 1862, what were the political and military strategies of the Confederate and Union leaders? Which side was the more successful and why?

Lee Moves North: Antietam Hoping for victories that would humiliate Lincoln's government, Lee went on the offensive. Joining with Jackson in northern

In September 1862, Union forces halted the Confederate invasion of Maryland with victories at South Mountain and Antietam (11 and 12).

To relieve pressure on Richmond, Confederate troops under General Stonewall Jackson made a run up the Shenandoah Valley, threatening Washington (4, 5, and 7).

The only major battle of 1861—Bull Run—took place about 30 miles southwest of the Union's capital. It left both armies in disarray.

At Fredericksburg (13) in December 1862, Confederate forces repulsed another Union thrust into the heart of Virginia.

The Peninsular Campaign (2 and 3; 6 and 8) began in May 1862 as an attempt by the Union armies to take Richmond by moving up the peninsula between the James and York rivers.

Assisted by Jackson's attacks, Lee repulsed the Union assault on Richmond and then advanced toward Washington. After another Confederate victory in the Second Battle of Bull Run (10) in August 1862, Lee's army moved into Maryland.

To help you to follow the sequence of the major battles of the eastern campaigns of 1862, each battle is dated and its place in the chronology denoted by a number in a circle.

Union Movements

- McDowell
- McClellan
- Frémont
- Banks
- Shields
- Pope
- Burnside
- ✴ Union victory

Confederate Movements

- Johnston
- Holmes
- Jackson
- Lee
- ✴ Confederate victory
- +++++ Railroad
- ❶ Sequence of battles

MAP 14.2

The Eastern Campaigns of 1862

Many of the great battles of the Civil War took place in the 125 miles separating the Union capital, Washington, D.C., and the Confederate capital, Richmond, Virginia. During 1862, Confederate generals Thomas Jonathan "Stonewall" Jackson and Robert E. Lee won battles that defended the Confederate capital (3, 6, 8, and 13) and launched offensive strikes against Union forces guarding Washington (1, 4, 5, 7, 9, and 10). They also suffered a defeat—at Antietam (12), in Maryland—that was almost fatal to the Confederate cause. As was often the case in the Civil War, the victors in these battles were either too bloodied or too timid to exploit their advantage.

Virginia, he routed Union troops in the Second Battle of Bull Run (August 1862) and then struck north through western Maryland. There, he nearly met with disaster. When the Confederate commander divided his force, sending Jackson to capture Harpers Ferry in West Virginia, a copy of Lee's orders fell into McClellan's hands. The Union general again failed to exploit his advantage, delaying an attack against Lee's depleted army, thereby allowing it to secure a strong defensive position west of Antietam Creek, near Sharpsburg,

Maryland. Outnumbered 87,000 to 50,000, Lee desperately fought off McClellan's attacks until Jackson's troops arrived and saved the Confederates from a major defeat. Appalled by the Union casualties, McClellan allowed Lee to retreat to Virginia.

The fighting at Antietam was savage. A Wisconsin officer described his men "loading and firing with demoniacal fury and shouting and laughing hysterically." A sunken road — nicknamed Bloody Lane — was filled with Confederate bodies two and three deep, and the advancing Union troops knelt on this "ghastly flooring" to shoot at the retreating Confederates. The battle at Antietam on September 17, 1862, remains the bloodiest single day in U.S. military history. Together,

the Confederate and Union dead numbered 4,800 and the wounded 18,500, of whom 3,000 soon died. (By comparison, there were 6,000 American casualties on D-Day, which began the invasion of Nazi-occupied France in World War II.)

In public, Lincoln claimed Antietam as a Union victory; privately, he criticized McClellan for not fighting Lee to the bitter end. A masterful organizer of men and supplies, McClellan refused to risk his troops, fearing that heavy casualties would undermine public support for the war. Lincoln worried more about the danger of a lengthy war. He dismissed McClellan and began a long search for an aggressive commanding general. His first choice, Ambrose E. Burnside, proved

The Battle of Pea Ridge, Arkansas, March 1862
Pea Ridge was the biggest battle of the Civil War fought west of the Mississippi and was of considerable strategic significance. By routing one Confederate army and holding another to a draw, outnumbered Union forces maintained their control of Missouri for the duration of the war. The lithograph, published in Chicago in 1889, commemorates the Union units — from Illinois and other midwestern states — who fought at Pea Ridge. Here the Union troops, half of whom were German immigrants, face a charging column of Confederate cavalry and infantry from Texas and Missouri and their Native American allies. Each side had about 1,000 men killed or wounded, with another 200 taken prisoner. Library of Congress.

to be more daring but less competent than McClellan. In December, after heavy losses in futile attacks against well-entrenched Confederate forces at Fredericksburg, Virginia, Burnside resigned his command, and Lincoln replaced him with Joseph "Fighting Joe" Hooker. As 1862 ended, Confederates were optimistic: they had won a stalemate in the East.

The War in the Mississippi Valley Meanwhile, Union commanders in the Upper South had been more successful (Map 14.3). Their goal was to control the Ohio, Mississippi, and Missouri rivers, dividing the Confederacy and reducing the mobility of its armies. Because Kentucky did not join the rebellion, the Union already dominated the Ohio River Valley. In February 1862, the Union army used an innovative tactic to take charge of the Tennessee and Mississippi rivers as well. General Ulysses S. Grant used riverboats clad with iron plates to capture Fort Donelson on the Cumberland River and Fort Henry on the Tennessee River. When Grant moved south toward Mississippi to seize critical railroad lines, Confederate troops led by Albert Sidney Johnston and P. G. T. Beauregard caught his army by surprise near a small log church at Shiloh, Tennessee. However, Grant relentlessly committed troops and forced a Confederate withdrawal. As the fighting at Shiloh ended on April 7, Grant surveyed a large field "so covered with dead that it would have been possible to walk over the clearing in any direction, stepping on dead bodies, without a foot touching the ground." The cost in lives was horrific, but Lincoln was resolute: "What I want . . . is generals who will fight battles and win victories."

Three weeks later, Union naval forces commanded by David G. Farragut struck the Confederacy from the Gulf of Mexico. They captured New Orleans, the South's financial center and largest city. The Union army also took control of fifteen hundred plantations and 50,000 slaves in the surrounding region, striking a strong blow against slavery. Workers on some plantations looted their owners' mansions; others refused to labor unless they were paid wages. "[Slavery there] is forever destroyed and worthless," declared one northern reporter. Union victories had significantly undermined Confederate strength in the Mississippi River Valley.

Toward Total War

The military carnage in 1862 revealed that the war would be long and costly. Grant later remarked that, after Shiloh, he "gave up all idea of saving the Union

except by complete conquest." Lincoln agreed. During the summer of 1862, he abandoned hope for a compromise peace that would restore the Union. Instead, he committed the nation to a **total war** that would mobilize all of society's resources — economic, political, and cultural — in support of the North's military effort and end slavery in the South. Aided by the Republican Party and a talented cabinet, Lincoln gradually organized an effective central government able to wage all-out war; and urged on by antislavery politicians and activists, he moved toward a controversial proclamation of emancipation. Jefferson Davis had less success at harnessing southern resources, because the eleven states of the Confederacy remained suspicious of centralized rule and southern yeomen grew increasingly skeptical of the war effort.

Mobilizing Armies and Civilians

Initially, patriotic fervor filled both armies with eager young volunteers. All he heard was "War! War! War!" one Union recruit recalled. Even those of sober minds joined up. "I don't think a young man ever went over all the considerations more carefully than I did," reflected William Saxton of Cincinnatus, New York. "It might mean sickness, wounds, loss of limb, and even life itself. . . . But my country was in danger." The southern call for volunteers was even more successful, thanks to its strong military tradition and a culture that stressed duty and honor. "Would you, My Darling, . . . be willing to leave your Children under such a [despotic Union] government?" James B. Griffin of Edgefield, South Carolina, asked his wife. "No — I know you would sacrifice every comfort on earth, rather than submit to it." However, enlistments declined as potential recruits learned the realities of mass warfare: epidemic diseases in the camps and wholesale death on the battlefields. Both governments soon faced the need for conscription.

The Military Draft The Confederacy acted first. In April 1862, following the bloodshed at Shiloh, the Confederate Congress imposed the first legally binding **draft (conscription)** in American history. New laws required existing soldiers to serve for the duration of the war and mandated three years of military service from all men between the ages of eighteen and thirty-five. In September 1862, after the heavy casualties at Antietam, the age limit jumped to forty-five. The South's draft had two loopholes, both controversial. First, it exempted one white man — the planter, a son, or an overseer — for each twenty slaves, allowing some

MAP 14.3

The Western Campaigns, 1861–1862

As the Civil War intensified in 1862, Union and Confederate military and naval forces sought control of the great valleys of the Ohio, Tennessee, and Mississippi rivers. From February through April 1862, Union armies moved south through western Tennessee (1–3 and 5). By the end of June, Union naval forces controlled the Mississippi River north of Memphis (4, 10, and 11) and from the Gulf of Mexico to Vicksburg (6, 7, 9, and 12). These military and naval victories gave the Union control of crucial transportation routes, kept Missouri in the Union, and carried the war to the borders of the states of the Lower South.

Kansas Volunteers, 1862
When they posed for this tintype photograph in 1862, these men from Company E, 8th Kansas Volunteer Infantry, had marched hundreds of miles through Kentucky and Tennessee in a largely fruitless pursuit of a Confederate army and wore the look of battle-hardened troops. Some of these volunteers appear to be in their thirties or forties, and perhaps were abolitionist veterans of the civil strife in Bloody Kansas during the 1850s. Kansas State Historical Society.

whites on large plantations to avoid military service. This provision, a Mississippi legislator warned Jefferson Davis, "has aroused a spirit of rebellion in some places." Second, draftees could hire substitutes. By the time the Confederate Congress closed this loophole in 1864, the price of a substitute had soared to $300 in gold, three times the annual wage of a skilled worker. Laborers and yeomen farmers angrily complained that it was "a rich man's war and a poor man's fight."

Consequently, some southerners refused to serve. Because the Confederate constitution vested sovereignty in the individual states, the government in Richmond could not compel military service. Independent-minded governors such as Joseph Brown of Georgia and Zebulon Vance of North Carolina simply ignored President Davis's first draft call in early 1862. Elsewhere, state judges issued writs of **habeas corpus** — legal instruments used to protect people from arbitrary arrest — and ordered the Confederate army to release reluctant draftees. However, the Confederate Congress

PLACE EVENTS IN CONTEXT
How did the Union and Confederacy mobilize their populations for war, and how effective were these methods?

overrode the judges' authority to free conscripted men, so the government was able to keep substantial armies in the field well into 1864.

The Union government acted more ruthlessly toward draft resisters and Confederate sympathizers. In Missouri and other border states, Union commanders levied special taxes on southern supporters. Lincoln went further, suspending habeas corpus and, over the course of the war, temporarily imprisoning about 15,000 southern sympathizers without trial. He also gave military courts jurisdiction over civilians who discouraged enlistments or resisted the draft, preventing acquittals by sympathetic local juries. However, most Union governments used incentives to lure recruits. To meet the local quotas set by the Militia Act of 1862, towns, counties, and states used cash bounties of as much as $600 (about $11,000 today) and signed up nearly 1 million men. The Union also allowed men to avoid military service by providing a substitute or paying a $300 fee.

When the Enrollment Act of 1863 finally initiated conscription, recent German and Irish immigrants often refused to serve. It was not their war, they said.

Northern Democrats used the furor over conscription to bolster support for their party, which increasingly criticized Lincoln's policies. They accused Lincoln of drafting poor whites to liberate enslaved blacks, who would then flood the cities and take their jobs. Slavery was nearly "dead, [but] the negro is not, there is the misfortune," declared a Democratic newspaper in Cincinnati. In July 1863, the immigrants' hostility to conscription and blacks sparked riots in New York City. For five days, Irish and German workers ran rampant, burning draft offices, sacking the homes of influential Republicans, and attacking the police. The rioters lynched and mutilated a dozen African Americans, drove hundreds of black families from their homes, and burned down the Colored Orphan Asylum. To suppress the mobs, Lincoln rushed in Union troops who had just fought at Gettysburg; they killed more than a hundred rioters.

The Union government won much stronger support from native-born middle-class citizens. In 1861, prominent New Yorkers established the U.S. Sanitary Commission to provide the troops with clothing, food, and medical services. Seven thousand local auxiliaries assisted the commission's work. "I almost weep," reported a local agent, "when these plain rural people come to send their simple offerings to absent sons and brothers." The commission also recruited battlefield nurses and doctors for the Union Army Medical Bureau. Despite these efforts, dysentery, typhoid, and malaria spread through the camps, as did mumps and measles, viruses that were often deadly to rural recruits. Diseases and infections killed about 250,000 Union soldiers, nearly twice the 135,000 who died in combat. Still, thanks to the Sanitary Commission, Union troops had a far lower mortality rate than soldiers fighting in nineteenth-century European wars. Confederate

The Business of Recruiting an Army

Even before the antidraft riots in New York City in July 1863, Union governments used monetary bonuses to induce men to join the army, and the payments increased as the war continued. George Law's painting shows a New York recruiting post in 1864. To meet the state's quota of 30,000 men, the county and state governments offered volunteers bounties of $300 and $75 — on top of a U.S. government bounty of $302. The total — some $677 — was serious money at a time when the average worker earned $1.70 for a ten-hour day. Anne S. K. Brown Military Collection, Brown University Library.

Hospital Nursing

Working as nurses in battlefront hospitals, thousands of Union and Confederate women gained firsthand experience of the horrors of war. A sense of calm prevails in this behind-the-lines Union hospital in Nashville, Tennessee, as nurse Anne Belle tends to the needs of soldiers recovering from their wounds. Most Civil War nurses were volunteers with little medical training; they spent time cooking and cleaning for their patients as well as tending their injuries. U.S. Army Military History Institute.

troops were less fortunate, despite the efforts of thousands of women who volunteered as nurses, because the Confederate army's health system was poorly organized. Scurvy was a special problem for southern soldiers; lacking vitamin C in their diets, they suffered muscle ailments and had low resistance to camp diseases (Thinking Like a Historian, p. 458).

So much death created new industries and cultural rituals. Embalmers devised a zinc chloride fluid to preserve soldiers' bodies, allowing them to be shipped home for burial, an innovation that began modern funeral practices. Military cemeteries with hundreds of crosses in neat rows replaced the landscaped "rural cemeteries" in vogue in American cities before the Civil War. As thousands of mothers, wives, and sisters mourned the deaths of fallen soldiers, they faced changed lives. Confronting utter deprivation, working-class women grieved for the loss of a breadwinner. Middle-class wives often had financial resources but, having embraced the affectionate tenets of domesticity, mourned the death of a loved one by wearing black crape "mourning" dresses and other personal accessories of death. The destructive war, in concert with the emerging consumer culture and ethic of domesticity,

produced a new "cult of mourning" among the middle and upper classes.

Women in Wartime As tens of thousands of wounded husbands and sons limped home, their wives and sisters helped them rebuild their lives. Another 200,000 women worked as volunteers in the Sanitary Commission and the Freedman's Aid Society, which collected supplies for liberated slaves.

The war also drew more women into the wage-earning workforce as nurses, clerks, and factory operatives. Dorothea Dix (Chapter 11) served as superintendent of female nurses and, by successfully combating the prejudice against women providing medical treatment to men, opened a new occupation to women. Thousands of educated Union women became government clerks, while southern women staffed the efficient Confederate postal service. In both societies, millions of women took over farm tasks; filled jobs in schools and offices; and worked in textile, shoe, and food-processing factories. A few even became spies, scouts, and (disguising themselves as men) soldiers. As Union nurse Clara Barton, who later founded the American Red Cross, recalled, "At the war's end, woman was at least fifty years in advance of the normal position which continued peace would have assigned her."

Mobilizing Resources

Wars are usually won by the side that possesses greater resources. In that regard, the Union had a distinct advantage. With nearly two-thirds of the nation's population, two-thirds of the railroad mileage, and almost 90 percent of the industrial output, the North's economy was far superior to that of the South (Figure 14.2). Furthermore, many of its arms factories were equipped for mass production.

Still, the Confederate position was far from weak. Virginia, North Carolina, and Tennessee had substantial industrial capacity. Richmond, with its Tredegar Iron Works, was an important manufacturing center, and in 1861 it acquired the gun-making machinery from the U.S. armory at Harpers Ferry. The production at the Richmond armory, the purchase of Enfield rifles from Britain, and the capture of 100,000 Union guns enabled the Confederacy to provide every infantryman with a modern rifle-musket by 1863.

Moreover, with 9 million people, the Confederacy could mobilize enormous armies. Enslaved blacks, one-third of the population, became part of the war effort by producing food for the army and raw cotton for export. Confederate leaders counted on **King**

FIGURE 14.2
Economies, North and South, 1860
The military advantages of the North were even greater than this chart suggests. The population figures for the South include slaves, whom the Confederacy feared to arm. Also, the South's commodity output was primarily in farm goods rather than manufactures. Finally, southern factories were much smaller on average than those in the North.

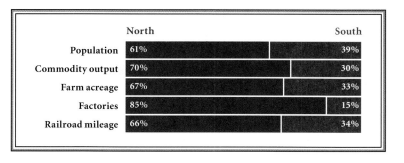

	North	South
Population	61%	39%
Commodity output	70%	30%
Farm acreage	67%	33%
Factories	85%	15%
Railroad mileage	66%	34%

Cotton—the leading American export and a crucial staple of the nineteenth-century economy—to purchase clothes, boots, blankets, and weapons from abroad. Leaders also saw cotton as a diplomatic weapon that would persuade Britain and France, which had large textile industries, to assist the Confederacy.

However, British manufacturers had stockpiled cotton and developed new sources in Egypt and India. Still, the South received some foreign support. Although Britain never recognized the Confederacy as an independent nation, it treated the rebel government as a belligerent power—with the right under international

Richmond: Capital City and Industrial Center
The Confederacy chose Richmond as its capital because of the historic importance of Virginia as the home of Washington, Jefferson, Madison, and Monroe. However, Richmond was also a major industrial center. Exploiting the city's location at the falls of the James River, the city's entrepreneurs had developed a wide range of industries: flour mills, tobacco factories, railroad and port facilities, and, most important, a substantial iron industry. In 1861, the Tredegar Iron Works employed nearly a thousand workers and, as the only facility in the South that could manufacture large machinery and heavy weapons, made a major contribution to the Confederate war effort. The Library of Virginia.

Military Deaths — and Lives Saved — During the Civil War

The Civil War, like all wars before and since, encouraged innovation in both the destruction and the saving of human life. More than 620,000 soldiers—360,000 on the Union side and 260,000 Confederates—died during the war, about 20 percent of those who served. However, thanks to advances in camp hygiene and battlefield treatment, the Union death rate was about 54–58 per 1,000 soldiers per year, less than half the level for British and French troops during the Crimean War of 1854–1855.

1. Report by surgeon Charles S. Tipler, medical director of the Army of the Potomac, January 4, 1862.

Most Civil War deaths came from disease. The major killers were bacterial intestinal diseases—typhoid fever, diarrhea, and dysentery—which spread because of unsanitary conditions in the camps.

The aggregate strength of the forces from which I have received reports is 142,577. Of these, 47,836 have been under treatment in the field and general hospitals, 35,915 of whom have been returned to duty, and 281 have died; 9,281 remained under treatment at the end of the month; . . .

The diseases from which our men have suffered most have been continued remittent and typhoid fevers, measles, diarrhea, dysentery, and the various forms of catarrh [heavy discharge of mucus from the nose]. Of all the scourges incident to armies in the field I suppose that chronic diarrheas and dysenteries have always been the most prevalent and the most fatal. I am happy to say that in this army they are almost unknown. We have but 280 cases of chronic diarrhea and 69 of chronic dysentery reported in the month of November.

2. Minie ball wounds: femur shot by Springfield 1862 rifle and Private George W. Lemon, 1867.

Ninety percent of battle casualties were the victims of a new technology: musket-rifles that fired lethal soft-lead bullets called minie balls (after their inventor, Claude-Étienne Minié). The rifle-musket revolutionized military strategy by enormously strengthening defensive forces. Infantrymen could now kill reliably at 300 yards — triple the previous range of muskets. Initially, the new technology baffled commanders, who continued to use the tactics perfected during the heyday of the musket and bayonet charge, sending waves of infantrymen against enemy positions.

A minie ball strike to the abdomen, chest, or head was usually fatal, but injuries to the limbs gave some hope of survival, given advances in battlefield surgery. When

Private George W. Lemon suffered a minie ball wound to his femur similar to the one shown here (below), surgeons amputated his leg below the hip and, after the war, fitted him with a prosthetic leg.

Source: National Museum of Health & Medicine, Armed Forces Institute of Pathology.

Source: Courtesy National Library of Medicine.

3. **Kate Cumming, April 23, 1862, journal entry on treating a Confederate victim after the Battle of Shiloh.** *Union surgeons performed 29,980 battlefield amputations during the Civil War. Confederate records are less complete, but surgeons apparently undertook about 28,000 amputations. They quickly removed limbs too shattered to mend, which increased the chances of survival. According to one witness, "surgeons and their assistants, stripped to the waist and bespattered with blood, stood around, some holding the poor fellows while others, armed with long, bloody knives and saws, cut and sawed away with frightful rapidity, throwing the mangled limbs on a pile nearby as soon as removed." This journal entry from a young Confederate nurse in Corinth, Mississippi, describes the plight of one such victim after the Battle of Shiloh.*

A young man whom I have been attending is going to have his arm cut off. Poor fellow! I am doing all I can to cheer him. He says that he knows that he will die, as all who have had limbs amputated in this hospital have died. . . . He lived only a few hours after his amputation.

4. **William Williams Keen, MD, "Surgical Reminiscences of the Civil War," 1905.** *Although 73 percent of the Union amputees survived the war, infected wounds—deadly gangrene—took the lives of most soldiers who suffered certain gunshot injuries in this pre-antibiotic, pre-antiseptic era. Keen, who later became the first brain surgeon in the United States, served as a surgeon in the Union army.*

Not more than one incontestable example of recovery from a gunshot wound of the stomach and not a single incontestable case of wound of the small intestines are recorded during the entire war among the almost 250,000 wounded. . . .

Of 852 amputations of the shoulder-joint, 236 died, a mortality of 28.5 per cent. Of 66 cases of amputation of the hip-joint, 55, or 83.3 per cent died. Of 155 cases of trephining [cutting a hole in the skull to relieve pressure], 60 recovered and 95 died, a mortality of over 61 per cent. Of 374 ligations of the femoral artery, 93 recovered and 281 died, a mortality of over 75 per cent.

These figures afford a striking evidence of the dreadful mortality of military surgery in the days before antisepsis and first-aid packages. Happily such death-rates can never again be seen, at least in civilized warfare.

5. **John Tooker, MD, "Aspects of Medicine, Nursing, and the Civil War," 2007.** *The Union doctor Jonathan Letterman pioneered a new method of battlefield triage that was adopted by the entire army in 1864.*

Letterman had devised an efficient and, for the times, modern system of mass casualty management, beginning with first aid adjacent to the battlefield, removal of the wounded by an organized ambulance system to field hospitals for urgent and stabilizing treatment, such as wound closure and amputation, and then referral to general hospitals for longer term definitive management. This three-stage approach to casualty management, strengthened by effective and efficient transport, earned Letterman the title of "The Father of Battlefield Medicine."

Sources: (1) *The War of the Rebellion: A Compilation of the Official Records of the Union and Confederate Armies* (Washington, DC: Government Printing Office, 1889), Series 1, Vol. 5 (Part V), 111–112; (3) Kate Cumming, *A Journal of Hospital Life in the Confederate Army of Tennessee* (Louisville, KY: John P. Morton & Company, 1866), 19; (4) William Williams Keen, "Surgical Reminiscences of the Civil War," in *Addresses and Other Papers* (Philadelphia: W. B. Saunders, 1905), 433–434; (5) John Tooker, "Antietam: Aspects of Medicine, Nursing, and the Civil War," National Center for Biotechnology Information, U.S. National Library of Medicine, National Institutes of Health.

ANALYZING THE EVIDENCE

1. Based on Tipler's report (source 1), would you say the Union army was healthy or unhealthy? Ready for battle or not?

2. Consider sources 2–4. How do you think the reentry of tens of thousands of maimed veterans into civil society affected American culture?

3. What do sources 3–5 suggest about the successes and limitations of battlefield medicine during the Civil War?

4. Consider the Civil War in the context of the Industrial Revolution. What was the impact of factory production and technological advances on the number of weapons and their killing power? And how might the organizational innovations of the Industrial Revolution pertain to the conflict? In this regard, what do you make of the new method of battlefield triage pioneered by Union doctor Jonathan Letterman (source 5)?

PUTTING IT ALL TOGETHER

As a "total war" the Civil War involved the citizenry as well as the military, marshaling all of the two societies' resources and ingenuity. Using your understanding of these documents and the textbook, write an essay that discusses the relation of the war to technology, medicine, public finance, and the lives of women on the battle lines and the home front.

law to borrow money and purchase weapons. The odds, then, did not necessarily favor the Union, despite its superior resources.

Republican Economic and Fiscal Policies

To mobilize northern resources, the Republican-dominated Congress enacted a neomercantilist program of government-assisted economic development that far surpassed Henry Clay's American System (Chapter 10). The Republicans imposed high tariffs (averaging nearly 40 percent) on various foreign goods, thereby encouraging domestic industries. To boost agricultural output, they offered "free land" to farmers. The Homestead Act of 1862 gave settlers the title to 160 acres of public land after five years of residence. To create an integrated national banking system (far more powerful than the First and Second Banks of the United States), Secretary of the Treasury Salmon P. Chase forced thousands of local banks to accept federal charters and regulations.

Finally, the Republican Congress implemented Clay's program for a nationally financed transportation system. Expansion to the Pacific, the California gold rush, and subsequent discoveries of gold, silver, copper, and other metals in Nevada, Montana, and other western lands had revived demands for such a network. Therefore, in 1862, Congress chartered the Union Pacific and Central Pacific companies to build a transcontinental railroad line and granted them lavish subsidies. This economic program won the allegiance of farmers, workers, and entrepreneurs and bolstered the Union's ability to fight a long war.

TRACE CHANGE OVER TIME

How did the economic policies of the Republican-controlled Congress redefine the character of the federal government?

New industries sprang up to provide the Union army — and its 1.5 million men — with guns, clothes, and food. Over the course of the war, soldiers consumed more than half a billion pounds of pork and other packed meats. To meet this demand, Chicago railroads built new lines to carry thousands of hogs and cattle to the city's stockyards and slaughterhouses. By 1862, Chicago had passed Cincinnati as the meatpacking capital of the nation, bringing prosperity to thousands of midwestern farmers and great wealth to Philip D. Armour and other meatpacking entrepreneurs.

Bankers and financiers likewise found themselves pulled into the war effort. The annual spending of the Union government shot up from $63 million in 1860 to more than $865 million in 1864. To raise that enormous sum, the Republicans created a modern system of public finance that secured funds in three ways. First, the government increased tariffs; placed high duties on alcohol and tobacco; and imposed direct taxes on business corporations, large inheritances, and the incomes of wealthy citizens. These levies paid about 20 percent of the cost. Second, interest-paying bonds issued by the U.S. Treasury financed another 65 percent. The National Banking Acts of 1863 and 1864 forced most banks to buy those bonds; and Philadelphia banker and Treasury Department agent Jay Cooke used newspaper ads and 2,500 subagents to persuade a million northern families to buy them.

The Union paid the remaining 15 percent by printing paper money. The Legal Tender Act of 1862 authorized $150 million in paper currency — soon known as **greenbacks** — and required the public to accept them as legal tender. Like the Continental currency of the Revolutionary era, greenbacks could not be exchanged for specie; however, the Treasury issued a limited amount of paper money, so it lost only a small part of its face value.

If a modern fiscal system was one result of the war, immense concentrations of capital in many industries — meatpacking, steel, coal, railroads, textiles, shoes — was another. The task of supplying the huge war machine, an observer noted, gave a few men "the command of millions of money." Such massed financial power threatened not only the prewar society of small producers but also the future of democratic self-government (America Compared, p. 461). Americans "are never again to see the republic in which we were born," lamented abolitionist and social reformer Wendell Phillips.

The South Resorts to Coercion and Inflation

The economic demands on the South were equally great, but, true to its states' rights philosophy, the Confederacy initially left most matters to the state governments. However, as the realities of total war became clear, Jefferson Davis's administration took extraordinary measures. It built and operated shipyards, armories, foundries, and textile mills; commandeered food and scarce raw materials such as coal, iron, copper, and lead; requisitioned slaves to work on fortifications; and directly controlled foreign trade.

The Confederate Congress and ordinary southern citizens opposed many of Davis's initiatives, particularly those involving taxes. The Congress refused to tax cotton exports and slaves, the most valuable property held by wealthy planters, and the urban middle classes and yeomen farm families refused to pay more than their fair share. Consequently, the Confederacy covered less than 10 percent of its expenditures through

War Debt: Britain and the United States, 1830–1900

Wars cost money, sometimes a lot of money, and nations often pay for them by issuing bonds and expanding the national debt. The British national debt grew enormously between 1750 and 1815 as it fought a great series of wars, all of which involved either its American colonies or the United States: the Great War for Empire (1754–1763), the War of American Independence (1776–1783), and the Wars of the French Revolution and Napoleon (1793–1815). Consequently, Britain's national debt peaked in 1815 at 260 percent of its gross domestic product (GDP). Even in 1830, after years of high taxation and economic growth, the debt amounted to 180 percent of British GDP.

By comparison, the United States in 1830 was virtually debt-free, as the policies of Jeffersonian Republicans reduced its debt from about 27 percent of GDP in 1790 to less than 5 percent. Ample tariff revenues and the frugal policies of Presidents Andrew Jackson and Martin Van Buren then cut the debt nearly to zero by the early 1840s. Even the war with Mexico barely raised the level of the debt, thanks to the return of prosperity and the growth of GDP between 1844 and 1857.

Then came the Civil War, which boosted the Union debt from $62 million in 1860 to $2.2 billion at the end of 1865, a 1,500 percent increase. (The Fourteenth Amendment, ratified in 1868, declared "illegal and void" all debts incurred by the Confederacy.) In relation to GDP, the U.S. national debt shot up to 27 percent, the same level as 1790, and then—thanks again to tariff revenue—decreased gradually to about 10 percent of GDP by 1900. By then, the British national debt had fallen to about 40 percent of its GDP, as the British—the world's strongest power—mostly avoided new wars and built a prosperous commercial and industrial economy. The cost of war, civil or international, may well be a high national debt.

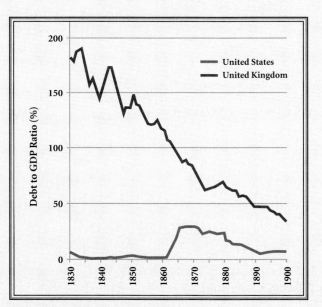

FIGURE 14.3
United States and United Kingdom National Debt as a Percentage of Gross Domestic Product, 1830–1900

QUESTIONS FOR ANALYSIS

1. In 1864, President Lincoln lamented: "This war of ours, in its magnitude and in its duration, is one of the most terrible. It has produced a national debt and taxation unprecedented, at least in this country." Given the relative size of the Union debt in relation to that of Britain, were Lincoln's worries exaggerated?

2. In 2012, the national debt of the United States—now the world's premier economic and military power—was nearly 100 percent of GDP and, since 1940, has averaged about 60 percent of GDP. Given those facts, and the evidence in this chart, is it fair to conclude that one of the costs of global power is a high national debt?

taxation. The government paid another 30 percent by borrowing, but wealthy planters and foreign bankers grew increasingly fearful that the South would never redeem its bonds.

Consequently, the Confederacy paid 60 percent of its war costs by printing paper money. The flood of currency created a spectacular inflation: by 1865, prices had risen to ninety-two times their 1861 level. As food prices soared, riots erupted in more than a dozen southern cities and towns. In Richmond, several hundred women broke into bakeries, crying, "Our children are starving while the rich roll in

A Southern Refugee Family

As Union and Confederate armies swept back and forth across northern Virginia and other war zones, the civilian population feared for its property and personal security. Here, two southern women—their husbands presumably away at war—have hitched up their mules and piled their goods and children on a farm wagon in order to flee the fighting. Lucky refugees had relatives in safe areas; others had to rely on the goodwill of strangers. National Archives.

wealth." In Randolph County, Alabama, women confiscated grain from a government warehouse "to prevent starvation of themselves and their families." As inflation spiraled upward, southerners refused to accept paper money, whatever the consequences. When South Carolina storekeeper Jim Harris refused the depreciated currency presented by Confederate soldiers, they raided his storehouse and, he claimed, "robbed it of about five thousand dollars worth of goods." Army supply officers likewise seized goods from merchants and offered payment in worthless IOUs. Facing a public that feared strong government and high taxation, the Confederacy could sustain the war effort only by seizing its citizens' property — and by championing white supremacy: President Davis warned that a Union victory would destroy slavery "and reduce the whites to the degraded position of the African race."

The Turning Point: 1863

By 1863, the Lincoln administration had created an efficient war machine and a set of strategic priorities. Henry Adams, the grandson of John Quincy Adams and a future novelist and historian, noted the change from his diplomatic post in London: "Little by little, one began to feel that, behind the chaos in Washington power was taking shape; that it was massed and guided as it had not been before." Slowly but surely, the tide of the struggle turned against the Confederacy.

Emancipation

When the war began, antislavery Republicans demanded that abolition be a goal of the war. The fighting should continue, said a Massachusetts abolitionist, "until the Slave power is completely subjugated, and *emancipation made certain*." Because slave-grown crops sustained the Confederacy, activists justified black emancipation on military grounds. As Frederick Douglass put it, "Arrest that hoe in the hands of the Negro, and you smite the rebellion in the very seat of its life."

"Contrabands" As abolitionists pressed their case, African Americans exploited wartime chaos to seize freedom for themselves. When three slaves reached the camp of Union general Benjamin Butler in Virginia in May 1861, he labeled them "contraband of war" (enemy property that can be legitimately seized, according to international law) and refused to return them. Butler's term stuck, and soon thousands of **"contrabands"** were camping with Union armies. Near Fredericksburg, Virginia, an average of 200 blacks appeared every day, "with their packs on their backs and handkerchiefs tied over their heads — men, women, little children, and babies." This influx created a humanitarian crisis; abolitionist Harriet Jacobs reported that hundreds of refugees were "[p]acked together in the most miserable quarters," where many died from smallpox and dysentery. To provide legal status to the refugees — some 400,000 by the war's end — in August 1861 Congress passed the Confiscation Act, which authorized the seizure of all property, including slave property, used to support the rebellion.

With the Confiscation Act, **Radical Republicans** — the members of the party who had been bitterly opposed to the "Slave Power" since the mid-1850s — began to use wartime legislation to destroy slavery. Their leaders were treasury secretary Salmon Chase, Senator Charles Sumner of Massachusetts, and Representative Thaddeus Stevens of Pennsylvania. A longtime member of Congress, Stevens was a masterful politician, skilled at fashioning legislation that could win majority support. In April 1862, Stevens and the Radicals persuaded Congress to end slavery in the District of Columbia by providing compensation for owners; in June, Congress outlawed slavery in the federal territories (finally enacting the Wilmot Proviso of 1846); and in July, it passed a second Confiscation Act, which declared "forever free" the thousands of refugee slaves and all slaves captured by the Union army. Emancipation had become an instrument of war.

The Emancipation Proclamation Initially, Lincoln rejected emancipation as a war aim, but faced with thousands of refugees and Radical Republican pressure, he moved cautiously toward that goal. The president

Eastman Johnson, *A Ride for Freedom — The Fugitive Slaves*, c. 1862

At the second battle of Manassas in September 1862, American genre painter Eastman Johnson (1824–1906) witnessed this "veritable incident" of an African American family fleeing slavery — and then painted it. A powerful, split-second image of the riders' silhouettes, Johnson's painting captures the father looking forward toward freedom, while the mother cradles a young child and looks back apprehensively for possible pursuers. By "freeing themselves," this family and thousands of blacks set the stage for Lincoln's Emancipation Proclamation. Brooklyn Museum of Art, New York, USA/The Bridgeman Art Library.

drafted a general proclamation of emancipation in July 1862, and he publicly linked black freedom with the preservation of the Union in August. "If I could save the Union without freeing any slave, I would do it," Lincoln told Horace Greeley of the *New York Tribune*, "and if I could save it by freeing all the slaves, I would do it."

Now he waited for a Union victory. Considering the Battle of Antietam "an indication of the Divine Will," Lincoln issued a preliminary proclamation of emancipation on September 22, 1862, basing its legal authority on his duty as commander in chief to suppress the rebellion. The proclamation legally abolished slavery in all states that remained out of the Union on January 1, 1863. The rebel states could preserve slavery by renouncing secession. None chose to do so.

The proclamation was politically astute. Lincoln conciliated slave owners in the Union-controlled border states, such as Maryland and Missouri, by leaving slavery intact in those states. It also permitted slavery to continue in areas occupied by Union armies: western and central Tennessee, western Virginia, and southern Louisiana. In Indian Territory, also under Union control, most mixed-blood Cherokee slave owners remained committed to the Confederacy and to bondage. They did not formally free their 4,000 slaves until July 1866, when a treaty with the U.S. government specified that their ex-slaves "shall have all the rights of native Cherokee."

Consequently, the **Emancipation Proclamation** did not immediately free a single slave. Yet, as abolitionist Wendell Phillips understood, Lincoln's proclamation had moved slavery to "the edge of Niagara," and would soon sweep it over the brink. Advancing Union troops became the agents of slavery's destruction. "I became free in 1863, in the summer, when the yankees come by and said I could go work for myself," recalled Jackson Daniel of Maysville, Alabama. As Lincoln now saw it, "the old South is to be destroyed and replaced by new propositions and ideas"—a system of free labor.

Hailed by reformers in Europe, emancipation was extraordinarily controversial in America. In the Confederacy, Jefferson Davis labeled it the "most execrable measure recorded in the history of guilty man"; in the North, white voters unleashed a racist backlash. During the elections of 1862, the Democrats denounced emancipation as unconstitutional, warned of slave uprisings, and predicted that freed blacks would take

white jobs. Every freed slave, suggested a nativist-minded New Yorker, should "shoulder an Irishman and leave the Continent." Such sentiments propelled Democrat Horatio Seymour into the governor's office in New York; if abolition was a war goal, Seymour argued, the South should not be conquered. In the November election, Democrats swept to victory in Pennsylvania, Ohio, and Illinois and gained thirty-four seats in Congress. However, Republicans still held a twenty-five-seat majority in the House and gained five seats in the Senate. Lincoln refused to retreat. Calling emancipation an "act of justice," he signed the final proclamation on New Year's Day 1863. "If my name ever goes into history," he said, "it was for this act."

 To see a longer excerpt of the Jefferson Davis document, along with other primary sources from this period, see *Sources for America's History*.

Vicksburg and Gettysburg

The Emancipation Proclamation's fate would depend on Republican political success and Union military victories, neither of which looked likely. Democrats had made significant gains in 1862, and popular support was growing for a negotiated peace. Two brilliant victories in Virginia by General Robert E. Lee, whose army defeated Union forces at Fredericksburg (December 1862) and Chancellorsville (May 1863), further eroded northern support for the war.

The Battle for the Mississippi   At this critical juncture, General Grant mounted a major offensive to split the Confederacy in two. Grant drove south along the west bank of the Mississippi in Arkansas and then crossed the river near Vicksburg, Mississippi. There, he defeated two Confederate armies and laid siege to the city. After repelling Union assaults for six weeks, the exhausted and starving Vicksburg garrison surrendered on July 4, 1863. Five days later, Union forces took Port Hudson, Louisiana (near Baton Rouge), and seized control of the entire Mississippi River. Grant had taken 31,000 prisoners; cut off Louisiana, Arkansas, and Texas from the rest of the Confederacy; and prompted thousands of slaves to desert their plantations. Confederate troops responded by targeting refugees for re-enslavement and massacre. "The battlefield was sickening," a Confederate officer reported from Arkansas, "no orders, threats or commands could restrain the men from vengeance on the negroes, and they were piled in great heaps about the wagons, in the tangled brushwood, and upon the muddy and trampled road."

UNDERSTAND POINTS OF VIEW

Some historians argue that slaves "freed themselves" by fleeing to Union armies, thereby forcing Lincoln to issue the Emancipation Proclamation. How persuasive is that argument?

As Grant had advanced toward Vicksburg in May, Confederate leaders had argued over the best strategic response. President Davis and other politicians wanted to send an army to Tennessee to relieve the Union pressure along the Mississippi River. General Lee, buoyed by his recent victories, favored a new invasion of the North. That strategy, Lee suggested, would either draw Grant's forces to the east or give the Confederacy a major victory that would destroy the North's will to fight.

Lee's Advance and Defeat Lee won out. In June 1863, he maneuvered his army north through Maryland into Pennsylvania. The Army of the Potomac moved along with him, positioning itself between Lee and Washington, D.C. On July 1, the two great armies met by accident at Gettysburg, Pennsylvania, in what became a decisive confrontation (Map 14.4). On the first day of battle, Lee drove the Union's advance guard to the south of town. There, Union commander George G. Meade placed his troops in well-defended hilltop positions and called up reinforcements. By the morning of July 2, Meade had 90,000 troops to Lee's 75,000. Lee knew he was outnumbered but was intent on victory; he ordered assaults on Meade's flanks but failed to turn them.

On July 3, Lee decided on a dangerous frontal assault against the center of the Union line. After the heaviest artillery barrage of the war, Lee sent General George E. Pickett and his 14,000 men to take Cemetery Ridge. When Pickett's men charged across a mile of open terrain, they faced deadly fire from artillery and massed riflemen; thousands suffered death, wounds, or capture. As the three-day battle ended, the Confederates counted 28,000 casualties, one-third of the Army of Northern Virginia, while 23,000 of Meade's soldiers lay

MAP 14.4

Lee Invades the North, 1863

After Lee's victories at Chancellorsville (1) in May and Brandy Station (2) in June, the Confederate forces moved northward, constantly shadowed by the Union army. On July 1, the two armies met accidentally near Gettysburg, Pennsylvania. In the ensuing battle (3), the Union army, commanded by General George Meade, emerged victorious, primarily because it was much larger than the Confederate force and held well-fortified positions along Cemetery Ridge, which gave its units a major tactical advantage.

EXPLAIN CONSEQUENCES
How did the battles at Gettysburg and Vicksburg significantly change the tide of war?

killed or wounded. Shocked by the bloodletting, Meade allowed the Confederate units to escape. Lincoln was furious at Meade's caution, perceiving that "the war will be prolonged indefinitely."

Still, Gettysburg was a great Union victory and, together with the simultaneous triumph at Vicksburg, marked a major military, political, and diplomatic turning point. As southern citizens grew increasingly critical of their government, the Confederate elections of 1863 went sharply against the politicians who supported Jefferson Davis. Meanwhile, northern citizens rallied to the Union, and Republicans swept state elections in Pennsylvania, Ohio, and New York. In Europe, the victories boosted the leverage of American diplomats. Since 1862, the British-built ironclad cruiser the *Alabama* had sunk or captured more than a hundred Union merchant ships, and the Confederacy was about to accept delivery of two more ironclads. With a Union victory increasingly likely, the British government decided to impound the warships and, subsequently, to pay $15.5 million for the depredations of the *Alabama*. British workers and reformers had long condemned slavery and praised emancipation; moreover, because of poor grain harvests, Britain depended on imports of wheat and flour from the American Midwest. King Cotton diplomacy had failed and King Wheat stood triumphant. "Rest not your hopes in foreign nations," President Jefferson Davis advised his people. "This war is ours; we must fight it ourselves."

The Union Victorious, 1864–1865

The Union victories of 1863 meant that the South could not win independence through a decisive military triumph. However, the Confederacy could still hope for a battlefield stalemate and a negotiated peace. To keep the Union in Republican hands, Lincoln faced the daunting task of conquering the South.

Soldiers and Strategy

The promotion of aggressive generals and the enlistment of African American soldiers allowed the Union to prosecute the war vigorously. As early as 1861, free African Americans and fugitive slaves had volunteered, both to end slavery and, as Frederick Douglass put it, to

win "the right to citizenship." Yet many northern whites refused to serve with blacks. "I am as much opposed to slavery as any of them," a New York soldier told his local newspaper, "but I am not willing to be put on a level with the negro and fight with them." Union generals also opposed the enlistment of African Americans, doubting they would make good soldiers. Nonetheless, free and contraband blacks formed volunteer regiments in New England, South Carolina, Louisiana, and Kansas.

The Impact of Black Troops The Emancipation Proclamation changed military policy and popular sentiment. The proclamation invited former slaves to serve in the Union army, and northern whites, having suffered thousands of casualties, now accepted that blacks should share in the fighting and dying. A heroic and costly attack by the 54th Massachusetts Infantry on Fort Wagner, South Carolina, in 1863 convinced Union officers of the value of black soldiers. By the spring of 1865, the Lincoln administration had recruited and armed nearly 200,000 African Americans. Without black soldiers, said Lincoln, "we would be compelled to abandon the war in three weeks."

Military service did not end racial discrimination. Black soldiers initially earned less than white soldiers ($10 a month versus $13) and died, mostly from disease, at higher rates than white soldiers. Nonetheless, African Americans continued to volunteer, seeking freedom and a new social order. "Hello, Massa," said one black soldier to his former master, who had been taken prisoner. "Bottom rail on top dis time." The worst fears of the secessionists had come true: through the disciplined agency of the Union army, African Americans had risen in a successful rebellion against slavery, just as six decades earlier enslaved Haitians had won emancipation in the army of Toussaint L'Ouverture (Chapter 7).

Capable Generals Take Command As African Americans bolstered the army's ranks, Lincoln finally found a ruthless commanding general. In March 1864, Lincoln placed General Ulysses S. Grant in charge of all Union armies; from then on, the president determined overall strategy and Grant implemented it. Lincoln favored a simultaneous advance against the major Confederate armies, a strategy Grant had long favored, in order to achieve a decisive victory before the election of 1864.

Grant knew how to fight a war that relied on industrial technology and targeted an entire society. At Vicksburg in July 1863, he had besieged the whole city

Black Soldiers in the Union Army
Determined to end racial slavery, tens of thousands of African Americans volunteered for service in the Union army in 1864 and 1865, boosting the northern war effort at a critical moment. These soldiers were members of the 107th Colored Infantry, stationed at Fort Corcoran near Washington, D.C. In January 1865, their regiment saw action in the daring capture of Fort Fisher, which protected Wilmington, North Carolina, the last Confederate port open to blockade runners. Library of Congress.

and forced its surrender. Then, in November, he had used railroads to rescue an endangered Union army near Chattanooga, Tennessee. Grant believed that the cautious tactics of previous Union commanders had prolonged the war. He was willing to accept heavy casualties, a stance that earned him a reputation as a butcher of enemy armies and his own men.

In May 1864, Grant ordered two major offensives. Personally taking charge of the 115,000-man Army of the Potomac, he set out to destroy Lee's force of 75,000 troops in Virginia. Grant instructed General William Tecumseh Sherman, who shared his harsh outlook, to invade Georgia and take Atlanta. "All that has gone before is mere skirmish," Sherman wrote as he prepared for battle. "The war now begins."

Grant advanced toward Richmond, hoping to force Lee to fight in open fields, where the Union's superior manpower and artillery would prevail. Remembering his tactical errors at Gettysburg, Lee remained in strong defensive positions and attacked only when he held an advantage. The Confederate general seized that opportunity twice in May 1864, winning costly victories at the battles of the Wilderness and Spotsylvania Court House. At Spotsylvania, the troops fought at point-blank range; an Iowa recruit recalled "lines of blue and grey [soldiers firing] into each other's faces; for an hour and a half." Despite heavy losses in these battles and then at Cold Harbor, Grant drove on (Map 14.5). His attacks severely eroded Lee's forces, which suffered 31,000 casualties, but Union losses were even higher: 55,000 killed or wounded.

EXPLAIN CONSEQUENCES
How did the Emancipation Proclamation and Grant's appointment as general in chief affect the course of the war?

Stalemate   The fighting took a heavy psychological toll. "Many a man has gone crazy since this campaign began from the terrible pressure on mind and body," observed a Union captain. As morale declined, soldiers deserted. In June 1864, Grant laid siege to Petersburg, an important railroad center near Richmond. As the siege continued, Union and Confederate soldiers built complex networks of trenches, tunnels, and artillery emplacements stretching for 40 miles along the eastern edge of Richmond and Petersburg, foreshadowing the devastating trench warfare in France in World War I. Invoking the intense imagery of the Bible, an officer described the continuous artillery barrages and sniping

Grant Planning a Strategic Maneuver

On May 21, 1864, the day this photograph was taken, Grant pulled his forces from Spotsylvania Court House, where a bitter two-week battle (May 8–21) resulted in 18,000 Union and 10,000 Confederate casualties. He moved his army to the southeast, seeking to outflank Lee's forces. Photographer Timothy H. O'Sullivan caught up to the Union army's high command at Massaponax Church, Virginia, and captured this image of Grant (to the left) leaning over a pew and reading a map held by General George H. Meade. As Grant plots the army's movement, his officers smoke their pipes and read reports of the war in newspapers that had just arrived from New York City. Intercepting Grant's forces, Lee took up fortified positions first at the North Anna River and then at Cold Harbor, where the Confederates scored their last major victory of the war (May 31–June 3). Library of Congress.

as "living night and day within the 'valley of the shadow of death.'" The stress was especially great for the out-numbered Confederate troops, who spent months in the muddy, hellish trenches without rotation to the rear.

As time passed, Lincoln and Grant felt pressures of their own. The enormous casualties and military stale-mate threatened Lincoln with defeat in the November election. The Republican outlook worsened in July, when Jubal Early's cavalry raided and burned the Pennsylvania town of Chambersburg and threatened Washington. To punish farmers in the Shenandoah Valley who had aided the Confederate raiders, Grant ordered General Philip H. Sheridan to turn the region into "a barren waste." Sheridan's troops conducted a **scorched-earth campaign**, destroying grain, barns, and gristmills and any other resource useful to the Confederates. These tactics, like Early's raid, violated the military norms of the day, which treated civilians as noncombatants. Rising desperation and anger were changing the definition of conventional warfare.

The Election of 1864 and Sherman's March

As the siege at Petersburg dragged on, Lincoln's hopes for reelection depended on General Sherman in Georgia. Sherman's army of 90,000 men had moved methodically toward Atlanta, a railway hub at the heart of the Confederacy. General Joseph E. Johnson's Confederate army of 60,000 stood in his way and, in June 1864, inflicted heavy casualties on Sherman's forces near Kennesaw Mountain, Georgia. By late July, the Union army stood on the northern outskirts of Atlanta, but the next month brought little gain. Like Grant, Sherman seemed bogged down in a hopeless campaign.

The National Union Party Versus the Peace Democrats Meanwhile, the presidential campaign of 1864 was heating up. In June, the Republican Party's convention rebuffed attempts to prevent Lincoln's renomination. It endorsed the president's war strategy, demanded the Confederacy's unconditional surrender, and called for a constitutional amendment to abolish slavery. The delegates likewise embraced Lincoln's political strategy. To attract border-state and Demo-cratic voters, the Republicans took a new name, the National Union Party, and chose Andrew Johnson, a Tennessee slave owner and Unionist Democrat, as Lincoln's running mate.

The Democratic Party met in August and nomi-nated General George B. McClellan for president. Lincoln had twice removed McClellan from military commands: first for an excess of caution and then for

MAP 14.5

The Closing Virginia Campaign, 1864–1865

Beginning in May 1864, General Ulysses S. Grant launched an all-out campaign against Richmond, trying to lure General Robert E. Lee into open battle. Lee avoided a major test of strength. Instead, he retreated to defensive positions and inflicted heavy casualties on Union attackers at the Wilderness, Spotsylvania Court House, North Anna, and Cold Harbor (1–4). From June 1864 to April 1865, the two armies faced each other across defensive fortifications outside Richmond and Petersburg (5). Grant finally broke this ten-month siege by a flanking maneuver at Five Forks (6). Lee's surrender followed shortly.

his opposition to emancipation. Like McClellan, the Democratic delegates rejected emancipation and condemned Lincoln's repression of domestic dissent, particularly the suspension of habeas corpus and the use of military courts to prosecute civilians. However, they split into two camps over war policy. **War Democrats** vowed to continue fighting until the rebellion ended, while **Peace Democrats** called for a "cessation of hostilities" and a constitutional convention to negotiate a peace settlement. Although personally a War Democrat, McClellan promised if elected to recommend to Congress an immediate armistice and a peace convention. Hearing this news, Confederate vice president Alexander Stephens celebrated "the first ray of real light I have seen since the war began." He predicted that if Atlanta and Richmond held out, Lincoln would be defeated and McClellan would eventually accept an independent Confederacy.

The Fall of Atlanta and Lincoln's Victory   Stephens's hopes collapsed on September 2, 1864, as Atlanta fell to Sherman's army. In a stunning move, the Union general pulled his troops from the trenches, swept around the city, and destroyed its rail links to the south. Fearing that Sherman would encircle his army, Confederate general John B. Hood abandoned the city. "Atlanta is ours, and fairly won," Sherman telegraphed Lincoln, sparking hundred-gun salutes and wild Republican

celebration. "We are gaining strength," Lincoln warned Confederate leaders, "and may, if need be, maintain the contest indefinitely."

A deep pessimism settled over the Confederacy. Mary Chesnut, a plantation mistress and general's wife, wrote in her diary, "I felt as if all were dead within me, forever," and foresaw the end of the Confederacy: "We are going to be wiped off the earth." Recognizing the dramatically changed military situation, McClellan repudiated the Democratic peace platform. The National Union Party went on the offensive, attacking McClellan's inconsistency and labeling Peace Democrats as "copperheads" (poisonous snakes) who were hatching treasonous plots. "A man must go for the Union at all hazards," declared a Republican legislator in Pennsylvania, "if he would entitle himself to be considered a loyal man."

Lincoln won a clear-cut victory in November. The president received 55 percent of the popular vote and won 212 of 233 electoral votes. Republicans and National Unionists captured 145 of the 185 seats in the House of Representatives and increased their Senate majority to 42 of 52 seats. Many Republicans owed their victory to the votes of Union troops, who wanted to crush the rebellion and end slavery.

Legal emancipation was already under way at the edges of the South. In 1864, Maryland and Missouri amended their constitutions to end slavery, and the

William Tecumseh Sherman

A man of nervous energy, Sherman smoked cigars and talked continuously. When seated, he crossed and uncrossed his legs incessantly, and a journalist described his fingers as constantly "twitching his red whiskers—his coat buttons—playing a tattoo on the table—or running through his hair." On the battlefield Sherman was a decisive general who commanded the loyalty of his troops. A photographer captured this image of Sherman in 1865, following his devastating march through Georgia and the Carolinas. Library of Congress.

three Confederate states occupied by the Union army — Tennessee, Arkansas, and Louisiana — followed suit. Still, abolitionists worried that the Emancipation Proclamation, based legally on the president's wartime powers, would lose its force at the end of the war. Urged on by Lincoln and the National Equal Rights League, in January 1865 the Republican Congress approved the Thirteenth Amendment, ending slavery, and sent it to the states for ratification. Slavery was nearly dead.

William Tecumseh Sherman: "Hard War" Warrior

Thanks to William Tecumseh Sherman, the Confederacy was nearly dead as well. As a young military officer stationed in the South, Sherman sympathized with the planter class and felt that slavery upheld social stability. However, Sherman believed in the Union. Secession meant "anarchy," he told his southern friends in early 1861: "If war comes . . . I must fight your people whom I best love." Serving under Grant, Sherman distinguished himself at Shiloh and Vicksburg. Taking command of the Army of the Tennessee, he developed the philosophy and tactics of **"hard war."** "When one nation is at war with another, all the people of one are enemies of the other," Sherman declared. When Confederate guerrillas fired on a boat carrying Unionist civilians near Randolph, Tennessee, Sherman sent a regiment to destroy the town, asserting, "We are justified in treating all inhabitants as combatants."

After capturing Atlanta, Sherman advocated a bold strategy. Instead of pursuing the retreating Confederate army northward into Tennessee, he proposed to move south, live off the land, and "cut a swath through to the sea." To persuade Lincoln and Grant to approve his unconventional plan, Sherman argued that his march would be "a demonstration to the world, foreign and domestic, that we have a power [Jefferson] Davis cannot resist." The Union general lived up to his pledge. "We are not only fighting hostile armies," Sherman wrote, "but a hostile people, and must make old and young, rich and poor, feel the hard hand of war." He left Atlanta in flames, and during his 300-mile **March to the Sea** (Map 14.6) his army consumed or demolished everything in its path. A Union veteran wrote, "[We] destroyed all we could not eat, stole their niggers, burned their cotton & gins, spilled their sorghum, burned & twisted their R.Roads and raised Hell generally." Although Sherman's army usually did not harm noncombatants who kept to their peaceful business, the havoc so demoralized Confederate soldiers that many deserted their units and returned home (American Voices, p. 472). When Sherman reached Savannah in mid-December, the city's 10,000 defenders left without a fight.

Georgia's African Americans treated Sherman as a savior. "They flock to me, old and young," he wrote. "[T]hey pray and shout and mix up my name with Moses . . . as well as 'Abram Linkom,' the Great Messiah of 'Dis Jubilee.'" To provide for the hundreds of blacks now following his army, Sherman issued Special Field Order No. 15, which set aside 400,000 acres of prime rice-growing land for the exclusive use of freedmen. By June 1865, about 40,000 blacks were cultivating "Sherman lands." Many freedmen believed that the lands were to be theirs forever, belated payment for generations of unpaid labor: "All the land belongs to the Yankees now and they gwine divide it out among de coloured people."

 To see more of Sherman's writing, along with other primary sources from this period, see *Sources for America's History*.

In February 1865, Sherman invaded South Carolina to punish the instigators of nullification and secession. His troops ravaged the countryside as they cut a narrow swath across the state. After capturing South Carolina's capital, Columbia, they burned the business district, most churches, and the wealthiest residential neighborhoods. "This disappointment to me is extremely bitter," lamented Jefferson Davis. By March, Sherman had reached North Carolina, ready to link up with Grant and crush Lee's army.

The Confederate Collapse   Grant's war of attrition in Virginia had already exposed a weakness in the Confederacy: rising class resentment among poor whites. Angered by slave owners' exemptions from military service and fearing that the Confederacy was doomed, ordinary southern farmers now repudiated the draft. "All they want is to git you . . . to fight for

their infurnal negroes," grumbled an Alabama hill farmer. More and more soldiers fled their units. "I am now going to work instead of to the war," vowed David Harris, another backcountry yeoman. By 1865, at least 100,000 men had deserted from Confederate armies, prompting reluctant Confederate leaders to approve the enlistment of black soldiers and promising them freedom. However, the fighting ended too soon to reveal whether any slaves would have fought for the Confederacy.

The symbolic end of the war took place in Virginia. In April 1865, Grant finally gained control of the crucial railroad junction at Petersburg and forced Lee to abandon Richmond. As Lincoln visited the ruins of the Confederate capital, greeted by joyful

PLACE EVENTS IN CONTEXT
To what extent were Grant and Sherman's military strategy and tactics responsible for defeat of the Confederacy?

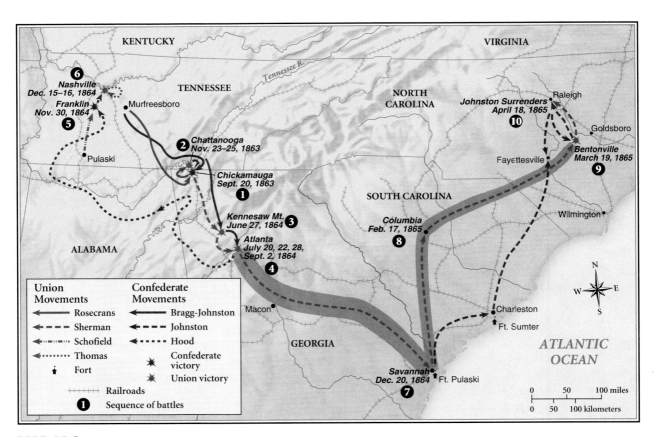

MAP 14.6

Sherman's March Through the Confederacy, 1864–1865

The Union victory in November 1863 at Chattanooga, Tennessee (2), was almost as critical as the victories in July at Gettysburg and Vicksburg, because it opened up a route of attack into the heart of the Confederacy. In mid-1864, General William Tecumseh Sherman advanced on the railway hub of Atlanta (3 and 4). After finally taking the city in September 1864, Sherman relied on other Union armies to stem General Hood's invasion of Tennessee (5 and 6) while he began his devastating March to the Sea. By December, he had reached Savannah (7); from there, he cut a swath through the Carolinas (8–10).

Gender, Class, and Sexual Terror in the Invaded South

When the white men of the South marched off to war, they left behind their wives and children. Soon, Confederate women in the border states confronted an enemy army of occupation. Later, when Union armies invaded the Confederacy, southern women—both black and white—faced an even more dangerous army of conquest and destruction.

Cornelia Peake McDonald
Journal

Cornelia Peake McDonald was the wife of an affluent lawyer in Winchester, Virginia, a town occupied by Union forces. She had nine children, born between 1848 and 1861.

[May 1863] 22nd . . . To day I received another intimation that my house would be wanted for a [Union] regimental hospital. I feel a sickening despair when I think of what will be my condition if they do take it. . . .

Major Butterworth . . . told me that he was a quarter master, and that he had been sent to inform me that I must give up the house, as they must have it for a hospital. . . . I lost no time in seeking [General] Milroy's presence. . . . "Gen. Milroy," said I. He looked around impatiently. "They have come to take my house from me." . . . [He replied,] "Why should you expect me to shelter you and your family, you who are a rebel, and whose husband and family are in arms against the best government the world ever saw?" . . . "But Gen. Milroy, you are commandant here . . . and you can suffer me to remain in mine, where at least I can have a shelter for my sick children." . . . At last he raised his head and looked in my face. "You can stay but I allow it at the risk of my commission."

Source: *A Woman's Civil War*, ed. Minrose C. Gwin (Madison: University of Wisconsin Press, 1992), 101, 150–153.

Judith White Brockenbrough McGuire
Diary

Judith White Brockenbrough McGuire, of Alexandria, Virginia, spent most of the war as a refugee in Richmond.

June 11, 1865
These particulars . . . I have [heard] from our nephew, J. P. [in occupied central Virginia. He reports that] . . . the Northern officers seemed disposed to be courteous to the ladies, in the little intercourse which they had with them. General Ferrera, who commanded the negro troops, was humane, in having a coffin made for a young Confederate officer. . . . The surgeons, too, assisted in attending to the Confederate wounded. An officer one morning sent for Mrs. N. [to return an item stolen by Union soldiers]. . . . She thanked him for his kindness. He seemed moved and said, "Mrs. N., I will do what I can for you, for I cannot be too thankful that my wife is not in an invaded country."

Source: Rod Gragg, *The Illustrated Confederate Reader* (New York: Harper & Row, 1989), 88–89.

Lieutenant Colonel Samuel J. Nasmith
Report, July 1, 1863

In June 1863, Confederate raiders attacked and burned twenty Union-run cotton plantations near Goodrich's Landing, Louisiana, along the Mississippi River. They captured 1,200 African American refugees and took vengeance on many others, including women and children. A report by Colonel Nasmith of the 25th Wisconsin Infantry related the gruesome details.

Major Farnan, commanding the cavalry, reports that the scenes witnessed by him . . . were of a character never before witnessed in a civilized country. . . . They spared neither age, sex, nor condition. In some instances the Negroes were shut up in their quarters, and literally roasted alive. The charred remains found in numerous instances testified to a degree of fiendish atrocity such as has no parallel either in civilized or savage warfare. Young children, only five or six years of age, were found skulking in the cane break with wounds, while helpless women were found shot down in the most inhumane manner. The whole country was destroyed, and every sign of civilization was given to the flames.

Source: *The War of the Rebellion: A Compilation of the Official Records of the Union and Confederate Armies* (Washington, DC: Government Printing Office, 1889), Series 1, Vol. 24 (Part II), 517.

Anna Maria Green
Diary

Twenty-year-old Anna Maria Green kept a diary as General William Tecumseh Sherman's army of 60,000 men approached Milledgeville, Georgia.

Saturday evening November 19th [1864] — Again we are in a state of excitement caused by the near approach to our town of the enemy. Last night they were two thousand strong at Monticello. . . . Minnie came in to call me to look at a fire in the west. My heart sank, and almost burst with grief as I beheld the horizon crimson and the desolation our hated foe was spreading. Great God! Deliver us, oh! Spare our city. . . .

Nov. 25th Friday evening . . . This morning the last of the vandals left our city and burned the bridge after them — leaving suffering and desolation behind them, and embittering every heart. The worst of their acts was committed to poor Mrs. Nichols — violence done, and atrocity committed that ought to make her husband an enemy unto death. Poor woman. I fear she has been driven crazy.

Source: Rod Gragg, *The Illustrated Confederate Reader* (New York: Harper & Row, 1989), 175–176.

Unknown Woman
Letter to Her Daughter

This letter was written by a woman in Columbia, South Carolina.

Columbia March 3, 1865
My dear Gracia

Doubtless your anxiety is very great to hear something about us after the great calamity that has befallen our town. We have lost everything, but thank God, our lives have been spared. Oh Gracia, what we have passed through no tongue can tell, it defies description! . . .

The first regiment sent into the city was what Sherman calls his "Tigers." Whenever he sends these men ahead, he intends to do his worst. . . . The first thing they did was break open the stores and distribute the goods right and left. They found liquor and all became heartily drunk. . . . When night came on, the soldiers . . . fired the houses. It was a fearful sight. . . .

We stayed all night in the street, protected by a Yankee Captain from Iowa who was very kind to us.

Source: Rod Gragg, *The Illustrated Confederate Reader* (New York: Harper & Row, 1989), 189–190.

Daniel Heyward Trezevant
Report

Daniel Heyward Trezevant, a doctor in Columbia, South Carolina, wrote a brief report after Sherman's departure.

The Yankees' gallantry, brutality and debauchery were afflicted on the negroes. . . . The case of Mr. Shane's old negro woman, who, after being subjected to the most brutal indecency from seven of the Yankees, was, at the proposition of one of them to "finish the old Bitch," put into a ditch and held under water until life was extinct. . . .

Mrs. T. B. C. was seized by one of the soldiers, an officer, and dragged by the hair and forced to the floor for the purpose of sensual enjoyment. She resisted as far as practical — held up her young infant as a plea for sparing her and succeeded, but they took her maid, and in her presence, threw her on the floor and had connection with her. . . . They pinioned Mrs. McCord and robbed her. They dragged Mrs. Gynn by the hair of her head about the house. Mrs. G. told me of a young lady about 16, Miss Kinsler, who . . . three officers brutally ravished and who became crazy.

Source: Rod Gragg, *The Illustrated Confederate Reader* (New York: Harper & Row, 1989), 192.

QUESTIONS FOR ANALYSIS

1. How might class loyalties and shared cultural values have influenced General Milroy's decision to let Cornelia McDonald stay in her home? How do the actions of the "Yankee Captain from Iowa" compare with Milroy's?

2. Although none of these writers used the word *rape* (why not?), we can assume that Mrs. Nichols was raped, as were Miss Kinsler and the enslaved African American maid in Columbia. What about Mrs. T. B. C., Mrs. McCord, and Mrs. Gynn? How should we evaluate the credibility of these sources (and other, similar accounts written by whites) when they assert or imply that Union troops raped enslaved women and spared white women?

3. How should we compare the brutal actions of Confederate soldiers toward fugitive blacks and the treatment of southern women by Sherman's troops? Explain why they do — or do not — represent the same kind of wartime military misconduct.

ex-slaves, Grant cut off Lee's escape route to North Carolina. On April 9, almost four years to the day after the attack on Fort Sumter, Lee surrendered at Appomattox Court House, Virginia. In return for their promise not to fight again, Grant allowed the Confederate officers and men to go home. By late May, all of the secessionist armies and governments had simply melted away (Map 14.7).

The hard and bitter conflict was finally over. Northern armies had preserved the Union and destroyed slavery; many of the South's factories, railroads, and cities lay in ruins; and its farms and plantations had suffered years of neglect. Almost 260,000 Confederate soldiers had paid for secession with their lives. On the other side, more than 360,000 northerners had died for the Union, and thousands more had been maimed. Was it all worth the price? Delivering his second inaugural address in March 1865 — less than a month before his assassination — Abraham Lincoln could justify the hideous carnage only by alluding to divine providence: "[S]o still it must be said 'the judgments of the Lord are true and righteous altogether.'"

What of the war's effects on society? A New York census taker suggested that the conflict had undermined "autocracy" and had an "equalizing effect." Slavery was gone from the South, he reflected, and in the North, "military men from the so called 'lower classes' now lead society, having been elevated by real merit and valor." However perceptive these remarks, they ignored the wartime emergence of a new financial aristocracy that would soon preside over what Mark Twain labeled the Gilded Age. Nor was the sectional struggle yet concluded. As the North began to reconstruct the South and the Union, it found those tasks to be almost as hard and bitter as the war itself.

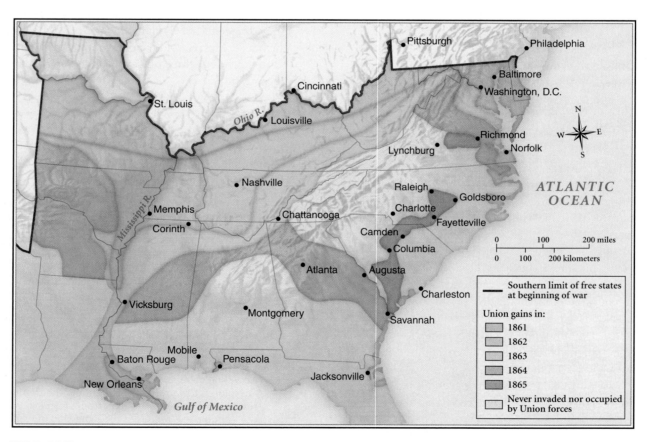

MAP 14.7

The Conquest of the South, 1861–1865

It took four years for the Union armies to defeat the Confederate forces. Until 1864, most of the South remained in Confederate hands; even at the end of the war, Union armies had never entered many parts of the rebellious states. Most of the Union's territorial gains came on the vast western front, where its control of strategic lines of communication (the Ohio and Mississippi rivers and major railroads) gave its forces a decisive advantage.

An Uncounted Casualty of the War

Many men who died in the war were husbands and fathers, leaving tens of thousands of widows—and even more children—to grieve over their loss. Dressed in mourning clothes, this unidentified, sad-faced young girl holds an image of her dead father, a cavalryman holding a sword and wearing a regulation dress hat. Library of Congress.

SUMMARY

In this chapter, we surveyed the dramatic events of the Civil War. Looking at the South, we watched the fire-eaters declare secession, form a new Confederacy, and attack Fort Sumter. Subsequently, we saw its generals repulse Union attacks against Richmond and go on the offensive. However, as the war continued, the inherent weaknesses of the Confederacy came to the fore. Enslaved workers fled or refused to work, and yeomen farmers refused to fight for an institution that primarily benefitted wealthy planters.

Examining the North, we witnessed its military shortcomings. Its generals—McClellan and Meade—moved slowly to attack and did not pursue their weakened foes. However, the Union's significant advantages in industrial output, financial resources, and military manpower became manifest over time. Congress created efficient systems of banking and war finance, Lincoln found efficient and ruthless generals, and the emancipation and recruitment of African Americans provided an abundant supply of soldiers determined to end slavery.

We explored the impact of the war on civilians in both regions: the imposition of conscription and high taxes, the increased workload of farm women, and the constant food shortages and soaring prices. Above all else, there was the omnipresent fact of death—a tragedy that touched nearly every family, North and South.

C H A P T E R   R E V I E W

MAKE IT STICK   Go to **LearningCurve** to retain what you've read.

TERMS TO KNOW   Identify and explain the significance of each term below.

Key Concepts and Events

Crittenden Compromise (p. 446)

total war (p. 452)

draft (conscription) (p. 452)

habeas corpus (p. 454)

King Cotton (p. 456)

greenbacks (p. 460)

"contrabands" (p. 463)

Radical Republicans (p. 463)

Emancipation Proclamation (p. 464)

scorched-earth campaign (p. 468)

War and Peace Democrats (p. 469)

"hard war" (p. 470)

March to the Sea (p. 470)

Key People

Abraham Lincoln (p. 444)

Jefferson Davis (p. 446)

Robert E. Lee (p. 448)

George McClellan (p. 449)

Ulysses S. Grant (p. 466)

William T. Sherman (p. 470)

REVIEW QUESTIONS   Answer these questions to demonstrate your understanding of the chapter's main ideas.

1. Based on the evidence presented in this chapter, did Lee's surrender at Appomattox and Grant's magnanimity to the defeated forces save the nation from a drawn-out guerrilla war, as some historians have argued? Or, as other scholars have suggested, did the events at Appomattox undermine black emancipation by giving a high priority to the reconciliation of northern and southern whites?

2. In 1860, the institution of slavery was firmly entrenched in the United States; by 1865, it was dead. How did this happen? How and why did Union policy toward slavery and enslaved people change over the course of the war?

3. **THEMATIC UNDERSTANDING** The thematic timeline for Part 5 (p. 409) lists six events or developments in the 1860s relating directly to the South's secession and the Civil War. Does that list capture the war's overwhelming importance to the history of nineteenth-century America? If not, is this deficiency inherent to timelines, or does it reflect a faulty construction of this specific timeline? How would you address this problem?

MAKING CONNECTIONS   Recognize the larger developments and continuities within and across chapters by answering these questions.

1. **ACROSS TIME AND PLACE** After reviewing the compromises over slavery at the Constitutional Convention (p. 469), in the Missouri Compromise (p. 269), and in the Compromise of 1850 (p. 429), write an essay analyzing why the opposing sides failed to compromise in 1861.

2. **VISUAL EVIDENCE** The photographs of the Southern Refugee Family (p. 462) and Grant Planning a Strategic Maneuver (p. 468) remind us of a world in which people, goods, and soldiers moved either on foot or on horses and mules. How did this limited mobility affect civilians — slave and free — and military forces during the Civil War?

MORE TO EXPLORE   Start here to learn more about the events discussed in this chapter.

Dora L. Costa and Matthew E. Kahn, *Heroes and Cowards: The Social Face of War* (2008). Demonstrates the role of friendship and community in soldiers' wartime behavior.

Drew Gilpin Faust, *This Republic of Suffering: Death and the American Civil War* (2008). Examines the cultural changes prompted by massive casualties.

William W. Freehling, *The South vs. the South* (2001). Explores anti-Confederate sentiment in the South.

Gary W. Gallagher, *The Confederate War* (1997). Views the fighting from the perspective of the secessionists.

Earl J. Hess, *The Union Soldier in Battle* (1997). Vividly describes the smell, sound, and feel of combat.

James M. McPherson, *The Battle Cry of Freedom* (1988). A fine narrative history of the Civil War.

TIMELINE   Ask yourself why this chapter begins and ends with these dates and then identify the links among related events.

1860	• Abraham Lincoln elected president (November 6) • South Carolina secedes (December 20)
1861	• Lincoln inaugurated (March 4) • Confederates fire on Fort Sumter (April 12) • Virginia leaves Union (April 17) • General Butler declares refugee slaves "contraband of war" (May) • Confederates win Battle of Bull Run (July 21) • First Confiscation Act (August)
1862	• Legal Tender Act authorizes greenbacks (February) • Union triumphs at Shiloh (April 6–7) • Confederacy introduces draft (April) • Congress passes Homestead Act and Transcontinental Railroad Act (May, July) • Union halts Confederates at Antietam (September 17) • Preliminary emancipation proclamation (September 22)
1863	• Lincoln signs Emancipation Proclamation (January 1) • Union wins battles at Gettysburg (July 1–3) and Vicksburg (July 4) • Union initiates draft (March), sparking riots in New York City (July)
1864	• Ulysses S. Grant named Union commander (March) • Grant advances on Richmond (May) • William Tecumseh Sherman takes Atlanta (September 2) • Lincoln reelected (November 8) • Sherman marches through Georgia (November and December)
1865	• Congress approves Thirteenth Amendment (January 31) • Robert E. Lee surrenders (April 9) • Lincoln assassinated (April 14) • Thirteenth Amendment ratified (December 6)

KEY TURNING POINTS: The Emancipation Proclamations (1862/1863); Union victories at Gettysburg and Vicksburg (1863); and Sherman's taking of Atlanta (1864): historians have seen all of these events as important turning points. Assume that *one* of these events did not happen. What difference would it have made in the military and political struggle between the Union and the Confederacy?

Reconstruction
1865–1877

O n the last day of April 1866, black soldiers in Memphis, Tennessee, turned in their weapons as they mustered out of the Union army. The next day, whites who resented the soldiers' presence provoked a clash. At a street celebration where African Americans shouted "Hurrah for Abe Lincoln," a white policeman responded, "Your old father, Abe Lincoln, is dead and damned." The scuffle that followed precipitated three days of white violence and rape that left forty-eight African Americans dead and dozens more wounded. Mobs burned black homes and churches and destroyed all twelve of the city's black schools.

Unionists were appalled. They had won the Civil War, but where was the peace? Ex-Confederates murdered freedmen and flagrantly resisted federal control. After the Memphis attacks, Republicans in Congress proposed a new measure that would protect African Americans by defining and enforcing U.S. citizenship rights. Eventually this bill became the most significant law to emerge from Reconstruction, the Fourteenth Amendment to the Constitution.

Andrew Johnson, however—the Unionist Democrat who became president after Abraham Lincoln's assassination—refused to sign the bill. In May 1865, while Congress was adjourned, Johnson had implemented his own Reconstruction plan. It extended amnesty to all southerners who took a loyalty oath, except for a few high-ranking Confederates. It also allowed states to reenter the Union as soon as they revoked secession, abolished slavery, and relieved their new state governments of financial burdens by repudiating Confederate debts. A year later, at the time of the Memphis carnage, all ex-Confederate states had met Johnson's terms. The president rejected any further intervention.

Johnson's vetoes, combined with ongoing violence in the South, angered Unionist voters. In the political struggle that ensued, congressional Republicans seized the initiative from the president and enacted a sweeping program that became known as Radical Reconstruction. One of its key achievements would have been unthinkable a few years earlier: voting rights for African American men.

Black Southeners, though, had additional, urgent priorities. "We have toiled nearly all our lives as slaves [and] have made these lands what they are," a group of South Carolina petitioners declared. They pleaded for "some provision by which we as Freedmen can obtain a Homestead." Though northern Republicans and freedpeople agreed that black southerners must have physical safety and the right to vote, former slaves also wanted economic independence. Northerners sought, instead, to revive cash-crop plantations with wage labor. Reconstruction's eventual failure stemmed from the conflicting goals of lawmakers, freedpeople, and relentlessly hostile ex-Confederates.

IDENTIFY THE BIG IDEA

What goals did Republican policymakers, ex-Confederates, and freedpeople pursue during Reconstruction? To what degree did each succeed?

CELEBRATION OF FIFTEENTH AMENDMENT MAY 19TH 1870.

LIBERTY PROTECTS THE MARRIAGE ALTAR.   THE BALLOT BOX IS OPEN TO US.   OUR REPRESENTATIVE SITS IN THE NATIONAL LEGISLATURE.

Celebrating the Fifteenth Amendment, 1870   This lithograph depicts a celebration in Baltimore on May 15, 1870. With perhaps 200,000 people attending, the grand parade and orations marked passage of the Fifteenth Amendment, which enfranchised men irrespective of "race, color, or previous condition of servitude." The heroes depicted at the top are Martin Delany, the first black man to become an officer in the U.S. Army; abolitionist Frederick Douglass, born in slavery on Maryland's eastern shore; and Mississippi senator Hiram Rhodes Revels. The images at the bottom carried the following captions: "Liberty Protects the Marriage Altar," "The Ballot Box is open to us," and "Our representative Sits in the National Legislature." Such lithographs, widely printed and sold, capture the pride, hope, and optimism of Reconstruction—but the optimism was not to last. Library of Congress.

The Struggle for National Reconstruction

Congress clashed with President Johnson, in part, because the framers of the Constitution did not anticipate a civil war or provide for its aftermath. Had Confederate states legally left the Union when they seceded? If so, then their reentry required action by Congress. If not—if even during secession they had retained U.S. statehood—then restoring them might be an administrative matter, best left to the president. Lack of clarity on this fundamental question made for explosive politics.

Presidential Approaches: From Lincoln to Johnson

As wartime president, Lincoln had offered a plan similar to Johnson's. It granted amnesty to most ex-Confederates and allowed each rebellious state to return to the Union as soon as 10 percent of its voters had taken a loyalty oath and the state had approved the Thirteenth Amendment, abolishing slavery. But even amid defeat, Confederate states rejected this **Ten Percent Plan**—an ominous sign for the

> **COMPARE AND CONTRAST**
> How did Lincoln and Johnson approach Reconstruction differently?

future. In July 1864, Congress proposed a tougher substitute, the **Wade-Davis Bill**, that required an oath of allegiance by a majority of each state's adult white men, new governments formed only by those who had never taken up arms against the Union, and permanent disenfranchisement of Confederate leaders. Lincoln defeated the Wade-Davis Bill with a pocket veto, leaving it unsigned when Congress adjourned. At the same time, he opened talks with key congressmen, aiming for a compromise.

We will never know what would have happened had Lincoln lived. His assassination in April 1865 plunged the nation into political uncertainty. As a special train bore the president's flag-draped coffin home to Illinois, thousands of Americans lined the railroad tracks in mourning. Furious and grief-stricken, many Unionists blamed all Confederates for the acts of southern sympathizer John Wilkes Booth and his accomplices in the murder. At the same time, Lincoln's death left the presidency in the hands of Andrew Johnson, a man utterly lacking in Lincoln's moral sense and political judgment.

Johnson was a self-styled "common man" from the hills of eastern Tennessee. Trained as a tailor, he built his political career on the support of farmers and laborers. Loyal to the Union, Johnson had refused to leave the U.S. Senate when Tennessee seceded. After federal forces captured Nashville in 1862, Lincoln appointed Johnson as Tennessee's military governor. In the election

Memphis Riot, 1866

Whites in postwar Memphis, as in much of the South, bitterly resented the presence in their city of former black soldiers mustered out of service with the U.S. Army. On April 30, 1866, when some black veterans—no longer protected by their uniforms—celebrated the end of their army service by drinking, violence broke out. For three days, whites burned black neighborhoods, churches, and schools, raped several African American women, and killed dozens of black residents. Two whites also died in the rioting, which hardened northern public opinion and prompted calls for stronger measures to put down ex-Confederate resistance. This tinted illustration is based on a lithograph that appeared in *Harper's Weekly*. *Harper's Weekly*/ Picture Research Consultants & Archives.

of 1864, placing Lincoln and this War Democrat on the ticket together had seemed a smart move, designed to promote unity. But after Lincoln's death, Johnson's disagreement with Republicans, combined with his belligerent and contradictory actions, wreaked political havoc.

The new president and Congress confronted a set of problems that would have challenged even Lincoln. During the war, Unionists had insisted that rebel leaders were a small minority and most white southerners wanted to rejoin the Union. With even greater optimism, Republicans hoped the defeated South would accept postwar reforms. Ex-Confederates, however, contested that plan through both violence and political action. New southern state legislatures, created under Johnson's limited Reconstruction plan, moved to restore slavery in all but name. In 1865, they enacted **Black Codes**, designed to force former slaves back to plantation labor. Like similar laws passed in other places after slavery ended, the codes reflected plantation owners' economic interests (America Compared, p. 482). They imposed severe penalties on blacks who did not hold full-year labor contracts and also set up procedures for taking black children from their parents and apprenticing them to former slave masters.

Faced with these developments, Johnson gave all the wrong signals. He had long talked tough against southern planters. But in practice, Johnson allied himself with ex-Confederate leaders, forgiving them when they appealed for pardons. White southern leaders were delighted. "By this wise and noble statesmanship," wrote a Confederate legislator, "you have become the benefactor of the Southern people." Northerners and freedmen were disgusted. The president had left Reconstruction "to the tender mercies of the rebels," wrote one Republican. An angry Union veteran in Missouri called Johnson "a traitor to the loyal people of the Union." Emboldened by Johnson's indulgence, ex-Confederates began to filter back into the halls of power. When Georgians elected Alexander Stephens, former vice president of the Confederacy, to represent them in Congress, many outraged Republicans saw this as the last straw.

Congress Versus the President

Under the Constitution, Congress is "the judge of the Elections, Returns and Qualifications of its own Members" (Article 1, Section 5). Using this power, Republican majorities in both houses had refused to admit southern delegations when Congress convened in December 1865, effectively blocking Johnson's

program. Hoping to mollify Congress, some southern states dropped the most objectionable provisions from their Black Codes. But at the same time, antiblack violence erupted in various parts of the South.

Congressional Republicans concluded that the federal government had to intervene. Back in March 1865, Congress had established the **Freedmen's Bureau** to aid displaced blacks and other war refugees. In early 1866, Congress voted to extend the bureau, gave it direct funding for the first time, and authorized its agents to investigate southern abuses. Even more extraordinary was the **Civil Rights Act of 1866**, which declared formerly enslaved people to be citizens and granted them equal protection and rights of contract, with full access to the courts.

These bills provoked bitter conflict with Johnson, who vetoed them both. Johnson's racism, hitherto publicly muted, now blazed forth: "This is a country for white men, and by God, as long as I am president, it shall be a government for white men." Galvanized, Republicans in Congress gathered two-thirds majorities and overrode both vetoes, passing the Civil Rights Act in April 1866 and the Freedmen's Bureau law four months later. Their resolve was reinforced by continued upheaval in the South. In addition to the violence in Memphis, twenty-four black political leaders and their allies in Arkansas were murdered and their homes burned.

Anxious to protect freedpeople and reassert Republican power in the South, Congress took further measures to sustain civil rights. In what became the **Fourteenth Amendment** (1868), it declared that "all persons born or naturalized in the United States" were citizens. No state could abridge "the privileges or immunities of citizens of the United States"; deprive "any person of life, liberty, or property, without due process of law"; or deny anyone "equal protection." In a stunning increase of federal power, the Fourteenth Amendment declared that when people's essential rights were at stake, national citizenship henceforth took priority over citizenship in a state.

Johnson opposed ratification, but public opinion had swung against him. In the 1866 congressional elections, voters gave Republicans a 3-to-1 majority in Congress. Power shifted to the so-called Radical Republicans, who sought sweeping transformations in the defeated South. Radicals' leader in the Senate was Charles Sumner of Massachusetts, the fiery abolitionist who in 1856 had been nearly beaten to death by South Carolina congressman Preston

PLACE EVENTS IN CONTEXT
Under what circumstances did the Fourteenth Amendment win passage, and what problems did its authors seek to address?

Labor Laws After Emancipation: Haiti and the United States

Many government officials agreed with former masters on the need to control rural workers. Often planters themselves or allied with the planter class, they believed that economic strength and public revenue depended on plantation export crops and that workers would not produce those without legal coercion.

This was true in the British Caribbean and also Haiti, which eventually, after a successful slave revolt ending in 1803, became an independent republic led by former slaves and, in particular, by propertied free men of color. In the passage below, a British observer describes a rural labor code adopted by Haiti's government in 1826. Despite the law, Haiti's large plantations did not revive; the island's economy, even more than that of the U.S. South, came to be dominated by small-scale, impoverished farmers.

The Code of Laws before us is one that could only have been framed by a legislature composed of proprietors of land, having at their command a considerable military power, of which they themselves were the leaders; for a population whom it was necessary to compel to labour. . . .

The choice of a master, altho' expressly reserved to the labourer, is greatly modified by the clauses which restrain the labourer from quitting the section of country to which he belongs; and from the absence of any clause compelling proprietors to engage him; so that the cultivator must consent to bind himself to whomsoever may be willing to engage him, or remain in prison, to be employed among convicts. . . .

The Code begins (Article 1) by declaring Agriculture to be the foundation of national prosperity; and then decrees (Article 3), That all persons, excepting soldiers, and civil servants of the State, professional persons, artizans, and domestic servants, shall cultivate the soil. The next clause (Article 4), forbids the inhabitants of the country quitting it to dwell in towns or villages; and every kind of wholesale or retail trade is forbidden (Article 7) to be exercised by persons dwelling in the country.

Further articles stipulate that any person dwelling in the country, not being the owner or occupier of land, and not having bound himself in the manner directed, . . . shall be considered a vagabond, be arrested, and taken before a Justice, who, after reading the Law to him, shall commit him to jail, until he consent to bind himself according to law.

. . . Those who are hired from a job-master [labor agent], . . . are entitled to receive half the produce, after deducting the expences of cultivation; [those who are bound to the proprietor directly], one-fourth of the gross produce of their labour. . . . Out of their miserable pittance, these Haitian labourers are to provide themselves and their children with almost every thing, and to lay by a provision for old age. . . .

These, with the regulations already detailed, clearly shew what is intended to be the condition of the labouring population of Haiti. I must not call it slavery; the word is objectionable; but few of the ingredients of slavery seem to be wanting.

QUESTIONS FOR ANALYSIS

1. Compare this Haitian law with the Black Codes briefly adopted by ex-Confederate states, and with the share-cropping system that evolved in the United States during Reconstruction (p. 491). What did these labor systems—or proposed systems—have in common? How did they differ?

2. Why would the Haitian government, led by men of color, enact such laws? What considerations other than race might have shaped their views, and why?

Brooks. Radicals in the House followed Thaddeus Stevens of Pennsylvania, a passionate advocate of freedmen's political and economic rights. With such men at the fore, and with congressional Republicans now numerous and united enough to override Johnson's vetoes on many questions, Congress proceeded to remake Reconstruction.

Radical Reconstruction

The **Reconstruction Act of 1867**, enacted in March, divided the conquered South into five military districts, each under the command of a U.S. general (Map 15.1). To reenter the Union, former Confederate states had to grant the vote to freedmen and deny it to

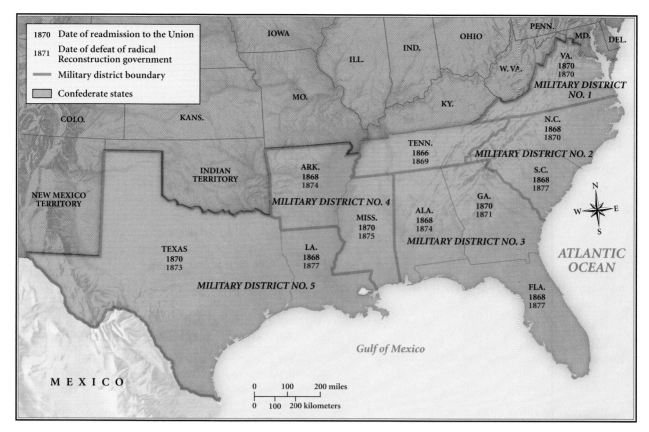

MAP 15.1

Reconstruction

The federal government organized the Confederate states into five military districts during Radical Reconstruction. For the states shown in this map, the first date indicates when that state was readmitted to the Union; the second date shows when Radical Republicans lost control of the state government. All the ex-Confederate states rejoined the Union between 1868 and 1870, but the periods of Radical government varied widely. Republicans lasted only a few months in Virginia; they held on until the end of Reconstruction in Louisiana, Florida, and South Carolina.

leading ex-Confederates. Each military commander was required to register all eligible adult males, black as well as white; supervise state constitutional conventions; and ensure that new constitutions guaranteed black suffrage. Congress would readmit a state to the Union once these conditions were met and the new state legislature ratified the Fourteenth Amendment. Johnson vetoed the Reconstruction Act, but Congress overrode his veto (Table 15.1).

The Impeachment of Andrew Johnson   In August 1867, Johnson fought back by "suspending" Secretary of War Edwin M. Stanton, a Radical, and replacing him with Union general Ulysses S. Grant, believing Grant would be a good soldier and follow orders. Johnson, however, had misjudged Grant, who publicly objected to the president's machinations. When the Senate overruled Stanton's suspension, Grant—now an open

enemy of Johnson—resigned so Stanton could resume his place as secretary of war. On February 21, 1868, Johnson formally dismissed Stanton. The feisty secretary of war responded by barricading himself in his office, precipitating a crisis.

Three days later, for the first time in U.S. history, legislators in the House of Representatives introduced articles of impeachment against the president, employing their constitutional power to charge high federal officials with "Treason, Bribery, or other high Crimes and Misdemeanors." The House serves, in effect, as the prosecutor in such cases, and the Senate serves as the court. The Republican majority brought eleven counts of misconduct against Johnson, most relating to infringement of the powers of Congress. After an eleven-week trial in the Senate, thirty-five senators voted for conviction—one vote short of the two-thirds majority required. Twelve Democrats and seven Republicans

TABLE 15.1

Primary Reconstruction Laws and Constitutional Amendments

Law (Date of Congressional Passage)	Key Provisions
Thirteenth Amendment (December 1865*)	Prohibited slavery
Civil Rights Act of 1866 (April 1866)	Defined citizenship rights of freedmen Authorized federal authorities to bring suit against those who violated those rights
Fourteenth Amendment (June 1866†)	Established national citizenship for persons born or naturalized in the United States Prohibited the states from depriving citizens of their civil rights or equal protection under the law Reduced state representation in House of Representatives by the percentage of adult male citizens denied the vote
Reconstruction Act of 1867 (March 1867)	Divided the South into five military districts, each under the command of a Union general Established requirements for readmission of ex-Confederate states to the Union
Tenure of Office Act (March 1867)	Required Senate consent for removal of any federal official whose appointment had required Senate confirmation
Fifteenth Amendment (February 1869‡)	Forbade states to deny citizens the right to vote on the grounds of race, color, or "previous condition of servitude"
Ku Klux Klan Act (April 1871)	Authorized the president to use federal prosecutions and military force to suppress conspiracies to deprive citizens of the right to vote and enjoy the equal protection of the law

*Ratified by three-fourths of all states in December 1865.
†Ratified by three-fourths of all states in July 1868.
‡Ratified by three-fourths of all states in March 1870.

voted for acquittal. The dissenting Republicans felt that removing a president for defying Congress was too damaging to the constitutional system of checks and balances. But despite the president's acquittal, Congress had shown its power. For the brief months remaining in his term, Johnson was largely irrelevant.

Election of 1868 and the Fifteenth Amendment

The impeachment controversy made Grant, already the Union's greatest war hero, a Republican idol as well. He easily won the party's presidential nomination in 1868. Although he supported Radical Reconstruction, Grant also urged sectional reconciliation. His Democratic opponent, former New York governor Horatio Seymour, almost declined the nomination because he understood that Democrats could not yet overcome the stain of disloyalty. Grant won by an overwhelming margin, receiving 214 out of 294 electoral votes. Republicans retained two-thirds majorities in both houses of Congress.

In February 1869, following this smashing victory, Republicans produced the era's last constitutional amendment, the Fifteenth. It protected male citizens' right to vote irrespective of race, color, or "previous condition of servitude." Despite Radical Republicans' protests, the amendment left room for a poll tax (paid for the privilege of voting) and literacy requirements. Both were concessions to northern and western states that sought such provisions to keep immigrants and

TRACE CHANGE OVER TIME
How and why did federal Reconstruction policies evolve between 1865 and 1870?

"We Accept the Situation"

This 1867 *Harper's Weekly* cartoon refers to the Military Reconstruction Act of 1867, which instructed ex-Confederate states to hold constitutional conventions and stipulated that the resulting constitutions must provide voting rights for black men. The two images here suggest white northerners' views of both ex-Confederates and emancipated slaves. How is each depicted? What does this suggest about the troubles that lay ahead for Reconstruction policy? The cartoonist was Thomas Nast (1840–1902), one of the most influential artists of his era. Nast first drew "Santa Claus" in his modern form, and it was he who began depicting the Democratic Party as a kicking donkey and Republicans as an elephant—suggesting (since elephants are supposed to have good memories) their long remembrance of the Civil War and emancipation. Library of Congress.

the "unworthy" poor from the polls. Congress required the four states remaining under federal control to ratify the measure as a condition for readmission to the Union. A year later, the **Fifteenth Amendment** became law.

Passage of the Fifteenth Amendment, despite its limitations, was an astonishing feat. Elsewhere in the Western Hemisphere, lawmakers had left emancipated slaves in a condition of semi-citizenship, with no voting rights. But, like almost all Americans, congressional Republicans had extraordinary faith in the power of the vote. Many African Americans agreed. "The colored people of these Southern states have cast their lot with the Government," declared a delegate to Arkansas's constitutional convention, "and with the great Republican Party. . . . The ballot is our only means of protection." In the election of 1870, hundreds of thousands of African Americans voted across the South, in an atmosphere of collective pride and celebration.

 To see a longer excerpt of the Arkansas delegate's document, along with other primary sources from this period, see *Sources for America's History*.

Woman Suffrage Denied

Passage of the Fifteenth Amendment was a bittersweet victory for one group of Union loyalists: women. Some formerly enslaved women believed they would win voting rights along with their men, until northern allies

corrected that impression. National women's rights leaders, who had campaigned for the ballot since the Seneca Falls convention of 1848, hoped to secure voting rights for women and African American men at the same time. As Elizabeth Cady Stanton put it, women could "avail ourselves of the strong arm and the blue uniform of the black soldier to walk in by his side." The protected categories for voting in the Fifteenth Amendment could have read "race, color, *sex*, or previous condition of servitude." But that word proved impossible to obtain.

Enfranchising black men had clear benefits for the authors of Reconstruction. It punished ex-Confederates and ensured Republican support in the South. But women's partisan loyalties were not so clear, and a substantial majority of northern voters—all men, of course—opposed women's enfranchisement. Even Radicals feared that this "side issue" would overburden their program. Influential abolitionists such as Wendell Philips refused to campaign for women's suffrage, fearing it would detract from the focus on black men. Philips criticized women's leaders for being "selfish." "Do you believe," Stanton hotly replied, "the African race is entirely composed of males?"

By May 1869, the former allies were at an impasse. At a convention of the Equal Rights Association, black abolitionist and women's rights advocate Frederick Douglass pleaded for white women to consider the situation in the South and allow black male suffrage to take priority. "When women, because they are women, are hunted down, . . . dragged from their homes and

OUT IN THE COLD.

"Out in the Cold"
Though many women, including African American activists in the South, went to the polls in the early 1870s to test whether the new Fourteenth Amendment had given them the vote, federal courts subsequently rejected women's voting rights. Only Wyoming and Utah territories fully enfranchised women. At the same time, revised naturalization laws allowed immigrant men of African descent—though not of Asian descent—to become citizens. With its crude Irish, African, and Chinese racial caricatures, this 1884 cartoon from the humor magazine *The Judge* echoes the arguments of some white suffragists: though men of races stereotyped as inferior had been enfranchised, white women were not. The woman knocking on the door is also a caricature, with her harsh appearance and masculine hat. Library of Congress.

UNDERSTAND POINTS OF VIEW

Abolitionists and women's suffrage advocates were generally close allies before 1865. What divisions emerged during Reconstruction and why?

hung upon lamp posts," Douglass said, "then they will have an urgency to obtain the ballot equal to our own." Some women's suffrage leaders joined Douglass in backing the Fifteenth Amendment without the word *sex*. But many, especially white women, rejected Douglass's plea. One African American woman remarked that they "all go for sex, letting race occupy a minor position." Embittered, Elizabeth Cady Stanton lashed out against "Patrick and Sambo and Hans and Ung Tung," maligning uneducated freedmen and immigrants who could vote while educated white women could not. Douglass's resolution in support of the Fifteenth Amendment failed, and the convention broke up.

At this searing moment, a rift opened in the women's movement. The majority, led by Lucy Stone, reconciled themselves to disappointment. Organized into the **American Woman Suffrage Association**, they remained loyal to the Republican Party in hopes that once Reconstruction had been settled, it would be women's turn. A group led by Elizabeth Cady Stanton and Susan B. Anthony struck out in a new direction. They saw that, once the Reconstruction Amendments had passed, women's suffrage was unlikely in the near future. Stanton declared that woman "must not put her trust in man." The new organization she headed,

the **National Woman Suffrage Association** (NWSA), focused exclusively on women's rights and took up the battle for a federal suffrage amendment.

In 1873, NWSA members decided to test the new constitutional amendments. Suffragists all over the United States, including some black women in the South, tried to register and vote. Most were turned away. In an ensuing lawsuit, suffrage advocate Virginia Minor of Missouri argued that the registrar who denied her a ballot had violated her rights under the Fourteenth Amendment. In *Minor v. Happersett* (1875), the Supreme Court dashed such hopes. It ruled that suffrage rights were not inherent in citizenship; women were citizens, but state legislatures could deny women the vote if they wished.

Despite these defeats, Radical Reconstruction had created the conditions for a nationwide women's rights movement. Some argued for suffrage as part of a broader expansion of democracy. Others, on the contrary, saw white women's votes as a possible counterweight to the votes of African American or Chinese men (while opponents pointed out that black and immigrant women would likely be enfranchised, too). When Wyoming Territory gave women full voting rights in 1869, its governor received telegrams of congratulation from around the world. Afterward, contrary to dire predictions, female voters in Wyoming did not appear to neglect their homes, abandon their children, or otherwise "unsex" themselves. Women's suffrage could no longer be dismissed as the absurd notion of a tiny minority. It had become a serious issue for national debate.

The Meaning of Freedom

While political leaders wrangled in Washington, emancipated slaves acted on their own ideas about freedom (American Voices, p. 488). Emancipation meant many things: the end of punishment by the lash; the ability to move around; reunion of families; and opportunities to build schools and churches and to publish and read newspapers. Foremost among freedpeople's demands were voting rights and economic autonomy. Former Confederates opposed these goals. Most southern whites believed the proper place for blacks was as "servants and inferiors," as a Virginia planter testified to Congress. Mississippi's governor, elected under President Johnson's plan, vowed that "ours is and it shall ever be, a government of white men." Meanwhile, as Reconstruction unfolded, it became clear that on economic questions, southern blacks and northern Republican policymakers did not see eye to eye.

The Quest for Land

During the Civil War, wherever Union forces had conquered portions of the South, rural black workers had formed associations that agreed on common goals and even practiced military drills. After the war, when resettlement became the responsibility of the Freedmen's Bureau, thousands of rural blacks hoped for land distributions. But Johnson's amnesty plan, which allowed pardoned Confederates to recover property seized during the war, blasted such hopes. In October 1865, for example, Johnson ordered General Oliver O. Howard, head of the Freedmen's Bureau, to restore plantations on South Carolina's Sea Islands to white property holders. Dispossessed blacks protested: "Why do you take away our lands? You take them from us who have always been true, always true to the Government! You give them to our all-time enemies! That is not right!" Former slaves resisted efforts to evict them. Led by black Union veterans, they fought pitched battles with former slaveholders and bands of ex-Confederate soldiers. But white landowners, sometimes aided by federal troops, generally prevailed.

Freed Slaves and Northerners: Conflicting Goals
On questions of land and labor, freedmen in the South and Republicans in Washington seriously differed. The economic revolution of the antebellum period had transformed New England and the Mid-Atlantic states. Believing similar development could revolutionize the South, most congressional leaders sought to restore cotton as the country's leading export, and they envisioned former slaves as wageworkers on cash-crop plantations, not independent farmers. Only a handful of radicals, like Thaddeus Stevens, argued that freed slaves had earned a right to land grants, through what Lincoln had referred to as "four hundred years of unrequited toil." Stevens proposed that southern plantations be treated as "forfeited estates of the enemy" and broken up into small farms for former slaves. "Nothing will make men so industrious and moral," Stevens declared, "as to let them feel that they are above want and are the owners of the soil which they till."

Today, most historians of Reconstruction agree with Stevens: policymakers did not do enough to ensure freedpeople's economic security. Without land, former slaves were left poor and vulnerable. At the time, though, Stevens had few allies. A deep veneration for private property lay at the heart of his vision, but others interpreted the same principle differently: they defined ownership by legal title, not by labor invested. Though often accused of harshness toward the defeated Confederacy, most Republicans — even Radicals — could not imagine "giving" land to former slaves. The same congressmen, of course, had no difficulty giving away homesteads on the frontier that had been taken from Indians. But they were deeply reluctant to confiscate white-owned plantations.

Some southern Republican state governments did try, without much success, to use tax policy to break up large landholdings and get them into the hands of poorer whites and blacks. In 1869, South Carolina established a land commission to buy property and resell it on easy terms to the landless; about 14,000 black families acquired farms through the program. But such initiatives were the exception, not the rule. Over time, some rural blacks did succeed in becoming small-scale landowners, especially in Upper South states such as Virginia, North Carolina, and Tennessee. But it was an uphill fight, and policymakers provided little aid.

Wage Labor and Sharecropping
Without land, most freedpeople had few options but to work for former slave owners. Landowners wanted to retain the old gang-labor system, with wages replacing the food, clothing, and shelter that slaves had once received. Southern planters — who had recently scorned the North for the cruelties of wage labor — now embraced

Freedom

Slavery meant one thing to slave masters, something altogether different to those enslaved. Emancipation exposed these radically different points of view.

Henry William Ravenel
Diary, March 8, 1865

Ravenel, from a (formerly) wealthy plantation family in South Carolina, wrote amid the Confederacy's collapse and the aftermath of defeat.

The breath of Emancipation has passed over the country, & we are now in that transition state between the new & the old systems — a state of chaos & disorder. Will the negro be materially benefitted by the change? Will the condition of the country in its productive resources, in material prosperity be improved? Will it be a benefit to the landed proprietors? These are questions which will have their solution in the future. They are in the hands of that Providence which over-ruleth all things for good. It was a strong conviction of my best judgment that the old relation of master & slave, had received the divine sanction & was the best condition in which the two races could live together for mutual benefit. There were many defects to be corrected & many abuses to be remedied. Among these defects I will enumerate the want of legislation to make the marriage contract binding — to prevent the separation of families, & to restrain the cupidity of cruel masters. Perhaps it is for neglecting these obligations that God has seen fit to dissolve that relation. I believe the negro must remain in this country & that his condition although a freed-man, must be to labour on the soil. Nothing but necessity will compel him to labour. Now the question is, will that necessity be so strong as to compel him to labour, which will be profitable to the landed proprietors. Will he make as much cotton, sugar, rice & tobacco for the world as he did previously? They will now have a choice *where* to labour. This will ensure good treatment & the best terms. The most humane, the most energetic & the most judicious managers have the best chances in the race for success. I expect to see a revolution in the ownership of landed estates. Those only can succeed who bring the best capacity for the business. Time will show.

Source: *The Civil War and Reconstruction: A Documentary Collection*, ed. William E. Gienapp (New York: W. W. Norton, 2001), 304–305.

Edward Barnell Heyward
Letter, January 22, 1866

In this letter to a friend in the North, the son of a South Carolina plantation owner made grim predictions for the future.

My dear Jim

Your letter of date July 1865, has just reached me and you will be relieved by my answers, to find that I am still alive, and extremely glad to hear from you. . . . I have served in the Army, my brother died in the Army, and every family has lost members. No one can know how reduced we are, particularly the refined & educated. . . .

My father had five plantations on the coast, and all the buildings were burnt, and the negroes, now left to themselves, are roaming in a starvation condition . . . like lost sheep, with no one to care for them.

They find the Yankee only a speculator, and they have no confidence in anyone. They very naturally, poor things, think that freedom means doing nothing, and this they are determined to do. They look to the government, to take care of them, and it will be many years, before this once productive country will be able to support itself. The former kind and just treatment of the slaves, and their docile and generous temper, make them now disposed to be [quiet] and obedient: but the determination of your Northern people to give them a place in the councils of the Country and make them the equal of the white man, will at last, bear its fruit, and we may *then* expect them, to rise against the whites, and in the end, be exterminated themselves.

I am now interested in a school for the negroes, who are around me, and will endeavor to do my duty, to them, as ever before, but I am afraid their best days are past. . . .

I feel now that I have *no country*, I *obey* like a subject, but I cannot love such a government. Perhaps the next letter, you get from me, will be from England. . . .

Source: Stanley I. Kutler, ed., *Looking for America: The People's History*, 2nd ed., 2 vols. (New York: W. W. Norton, 1979), 2: 4–6.

Isabella Soustan
Letter, July 10, 1865

Isabella Soustan, a freedwoman in Virginia, wrote to her former master not long after the Civil War ended.

I have the honor to appeal to you once more for assistance, Master. I am cramped hear nearly to death and no one ceares for me heare, and I want you if you please Sir, to Send for me. I dont care if I am free. I had rather live with you. I was as free while with you, as I wanted to be. Mas Man you know I was as well Satisfied with you as I wanted to be. . . . John is still hired out at the same and doing Well and well Satisfied only greaveing about home, he want to go home as bad as I do, if you ever Send for me I will Send for him immediately, and take him home to his kind Master. . . . Pleas to give my love to all of my friends, and especially to my young mistress don't forget to reserve a double portion for yourself. I Will close at present, hoping to bee at your Service Soon yes before yonder Sun Shal rise and set any more.

May I subscribe myself your Most affectionate humble friend and Servt.

Isabella A. Soustan

Source: Leon F. Litwack, *Been in the Storm So Long: The Aftermath of Slavery* (New York: Knopf, 1979), 332.

Jourdon Anderson
Letter, August 7, 1865

Anderson had escaped with his family from Tennessee and settled in Dayton, Ohio. He dictated this letter to a friend, and it later appeared in the *New York Tribune*. Folklorists have reported on ways that enslaved people found, even in bondage, for "puttin' down" masters. But only in freedom—and in a northern state—could Anderson's sarcasm be expressed so openly.

To My Old Master, Colonel P. H. Anderson, Big Spring, Tennessee.
Sir:

I got your letter, and was glad to find that you had not forgotten Jourdon. . . . I thought the Yankees would have hung you long before this, for harboring Rebs. . . .

I want to know particularly what the good chance is you propose to give me. I am doing tolerably well here. I get twenty-five dollars a month, with victuals and clothing; have a comfortable home for Mandy,—the folks here call her Mrs. Anderson,—and the children—Milly, Jane, and Grundy—go to school and are learning well. . . .

Mandy says she would be afraid to go back without some proof that you were disposed to treat us justly and kindly; and we have concluded to test your sincerity by asking you to send us our wages for the time we served you. This will make us forget and forgive old scores, and rely on your justice and friendship in the future. I served you faithfully for thirty-two years, and Mandy twenty years. At twenty-five dollars a month for me and two dollars a week for Mandy, our earnings would amount to eleven thousand six hundred and eighty dollars. Add to this the interest for the time our wages have been kept back, and deduct what you paid for our clothing, and three doctor's visits to me, and pulling a tooth for Mandy, and the balance will show what we are in justice entitled to. Please send the balance by Adams Express, in care of V. Winters, esq., Dayton, Ohio. If you do not pay us for faithful labors in the past we can have little faith in your promises in the future. . . .

In answering this letter, please state if there would be any safety for my Milly and Jane, who are now grown up, and both good-looking girls. . . . I would rather stay here and starve — and die, if it come to that — than have my girls brought to shame by the violence and wickedness of their young masters. You will also please state if there has been any schools opened for the colored children in your neighborhood. The great desire of my life now is to give my children an education, and have them form virtuous habits.

From your old servant,
Jourdon Anderson
P.S. Say howdy to George Carter, and thank him for taking the pistol from you when you were shooting at me.

Source: Leon F. Litwack, *Been in the Storm So Long: The Aftermath of Slavery* (New York: Knopf, 1979), 333–335.

QUESTIONS FOR ANALYSIS

1. Compare Ravenel's and Heyward's attitudes toward freedmen and freedwomen. How did their views differ, and on what points did they agree?

2. What predictions did Ravenel and Heyward make about the South's postwar future? How might their expectations have shaped their own actions?

3. Soustan and Anderson both wrote to men who had formerly claimed them as property. How do you account for their different outlooks and approaches? What conditions of life does each mention? What inferences might be drawn from this about the varied postwar experiences of freedpeople?

Sharecroppers in Georgia

This photograph shows a Georgia sharecropping family in front of their cabin at cotton-harvesting time. The man in the buggy behind them is probably the landowner. What does this photograph reveal about the condition of sharecroppers? Is there evidence that they might have considered themselves to be doing fairly well—as well as evidence of limits on their success and independence? Note that cotton is growing all the way up to the house, suggesting that the family left little room for a garden or livestock. Through the relentless pressure of loans and debt, sharecropping forced southern farmers into a cash-crop monoculture. Brown Brothers.

wage work with apparent satisfaction. Maliciously comparing black workers to free-roaming pigs, landowners told them to "root, hog, or die." Former slaves found themselves with rock-bottom wages; it was a shock to find that emancipation and "free labor" did not prevent a hardworking family from nearly starving.

African American workers used a variety of tactics to fight back. As early as 1865, alarmed whites across the South reported that former slaves were holding mass meetings to agree on "plans and terms for labor." Such meetings continued through the Reconstruction years. Facing limited prospects at home, some workers left the fields and traveled long distances to seek better-paying jobs on the railroads or in turpentine and lumber camps. Others—from rice cultivators to laundry workers—organized strikes.

At the same time, struggles raged between employers and freedpeople over women's work. In slavery, African American women's bodies had been the sexual property of white men. Protecting black women from such abuse, as much as possible, was a crucial priority for freedpeople. When planters demanded that black women go back into the fields, African Americans resisted resolutely. "I seen on some plantations," one freedman recounted, "where the white men would . . . tell colored men that their wives and children could not live on their places unless they work in the fields. The colored men [answered that] whenever they wanted their wives to work they would tell them themselves."

There was a profound irony in this man's definition of freedom: it designated a wife's labor as her husband's property. Some black women asserted their independence and headed their own households, though this was often a matter of necessity rather than choice. For many freedpeople, the opportunity for a stable family life was one of the greatest achievements of emancipation. Many enthusiastically accepted the northern ideal of domesticity. Missionaries, teachers, and editors of black newspapers urged men to work diligently and support their families, and they told women (though many worked for wages) to devote themselves to motherhood and the home.

Even in rural areas, former slaves refused to work under conditions that recalled slavery. There would be no gang work, they vowed: no overseers, no whippings, no regulation of their private lives. Across the South, planters who needed labor were forced to yield to what one planter termed the "prejudices of the freedmen,

who desire to be masters of their own time." In a few areas, wage work became the norm — for example, on the giant sugar plantations of Louisiana financed by northern capital. But cotton planters lacked money to pay wages, and sometimes, in lieu of a wage, they offered a share of the crop. Freedmen, in turn, paid their rent in shares of the harvest.

Thus the Reconstruction years gave rise to a distinctive system of cotton agriculture known as **sharecropping**, in which freedmen worked as renters, exchanging their labor for the use of land, house, implements, and sometimes seed and fertilizer. Sharecroppers typically turned over half of their crops to the landlord (Map 15.2). In a credit-starved agricultural region that grew crops for a world economy, sharecropping was an effective strategy, enabling laborers and landowners to share risks and returns. But it was a very

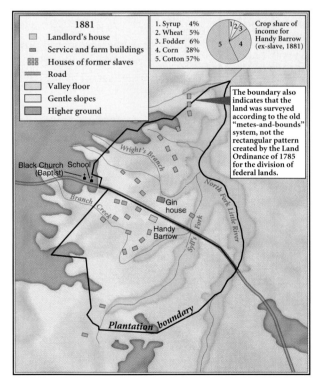

MAP 15.2

The Barrow Plantation, 1860 and 1881

This map is a modern redrawing of one that first appeared in the popular magazine *Scribner's Monthly* in April 1881, accompanying an article about the Barrow plantation. Comparing the 1860 map of this central Georgia plantation with the 1881 map reveals the impact of sharecropping on patterns of black residence. In 1860, the slave quarters were clustered near the planter's house. In contrast, by 1881 the sharecroppers were scattered across the plantation's 2,000 acres, having built cabins on the ridges between the low-lying streams. The surname *Barrow* was common among the sharecropping families, which means almost certainly that they had been slaves who, years after emancipation, still had not moved on. For sharecroppers, freedom meant not only their individual lots and cabins but also the school and church shown on the map.

unequal relationship. Starting out penniless, share-croppers had no way to make it through the first grow-ing season without borrowing for food and supplies.

Country storekeepers stepped in. Bankrolled by northern suppliers, they furnished sharecroppers with provisions and took as collateral a lien on the crop, effectively assuming ownership of croppers' shares and leaving them only what remained after debts had been paid. Crop-lien laws enforced lenders' ownership rights to the crop share. Once indebted at a store, share-croppers became easy targets for exorbitant prices, unfair interest rates, and crooked bookkeeping. As cot-ton prices declined in the 1870s, more and more share-croppers fell into permanent debt. If the merchant was also the landowner or conspired with the landowner, debt became a pretext for forced labor, or peonage.

Sharecropping arose in part because it was a good fit for cotton agriculture. Cotton, unlike sugarcane, could be raised efficiently by small farmers (provided they had the lash of indebtedness always on their backs). We can see this in the experience of other regions that became major pro-ducers in response to the global cotton shortage set off by the Civil War. In India, Egypt, Brazil, and West Africa, variants of the sharecropping system emerged. Everywhere international merchants and bankers, who put up cap-ital, insisted on passage of crop-lien laws. Indian and Egyptian villagers ended up, like their American coun-terparts, permanently under the thumb of furnishing merchants.

By 1890, three out of every four black farmers in the South were tenants or sharecroppers; among white farmers, the ratio was one in three. For freedmen, sharecropping was not the worst choice, in a world where former masters threatened to impose labor con-ditions that were close to slavery. But the costs were devastating. With farms leased on a year-to-year basis, neither tenant nor owner had much incentive to improve the property. The crop-lien system rested on expensive interest payments—money that might otherwise have gone into agricultural improvements or to meet human needs. And sharecropping committed the South inflexibly to cotton, a crop that generated the cash required by landlords and furnishing merchants. The result was a stagnant farm economy that blighted the South's future. As Republican governments tried to remake the region, they confronted not only wartime destruction but also the failure of their hopes that free

IDENTIFY CAUSES
Why did sharecropping emerge, and how did it affect freedpeople and the southern economy?

Cotton Farmers, Marietta, Georgia, c. 1880

Before the Civil War, the South had proudly called itself the "Cotton Kingdom." After the war, cotton was still king, but few southerners got rich on cot-ton profits. Instead, thousands of small-scale farmers, white and black, struggled with plunging crop prices, debt, and taxes on land to support an array of ambitious Reconstruction pro-grams. The farmers here have baled their cotton for market and pose with their wagons in Marietta's courthouse square.
Courtesy Georgia Vanishing Archives Collection, cob262.

labor would create a modern, prosperous South, built in the image of the industrializing North. Instead, the South's rural economy remained mired in widespread poverty and based on an uneasy compromise between landowners and laborers.

Republican Governments in the South

Between 1868 and 1871, all the former Confederate states met congressional stipulations and rejoined the Union. Protected by federal troops, Republican administrations in these states retained power for periods ranging from a few months in Virginia to nine years in South Carolina, Louisiana, and Florida. These governments remain some of the most misunderstood institutions in all U.S. history. Ex-Confederates never accepted their legitimacy. Many other whites agreed, focusing particularly on the role of African Americans who began to serve in public office. "It is strange, abnormal, and unfit," declared one British visitor to Louisiana, "that a *negro* Legislature should deal . . . with the gravest commercial and financial interests." During much of the twentieth century, historians echoed such critics, condemning Reconstruction leaders as ignorant and corrupt. These historians shared the racial prejudices of the British observer: Blacks were simply unfit to govern.

In fact, Reconstruction governments were ambitious. They were hated, in part, because they undertook impressive reforms in public education, family law, social services, commerce, and transportation. Like their northern allies, southern Republicans admired the economic and social transformations that had occurred in the North before the Civil War and worked energetically to import them.

The southern Republican Party included former Whigs, a few former Democrats, black and white newcomers from the North, and southern African Americans. From the start, its leaders faced the dilemma of racial prejudice. In the upcountry, white Unionists were eager to join the party but sometimes reluctant to work with black allies. In most areas, the Republicans also desperately needed African Americans, who constituted a majority of registered voters in Alabama, Florida, South Carolina, and Mississippi.

For a brief moment in the late 1860s, black and white Republicans joined forces through the **Union League**, a secret fraternal order. Formed in border states and northern cities during the Civil War, the league became a powerful political association that spread through the former Confederacy. Functioning as a grassroots wing of Radical Republicanism, it

pressured Congress to uphold justice for freedmen. After blacks won voting rights, the league organized meetings at churches and schoolhouses to instruct freedmen on political issues and voting procedures. League clubs held parades and military drills, giving a public face to the new political order.

The Freedmen's Bureau also supported grassroots Reconstruction efforts. Though some bureau officials sympathized with planters, most were dedicated, idealistic men who tried valiantly to reconcile opposing interests. Bureau men kept a sharp eye out for unfair labor contracts and often forced landowners to bargain with workers and tenants. They advised freedmen on economic matters; provided direct payments to desperate families, especially women and children; and helped establish schools. In cooperation with northern aid societies, the bureau played a key role in founding African American colleges and universities such as Fisk, Tougaloo, and the Hampton Institute. These institutions, in turn, focused on training teachers. By 1869, there were more than three thousand teachers instructing freedpeople in the South. More than half were themselves African Americans.

Ex-Confederates viewed the Union League, Freedmen's Bureau, and Republican Party as illegitimate forces in southern affairs, and they resented the political education of freedpeople. They referred to southern whites who supported Reconstruction as **scalawags** — an ancient Scots-Irish term for worthless animals — and denounced northern whites as **carpetbaggers**, self-seeking interlopers who carried all their property in cheap suitcases called carpetbags. Such labels glossed over the actual diversity of white Republicans. Many arrivals from the North, while motivated by personal profit, also brought capital and skills. Interspersed with ambitious schemers were reformers hoping to advance freedmen's rights. So-called scalawags were even more varied. Some southern Republicans were former slave owners; others were ex-Whigs or even ex-Democrats who hoped to attract northern capital. But most hailed from the backcountry and wanted to rid the South of its slaveholding aristocracy, believing slavery had victimized whites as well as blacks.

Southern Democrats' contempt for black politicians, whom they regarded as ignorant field hands, was just as misguided as their stereotypes about white Republicans. Many African American leaders in the South came from the ranks of antebellum free blacks. Others were skilled men like Robert Smalls of South Carolina, who as a slave had worked for wages that he turned over to his master. Smalls, a steamer pilot in

Hiram R. Revels
In 1870, Hiram Rhoades Revels (1827–1901) was elected to the U.S. Senate from Mississippi to fill Jefferson Davis's former seat. Revels was a free black from North Carolina who had moved to the North and attended Knox College in Illinois. During the Civil War he had recruited African Americans for the Union army and, as an ordained Methodist minister, served as chaplain of a black regiment in Mississippi, where he settled after the war. The Granger Collection, New York.

Charleston harbor, had become a war hero when he escaped with his family and other slaves and brought his ship to the Union navy. Buying property in Beaufort after the war, Smalls became a state legislator and later a congressman. Blanche K. Bruce, another former slave, had been tutored on a Virginia plantation by his white father; during the war, he escaped and established a school for freedmen in Missouri. In 1869, he moved to Mississippi and became, five years later, Mississippi's second black U.S. senator. Political leaders such as Smalls and Bruce were joined by northern blacks — including ministers, teachers, and Union veterans — who moved south to support Reconstruction.

During Radical Reconstruction, such men fanned out into plantation districts and recruited former slaves to participate in politics. Literacy helped freedman Thomas Allen, a Baptist minister and shoemaker, win election to the Georgia legislature. "The colored people came to me," Allen recalled, "and I gave them the best instructions I could. I took the *New York Tribune* and

PLACE EVENTS IN CONTEXT
What policies did southern Reconstruction legislators pursue, and what needs of the postwar South did they seek to serve?

other papers, and in that way I found out a great deal, and I told them whatever I thought was right." Though never proportionate to their numbers in the population, blacks became officeholders across the South. In South Carolina, African Americans constituted a majority in the lower house of the legislature in 1868. Over the course of Reconstruction, twenty African Americans served in state administrations as governor, lieutenant governor, secretary of state, or lesser offices. More than six hundred became state legislators, and sixteen were congressmen.

Both white and black Republicans had big plans. Their southern Reconstruction governments eliminated property qualifications for the vote and abolished Black Codes. Their new state constitutions expanded the rights of married women, enabling them to own their own property and wages — "a wonderful reform," one white woman in Georgia wrote, for "the cause of Women's Rights." Like their counterparts in the North, southern Republicans also believed in using government to foster economic growth. Seeking to diversify the economy beyond cotton agriculture, they poured money into railroads and other projects.

In myriad ways, Republicans brought southern state and city governments up to date. They outlawed corporal punishments such as whipping and branding. They established hospitals and asylums for orphans and the disabled. South Carolina offered free public health services, while Alabama provided free legal representation for defendants who could not pay. Some municipal governments paved streets and installed streetlights. Petersburg, Virginia, established a board of health that offered free medical care during the smallpox epidemic of 1873. Nashville, Tennessee, created soup kitchens for the poor.

Most impressive of all were achievements in public education, where the South had lagged woefully. Republicans viewed education as the foundation of a true democratic order. By 1875, over half of black children were attending school in Mississippi, Florida, and South Carolina. African Americans of all ages rushed to the newly established schools, even when they had to pay tuition. They understood why slaveholders had criminalized slave literacy: the practice of freedom rested on the ability to read newspapers, labor contracts, history books, and the Bible. A school official in Virginia reported that freedpeople were "*crazy* to learn." One Louisiana man explained why he was sending his children to school, even though he needed their help in the field. It was "better than leaving them a fortune; because if you left them even five hundred dollars, some man having more education than they had would come along and cheat them out of it all."

Thousands of white children, particularly girls and the sons of poor farmers and laborers, also benefitted from new public education systems. Young white women's graduation from high school, an unheard-of occurrence before the Civil War, became a celebrated event in southern cities and towns.

Southern Reconstruction governments also had their flaws — flaws that would become more apparent as the 1870s unfolded. In the race for economic development, for example, state officials allowed private companies to hire out prisoners to labor in mines and other industries, in a notorious system known as **convict leasing**. Corruption was rife and conditions horrific. In 1866, Alabama's governor leased 200 state convicts to a railroad construction company for the grand total of $5. While they labored to build state-subsidized lines such as the Alabama and Chattanooga, prisoners were housed at night in open, rolling cages. Physical abuse was common and medical care nonexistent. At the start of 1869, Alabama counted 263 prisoners available for leasing; by the end of the year, a staggering 92 of them had died. While convict leasing expanded in later decades, it began during Reconstruction, supported by both Republicans and Democrats.

Building Black Communities

In slavery days, African Americans had built networks of religious worship and mutual aid, but these operated largely in secret. After emancipation, southern blacks could engage in open community building. In doing so, they cooperated with northern missionaries and teachers, both black and white, who came to help in the great work of freedom. "Ignorant though they may be, on account of long years of oppression, they exhibit a desire to hear and to learn, that I never imagined," reported African American minister Reverend James Lynch, who traveled from Maryland to the Deep South. "Every word you say while preaching, they drink down and respond to, with an earnestness that sets your heart all on fire."

COMPARE AND CONTRAST
Compare the results of African Americans' community building with their struggles to obtain better working conditions. What links do you see between these efforts?

Independent churches quickly became central community institutions, as blacks across the South left white-dominated congregations, where they had sat in segregated balconies, and built churches of their own. These churches joined their counterparts in the North to become national denominations, including, most prominently, the National Baptist Convention and the African Methodist Episcopal Church. Black churches served not only as sites of worship but also as schools, social centers, and meeting halls. Ministers were often political spokesmen as well. As Charles H. Pearce, a black Methodist pastor in Florida, declared, "A man in this State cannot do his whole duty as a minister except he looks out for the political interests of his people." Religious leaders articulated the special destiny of freedpeople as the new "Children of Israel."

The flowering of black churches, schools, newspapers, and civic groups was one of the most enduring initiatives of the Reconstruction era. Dedicated teachers and charity leaders embarked on a project of "race uplift" that never ceased thereafter, while black

Freedmen's School, Petersburg, Virginia, 1870s

A Union veteran, returning to Virginia in the 1870s to photograph battlefields, captured this image of an African American teacher and her students at a freedmen's school. Note the difficult conditions in which they study: many are barefoot, and there are gaps in the walls and floor of the school building. Nonetheless, the students have a few books. Despite poverty and relentless hostility from many whites, freedpeople across the South were determined to get a basic education for themselves and their children. William L. Clements Library, University of Michigan.

Fisk Jubilee Singers, 1873
Fisk University in Nashville, Tennessee, was established in 18€5 to provide higher education for African Americans from all across the South. When university funds ran short in 1871, the Jubilee Singers choral group was formed and began touring to raise money for the school. They performed African American spirituals and folksongs, such as "Swing Low, Sweet Chariot," arranged in ways that appealed to white audiences, making this music nationally popular for the first time. In 1872, the group performed for President Grant at the White House. Money raised by this acclaimed chorale saved Fisk from bankruptcy. Edmund Havel's portrait of the group was painted during their first European tour. Fisk University Art Galleries.

entrepreneurs were proud to build businesses that served their communities. The issue of desegregation—sharing public facilities with whites—was a trickier one. Though some black leaders pressed for desegregation, they were keenly aware of the backlash this was likely to provoke. Others made it clear that they preferred their children to attend all-black schools, especially if they encountered hostile or condescending white teachers and classmates. Many had pragmatic concerns. Asked whether she wanted her boys to attend an integrated school, one woman in New Orleans said no: "I don't want my children to be pounded by . . . white boys. I don't send them to school to fight, I send them to learn."

At the national level, congressmen wrestled with similar issues as they debated an ambitious civil rights bill championed by Radical Republican senator Charles Sumner. Sumner first introduced his bill in 1870, seeking to enforce, among other things, equal access to schools, public transportation, hotels, and churches. Despite a series of defeats and delays, the bill remained on Capitol Hill for five years. Opponents charged that shared public spaces would lead to race mixing and intermarriage. Some sympathetic Republicans feared a backlash, while others questioned whether, because of the First Amendment, the federal government had the right to regulate churches. On his deathbed in 1874, Sumner exhorted a visitor to remember the civil rights bill: "Don't let it fail." In the end, the Senate removed Sumner's provision for integrated churches, and the House removed the clause requiring integrated schools. But to honor the great Massachusetts abolitionist, Congress passed the **Civil Rights Act of 1875**. The law required "full and equal" access to jury service and to transportation and public accommodations, irrespective of race. It was the last such act for almost a hundred years—until the Civil Rights Act of 1964.

The Undoing of Reconstruction

Sumner's death marked the waning of Radical Reconstruction. That movement had accomplished more than anyone dreamed a few years earlier. But a chasm had opened between the goals of freedmen, who wanted autonomy, and policymakers, whose first priorities were to reincorporate ex-Confederates into the nation and build a powerful national economy. Meanwhile, the North was flooded with one-sided, racist reports such as James M. Pike's influential book *The Prostrate State* (1873), which claimed South Carolina was in the grip of "black barbarism." Events of the 1870s deepened the northern public's disillusionment. Scandals rocked the Grant administration, and an economic depression curbed both private investment and public spending. At the same time, northern resolve was worn down by continued ex-Confederate resistance and violence. Only full-scale military intervention could reverse the situation in the South, and by the mid-1870s the North had no political willpower to renew the occupation.

The Republicans Unravel

Republicans had banked on economic growth to underpin their ambitious program, but their hopes were dashed in 1873 by the sudden onset of a severe worldwide depression. In the United States, the initial panic was triggered by the bankruptcy of the Northern Pacific Railroad, backed by leading financier Jay Cooke. Cooke's supervision of Union finances during the Civil War had made him a national hero; his downfall was a shock, and since Cooke was so well connected in Washington, it raised suspicions that Republican financial manipulation had caused the depression. Officials in the Grant administration deepened public resentment toward their party when they rejected pleas to increase the money supply and provide relief from debt and unemployment.

The impact of the depression varied in different parts of the United States. Farmers suffered a terrible plight as crop prices plunged, while industrial workers faced layoffs and sharp wage reductions. Within a year, 50 percent of American iron manufacturing had stopped. By 1877, half the nation's railroad companies had filed for bankruptcy. Rail construction halted. With hundreds of thousands thrown out of work, people took to the road. Wandering "tramps," who camped by railroad tracks and knocked on doors to beg for work and food, terrified prosperous Americans.

In addition to discrediting Republicans, the depression directly undercut their policies, most dramatically in the South. The ex-Confederacy was still recovering from the ravages of war, and its new economic and social order remained fragile. The bold policies of southern Republicans — for education, public health, and grants to railroad builders — cost a great deal of money. Federal support, through programs like the Freedmen's Bureau, had begun to fade even before 1873. Republicans had banked on major infusions of northern and foreign investment capital; for the most part, these failed to materialize. Investors who had sunk money into Confederate bonds, only to have those repudiated, were especially wary. The South's economy grew more slowly than Republicans had hoped, and after 1873, growth screeched to a halt. State debts mounted rapidly, and as crushing interest on bonds fell due, public credit collapsed.

Not only had Republican officials failed to anticipate a severe depression; during the era of generous spending, considerable funds had also been wasted or had ended up in the pockets of corrupt officials. Two swindlers in North Carolina, one of them a former Union general, were found to have distributed more than $200,000 in bribes and loans to legislators to gain millions in state funds for rail construction. Instead of building railroads, they used the money to travel to Europe and speculate in stocks and bonds. Not only Republicans were on the take. "You are mistaken," wrote one southern Democrat to a northern friend, "if you suppose that all the evils . . . result from the carpetbaggers and negroes. The Democrats are leagued with them when anything is proposed that promises to pay." In South Carolina, when African American congressman Robert Smalls was convicted of taking a bribe, the Democratic governor pardoned him — in exchange for an agreement that federal officials would drop an investigation of Democratic election frauds.

One of the depression's most tragic results was the failure of the **Freedman's Savings and Trust Company.** This private bank, founded in 1865, had worked closely with the Freedmen's Bureau and Union army across the South. Former slaves associated it with the party of Lincoln, and thousands responded to northerners' call for thrift and savings by bringing their small deposits to the nearest branch. African American farmers, entrepreneurs, churches, and charitable groups opened accounts at the bank. But in the early 1870s, the bank's directors sank their money into risky loans and speculative investments. In June 1874, the bank failed.

Some Republicans believed that, because the bank had been so closely associated with the U.S. Army and federal agencies, Congress had a duty to step in. Even one southern Democrat argued that the government was "morally bound to see to it that not a dollar is lost." But in the end, Congress refused to compensate the 61,000 depositors. About half recovered small amounts — averaging $18.51 — but the others received nothing. The party of Reconstruction was losing its moral gloss.

The Disillusioned Liberals

As a result of the depression and rising criticism of postwar activist government, a revolt emerged in the Republican Party. It was led by influential intellectuals, journalists, and businessmen who believed in **classical liberalism**: free trade, small government, low property taxes, and limitation of voting rights to men of education and property. Liberals responded to the massive increase in federal power, during the Civil War and Reconstruction, by urging a policy of *laissez faire*, in which government "let alone" business and the economy. In the postwar decades, *laissez faire* advocates never succeeded in ending federal policies such as the protective tariff and national banking system (Chapter 16), but their arguments helped roll back Reconstruction. Unable to block Grant's renomination for the presidency in 1872, the dissidents broke away and formed a new party under the name Liberal Republican. Their candidate was Horace Greeley, longtime publisher of the *New York Tribune* and veteran reformer and abolitionist. The Democrats, still in disarray, also nominated Greeley, notwithstanding his editorial diatribes against them. A poor campaigner, Greeley was assailed so severely that, as he said, "I hardly knew whether I was running for the Presidency or the penitentiary."

Grant won reelection overwhelmingly, capturing 56 percent of the popular vote and every electoral vote. Yet Liberal Republicans had shifted the terms of debate. The agenda they advanced — smaller government, restricted voting rights, and reconciliation with ex-Confederates — resonated with Democrats, who had long advocated limited government and were working to reclaim their status as a legitimate national party. Liberalism thus crossed party lines, uniting disillusioned conservative Republicans with Democrats who denounced government activism. E. L. Godkin of *The Nation* and other classical liberal editors played key roles in turning northern public opinion against Reconstruction. With unabashed elitism, Godkin and others claimed that freedmen were unfit to vote. They denounced universal suffrage, which "can only mean in plain English the government of ignorance and vice."

The second Grant administration gave liberals plenty of ammunition. The most notorious scandal involved **Crédit Mobilier**, a sham corporation set up by shareholders in the Union Pacific Railroad to secure government grants at an enormous profit. Organizers of the scheme protected it from investigation by providing gifts of Crédit Mobilier stock to powerful members of Congress. Another scandal involved the Whiskey Ring, a network of liquor distillers and treasury agents who defrauded the government of millions of dollars of excise taxes on whiskey. The ringleader was Grant's private secretary, Orville Babcock. Others went to prison, but Grant stood by Babcock, possibly perjuring himself to save his secretary from jail. The stench of scandal permeated the White House.

Counterrevolution in the South

While northerners became preoccupied with scandals and the shock of economic depression, ex-Confederates seized power in the South. Most believed (as northern liberals had also begun to argue) that southern Reconstruction governments were illegitimate "regimes." Led by the planters, ex-Confederates staged a massive insurgency to take back the South.

When they could win at the ballot box, southern Democrats took that route. They got ex-Confederate voting rights restored and campaigned against "negro rule." But when force was necessary, southern Democrats used it. Present-day Americans, witnessing political violence in other countries, seldom remember that our own history includes the overthrow of elected governments by paramilitary groups. But this is exactly how Reconstruction ended in many parts of the South. Ex-Confederates terrorized Republicans, especially in districts with large proportions of black voters. Black political leaders were shot, hanged, beaten to death, and in one case even beheaded. Many Republicans, both black and white, went into hiding or fled for their lives. Southern Democrats called this violent process **"Redemption"** — a heroic name that still sticks today, even though this seizure of power was murderous and undemocratic.

No one looms larger in this bloody story than Nathan Bedford Forrest, a decorated Confederate general. Born in poverty in 1821, Forrest had risen to become a big-time slave trader and Mississippi planter. A fiery secessionist, Forrest had formed a Tennessee

UNDERSTAND POINTS OF VIEW
How did ex-Confederates, freedpeople, Republicans, and classical liberals view the end of Reconstruction?

Confederate cavalry regiment, fought bravely at the battle of Shiloh, and won fame as a daring raider. On April 12, 1864, his troops perpetrated one of the war's worst atrocities, the massacre at Fort Pillow, Tennessee, of black Union soldiers who were trying to surrender.

After the Civil War, Forrest's determination to uphold white supremacy altered the course of Reconstruction. William G. Brownlow, elected as Tennessee's Republican governor in 1865, was a tough man, a former prisoner of the Confederates who was not shy about calling his enemies to account. Ex-Confederates struck back with a campaign of terror, targeting especially Brownlow's black supporters. Amid the mayhem, ex-Confederates formed the first **Ku Klux Klan** group in late 1865 or early 1866. As it proliferated across the state, the Klan turned to Forrest, who had been trying, unsuccessfully, to rebuild his prewar fortune. Late in 1866, at a secret meeting in Nashville, Forrest donned the robes of Grand Wizard. His activities are mostly cloaked in mystery, but there is no mistake about his goals: the Klan would strike blows against the despised Republican government of Tennessee.

In many towns, the Klan became virtually identical to the Democratic Party. Klan members — including Forrest — dominated Tennessee's delegation to the Democratic national convention of 1868. At home, the Klan unleashed a murderous campaign of terror, and though Governor Brownlow responded resolutely, in the end Republicans cracked. The Klan and similar groups — organized under such names as the White League and Knights of the White Camelia — arose in other states. Vigilantes burned freedmen's schools, beat teachers, attacked Republican gatherings, and murdered political opponents. By 1870, Democrats had seized power in Georgia and North Carolina and were making headway across the South. Once they took power, they slashed property taxes and passed other laws favorable to landowners. They terminated Reconstruction programs and cut funding for schools, especially those teaching black students.

In responding to the Klan between 1869 and 1871, the federal government showed it could still exert power effectively in the South. Determined to end Klan violence, Congress held extensive hearings and in 1870 passed laws designed to protect freedmen's rights under the Fourteenth and Fifteenth Amendments. These so-called **Enforcement Laws** authorized federal prosecutions, military intervention, and martial law to suppress terrorist activity. Grant's administration made full use of these new powers. In South Carolina, where the Klan was deeply entrenched, U.S. troops occupied

Ku Klux Klan Mask

White supremacists of the 1870s organized under many names and wore many costumes, not simply (or often) the white cone-shaped hats that were made famous later, in the 1920s, when the Klan underwent a nationwide resurgence. Few masks from the 1870s have survived. The horns and fangs on this one, from North Carolina, suggest how Klan members sought to strike terror in their victims, while also hiding their own identities. North Carolina Museum of History.

nine counties, made hundreds of arrests, and drove as many as 2,000 Klansmen from the state.

This assault on the Klan, while raising the spirits of southern Republicans, revealed how dependent they were on Washington. "No such law could be enforced by state authority," one Mississippi Republican observed, "the local power being too weak." But northern Republicans were growing disillusioned with Reconstruction, while in the South, prosecuting Klansmen was an uphill battle against all-white juries and unsympathetic federal judges. After 1872, prosecutions dropped off. In the meantime, the Texas government fell to the Democrats in 1873 and Alabama and Arkansas in 1874.

Reconstruction Rolled Back

As divided Republicans debated how to respond, voters in the congressional election of 1874 handed them one of the most stunning defeats of the nineteenth century. Responding especially to the severe depression that gripped the nation, they removed almost half of the party's 199 representatives in the House. Democrats, who had held 88 seats, now commanded an overwhelming majority of 182. "The election is not merely a victory but a revolution," exulted a Democratic newspaper in New York.

After 1874, with Democrats in control of the House, Republicans who tried to shore up their southern wing had limited options. Bowing to election results, the Grant administration began to reject southern Republicans' appeals for aid. Events in Mississippi showed the outcome. As state elections neared there in 1875, paramilitary groups such as the Red Shirts operated openly. Mississippi's Republican governor, Adelbert Ames, a Union veteran from Maine, appealed for U.S. troops, but Grant refused. "The whole public are tired out with these annual autumnal outbreaks in the South," complained a Grant official, who told southern Republicans that they were responsible for their own fate. Facing a rising tide of brutal murders, Governor Ames—realizing that only further bloodshed could result—urged his allies to give up the fight. Brandishing guns and stuffing ballot boxes, Democratic "Redeemers" swept the 1875 elections and took control of Mississippi. By 1876, Reconstruction was largely over. Republican governments, backed by token U.S. military units, remained in only three southern states: Louisiana, South Carolina, and Florida. Elsewhere, former Confederates and their allies took power.

The Supreme Court Rejects Equal Rights

Though ex-Confederates seized power in southern states, new landmark constitutional amendments and federal laws remained in force. If the Supreme Court had left these intact, subsequent generations of civil rights advocates could have used the federal courts to combat racial discrimination and violence. Instead, the Court closed off this avenue for the pursuit of justice, just as it dashed the hopes of women's rights advocates.

As early as 1873, in a group of decisions known collectively as the *Slaughter-House Cases*, the Court began to undercut the power of the Fourteenth Amendment. In this case and a related ruling, *U.S. v. Cruikshank* (1876), the justices argued that the Fourteenth Amendment offered only a few, rather trivial federal protections to citizens (such as access to navigable waterways). In *Cruikshank*—a case that emerged from a gruesome killing of African American farmers by ex-Confederates in Colfax, Louisiana, followed by a Democratic political coup—the Court ruled that voting rights remained a state matter unless the state *itself* violated those rights. If former slaves' rights were violated by individuals or private groups (including the Klan), that lay beyond federal jurisdiction. The Fourteenth Amendment did not protect citizens from armed vigilantes, even when those vigilantes seized

political power. The Court thus gutted the Fourteenth Amendment. In the *Civil Rights Cases* (1883), the justices also struck down the Civil Rights Act of 1875, paving the way for later decisions that sanctioned segregation. The impact of these decisions endured well into the twentieth century.

The Political Crisis of 1877

After the grim election results of 1874, Republicans faced a major battle in the presidential election of 1876. Abandoning Grant, they nominated Rutherford B. Hayes, a former Union general who was untainted by corruption and—even more important—hailed from the key swing state of Ohio. Hayes's Democratic opponent was New York governor Samuel J. Tilden, a Wall Street lawyer with a reform reputation. Tilden favored home rule for the South, but so, more discreetly, did Hayes. With enforcement on the wane, Reconstruction did not figure prominently in the campaign, and little was said about the states still led by Reconstruction governments: Florida, South Carolina, and Louisiana.

Once returns started coming in on election night, however, those states loomed large. Tilden led in the popular vote and seemed headed for victory until sleepless politicians at Republican headquarters realized that the electoral vote stood at 184 to 165, with the 20 votes from Florida, South Carolina, and Louisiana still uncertain. If Hayes took those votes, he would win by a margin of 1. Citing ample evidence of Democratic fraud and intimidation, Republican officials certified all three states for Hayes. "Redeemer" Democrats who had taken over the states' governments submitted their own electoral votes for Tilden. When Congress met in early 1877, it confronted two sets of electoral votes from those states.

The Constitution does not provide for such a contingency. All it says is that the president of the Senate (in 1877, a Republican) opens the electoral certificates before the House (Democratic) and the Senate (Republican) and "the Votes shall then be counted" (Article 2, Section 1). Suspense gripped the country. There was talk of inside deals or a new election—even a violent coup. Finally, Congress appointed an electoral commission to settle the question. The commission included seven Republicans, seven Democrats, and, as the deciding member, David Davis, a Supreme Court justice not known to have fixed party loyalties. Davis, however, disqualified himself by accepting an Illinois Senate seat. He was replaced by Republican justice Joseph P. Bradley, and by a vote of 8 to 7, on party lines, the commission awarded the election to Hayes.

In the House of Representatives, outraged Democrats vowed to stall the final count of electoral votes so

"Grantism"

President Grant was lampooned on both sides of the Atlantic for the problems of his scandal-ridden administration. The British magazine *Puck* shows Grant barely defying gravity to keep himself and his corrupt subordinates aloft and out of jail. To a great extent, however, the hero of the Union army remained personally popular at home and abroad. The British public welcomed Grant with admiration on his triumphant foreign tour in 1877. Library of Congress.

as to prevent Hayes's inauguration on March 4. But in the end, they went along — partly because Tilden himself urged that they do so. Hayes had publicly indicated his desire to offer substantial patronage to the South, including federal funds for education and internal improvements. He promised "a complete change of men and policy" — naively hoping, at the same time, that he could count on support from old-line southern Whigs and protect black voting rights. Hayes was inaugurated on schedule. He expressed hope in his inaugural address that the federal government could serve "the interests of both races carefully and equally." But,

setting aside the U.S. troops who were serving on border duty in Texas, only 3,000 Union soldiers remained in the South. As soon as the new president ordered them back to their barracks, the last Republican administrations in the South collapsed. Reconstruction had ended.

Lasting Legacies

In the short run, the political events of 1877 had little impact on most southerners. Much of the work of "Redemption" had already been done. What mattered

The South's "Lost Cause"

After Reconstruction ended, many white southerners celebrated the Confederacy as a heroic "Lost Cause." Through organizations such as the Sons of Confederate Veterans and United Daughters of the Confederacy, they profoundly influenced the nation's memories of slavery, the Civil War, and Reconstruction.

---

1. **Commemorative postcard of living Confederate flag, Robert E. Lee Monument, Richmond, Virginia, 1907.** *An estimated 150,000 people gathered in 1890 to dedicate this statue—ten times more than had attended earlier memorial events.*

Source: The Library of Virginia.

2. **From the United Daughters of the Confederacy Constitution, 1894.** *The United Daughters of the Confederacy (UDC), founded in 1894, grew in three years to 136 chapters and by the late 1910s counted a membership of 100,000.*

The objects of this association are historical, educational, memorial, benevolent, and social: To fulfill the duties of sacred charity to the survivors of the war and those dependent on them; to collect and preserve material for a truthful history of the war; to protect historic places of the Confederacy; to record the part taken by the Southern women . . . in patient endurance of hardship and patriotic devotion during the struggle; to perpetuate the memory of our Confederate heroes and the glorious cause for which they fought; to cherish the ties of friendship among members of this Association; to endeavor to have used in all Southern schools only such histories as are just and true.

3. **McNeel Marble Co. advertisement in *Confederate Veteran* magazine, 1905.**

To the Daughters of the Confederacy: In regard to that Confederate monument which your Chapter has been talking about and planning for since you first got organized. Why not buy it NOW and have it erected before all the old veterans have answered the final roll call? Why wait and worry about raising funds? Our terms to U.D.C. Chapters are so liberal and our plans for raising funds are so effective as to obviate the necessity of either waiting or worrying. During the last three or four years we have sold Confederate monuments to thirty-seven of your sister Chapters. . . . Our designs, our prices, our work, our business methods have pleased them, and we can please you. What your sister Chapters have done, you can do. . . . WRITE TO-DAY.

4. Confederate veteran's letter, *Confederate Veteran* magazine, 1910. *An anonymous Georgian who had served in Lee's army sent the following letter to the veterans' magazine after attending a reunion in Memphis.*

Reunion gatherings are supposed to be for the benefit of the old veterans; but will you show us where the privates, the men who stood the hardships and did the fighting, have any consideration when they get to the city that is expected to entertain them? . . . [In Memphis, I] stopped at the school building, where there were at least twenty-five or thirty old veterans lying on the ground, and had been there all night. All this while the officers were being banqueted, wined, dined, and quartered in the very best hotels; but the private must shift for himself, stand around on the street, or sit on the curbstone. He must march if he is able, but the officers ride in fine carriages. Pay more attention to the men of the ranks — men who did service! I always go prepared to pay my way; but I do not like to be ignored.

5. Matthew Page Andrews, *The Women of the South in War Times*, 1923. *Matthew Page Andrews's* The Women of the South in War Times, *approved by the UDC, was a popular textbook for decades in schools throughout the South.*

The Southern people of the "old regime" have been pictured as engaged primarily in a protracted struggle for the maintenance of negro slavery. . . . Fighting on behalf of slavery was as far from the minds of these Americans as going to war in order to free the slaves was from the purpose of Abraham Lincoln, whose sole object, frequently expressed by him, was to "preserve the Union." . . .

That, in the midst of war, there were almost no instances of arson, murder, or outrage committed by the negroes of the South is an everlasting tribute to the splendid character of the dominant race and their moral uplift of a weaker one. . . . When these negroes were landed on American shores, almost all were savages taken from the lowest forms of jungle life. It was largely the women of the South who trained these heathen people, molded their characters, and, in the second and third generations, lifted them up a thousand years in the scale of civilization.

6. Susie King Taylor, *Reminiscences of My Life in Camp with the 33d United States Colored Troops, Late 1st S.C. Volunteers*, 1902. *Susie King Taylor, born in slavery in Georgia in 1848, fled with her uncle during the Civil War and served as a nurse in the Union army.*

I read an article, which said the ex-Confederate Daughters had sent a petition to the managers of the local theatres in Tennessee to prohibit the performance of "Uncle Tom's Cabin," claiming it was exaggerated (that is, the treatment of the slaves), and would have a very bad effect on the children who might see the drama. I paused and thought back a few years of the heart-rending scenes I have witnessed. . . . I remember, as if it were yesterday, seeing droves of negroes going to be sold, and I often went to look at them, and I could hear the auctioneer very plainly from my house, auctioning these poor people off.

Do these Confederate Daughters ever send petitions to prohibit the atrocious lynchings and wholesale murdering and torture of the negro? Do you ever hear of them fearing this would have a bad effect on the children? Which of these two, the drama or the present state of affairs, makes a degrading impression upon the minds of our young generation? In my opinion it is not "Uncle Tom's Cabin." . . . It does not seem as if our land is yet civilized.

Sources: (2) *Minutes of the Seventh Annual Meeting of the United Daughters of the Confederacy* (Nashville, TN.: Press of Foster & Webb, Printers, 1901), 235; (3) *Confederate Veteran*, 1905; (4) *Confederate Veteran*, Vol. XVIII (Nashville, TN.: S. A. Cunningham, 1910); (5) Matthew Page Andrews, ed., *The Women of the South in War Times* (Baltimore: The Norman, Remington Co., 1923), 3–4, 9–10; (6) Susie King Taylor, *Reminiscences of My Life in Camp* (Boston: Published by the author, 1902), 65–66.

ANALYZING THE EVIDENCE

1. What do sources 2 and 3 tell us about the work of local UDC chapters? What does the advertisement suggest about the economy of the postwar South?

2. What can you infer from these sources about the situation in the South after the Civil War? Why might women have played a particularly important role in memorial associations?

3. Compare and contrast sources 4 and 6. Who did "Lost Cause" associations serve, and how is this connected to issues of class and race?

4. How does source 5 depict slaves? Slaveholders? Is this an accurate account of the history of the South, and how does this compare to source 4? What do these different interpretations suggest about the legacy of "Redemption"?

PUTTING IT ALL TOGETHER

"Lost Cause" advocates often stated that their work was not political. To what extent was this true, based on the evidence here? What do these documents suggest about the influence of the Lost Cause, and also the limitations and challenges it faced? What do they tell us about the legacies of Reconstruction more broadly?

was the long, slow decline of Radical Republican power and the corresponding rise of Democrats in the South and nationally. It was obvious that so-called Redeemers in the South had assumed power through violence. But many Americans—including prominent classical liberals who shaped public opinion—believed the Democrats had overthrown corrupt, illegitimate governments; thus the end justified the means. After 1874, those who deplored the results had little political traction. The only remaining question was how far Reconstruction would be rolled back.

The South never went back to the antebellum status quo. Sharecropping, for all its flaws and injustices, was not slavery. Freedmen and freedwomen managed to resist gang labor and work on their own terms. They also established their right to marry, read and write, worship as they pleased, and travel in search of a better life—rights that were not easily revoked. Across the South, black farmers overcame great odds to buy and work their own land. African American businessmen built thriving enterprises. Black churches and community groups sustained networks of mutual aid. Parents sacrificed to send their children to school, and a few proudly watched their sons and daughters graduate from college.

Reconstruction had also shaken, if not fully overturned, the legal and political framework that had made the United States a white man's country. This was a stunning achievement, and though hostile courts and political opponents undercut it, no one ever repealed the Thirteenth, Fourteenth, and Fifteenth Amendments. They remained in the Constitution, and the civil rights movement of the twentieth century would return and build on this framework (Chapter 26).

Still, in the final reckoning, Reconstruction failed. The majority of freedpeople remained in poverty, and by the late 1870s their political rights were also eroding. Vocal advocates of smaller government argued that Reconstruction had been a mistake; pressured by economic hardship, northern voters abandoned their southern Unionist allies. One of the enduring legacies of this process was the way later Americans remembered Reconstruction itself. After "Redemption," generations of schoolchildren were taught that ignorant, lazy blacks and corrupt whites had imposed illegitimate Reconstruction "regimes" on the South. White southerners won national support for their celebration of a heroic Confederacy (Thinking Like a Historian, p. 502).

One of the first historians to challenge these views was the great African American intellectual W. E. B. Du Bois. In *Black Reconstruction in America* (1935),

Du Bois meticulously documented the history of African American struggle, white vigilante violence, and national policy failure. If Reconstruction, he wrote, "had been conceived as a major national program . . . whose accomplishment at any price was well worth the effort, we should be living today in a different world." His words still ring true, but in 1935 historians ignored him. Not a single scholarly journal reviewed Du Bois's important book. Ex-Confederates had lost the war, but they won control over the nation's memory of Reconstruction.

Meanwhile, though their programs failed in the South, Republicans carried their nation-building project into the West, where their policies helped consolidate a continental empire. There, the federal power that had secured emancipation created the conditions for the United States to become an industrial power and a major leader on the world stage.

SUMMARY

Postwar Republicans faced two tasks: restoring rebellious states to the Union and defining the role of emancipated slaves. After Lincoln's assassination, his successor, Andrew Johnson, hostile to Congress, unilaterally offered the South easy terms for reentering the Union. Exploiting this opportunity, southerners adopted oppressive Black Codes and put ex-Confederates back in power. Congress impeached Johnson and, though failing to convict him, seized the initiative and placed the South under military rule. In this second, or radical, phase of Reconstruction, Republican state governments tried to transform the South's economic and social institutions. Congress passed innovative civil rights acts and funded new agencies like the Freedmen's Bureau. The Fourteenth Amendment defined U.S. citizenship and asserted that states could no longer supersede it, and the Fifteenth Amendment gave voting rights to formerly enslaved men. Debate over this amendment precipitated a split among women's rights advocates, since women did not win inclusion.

Freedmen found that their goals conflicted with those of Republican leaders, who counted on cotton to fuel economic growth. Like southern landowners, national lawmakers envisioned former slaves as wageworkers, while freedmen wanted their own land. Sharecropping, which satisfied no one completely, emerged as a compromise suited to the needs of the cotton market and an impoverished, credit-starved region.

Nothing could reconcile ex-Confederates to Republican government, and they staged a violent counter-revolution in the name of white supremacy and "Redemption." Meanwhile, struck by a massive economic depression, northern voters handed Republicans a crushing defeat in the election of 1874. By 1876, Reconstruction was dead. Rutherford B. Hayes's narrow victory in the presidential election of that year resulted in withdrawal of the last Union troops from the South. A series of Supreme Court decisions also undermined the Fourteenth Amendment and civil rights laws, setting up legal parameters through which, over the long term, disenfranchisement and segregation would flourish.

C H A P T E R   R E V I E W

MAKE IT STICK   Go to **LearningCurve** to retain what you've read.

TERMS TO KNOW   Identify and explain the significance of each term below.

Key Concepts and Events

Ten Percent Plan (p. 480)
Wade-Davis Bill (p. 480)
Black Codes (p. 481)
Freedmen's Bureau (p. 481)
Civil Rights Act of 1866 (p. 481)
Fourteenth Amendment (p. 481)
Reconstruction Act of 1867 (p. 482)
Fifteenth Amendment (p. 485)
American Woman Suffrage Association (p. 486)
National Woman Suffrage Association (p. 486)
Minor v. Happersett (p. 486)
sharecropping (p. 491)
Union League (p. 493)

scalawags (p. 493)
carpetbaggers (p. 493)
convict leasing (p. 495)
Civil Rights Act of 1875 (p. 496)
Freedman's Savings and Trust Company (p. 497)
classical liberalism (p. 498)
laissez faire (p. 498)
Crédit Mobilier (p. 498)
"Redemption" (p. 498)
Ku Klux Klan (p. 499)
Enforcement Laws (p. 499)
Slaughter-House Cases (p. 500)
U.S. v. Cruikshank (p. 500)
Civil Rights Cases (p. 500)

Key People

Andrew Johnson (p. 480)
Charles Sumner (p. 481)
Thaddeus Stevens (p. 482)
Ulysses S. Grant (p. 483)
Elizabeth Cady Stanton (p. 486)
Robert Smalls (p. 493)
Blanche K. Bruce (p. 494)
Nathan Bedford Forrest (p. 498)

REVIEW QUESTIONS   Answer these questions to demonstrate your understanding of the chapter's main ideas.

1. How did U.S. presidents and Congress seek to reintegrate the Confederacy into the Union? What different approaches did they take, and what were the results?

2. Compare the goals of Radical Republicans, freedpeople, and ex-Confederates during Reconstruction. What conflicts ensued from their differing agendas?

3. Why did Reconstruction falter? To what extent was its failure the result of events in the South, the North, and Washington, D.C.?

4. Some of the language historians use to describe Reconstruction still reflects the point of view of ex-Confederates, who spoke of "Redemption." What other names might we use for that process? What difference (if any) would it make if scholars called it something else?

5. THEMATIC UNDERSTANDING   Look again at the events listed under "Politics and Power" and "Identity" on the thematic timeline on page 409. Some historians have argued that, during this era, the United States moved, politically and socially, from being a loose union of states to being a more unified and inclusive *nation*. To what extent do you agree? Use the events of Reconstruction as evidence in making your case.

MAKING CONNECTIONS

Recognize the larger developments and continuities within and across chapters by answering these questions.

1. ACROSS TIME AND PLACE   Ex-Confederates were not the first Americans to engage in violent protest against what they saw as tyrannical government power. Imagine, for example, a conversation between a participant in Shays's Rebellion (Chapter 6) and a southern Democrat who participated in the overthrow of a Republican government in his state. How would each describe his grievances? Who would he name as enemies? Compare and contrast the tactics of these and other violent protests against government power in the United States. To what extent did these groups succeed?

2. VISUAL EVIDENCE   Return to the image at the start of this chapter (p. 479), which shows a celebration in Baltimore after ratification of the Fifteenth Amendment. Note the distinguished African American heroes depicted at the top and the three scenes at the bottom. In the complete version of this popular lithograph, additional images appear on the left and right: black Union soldiers in battle; an African American minister preaching at an independent black church; a teacher and her students in a freedpeople's school; an African American farmer in a wheat field; and a drawing of a proud black family on their farm with the caption "We till our own fields." If a freedperson and a former slave owner had seen this image in 1870, how might each have responded? Imagine that an African American family had placed the picture in their home in 1870. How might they have reflected differently, twenty years later, on its significance?

MORE TO EXPLORE

Start here to learn more about the events discussed in this chapter.

American Social History Project, *Freedom's Unfinished Revolution* (1996). A wonderful collection of images and eyewitness accounts.

Philip Dray, *Capitol Men* (2008). A readable history of Reconstruction from the perspective of the first African American congressmen.

Faye E. Dudden, *Fighting Chance: The Struggle over Woman Suffrage and Black Suffrage in Reconstruction America* (2011). A thoughtful exploration of the split among radical reformers.

Eric Foner, *A Short History of Reconstruction* (1990). The best short overview of events in this decade, combining grassroots and political perspectives.

Steven Hahn, *A Nation Under Our Feet* (2003). Hahn's groundbreaking study of the rural South shows how African Americans' strategies during Reconstruction were built on earlier experiences during slavery and the Civil War.

Brooks D. Simpson, *The Reconstruction Presidents* (1998). A lively assessment of presidential politics from Lincoln through Hayes, full of entertaining quotations.

TIMELINE

Ask yourself why this chapter begins and ends with these dates and then identify the links among related events.

1864	• Wade-Davis Bill passed by Congress but killed by Lincoln's pocket veto
1865	• Freedmen's Bureau established • Lincoln assassinated; Andrew Johnson succeeds him as president • Johnson implements restoration plan • Ex-Confederate states pass Black Codes to limit freedpeople's rights
1866	• Civil Rights Act passes over Johnson's veto • Major Republican gains in congressional elections
1867	• Reconstruction Act
1868	• Impeachment of Andrew Johnson • Fourteenth Amendment ratified • Ulysses S. Grant elected president
1870	• Ku Klux Klan at peak of power • Congress passes Enforcement Laws to suppress Klan • Fifteenth Amendment ratified
1872	• Grant reelected; Crédit Mobilier scandal emerges
1873	• Panic of 1873 ushers in severe economic depression
1874	• Sweeping Democratic gains in congressional elections
1875	• Whiskey Ring and other scandals undermine Grant administration • *Minor v. Happersett*: Supreme Court rules that Fourteenth Amendment does not extend voting rights to women
1876	• Supreme Court severely curtails Reconstruction in *U.S. v. Cruikshank*
1877	• Rutherford B. Hayes becomes president • Reconstruction officially ends

KEY TURNING POINTS: Identify two crucial turning points in the course of Reconstruction. What caused those shifts in direction, and what were the results?

16
CHAPTER

Conquering a Continent
1854–1890

O n May 10, 1869, Americans poured into the streets for a giant party. In big cities, the racket was incredible. Cannons boomed and train whistles shrilled. New York fired a hundred-gun salute at City Hall. Congregations sang anthems, while the less religious gathered in saloons to celebrate with whiskey. Philadelphia's joyful throngs reminded an observer of the day, four years earlier, when news had arrived of Lee's surrender. The festivities were prompted by a long-awaited telegraph message: executives of the Union Pacific and Central Pacific railroads had driven a golden spike at Promontory Point, Utah, linking up their lines. Unbroken track now stretched from the Atlantic to the Pacific. A journey across North America could be made in less than a week.

The first **transcontinental railroad** meant jobs and money. San Francisco residents got right to business: after firing a salute, they loaded Japanese tea on a train bound for St. Louis, marking California's first overland delivery to the East. In coming decades, trade and tourism fueled tremendous growth west of the Mississippi. San Francisco, which in 1860 had handled $7.4 million in imports, increased that figure to $49 million over thirty years. The new railroad would, as one speaker predicted in 1869, "populate our vast territory" and make America "the highway of nations."

The railroad was also a political triumph. Victorious in the Civil War, Republicans saw themselves as heirs to the American System envisioned by antebellum Whigs. They believed government intervention in the economy was the key to nation building. But unlike Whigs, whose plans had met stiff Democratic opposition, Republicans enjoyed a decade of unparalleled federal power. They used it vigorously: U.S. government spending per person, after skyrocketing in the Civil War, remained well above earlier levels. Republicans believed that national economic integration was the best guarantor of lasting peace. As a New York minister declared, the federally supported transcontinental railroad would "preserve the Union."

The minister was wrong on one point. He claimed the railroad was a peaceful achievement, in contrast to military battles that had brought "devastation, misery, and woe." In fact, creating a continental empire caused plenty of woe. Regions west of the Mississippi could only be incorporated if the United States subdued native peoples and established favorable conditions for international investors—often at great domestic cost. And while conquering the West helped make the United States into an industrial power, it also deepened America's rivalry with European empires and created new patterns of exploitation.

IDENTIFY THE BIG IDEA
How did U.S. policymakers seek to stimulate the economy and integrate the trans-Mississippi west into the nation, and how did this affect people living there?

THE GREAT WEST

The Great West In the wake of the Civil War, Americans looked westward. Republicans implemented an array of policies to foster economic development in the "Great West." Ranchers, farmers, and lumbermen cast hungry eyes on the remaining lands held by Native Americans. Steamboats and railroads, both visible in the background of this image, became celebrated as symbols of the expanding reach of U.S. economic might. This 1881 promotional poster illustrates the bountiful natural resources to be found out west, as well as the land available for ranching, farming, and commerce. The men in the lower left corner are surveying land for sale. Library of Congress.

509

The Republican Vision

Reshaping the former Confederacy was only part of Republicans' plan for a reconstructed nation. They remembered the era after Andrew Jackson's destruction of the Second National Bank as one of economic chaos, when the United States had become vulnerable to international creditors and market fluctuations. Land speculation on the frontier had provoked extreme cycles of boom and bust. Failure to fund a transcontinental railroad had left different regions of the country disconnected. This, Republicans believed, had helped trigger the Civil War, and they were determined to set a new direction.

Even while the war raged, Congress made vigorous use of federal power, launching the transcontinental rail project and a new national banking system. Congress also raised the **protective tariff** on a range of manufactured goods, from textiles to steel, and on some agricultural products, like wool and sugar. At federal customhouses in each port, foreign manufacturers who brought merchandise into the United States had to pay import fees. These tariff revenues gave U.S. manufacturers, who did not pay the fees, a competitive advantage in America's vast domestic market.

EXPLAIN CONSEQUENCES

In what ways did Republicans use federal power on the world stage, and in what ways did they continue policies from the pre–Civil War era?

The economic depression that began in 1873 set limits on Republicans' economic ambitions, just as it hindered their Reconstruction plans in the South. But their policies continued to shape the economy. Though some historians argue that the late nineteenth century was an era of *laissez faire* or unrestrained capitalism, in which government sat passively by, the industrial United States was actually the product of a massive public-private partnership in which government played critical roles.

The New Union and the World

The United States emerged from the Civil War with new leverage in its negotiation with European countries, especially Great Britain, whose navy dominated the seas. Britain, which had allowed Confederate raiding ships such as CSS *Alabama* to be built in its shipyards, submitted afterward to arbitration and paid the United States $15.5 million in damages. Flush with victory, many Americans expected more British and Spanish territories to drop into the Union's lap. Senator Charles Sumner proposed, in fact, that Britain settle the *Alabama* claims by handing over Canada.

Such dreams were a logical extension of pre–Civil War conquests, especially in the Mexican War. With the coasts now linked by rail, merchants and manufacturers looked across the Pacific, hungry for trade with Asia. Americans had already established a dominant presence in Hawaii, where U.S. whalers and merchant ships stopped for food and repairs. With the advent of steam-powered vessels, both the U.S. Navy and private shippers wanted more refueling points in the Caribbean and Pacific.

Even before the Civil War, these commercial aims had prompted the U.S. government to force Japan to open trade. For centuries, since unpleasant encounters with Portuguese traders in the 1600s, Japanese leaders had adhered to a policy of strict isolation. Americans, who wanted coal stations in Japan, argued that trade would extend what one missionary called "commerce, knowledge, and Christianity, with their multiplied blessings." Whether or not Japan wanted these blessings was irrelevant. In 1854, Commodore Matthew Perry succeeded in getting Japanese officials to sign the **Treaty of Kanagawa**, allowing U.S. ships to refuel at two ports. By 1858, America and Japan had commenced trade, and a U.S. consul took up residence in Japan's capital, Edo (now known as Tokyo).

Union victory also increased U.S. economic influence in Latin America. While the United States was preoccupied with its internal war, France had deposed Mexico's government and installed an emperor. On May 5, 1867, Mexico overthrew the French invaders and executed Emperor Maximilian. But while Mexico regained independence, it lay open to the economic designs of its increasingly powerful northern neighbor.

A new model emerged for asserting U.S. power in Latin America and Asia: not by direct conquest, but through trade. The architect of this vision was William Seward, secretary of state from 1861 to 1869 under presidents Abraham Lincoln and Andrew Johnson. A New Yorker of grand ambition and ego, Seward believed, like many contemporaries, that Asia would become "the chief theatre of [world] events" and that commerce there was key to America's prosperity. He urged the Senate to purchase sites in both the Pacific and the Caribbean for naval bases and refueling stations. When Japan changed policy and tried to close its ports to foreigners, Seward dispatched U.S. naval vessels to join those of Britain, France, and the Netherlands in reopening trade by force. At the same time, Seward urged annexation of Hawaii. He also predicted that the

An American Merchant Ship in Yokohama Harbor, 1861

After the United States forcibly "opened" Japan to foreign trade in 1854, American and European ships and visitors became a familiar sight in the port of Yokohama. In these 1861 prints—two panels of a five-panel series—artist Hashimoto Sadahide meticulously details activity in Yokohama Harbor. On the left, goods are carried onto an American merchant ship; on the right, two women dressed in Western style watch the arrival of another boat. In the background, a steamship flies the Dutch flag; a rowboat heading to or from another (unseen) ship carries the flag of France. Library of Congress.

United States would one day claim the Philippines and build a Panama canal.

Seward's short-term achievements were modest. Exhausted by civil war, Americans had little enthusiasm for further military exploits. Seward achieved only two significant victories. In 1868, he secured congressional approval for the **Burlingame Treaty** with China, which guaranteed the rights of U.S. missionaries in China and set official terms for the emigration of Chinese laborers, some of whom were already clearing farmland and building railroads in the West. That same year, Seward negotiated the purchase of Alaska from Russia. After the Senate approved the deal, Seward waxed poetic:

> Our nation with united interests blest
> Not now content to poise, shall sway the rest;
> Abroad our empire shall no limits know,
> But like the sea in endless circles flow.

Many Americans scoffed at the purchase of Alaska, a frigid arctic tract that skeptics nicknamed "Seward's Icebox." But the secretary of state mapped out a path his Republican successors would follow thirty years later in an aggressive bid for global power.

Integrating the National Economy

Closer to home, Republicans focused on transportation infrastructure. Railroad development in the United States began well before the Civil War, with the first locomotives arriving from Britain in the early 1830s. Unlike canals or roads, railroads offered the promise of year-round, all-weather service. Locomotives could run in the dark and never needed to rest, except to take on coal and water. Steam engines crossed high mountains and rocky gorges where pack animals could find no fodder and canals could never reach. West of the Mississippi, railroads opened vast regions for farming, trade, and tourism. A transcontinental railroad executive was only half-joking when he said, "The West is purely a railroad enterprise."

Governments could choose to build and operate railroads themselves or promote construction by

Building the Central Pacific Railroad

In 1865, Chinese workers had labored to build the 1,100-foot-long, 90-foot-high trestle over the divide between the American and Bear rivers at Secret Town in the Sierra Nevada Mountains. In 1877, the Chinese workers shown in this photograph by Carleton Watkins were again at work on the site, burying the trestle to avoid replacement of the aging timbers, which had become a fire hazard. University of California at Berkeley, Bancroft Library.

private companies. Unlike most European countries, the United States chose the private approach. The federal government, however, provided essential loans, subsidies, and grants of public land. States and localities also lured railroads with offers of financial aid, mainly by buying railroad bonds. Without this aid, rail networks would have grown much more slowly and would probably have concentrated in urban regions. With it, railroads enjoyed an enormous — and reckless — boom. By 1900, virtually no corner of the country lacked rail service (Map 16.1). At the same time, U.S. railroads built across the border into Mexico (America Compared, p. 514).

Railroad companies transformed American capitalism. They adopted a legal form of organization, the corporation, that enabled them to raise private capital in prodigious amounts. In earlier decades, state legislatures had chartered corporations for specific public purposes, binding these creations to government goals and oversight. But over the course of the nineteenth century, legislatures gradually began to allow any business to become a corporation by simply applying for a state charter. Among the first corporations to become large interstate enterprises, private railroads were much freer than earlier companies to do as they pleased. After the Civil War, they received lavish public aid with few strings attached. Their position was like that of American banks in late 2008 after the big federal bailout: even critics acknowledged that public aid to these giant companies was good for the economy, but they observed that it also lent government support to fabulous accumulations of private wealth.

Tariffs and Economic Growth   Along with the transformative power of railroads, Republicans' protective tariffs helped build other U.S. industries, including textiles and steel in the Northeast and Midwest and, through tariffs on imported sugar and wool, sugar beet farming and sheep ranching in the West. Tariffs also funded government itself. In an era when the United States did

MAP 16.1

Expansion of the Railroad System, 1870–1890

In 1860, the nation had 30,000 miles of rail track; by 1890, it had 167,000 miles. The tremendous burst of construction during the last twenty years of that period essentially completed the nation's rail network, although there would be additional expansion for the next two decades. The main areas of growth were in the South and in lands west of the Mississippi. Time zones—introduced by the railroad companies in 1883—are marked by the gray lines.

not levy income taxes, tariffs provided the bulk of treasury revenue. The Civil War had left the Union with a staggering debt of $2.8 billion. Tariff income erased that debt and by the 1880s generated huge budget *surpluses*—a circumstance hard to imagine today.

As Reconstruction faltered, tariffs came under political fire. Democrats argued that tariffs taxed American consumers by denying them access to low-cost imported goods and forcing them to pay subsidies to U.S. manufacturers. Republicans claimed, conversely, that tariffs benefitted workers because they created jobs, blocked low-wage foreign competition, and safeguarded America from the kind of industrial poverty that had arisen in Europe. According to this argument, tariffs helped American men earn enough to support their families; wives could devote themselves to homemaking, and children could go to school, not the

factory. For protectionist Republicans, high tariffs were akin to the abolition of slavery: they protected and uplifted the most vulnerable workers.

In these fierce debates, both sides were partly right. Protective tariffs did play a powerful role in economic growth. They helped transform the United States into a global industrial power. Eventually, though, even protectionist Republicans had to admit that Democrats had a point: tariffs had not prevented industrial poverty in the United States. Corporations accumulated massive benefits from tariffs but failed to pass them along to workers, who often toiled long hours for low wages. Furthermore, tariffs helped foster trusts, corporations that dominated whole sectors of the economy and wielded near-monopoly power. The rise of large private corporations and trusts generated enduring political problems.

The Santa Fe Railroad in Mexico and the United States

This map, based on an 1885 traveler's guide published by the Atchison, Topeka, and Santa Fe Railroad, includes the company's U.S. lines and also those of its Mexican Central Railroad, an ATSF subsidiary that crossed the border and terminated at Guaymas and Mexico City, Mexico. The dots represent the many stops that the trains made along the routes between major cities. Most Mexican railroads in this era were built and operated by U.S. companies. As you analyze this map, consider how residents of the two countries may have experienced the railroad's arrival in different ways.

MAP 16.2
The Santa Fe Railroad System, 1885

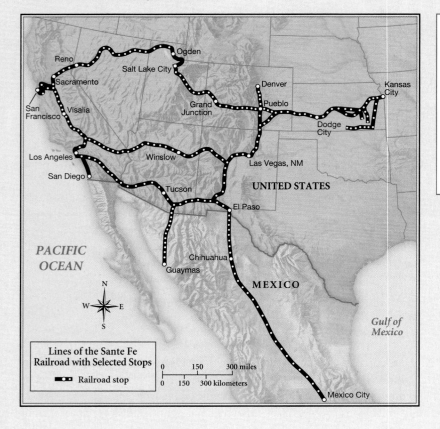

QUESTIONS FOR ANALYSIS

1. In what directions could passengers and freight travel on ATSF lines in each country? What does this suggest about the objectives of railroad companies like this one?

2. Based on this evidence, how might Mexicans have experienced the arrival of railroads differently from residents of the western United States?

The Role of Courts While fostering growth, most historians agree, Republicans did not give government enough regulatory power over the new corporations. State legislatures did pass hundreds of regulatory laws after the Civil War, but interstate companies challenged them in federal courts. In ***Munn v. Illinois*** (1877), the Supreme Court affirmed that states could regulate key businesses, such as railroads and grain elevators, that were "clothed in the public interest." However, the justices feared that too many state and local regulations would impede business and fragment the national marketplace. Starting in the 1870s, they interpreted the "due process" clause of the new Fourteenth Amendment — which dictated that no state could "deprive any person of life, liberty, or property, without due process of law" — as shielding corporations from excessive regulation. Ironically, the Court refused to use the same amendment to protect the rights of African Americans.

In the Southwest as well, federal courts promoted economic development at the expense of racial justice. Though the United States had taken control of New Mexico and Arizona after the Mexican War, much land remained afterward in the hands of Mexican farmers and ranchers. Many lived as *peónes*, under long-standing agreements with landowners who held large tracts originally granted by the Spanish crown. The post–Civil War years brought railroads and an influx of land-hungry Anglos. New Mexico's governor reported indignantly that Mexican shepherds were often "asked" to leave their ranges "by a cowboy or cattle herder with a brace of pistols at his belt and a Winchester in his hands."

Existing land claims were so complex that Congress eventually set up a special court to rule on land titles. Between 1891 and 1904, the court invalidated most traditional claims, including those of many New Mexico *ejidos*, or villages owned collectively by their communities. Mexican Americans lost about 64 percent of the contested lands. In addition, much land was sold or appropriated through legal machinations like those of a notorious cabal of politicians and lawyers known as the Santa Fe Ring. The result was displacement of thousands of Mexican American villagers and farmers. Some found work as railroad builders or mine workers; others, moving into the sparse high country of the Sierras and Rockies where cattle could not survive, developed sheep raising into a major enterprise.

Silver and Gold   In an era of nation building, U.S. and European policymakers sought new ways to rationalize markets. Industrializing nations, for example, tried to develop an international system of standard measurements and even a unified currency. Though these proposals failed as each nation succumbed to self-interest, governments did increasingly agree that, for "scientific" reasons, money should be based on gold, which was thought to have an intrinsic worth above other metals. Great Britain had long held to the **gold standard**, meaning that paper notes from the Bank of England could be backed by gold held in the bank's vaults. During the 1870s and 1880s, the United States, Germany, France, and other countries also converted to gold.

Beforehand, these nations had been on a bimetallic standard: they issued both gold and silver coins, with respective weights fixed at a relative value. The United States switched to the gold standard in part because treasury officials and financiers were watching developments out west. Geologists accurately predicted the discovery of immense silver deposits, such as Nevada's Comstock Lode, without comparable new gold strikes. A massive influx of silver would clearly upset the long-

standing ratio. Thus, with a law that became infamous to later critics as the "**Crime of 1873**," Congress chose gold. It directed the U.S. Treasury to cease minting silver dollars and, over a six-year period, retire Civil War–era greenbacks (paper dollars) and replace them with notes from an expanded system of national banks. After this process was complete in 1879, the treasury exchanged these notes for gold on request. (Advocates of bimetallism did achieve one small victory: the Bland-Allison Act of 1878 required the U.S. Mint to coin a modest amount of silver.)

By adopting the gold standard, Republican policymakers sharply limited the nation's money supply, to the level of available gold. The amount of money circulating in the United States had been $30.35 per person in 1865; by 1880, it fell to only $19.36 per person. Today, few economists would sanction such a plan, especially for an economy growing at breakneck speed. They would recommend, instead, increasing money supplies to keep pace with development. But at the time, policymakers remembered rampant antebellum speculation and the hardships of inflation during the Civil War. The United States, as a developing country, also needed to attract investment capital from Britain, Belgium, and other European nations that were on the gold standard. Making it easy to exchange U.S. bonds and currency for gold encouraged European investors to send their money to the United States.

Republican policies fostered exuberant growth and a breathtakingly rapid integration of the economy. Railroads and telegraphs tied the nation together. U.S. manufacturers amassed staggering amounts of capital and built corporations of national and even global scope. With its immense, integrated marketplace of workers, consumers, raw materials, and finished products, the United States was poised to become a mighty industrial power.

> **IDENTIFY CAUSES**
> What federal policies contributed to the rise of America's industrial economy, and what were their results?

Incorporating the West

Republicans wanted farms as well as factories. As early as 1860, popular lyrics hailed the advent of "Uncle Sam's Farm":

> A welcome, warm and hearty, do we give the sons of toil,
> To come west and settle and labor on Free Soil;
> We've room enough and land enough, they needn't feel alarmed —
> Oh! Come to the land of Freedom and vote yourself a farm.

The **Homestead Act** (1862) gave 160 acres of federal land to any applicant who occupied and improved the property. Republicans hoped the bill would help build up the interior West, which was inhabited by Indian peoples but remained "empty" on U.S. government survey maps.

Implementing this plan required innovative policies. The same year it passed the Homestead Act, Congress also created the federal Department of Agriculture and, through the **Morrill Act**, set aside 140 million federal acres that states could sell to raise money for public universities. The goal of these **land-grant colleges** was to broaden educational opportunities and foster technical and scientific expertise. After the Civil War, Congress also funded a series of geological surveys, dispatching U.S. Army officers, scientists, and photographers to chart unknown western terrain and catalog resources.

To a large extent, these policies succeeded in incorporating lands west of the Mississippi. The United States began to exploit its western empire for minerals, lumber, and other raw materials. But for ordinary Americans who went west, dreams often outran reality. Well-financed corporations, not individual prospectors, reaped most of the profits from western mines, while the Great Plains environment proved resistant to ranching and farming.

Mining Empires

In the late 1850s, as easy pickings in the California gold rush diminished, prospectors scattered in hopes of finding riches elsewhere. They found gold at many sites, including Nevada, the Colorado Rockies, and South Dakota's Black Hills (Map 16.3). As news of each strike spread, remote areas turned overnight into mob scenes of prospectors, traders, prostitutes, and saloon keepers. At community meetings, white prospectors made their own laws, often using them as an instrument for excluding Mexicans, Chinese, and blacks.

The silver from Nevada's **Comstock Lode**, discovered in 1859, built the boomtown of Virginia City,

Hydraulic Mining

When surface veins of gold played out, miners turned to hydraulic mining, the modern form of which was invented in California in 1853. The technology was simple, using high-pressure streams of water to wash away hillsides of gold-bearing soil. Although building the reservoirs, piping systems, and sluices cost money, the profits from hydraulic mining helped transform western mining into big business. But, as this daguerreotype suggests, the large scale on which hydraulic mining was done wreaked large-scale havoc on the environment. Collection of Matthew Isenburg.

MAP 16.3
Mining Frontiers, 1848–1890

The Far West was America's gold country because of its geological history. Veins of gold and silver form when molten material from the earth's core is forced up into fissures caused by the tectonic movements that create mountain ranges, such as the ones that dominate the far western landscape. It was these veins, the product of mountain-forming activity many thousands of years earlier, that prospectors began to discover after 1848 and furiously exploit. Although widely dispersed across the Far West, the lodes that they found followed the mountain ranges bisecting the region and bypassing the great plateaus not shaped by the ancient tectonic activity.

which soon acquired fancy hotels, a Shakespearean theater, and even its own stock exchange. In 1870, a hundred saloons operated in Virginia City, brothels lined D Street, and men outnumbered women 2 to 1. In the 1880s, however, as the Comstock Lode played out, Virginia City suffered the fate of many mining camps: it became a ghost town. What remained was a ravaged landscape with mountains of debris, poisoned water sources, and surrounding lands stripped of timber.

In hopes of encouraging development of western resources, Congress passed the General Mining Act of 1872, which allowed those who discovered minerals on

federally owned land to work the claim and keep all the proceeds. (The law — including the $5-per-acre fee for filing a claim — remains in force today.) Americans idealized the notion of the lone, hardy mining prospector with his pan and his mule, but digging into deep veins of underground ore required big money. Consortiums of powerful investors, bringing engineers and advanced equipment, generally extracted the most wealth. This was the case for the New York trading firm Phelps Dodge, which invested in massive copper mines and smelting operations on both sides of the U.S.-Mexico border. The mines created jobs in new towns like Bisbee and Morenci, Arizona — but with dangerous conditions and low pay, especially for those who received the segregated "Mexican wage." Anglos, testified one Mexican mine worker, "occupied decorous residences . . . and had large amounts of money," while "the Mexican population and its economic condition offered a pathetic contrast." He protested this affront to "the most elemental principles of justice."

The rise of western mining created an insatiable market for timber and produce from the Pacific Northwest (Map 16.4). Seattle and Portland grew rapidly as

MAP 16.4
Settlement of the Pacific Slope, 1860–1890

In 1860, the economic development of the Pacific slope was remarkably uneven — fully under way in northern California and scarcely begun anywhere else. By 1890, a new pattern had begun to emerge, with the swift growth of southern California foreshadowed and the Pacific Northwest incorporated into the regional and national economy.

supply centers, especially during the great gold rushes of California (after 1849) and the Klondike in Canada's Yukon Territory (after 1897). Residents of Tacoma, Washington, claimed theirs was the "City of Destiny" when it became the Pacific terminus for the Northern Pacific, the nation's third transcontinental railroad, in 1887. But rival businessmen in Seattle succeeded in promoting their city as the gateway to Alaska and the Klondike. Seattle, a town with 1,000 residents in 1870, grew over the next forty years to a population of a quarter million.

Cattlemen on the Plains

While boomtowns arose across the West, hunters began transforming the plains. As late as the Civil War years, great herds of bison still roamed this region. But overhunting and the introduction of European animal afflictions, like the bacterial disease brucellosis, were already decimating the herds. In the 1870s, hide hunters finished them off so thoroughly that at one point fewer than two hundred bison remained in U.S. territory. Hunters hidden downwind, under the right conditions, could kill four dozen at a time without moving from the spot. They took hides but left the meat to rot, an act of vast wastefulness that shocked native peoples.

Removal of the bison opened opportunities for cattle ranchers. South Texas provided an early model for their ambitious plans. By the end of the Civil War, about five million head of longhorn cattle grazed on Anglo ranches there. In 1865, the Missouri Pacific Railroad reached Sedalia, Missouri, far enough west to be accessible as Texas reentered the Union. A longhorn worth $3 in Texas might command $40 at Sedalia.

Cowboys, Real and Mythic

As early as the 1860s, popular dime novels such as this one (right) celebrated the alleged ruggedness, individual freedoms, and gun-slinging capabilities of western cowboys. (Note that this 1888 story, like most dime novels, was published in New York.) Generations of young Americans grew up on stories of frontier valor and "Cowboys versus Indians." In fact, cowboys like the ones depicted in the photograph were really wageworkers on horseback. An ethnically diverse group, including many blacks and Hispanics, they earned perhaps $25 a month, plus meals and a bed in the bunkhouse, in return for long hours of grueling, lonesome work. Library of Congress; Denver Public Library/Bridgeman Art Library.

Advertisement for Silver Pine Healing Oil, c. 1880s

Conquest of the Great Plains was made possible in part by the invention of barbed wire, which could cheaply enclose wide areas, even where trees and wood were scarce. Inventor Joseph Glidden received a patent in 1874 for the most familiar form of barbed wire. His wire proved durable, and Glidden invented machinery to mass-produce it—while his business associates skillfully promoted the product to farmers in the West. By 1880, Glidden's company sold 80 million pounds of barbed wire a year. This image shows, however, that the new "thorny fence" also had a downside. Other businessmen profited by healing the injuries that barbed wire caused to valuable animals. Picture Research Consultants & Archives.

With this incentive, ranchers inaugurated the **Long Drive**, hiring cowboys to herd cattle hundreds of miles north to the new rail lines, which soon extended into Kansas. At Abilene and Dodge City, Kansas, ranchers sold their longhorns and trail-weary cowboys crowded into saloons. These cow towns captured the nation's imagination as symbols of the Wild West, but the reality was much less exciting. Cowboys, many of them African Americans and Latinos, were really farmhands on horseback who worked long, harsh hours for low pay.

North of Texas, public grazing lands drew investors and adventurers eager for a taste of the West. By the early 1880s, as many as 7.5 million cattle were overgrazing the plains' native grasses. A cycle of good weather postponed disaster, which arrived in 1886: record blizzards and bitter cold. An awful scene of rotting carcasses greeted cowboys as they rode onto the range that spring. Further hit by a severe drought the following summer, the cattle boom collapsed.

Thanks to new strategies, however, cattle ranching survived and became part of the integrated national economy. As railroads reached Texas and ranchers there abandoned the Long Drive, the invention of barbed wire—which enabled ranchers and farmers to fence large areas cheaply and easily on the plains, where wood was scarce and expensive—made it easier for northern cattlemen to fence small areas and feed animals on hay. Stockyards appeared beside the rapidly extending railroad tracks, and trains took these gathered cattle to giant slaughterhouses in cities like Chicago, which turned them into cheap beef for customers back east.

Homesteaders

Republicans envisioned the Great Plains dotted with small farms, but farmers had to be persuaded that crops would grow there. Powerful interests worked hard to overcome the popular idea that the grassland was the Great American Desert. Railroads, eager to sell land the government had granted them, advertised aggressively. Land speculators, transatlantic steamship lines, and western states and territories joined the campaign.

Newcomers found the soil beneath the native prairie grasses deep and fertile. Steel plows enabled them to break through the tough roots, while barbed wire provided cheap, effective fencing against roaming cattle. European immigrants brought strains of hard-kernel wheat that tolerated the extreme temperatures of the plains. As if to confirm promoters' optimism, a wet cycle occurred between 1878 and 1886, increasing rainfall in the arid regions east of the Rockies. Americans decided that **"rain follows the plow"**: settlement was increasing rainfall. Some attributed the rain to soil cultivation and tree planting, while others credited God. One Harvard professor proposed that

Family on the L. W. Hall Farm, Buffalo County, Nebraska, 1903

This family has moved from their original sod house into a new frame house. Perhaps they asked the photographer to include in his image the windmill, a key to their prosperity. Other photographs on this property, some taken in 1907, show thriving young trees and a woman proudly posed with her new hand-cranked washing machine. How might this family have responded to the argument, made in this textbook chapter and by some critics at the time, that farming was a failure on the arid Great Plains? What different story might they tell about their hardships and successes? Nebraska State Historical Society.

steel railroad tracks attracted moisture. Such optimists would soon learn their mistake.

The motivation for most settlers, American or immigrant, was to better themselves economically. Union veterans, who received favorable terms in staking homestead claims, played a major role in settling Kansas and other plains states. When severe depression hit northern Europe in the 1870s, Norwegians and Swedes joined German emigrants in large numbers. At the peak of "American fever" in 1882, more than 105,000 Scandinavians left for the United States. Swedish and Norwegian became the primary languages in parts of Minnesota and the Dakotas.

For some African Americans, the plains represented a promised land of freedom. In 1879, a group of black communities left Mississippi and Louisiana in a quest to escape poverty and white violence. Some 6,000 blacks departed together, most carrying little but the clothes on their backs and faith in God. They called themselves **Exodusters**, participants in a great exodus to Kansas. The 1880 census reported 40,000 blacks there, by far the largest African American concentration in the West aside from Texas, where the expanding cotton frontier attracted hundreds of thousands of black migrants.

For newcomers, taming the plains differed from pioneering in antebellum Iowa or Oregon. Dealers sold big new machines to help with plowing and harvesting.

Western wheat traveled by rail to giant grain elevators and traded immediately on world markets. Hoping frontier land values would appreciate rapidly, many farmers planned to profit from selling acres as much as (or more than) from their crops. In boom times, many rushed into debt to acquire more land and better equipment. All these enthusiasms—for cash crops, land speculation, borrowed money, and new technology—bore witness to the conviction that farming was, as one agricultural journal remarked, a business "like all other business."

Women in the West Early miners, lumbermen, and cowboys were overwhelmingly male, but homesteading was a family affair. The success of a farm depended on the work of wives and children who tended the garden and animals, preserved food, and helped out at harvest time. Some women struck out on their own: a study of North Dakota found between 5 and 20 percent of homestead claims filed by single women, often working land adjacent to that of sisters, brothers, and parents. Family members thus supported one another in the difficult work of farming, while easing the loneliness many newcomers felt. Looking back with pride on her homesteading days, one Dakota woman said simply, "It was a place to stay and it was mine."

While promoting farms in the West, Republicans clashed with the distinctive religious group that had already settled Utah: Mormons, or members of the Church of Jesus Christ of Latter-day Saints (LDS). After suffering persecution in Missouri and Illinois, Mormons had moved west to Utah in the 1840s, attracting many working-class converts from England as well. Most Americans at the time were deeply hostile to Mormonism, especially the LDS practice of plural marriage — sanctioned by church founder Joseph Smith — through which some Mormon men married more than one wife.

Mormons had their own complex view of women's role, illustrated by the career of Mormon leader Emmeline Wells. Born in New Hampshire, Emmeline converted to Mormonism at age thirteen along with her mother and joined the exodus to Utah in 1848. After her first husband abandoned her when he left the church, Emmeline became the seventh wife of church elder Daniel Wells. In 1870, due in part to organized pressure from Wells and other Mormon women, the Utah legislature granted full voting rights to women, becoming the second U.S. territory to do so (after Wyoming, in 1869). The measure increased LDS control, since most Utah women were Mormons, while non-Mormons in mining camps were predominantly male. It also recognized the central role of women in Mormon life.

Amid the constitutional debates of Reconstruction, polygamy and women's voting rights became intertwined issues (American Voices, p. 522). Encouraged by other plural wives, Emmeline Wells began in 1877 to write for a Salt Lake City newspaper, the *Woman's Exponent*. She served as editor for forty years and led local women's rights groups. At first, Utah's legislature blocked Wells's candidacy in a local election, based on her sex. But when Utah won statehood in 1896, Wells had the pleasure of watching several women win seats in the new legislature, including Dr. Martha Hughes Cannon, a physician and Mormon plural wife who became the first American woman to serve in a state senate. Like their counterparts in other western states, Utah's women experienced a combination of severe frontier hardships and striking new opportunities.

Environmental Challenges   Homesteaders faced a host of challenges, particularly the natural environment of the Great Plains. Clouds of grasshoppers could descend and destroy a crop in a day; a prairie fire or hailstorm could do the job in an hour. In spring, homesteaders faced sudden, terrifying tornados, while their winter experiences in the 1870s added the word *blizzard* to America's vocabulary. On the plains, also, water and lumber were hard to find. Newly arrived families often cut dugouts into hillsides and then, after a season or two, erected houses made of turf cut from the ground.

Over the long term, homesteaders discovered that the western grasslands did not receive enough rain to grow wheat and other grains. As the cycle of rainfall shifted from wet to dry, farmers as well as ranchers suffered. "A wind hot as an oven's fury . . . raged like a pestilence," reported one Nebraskan, leaving "farmers helpless, with no weapon against this terrible and inscrutable wrath of nature." By the late 1880s, some recently settled lands emptied as homesteaders fled in defeat — 50,000 from the Dakotas alone. It became obvious that farming in the arid West required methods other than those used east of the Mississippi.

Clearly, 160-acre homesteads were the wrong size for the West: farmers needed either small irrigated plots or immense tracts for dry farming, which involved deep planting to bring subsoil moisture to the roots and quick harrowing after rainfalls to slow evaporation. Dry farming developed most fully on huge corporate farms in the Red River Valley of North Dakota. But even family farms, the norm elsewhere, could not survive on less than 300 acres of grain. Crop prices were too low, and the climate too unpredictable, to allow farmers to get by on less.

In this struggle, settlers regarded themselves as nature's conquerors, striving, as one pioneer remarked, "to get the land subdued and the wilde nature out of it." Much about its "wilde nature" was hidden to the newcomers. They did not know that destroying biodiversity, which was what farming the plains really meant, opened pathways for exotic, destructive pests and weeds, and that removing native grasses left the soil vulnerable to erosion. By the turn of the twentieth century, about half the nation's cattle and sheep, one-third of its cereal crops, and nearly three-fifths of its wheat came from the Great Plains. But in the drier parts of the region, it was not a sustainable achievement. This renowned breadbasket was later revealed to be, in the words of one historian, "the largest, longest-run agricultural and environmental miscalculation in American history."

John Wesley Powell, a one-armed Union veteran, predicted the catastrophe from an early date. Powell, employed by the new U.S. Geological Survey, led a famous expedition in the West in which his team navigated the rapids of the Colorado River through the Grand Canyon in wooden boats. In his *Report on the*

COMPARE AND CONTRAST
Compare the development of mining, ranching, and farming in the West. How did their environmental consequences differ?

Women's Rights in the West

In 1870, Utah's territorial legislature granted voting rights to women. The decision was a shock to advocates of women's suffrage in the East: they expected their first big victories would come in New England. Furthermore, Utah was overwhelmingly peopled by Mormons—members of the Church of Jesus Christ of Latter-day Saints (LDS). Critics saw Mormonism as a harshly patriarchal religion. They especially loathed the Mormon practice of "plural marriage," in which some Mormon men took more than one wife. Most easterners thought this practice was barbaric and demeaning to women. Over the next two decades, Republicans pressured Mormons to abolish plural marriage. They also disenfranchised Mormon women and required men to take an anti-polygamy oath; Congress refused to admit Utah as a state. Only after 1890, when the LDS church officially abolished plural marriage, was Utah statehood possible. In 1896, when Utah became a state, women's voting rights were finally reinstated.

Fanny Stenhouse

Exposé of Polygamy: A Lady's Life Among the Mormons (1872)

An Englishwoman who converted to the faith and moved to Utah, Stenhouse became disillusioned and published her book to criticize the practice of Mormon polygamy.

How little do the Mormon men of Utah know what it is, in the truest sense, to have a wife, though they have so many "wives," after their own fashion. Almost imperceptibly to the husband, and even the wife herself, a barrier rises between them the very day that he marries another woman. It matters not how much she believes in the doctrine of plural marriages, or how willing she may be to submit to it; the fact remains the same. The estrangement begins by her trying to hide from him all secret sorrow; for she feels that what has been can not be undone now, and she says, "I cannot change it; neither would I if I could, because it is the will of God, and I must bear it; besides, what good will it do to worry my husband with all my feelings?"

... A man may have a dozen wives; but from the whole of them combined he will not receive as much real love and devotion as he might from one alone, if he had made her feel that she had his undivided affection and confidence. How terribly these men deceive themselves! When peace, or rather quiet, reigns in their homes, they think that the spirit of God is there. But it is not so! It is a calm, not like the gentle silence of sleep, but as the horrible stillness of death — the death of the heart's best affections, and all that is worth calling love. All true love has fled, and indifference has taken its place. The very children feel it. What do they — what can they care about their fathers? They seldom see them.

Whatever, in the providence of God, may be the action of Congress toward Utah, if the word of a feeble woman can be listened to, let me respectfully ask the Honorable Senators and Representatives of the United States that, in the abolition of Polygamy, if such should be the decree of the nation, let no compromise be made where subtlety can bind the woman now living in Polygamy to remain in that condition.

Source: *Exposé of Polygamy: A Lady's Life Among the Mormons*, ed. Linda Wilcox DeSimone (Logan: Utah State University Press, 2008), 72–73, 155.

Eliza Snow, Harriet Cook Young, Phoebe Woodruff

A Defense of Plural Marriage

The vast majority of Mormon women defended their faith and the practice of plural marriage. The statements by Eliza Snow, Harriet Cook Young, and Phoebe Woodruff, below, were made at a public protest meeting in Salt Lake City in 1870. LDS women pointed proudly to their new suffrage rights as proof of their religion's just treatment of women. Why did Mormons, who dominated the Utah legislature, give women full voting rights? In part, they sought to protect their church by increasing Mormon voting power: most of the non-Mormons were single men who worked on ranches or in mining camps. But the LDS Church also celebrated women's central role in the family and community. Some women achieved prominence as midwives, teachers, and professionals.

Eliza Snow: Our enemies pretend that, in Utah, woman is held in a state of vassalage — that she does not act from choice, but by coercion — that we would even prefer life elsewhere, were it possible for us to make our escape. What nonsense! We all know that if we wished we could leave at any time — either go singly, or to rise en masse, and there is no power here that could, or would wish to, prevent us. I will now ask this assemblage of intelligent ladies, do you know of anyplace on the face of the earth, where woman has more liberty, and where she enjoys such high and glorious privileges as she does here, as a latter-day saint? No! The very idea of woman here in a state of slavery is a burlesque on good common sense.

Harriet Cook Young: Wherever monogamy reigns, adultery, prostitution and foeticide, directly or indirectly, are its concomitants. . . . The women of Utah comprehend this; and they see, in the principle of plurality of wives, the only safeguard against adultery, prostitution, and the reckless waste of pre-natal life, practiced throughout the land.

Phoebe Woodruff: God has revealed unto us the law of the patriarchal order of marriage, and commanded us to obey it. We are sealed to our husbands for time and eternity, that we may dwell with them and our children in the world to come; which guarantees unto us the greatest blessing for which we are created. If the rulers of the nation will so far depart from the spirit and letter of our glorious constitution as to deprive our prophets, apostles and elders of citizenship, and imprison them for obeying this law, let them grant this, our last request, to make their prisons large enough to hold their wives, for where they go we will go also.

Source: Edward W. Tullidge, *Women of Mormondom* (New York: Tullidge & Crandall, 1877), 390–391, 396, 400.

Susan B. Anthony
Letter to *The Revolution*, July 5, 1871

National women's suffrage leaders responded awkwardly to the Utah suffrage victory. Being associated with Mormons, they understood, damaged their fragile new movement in the eyes of most Americans. But they tried tentatively to forge alliances with Mormon women they viewed as progressive, as well as dissidents in the church. Suffrage leader Susan B. Anthony traveled to Salt Lake City in 1871 to try to forge alliances with Mormon women, especially dissidents such as Fanny Stenhouse. Anthony expressed strong disapproval of polygamy, but she also

tried to change the debate to focus on the vulnerability of all married women to exploitation by their husbands. Her report from Utah, published in her journal *The Revolution*, is below.

Woman's work in monogamy and polygamy is essentially one and the same — that of planting her feet on the solid ground of self-support; . . . there is and can be no salvation for womanhood but in the possession of power over her own subsistence.

The saddest feature here is that there really is nothing by which these women can earn an independent livelihood for themselves and children. No manufacturing establishments; no free schools to teach. Women here, as everywhere, must be able to live honestly and honorably without men, before it can be possible to save the masses of them from entering into polygamy or prostitution, legal or illegal. Whichever way I turn, whatever phase of social life presents itself, the same conclusion comes — independent bread alone can redeem woman from her sure subjection to man. . . .

Here is missionary ground. Not for "thus saith the Lord," divine rights, canting priests, or echoing priestesses of any sect whatsoever; but for great, god-like, humanitarian men and women, who "feel for them in bonds as bound with them," . . . a simple, loving, sisterly clasp of hands with these struggling women, and an earnest work with them. Not to modify nor ameliorate, but to ABOLISH the whole system of woman's subjection to man in both polygamy and monogamy.

Source: *The Revolution*, July 20, 1871.

QUESTIONS FOR ANALYSIS

1. What arguments did the Mormon women make in defense of plural marriage? On what grounds did Stenhouse argue for its abolition?

2. Susan B. Anthony's letter was published in Boston. How might Mormon women have reacted to it? How might non-Mormon women have reacted to the statements by Snow, Young, and Woodruff?

3. Compare the experiences of plural marriage described by Stenhouse, on the one hand, and Snow, Young, and Woodruff, on the other. How do you account for these very different perspectives?

Lands of the Arid Region of the United States (1879), Powell told Congress bluntly that 160-acre homesteads would not work in dry regions. Impressed with the success of Mormon irrigation projects in Utah, Powell urged the United States to follow their model. He proposed that the government develop the West's water resources, building dams and canals and organizing landowners into local districts to operate them. Doubting that rugged individualism would succeed in the West, Powell proposed massive cooperation under government control.

After heated debate, Congress rejected Powell's plan. Critics accused him of playing into the hands of large ranching corporations; boosters were not yet willing to give up the dream of small homesteads. But Powell turned out to be right. Though environmental historians do not always agree with Powell's proposed solutions, they point to his *Report on Arid Lands* as a cogent critique of what went wrong on the Great Plains. Later, federal funding paid for dams and canals that supported intensive agriculture in many parts of the West.

IDENTIFY CAUSES
What factors led to the creation of the first national parks?

The First National Park

Powell was not the only one rethinking land use. The West's incorporation into the national marketplace occurred with such speed that some Americans began to fear rampant overdevelopment. Perhaps the federal government should not sell off all its public land, but instead hold and manage some of it. Amid the heady initiatives of Reconstruction, Congress began to preserve sites of unusual natural splendor. As early as 1864, Congress gave 10 square miles of the Yosemite Valley to California for "public use, resort, and recreation." (In 1890, Yosemite reverted to federal control.) In 1872, it set aside 2 million acres of Wyoming's Yellowstone Valley as the world's first national park: preserved as a public holding, it would serve as "a public park or pleasuring ground for the benefit and enjoyment of the people."

The Yo-Hamite Falls, 1855

This is one of the earliest artistic renderings of the Yosemite Valley, drawn, in fact, before the place came to be called Yosemite. The scale of the waterfall, which drops 2,300 feet to the valley below, is dramatized by artist Thomas A. Ayres's companions in the foreground. In this romantic lithograph, one can already see the grandeur of the West that Yosemite came to represent for Americans. University of California at Berkeley, Bancroft Library.

Railroad tourism, which developed side by side with other western industries, was an important motive for the creation of **Yellowstone National Park**. The Northern Pacific Railroad lobbied Congress vigorously to get the park established. Soon, luxury Pullman cars ushered visitors to Yellowstone's hotel, operated by the railroad itself. But creation of the park was fraught with complications. Since no one knew exactly what a "national park" was or how to operate it, the U.S. Army was dispatched to take charge; only in the early 1900s, when Congress established many more parks in the West, did consistent management policies emerge. In the meantime, soldiers spent much of their time arresting native peoples who sought to hunt on Yellowstone lands.

The creation of Yellowstone was an important step toward an ethic of respect for land and wildlife. So was the 1871 creation of a **U.S. Fisheries Commission**, which made recommendations to stem the decline in wild fish; by the 1930s, it merged with other federal wildlife bureaus to become the U.S. Fish and Wildlife Service. At the same time, eviction of Indians showed that defining small preserves of "uninhabited wilderness" was part of conquest itself. In 1877, for example, the federal government forcibly removed the Nez Perce tribe from their ancestral land in what is now Idaho, Washington, and Oregon. Under the leadership of young Chief Joseph, the Nez Perces tried to flee to Canada. After a journey of 1,100 miles, they were forced to surrender just short of the border. During their trek, five bands crossed Yellowstone; as a Nez Perce named Yellow Wolf recalled, they "knew that

country well." For thirteen days, Nez Perce men raided the valley for supplies, waylaying several groups of tourists. The conflict made national headlines. Easterners, proud of their new "pleasuring ground," were startled to find that it remained a site of native resistance. Americans were not settling an empty West. They were *un*settling it by taking it from native peoples who already lived there.

A Harvest of Blood: Native Peoples Dispossessed

Before the Civil War, when most Americans believed the prairie could not be farmed, Congress reserved the Great Plains for Indian peoples. But in the era of steel plows and railroads, policymakers suddenly had the power and desire to incorporate the whole region. The U.S. Army fought against the loosely federated Sioux — the major power on the northern grasslands — as well as other peoples who had agreed to live on reservations but found conditions so desperate that they fled (Map 16.5). These "reservation wars," caused largely by local violence and confused federal policies, were messy and bitter. Pointing to failed military campaigns, army atrocities, and egregious corruption in the Indian Bureau, reformers called for new policies that would destroy native people's traditional lifeways and "civilize" them — or, as one reformer put it, "kill the Indian and save the man."

Killing the Bison

This woodcut shows passengers shooting bison from a Kansas Pacific Railroad train—a small thrill added to the modern convenience of traveling west by rail. By the end of the 1870s, the plains bison shown here, which once numbered in the tens of millions and had been a large part of the Plains Indians' way of life, had been hunted almost to extinction. North Wind Picture Archives.

MAP 16.5

Indian Country in the West, to 1890

As settlement pushed onto the Great Plains after the Civil War, native peoples put up bitter resistance but ultimately to no avail. Over a period of decades, they ceded most of their lands to the federal government, and by 1890 they were confined to scattered reservations.

The Civil War and Indians on the Plains

In August 1862, the attention of most Unionists and Confederates was riveted on General George McClellan's failing campaign in Virginia. But in Minnesota, the Dakota Sioux were increasingly frustrated. In 1858, the year Minnesota secured statehood, they had agreed to settle on a strip of land reserved by the government, in exchange for receiving regular payments and supplies. But Indian agents, contractors, and even Minnesota's territorial governor pocketed most of the funds. When the Dakotas protested that their children were starving, state officials dismissed their appeals. Corruption was so egregious that one

leading Minnesotan, Episcopal bishop Henry Whipple, wrote an urgent appeal to President James Buchanan. "A nation which sows robbery," he warned, "will reap a harvest of blood."

Whipple's prediction proved correct. During the summer of 1862, a decade of anger boiled over. In a surprise attack, Dakota fighters fanned out through the Minnesota countryside, killing immigrants and burning farms. They planned to sweep eastward to St. Paul but were stopped at Fort Ridgely. In the end, more than four hundred whites lay dead, including women and children from farms and small towns. Thousands fled; panicked officials telegraphed for aid, spreading hysteria from Wisconsin to Colorado.

Enclosed Dakota Camp at Fort Snelling, Minnesota, 1862

During the trial of Dakota warriors involved in the 1862 rebellion, and through the harsh Minnesota winter that followed, more than a thousand members of the tribe were imprisoned in an enormous enclosure on Pike Island, near St. Paul. A measles epidemic broke out in the crowded camp and dozens died, especially children. Though U.S. soldiers were often unfriendly toward their captives, local sentiment was even more hostile; troops regularly marched through the camp, in part to protect the Dakotas from vigilante violence. In 1863 all members of the tribe were forcibly removed from the state. In November 1862, photographer Benjamin Franklin Upton captured this image of Dakota tents in the Pike Island enclosure. Minnesota Historical Society.

Minnesotans' ferocious response to the uprising set the stage for further conflict. A hastily appointed military court, bent on revenge, sentenced 307 Dakotas to death, making it clear that rebellious Indians would be treated as criminals rather than warriors. President Abraham Lincoln reviewed the trial records and commuted most of the sentences but authorized the deaths of 38 Dakota men. They were hanged just after Christmas 1862 in the largest mass execution in U.S. history. Two months later, Congress canceled all treaties with the Dakotas, revoked their annuities, and expelled them from Minnesota. The scattered bands fled west to join nonreservation allies.

As the uprising showed, the Civil War created two dangerous conditions in the West, compounding the problems already caused by corruption. With the Union army fighting the Confederacy, western whites felt vulnerable to Indian attacks. They also discovered they could fight Indians with minimal federal oversight. In the wake of the Dakota uprising, worried Coloradans favored a military campaign against the Cheyennes — allies of the Sioux — even though the Cheyennes had shown little evidence of hostility. Colorado militia leader John M. Chivington, an aspiring politician, determined to quell public anxiety and make his career.

In May 1864, Cheyenne chief Black Kettle, fearing his band would be attacked, consulted with U.S. agents, who instructed him to settle along Sand Creek in eastern Colorado until a treaty could be signed. On November 29, 1864, Chivington's Colorado militia attacked the camp while most of the men were out hunting, slaughtering more than a hundred women and children. "I killed all I could," one officer testified later. "I think and earnestly believe the Indian to be an obstacle to civilization and should be exterminated." Captain Silas Soule, who served under Chivington but refused to give his men the order to fire, dissented. "It was hard to see little children on their knees," he wrote later, "having their brains beat out by men professing to be civilized." Chivington's men rode back for a celebration in Denver, where they hung Cheyenne scalps (and women's genitals) from the rafters of the Apollo Theater.

The northern plains exploded in conflict. Infuriated by the **Sand Creek massacre**, Cheyennes carried war pipes to the Arapahos and Sioux, who attacked and burned white settlements along the South Platte River. Ordered to subdue these peoples, the U.S. Army failed

IDENTIFY CAUSES
What factors led to warfare between whites and native peoples on the plains?

miserably: officers could not even locate the enemy, who traveled rapidly in small bands and knew the country well. A further shock occurred in December 1866 when 1,500 Sioux warriors executed a perfect ambush, luring Captain William Fetterman and 80 soldiers from a Wyoming fort and wiping them out. With the **Fetterman massacre**, the Sioux succeeded in closing the Bozeman Trail, a private road under army protection that had served as the main route into Montana.

General William Tecumseh Sherman, now commanding the army in the West, swore to defeat defiant Indians. But the Union hero met his match on the plains. Another year of fighting proved expensive and inconclusive. In 1868, the Sioux, led by the Oglala band under Chief Red Cloud, told a peace commission they would not sign any treaty unless the United States pledged to abandon all its forts along the Bozeman Trail. The commission agreed. Red Cloud had won.

In the wake of these events, eastern public opinion turned against the Indian wars, which seemed at best ineffective, at worst brutal. Congress held hearings on the slaughter at Sand Creek. Though Chivington, now a civilian, was never prosecuted, the massacre became an infamous example of western vigilantism. By the time Ulysses Grant entered the White House in 1869, the authors of Reconstruction in the South also began to seek solutions to what they called the "Indian problem."

Grant's Peace Policy

Grant inherited an Indian policy in disarray. Federal incompetence was highlighted by yet another mass killing of friendly Indians in January 1870, this time on the Marias River in Montana, by an army detachment that shot and burned to death 173 Piegans (Blackfeet). Having run out of other options, Grant introduced a peace policy, based on recommendations from Christian advisors. He offered selected appointments to the reformers — including many former abolitionists — who had created such groups as the Indian Rights Association and the Women's National Indian Association.

Rejecting the virulent anti-Indian stance of many westerners, reformers argued that native peoples had the innate capacity to become equal with whites. They believed, however, that Indians could achieve this only if they embraced Christianity and white ways. Reformers thus aimed to destroy native languages, cultures, and religions. Despite humane intentions, their condescension was obvious. They ignored dissenters like Dr. Thomas Bland of the National Indian Defense

Association, who suggested that instead of an "Indian problem" there might be a "white problem" — refusal to permit Indians to follow their own lifeways. To most nineteenth-century Americans, such a notion was shocking and uncivilized. Increasingly dismissive of blacks' capacity for citizenship and hostile toward "heathen" Chinese immigrants, white Americans were even less willing to understand and respect Indian cultures. They believed that in the modern world, native peoples were fated for extinction (Thinking Like a Historian, p. 530).

Indian Boarding Schools   Reformers focused their greatest energy on educating the next generation. Realizing that acculturation — adoption of white ways — was difficult when children lived at home, agents and missionaries created off-reservation schools. Native families were exhorted, bullied, and bribed into sending their children to these schools, where, in addition to school lessons, boys learned farming skills and girls practiced housekeeping. "English only" was the rule; students were punished if they spoke their own languages. Mourning Dove, a Salish girl from what is now Washington State, remembered that her school "ran strictly. We never talked during meals without permission, given only on Sunday or special holidays. Otherwise there was silence — a terrible silent silence. I was used to the freedom of the forest, and it was hard to learn this strict discipline. I was punished many times before I learned." The Lakota boy Plenty Kill, who at boarding school received the new name Luther, remembered his loneliness and fear upon arrival: "The big boys would sing brave songs, and that would start the girls to crying. . . . The girls' quarters were about a hundred and fifty yards from ours, so we could hear them." After having his hair cut short, Plenty Kill felt a profound change in his identity. "None of us slept well that night," he recalled. "I felt that I was no more Indian, but would be an imitation of a white man."

 To see a longer excerpt of Mourning Dove's autobiography, along with other primary sources from this period, see *Sources for America's History*.

Even in the first flush of reform zeal, Grant's policies faced major hurdles. Most Indians had been pushed off traditional lands and assigned to barren ground that would have defeated the most enterprising farmer. Poverty and dislocation left Indians especially vulnerable to the ravages of infectious diseases like measles and scarlet fever. At the same time, Quaker, Presbyterian, and Methodist reformers fought turf

Red Cloud's Bedroom, 1891

Taken on the Pine Ridge Reservation in South Dakota by photographer C. G. Morledge, this photograph shows the bedroom of Red Cloud, a distinguished Oglala Lakota leader. Red Cloud had won a war against the U.S. Army just after the Civil War. He negotiated so tenaciously and shrewdly, afterward, with what he saw as meddlesome Indian agents, that his people nicknamed Pine Ridge "The Place Where Everything Is Disputed." Some of the contents of Red Cloud's bedroom may surprise you. How do you interpret the presence of five American flags? The visual images on the walls? What strategies and ways of life, blending old and new, does the photograph suggest? Compare it to Edward S. Curtis, "Little Plume and Yellow Kidney" (p. 533). In what ways did Morledge and Curtis craft different representations of Indian life? Denver Public Library/Bridgeman Art Library.

battles among themselves and with Catholic missionaries. Many traders and agents also continued to steal money and supplies from people they were supposed to protect. In the late 1870s, Rutherford B. Hayes's administration undertook more housecleaning at the Bureau of Indian Affairs, but corruption lingered.

From the Indians' point of view, reformers often became just another interest group in a crowded field of whites sending hopelessly mixed messages. The attitudes of individual army representatives, agents, and missionaries ranged from courageous and sympathetic to utterly ruthless. Many times, after chiefs thought they had reached a face-to-face agreement, they found it drastically altered by Congress or Washington bureaucrats. Nez Perce leader Joseph observed that "white people have too many chiefs. They do not understand each other. . . . I cannot understand why so

many chiefs are allowed to talk so many different ways, and promise so many different things." A Kiowa chief agreed: "We make but few contracts, and them we remember well. The whites make so many they are liable to forget them. The white chief seems not to be able to govern his braves."

Native peoples were nonetheless forced to accommodate, as independent tribal governance and treaty making came to an end. Back in the 1830s, the U.S. Supreme Court had declared Indians no longer sovereign but rather "domestic dependent nations." On a practical basis, however, both the U.S. Senate and agents in the field continued to negotiate treaties as late as 1869. Two years later, the House of Representatives,

UNDERSTAND POINTS OF VIEW
How did post–Civil War reformers believe they were improving U.S. Indian policies, and in what ways did that prove to be true and untrue?

Representing Indians

The documents below, designed for white audiences, all depict American Indians in the West.

1. **Buffalo Bill Cody's Wild West advertisement, 1899.** *Cody never called the Wild West a "show," placing tremendous emphasis on its allegedly authentic reenactments of events.*

Superstock.

2. **Lewis Henry Morgan, *Ancient Society*, 1877.**
   Morgan, a leading American anthropologist, studied the Iroquois and other native peoples. In 1877 he published an influential theory of human development, ranking various peoples in their "progress" from the "lowest stage of savagery" through the pinnacle of "civilization"—northern Europeans.

Some tribes and families have been left in geographical isolation to work out the problems of progress. . . . [Others] have been adulterated through external influence. Thus, while Africa was and is an ethnical chaos of savagery and barbarism, Australia and Polynesia were in savagery, pure and simple. . . . The Indian family of America, unlike any other existing family, exemplified the condition of mankind in three successive ethnical

TABLE 16.1

Status of Civilization (from Morgan, *Ancient Society*, 1877)

I. Lower Status of Savagery	From the Infancy of the Human Race to the commencement of the next Period.
II. Middle Status of Savagery	From the acquisition of a fish subsistence and a knowledge of the use of fire . . .
III. Upper Status of Savagery	From the Invention of the Bow and Arrow . . .
IV. Lower Status of Barbarism	From the Invention of the Art of Pottery . . .
V. Middle Status of Barbarism	From the Domestication of animals on the Eastern hemisphere, and in the Western from the cultivation of maize and plants by Irrigation . . .
VI. Upper Status of Barbarism	From the Invention of the process of Smelting Iron Ore, with the use of iron tools . . .
VII. Civilization	From the Invention of writing, to the present time.

periods. . . . The far northern Indians and some of the coast tribes of North and South America were in the Upper Status of savagery; the partially Village Indians east of the Mississippi were in the Lower Status of barbarism, and the Village Indians of North and South America were in the Middle Status. . . .

Commencing, then, with the Australians and Polynesians, following with the American Indian tribes, and concluding with the Roman and Grecian, who afford the highest exemplifications respectively of the six great stages of human progress, the sum of their united experiences may be supposed fairly to represent that of the human family. . . . We are dealing substantially, with the ancient history and condition of our own remote ancestors.

3. **Touring Indian Country, 1888 and 1894.** *Hoping to lure eastern tourists, the Northern Pacific Railroad published an annual journal,* Wonderland, *describing the natural splendors and economic progress of the West, as seen from its rail lines.*

We are now in the far-famed Yellowstone Valley. . . . There are but few Indians now to be seen along the line of the railroad, and those are engaged in agricultural and industrial pursuits. The extinction of the buffalo has rendered the Indian much more amenable to the civilizing influences brought to bear upon him than he formerly was, and very fair crops of grain are being raised at some of the agencies. At the Devil's Lake agency, for example, 60,000 bushels of wheat have been raised by the [Sioux and Chippewa] Indians in a single season. . . .

[The Crows'] great reservation is probably the garden spot of Montana, and the throwing open of a large portion of it to [white] settlement, which cannot long be delayed, will assuredly give an immense impetus to the agricultural interests of the Territory. . . .

The Flatheads have probably 10,000 or more horses and 5,000 or 6,000 cattle. . . . As ranchers and farmers the Flatheads are a success. It would be a matter of surprise to some people who think that the only good Indian is a dead Indian, to see the way some of the women handle sewing machines.

Sources: (2) Lewis H. Morgan, *Ancient Society* (New York: Henry Holt and Company, 1878), 12–13, 16–18; (3) John Hyde, *Wonderland* (St. Paul, 1888), 21, and 1894, 27.

4. **Gertrude Käsebier, photograph of Joe Black Fox, 1898.** *One of the first women to become a professional photographer, Käsebier here depicts Joe Black Fox relaxing with a cigarette. Black Fox, an Oglala Sioux, toured with Buffalo Bill's Wild West in 1900.*

Photographic History Collection, National Museum of American History, Smithsonian Institution 69.236.22, 2004-57801

ANALYZING THE EVIDENCE

1. Compare the depiction of the Plains Indians and Buffalo Bill Cody in source 1. How does source 4 differ from source 1? From Edward Curtis's "In a Piegan Lodge" (p. 533), in which all traces of modern life were erased? How might these depictions of "actual life" have shaped their audience's understanding of the West?

2. What bases did Morgan use for his rankings in source 2? How did he define the relationship between American Indians and whites (whom he refers to, in this passage, as "we")? Why did he suggest that Indians offered a unique opportunity for study?

3. Imagine that you were a wealthy, well-educated tourist preparing to travel west in 1900. Which of these documents would you most likely have encountered in advance? How might they have shaped your expectations and experiences?

4. These documents had different creators: an artist, a scholar, and two sets of entrepreneurs. What audiences did they have in mind? How do you think this affected their messages?

PUTTING IT ALL TOGETHER

Many nineteenth-century commentators claimed that American Indians were "vanishing": that is, they could not adapt to modernity and would die out. This proved untrue, of course, but the idea circulated widely. Which of these sources lend support to the idea of the "vanishing Indian"? Which suggest counter-stories of survival and endurance? Using these sources and your knowledge of the period, analyze the myths and realities of Native American life in the late nineteenth century.

jealous of Senate privileges, passed a bill to abolish all treaty making with Indians. The Senate agreed, provided that existing treaties remained in force. It was one more step in a long, torturous erosion of native rights. Eventually, the U.S. Supreme Court ruled in **Lone Wolf v. Hitchcock** (1903) that Congress could make whatever Indian policies it chose, ignoring all existing treaties. That same year, in *Ex Parte Crow Dog*, the Court ruled that no Indian was a citizen unless Congress designated him so. Indians were henceforth wards of the government. These rulings remained in force until the New Deal of the 1930s.

Breaking Up Tribal Lands   Reformers' most sweeping effort to assimilate Indians was the **Dawes Severalty Act** (1887), the dream of Senator Henry L. Dawes of Massachusetts, a leader in the Indian Rights Association. Dawes saw the reservation system as an ugly relic of the past. Through severalty—division of tribal lands—he hoped to force Indians onto individual landholdings, partitioning reservations into homesteads, just like those of white farmers. Supporters of the plan believed that landownership would encourage Indians to assimilate. It would lead, as Dawes wrote, to "a personal sense of independence." Individual property, echoed another reformer, would make the Indian man "intelligently selfish, . . . with a *pocket that aches to be filled with dollars!*"

The Dawes Act was a disaster. It played into the hands of whites who coveted Indian land and who persuaded the government to sell them land that was not needed for individual allotments. In this and other ways, the Bureau of Indian Affairs (BIA) implemented the law carelessly, to the outrage of Dawes. In Indian Territory, a commission seized more than 15 million "surplus" acres from native tribes by 1894, opening the way for whites to convert the last federal territory set aside for native peoples into the state of Oklahoma. In addition to catastrophic losses of collectively held property, native peoples lost 66 percent of their individually allotted lands between the 1880s and the 1930s, through fraud, BIA mismanagement, and pressure to sell to whites.

The End of Armed Resistance

As the nation consolidated control of the West in the 1870s, Americans hoped that Grant's peace policy was solving the "Indian problem." In the Southwest, such formidable peoples as the Kiowas and Comanches had been forced onto reservations. The Diné or Navajo nation, exiled under horrific conditions during the

Civil War but permitted to reoccupy their traditional land, gave up further military resistance. An outbreak among California's Modoc people in 1873—again, humiliating to the army—was at last subdued. Only Sitting Bull, a leader of the powerful Lakota Sioux on the northern plains, openly refused to go to a reservation. When pressured by U.S. troops, he repeatedly crossed into Canada, where he told reporters that "the life of white men is slavery. . . . I have seen nothing that a white man has, houses or railways or clothing or food, that is as good as the right to move in open country and live in our own fashion."

In 1874, the Lakotas faced direct provocation. Lieutenant Colonel George Armstrong Custer, a brash self-promoter who had graduated last in his class at West Point, led an expedition into South Dakota's Black Hills and loudly proclaimed the discovery of gold. Amid the severe depression of the 1870s, prospectors rushed in. The United States, wavering on its 1868 treaty, pressured Sioux leaders to sell the Black Hills. The chiefs said no. Ignoring this answer, the government demanded in 1876 that all Sioux gather at the federal agencies. The policy backfired: not only did Sitting Bull refuse to report, but other Sioux, Cheyennes, and Arapahos slipped away from reservations to join him. Knowing they might face military attack, they agreed to live together for the summer in one great village numbering over seven thousand people. By June, they were camped on the Little Big Horn River in what is now southeastern Montana. Some of the young men wanted to organize raiding parties, but elders counseled against it. "We [are] within our treaty rights as hunters," they argued. "We must keep ourselves so."

The U.S. Army dispatched a thousand cavalry and infantrymen to drive the Indians back to the reservation. Despite warnings from experienced scouts— including Crow Indian allies—most officers thought the job would be easy. Their greatest fear was that the Indians would manage to slip away. But amid the nation's centennial celebration on the Fourth of July 1876, Americans received dreadful news. On June 26 and 27, Lieutenant Colonel Custer, leading the 7th Cavalry as part of a three-pronged effort to surround the Indians, had led 210 men in an ill-considered assault on Sitting Bull's camp. The Sioux and their allies had killed the attackers to the last man. "The Indians," one Oglala woman remembered, "acted just like they were driving buffalo to a good place where they could be easily slaughtered."

As retold by the press in sensational (and often fictionalized) accounts, the story of Custer's "last stand" quickly served to justify American conquest of Indian

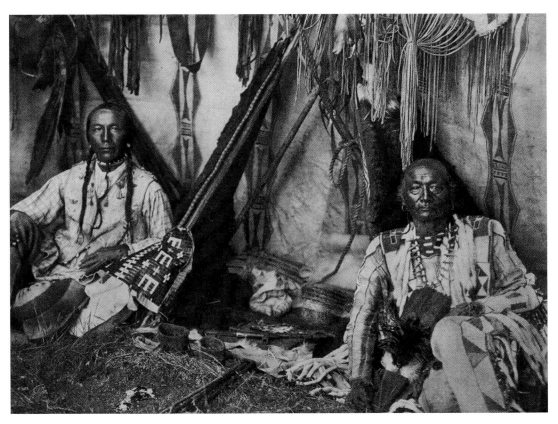

Little Plume and Yellow Kidney

Photographer Edward S. Curtis took this photograph of the Piegan (Blackfeet) leader Little Plume and his son Yellow Kidney. Curtis's extensive collection of photographs of Native Americans remains a valuable resource for historians. However, Curtis altered his images to make his native subjects seem more "authentic": though Indians made widespread use of nonnative furniture, clothes, and other consumer goods (such as Singer sewing machines), Curtis removed those from the frame. He also retouched photographs to remove items such as belts and watches. Note the circular "shadow" here, against the lodge wall, near Little Plume's right arm: the original photograph included a clock. Library of Congress.

"savages." Long after Americans forgot the massacres of Cheyenne women and children at Sand Creek and of Piegan people on the Marias River, prints of the **Battle of Little Big Horn** hung in barrooms across the country. William F. "Buffalo Bill" Cody, in his traveling Wild West performances, enacted a revenge killing of a Cheyenne man named Yellow Hand in a tableau Cody called "first scalp for Custer." Notwithstanding that the tableau featured a white man scalping a Cheyenne, Cody depicted it as a triumph for civilization.

Little Big Horn proved to be the last military victory of Plains Indians against the U.S. Army. Pursued relentlessly after Custer's death and finding fewer and fewer bison to sustain them, Sioux parents watched their children starve through a bitter winter. Slowly, families trickled into the agencies and accommodated themselves to reservation life (Map 16.6). The next year,

the Nez Perces, fleeing for the Canadian border, also surrendered. The final holdouts fought in the Southwest with Chiricahua Apache leader Geronimo. Like many others, Geronimo had accepted reservation life but found conditions unendurable. Describing the desolate land the tribe had been allotted, one Apache said it had "nothing but cactus, rattlesnakes, heat, rocks, and insects. . . . Many, many of our people died of starvation." When Geronimo took up arms in protest, the army recruited other Apaches to track him and his band into the hills; in September 1886, he surrendered for the last time. The Chiricahua Apaches never returned to their homeland. The United States had completed its military conquest of the West.

EXPLAIN CONSEQUENCES

How did Grant's peace policy fail to consider the needs of Native Americans in the West, and what were its results?

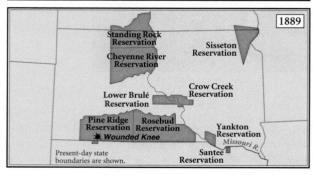

MAP 16.6

The Sioux Reservations in South Dakota, 1868–1889

In 1868, when they bent to the demand that they move onto the reservation, the Sioux thought they had gained secure rights to a substantial part of their ancestral hunting grounds. But harsh conditions on reservations led to continuing military conflicts. Land-hungry whites exerted continuous local pressure, and officials in Washington repeatedly changed the terms of Sioux land holdings—always eroding native claims.

Strategies of Survival

Though the warpath closed, many native peoples continued secretly to practice traditional customs. Away from the disapproving eyes of agents and teachers, they passed on their languages, histories, and traditional arts and medicine to younger generations. Frustrated missionaries often concluded that little could be accomplished because bonds of kinship and

TRACE CHANGE OVER TIME

In what ways did the outlook of native peoples change in the era after armed resistance had ended?

custom were so strong. Parents also hated to relinquish their children to off-reservation boarding schools. Thus more and more Indian schools ended up on or near reservations; white teachers had to accept their pupils' continued participation in the rhythms of Indian community life.

Selectively, most native peoples adopted some white ways. Many parents urged their sons and daughters to study hard, learn English, and develop skills to help them succeed in the new world they confronted. Even Sitting Bull announced in 1885 that he wanted his children "to be educated like the white children are." Some Indian students grew up to be lawyers, doctors, and advocates for their people, including writers and artists who interpreted native experiences for national audiences. One of the most famous was a Santee Sioux boy named Ohiyesa, who became Dr. Charles Eastman. Posted to the Pine Ridge Reservation in South Dakota, Eastman practiced medicine side by side with traditional healers, whom he respected, and wrote popular books under his Sioux name. He remembered that when he left for boarding school, his father had said, "We have now entered upon this life, and there is no going back. . . . Remember, my boy, it is the same as if I sent you on your first war-path. I shall expect you to conquer."

Nothing exemplified this syncretism, or cultural blending, better than the **Ghost Dance movement** of the late 1880s and early 1890s, which fostered native peoples' hope that they could, through sacred dances, resurrect the bison and call a great storm to drive whites back across the Atlantic. The Ghost Dance drew on Christian elements as well as native ones. As the movement spread from reservation to reservation—Paiutes, Arapahos, Sioux—native peoples developed new forms of pan-Indian identity and cooperation.

White responses to the Ghost Dance showed continued misunderstanding and lethal exertion of authority. In 1890, when a group of Lakota Sioux Ghost Dancers left their South Dakota reservation, they were pursued by the U.S. Army, who feared that further spread of the religion would provoke war. On December 29, at **Wounded Knee**, the 7th Cavalry caught up with fleeing Lakotas and killed at least 150—perhaps as many as 300. Like other massacres, this one could have been avoided. The deaths at Wounded Knee stand as a final indictment of decades of relentless U.S. expansion, white ignorance and greed, chaotic and conflicting policies, and bloody mistakes.

Western Myths and Realities

The post–Civil War frontier produced mythic figures who have played starring roles in America's national folklore ever since: "savage" Indians, brave pioneers, rugged cowboys, and gun-slinging sheriffs. Far from being invented by Hollywood in the twentieth century, these oversimplified characters emerged in the era when the nation incorporated the West. Pioneers helped develop the mythic ideal. As one Montana woman claimed, they had come west "at peril of their lives" and faced down "scalp dances" and other terrors; in the end, they "conquered the wilderness and transformed it into a land of peace and plenty." Some former cowboys, capitalizing on the popularity of dime novel Westerns, spiced up their memoirs for sale. Eastern readers were eager for stories like *The Life and Adventures of Nat Love* (1907), written by a Texas cowhand who had been born in slavery in Tennessee and who, as a rodeo star in the 1870s, had won the nickname "Deadwood Dick."

No myth-maker proved more influential than Buffalo Bill Cody. Unlike those who saw the West as free or empty, Bill understood that the United States had taken it by conquest. Ironically, his famous Wild West, which he insisted was not a "show" but an authentic representation of frontier experience, provided one of the few employment options for Plains Indians. To escape harsh reservation conditions, Sioux and Cheyenne men signed on with Bill and demonstrated their riding skills for cheering audiences across the United States and Europe, chasing buffalo and attacking U.S. soldiers and pioneer wagons in the arena. Buffalo Bill proved to be a good employer. Black Elk, a Sioux man who joined Cody's operation, recalled that Bill was generous and "had a strong heart." But Black Elk had a mixed reaction to the Wild West. "I liked the part of the show we made," he told an interviewer, "but not the part the Wasichus [white people] made." As he observed, the Wild West of the 1880s was at its heart a celebration of U.S. military conquest.

At this same moment of transition, a young historian named Frederick Jackson Turner reviewed recent census data and proclaimed the end of the frontier. Up to 1890, he wrote, a clear, westward-moving line had existed between "civilization and savagery." The frontier experience, Turner argued, shaped Americans' national character. It left them a heritage of "coarseness and strength, combined with acuteness and inquisitiveness," as well as "restless, nervous energy."

Today, historians reject Turner's depiction of Indian "savagery"—and his contradictory idea that white pioneers in the West claimed empty "free land." Many scholars have noted that frontier conquest was both violent and incomplete. The Dust Bowl of the 1930s, as well as more recent cycles of drought, have repeated late-nineteenth-century patterns of hardship and depopulation on the plains. During the 1950s and 1960s, also, uranium mining rushes in the West mimicked earlier patterns of boom and bust, leaving ghost towns in their wake. Turner himself acknowledged that the frontier had both good and evil elements. He noted that in the West, "frontier liberty was sometimes confused with absence of all effective government." But in 1893, when Turner first published "The Significance of the Frontier in American History," eager listeners heard only the positives. They saw pioneering in the West as evidence of American exceptionalism: of the nation's unique history and destiny. They claimed that "peaceful" American expansion was the opposite of European empires—ignoring the many military and economic similarities. Although politically the American West became a set of states rather than a colony, historians today emphasize the legacy of conquest that is central to its (and America's) history.

Less than two months after the massacre at Wounded Knee, General William T. Sherman died in New York. As the nation marked his passing with pomp and oratory, commentators noted that his career reflected a great era of conquest and consolidation of national power. Known primarily for his role in defeating the Confederacy, Sherman's first military exploits had been against Seminoles in Florida. Later, during the Mexican War (1846–1848), he had gone west with the U.S. Army to help claim California. After the Civil War, the general went west again, supervising the forced removal of Sioux and Cheyennes to reservations.

When Sherman graduated from West Point in 1840, the United States had counted twenty-six states, none of them west of Missouri. At his death in 1891, the nation boasted forty-four states, stretching to the Pacific coast. The United States now rivaled Britain and Germany as an industrial giant, and its dynamic economy was drawing immigrants from around the world. Over the span of Sherman's career, the United States had become a major player on the world stage. It had done so through the kind of fierce military conquest that Sherman made famous, as well as through bold expansions of federal authority to foster economic expansion. From the wars and policies of Sherman's lifetime, the children and grandchildren of Civil War heroes inherited a vast empire. In the coming decades, it would be up to them to decide how they would use the nation's new power.

SUMMARY

Between 1861 and 1877, the United States completed its conquest of the continent. After the Civil War, expansion of railroads fostered integration of the national economy. Republican policymakers promoted this integration through protective tariffs, while federal court rulings facilitated economic growth and strengthened corporations. To attract foreign investment, Congress placed the nation on the gold standard. Federal officials also pursued a vigorous foreign policy, acquiring Alaska and asserting U.S. power indirectly through control of international trade in Latin America and Asia.

An important result of economic integration was incorporation of the Great Plains. Cattlemen built an industry linked to the integrated economy, in the process nearly driving the native bison to extinction. Homesteaders confronted harsh environmental conditions as they converted the grasslands for agriculture. Republicans championed homesteader families as representatives of domesticity, an ideal opposed to Mormon plural marriage in Utah. Homesteading accelerated the rapid, often violent, transformation of western environments. Perceiving this transformation, federal officials began setting aside natural preserves such as Yellowstone, often clashing with Native Americans who wished to hunt there.

Conflicts led to the dispossession of Native American lands. During the Civil War, whites clashed with the Sioux and their allies. Grant's peace policy sought to end this conflict by forcing Native Americans to acculturate to European-style practices. Indian armed resistance continued through the 1880s, ending with Geronimo's surrender in 1886. Thereafter, Native Americans survived by secretly continuing their traditions and selectively adopting white ways. Due in part to the determined military conquest of this period, the United States claimed a major role on the world stage. Frontier myths shaped Americans' view of themselves as rugged individualists with a unique national destiny.

CHAPTER REVIEW

 MAKE IT STICK   Go to **LearningCurve** to retain what you've read.

TERMS TO KNOW   Identify and explain the significance of each term below.

Key Concepts and Events

transcontinental railroad (p. 508)
protective tariff (p. 510)
Treaty of Kanagawa (p. 510)
Burlingame Treaty (p. 511)
Munn v. Illinois (p. 514)
gold standard (p. 515)
Crime of 1873 (p. 515)
Homestead Act (p. 516)
Morrill Act (p. 516)
land-grant colleges (p. 516)
Comstock Lode (p. 516)
Long Drive (p. 519)
"rain follows the plow" (p. 519)

Exodusters (p. 520)
Yellowstone National Park (p. 525)
U.S. Fisheries Commission (p. 525)
Sand Creek massacre (p. 527)
Fetterman massacre (p. 528)
Lone Wolf v. Hitchcock (p. 532)
Dawes Severalty Act (p. 532)
Battle of Little Big Horn (p. 533)
Ghost Dance movement (p. 534)
Wounded Knee (p. 534)

Key People

William Seward (p. 510)
Emmeline Wells (p. 521)
John Wesley Powell (p. 521)
Chief Joseph (p. 525)
Sitting Bull (p. 532)
George Armstrong Custer (p. 532)
Geronimo (p. 533)
Ohiyesa (Dr. Charles Eastman) (p. 534)
Buffalo Bill Cody (p. 535)
Frederick Jackson Turner (p. 535)

REVIEW QUESTIONS   Answer these questions to demonstrate your understanding of the chapter's main ideas.

1. What national policies did Republicans pursue during the Civil War and Reconstruction to stimulate economic growth and consolidate a continental empire? What were the resulting achievements and costs?

2. How did the trans-Mississippi west develop economically in this era? What problems and conflicts resulted?

3. Why did U.S. policies toward Native Americans in this era result in so much violence? Why did armed struggle continue as late as 1890, despite the U.S. "peace policy" that was proclaimed in the 1870s?

4. **THEMATIC UNDERSTANDING** Review the events listed under "Peopling" on the thematic timeline on page 409. Between the 1840s and the 1870s, what distinctive patterns of racial and ethnic conflict occurred along the northeastern seaboard and in the West? What were the results for immigrants in the Northeast, and for different ethnic and racial groups in the West?

MAKING CONNECTIONS   Recognize the larger developments and continuities within and across chapters by answering these questions.

1. **ACROSS TIME AND PLACE** During the Reconstruction years, Republican policymakers made sweeping policy decisions — especially having to do with land rights, voting rights, and education — that shaped the future of African Americans in the South and American Indians in the West. In an essay, compare U.S. policies toward the two groups. What assumptions and goals underlay each effort to incorporate racial minorities into the United States? To what extent did each effort succeed or fail, and why? How did the actions of powerful whites in each region shape the results?

2. **VISUAL EVIDENCE** Review the images in this chapter. Find two that show how Americans of the era thought the landscapes of the West *ought* to look when settlement was complete. Identify at least three others that show what the natural and built environments of the West *really* looked like. What do you conclude from this comparison about the ambitions and limits of westward expansion?

MORE TO EXPLORE   Start here to learn more about the events discussed in this chapter.

David Wallace Adams, *Education for Extinction* (1995). A powerful history of American Indian boarding schools.

American Experience (PBS), "Last Stand at Little Big Horn." A nuanced one-hour documentary about the famous battle.

Sarah Barringer Gordon, *The Mormon Question* (2002). An exploration of plural marriage debates in national politics.

Joy S. Kasson, *Buffalo Bill's Wild West* (2001). A wonderful study of Buffalo Bill's performances and their role in shaping mythologies of the West.

Patricia Nelson Limerick, *The Legacy of Conquest* (1987) and *Something in the Soil* (2000). Limerick's lively, accessible books are an excellent introduction to historians' recent rethinking of western history.

María Montoya, *Translating Property* (2002). Tells the story of the displacement of Mexican Americans (and their neighbors) in struggles over the Maxwell Land Grant in New Mexico and Colorado.

TIMELINE

Ask yourself why this chapter begins and ends with these dates and then identify the links among related events.

1854	• United States "opens" Japan to trade
1859	• Comstock silver lode discovered in Nevada
1862	• Homestead Act • Dakota Sioux uprising in Minnesota • Morrill Act funds public state universities
1864	• Sand Creek massacre of Cheyennes in Colorado • Yosemite Valley reserved as public park
1865	• Long Drive of Texas longhorns begins
1866	• Fetterman massacre
1868	• Burlingame Treaty with China
1869	• Transcontinental railroad completed • Wyoming women's suffrage
1870	• Utah women's suffrage
1872	• General Mining Act • Yellowstone National Park created
1873	• United States begins move to gold standard
1876	• Battle of Little Big Horn
1877	• Nez Perces forcibly removed from ancestral homelands in Northwest • *Munn v. Illinois* Supreme Court decision
1879	• Exoduster migration to Kansas • John Wesley Powell presents *Report on the Lands of the Arid Region of the United States*
1880s	• Rise of the Ghost Dance movement
1885	• Sitting Bull tours with Buffalo Bill's Wild West
1886	• Dry cycle begins on the plains • Chiricahua Apache leader Geronimo surrenders
1887	• Dawes Severalty Act
1890	• Massacre of Sioux Ghost Dancers at Wounded Knee, South Dakota

KEY TURNING POINTS: The military, political, and economic events of the Civil War years (1861–1865) are often treated as largely occurring in the Northeast and South — at places such as Shiloh, Gettysburg, and Washington, D.C. What impact did these developments have on the West, and what were their legacies?

Documents

The Declaration of Independence

In Congress, July 4, 1776,
The Unanimous Declaration of the Thirteen United States of America

When in the Course of human events, it becomes necessary for one people to dissolve the political bands which have connected them with another, and to assume among the Powers of the earth, the separate and equal station to which the Laws of Nature and of Nature's God entitle them, a decent respect to the opinions of mankind requires that they should declare the causes which impel them to the separation.

We hold these truths to be self-evident, that all men are created equal, that they are endowed by their Creator with certain unalienable rights, that among these are Life, Liberty, and the pursuit of Happiness. That to secure these rights, Governments are instituted among Men, deriving their just powers from the consent of the governed. That whenever any Form of Government becomes destructive of these ends, it is the Right of the People to alter or to abolish it, and to institute new Government, laying its foundation on such principles and organizing its powers in such form, as to them shall seem most likely to effect their Safety and Happiness. Prudence, indeed, will dictate that Governments long established should not be changed for light and transient causes; and accordingly all experience hath shown, that mankind are more disposed to suffer, while evils are sufferable, than to right themselves by abolishing the forms to which they are accustomed. But when a long train of abuses and usurpations, pursuing invariably the same Object evinces a design to reduce them under absolute Despotism, it is their right, it is their duty, to throw off such Government, and to provide new Guards for their future security. — Such has been the patient sufferance of these Colonies; and such is now the necessity which constrains them to alter their former Systems of Government. The history of the present King of Great Britain is a history of repeated injuries and usurpations, all having in direct object the establishment of an absolute Tyranny over these States. To prove this, let Facts be submitted to a candid world.

He has refused his Assent to Laws, the most wholesome and necessary for the public good.

He has forbidden his Governors to pass Laws of immediate and pressing importance, unless suspended in their operation till his Assent should be obtained; and, when so suspended, he has utterly neglected to attend to them.

He has refused to pass other Laws for the accommodation of large districts of people, unless those people would relinquish the right of Representation in the Legislature, a right inestimable to them and formidable to tyrants only.

He has called together legislative bodies at places unusual, uncomfortable, and distant from the depository of their public Records, for the sole purpose of fatiguing them into compliance with his measures.

He has dissolved Representative Houses repeatedly, for opposing with manly firmness his invasions on the rights of the people.

He has refused for a long time, after such dissolutions, to cause others to be elected; whereby the Legislative powers, incapable of Annihilation, have returned to the People at large for their exercise; the State remaining in the mean time exposed to all the dangers of invasion from without and convulsions within.

He has endeavoured to prevent the population of these States; for that purpose obstructing the Laws of Naturalization of Foreigners; refusing to pass others to encourage their migrations hither, and raising the conditions of new Appropriations of Lands.

He has obstructed the Administration of Justice, by refusing his Assent to Laws for establishing Judiciary powers.

He has made Judges dependent on his Will alone, for the tenure of their offices, and the amount and payment of their salaries.

He has erected a multitude of New Offices, and sent hither swarms of Officers to harass our People, and eat out their substance.

He has kept among us, in times of peace, Standing Armies without the Consent of our legislature.

He has combined with others to subject us to a jurisdiction foreign to our constitution, and unacknowledged by our laws; giving his Assent to their Acts of pretended Legislation:

For quartering large bodies of armed troops among us:

For protecting them, by a mock Trial, from Punishment for any Murders which they should commit on the Inhabitants of these States:

For cutting off our Trade with all parts of the world:

For imposing taxes on us without our Consent:

For depriving us, in many cases, of the benefits of Trial by jury:

For transporting us beyond Seas to be tried for pretended offences:

For abolishing the free System of English Laws in a neighbouring Province, establishing therein an Arbitrary government, and enlarging its Boundaries so as to render it at once an example and fit instrument for introducing the same absolute rule into these Colonies:

For taking away our Charters, abolishing our most valuable Laws, and altering fundamentally the Forms of our Governments:

For suspending our own Legislatures, and declaring themselves invested with Power to legislate for us in all cases whatsoever.

He has abdicated Government here, by declaring us out of his Protection and waging War against us.

He has plundered our seas, ravaged our Coasts, burnt our towns, and destroyed the lives of our people.

He is at this time transporting large armies of foreign mercenaries to compleat the works of death, desolation, and tyranny, already begun with circumstances of Cruelty & perfidy scarcely paralleled in the most barbarous ages, and totally unworthy the Head of a civilized nation.

He has constrained our fellow Citizens taken Captive on the high Seas to bear Arms against their Country, to become the executioners of their friends and Brethren, or to fall themselves by their Hands.

He has excited domestic insurrections amongst us, and has endeavoured to bring on the inhabitants of our frontiers, the merciless Indian Savages, whose known rule of warfare, is an undistinguished destruction of all ages, sexes, and conditions.

In every stage of these Oppressions We have Petitioned for Redress in the most humble terms: Our repeated Petitions have been answered only by repeated injury. A Prince, whose character is thus marked by every act which may define a Tyrant, is unfit to be the ruler of a free people.

Nor have We been wanting in attention to our British brethren. We have warned them from time to time of attempts by their legislature to extend an unwarrantable jurisdiction over us. We have reminded them of the circumstances of our emigration and settlement here. We have appealed to their native justice and magnanimity, and we have conjured them by the ties of our common kindred to disavow these usurpations, which would inevitably interrupt our connections and correspondence. They too have been deaf to the voice of justice and of consanguinity. We must, therefore, acquiesce in the necessity, which denounces our Separation, and hold them, as we hold the rest of mankind, Enemies in War, in Peace Friends.

We, therefore, the Representatives of the United States of America, in General Congress, Assembled, appealing to the Supreme Judge of the world for the rectitude of our intentions, do, in the Name, and by Authority of the good People of these Colonies, solemnly publish and declare, That these United Colonies are, and of Right ought to be FREE AND INDEPENDENT STATES; that they are Absolved from all Allegiance to the British Crown, and that all political connection between them and the State of Great Britain, is and ought to be totally dissolved; and that as Free and Independent States, they have full Power to levy War, conclude Peace, contract Alliances, establish Commerce, and to do all other Acts and Things which Independent States may of right do. And for the support of this Declaration, with a firm reliance on the Protection of Divine Providence, we mutually pledge to each other our Lives, our Fortunes, and our sacred Honor.

John Hancock

Button Gwinnett	**George Wythe**	**James Wilson**	**Josiah Bartlett**
Lyman Hall	**Richard Henry Lee**	**Geo. Ross**	**Wm. Whipple**
Geo. Walton	**Th. Jefferson**	**Caesar Rodney**	**Matthew Thornton**
Wm. Hooper	**Benja. Harrison**	**Geo. Read**	**Saml. Adams**
Joseph Hewes	**Thos. Nelson, Jr.**	**Thos. M'Kean**	**John Adams**
John Penn	**Francis Lightfoot Lee**	**Wm. Floyd**	**Robt. Treat Paine**
Edward Rutledge	**Carter Braxton**	**Phil. Livingston**	**Elbridge Gerry**
Thos. Heyward, Junr.	**Robt. Morris**	**Frans. Lewis**	**Step. Hopkins**
Thomas Lynch, Junr.	**Benjamin Rush**	**Lewis Morris**	**William Ellery**
Arthur Middleton	**Benja. Franklin**	**Richd. Stockton**	**Roger Sherman**
Samuel Chase	**John Morton**	**John Witherspoon**	**Sam'el Huntington**
Wm. Paca	**Geo. Clymer**	**Fras. Hopkinson**	**Wm. Williams**
Thos. Stone	**Jas. Smith**	**John Hart**	**Oliver Wolcott**
Charles Carroll of Carrollton	**Geo. Taylor**	**Abra. Clark**	

The Constitution of the United States of America

Agreed to by Philadelphia Convention, September 17, 1787
Implemented March 4, 1789

We the People of the United States, in Order to form a more perfect Union, establish Justice, insure domestic Tranquility, provide for the common defence, promote the general Welfare, and secure the Blessings of Liberty to ourselves and our Posterity, do ordain and establish this Constitution for the United States of America.

Article I

Section 1. All legislative Powers herein granted shall be vested in a Congress of the United States, which shall consist of a Senate and a House of Representatives.

Section 2. The House of Representatives shall be composed of Members chosen every second Year by the People of the several States, and the Electors in each State shall have the Qualifications requisite for Electors of the most numerous Branch of the State Legislature.

No Person shall be a Representative who shall not have attained to the Age of twenty-five Years, and been seven Years a Citizen of the United States, and who shall not, when elected, be an Inhabitant of that State in which he shall be chosen.

Representatives and direct Taxes shall be apportioned among the several States which may be included within this Union, according to their respective Numbers, *which shall be determined by adding to the whole Number of free Persons, including those bound to Service for a Term of Years, and excluding Indians not taxed, three fifths of all other Persons.** The actual Enumeration shall be made within three Years after the first Meeting of the Congress of the United States, and within every subsequent Term of ten Years, in such Manner as they shall by Law direct. The Number of Representatives shall not exceed one for every thirty Thousand, but each State shall have at Least one Representative; and *until such enumeration shall be made, the State of New Hampshire shall be entitled to chuse three, Massachusetts eight, Rhode Island and Providence Plantations one, Connecticut five, New York six, New Jersey four, Pennsylvania eight, Delaware one, Maryland six, Virginia ten, North Carolina five, South Carolina five, and Georgia three.*

When vacancies happen in the Representation from any State, the Executive Authority thereof shall issue Writs of Election to fill such Vacancies.

The House of Representatives shall chuse their Speaker and other Officers; and shall have the sole Power of Impeachment.

Section 3. The Senate of the United States shall be composed of two Senators from each State, *chosen by the Legislature thereof,*† for six Years; and each Senator shall have one Vote.

Immediately after they shall be assembled in Consequence of the first Election, they shall be divided as equally as may be into three Classes. The Seats of the Senators of the first Class shall be vacated at the Expiration of the second Year, of the second Class at the Expiration of the fourth Year, and of the third Class at the Expiration of the sixth Year, so that one-third may be chosen every second Year; and if Vacancies happen by Resignation, or otherwise, during the Recess of the Legislature of any State, the Executive thereof may make temporary Appointments until the next Meeting of the Legislature, which shall then fill such Vacancies.‡

No person shall be a Senator who shall not have attained to the Age of thirty Years, and been nine Years a Citizen of the United States, and who shall not, when elected, be an Inhabitant of that State for which he shall be chosen.

The Vice President of the United States shall be President of the Senate, but shall have no Vote, unless they be equally divided.

The Senate shall chuse their other Officers, and also a President pro tempore, in the absence of the Vice President, or when he shall exercise the Office of President of the United States.

The Senate shall have the sole Power to try all Impeachments. When sitting for that Purpose, they shall be on Oath or Affirmation. When the President of the United States is tried, the Chief Justice shall preside: And no Person shall be convicted without the Concurrence of two-thirds of the Members present.

Judgment in Cases of Impeachment shall not extend further than to removal from Office, and disqualification to hold and enjoy any Office of honor, Trust or Profit under the United States: but the Party convicted shall nevertheless be liable and subject to Indictment, Trial, Judgment and Punishment, according to Law.

Note: The Constitution became effective March 4, 1789. Provisions in italics are no longer relevant or have been changed by constitutional amendment.
*Changed by Section 2 of the Fourteenth Amendment.

†Changed by Section 1 of the Seventeenth Amendment.
‡Changed by Clause 2 of the Seventeenth Amendment.

Section 4. The Times, Places and Manner of holding Elections for Senators and Representatives, shall be prescribed in each State by the Legislature thereof; but the Congress may at any time by Law make or alter such Regulations, except as to the Places of Chusing Senators.

The Congress shall assemble at least once in every Year, and such Meeting *shall be on the first Monday in December, unless they shall by Law appoint a different Day.**

Section 5. Each House shall be the Judge of the Elections, Returns and Qualifications of its own Members, and a Majority of each shall constitute a Quorum to do Business; but a smaller number may adjourn from day to day, and may be authorized to compel the Attendance of absent Members, in such Manner, and under such Penalties, as each House may provide.

Each House may determine the Rules of its Proceedings, punish its Members for disorderly Behavior, and, with the Concurrence of two-thirds, expel a Member.

Each House shall keep a Journal of its Proceedings, and from time to time publish the same, excepting such Parts as may in their Judgment require Secrecy; and the Yeas and Nays of the Members of either House on any question shall, at the Desire of one-fifth of those Present, be entered on the Journal.

Neither House, during the Session of Congress, shall, without the Consent of the other, adjourn for more than three days, nor to any other Place than that in which the two Houses shall be sitting.

Section 6. The Senators and Representatives shall receive a Compensation for their Services, to be ascertained by Law, and paid out of the Treasury of the United States. They shall in all Cases, except Treason, Felony and Breach of the Peace, be privileged from Arrest during their Attendance at the Session of their respective Houses, and in going to and returning from the same; and for any Speech or Debate in either House, they shall not be questioned in any other Place.

No Senator or Representative shall, during the Time for which he was elected, be appointed to any civil Office under the Authority of the United States, which shall have been created, or the Emoluments whereof shall have been increased, during such time; and no Person holding any Office under the United States, shall be a Member of either House during his Continuance in Office.

Section 7. All Bills for raising Revenue shall originate in the House of Representatives; but the Senate may propose or concur with Amendments as on other Bills.

Every Bill which shall have passed the House of Representatives and the Senate, shall, before it becomes a Law, be presented to the President of the United States; If he approve he shall sign it, but if not he shall return it, with his Objections to that House in which it shall have originated, who shall enter the Objections at large on their Journal, and proceed to reconsider it. If after such Reconsideration two-thirds of that House shall agree to pass the Bill, it shall be sent, together with the Objections, to the other House, by which it shall likewise be reconsidered, and if approved by two-thirds of that House, it shall become a Law. But in all such Cases the Votes of both Houses shall be determined by Yeas and Nays, and the Names of the Persons voting for and against the Bill shall be entered on the Journal of each House respectively. If any Bill shall not be returned by the President within ten Days (Sundays excepted) after it shall have been presented to him, the Same shall be a Law, in like Manner as if he had signed it, unless the Congress by their Adjournment prevent its Return, in which Case it shall not be a Law.

Every Order, Resolution, or Vote to which the Concurrence of the Senate and the House of Representatives may be necessary (except on a question of Adjournment) shall be presented to the President of the United States; and before the Same shall take Effect, shall be approved by him, or being disapproved by him, shall be repassed by two-thirds of the Senate and House of Representatives, according to the Rules and Limitations prescribed in the Case of a Bill.

Section 8. The Congress shall have Power To lay and collect Taxes, Duties, Imposts and Excises, to pay the Debts and provide for the common Defence and general Welfare of the United States; but all Duties, Imposts and Excises shall be uniform throughout the United States;

To borrow money on the credit of the United States;

To regulate Commerce with foreign Nations, and among the several States, and with the Indian Tribes;

To establish an uniform Rule of Naturalization, and uniform Laws on the subject of Bankruptcies throughout the United States;

To coin Money, regulate the Value thereof, and of foreign Coin, and fix the Standard of Weights and Measures;

To provide for the Punishment of counterfeiting the Securities and current Coin of the United States;

To establish Post Offices and post Roads;

To promote the Progress of Science and useful Arts, by securing for limited Times to Authors and Inventors the exclusive Right to their respective Writings and Discoveries;

To constitute Tribunals inferior to the supreme Court;

To define and punish Piracies and Felonies committed on the high Seas, and Offenses against the Law of Nations;

To declare War, grant Letters of Marque and Reprisal, and make Rules concerning Captures on Land and Water;

---

*Changed by Section 2 of the Twentieth Amendment.

To raise and support Armies, but no Appropriation of Money to that Use shall be for a longer Term than two Years;

To provide and maintain a Navy;

To make Rules for the Government and Regulation of the land and naval Forces;

To provide for calling forth the Militia to execute the Laws of the Union, suppress Insurrections and repel Invasions;

To provide for organizing, arming, and disciplining the Militia, and for governing such Part of them as may be employed in the Service of the United States, reserving to the States respectively, the Appointment of the Officers, and the Authority of training the Militia according to the discipline prescribed by Congress;

To exercise exclusive Legislation in all Cases whatsoever, over such District (not exceeding ten Miles square) as may, by Cession of particular States, and the acceptance of Congress, become the Seat of Government of the United States, and to exercise like Authority over all Places purchased by the Consent of the Legislature of the State in which the Same shall be, for the Erection of Forts, Magazines, Arsenals, dock-Yards, and other needful Buildings; — And

To make all Laws which shall be necessary and proper for carrying into Execution the foregoing Powers, and all other Powers vested by this Constitution in the Government of the United States, or in any Department or Officer thereof.

Section 9. The Migration or Importation of such Persons as any of the States now existing shall think proper to admit, shall not be prohibited by the Congress prior to the Year one thousand eight hundred and eight but a tax or duty may be imposed on such Importation, not exceeding ten dollars for each Person.

The privilege of the Writ of Habeas Corpus shall not be suspended, unless when in Cases of Rebellion or Invasion the public Safety may require it.

No Bill of Attainder or ex post facto Law shall be passed.

No capitation, or other direct, Tax shall be laid, unless in Proportion to the Census or Enumeration herein before directed to be taken.*

No Tax or Duty shall be laid on Articles exported from any State.

No Preference shall be given by any Regulation of Commerce or Revenue to the Ports of one State over those of another: nor shall Vessels bound to, or from, one State, be obliged to enter, clear, or pay Duties in another.

No Money shall be drawn from the Treasury, but in Consequence of Appropriations made by law; and a regular Statement and Account of the Receipts and Expenditures of all public Money shall be published from time to time.

*Changed by the Sixteenth Amendment.

No Title of Nobility shall be granted by the United States: And no Person holding any Office of Profit or Trust under them, shall, without the Consent of the Congress, accept of any present, Emolument, Office, or Title, of any kind whatever, from any King, Prince, or foreign State.

Section 10. No State shall enter into any Treaty, Alliance, or Confederation; grant Letters of Marque and Reprisal; coin Money; emit Bills of Credit; make any Thing but gold and silver Coin a Tender in Payment of Debts; pass any Bill of Attainder, ex post facto Law, or Law impairing the Obligation of Contracts, or grant any Title of Nobility.

No State shall, without the Consent of the Congress, lay any Imposts or Duties on Imports or Exports, except what may be absolutely necessary for executing its inspection Laws: and the net Produce of all Duties and Imposts, laid by any State on Imports or Exports, shall be for the Use of the Treasury of the United States; and all such Laws shall be subject to the Revision and Control of the Congress.

No State shall, without the Consent of the Congress, lay any duty of Tonnage, keep Troops, or Ships of War in time of Peace, enter into any Agreement or Compact with another State, or with a foreign Power, or engage in War, unless actually invaded, or in such imminent Danger as will not admit of delay.

Article II

Section 1. The executive Power shall be vested in a President of the United States of America. He shall hold his Office during the Term of four Years, and, together with the Vice President, chosen for the same Term, be elected, as follows:

Each State shall appoint, in such Manner as the Legislature thereof may direct, a Number of Electors, equal to the whole Number of Senators and Representatives to which the State may be entitled in the Congress; but no Senator or Representative, or Person holding an Office of Trust or Profit under the United States, shall be appointed an Elector.

The Electors shall meet in their respective States, and vote by Ballot for two Persons, of whom one at least shall not be an Inhabitant of the same State with themselves. And they shall make a List of all the Persons voted for, and of the Number of Votes for each; which List they shall sign and certify, and transmit sealed to the Seat of the Government of the United States, directed to the President of the Senate. The President of the Senate shall, in the Presence of the Senate and House of Representatives, open all the Certificates, and the Votes shall then be counted. The Person having the greatest Number of Votes shall be the President, if such Number be a Majority of the whole Number of Electors appointed; and if there be more than one who have such Majority, and have an equal Number of Votes, then the House of Representatives shall immediately chuse by

*Ballot one of them for President; and if no Person have a Majority, then from the five highest on the List the said House shall in like Manner chuse the President. But in chusing the President, the Votes shall be taken by States, the Representation from each State having one Vote; a quorum for this Purpose shall consist of a Member or Members from two thirds of the States, and a Majority of all the States shall be necessary to a Choice. In every Case, after the Choice of the President, the Person having the greatest Number of Votes of the Electors shall be the Vice President. But if there should remain two or more who have equal Votes, the Senate shall chuse from them by Ballot the Vice President.**

The Congress may determine the Time of chusing the Electors, and the Day on which they shall give their Votes; which Day shall be the same throughout the United States.

No Person except a natural born Citizen, or a Citizen of the United States, at the time of the Adoption of this Constitution, shall be eligible to the Office of President; neither shall any Person be eligible to that Office who shall not have attained to the Age of thirty five Years, and been fourteen Years a Resident within the United States.

In Case of the Removal of the President from Office, or of his Death, Resignation, or Inability to discharge the Powers and Duties of the said Office, the same shall devolve on the Vice President, *and the Congress may by Law provide for the Case of Removal, Death, Resignation, or Inability, both of the President and Vice President, declaring what Officer shall then act as President, and such Officer shall act accordingly, until the Disability be removed, or a President shall be elected.*†

The President shall, at stated Times, receive for his Services a Compensation, which shall neither be increased nor diminished during the Period for which he shall have been elected, and he shall not receive within that Period any other Emolument from the United States, or any of them.

Before he enter on the Execution of his Office, he shall take the following Oath or Affirmation: — "I do solemnly swear (or affirm) that I will faithfully execute the Office of President of the United States, and will to the best of my Ability, preserve, protect and defend the Constitution of the United States."

Section 2. The President shall be Commander in Chief of the Army and Navy of the United States, and of the Militia of the several States, when called into the actual Service of the United States; he may require the Opinion, in writing, of the principal Officer in each of the executive Departments, upon any Subject relating to the Duties of their respective Offices, and he shall have Power to Grant Reprieves and Pardons for Offences against the United States, except in Cases of Impeachment.

He shall have Power, by and with the Advice and Consent of the Senate, to make Treaties, provided two thirds of the Senators present concur; and he shall nominate, and by and with the Advice and Consent of the Senate, shall appoint Ambassadors, other public Ministers and Consuls, Judges of the supreme Court, and all other Officers of the United States, whose Appointments are not herein otherwise provided for, and which shall be established by Law: but the Congress may by Law vest the Appointment of such inferior Officers, as they think proper, in the President alone, in the Courts of Law, or in the Heads of Departments.

The President shall have Power to fill up all Vacancies that may happen during the Recess of the Senate, by granting Commissions which shall expire at the End of their next Session.

Section 3. He shall from time to time give to the Congress Information of the State of the Union, and recommend to their Consideration such Measures as he shall judge necessary and expedient; he may, on extraordinary Occasions, convene both Houses, or either of them, and in Case of Disagreement between them, with Respect to the Time of Adjournment, he may adjourn them to such Time as he shall think proper; he shall receive Ambassadors and other public Ministers; he shall take Care that the Laws be faithfully executed, and shall Commission all the Officers of the United States.

Section 4. The President, Vice President and all civil Officers of the United States, shall be removed from Office on Impeachment for, and Conviction of, Treason, Bribery, or other high Crimes and Misdemeanors.

Article III

Section 1. The judicial Power of the United States, shall be vested in one supreme Court, and in such inferior Courts as the Congress may from time to time ordain and establish. The Judges, both of the supreme and inferior Courts, shall hold their Offices during good Behaviour, and shall, at stated Times, receive for their Services a Compensation, which shall not be diminished during their Continuance in Office.

Section 2. The judicial Power shall extend to all Cases, in Law and Equity, arising under this Constitution, the Laws of the United States, and Treaties made, or which shall be made, under their Authority; — to all Cases affecting Ambassadors, other public Ministers and Consuls; — to all Cases of admiralty and maritime Jurisdiction; — to Controversies to which the United States shall be a Party; — to Controversies between two or more States; — *between a State and Citizens of another State;*‡ — between Citizens of different States; — between Citizens of the same State claiming Lands under

---

*Superseded by the Twelfth Amendment.
†Modified by the Twenty-fifth Amendment.

‡Restricted by the Eleventh Amendment.

Grants of different States, and between a State, or the Citizens thereof, and foreign States, Citizens or Subjects.

In all Cases affecting Ambassadors, other public Ministers and Consuls, and those in which a State shall be Party, the supreme Court shall have original Jurisdiction. In all the other Cases before mentioned, the supreme Court shall have appellate Jurisdiction, both as to Law and Fact, with such Exceptions, and under such Regulations as the Congress shall make.

The trial of all Crimes, except in Cases of Impeachment, shall be by Jury; and such Trial shall be held in the State where said Crimes shall have been committed; but when not committed within any State, the Trial shall be at such Place or Places as the Congress may by Law have directed.

Section 3. Treason against the United States, shall consist only in levying War against them, or in adhering to their Enemies, giving them Aid and Comfort. No Person shall be convicted of Treason unless on the Testimony of two Witnesses to the same overt Act, or on Confession in open Court.

The Congress shall have Power to declare the Punishment of Treason, but no Attainder of Treason shall work Corruption of Blood, or Forefeiture except during the Life of the Person attainted.

Article IV

Section 1. Full Faith and Credit shall be given in each State to the public Acts, Records, and judicial Proceedings of every other State. And the Congress may by general Laws prescribe the Manner in which such Acts, Records, and Proceedings shall be proved, and the Effect thereof.

Section 2. The Citizens of each State shall be entitled to all Privileges and Immunities of Citizens in the several States.

A Person charged in any State with Treason, Felony, or other Crime, who shall flee from Justice, and be found in another State, shall on demand of the executive Authority of the State from which he fled, be delivered up, to be removed to the State having Jurisdiction of the Crime.

No Person held to Service or Labour in one State, under the Laws thereof, escaping into another, shall, in Consequence of any Law or Regulation therein, be discharged from such Service or Labour, but shall be delivered up on Claim of the Party to whom such Service or Labour may be due.*

Section 3. New States may be admitted by the Congress into this Union; but no new State shall be formed or erected within the Jurisdiction of any other State; nor any State be formed by the Junction of two or more States, or parts of States, without the Consent of the Legislatures of the States concerned as well as of the Congress.

The Congress shall have Power to dispose of and make all needful Rules and Regulations respecting the Territory or other Property belonging to the United States; and nothing in this Constitution shall be so construed as to Prejudice any Claims of the United States, or of any particular State.

Section 4. The United States shall guarantee to every State in this Union a Republican Form of Government, and shall protect each of them against Invasion; and on Application of the Legislature, or of the Executive (when the Legislature cannot be convened) against domestic Violence.

Article V

The Congress, whenever two-thirds of both Houses shall deem it necessary, shall propose Amendments to this Constitution, or, on the Application of the Legislatures of two-thirds of the several States, shall call a Convention for proposing Amendments, which, in either Case, shall be valid to all Intents and Purposes, as Part of this Constitution, when ratified by the Legislatures of three-fourths of the several States, or by Conventions in three-fourths thereof, as the one or the other Mode of Ratification may be proposed by the Congress; *Provided that no Amendment which may be made prior to the Year One thousand eight hundred and eight shall in any Manner affect the first and fourth Clauses in the Ninth Section of the first Article; and* that no State, without its Consent, shall be deprived of its equal Suffrage in the Senate.

Article VI

All Debts contracted and Engagements entered into, before the Adoption of this Constitution, shall be as valid against the United States under this Constitution, as under the Confederation.

This Constitution, and the Laws of the United States which shall be made in Pursuance thereof; and all Treaties made, or which shall be made, under the Authority of the United States, shall be the supreme Law of the Land; and the Judges in every State shall be bound thereby, any Thing in the Constitution or Laws of any State to the Contrary notwithstanding.

The Senators and Representatives before mentioned, and the Members of the several State Legislatures, and all executive and judicial Officers, both of the United States and of the several States, shall be bound by Oath or Affirmation, to support this Constitution; but no religious Test shall ever be required as a Qualification to any Office or public Trust under the United States.

*Superseded by the Thirteenth Amendment.

Article VII

The Ratification of the Conventions of nine States shall be sufficient for the Establishment of this Constitution between the States so ratifying the Same.

Done in Convention by the Unanimous Consent of the States present the Seventeenth Day of September in the Year of our Lord one thousand seven hundred and Eighty seven and of the Independence of the United States of America the Twelfth. In Witness whereof We have hereunto subscribed our Names.

Go. Washington
President and deputy from Virginia

New Hampshire
John Langdon
Nicholas Gilman

Massachusetts
Nathaniel Gorham
Rufus King

Connecticut
Wm. Saml. Johnson
Roger Sherman

New York
Alexander Hamilton

New Jersey
Wil. Livingston
David Brearley
Wm. Paterson
Jona. Dayton

Pennsylvania
B. Franklin
Thomas Mifflin
Robt. Morris
Geo. Clymer
Thos. FitzSimons
Jared Ingersoll
James Wilson
Gouv. Morris

Delaware
Geo. Read
Gunning Bedford jun
John Dickinson
Richard Bassett
Jaco. Broom

Maryland
James McHenry
Dan. of St. Thos. Jenifer
Danl. Carroll

Virginia
John Blair
James Madison, Jr.

North Carolina
Wm. Blount
Richd. Dobbs Spaight
Hu Williamson

South Carolina
J. Rutledge
Charles Cotesworth
　Pinckney
Pierce Butler

Georgia
William Few
Abr. Baldwin

Amendments to the Constitution (Including the Six Unratified Amendments)

Amendment I [1791]*

Congress shall make no law respecting an establishment of religion, or prohibiting the free exercise thereof; or abridging the freedom of speech, or of the press; or the right of the people peaceably to assemble, and to petition the Government for a redress of grievances.

Amendment II [1791]

A well regulated Militia, being necessary to the security of a free State, the right of the people to keep and bear Arms shall not be infringed.

Amendment III [1791]

No Soldier shall, in time of peace, be quartered in any house, without the consent of the Owner, nor in time of war, but in a manner to be prescribed by law.

Amendment IV [1791]

The right of the people to be secure in their persons, houses, papers, and effects, against unreasonable searches and seizures, shall not be violated, and no Warrants shall issue, but upon probable cause, supported by Oath or affirmation, and particularly describing the place to be searched, and the persons or things to be seized.

Amendment V [1791]

No person shall be held to answer for a capital or otherwise infamous crime, unless on a presentment or indictment of a Grand Jury, except in cases arising in the land or naval forces, or in the Militia, when in actual service in time of War or public danger; nor shall any person be subject for the same offence to be twice put in jeopardy of life or limb; nor shall be compelled in any criminal case to be a witness against himself, nor be deprived of life, liberty, or property, without due process of law; nor shall private property be taken for public use, without just compensation.

Amendment VI [1791]

In all criminal prosecutions, the accused shall enjoy the right to a speedy and public trial, by an impartial jury of the State and district wherein the crime shall have been committed, which district shall have been previously ascertained by law, and to be informed of the nature and cause of the accusation; to be confronted with the witnesses against him; to have compulsory process for obtaining witnesses in his favor, and to have the Assistance of Counsel for his defence.

Amendment VII [1791]

In suits at common law, where the value in controversy shall exceed twenty dollars, the right of trial by jury shall be preserved, and no fact tried by a jury, shall be otherwise reexamined in any Court of the United States, than according to the Rules of the common law.

Amendment VIII [1791]

Excessive bail shall not be required, nor excessive fines imposed, nor cruel and unusual punishments inflicted.

Amendment IX [1791]

The enumeration in the Constitution, of certain rights, shall not be construed to deny or disparage others retained by the people.

Amendment X [1791]

The powers not delegated to the United States by the Constitution, nor prohibited by it to the States, are reserved to the States respectively, or to the people.

Unratified Amendment

Reapportionment Amendment (proposed by Congress September 25, 1789, along with the Bill of Rights)

After the first enumeration required by the first article of the Constitution, there shall be one Representative for every thirty thousand, until the number shall amount to one hundred, after which the proportion shall be so regulated by Congress, that there shall be not less than one hundred Representatives, nor less than one Representative for every forty thousand persons, until the number of Representatives shall amount to two hundred; after which the proportion shall be so regulated by Congress, that there shall not be less than two hundred Representatives, nor more than one Representative for every fifty thousand persons.

Amendment XI [1798]

The Judicial power of the United States shall not be construed to extend to any suit in law or equity, commenced or prosecuted against one of the United States by Citizens of another State, or by Citizens or subjects of any foreign state.

*The dates in brackets indicate when the amendment was ratified.

Amendment XII [1804]

The Electors shall meet in their respective States and vote by ballot for President and Vice-President, one of whom, at least, shall not be an inhabitant of the same State with themselves; they shall name in their ballots the person voted for as President, and in distinct ballots the person voted for as Vice-President, and they shall make distinct lists of all persons voted for as President, and of all persons voted for as Vice-President, and of the number of votes for each, which lists they shall sign and certify, and transmit sealed to the seat of government of the United States, directed to the President of the Senate; — the President of the Senate shall, in the presence of the Senate and House of Representatives, open all the certificates and the votes shall then be counted; — The person having the greatest number of votes for President, shall be the President, if such number be a majority of the whole number of Electors appointed; and if no person have such majority, then from the persons having the highest numbers not exceeding three on the list of those voted for as President, the House of Representatives shall choose immediately, by ballot, the President. But in choosing the President, the votes shall be taken by States, the representation from each State having one vote; a quorum for this purpose shall consist of a member or members from two-thirds of the States, and a majority of all the States shall be necessary to a choice. And if the House of Representatives shall not choose a President whenever the right of choice shall devolve upon them, before *the fourth day of March* next following, then the Vice-President shall act as President, as in the case of the death or other constitutional disability of the President.* — The person having the greatest number of votes as Vice-President, shall be the Vice-President, if such number be a majority of the whole number of Electors appointed; and if no person have a majority, then from the two highest numbers on the list, the Senate shall choose the Vice-President; a quorum for the purpose shall consist of two-thirds of the whole number of Senators, and a majority of the whole number shall be necessary to a choice. But no person constitutionally ineligible to the office of President shall be eligible to that of Vice-President of the United States.

Unratified Amendment
Titles of Nobility Amendment (proposed by Congress May 1, 1810)

If any citizen of the United States shall accept, claim, receive or retain any title of nobility or honor or shall, without the consent of Congress, accept and retain any present, pension, *office or emolument of any kind whatever, from any emperor, king, prince or foreign power, such person shall cease to be a citizen of the United States, and shall be incapable of holding any office of trust or profit under them, or either of them.*

Unratified Amendment
Corwin Amendment (proposed by Congress March 2, 1861)

No amendment shall be made to the Constitution which will authorize or give to Congress the power to abolish or interfere, within any State, with the domestic institutions thereof, including that of persons held to labor or service by the laws of said State.

Amendment XIII [1865]

Section 1. Neither slavery nor involuntary servitude, except as a punishment for crime whereof the party shall have been duly convicted, shall exist within the United States, or any place subject to their jurisdiction.

Section 2. Congress shall have power to enforce this article by appropriate legislation.

Amendment XIV [1868]

Section 1. All persons born or naturalized in the United States, and subject to the jurisdiction thereof, are citizens of the United States and of the State wherein they reside. No State shall make or enforce any law which shall abridge the privileges or immunities of citizens of the United States; nor shall any State deprive any person of life, liberty, or property, without due process of law; nor deny to any person within its jurisdiction the equal protection of the laws.

Section 2. Representatives shall be apportioned among the several States according to their respective numbers, counting the whole number of persons in each State, excluding Indians not taxed. But when the right to vote at any election for the choice of electors for President and Vice-President of the United States, Representatives in Congress, the Executive and Judicial officers of a State, or the members of the Legislature thereof, is denied to any of the *male* inhabitants of such State, being *twenty-one* years of age and citizens of the United States, or in any way abridged, except for participation in rebellion, or other crime, the basis of representation therein shall be reduced in the proportion which the number of such *male* citizens shall bear to the whole number of *male* citizens *twenty-one* years of age in such State.

Section 3. No person shall be a Senator or Representative in Congress, or Elector of President and Vice-President, or hold any office, civil or military, under the United States, or under any State, who, having previously taken an oath, as a member of Congress, or as an officer of the United States, or as a member of any State legislature, or as an executive or judicial officer of any State, to support the Constitution of the

---

*Superseded by Section 3 of the Twentieth Amendment.

United States, shall have engaged in insurrection or rebellion against the same, or given aid or comfort to the enemies thereof. Congress may, by a vote of two-thirds of each house, remove such disability.

Section 4. The validity of the public debt of the United States, authorized by law, including debts incurred for payment of pensions and bounties for services in suppressing insurrection or rebellion, shall not be questioned. But neither the United States nor any State shall assume or pay any debt or obligation incurred in aid of insurrection or rebellion against the United States, or any claim for the loss or emancipation of any slave; but all such debts, obligations, and claims shall be held illegal and void.

Section 5. The Congress shall have power to enforce, by appropriate legislation, the provisions of this article.

Amendment XV [1870]

Section 1. The right of citizens of the United States to vote shall not be denied or abridged by the United States or by any State on account of race, color, or previous condition of servitude —

Section 2. The Congress shall have power to enforce this article by appropriate legislation.

Amendment XVI [1913]

The Congress shall have power to lay and collect taxes on incomes, from whatever source derived, without apportionment among the several States, and without regard to any census or enumeration.

Amendment XVII [1913]

Section 1. The Senate of the United States shall be composed of two Senators from each State, elected by the people thereof, for six years; and each Senator shall have one vote. The electors in each State shall have the qualifications requisite for electors of [voters for] the most numerous branch of the State legislatures.

Section 2. When vacancies happen in the representation of any State in the Senate, the executive authority of such State shall issue writs of election to fill such vacancies: Provided, that the Legislature of any State may empower the executive thereof to make temporary appointments until the people fill the vacancies by election as the Legislature may direct.

Section 3. This amendment shall not be so construed as to affect the election or term of any Senator chosen before it becomes valid as part of the Constitution.

Amendment XVIII [1919; repealed 1933 by Amendment XXI]

Section 1. After one year from the ratification of this article the manufacture, sale, or transportation of intoxicating liquors within, the importation thereof into, or the exportation thereof from the United States and all territory subject to the jurisdiction thereof, for beverage purposes, is hereby prohibited.

Section 2. The Congress and the several States shall have concurrent power to enforce this article by appropriate legislation.

Section 3. This article shall be inoperative unless it shall have been ratified as an amendment to the Constitution by the legislatures of the several States, as provided by the Constitution, within seven years from the date of the submission thereof to the States by the Congress.

Amendment XIX [1920]

Section 1. The right of citizens of the United States to vote shall not be denied or abridged by the United States or by any State on account of sex.

Section 2. Congress shall have the power to enforce this article by appropriate legislation.

Unratified Amendment
Child Labor Amendment
(proposed by Congress June 2, 1924)

Section 1. The Congress shall have power to limit, regulate, and prohibit the labor of persons under eighteen years of age.

Section 2. The power of the several States is unimpaired by this article except that the operation of State laws shall be suspended to the extent necessary to give effect to legislation enacted by Congress.

Amendment XX [1933]

Section 1. The terms of the President and Vice-President shall end at noon on the 20th day of January, and the terms of Senators and Representatives at noon on the 3rd day of January, of the years in which such terms would have ended if this article had not been ratified; and the terms of their successors shall then begin.

Section 2. The Congress shall assemble at least once in every year, and such meeting shall begin at noon on the 3rd day of January, unless they shall by law appoint a different day.

Section 3. If, at the time fixed for the beginning of the term of the President, the President-elect shall have died, the Vice-President-elect shall become President. If a President shall not have been chosen before the time fixed for the beginning of his term, or if the President-elect shall have failed to qualify, then the Vice-President-elect shall act as President until a President shall have qualified; and the Congress may by law provide for the case wherein neither a President-elect nor a Vice-President-elect shall have qualified, declaring who shall then act as President, or the manner in which one who is to act shall be selected, and such person shall act accordingly until a President or Vice-President shall have qualified.

Section 4. The Congress may by law provide for the case of the death of any of the persons from whom the House of Representatives may choose a President whenever the right of choice shall have devolved upon them, and for the case of the death of any of the persons from whom the Senate may choose a Vice-President whenever the right of choice shall have devolved upon them.

Section 5. Sections 1 and 2 shall take effect on the 15th day of October following the ratification of this article.

Section 6. This article shall be inoperative unless it shall have been ratified as an amendment to the Constitution by the Legislatures of three-fourths of the several States within seven years from the date of its submission.

Amendment XXI [1933]

Section 1. The eighteenth article of amendment to the Constitution of the United States is hereby repealed.

Section 2. The transportation or importation into any State, Territory, or Possession of the United States for delivery or use therein of intoxicating liquors, in violation of the laws thereof, is hereby prohibited.

Section 3. This article shall be inoperative unless it shall have been ratified as an amendment to the Constitution by conventions in the several States, as provided in the Constitution, within seven years from the date of the submission thereof to the States by the Congress.

Amendment XXII [1951]

Section 1. No person shall be elected to the office of the President more than twice, and no person who has held the office of President, or acted as President, for more than two years of a term to which some other person was elected President shall be elected to the office of President more than once. But this article shall not apply to any person holding the office of President when this Article was proposed by the Congress, and shall not prevent any person who may be holding the office of President, or acting as President, during the term within which this Article becomes operative from holding the office of President or acting as President during the remainder of such term.

Section 2. This article shall be inoperative unless it shall have been ratified as an amendment to the Constitution by the legislatures of three-fourths of the several States within seven years from the date of its submission to the States by the Congress.

Amendment XXIII [1961]

Section 1. The District constituting the seat of Government of the United States shall appoint in such manner as the Congress may direct: A number of electors of President and Vice-President equal to the whole number of Senators and Representatives in Congress to which the District would be entitled if it were a State, but in no event more than the least populous State; they shall be in addition to those appointed by the States, but they shall be considered for the purposes of the election of President and Vice-President, to be electors appointed by a State; and they shall meet in the District and perform such duties as provided by the twelfth article of amendment.

Section 2. The Congress shall have the power to enforce this article by appropriate legislation.

Amendment XXIV [1964]

Section 1. The right of citizens of the United States to vote in any primary or other election for President or Vice-President, for electors for President or Vice-President, or for Senator or Representative in Congress, shall not be denied or abridged by the United States or any State by reason of failure to pay any poll tax or other tax.

Section 2. The Congress shall have the power to enforce this article by appropriate legislation.

Amendment XXV [1967]

Section 1. In case of the removal of the President from office or of his death or resignation, the Vice-President shall become President.

Section 2. Whenever there is a vacancy in the office of the Vice-President, the President shall nominate a Vice-President who shall take office upon confirmation by a majority vote of both Houses of Congress.

Section 3. Whenever the President transmits to the President pro tempore of the Senate and the Speaker of the House of Representatives his written declaration that he is unable to discharge the powers and duties of his office, and until he transmits to them a written declaration to the contrary, such powers and duties shall be discharged by the Vice-President as Acting President.

Section 4. Whenever the Vice-President and a majority of either the principal officers of the executive departments or of such other body as Congress may by law provide, transmit to the President pro tempore of the Senate and the Speaker of the House of Representatives their written declaration that the President is unable to discharge the powers and duties of his office, the Vice-President shall immediately assume the powers and duties of the office as Acting President.

Thereafter, when the President transmits to the President pro tempore of the Senate and the Speaker of the House of Representatives his written declaration that no inability exists, he shall resume the powers and duties of his office unless the Vice-President and a majority of either the principal officers of the executive department[s] or of such other body as Congress may by law provide, transmit within four days to the President pro tempore of the Senate and the Speaker of the House of Representatives their written declaration that the President is unable to discharge the powers and duties of his office. Thereupon Congress shall decide the issue, assembling within forty-eight hours for that purpose if not in session. If the Congress, within twenty-one days after receipt of the latter written declaration, or, if Congress is not in session, within twenty-one days after Congress is required to assemble, determines by two-thirds vote of both Houses that the President is unable to discharge the powers and duties of his office, the Vice-President shall continue to discharge the same as Acting President; otherwise, the President shall resume the powers and duties of his office.

Amendment XXVI [1971]

Section 1. The right of citizens of the United States, who are eighteen years of age or older, to vote shall not be denied or abridged by the United States or by any State on account of age.

Section 2. The Congress shall have power to enforce this article by appropriate legislation.

Unratified Amendment

Equal Rights Amendment (proposed by Congress March 22, 1972; seven-year deadline for ratification extended to June 30, 1982)

Section 1. Equality of rights under the law shall not be denied or abridged by the United States or by any State on account of sex.

Section 2. The Congress shall have the power to enforce, by appropriate legislation, the provisions of this article.

Section 3. This amendment shall take effect two years after the date of ratification.

Unratified Amendment

District of Columbia Statehood Amendment (proposed by Congress August 22, 1978)

Section 1. For purposes of representation in the Congress, election of the President and Vice President, and article V of this Constitution, the District constituting the seat of government of the United States shall be treated as though it were a State.

Section 2. The exercise of the rights and powers conferred under this article shall be by the people of the District constituting the seat of government, and as shall be provided by Congress.

Section 3. The twenty-third article of amendment to the Constitution of the United States is hereby repealed.

Section 4. This article shall be inoperative, unless it shall have been ratified as an amendment to the Constitution by the legislatures of three-fourths of the several states within seven years from the date of its submission.

Amendment XXVII [1992]

No law varying the compensation for the services of the Senators and Representatives, shall take effect, until an election of Representatives shall have intervened.

Appendix

The American Nation

Admission of States into the Union

State	Date of Admission	State	Date of Admission	State	Date of Admission
1. Delaware	December 7, 1787	18. Louisiana	April 30, 1812	35. West Virginia	June 20, 1863
2. Pennsylvania	December 12, 1787	19. Indiana	December 11, 1816	36. Nevada	October 31, 1864
3. New Jersey	December 18, 1787	20. Mississippi	December 10, 1817	37. Nebraska	March 1, 1867
4. Georgia	January 2, 1788	21. Illinois	December 3, 1818	38. Colorado	August 1, 1876
5. Connecticut	January 9, 1788	22. Alabama	December 14, 1819	39. North Dakota	November 2, 1889
6. Massachusetts	February 6, 1788	23. Maine	March 15, 1820	40. South Dakota	November 2, 1889
7. Maryland	April 28, 1788	24. Missouri	August 10, 1821	41. Montana	November 8, 1889
8. South Carolina	May 23, 1788	25. Arkansas	June 15, 1836	42. Washington	November 11, 1889
9. New Hampshire	June 21, 1788	26. Michigan	January 26, 1837	43. Idaho	July 3, 1890
10. Virginia	June 25, 1788	27. Florida	March 3, 1845	44. Wyoming	July 10, 1890
11. New York	July 26, 1788	28. Texas	December 29, 1845	45. Utah	January 4, 1896
12. North Carolina	November 21, 1789	29. Iowa	December 28, 1846	46. Oklahoma	November 16, 1907
13. Rhode Island	May 29, 1790	30. Wisconsin	May 29, 1848	47. New Mexico	January 6, 1912
14. Vermont	March 4, 1791	31. California	September 9, 1850	48. Arizona	February 14, 1912
15. Kentucky	June 1, 1792	32. Minnesota	May 11, 1858	49. Alaska	January 3, 1959
16. Tennessee	June 1, 1796	33. Oregon	February 14, 1859	50. Hawaii	August 21, 1959
17. Ohio	March 1, 1803	34. Kansas	January 29, 1861		

Presidential Elections

Year	Candidates	Parties	Percentage of Popular Vote*	Electoral Vote
1789	**George Washington**	No party designations		69
	John Adams[†]			34
	Other candidates			35
1792	**George Washington**	No party designations		132
	John Adams			77
	George Clinton			50
	Other candidates			5

SOURCES: U.S. Bureau of the Census, *Historical Statistics of the United States, Colonial Times to 1970* (1975); *Statistical Abstract of the United States, 2001; Statistical Abstract of the United States, 2006.*

*Prior to 1824, most presidential electors were chosen by state legislators rather than by popular vote. For elections after 1824, candidates receiving less than 1.0 percent of the popular vote have been omitted from this chart. Hence the popular vote does not total 100 percent for all elections.

†Before the Twelfth Amendment was passed in 1804, the electoral college voted for two presidential candidates; the runner-up became vice president.

Year	Candidates	Parties	Percentage of Popular Vote	Electoral Vote
1796	**John Adams**	Federalist		71
	Thomas Jefferson	Democratic-Republican		68
	Thomas Pinckney	Federalist		59
	Aaron Burr	Democratic-Republican		30
	Other candidates			48
1800	**Thomas Jefferson**	Democratic-Republican		73
	Aaron Burr	Democratic-Republican		73
	John Adams	Federalist		65
	Charles C. Pinckney	Federalist		64
	John Jay	Federalist		1
1804	**Thomas Jefferson**	Democratic-Republican		162
	Charles C. Pinckney	Federalist		14
1808	**James Madison**	Democratic-Republican		122
	Charles C. Pinckney	Federalist		47
	George Clinton	Democratic-Republican		6
1812	**James Madison**	Democratic-Republican		128
	DeWitt Clinton	Federalist		89
1816	**James Monroe**	Democratic-Republican		183
	Rufus King	Federalist		34
1820	**James Monroe**	Democratic-Republican		231
	John Quincy Adams	Independent Republican		1
1824	**John Quincy Adams**	Democratic-Republican	30.5	84
	Andrew Jackson	Democratic-Republican	43.1	99
	Henry Clay	Democratic-Republican	13.2	37
	William H. Crawford	Democratic-Republican	13.1	41
1828	**Andrew Jackson**	Democratic	56.0	178
	John Quincy Adams	National Republican	44.0	83
1832	**Andrew Jackson**	Democratic	54.5	219
	Henry Clay	National Republican	37.5	49
	William Wirt	Anti-Masonic	8.0	7
	John Floyd	Democratic	‡	11
1836	**Martin Van Buren**	Democratic	50.9	170
	William H. Harrison	Whig	49.1	73
	Hugh L. White	Whig		26
	Daniel Webster	Whig		14
	W. P. Mangum	Whig		11
1840	**William H. Harrison**	Whig	53.1	234
	Martin Van Buren	Democratic	46.9	60
1844	**James K. Polk**	Democratic	49.6	170
	Henry Clay	Whig	48.1	105
	James G. Birney	Liberty	2.3	
1848	**Zachary Taylor**	Whig	47.4	163
	Lewis Cass	Democratic	42.5	127
	Martin Van Buren	Free Soil	10.1	

‡Independent Democrat John Floyd received the 11 electoral votes of South Carolina; that state's presidential electors were still chosen by its legislature, not by popular vote.

Year	Candidates	Parties	Percentage of Popular Vote	Electoral Vote
1852	**Franklin Pierce**	Democratic	50.9	254
	Winfield Scott	Whig	44.1	42
	John P. Hale	Free Soil	5.0	
1856	**James Buchanan**	Democratic	45.3	174
	John C. Frémont	Republican	33.1	114
	Millard Fillmore	American	21.6	8
1860	**Abraham Lincoln**	Republican	39.8	180
	Stephen A. Douglas	Democratic	29.5	12
	John C. Breckinridge	Democratic	18.1	72
	John Bell	Constitutional Union	12.6	39
1864	**Abraham Lincoln**	Republican	55.0	212
	George B. McClellan	Democratic	45.0	21
1868	**Ulysses S. Grant**	Republican	52.7	214
	Horatio Seymour	Democratic	47.3	80
1872	**Ulysses S. Grant**	Republican	55.6	286
	Horace Greeley	Democratic	43.9	
1876	**Rutherford B. Hayes**	Republican	48.0	185
	Samuel J. Tilden	Democratic	51.0	184
1880	**James A. Garfield**	Republican	48.5	214
	Winfield S. Hancock	Democratic	48.1	155
	James B. Weaver	Greenback-Labor	3.4	
1884	**Grover Cleveland**	Democratic	48.5	219
	James G. Blaine	Republican	48.2	182
	Benjamin F. Butler	Greenback-Labor	1.8	
	John P. St. John	Prohibition	1.5	
1888	**Benjamin Harrison**	Republican	47.9	233
	Grover Cleveland	Democratic	48.6	168
	Clinton P. Fisk	Prohibition	2.2	
	Anson J. Streeter	Union Labor	1.3	
1892	**Grover Cleveland**	Democratic	46.1	277
	Benjamin Harrison	Republican	43.0	145
	James B. Weaver	People's	8.5	22
	John Bidwell	Prohibition	2.2	
1896	**William McKinley**	Republican	51.1	271
	William J. Bryan	Democratic	47.7	176
1900	**William McKinley**	Republican	51.7	292
	William J. Bryan	Democratic; Populist	45.5	155
	John C. Wooley	Prohibition	1.5	
1904	**Theodore Roosevelt**	Republican	57.4	336
	Alton B. Parker	Democratic	37.6	140
	Eugene V. Debs	Socialist	3.0	
	Silas C. Swallow	Prohibition	1.9	
1908	**William H. Taft**	Republican	51.6	321
	William J. Bryan	Democratic	43.1	162
	Eugene V. Debs	Socialist	2.8	
	Eugene W. Chafin	Prohibition	1.7	

Year	Candidates	Parties	Percentage of Popular Vote	Electoral Vote
1912	**Woodrow Wilson**	Democratic	41.9	435
	Theodore Roosevelt	Progressive	27.4	88
	William H. Taft	Republican	23.2	8
	Eugene V. Debs	Socialist	6.0	
	Eugene W. Chafin	Prohibition	1.4	
1916	**Woodrow Wilson**	Democratic	49.4	277
	Charles E. Hughes	Republican	46.2	254
	A. L. Benson	Socialist	3.2	
	J. Frank Hanly	Prohibition	1.2	
1920	**Warren G. Harding**	Republican	60.4	404
	James M. Cox	Democratic	34.2	127
	Eugene V. Debs	Socialist	3.4	
	P. P. Christensen	Farmer-Labor	1.0	
1924	**Calvin Coolidge**	Republican	54.0	382
	John W. Davis	Democratic	28.8	136
	Robert M. La Follette	Progressive	16.6	13
1928	**Herbert C. Hoover**	Republican	58.2	444
	Alfred E. Smith	Democratic	40.9	87
1932	**Franklin D. Roosevelt**	Democratic	57.4	472
	Herbert C. Hoover	Republican	39.7	59
	Norman Thomas	Socialist	2.2	
1936	**Franklin D. Roosevelt**	Democratic	60.8	523
	Alfred M. Landon	Republican	36.5	8
	William Lemke	Union	1.9	
1940	**Franklin D. Roosevelt**	Democratic	54.8	449
	Wendell L. Willkie	Republican	44.8	82
1944	**Franklin D. Roosevelt**	Democratic	53.5	432
	Thomas E. Dewey	Republican	46.0	99
1948	**Harry S. Truman**	Democratic	49.6	303
	Thomas E. Dewey	Republican	45.1	189
	J. Strom Thurmond	States' Rights	2.4	
	Henry Wallace	Progressive	2.4	
1952	**Dwight D. Eisenhower**	Republican	55.1	442
	Adlai E. Stevenson	Democratic	44.4	89
1956	**Dwight D. Eisenhower**	Republican	57.6	457
	Adlai E. Stevenson	Democratic	42.1	73
1960	**John F. Kennedy**	Democratic	49.7	303
	Richard M. Nixon	Republican	49.5	219
1964	**Lyndon B. Johnson**	Democratic	61.1	486
	Barry M. Goldwater	Republican	38.5	52
1968	**Richard M. Nixon**	Republican	43.4	301
	Hubert H. Humphrey	Democratic	42.7	191
	George C. Wallace	American Independent	13.5	46

Year	Candidates	Parties	Percentage of Popular Vote	Electoral Vote
1972	**Richard M. Nixon**	Republican	60.7	520
	George S. McGovern	Democratic	37.5	17
	John G. Schmitz	American	1.4	
1976	**Jimmy Carter**	Democratic	50.1	297
	Gerald R. Ford	Republican	48.0	240
1980	**Ronald W. Reagan**	Republican	50.7	489
	Jimmy Carter	Democratic	41.0	49
	John B. Anderson	Independent	6.6	0
	Ed Clark	Libertarian	1.1	
1984	**Ronald W. Reagan**	Republican	58.4	525
	Walter F. Mondale	Democratic	41.6	13
1988	**George H. W. Bush**	Republican	53.4	426
	Michael Dukakis	Democratic	45.6	111*
1992	**Bill Clinton**	Democratic	43.7	370
	George H. W. Bush	Republican	38.0	168
	H. Ross Perot	Independent	19.0	0
1996	**Bill Clinton**	Democratic	49	379
	Robert J. Dole	Republican	41	159
	H. Ross Perot	Reform	8	0
2000	**George W. Bush**	Republican	47.8	271
	Albert Gore	Democratic	48.4	267
	Ralph Nader	Green	2.7	0
2004	**George W. Bush**	Republican	50.7	286
	John Kerry	Democratic	48.3	252
2008	**Barack Obama**	Democratic	52.9	365
	John McCain	Republican	45.7	173
2012	**Barack Obama**	Democratic	51	332
	Mitt Romney	Republican	41.2	206

*One Dukakis elector cast a vote for Lloyd Bentsen.

Population Growth*

Year	Population	Percentage Increase	Year	Population	Percentage Increase
1610	350	—	1820	9,638,453	33.1
1620	2,300	557.1	1830	12,866,020	33.5
1630	4,600	100.0	1840	17,069,453	32.7
1640	26,600	478.3	1850	23,191,876	35.9
1650	50,400	90.8	1860	31,443,321	35.6
1660	75,100	49.0	1870	39,818,449	26.6
1670	111,900	49.0	1880	50,155,783	26.0
1680	151,500	35.4	1890	62,947,714	25.5
1690	210,400	38.9	1900	75,994,575	20.7
1700	250,900	19.2	1910	91,972,266	21.0
1710	331,700	32.2	1920	105,710,620	14.9
1720	466,200	40.5	1930	122,775,046	16.1
1730	629,400	35.0	1940	131,669,275	7.2
1740	905,600	43.9	1950	150,697,361	14.5
1750	1,170,800	29.3	1960	179,323,175	19.0
1760	1,593,600	36.1	1970	203,235,298	13.3
1770	2,148,100	34.8	1980	226,545,805	11.5
1780	2,780,400	29.4	1990	248,709,873	9.8
1790	3,929,214	41.3	2000	281,421,906	13.2
1800	5,308,483	35.1	2010	308,745,538	9.7
1810	7,239,881	36.4			

SOURCES: U.S. Bureau of the Census, *Historical Statistics of the United States, Colonial Times to 1970* (1975); *Statistical Abstract of the United States, 2010*.

*Note: Until 1890, census takers never made any effort to count the Native American people who lived outside their reserved political areas and compiled only casual and incomplete enumerations of those living within their jurisdictions. In 1890, the federal government attempted a full count of the Indian population: the Census found 125,719 Indians in 1890, compared with only 12,543 in 1870 and 33,985 in 1880.

Immigration by Decade

Year	Number	Immigrants During this Decade as a Percentage of Total Population	Year	Number	Immigrants During this Decade as a Percentage of Total Population
1821–1830	151,824	1.6	1921–1930	4,107,209	3.9
1831–1840	599,125	4.6	1931–1940	528,431	0.4
1841–1850	1,713,251	10.0	1941–1950	1,035,039	0.7
1851–1860	2,598,214	11.2	1951–1960	2,515,479	1.6
1861–1870	2,314,824	7.4	1961–1970	3,321,677	1.8
1871–1880	2,812,191	7.1	1971–1980	4,493,000	2.2
1881–1890	5,246,613	10.5	1981–1990	7,338,000	3.0
1891–1900	3,687,546	5.8	1991–2000	9,095,083	3.7
1901–1910	8,795,386	11.6	**Total**	**32,433,918**	
1911–1920	5,735,811	6.2			
Total	**33,654,785**		1821–2000		
			GRAND TOTAL	**66,088,703**	

SOURCES: U.S. Bureau of the Census, *Historical Statistics of the United States, Colonial Times to 1970* (1975), part 1, 105–106; *Statistical Abstract of the United States, 2001*.

Regional Origins

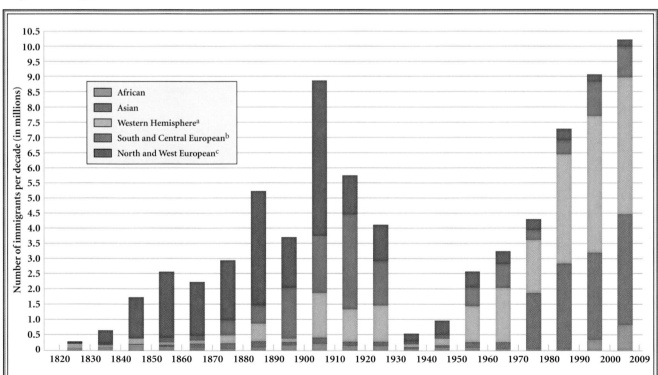

Legend:
- African
- Asian
- Western Hemisphere[a]
- South and Central European[b]
- North and West European[c]

Y-axis: Number of immigrants per decade (in millions)
X-axis: 1820, 1830, 1840, 1850, 1860, 1870, 1880, 1890, 1900, 1910, 1920, 1930, 1940, 1950, 1960, 1970, 1980, 1990, 2000, 2009

[a] Canada and all countries in South America and Central America.
[b] Italy, Spain, Portugal, Greece, Germany (Austria included, 1938–1945), Poland, former Czechoslovakia (since 1920), former Yugoslavia (since 1920), Hungary (since 1861), Austria (since 1861, except 1938–1945), former USSR (excludes Asian USSR between 1931 and 1963), Latvia, Estonia, Lithuania, Finland, Romania, Bulgaria, Turkey (in Europe), and other European countries not classified elsewhere.
[c] Great Britain, Ireland, Norway, Sweden, Denmark, Iceland, Netherlands, Belgium, Luxembourg, Switzerland, France.
Sources: Stephan Thernstrom, ed., *Harvard Encyclopedia of American Ethnic Groups* (1980), 480; U.S. Bureau of the Census, *Statistical Abstract of the United States, 1991*; U.S. Department of Homeland Security, *Yearbook of Immigration Statistics, 2009*.

Glossary

abolitionism: The social reform movement to end slavery immediately and without compensation that began in the United States in the 1830s. (p. 357)

Adams-Onís Treaty: An 1819 treaty in which John Quincy Adams persuaded Spain to cede the Florida territory to the United States. In return, the American government accepted Spain's claim to Texas and agreed to a compromise on the western boundary for the state of Louisiana. (p. 243)

Alamo: The 1836 defeat by the Mexican army of the Texan garrison defending the Alamo in San Antonio. Newspapers urged Americans to "Remember the Alamo," and American adventurers, lured by offers of land grants, flocked to Texas to join the rebel forces. (p. 391)

amalgamation: A term for racial mixing and intermarriage, almost universally opposed by whites in the nineteenth-century United States. (p. 364)

American, or Know-Nothing, Party: A political party formed in 1851 that drew on the anti-immigrant and anti-Catholic movements of the 1840s. In 1854, the party gained control of the state governments of Massachusetts and Pennsylvania. (p. 432)

American Colonization Society: A society founded by Henry Clay and other prominent citizens in 1817. The society argued that slaves had to be freed and then resettled, in Africa or elsewhere. (p. 267)

American Renaissance: A literary explosion during the 1840s inspired in part by Emerson's ideas on the liberation of the individual. (p. 346)

American System: The mercantilist system of national economic development advocated by Henry Clay and adopted by John Quincy Adams, with a national bank to manage the nation's financial system; protective tariffs to provide revenue and encourage industry; and a nationally funded network of roads, canals, and railroads. (p. 319)

American Temperance Society: A society invigorated by evangelical Protestants in 1832 that set out to curb the consumption of alcoholic beverages. (p. 310)

American Woman Suffrage Association: A women's suffrage organization led by Lucy Stone, Henry Blackwell, and others who remained loyal to the Republican Party, despite its failure to include women's voting rights in the Reconstruction Amendments. Stressing the urgency of voting rights for African American men, AWSA leaders held out hope that once Reconstruction had been settled, it would be women's turn. (p. 486)

animism: Spiritual beliefs that center on the natural world. Animists do not worship a supernatural God; instead, they pay homage to spirits and spiritual forces that they believe dwell in the natural world. (p. 17)

Antifederalists: Opponents of ratification of the Constitution. Antifederalists feared that a powerful and distant central government would be out of touch with the needs of citizens. They also complained that it failed to guarantee individual liberties in a bill of rights. (p. 207)

Articles of Confederation: The written document defining the structure of the government from 1781 to 1788, under which the Union was a confederation of equal states, with no executive and limited powers, existing mainly to foster a common defense. (p. 200)

artisan republicanism: An ideology that celebrated small-scale producers, men and women who owned their own shops (or farms). It defined the ideal republican society as one constituted by, and dedicated to the welfare of, independent workers and citizens. (p. 291)

Bank of the United States: A bank chartered in 1790 and jointly owned by private stockholders and the national government. Alexander Hamilton argued that the bank would provide stability to the specie-starved American economy by making loans to merchants, handling government funds, and issuing bills of credit. (p. 218)

Battle of Little Big Horn: The 1876 battle begun when American cavalry under George Armstrong Custer attacked an encampment of Sioux, Arapaho, and Cheyenne Indians who resisted removal to a reservation. Custer's force was annihilated, but with whites calling for U.S. soldiers to retaliate, the Native American military victory was short-lived. (p. 533)

Battle of Long Island (1776): First major engagement of the new Continental army, defending against 32,000 British troops outside of New York City. (p. 184)

Battle of Saratoga (1777): A multistage battle in New York ending with the surrender of British general John Burgoyne. The victory ensured the diplomatic success of American representatives in Paris, who won a military alliance with France. (p. 187)

Battle of Tippecanoe: An attack on Shawnee Indians at Prophetstown on the Tippecanoe River in 1811 by American forces headed by William Henry Harrison, Indiana's territorial governor. The governor's troops traded heavy casualties with the confederacy's warriors and then destroyed the holy village. (p. 236)

Battle of Yorktown (1781): A battle in which French and American troops and a French fleet trapped the British army under the command of General Charles Cornwallis at Yorktown, Virginia. The Franco-American victory broke the resolve of the British government. (p. 195)

Benevolent Empire: A broad-ranging campaign of moral and institutional reforms inspired by evangelical Christian ideals and endorsed by upper-middle-class men and women in the 1820s and 1830s. (p. 305)

benevolent masters: Slave owners who considered themselves committed to the welfare of their slaves. (p. 382)

Bill of Rights: The first ten amendments to the Constitution, officially ratified by 1791. The amendments safeguarded fundamental personal rights, including freedom of speech and religion, and mandated legal procedures, such as trial by jury. (p. 216)

Black Codes: Laws passed by southern states after the Civil War that denied ex-slaves the civil rights enjoyed by whites, punished vague crimes such as "vagrancy" or failing to have a labor contract, and tried to force African Americans back to plantation labor systems that closely mirrored those in slavery times. (p. 481)

black Protestantism: A form of Protestantism that was devised by Christian slaves in the Chesapeake and spread to the Cotton South as a result of the domestic slave trade. It emphasized the evangelical message of emotional conversion, ritual baptism, communal spirituality, and the idea that blacks were "children of God" and should be treated accordingly. (p. 395)

"Bleeding Kansas": Term for the bloody struggle between proslavery and antislavery factions in Kansas following its organization as a territory in the fall of 1854. (p. 433)

Burlingame Treaty: An 1868 treaty that guaranteed the rights of U.S. missionaries in China and set official terms for the emigration of Chinese laborers to work in the United States. (p. 511)

Californios: The elite Mexican ranchers in the province of California. (p. 415)

carpetbaggers: A derisive name given by ex-Confederates to northerners who, motivated by idealism or the search for personal opportunity or profit, moved to the South during Reconstruction. (p. 493)

caucus: A meeting held by a political party to choose candidates, make policies, and enforce party discipline. (p. 318)

chattel principle: A system of bondage in which a slave has the legal status of property and so can be bought and sold. (p. 381)

chattel slavery: A system of bondage in which a slave has the legal status of property and so can be bought and sold like property. (p. 40)

Christianity: A religion that holds the belief that Jesus Christ was himself divine. For centuries, the Roman Catholic Church was the great unifying institution in Western Europe, and it was from Europe that Christianity spread to the Americas. (p. 21)

civic humanism: The belief that individuals owe a service to their community and its government. During the Renaissance, political theorists argued that selfless service to the polity was of critical importance in a self-governing republic. (p. 20)

Civil Rights Act of 1866: Legislation passed by Congress that nullified the Black Codes and affirmed that African Americans should have equal benefit of the law. (p. 481)

Civil Rights Act of 1875: A law that required "full and equal" access to jury service and to transportation and public accommodations, irrespective of race. (p. 496)

Civil Rights Cases: A series of 1883 Supreme Court decisions that struck down the Civil Rights Act of 1875, rolling back key Reconstruction laws and paving the way for later decisions that sanctioned segregation. (p. 500)

classical liberalism: The idea that the less government does, the better, particularly in reference to economic policies such as tariffs and incentives for industrial development. Attacking corruption and defending private property, late-nineteenth-century liberals generally called for elite governance and questioned the advisability of full democratic participation. (p. 498)

coastal trade: The domestic slave trade with routes along the Atlantic coast that sent thousands of slaves to sugar plantations in Louisiana and cotton plantations in the Mississippi Valley. (p. 380)

Coercive Acts: Four British acts of 1774 meant to punish Massachusetts for the destruction of three shiploads of tea. Known in America as the Intolerable Acts, they led to open rebellion in the northern colonies. (p. 168)

Columbian Exchange: The massive global exchange of living things, including people, animals, plants, and diseases, between the Eastern and Western Hemispheres that began after the voyages of Columbus. (p. 43)

committees of correspondence: A communications network established among towns in the colonies, and among colonial assemblies, between 1772 and 1773 to provide for rapid dissemination of news about important political developments. (p. 168)

Commonwealth System: The republican system of political economy created by state governments by 1820, whereby states funneled aid to private businesses whose projects would improve the general welfare. (p. 256)

companionate marriage: A marriage based on the republican values of equality and mutual respect. Although husbands in these marriages retained significant legal power, they increasingly came to see their wives as loving partners rather than as inferiors or dependents. (p. 258)

competency: The ability of a family to keep a household solvent and independent and to pass that ability on to the next generation. (p. 117)

Compromise of 1850: Laws passed in 1850 that were meant to resolve the dispute over the status of slavery in the territories. Key elements included the admission of California as a free state and the Fugitive Slave Act. (p. 429)

Comstock Lode: Immense silver ore deposit discovered in 1859 in Nevada that touched off a mining rush, bringing a diverse population into the region and leading to the establishment of boomtowns. (p. 516)

conscience Whigs: Whig politicians who opposed the Mexican War (1846–1848) on moral grounds, maintaining that the purpose of the war was to expand and perpetuate control of the national government. (p. 421)

"consolidated government": A term meaning a powerful and potentially oppressive national government. (p. 320)

constitutional monarchy: A monarchy limited in its rule by a constitution. (p. 87)

consumer revolution: An increase in consumption in English manufactures in Britain and the British colonies fueled by the Industrial Revolution. Although the consumer revolution raised living standards, it landed many consumers — and the colonies as a whole — in debt. (p. 141)

Continental Association: An association established in 1774 by the First Continental Congress to enforce a boycott of British goods. (p. 171)

Continental Congress: September 1774 gathering of colonial delegates in Philadelphia to discuss the crisis precipitated by the Coercive Acts. The Congress produced a declaration of rights and an agreement to impose a limited boycott of trade with Britain. (p. 169)

"contrabands": Slaves who fled plantations and sought protection behind Union lines during the Civil War. (p. 463)

convict leasing: Notorious system, begun during Reconstruction, whereby southern state officials allowed private companies to hire out prisoners to labor under brutal conditions in mines and other industries. (p. 495)

corrupt bargain: A term used by Andrew Jackson's supporters for the appointment by President John Quincy Adams of Henry Clay as his secretary of state, the traditional stepping-stone to the presidency. Clay had used his influence as Speaker of the House to elect Adams rather than Jackson in the election in 1824. (p. 319)

Counter-Reformation: A reaction in the Catholic Church triggered by the Reformation that sought change from within and created new monastic and missionary orders, including the Jesuits (founded in 1540), who saw themselves as soldiers of Christ. (p. 22)

Covenant Chain: The alliance of the Iroquois, first with the colony of New York, then with the British Empire and its other colonies. The Covenant Chain became a model for relations between the British Empire and other Native American peoples. (p. 89)

covenant of grace: The Christian idea that God's elect are granted salvation as a pure gift of grace. This doctrine holds that nothing people do can erase their sins or earn them a place in heaven. (p. 62)

covenant of works: The Christian idea that God's elect must do good works in their earthly lives to earn their salvation. (p. 62)

Crédit Mobilier: A sham corporation set up by shareholders in the Union Pacific Railroad to secure government grants at an enormous profit. Organizers of the scheme protected it from investigation by providing gifts of its stock to powerful members of Congress. (p. 498)

Crime of 1873: A term used by those critical of an 1873 law directing the U.S. Treasury to cease minting silver dollars, retire Civil War–era greenbacks, and replace them with notes backed by the gold standard from an expanded system of national banks. (p. 515)

Crittenden Compromise: A plan proposed by Senator John J. Crittenden for a constitutional amendment to protect slavery from federal interference in any state where it already existed and for the westward extension of the Missouri Compromise line to the California border. (p. 446)

Crusades: A series of wars undertaken by Christian armies between A.D. 1096 and 1291 to reverse the Muslim advance in Europe and win back the holy lands where Christ had lived. (p. 22)

currency tax: A hidden tax on the farmers and artisans who accepted Continental bills in payment for supplies and on the thousands of soldiers who took them as pay. Because of rampant inflation, Continental currency lost much of its value during the war; thus, the implicit tax on those who accepted it as payment. (p. 196)

Dawes Severalty Act: The 1887 law that gave Native Americans severalty (individual ownership of land) by dividing reservations into homesteads. The law was a disaster for native peoples, resulting over several decades in the loss of 66 percent of lands held by Indians at the time of the law's passage. (p. 532)

Declaration of Independence: A document containing philosophical principles and a list of grievances that declared separation from Britain. Adopted by the Second Continental Congress on July 4, 1776, it ended a period of intense debate with moderates still hoping to reconcile with Britain. (p. 178)

Declaratory Act of 1766: Law issued by Parliament to assert Parliament's unassailable right to legislate for its British colonies "in all cases whatsoever," putting Americans on notice that the simultaneous repeal of the Stamp Act changed nothing in the imperial powers of Britain. (p. 160)

deism: The Enlightenment-influenced belief that the Christian God created the universe and then left it to run according to natural laws. (p. 128)

demographic transition: The sharp decline in birthrate in the United States beginning in the 1790s that was caused by changes in cultural behavior, including the use of birth control. The migration of thousands of young men to the trans-Appalachian west was also a factor in this decline. (p. 259)

division of labor: A system of manufacture that divides production into a series of distinct and repetitive tasks performed by machines or workers. (p. 286)

domestic slavery: A term referring to the assertion by Elizabeth Cady Stanton and other female abolitionists that traditional gender roles and legal restrictions created a form of slavery for married women. (p. 370)

Dominion of New England: A royal province created by King James II in 1686 that would have absorbed Connecticut, Rhode Island, Massachusetts Bay, Plymouth, New York, and New Jersey into a single, vast colony and eliminated their assemblies and other chartered rights. James's plan was canceled by the Glorious Revolution in 1688, which removed him from the throne. (p. 85)

draft (conscription): The system for selecting individuals for conscription, or compulsory military service, first implemented during the Civil War. (p. 452)

Dred Scott v. Sandford: The 1857 Supreme Court decision that ruled the Missouri Compromise unconstitutional. The Court ruled against slave Dred Scott, who claimed that travels with his master into free states and territories made him and his family free. The decision also denied the federal government the right to exclude slavery from the territories and declared that African Americans were not citizens. (p. 433)

Dunmore's War: A 1774 war led by Virginia's royal governor, the Earl of Dunmore, against the Ohio Shawnees, who had a long-standing claim to Kentucky as a hunting ground. The Shawnees were defeated and Dunmore and his militia forces claimed Kentucky as their own. (p. 175)

Emancipation Proclamation: President Abraham Lincoln's proclamation issued on January 1, 1863, that legally abolished slavery in all states that remained out of the Union. While the Emancipation Proclamation did not immediately free a single slave, it signaled an end to the institution of slavery. (p. 464)

Embargo Act of 1807: An act of Congress that prohibited U.S. ships from traveling to foreign ports and effectively banned overseas trade in an attempt to deter Britain from halting U.S. ships at sea. The embargo caused grave hardships for Americans engaged in overseas commerce. (p. 234)

encomienda: A grant of Indian labor in Spanish America given in the sixteenth century by the Spanish kings to prominent men. *Encomenderos* extracted tribute from these Indians in exchange for granting them protection and Christian instruction. (p. 42)

Enforcement Laws: Acts passed in Congress in 1870 and signed by President U. S. Grant that were designed to protect freedmen's rights under the Fourteenth and Fifteenth Amendments. Authorizing federal prosecutions, military intervention, and martial law to suppress terrorist activity, the Enforcement Laws largely succeeded in shutting down Klan activities. (p. 499)

English common law: The centuries-old body of legal rules and procedures that protected the lives and property of the British monarch's subjects. (p. 159)

Enlightenment: An eighteenth-century philosophical movement that emphasized the use of reason to reevaluate previously accepted doctrines and traditions and the power of reason to understand and shape the world. (p. 126)

Erie Canal: A 364-mile waterway connecting the Hudson River and Lake Erie. The Erie Canal brought prosperity to the entire Great Lakes region, and its benefits prompted civic and business leaders in Philadelphia and Baltimore to propose canals to link their cities to the Midwest. (p. 293)

established church: A church given privileged legal status by the government. Historically, such established churches in Europe and America were supported by public taxes and were often the only legally permitted religious institutions. (p. 270)

ethnocultural politics: Refers to the fact that the political allegiance of many American voters was determined less by party policy than by their membership in a specific ethnic or religious group. (p. 340)

Exodusters: African Americans who walked or rode out of the Deep South following the Civil War, many settling on farms in Kansas in hopes of finding peace and prosperity. (p. 520)

Federalist No. 10: An essay by James Madison in *The Federalist* (1787–1788) that challenged the view that republican governments only worked in small polities; it argued that a geographically expansive national government would better protect republican liberty. (p. 210)

Federalists: Supporters of the Constitution of 1787, which created a strong central government; their opponents, the Antifederalists, feared that a strong central government would corrupt the nation's newly won liberty. (p. 207)

Fetterman massacre: A massacre in December 1866 in which 1,500 Sioux warriors lured Captain William Fetterman and 80 soldiers from a Wyoming fort and attacked them. With the Fetterman massacre the Sioux succeeded in closing the Bozeman Trail, the main route into Montana. (p. 528)

Fifteenth Amendment: Constitutional amendment ratified in 1869 that forbade states to deny citizens the right to vote on grounds of race, color, or "previous condition of servitude." (p. 485)

"Fifty-four forty or eight!": Democratic candidate Governor James K. Polk's slogan in the election of 1844 calling for American sovereignty over the entire Oregon Country, stretching from California to Russian-occupied Alaska and presently shared with Great Britain. (p. 418)

forty-niners: The more than 80,000 settlers who arrived in California in 1849 as part of that territory's gold rush. (p. 425)

Fourteenth Amendment: Constitutional amendment ratified in 1868 that made all native-born or naturalized persons U.S. citizens and prohibited states from abridging the rights of national citizens, thus giving primacy to national rather than state citizenship. (p. 481)

franchise: The right to vote. Between 1820 and 1860, most states revised their constitutions to extend the vote to all adult white males. Black adult men gained the right to vote with the passage of the Fourteenth Amendment (1868). The Nineteenth Amendment (1920) granted adult women the right to vote. (p. 316)

Freedmen's Bureau: Government organization created in March 1865 to aid displaced blacks and other war refugees. Active until the early 1870s, it was the first federal agency in history that provided direct payments to assist those in poverty and to foster social welfare. (p. 481)

Freedman's Savings and Trust Company: A private bank founded in 1865 that had worked closely with the Freedmen's Bureau and Union army across the South. In June 1874, when the bank failed, Congress refused to compensate its 61,000 depositors, including many African Americans. (p. 497)

freeholds: Land owned in its entirety, without feudal dues or landlord obligations. Freeholders had the legal right to improve, transfer, or sell their landed property. (p. 53)

Freeport Doctrine: The argument presented by Senator Stephen A. Douglas that a territory's residents could exclude slavery by not adopting laws to protect it. (p. 438)

free-soil movement: A political movement that opposed the expansion of slavery. In 1848 the free-soilers organized the Free-Soil Party, which depicted slavery as a threat to republicanism and to the Jeffersonian ideal of a freeholder society, arguments that won broad support among aspiring white farmers. (p. 421)

French Revolution: A 1789 revolution in France that was initially welcomed by most Americans because it abolished feudalism and established a constitutional monarchy, but eventually came to seem too radical to many. (p. 219)

Gadsden Purchase: A small slice of land (now part of Arizona and New Mexico) purchased by President Franklin Pierce in 1853 for the purpose of building a transcontinental rail line from New Orleans to Los Angeles. (p. 431)

gag rule: A procedure in the House of Representatives from 1836 to 1844 by which antislavery petitions were automatically tabled when they were received so that they could not become the subject of debate. (p. 365)

gang-labor system: A system of work discipline used on southern cotton plantations in the mid-nineteenth century in which white overseers or black drivers supervised gangs of enslaved laborers to achieve greater productivity. (p. 388)

gentility: A refined style of living and elaborate manners that came to be highly prized among well-to-do English families after 1600 and strongly influenced leading colonists after 1700. (p. 102)

Ghost Dance movement: Religion of the late 1880s and early 1890s that combined elements of Christianity and traditional Native American religion. It fostered Plains Indians' hope that they could, through sacred dances, resurrect the great bison herds and call up a storm to drive whites back across the Atlantic. (p. 534)

Glorious Revolution: A quick and nearly bloodless coup in 1688 in which James II of England was overthrown by William of Orange. Whig politicians forced the new King William and Queen Mary to accept the Declaration of Rights, creating a constitutional monarchy that enhanced the powers of the House of Commons at the expense of the crown. (p. 86)

gold standard: The practice of backing a country's currency with its reserves of gold. In 1873 the United States, following Great Britain and other European nations, began converting to the gold standard. (p. 515)

greenbacks: Paper money issued by the U.S. Treasury during the Civil War to finance the war effort. (p. 460)

guilds: Organizations of skilled workers in medieval and early modern Europe that regulated the entry into, and the practice of, a trade. (p. 20)

habeas corpus: A legal writ forcing government authorities to justify their arrest and detention of an individual. During the Civil War, Lincoln suspended habeas corpus to stop protests against the draft and other anti-Union activities. (p. 454)

Haitian Revolution: The 1791 conflict involving diverse Haitian participants and armies from three European countries. At its end, Haiti became a free, independent nation in which former slaves were citizens. (p. 222)

"hard war": The philosophy and tactics used by Union general William Tecumseh Sherman, by which he treated civilians as combatants. (p. 470)

headright system: A system of land distribution, pioneered in Virginia and used in several other colonies, that granted land — usually 50 acres — to anyone who paid the passage of a new arrival. By this means, large planters amassed huge landholdings as they imported large numbers of servants and slaves. (p. 54)

heresy: A religious doctrine that is inconsistent with the teachings of a church. (p. 22)

herrenvolk **republic:** A republic based on the principle of rule by a master race. To preserve their privileged social position, southern leaders restricted individual liberty and legal equality to whites. (p. 266)

Homestead Act: The 1862 act that gave 160 acres of free western land to any applicant who occupied and improved the property. This policy led to the rapid development of the American West after the Civil War; facing arid conditions in the West, however, many homesteaders found themselves unable to live on their land. (p. 516)

House of Burgesses: Organ of government in colonial Virginia made up of an assembly of representatives elected by the colony's inhabitants. (p. 52)

household mode of production: The system of exchanging goods and labor that helped eighteenth-century New England freeholders survive on ever-shrinking farms as available land became more scarce. (p. 120)

indentured servitude: Workers contracted for service for a specified period. In exchange for agreeing to work for four or five years (or more) without wages in the colonies, indentured workers received passage across the Atlantic, room and board, and status as a free person at the end of the contract period. (p. 54)

Indian Removal Act of 1830: Act that directed the mandatory relocation of eastern tribes to territory west of the Mississippi. Jackson insisted that his goal was to save the Indians and their culture. Indians resisted the controversial act, but in the end most were forced to comply. (p. 327)

individualism: Word coined by Alexis de Tocqueville in 1835 to describe Americans as people no longer bound by social attachments to classes, castes, associations, and families. (p. 346)

Industrial Revolution: A burst of major inventions and economic expansion based on water and steam power and the use of machine technology that transformed certain industries, such as cotton textiles and iron, between 1790 and 1860. (p. 286)

inland system: The slave trade system in the interior of the country that fed slaves to the Cotton South. (p. 380)

internal improvements: Public works such as roads and canals. (p. 319)

Islam: A religion that considers Muhammad to be God's last prophet. Following the death of Muhammad in A.D. 632, the newly converted Arab peoples of North Africa used force and fervor to spread the Muslim faith into sub-Saharan Africa, India, Indonesia, Spain, and the Balkan regions of Europe. (p. 22)

Jacobins: A political faction in the French Revolution. Many Americans embraced the democratic ideology of the radical Jacobins and, like them, formed political clubs and began to address one another as "citizen." (p. 219)

Jay's Treaty: A 1795 treaty between the United States and Britain, negotiated by John Jay. The treaty accepted Britain's right to stop neutral ships. In return, it allowed Americans to submit claims for illegal seizures and required the British to remove their troops and Indian agents from the Northwest Territory. (p. 222)

joint-stock corporation: A financial organization devised by English merchants around 1550 that facilitated the colonization of North America. In these companies, a number of investors pooled their capital and received shares of stock in the enterprise in proportion to their share of the total investment. (p. 62)

Judiciary Act of 1789: Act that established a federal district court in each state and three circuit courts to hear appeals from the districts, with the Supreme Court having the final say. (p. 216)

Kansas-Nebraska Act: A controversial 1854 law that divided Indian Territory into Kansas and Nebraska, repealed the Missouri Compromise, and left the new territories to decide the issue of slavery on the basis of popular sovereignty. (p. 432)

King Cotton: The Confederate belief during the Civil War that their cotton was so important to the British and French economies that those governments would recognize the South as an independent nation and supply it with loans and arms. (p. 456)

Ku Klux Klan: A white supremacist group that arose in the South after the Civil War. The Klan terrorized Republican leaders and voters and sought to roll back Reconstruction, for example, by policing interracial sexual relationships and attacking teachers in African American schools. (p. 499)

labor theory of value: The belief that human labor produces economic value. Adherents argued that the price of a product should be determined not by the market (supply and demand) but by the amount of work required to make it, and that most of the price should be paid to the person who produced it. (p. 292)

laissez faire: French for "let do" or "leave alone." A doctrine espoused by classical liberals that the less the government does, the better, particularly in reference to the economy. (p. 498)

land banks: An institution, established by a colonial legislature, that printed paper money and lent it to farmers, taking a lien on their land to ensure repayment. (p. 107)

land-grant colleges: Public universities founded to broaden educational opportunities and foster technical and scientific expertise. These universities were funded by the Morrill Act, which authorized the sale of federal lands to raise money for higher education. (p. 516)

Lone Wolf v. Hitchcock: A 1903 Supreme Court ruling that Congress could make whatever Indian policies it chose, ignoring all existing treaties. (p. 532)

Long Drive: Facilitated by the completion of the Missouri Pacific Railroad in 1865, a system by which cowboys herded cattle hundreds of miles north from Texas to Dodge City and the other cow towns of Kansas. (p. 519)

Louisiana Purchase: The 1803 purchase of French territory west of the Mississippi River that stretched from the Gulf of Mexico to Canada. The Louisiana Purchase nearly doubled the size of the United States and opened the way for future American expansion west. The purchase required President Thomas Jefferson to exercise powers not explicitly granted to him by the Constitution. (p. 233)

machine tools: Cutting, boring, and drilling machines used to produce standardized metal parts, which were then assembled into products such as textile looms and sewing machines. The rapid development of machine tools by American inventors in the early nineteenth century was a factor in the rapid spread of industrialization. (p. 290)

Manifest Destiny: A term coined by John L. O'Sullivan in 1845 to express the idea that Euro-Americans were fated by God to settle the North American continent from the Atlantic to the Pacific Ocean. (p. 412)

manumission: The legal act of relinquishing property rights in slaves. Worried that a large free black population would threaten the institution of slavery, the Virginia assembly repealed Virginia's 1782 manumission law in 1792. (p. 265)

Marbury v. Madison **(1803):** A Supreme Court case that established the principle of judicial review in finding that parts of the Judiciary Act of 1789 were in conflict with the Constitution. For the first time, the Supreme Court assumed legal authority to overrule acts of other branches of the government. (p. 231)

March to the Sea: Military campaign from September through December 1864 in which Union forces under General Sherman marched from Atlanta, Georgia, to the coast at Savannah. Carving a path of destruction as it progressed, Sherman's army aimed at destroying white southerners' will to continue the war. (p. 470)

Market Revolution: The dramatic increase between 1820 and 1850 in the exchange of goods and services in market transactions. The Market Revolution reflected the increased output of farms and factories, the entrepreneurial activities of traders and merchants, and the creation of a transportation network of roads, canals, and railroads. (p. 293)

married women's property laws: Laws enacted between 1839 and 1860 in New York and other states that permitted married women to own, inherit, and bequeath property. (p. 371)

matriarchy: A gendered power structure in which social identity and property descend through the female line. (p. 15)

McCulloch v. Maryland **(1819):** A Supreme Court case that asserted the dominance of national over state statutes. (p. 241)

mechanics: A term used in the nineteenth century to refer to skilled craftsmen and inventors who built and improved machinery and machine tools for industry. (p. 287)

mercantilism: A system of political economy based on government regulation. Beginning in 1650, Britain enacted Navigation Acts that controlled colonial commerce and manufacturing for the enrichment of Britain. (p. 45)

middle class: An economic group of prosperous farmers, artisans, and traders that emerged in the early nineteenth century. Its rise reflected a dramatic increase in prosperity. This surge in income, along with an abundance of inexpensive mass-produced goods, fostered a distinct middle-class urban culture. (p. 302)

Middle Passage: The brutal sea voyage from Africa to the Americas that took the lives of nearly two million enslaved Africans. (p. 94)

mineral-based economy: An economy based on coal and metal that began to emerge in the 1830s, as manufacturers increasingly ran machinery fashioned from metal with coal-burning stationary steam engines rather than with water power. (p. 287)

Minor v. Happersett: A Supreme Court decision in 1875 that ruled that suffrage rights were not inherent in citizenship and had not been granted by the Fourteenth Amendment, as some women's rights advocates argued. Women were citizens, the Court ruled, but state legislatures could deny women the vote if they wished. (p. 486)

minstrelsy: Popular theatrical entertainment begun around 1830, in which white actors in blackface presented comic routines that combined racist caricature and social criticism. (p. 356)

Minutemen: Colonial militiamen who stood ready to mobilize on short notice during the imperial crisis of the 1770s. These volunteers formed the core of the citizens' army that met British troops at Lexington and Concord in April 1775. (p. 175)

Missouri Compromise: A series of political agreements devised by Speaker of the House Henry Clay. Maine entered the Union as a free state in 1820 and Missouri followed as a slave state in 1821, preserving a balance in the Senate between North and South and setting a precedent for future admissions to the Union. Most importantly, this bargain set the northern boundary of slavery in the lands of the Louisiana Purchase at the southern boundary of Missouri, with the exception of that state. (p. 269)

mixed government: John Adams's theory from *Thoughts on Government* (1776), which called for three branches of government, each representing one function: executive, legislative, and judicial. This system of dispersed authority was devised to maintain a balance of power and ensure the legitimacy of governmental procedures. (p. 198)

Monroe Doctrine: The 1823 declaration by President James Monroe that the Western Hemisphere was closed to any further colonization or interference by European powers. In exchange, Monroe pledged that the United States would not become involved in European struggles. (p. 244)

moral free agency: The doctrine of free will that was the central message of Presbyterian minister Charles Grandison Finney. It was particularly attractive to members of the new middle class, who had accepted personal responsibility for their lives, improved their material condition, and welcomed Finney's assurance that heaven was also within their grasp. (p. 306)

Mormonism: The religion of members of the Church of Jesus Christ of Latter-day Saints, founded by Joseph Smith in 1830. After Smith's death at the hands of an angry mob, Brigham Young led many followers of Mormonism to lands in present-day Utah in 1846. (p. 352)

Morrill Act: An 1862 act that set aside 140 million federal acres that states could sell to raise money for public universities. (p. 516)

Munn v. Illinois: An 1877 Supreme Court case that affirmed that states could regulate key businesses, such as railroads and grain elevators, if those businesses were "clothed in the public interest." (p. 514)

National Woman Suffrage Association: A suffrage group headed by Elizabeth Cady Stanton and Susan B. Anthony that stressed the need for women to lead organizations on their own behalf. The NWSA focused exclusively on women's rights — sometimes denigrating men of color, in the process — and took up the battle for a federal women's suffrage amendment. (p. 486)

nativist movements: Antiforeign sentiment in the United States that fueled anti-immigrant and immigration-restriction policies against the Irish and Germans in the 1840s and the 1850s and against other ethnic immigrants in subsequent decades. (p. 310)

natural rights: The rights to life, liberty, and property. According to the English philosopher John Locke in *Two Treatises of Government* (1690), political authority was not given by God to monarchs. Instead, it derived from social compacts that people made to preserve their natural rights. (p. 127)

Naturalization, Alien, and Sedition Acts: Three laws passed in 1798 that limited individual rights and threatened the fledgling party system. The Naturalization Act lengthened the residency requirement for citizenship, the Alien Act authorized the deportation of foreigners, and the Sedition Act prohibited the publication of insults or malicious attacks on the president or members of Congress. (p. 224)

Navigation Acts: English laws passed, beginning in the 1650s and 1660s, requiring that certain English colonial goods be shipped through English ports on English ships manned primarily by English sailors in order to benefit English merchants, shippers, and seamen. (p. 83)

neo-Europes: Term for colonies in which colonists sought to replicate, or at least approximate, economies and social structures they knew at home. (p. 40)

"neomercantilist": A system of government-assisted economic development embraced by republican state legislatures throughout the nation, especially in the Northeast. This system of activist government encouraged private entrepreneurs to seek individual opportunity and the public welfare through market exchange. (p. 250)

New Jersey Plan: Alternative to the Virginia Plan drafted by delegates from small states, retaining the confederation's single-house congress with one vote per state. It shared with the Virginia Plan enhanced congressional powers to raise revenue, control commerce, and make binding requisitions on the states. (p. 206)

New Lights: Evangelical preachers, many of them influenced by John Wesley, the founder of English Methodism, and George Whitefield, the charismatic itinerant preacher who brought his message to Britain's American colonies. They decried a Christian faith that was merely intellectual and emphasized the importance of a spiritual rebirth. (p. 132)

nonimportation movement: Colonists attempted nonimportation agreements three times: in 1766, in response to the Stamp Act;

in 1768, in response to the Townshend duties; and in 1774, in response to the Coercive Acts. In each case, colonial radicals pressured merchants to stop importing British goods. In 1774 nonimportation was adopted by the First Continental Congress and enforced by the Continental Association. American women became crucial to the movement by reducing their households' consumption of imported goods and producing large quantities of homespun cloth. (p. 161)

Northwest Ordinance of 1787: A land act that provided for orderly settlement and established a process by which settled territories would become the states of Ohio, Indiana, Illinois, Michigan, and Wisconsin. It also banned slavery in the Northwest Territory. (p. 201)

notables: Northern landlords, slave-owning planters, and seaport merchants who dominated the political system of the early nineteenth century. (p. 316)

nullification: The constitutional argument advanced by John C. Calhoun that a state legislature or convention could void a law passed by Congress. (p. 324)

Old Lights: Conservative ministers opposed to the passion displayed by evangelical preachers; they preferred to emphasize the importance of cultivating a virtuous Christian life. (p. 132)

Ostend Manifesto: An 1854 manifesto that urged President Franklin Pierce to seize the slave-owning province of Cuba from Spain. Northern Democrats denounced this aggressive initiative, and the plan was scuttled. (p. 431)

outwork: A system of manufacturing, also known as putting out, used extensively in the English woolen industry in the sixteenth and seventeenth centuries. Merchants bought wool and then hired landless peasants who lived in small cottages to spin and weave it into cloth, which the merchants would sell in English and foreign markets. (p. 45)

Panic of 1819: First major economic crisis of the United States. Farmers and planters faced an abrupt 30 percent drop in world agricultural prices, and as farmers' income declined, they could not pay debts owed to stores and banks, many of which went bankrupt. (p. 251)

Panic of 1837: Second major economic crisis of the United States, which led to hard times from 1837 to 1843. (p. 334)

patriarchy: A gendered power structure in which social identity and property descend through the male line and male heads of family rule over women and children. (p. 18)

patronage: The power of elected officials to grant government jobs and favors to their supporters; also the jobs and favors themselves. (p. 106)

peasants: The traditional term for farmworkers in Europe. Some peasants owned land, while others leased or rented small plots from landlords. (p. 18)

Pennsylvania constitution of 1776: A constitution that granted all taxpaying men the right to vote and hold office and created a unicameral (one-house) legislature with complete power; there was no governor to exercise a veto. Other provisions mandated a system of elementary education and protected citizens from imprisonment for debt. (p. 198)

perfectionism: Christian movement of the 1830s that believed people could achieve moral perfection in their earthly lives because the Second Coming of Christ had already occurred. (p. 352)

personal-liberty laws: Laws enacted in many northern states that guaranteed to all residents, including alleged fugitives, the right to a jury trial. (p. 431)

Philipsburg Proclamation: A 1779 proclamation that declared that any slave who deserted a rebel master would receive protection, freedom, and land from Great Britain. (p. 190)

Pietism: A Christian revival moment characterized by Bible study, the conversion experience, and the individual's personal relationship with God. It began as an effort to reform the German Lutheran Church in the mid-seventeenth century and became widely influential in Britain and its colonies in the eighteenth century. (p. 126)

Pilgrims: One of the first Protestant groups to come to America, seeking a separation from the Church of England. They founded Plymouth, the first permanent community in New England, in 1620. (p. 60)

political machine: A highly organized group of insiders that directs a political party. As the power of notables waned in the 1820s, disciplined political parties usually run by professional politicians appeared in a number of states. (p. 317)

popular sovereignty: The principle that ultimate power lies in the hands of the electorate. (p. 179)

"positive good" argument: An argument in the 1830s that the institution of slavery was a "positive good" because it subsidized an elegant lifestyle for the white elite and provided tutelage for genetically inferior Africans. (p. 386)

predestination: The Protestant Christian belief that God chooses certain people for salvation before they are born. Sixteenth-century theologian John Calvin was the main proponent of this doctrine, which became a fundamental tenet of Puritan theology. (p. 22)

primogeniture: The practice of passing family land, by will or by custom, to the eldest son. (p. 18)

Proclamation of Neutrality: A proclamation issued by President George Washington in 1793, allowing U.S. citizens to trade with all belligerents in the war between France and Great Britain. (p. 219)

proprietorship: A colony created through a grant of land from the English monarch to an individual or group, who then set up a form of government largely independent from royal control. (p. 82)

protective tariff: A tax or duty on foreign producers of goods coming into or imported into the United States; tariffs gave U.S. manufacturers a competitive advantage in America's gigantic domestic market. (p. 510)

Protestant Reformation: The reform movement that began in 1517 with Martin Luther's critiques of the Roman Catholic Church and that precipitated an enduring schism that divided Protestants from Catholics. (p. 22)

Puritans: Dissenters from the Church of England who wanted a genuine Reformation rather than the partial Reformation sought by Henry VIII. The Puritans' religious principles emphasized the importance of an individual's relationship with God developed through Bible study, prayer, and introspection. (p. 61)

Quakers: Epithet for members of the Society of Friends. Their belief that God spoke directly to each individual through an "inner light" and that neither ministers nor the Bible was essential to discovering God's Word put them in conflict with both the Church of England and orthodox Puritans. (p. 82)

Quartering Act of 1765: A British law passed by Parliament at the request of General Thomas Gage, the British military commander in America, that required colonial governments to provide barracks and food for British troops. (p. 157)

Radical Republicans: The members of the Republican Party who were bitterly opposed to slavery and to southern slave owners since the mid-1850s. With the Confiscation Act in 1861, Radical Republicans began to use wartime legislation to destroy slavery. (p. 463)

"rain follows the plow": An unfounded theory that settlement of the Great Plains caused an increase in rainfall. (p. 519)

reconquista: The campaign by Spanish Catholics to drive North African Moors (Muslim Arabs) from the European mainland. After a centuries-long effort to recover their lands, the Spaniards defeated the Moors at Granada in 1492 and secured control of all of Spain. (p. 31)

Reconstruction Act of 1867: An act that divided the conquered South into five military districts, each under the command of a U.S. general. To reenter the Union, former Confederate states had to grant the vote to freedmen and deny it to leading ex-Confederates. (p. 482)

"Redemption": A term used by southern Democrats for the overthrow of elected governments that ended Reconstruction in many parts of the South. So-called Redeemers terrorized Republicans, especially in districts with large proportions of black voters, and killed and intimidated their opponents to regain power. (p. 498)

redemptioner: A common type of indentured servant in the Middle colonies in the eighteenth century. Unlike other indentured servants, redemptioners did not sign a contract before leaving Europe. Instead, they found employers after arriving in America. (p. 124)

Regulators: Landowning protestors who organized in North and South Carolina in the 1760s and 1770s to demand that the eastern-controlled government provide western districts with more courts, fairer taxation, and greater representation in the assembly. (p. 142)

Renaissance: A cultural transformation in the arts and learning that began in Italy in the fourteenth century and spread through much of Europe. Its ideals reshaped art and architecture and gave rise to civic humanism. (p. 20)

Report on Manufactures: A proposal by treasury secretary Alexander Hamilton in 1791 calling for the federal government to urge the expansion of American manufacturing while imposing tariffs on foreign imports. (p. 218)

Report on the Public Credit: Alexander Hamilton's 1790 report recommending that the federal government should assume all state debts and fund the national debt — that is, offer interest on it rather than repaying it — at full value. Hamilton's goal was to make the new country creditworthy, not debt-free. (p. 216)

republic: A state without a monarch or prince that is governed by representatives of the people. (p. 19)

republican aristocracy: The Old South gentry that built impressive mansions, adopted the manners and values of the English landed gentry, and feared federal government interference with their slave property. (p. 386)

republican motherhood: The idea that the primary political role of American women was to instill a sense of patriotic duty and republican virtue in their children and mold them into exemplary republican citizens. (p. 259)

revival: A renewal of religious enthusiasm in a Christian congregation. In the eighteenth century, revivals were often inspired by evangelical preachers who urged their listeners to experience a rebirth. (p. 129)

royal colony: In the English system, a royal colony was chartered by the crown. The colony's governor was appointed by the crown and served according to the instructions of the Board of Trade. (p. 52)

Sabbatarian movement: A movement to preserve the Sabbath as a holy day. These reformers believed that declining observance by Christians of the Sabbath (Sunday) was the greatest threat to religion in the United States. (p. 306)

salutary neglect: A term used to describe British colonial policy during the reigns of George I (r. 1714–1727) and George II (r. 1727–1760). By relaxing their supervision of internal colonial affairs, royal bureaucrats inadvertently assisted the rise of self-government in North America. (p. 106)

Sand Creek massacre: The November 29, 1864, massacre of more than a hundred peaceful Cheyennes, largely women and children, by John M. Chivington's Colorado militia. (p. 527)

scalawags: Southern whites who supported Republican Reconstruction and were ridiculed by ex-Confederates as worthless traitors. (p. 493)

scorched-earth campaign: A campaign in the Shenandoah Valley of Virginia by Union general Philip H. Sheridan's troops. The troops destroyed grain, barns, and other useful resources to punish farmers who had aided Confederate raiders. (p. 468)

Second Bank of the United States: National bank with multiple branches chartered in 1816 for twenty years. Intended to help regulate the economy, the bank became a major issue in Andrew Jackson's reelection campaign in 1832. (p. 325)

Second Continental Congress: Legislative body that governed the United States from May 1775 through the war's duration. It established an army, created its own money, and declared independence once all hope for a peaceful reconciliation with Britain was gone. (p. 176)

Second Great Awakening: Unprecedented religious revival that swept the nation between 1790 and 1850; it also proved to be a major impetus for the reform movements of the era. (p. 271)

Second Hundred Years' War: An era of warfare beginning with the War of the League of Augsburg in 1689 and lasting until the defeat of Napoleon at Waterloo in 1815. In that time, England fought in seven major wars; the longest era of peace lasted only twenty-six years. (p. 88)

secret ballot: Form of voting that allows the voter to enter a choice in privacy without having to submit a recognizable ballot or to voice the choice out loud to others. (p. 393)

self-made man: A nineteenth-century ideal that celebrated men who rose to wealth or social prominence from humble origins through self-discipline, hard work, and temperate habits. (p. 304)

Seneca Falls Convention: The first women's rights convention in the United States. Held in Seneca Falls, New York, in 1848, it resulted in a manifesto extending to women the egalitarian republican ideology of the Declaration of Independence. (p. 371)

sentimentalism: A way of experiencing the world that emphasized emotions and a sensuous appreciation of God, nature, and people. Part of the Romantic movement, it spread to the United States from Europe in the late eighteenth century. (p. 258)

separate sphere: A term used by historians to describe the nineteenth-century view that men and women have different gender-defined characteristics and, consequently, that men should dominate the public sphere of politics and economics, while women should manage the private sphere of home and family. (p. 367)

sharecropping: The labor system by which landowners and impoverished southern farmworkers, particularly African Americans, divided the proceeds from crops harvested on the landowner's property. With local merchants providing supplies — in exchange for a lien on the crop — sharecropping pushed farmers into cash-crop production and often trapped them in long-term debt. (p. 491)

Shays's Rebellion: A 1786–1787 uprising led by dissident farmers in western Massachusetts, many of them Revolutionary War veterans, protesting the taxation policies of the eastern elites who controlled the state's government. (p. 204)

Slaughter-House Cases: A group of decisions begun in 1873 in which the Court began to undercut the power of the Fourteenth Amendment to protect African American rights. (p. 500)

slave society: A society in which the institution of slavery affects all aspects of life. (p. 388)

"slavery follows the flag": The assertion by John C. Calhoun that planters could by right take their slave property into newly opened territories. (p. 428)

socialism: A system of social and economic organization based on the common ownership of goods or state control of the economy. (p. 351)

Sons of Liberty: Colonists — primarily middling merchants and artisans — who banded together to protest the Stamp Act and other imperial reforms of the 1760s. The group originated in Boston in 1765 but soon spread to all the colonies. (p. 158)

South Atlantic System: A new agricultural and commercial order that produced sugar, tobacco, rice, and other tropical and subtropical products for an international market. Its plantation societies were ruled by European planter-merchants and worked by hundreds of thousands of enslaved Africans. (p. 90)

Specie Circular: An executive order in 1836 that required the Treasury Department to accept only gold and silver in payment for lands in the national domain. (p. 338)

spoils system: The widespread award of public jobs to political supporters after an electoral victory. In 1829, Andrew Jackson instituted the system on the national level, arguing that the rotation of officeholders was preferable to a permanent group of bureaucrats. (p. 318)

squatter: Someone who settles on land he or she does not own or rent. Many eighteenth-century settlers established themselves on land before it was surveyed and entered for sale, requesting the first right to purchase the land when sales began. (p. 121)

squatter sovereignty: A plan promoted by Democratic candidate Senator Lewis Cass under which Congress would allow settlers in each territory to determine its status as free or slave. (p. 424)

Stamp Act Congress: A congress of delegates from nine assemblies that met in New York City in October 1765 to protest the loss of American "rights and liberties," especially the right to trial by jury. The congress challenged the constitutionality of both the Stamp and Sugar Acts by declaring that only the colonists' elected representatives could tax them. (p. 158)

Stamp Act of 1765: British law imposing a tax on all paper used in the colonies. Widespread resistance to the Stamp Act prevented it from taking effect and led to its repeal in 1766. (p. 157)

states' rights: An interpretation of the Constitution that exalts the sovereignty of the states and circumscribes the authority of the national government. (p. 324)

Stono Rebellion: Slave uprising in 1739 along the Stono River in South Carolina in which a group of slaves armed themselves, plundered six plantations, and killed more than twenty colonists. Colonists quickly suppressed the rebellion. (p. 101)

Sugar Act of 1764: British law that decreased the duty on French molasses, making it more attractive for shippers to obey the law, and at the same time raised penalties for smuggling. The act enraged New England merchants, who opposed both the tax and the fact that prosecuted merchants would be tried by British-appointed judges in a vice-admiralty court. (p. 155)

Tariff of Abominations: A tariff enacted in 1828 that raised duties significantly on raw materials, textiles, and iron goods. New York senator Van Buren hoped to win the support of farmers in New York, Ohio, and Kentucky with the tariff, but it enraged the South, which had no industries that needed tariff protection and resented the higher cost of imported dutied goods. (p. 320)

task system: A system of labor common in the rice-growing regions of South Carolina in which a slave was assigned a daily task to complete and allowed to do as he wished upon its completion. (p. 397)

Tea Act of May 1773: British act that lowered the existing tax on tea and granted exemptions to the East India Company to make their tea cheaper in the colonies and entice boycotting Americans to buy it. Resistance to the Tea Act led to the passage of the Coercive Acts and imposition of military rule in Massachusetts. (p. 168)

Ten Percent Plan: A plan proposed by President Abraham Lincoln during the Civil War, but never implemented, that would have granted amnesty to most ex-Confederates and allowed each rebellious state to return to the Union as soon as 10 percent of its voters had taken a loyalty oath and the state had approved the Thirteenth Amendment. (p. 480)

tenancy: The rental of property. To attract tenants in New York's Hudson River Valley, Dutch and English manorial lords granted long tenancy leases, with the right to sell improvements — houses and barns, for example — to the next tenant. (p. 116)

toleration: The allowance of different religious practices. Lord Baltimore persuaded the Maryland assembly to enact the Toleration Act (1649), which granted all Christians the right to follow their beliefs and hold church services. The crown imposed toleration on Massachusetts Bay in its new royal charter of 1691. (p. 62)

total war: A form of warfare that mobilizes all of a society's resources — economic, political, and cultural — in support of the military effort. (p. 452)

town meeting: A system of local government in New England in which all male heads of households met regularly to elect selectmen, levy local taxes, and regulate markets, roads, and schools. (p. 64)

Townshend Act of 1767: British law that established new duties on tea, glass, lead, paper, and painters' colors imported into the colonies. The Townshend duties led to boycotts and heightened tensions between Britain and the American colonies. (p. 161)

Trail of Tears: Forced westward journey of Cherokees from their lands in Georgia to present-day Oklahoma in 1838. Nearly a quarter of the Cherokees died en route. (p. 331)

transcendentalism: A nineteenth-century intellectual movement that posited the importance of an ideal world of mystical knowledge and harmony beyond the immediate grasp of the senses. Transcendentalists Ralph Waldo Emerson and Henry David Thoreau called for the critical examination of society and emphasized individuality, self-reliance, and nonconformity. (p. 346)

transcontinental railroad: The railway line completed on May 10, 1869, that connected the Central Pacific and Union Pacific lines, enabling goods to move by railway from the eastern United States all the way to California. (p. 508)

trans-Saharan trade: The primary avenue of trade for West Africans before European traders connected them to the Atlantic World. Controlled in turn by the Ghana, Mali, and Songhai empires, it carried slaves and gold to North Africa in exchange for salt and other goods. (p. 23)

Treaty of Ghent: The treaty signed on Christmas Eve 1814 that ended the War of 1812. It retained the prewar borders of the United States. (p. 241)

Treaty of Greenville: A 1795 treaty between the United States and various Indian tribes in Ohio. American negotiators acknowledged Indian ownership of the land, and, in return for various payments, the Western Confederacy ceded most of Ohio to the United States. (p. 226)

Treaty of Kanagawa: An 1854 treaty that, in the wake of a show of military force by U.S. Commodore Matthew Perry, allowed American ships to refuel at two ports in Japan. (p. 510)

Treaty of Paris of 1783: The treaty that ended the Revolutionary War. In the treaty, Great Britain formally recognized American independence and relinquished its claims to lands south of the Great Lakes and east of the Mississippi River. (p. 196)

tribalization: The adaptation of stateless peoples to the demands imposed on them by neighboring states. (p. 88)

tribute: The practice of collecting goods from conquered peoples. The Aztecs and Incas relied on systems of tribute before they were conquered by Spain; after the conquest, Spanish officials adapted indigenous tribute systems to their own needs by binding Indian labor to powerful men through the *encomienda* and *mita* systems. (p. 8)

U.S. Fisheries Commission: A federal bureau established in 1871 that made recommendations to stem the decline in wild fish. Its creation was an important step toward wildlife conservation and management. (p. 525)

U.S. v. Cruikshank: A decision in which the Supreme Court ruled that voting rights remained a state matter unless the state itself violated those rights. If former slaves' rights were violated by individuals or private groups, that lay beyond federal jurisdiction. Like the *Slaughter-House Cases*, the ruling undercut the power of the Fourteenth Amendment to protect African American rights. (p. 500)

"unchurched": Irreligious Americans, who probably constituted a majority of the population in 1800. Evangelical Methodist and Baptist churches were by far the most successful institutions in attracting new members from the unchurched. (p. 270)

Underground Railroad: An informal network of whites and free blacks in the South that assisted fugitive slaves to reach freedom in the North. (p. 362)

Union League: A secret fraternal order in which black and white Republicans joined forces in the late 1860s. The League became a powerful political association that spread through the former Confederacy, pressuring Congress to uphold justice for freedmen. (p. 493)

unions: Organizations of workers that began during the Industrial Revolution to bargain with employers over wages, hours, benefits, and control of the workplace. (p. 291)

utopias: Communities founded by reformers and transcendentalists to help realize their spiritual and moral potential and to escape from the competition of modern industrial society. (p. 349)

Valley Forge: A military camp in which George Washington's army of 12,000 soldiers and hundreds of camp followers suffered horribly in the winter of 1777–1778. (p. 189)

vice-admiralty court: A maritime tribunal presided over by a royally appointed judge, with no jury. (p. 156)

Virginia and Kentucky Resolutions: Resolutions of 1798 condemning the Alien and Sedition Acts that were submitted to the federal government by the Virginia and Kentucky state legislatures. The resolutions tested the idea that state legislatures could judge the constitutionality of federal laws and nullify them. (p. 225)

Virginia Plan: A plan drafted by James Madison that was presented at the Philadelphia Constitutional Convention. It designed a powerful three-branch government, with representation in both houses of the congress tied to population; this plan would have eclipsed the voice of small states in the national government. (p. 205)

virtual representation: The claim made by British politicians that the interests of the American colonists were adequately represented in Parliament by merchants who traded with the colonies and by absentee landlords (mostly sugar planters) who owned estates in the West Indies. (p. 157)

voluntarism: The funding of churches by their members. It allowed the laity to control the clergy, while also supporting the republican principle of self-government. (p. 270)

Wade-Davis Bill: A bill proposed by Congress in July 1864 that required an oath of allegiance by a majority of each state's adult white men, new governments formed only by those who had never taken up arms against the Union, and permanent disenfranchisement of Confederate leaders. The plan was passed but pocket vetoed by President Abraham Lincoln. (p. 480)

Waltham-Lowell System: A system of labor using young women recruited from farm families to work in factories in Lowell, Chicopee, and other sites in Massachusetts and New Hampshire. The women lived in company boardinghouses with strict rules and curfews and were often required to attend church. (p. 288)

War and Peace Democrats: Members of the Democratic Party that split into two camps over war policy during the Civil War. War Democrats vowed to continue fighting until the rebellion ended, while Peace Democrats called for a constitutional convention to negotiate a peace settlement. (p. 469)

Whigs: The second national party, the Whig Party arose in 1834 when a group of congressmen contested Andrew Jackson's policies and conduct. The party identified itself with the pre-Revolutionary American and British parties — also called Whigs — that had opposed the arbitrary actions of British monarchs. (p. 332)

Whiskey Rebellion: A 1794 uprising by farmers in western Pennsylvania in response to enforcement of an unpopular excise tax on whiskey. (p. 219)

Wilmot Proviso: The 1846 proposal by Representative David Wilmot of Pennsylvania to ban slavery in territory acquired from the Mexican War. (p. 421)

Wounded Knee: The 1890 massacre of Sioux Indians by American cavalry at Wounded Knee Creek, South Dakota. Sent to suppress the Ghost Dance, soldiers caught up with fleeing Lakotas and killed as many as 300. (p. 534)

XYZ Affair: A 1797 incident in which American negotiators in France were rebuffed for refusing to pay a substantial bribe. The incident led the United States into an undeclared war that curtailed American trade with the French West Indies. (p. 223)

Yellowstone National Park: Established in 1872 by Congress, Yellowstone was the United States's first national park. (p. 525)

Index

About the authors

James A. Henretta is Professor Emeritus of American History at the University of Maryland, College Park. His publications include *"Salutary Neglect": Colonial Administration under the Duke of Newcastle; The Origins of American Capitalism*; and an edited volume, *Republicanism and Liberalism in America and the German States, 1750–1850*. His most recent publication is a long article, "Charles Evans Hughes and the Strange Death of Liberal America," in *Law and History Review*, derived from his ongoing research on the liberal state in America, and in particular New York, 1820–1975.

Eric Hinderaker is Professor of History and Director of Graduate Studies at the University of Utah. His research explores early modern imperialism, relations between Europeans and Native Americans, and comparative colonization. His publications include *The Two Hendricks: Unraveling a Mohawk Mystery*, which won the Dixon Ryan Fox Prize; *Elusive Empires: Constructing Colonialism in the Ohio Valley, 1673–1800*; and, with Peter C. Mancall, *At the Edge of Empire: The Backcountry in British North America*. He is currently working on two books, one about the Boston Massacre and another, with Rebecca Horn, on patterns of European colonization in the Americas.

Rebecca Edwards is Eloise Ellery Professor of History at Vassar College, where she teaches courses on the Civil War era, the West, environmental history, and the history of women and gender roles. She is the author of, among other publications, *Angels in the Machinery: Gender in American Party Politics from the Civil War to the Progressive Era*; *New Spirits: Americans in the "Gilded Age," 1865–1905*; and the essay "Women's and Gender History" in *The New American History*. She is currently researching the connections between westward expansion, high frontier fertility, and nineteenth-century political ideologies.

Robert O. Self is Professor of History at Brown University. His research focuses on urban history, American politics, and the post-1945 United States. He is the author of *American Babylon: Race and the Struggle for Postwar Oakland*, which won four professional prizes, including the James A. Rawley Prize from the Organization of American Historians, and *All in the Family: The Realignment of American Democracy Since the 1960s*. He is currently at work on a book about the centrality of houses, cars, and children to family consumption in the twentieth-century United States.